$$\sum_{x} f[x] \Leftrightarrow \text{sum}(x)$$

Technical Computation and Visualization in MATLAB for Engineers and Scientists

\>>

Mohammad Nuruzzaman
Electrical Engineering Department
King Fahd University of Petroleum and Minerals
Dhahran, Saudi Arabia

Bloomington, IN authorHOUSE® Milton Keynes, UK

AuthorHouse™
1663 Liberty Drive, Suite 200
Bloomington, IN 47403
www.authorhouse.com
Phone: 1-800-839-8640

AuthorHouse™ UK Ltd.
500 Avebury Boulevard
Central Milton Keynes, MK9 2BE
www.authorhouse.co.uk
Phone: 08001974150

©2007 Mohammad Nuruzzaman. All rights reserved.

No part of this book may be reproduced, stored in a retrieval system, or transmitted by any means without the written permission of the author.

First published by AuthorHouse 01/17/2007

ISBN: 978-1-4259-7738-2 (sc)

Printed in the United States of America
Bloomington, Indiana

This book is printed on acid-free paper.

To my parents

PREFACE

Bits and pieces of isolated idea-information-implementation when organized in a unified way – a book in compact form is born. "*Technical Computation and Visualization in MATLAB for Engineers and Scientists*" allows users to compute and visualize many scientific and engineering problems in an easeful way in MATLAB. MATLAB which is the short for matrix laboratory is not just a software, it is a great tool for studying and analyzing technical problems with great confidence. Our style in the text is to attack a scientific problem straightforwardly, mostly from pure mathematics context, and find its MATLAB solution for this reason we have maintained "let us be engaged" approach throughout the text.

MATLAB's familiarity is ever increasing among engineers and scientists for a number of reasons. Contemporary MATLAB compilers provide easy to use workspace, debugging convenience, fully featured graphics environment, and extensive help facilities. Besides, access to graphical user interface (GUI), interactive system planning, and model design and development had never been as facile as it is executed nowadays in MATLAB. Whether we concentrate on computation or visualization, one word or few words MATLAB command bypass traditional programming, compiling, and debugging as conducted in FORTRAN, PASCAL, or C – that is the amazing aspect of working in MATLAB.

Although the text is devised to meet the needs for the undergraduate and graduate students of science and engineering, it holds immense attention for the practicing engineering and scientific professionals because the advent of the package had not been long ago. MATLAB can be viewed as the album of thousands of function files experienced and utilized by the engineers and scientists all over the world. Relying on the current practice and end-result, one can quickly develop the solution, extend any methodology, or modify ongoing algorithm and technique for any scientific problem. Neoteric features are being appended almost every year ever since the package was evolved. Nevertheless, discipline-specific function set which is called Toolbox (such as Statistical Toolbox, Signal Processing Toolbox, Image Processing Toolbox, Optimization Toolbox, System Identification Toolbox, etc) enhanced the applicability of the package in various dimensions since there are dozens of embedded Toolboxes. Furthermore, industrial design, process, and manufacturing also make use of the package along with the academia. Science and engineering disciplines call for quantitative research which always confronts huge amounts of numerical data that is collected from explorations, experiments, and surveys. MATLAB is a powerful tool in handling matrix-oriented calculations and manipulations. In this sense the package keeps great promise for the study-research-analysis of any scientific and engineering problem. Another unique feature of the package is the integration of data-manipulation, program writing, and graphics drawing – a complete companion software indeed.

The text contains chapter titles similar to the ones often viewed in pure mathematics. We believe this is an effective introduction to the general ideas involved. So long as one can implement the problems in pure mathematics context, execution of the practical scientific problem which is often modeled by pure mathematical equations and concepts is by no means a complicated task. Commencing with the elementary examples, we developed the steps required for MATLAB solution for various mathematical problems. Mathematical details or algorithms behind any execution are not addressed because we are focused on the implementation not on the theory of the computation which the reader can access through the reference cited at the end. Ample number of implementations enables the average reader to follow without any difficulty. Article headings in any chapter obviously describe the problems to be solved or implemented.

Rather than devote a MATLAB-based article, a reader may prefer to have the reading material organized in consistent with the traditional theory. For this reason our material accumulation is rendered in formal mathematics title. Chapters 1 and 2 present a quick introduction to MATLAB's opening features and elementary matrix implementations respectively. Even though elementary algebraic, trigonometric, and geometric problems would not have appeared as chapter 3, the easy computational tactics presented in the chapter will make the mathematics simple. Despite simple matrix arithmetic introduction in chapter 2, in-depth matrix algebra problems are covered in the chapter 4. Differential and integral calculus problems are part and parcel of scientific computation which we focused in the chapters 5 and 6 respectively. Differential equation and transform-oriented analyses follow a large variety of engineering systems for which the chapters 7 and 8 are dedicated. Few introductory statistical problems are addressed in chapter 9 in view of the fact that statistics and probability are becoming increasingly important in applied sciences. Besides the title specific solutions, miscellaneous functions sampled from thousands are presented in chapter 10 just to show the computational capability of MATLAB in various disciplines. Optimization techniques have obvious applications in engineering process and operation management which we highlighted in chapter 11. Advanced engineering needs to solve the partial differential equations which is seen in chapter 12. MATLAB not only computes the toilsome numeric and symbolic problems quickly but also displays the results graphically in a variety of picturesque representations. Graphical analysis is a momentous procedure for visualizing results and solutions from final outcome in scientific and engineering research. Chapter 13 solely describes the graphing in MATLAB. Finally chapter 14 handles the issues of programming which are very vital for user-defined problem solving.

My words of acknowledgement are due to the King Fahd University of Petroleum and Minerals (KFUPM). Thanks to the printing and library facilities of the King Fahd University. All illustrative problems cited in the text have been given MATLAB codes and implemented in a Pentium Personal Computer on Microsoft Windows operated system.

Mohammad Nuruzzaman

CONTENTS

Chapter 1
Introduction to MATLAB
1.1 What is MATLAB? 1
1.2 MATLAB's opening window features 1
1.3 How to get started? 3
1.4 Some queries about MATLAB environment 6
1.5 How to get help? 8

Chapter 2
Matrix Fundamentals
2.1 Matrix addition and subtraction 9
2.2 Matrix multiplication 10
2.3 Simple matrix arithmetic 12
2.4 Matrix data flipping 13
2.5 Power operations on matrix elements 14
2.6 Indexing and coloning of arrays or matrices 15
2.7 Appending, deleting, and editing matrix elements 16
2.8 Summing and producting matrix elements 19
2.9 Finding the maximum/minimum and data sorting 20
2.10 Array or matrix manipulation 20
2.11 Rounding, remainder after integer division, and factoring 22
2.12 Matrix element testing and dimension finding 23
2.13 Position indexes of matrix elements with conditions 24
2.14 Matrix of ones, zeroes, and constants 25
2.15 Inner product, outer product, and array extension 25

Chapter 3
Algebraic, Trigonometric, and Geometric Problems
3.1 Polynomial representation and its roots 27
3.2 Polynomial related computations 29
3.3 Partial fraction in symbolic and coefficient forms 30
3.4 Numerator and denominator from an expression 32
3.5 LCM and GCD of integers and functions 33
3.6 Algebraic substitution and variable elimination 33
3.7 Complete square from an expression 34
3.8 Solving algebraic equations 34
3.9 Expansion of trigonometric functions 37
3.10 Computations of expressions 37
- 3.10.1 Functions of one variable 37
- 3.10.2 Functions of two variables 38

3.11 Geometric problems 39
- 3.11.1 Defining a geometric object 39
- 3.11.2 Area of a geometric object 42
- 3.11.3 Rotation of a geometric object 43
- 3.11.4 Reflection of a geometric object 44
- 3.11.5 Miscellaneous geometric problems 44
- 3.11.6 Help about the geometry package 49

Chapter 4

Matrix Algebra

4.1 Formation of identity and diagonal matrices 51
4.2 Reduced row echelon form of a matrix 52
4.3 Pivoting about an element and minor of a matrix 52
4.4 Adjoint of a square matrix 53
4.5 Gaussian elimination of a matrix 53
4.6 Rank of matrices 53
4.7 Determinant of a square matrix 54
4.8 Power of a square matrix and matrix polynomial 54
4.9 Inverse of a square matrix 54
4.10 Characteristic polynomial and matrix of a square matrix 55
4.11 Eigenvalues and eigenvectors of a square matrix 55
4.12 Basis and null space of some vectors 56
4.13 Singular value decomposition and condition number 57
4.14 Matrix norms and trace 58
4.15 Linearly and logarithmically spaced vectors and normalization 59
4.16 Pseudoinverse of a rectangular matrix 60
4.17 Bilinear and quadratic forms 60
4.18 Orthonormalization of a matrix 61
4.19 Minimal polynomial and matrix exponential of a square matrix 62
4.20 LU triangular factorization of a square matrix 62
4.21 QR decomposition of a matrix 63
4.22 Jordan form decomposition of a square matrix 63
4.23 Cholesky decomposition of a square matrix 64
4.24 Special matrices 65
4.25 Generating equations from coefficient matrices or vice versa 67

Chapter 5

Problems on Differential Calculus

5.1 Limit of a function 69
5.2 Derivatives of polynomials using coefficients 70
5.3 Symbolic differentiation of functions 71
5.4 Partial differentiation of functions 74
5.5 Derivatives of parametric and implicit equations 74
5.6 Taylor series expansion of a function 75
5.7 Jacobian and Hessian matrices of some function 77
5.8 Gradient, divergence, and curl of different fields 78
5.9 Laplacian of a scalar field 80
5.10 Average, arc length, and tangent of a curve 80
5.11 Minimum and maximum from a function 81

Chapter 6

Problems on Integral Calculus

6.1 Symbolic integration of functions 83
    6.1.1 Single indefinite integration 84
    6.1.2 Double indefinite integration 84
    6.1.3 Triple indefinite integration 85
6.2 Symbolic definite integration 85
    6.2.1 Single definite integration 85
    6.2.2 Double definite integration 86
    6.2.3 Triple definite integration 86
6.3 Numerical integration 87
    6.3.1 Single integration 87
    6.3.2 Double integration 87
    6.3.3 Triple integration 88
6.4 Summation of a series 88
6.5 Volume of a solid and surface of revolution 89
6.6 Some integral calculus functions 90

Chapter 7

Ordinary Differential Equations

7.1 Ordinary differential equations 93
7.2 Symbolic solution of ordinary differential equations 94
7.2.1 First order ordinary differential equations 94
7.2.2 Second order ordinary differential equations 95
7.2.3 Higher order ordinary differential equations 95
7.2.4 System of differential equations 96
7.2.5 Nonlinear differential equations 97
7.3 Numerical solution of ordinary differential equations 98
7.3.1 First order differential equations 99
7.3.2 Second order differential equations 100
7.3.3 Higher order differential equations 101
7.3.4 System of differential equations 102
7.3.5 Some factors to be considered for the ODE solution 103
7.3.6 Graphing the ODE solution 104

Chapter 8

Continuous and Discrete Transforms

8.1 What is Fourier analysis? 105
8.2 Fourier series of continuous periodic functions 105
8.2.1 Symbolic Fourier series coefficients 106
8.2.2 Numeric Fourier series coefficients 108
8.2.3 Graphing Fourier series coefficients 109
8.2.4 Reconstruction from Fourier series coefficients 110
8.3 Fourier transform of nonperiodic functions 111
8.3.1 Forward Fourier transform 112
8.3.2 Inverse Fourier transform 113
8.3.3 Graphing the Fourier transform 114
8.4 Discrete Fourier transform of discrete functions 116
8.4.1 Graphing the discrete Fourier transform 117
8.4.2 DFT implications on discrete sine function 118
8.4.3 Half index flipping of the DFT 119
8.5 Laplace transform 121
8.5.1 Forward Laplace transform of continuous functions 121
8.5.2 Inverse Laplace transform 124
8.5.3 Integrodifferential equations using Laplace transform 125
8.6 Z transform 126
8.6.1 Forward Z transform of discrete functions 126
8.6.2 Inverse Z transforms 128
8.6.3 Z transform on difference equations 130

Chapter 9

Problems on Statistics

9.1 Random number generators 131
9.2 Frequency table from positive integers 133
9.3 Mean, geometric mean, and harmonic mean of a sample 133
9.4 Range, variance, and standard deviation of a sample 134
9.5 Mean absolute deviation, median, and moment of a sample 135
9.6 Covariance and correlation of random variables 136
9.7 Probability density functions 139
9.8 Statistics from a given distribution 139
9.9 Cumulative distribution functions 140
9.10 Inverse cumulative distribution functions or critical values 141
9.11 Best-fit straight line/curve of higher degree 141
9.12 Regression analysis 143
9.13 Principal component analysis 143
9.14 Mahalanobis distance 144
9.15 Crosscorrelation of random processes 145
9.16 Help about other statistical functions 146

Chapter 10

Miscellaneous Functions

10.1 Some classical functions 147
10.2 Complex number basics 149
10.3 Complex number based computations 150
10.4 Complex expression computation 153
10.5 Conversion of numbers from one base to other 154
10.6 Dot and cross products of vectors 154
10.7 Inverse of a function 155
10.8 Polynomial interpolation 155
10.9 Orthogonal polynomials 156
10.10 Piecewise continuous function 156
10.11 Set theory functions 157
10.12 Nonperiodic continuous functional data generation 159
10.12.1 Functions from mathematical expressions 159
10.12.2 Functions from graphical representations 160
10.12.3 Functions applying M-file descriptions 162
10.13 Some periodic functional data generation 163

Chapter 11

Problems on Optimizations

11.1 Optimization in symbolic sense 167
11.1.1 Linear objective functions 168
11.1.2 Other objective functions 168
11.2 Optimization in numeric sense 169
11.2.1 Linear programming 169
11.2.2 Quadratic programming 170
11.2.3 M-file based optimization without constraint 171
11.2.4 M-file based optimization with constraint 172
11.2.5 Multiple objective functions with some goals 176
11.2.6 Minimax optimization problems 177
11.2.7 Help about other optimization problems 178

Chapter 12

Partial Differential Equations

12.1 Partial differential equations 179
12.2 Symbolic solution of PDEs 180
12.2.1 First order partial differential equations 180
12.2.2 Second order partial differential equations 181
12.3 Numerical solution of PDEs 182
12.4 PDE with one space variable and time 183
12.4.1 How to write the code of the PDE? 183
12.4.2 Model examples on the PDE 185
12.4.3 Graphing the PDE solution 187
12.5 PDE with two space variables 187
12.5.1 Definition of a second order PDE on implementation context 187
12.5.2 Domain description for the PDE solution 188
12.5.3 Graphical User Interface (GUI) for the PDE solving 190
12.5.4 Model examples on two space variable PDE 196
12.5.5 Nonlinear PDEs with two space variables 199
12.5.6 Accessibility to and graphing the PDE solution 200

Chapter 13

Graphing in MATLAB

13.1 Graphing from symbolic functions 203
13.1.1 Functions of the form $y = f(x)$ 204
13.1.2 Implicit functions of the form $f(x, y) = 0$ 204

13.1.3 Parametric equations of the form $x = f(t)$ and $y = g(t)$ 205
13.1.4 Contour plot from $f(x, y)$ 206
13.1.5 Polar curve of the form $r = f(\theta)$ 207
13.1.6 Surface plot for $f(x, y)$ 207
13.2 Graphing from numerical data 209
13.2.1 y versus x data 209
13.2.2 Multiple y data versus common x data 210
13.2.3 Two dissimilar y data on common x 210
13.2.4 Piecewise continuous functions 211
13.2.5 Contour plot from sampled $f(x, y)$ data 211
13.2.6 Surface plot from sampled $f(x, y)$ data 212
13.2.7 Multiple graphs in the same window 213
13.2.8 Scatter data plot using small circles 214
13.2.9 Discrete function or data plotting using vertical lines 214
13.2.10 Pie chart from some data 215
13.2.11 Logarithmic plots 215
13.2.12 Three dimensional curve plotting 216
13.2.13 Bar graph from some x-y data 216
13.2.14 Intensity image plot of some matrix data 216
13.3 Some troubleshooting while graphing 217

Chapter 14

Programming Issues

14.1 What is an M-file? 221
14.2 MATLAB coding of functions 221
14.3 Control statements of M-file programming 223
14.3.1 Comparative and logical operators 223
14.3.2 Suppressing any execution 224
14.3.3 For-loop syntax 224
14.3.4 Simple if / if-else / nested if syntax 226
14.3.5 User input during the run time of an M-file 227
14.3.6 Switch-case-otherwise syntax 228
14.3.7 While-end syntax 228
14.3.8 Comment on executable statements 229
14.3.9 Break statement 229
14.3.10 String and its related functions 229
14.4 Three dimensional, structure, and cell arrays 230
14.4.1 Three dimensional arrays 230
14.4.2 Structure arrays 232
14.4.3 Cell arrays 233
14.5 Creating a function file 235
14.6 Saving, importing, and exporting data 236

Appendix A. MATLAB functions exercised in the text 239
Appendix B. Some symbols presented in the text 245
References 246
Subject Index 248

Chapter 1

MATLAB is a computational software, which offers the quickest and easiest way to compute the scientific and technical problems and visualize the solutions. As worldly standard for the simulation and analysis, engineers, scientists, and researchers are becoming more and more affiliated with MATLAB. The general questionnaires about the MATLAB platform before one gets started with are the contents of this chapter. We explain some introductory features of the package when one starts navigating in MATLAB. Our highlight covers the following:

- MATLAB and its features found in the MATLAB command window
- The easiest and quickest way to get started in MATLAB beginning from scratch
- Frequently encountered questions when one starts working in MATLAB environment
- Different forms of assistance about MATLAB and the implanted functions in it

1.1 What is MATLAB?

MATLAB is mainly a scientific and technical computing software whose elaboration is matrix laboratory. The command prompt of MATLAB (>>) provides an interactive system. In the workspace of MATLAB, most data element is dealt as a matrix without dimensioning. The package is incredibly advantageous for the matrix-oriented computations. MATLAB's easy-to-use platform enables us to compute and manipulate matrices, perform numerical analysis, and visualize different variety of one/two/three dimensional graphics in a matter of second or seconds without conventional programming in FORTRAN, PASCAL, or C.

1.2 MATLAB's opening window features

If you do not have MATLAB installed in your personal computer, contact MathWorks (owner and developer, www.mathworks.com) for the installation CD. If you know how to get in MATLAB and its basics, you can skip the chapter. Assuming the package is installed in your system, run MATLAB from the Start of the Microsoft Windows. Let us get familiarized with MATLAB's opening window features. Figure 1.1(a) shows a typical firstly opened MATLAB window. Depending on the desktop setting or MATLAB version, your MATLAB window may not look like the figure 1.1(a) but the descriptions of the features by and large are appropriate.

❖❖ Command prompt of MATLAB

Command prompt means that you tell MATLAB to do something from here. As an interactive system, MATLAB responds to user through this prompt. MATLAB cursor will be blinking after >> prompt once you open MATLAB that says MATLAB is ready to take your commands. To enter any command, type executable MATLAB statements from keyboard and to execute that, press the Enter key (the symbol ↵ for the 'Hit the Enter Key' operation).

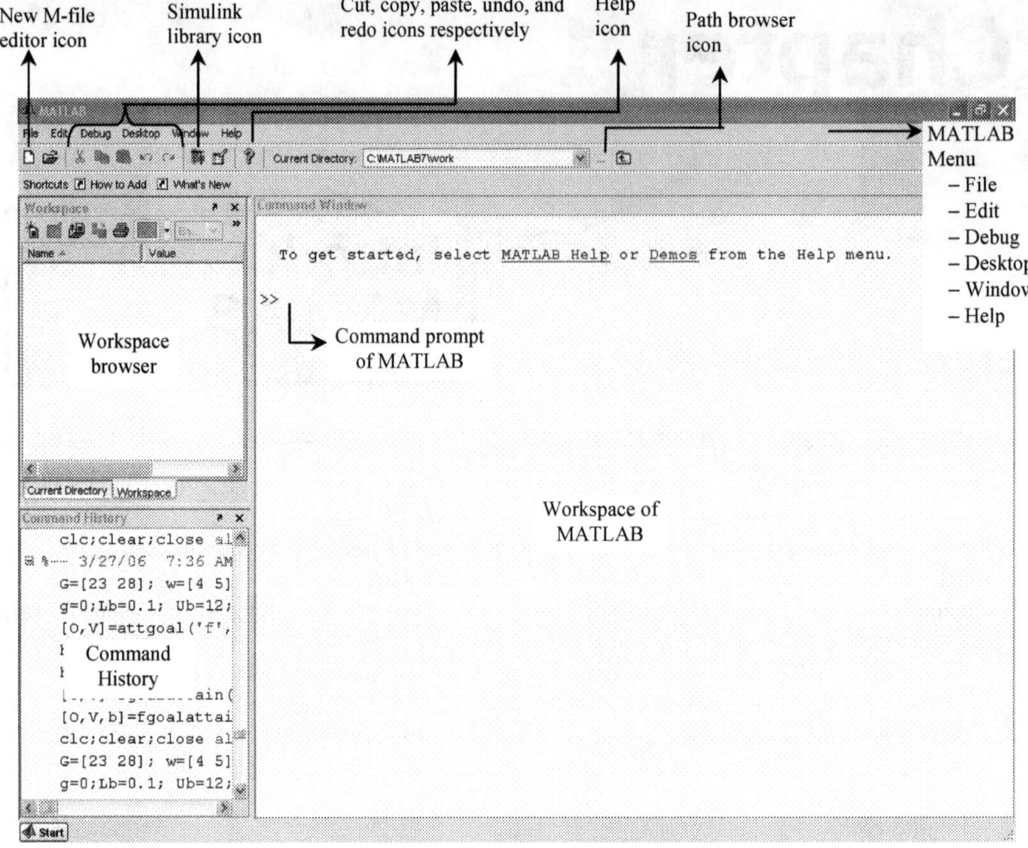

Figure 1.1(a) Typical features of MATLAB's firstly opened window

❖❖ MATLAB Menu

MATLAB is accompanied with six submenus namely File, Edit, Debug, Desktop, Window, and Help. Each submenu has its own features. Use the mouse to click different submenus and their brief descriptions are as follows:

Submenu File: It (figure 1.1(b)) opens a new M-file, figure, model, or Graphical User Interface (GUI) layout maker, opens a file which was saved before, loads a saved workspace, imports data from a file, saves the workspace variables, sets the required path to execute a file, prints the workspace, and keeps the provision for changing the command window property.

Submenu Edit: The second submenu Edit (figure 1.1(c)) includes cutting, copying, pasting, undoing, and clearing operations. These operations are useful when you frequently work at the command prompt.

Submenu Debug: The submenu Debug (figure 1.1(d)) is mainly related with the text mode or M-file programming.

Figure 1.1(b) Submenu File

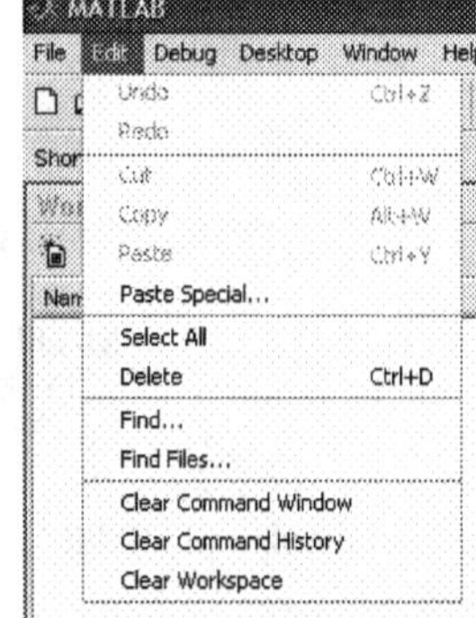

Figure 1.1(c) Submenu Edit

Submenu Desktop: The fourth submenu Desktop (figure 1.1(e)) is accompanied with MATLAB command window viewing functions such as displaying the workspace variable information, current directory information, command history, etc.

Submenu Window: You may open some graphics window from MATLAB command prompt or running some M-files. From the fifth submenu Window (figure 1.1(f)), one can see how many graphics window under MATLAB are open and can switch from one window to another clicking the mouse to the required window.

Submenu Help: MATLAB holds abundant help facilities. The last submenu shows Help (figure 1.1(g)) in different ways. Latter in this chapter, we mention how one gets specific help. The submenu also provides the easiness to get connected with the MathWorks Website assuming that your system is connected with Internet.

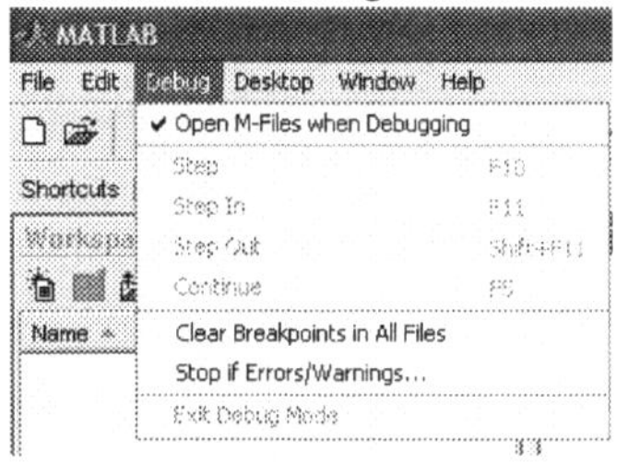

Figure 1.1(d) Submenu Debug

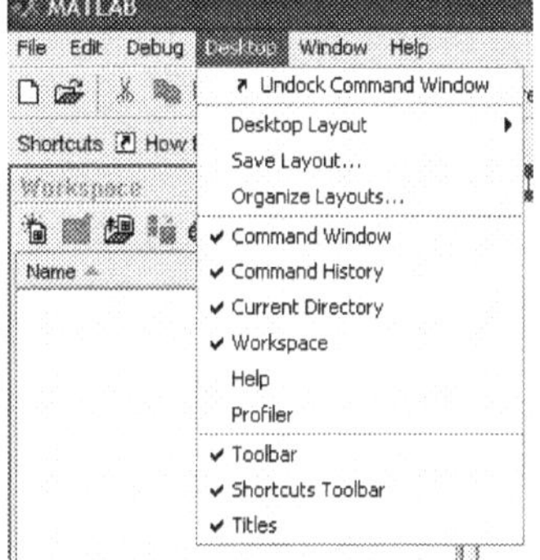

Figure 1.1(e) Submenu Desktop

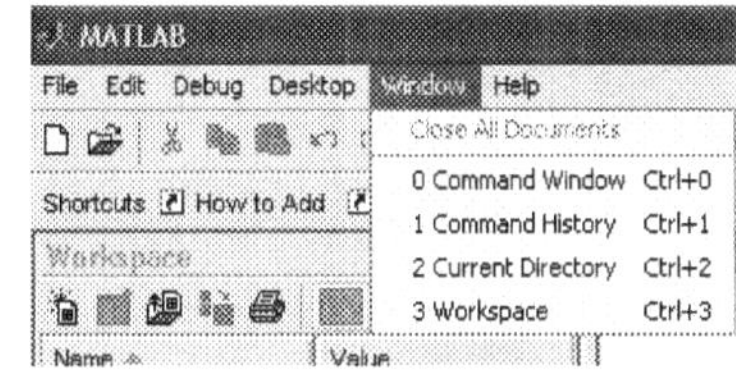

Figure 1.1(f) Submenu Window

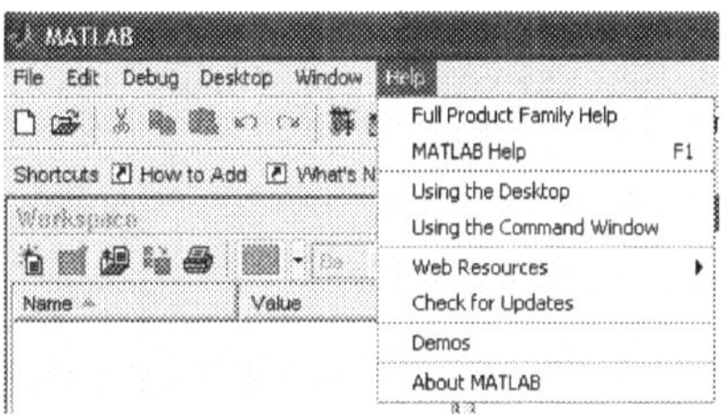

Figure 1.1(g) Submenu Help

❖ Icons

Available icons are shown in the icon bar (down the menu bar) of the figure 1.1(a). Frequently used operations such as opening a new file, opening an existing file, getting help, etc are found in the icon bar so that the user does not have to go through the menu bar over and over.

❖ MATLAB workspace

Workspace (figure 1.1(a)) is the platform of MATLAB where one executes MATLAB commands. During execution of commands, one may have to deal with some input and output variables. These variables can be one-dimensional array, multi-dimensional array, characters, symbolic objects, etc. Again to deal with graphics window, we have texts, graphics, or object handles. Workspace holds all those variables or handles for you. As a subwindow of the figure 1.1(a), its browser exhibits the types or properties of those variables or handles. If the browser is not seen in the opening window of MATLAB, click the Desktop down Workspace to bring the subwindow (figure 1.1(e)).

❖ MATLAB command history

There is a subwindow in the figure 1.1(a) called Command History which holds all previously used commands at the command prompt. Depending on the desktop setting, it may or may not appear during the opening of MATLAB. If it is not, click the Command History from the figure 1.1(e) under the Desktop.

1.3 How to get started?

New MATLAB users face a common question how one gets started in MATLAB. This tutorial is for the beginners in MATLAB. Here we address the terms under the following bold headings.

❖ How one can enter a vector/matrix

The first step is the user has to be in the command window of MATLAB. Look for the command prompt >> in the command window. One can type anything from the keyboard at the command prompt. Row or column matrices are termed as vectors. We intend to enter the row matrix R=[2 3 4 −2 0] into the workspace of MATLAB. Type the following from the keyboard at the command prompt:

>>R=[2 3 4 -2 0] ← Arial font set is used for the executable commands in the whole text i.e. R⇔R

There is one space gap between two elements of the matrix R but no space gap at the edge elements. All elements are placed under the [ ]. Press Enter key after the third brace] from the keyboard and we see

```
R =
      2   3   4  -2   0
>>
```

← command prompt is ready again

It means we assigned the row matrix to the workspace variable R. Whenever we call R, MATLAB understands the whole row matrix. Matrix R is having five elements. Even if R had 100 elements, it would understand the whole matrix that is one of many appreciative features of MATLAB. Next we wish to enter the column matrix C= $\begin{bmatrix} 7 \\ 8 \\ 10 \\ -11 \end{bmatrix}$. Again type the following from the keyboard at the blinking cursor:

>>C=[7;8;10;-11] ↵ you will see (↵ means 'Press the Enter Key'),

```
C =
    7
    8
   10
  −11
>>                     ← command prompt is ready again
```

This time we also assigned the column matrix to the workspace variable C. For the column matrix, there is one semicolon ; between two consecutive elements of the matrix C but no space gap is necessary. As another option, the matrix C could have been entered by writing C=[7 8 10 -11]'. The operator ' of the keyboard is the matrix transposition operator in MATLAB. As if you entered a row matrix but at the end just the transpose operator ' is attached. After that the rectangular matrix $A=\begin{bmatrix} 20 & 6 & 7 \\ 5 & 12 & -3 \\ 1 & -1 & 0 \\ 19 & 3 & 2 \end{bmatrix}$ is to be entered:

>>A=[20 6 7;5 12 -3;1 -1 0;19 3 2] ↵ you will see,

```
A =

    20    6    7
     5   12   −3
     1   −1    0
    19    3    2
```

Two consecutive rows of A are separated by semicolon ; and consecutive elements in a row are separated by one space gap. Instead of typing all elements in a row, one can type the first row, press Enter key, the cursor blinks in the next line, type the second row, and so on.

♦♦ How one can use the colon and semicolon operators

The operators semicolon ; and colon : have special significance in MATLAB. Most MATLAB statements and M-file programming use these two operators almost in every line. Generation of vectors can easily be performed by the colon operator no matter how many elements we need. Let us carry out the following at the command prompt to see the importance of the colon operator:

>>A=1:4 ↵ you will see,

```
A =

    1   2   3   4
```

← We created a vector A or row matrix where A=[1 2 3 4]

Let us interact with MATLAB by the following commands:

>>R=1:3:10 ↵ you will see,

```
R =

    1   4   7   10
```

← We created a vector or row matrix R whose elements form an arithmetic progression with first element 1, last element 10, and common difference or increment 3

Vector with decrement can also be generated:

>>C=[0:-2:-10]' ↵ you will see,

```
C =

     0
    −2
    −4
    −6
    −8
   −10
```

← We created a vector or column matrix C whose consecutive elements have the decrement 2 with the first element 0 and the last element −10

MATLAB is also capable of producing vectors whose elements are decimal numbers. Let us form a row matrix R whose first element is 3, last element is 6, and increment is 0.5 and which we accomplish as follows:

>>R=3:0.5:6 ↵ you will see,

```
R =

   3.0000   3.5000   4.0000   4.5000   5.0000   5.5000   6.0000
```

The reader is referred to section 2.6 for more about the colon operator. Then, what is the use of the semicolon operator? Append a semicolon at the end in the last command and execute that:

>>R=3:0.5:6; ↵ you will see,

>> ← Assignment is not shown

Type R at the command prompt and press Enter:

```
>>R ↵

R =
        3.0000   3.5000   4.0000   4.5000   5.0000   5.5000   6.0000
```

It indicates that the semicolon operator prevents MATLAB from displaying the contents of the workspace variable R.

◆◆ How one can call a built-in MATLAB function

In MATLAB, thousands of M-files or built-in function files are functioning. Knowing the descriptions of the function, the numbers of input and output arguments, and the nature of the arguments is mandatory in order to execute a built-in function file at the command prompt. Let us start with a simplest example. We intend to find $\sin x$ for $x=\frac{3\pi}{2}$ which should be −1. The MATLAB counterpart (section 14.2) of $\sin x$ is sin(x) where x can be any real or complex number in radians and can be a matrix too. The angle $\frac{3\pi}{2}$ is written as 3*pi/2(π is coded by pi) and let us perform it as follows:

```
>>sin(3*pi/2) ↵

ans =
        -1
```

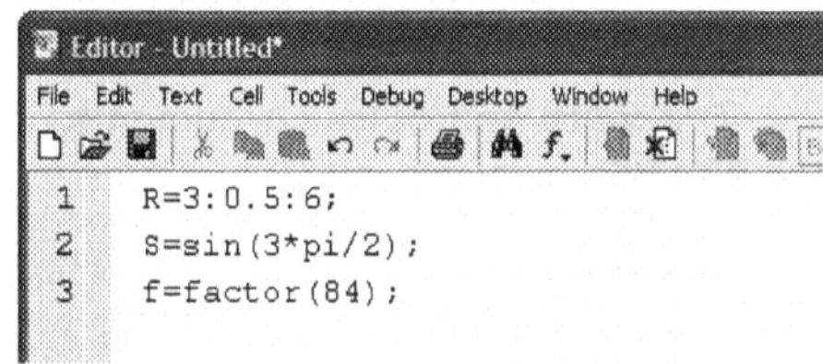

Figure 1.2(a) Last three executed statements are typed in the M-file editor of MATLAB

By default the return from any function is assigned to workspace ans. If you wanted to assign the return to S, you would write S=sin(3*pi/2);. As another example, let us factorize the integer 84 (84=2×2×3×7). The MATLAB built-in function factor finds the factors of an integer and the implementation is as follows:

```
>>f=factor(84) ↵

f =
        2   2   3   7
```

The output of the factor is a row matrix which we assigned to workspace f in fact the f can be any user-given name. Thus you can call any other built-in function from the command prompt provided that you have the knowledge about the calling of inputs to and outputs from the function.

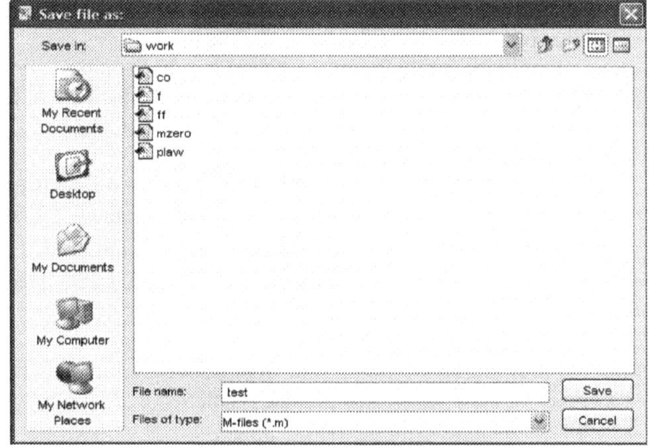

Figure 1.2(b) Save dialog window for naming the M-file

◆◆ How one can open and execute an M-file

This is the most important start up for the beginners. An M-file can be regarded as a text or script file. A collection of executable MATLAB statements are the contents of an M-file. Ongoing discussion made you familiarize with entering a matrix, computing a sine value, and factorizing an integer. These three executions took place at the command prompt. They can be executed from an M-file as well. This necessitates opening the M-file editor. Referring to the figure 1.1(b), you find the link for the M-file editor as **File → New → M-file** and click it to see the new untitled M-file editor. Another option is click the New M-file editor icon of the figure 1.1(a). However after opening the new M-file editor, we type the last three executable statements in the untitled file as shown in the figure 1.2(a). The next step is to save the untitled file clicking the Save icon or from the File Menu of the M-file editor window. Figure 1.2(b) presents the File Save dialog window. We type the file name as the test (can be any name of your choice) in the slot of the File name in the window. The M-file has the file extension .m but we do not type .m only the file name is enough. After saving the file, let us move on to the MATLAB command prompt and conduct the following:

>>test ↵

>> ← command prompt is ready again

It indicates that MATLAB executed the M-file by the name test and is ready for the next command. We can check calling the assignees whether the previously performed executions occurred exactly as follows:

```
>>R ↵

R =
     3.0000   3.5000   4.0000   4.5000   5.0000   5.5000   6.0000
>>S ↵

S =
     -1
```

```
>>f ↵

f =
     2   2   3   7
```

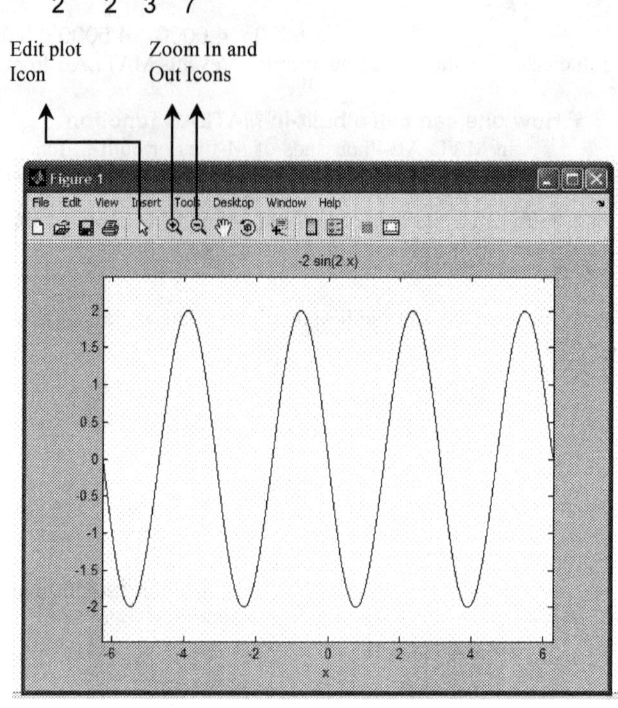

Figure 1.2(c) Graph of $-2\sin 2x$ versus x

This is what we found before. Thus one can run any executable statements in the M-file. The reader might ask in which folder or path the file **test** was saved. Figure 1.1(a) shows one slot for the Current Directory in the upper middle portion of the window. That is the location of your file. If you want to save the M-file in other folder or directory, change your path clicking the path browser icon (figure 1.1(a)) before saving the file. When you call the **test** or any other file from the command prompt of MATLAB, the command prompt must be in the same directory where the file is in or its path must be defined to MATLAB.

◆◆ The input and output arguments of a function file

MATLAB is a collection of thousands of M-files. Some files just execute the command without any return and some return results which are called function files (section 14.5). You have seen the use of function sin(x) before which has one input argument x. The statement test(x,y) means that the test is a function file which has two input arguments – x and y. Again the test(x,y,z) means the test is a function file which needs three input arguments – x, y, and z. Similar style also follows for the return but under the third brace. The [a,b]=test(x,y) means there are two output arguments from the test which are a and b and the [a,b,c]=test(x,y) means three returns from the test which are a, b, and c.

◆◆ How one can plot a graph

MATLAB is very convenient for plotting different sorts of graphs. The graphs are plotted either from the mathematical expression or from the data. Let us plot the function $y = -2\sin 2x$. The MATLAB function **ezplot** plots y versus x type graph taking the expression as its input argument. The MATLAB code (section 14.2) for the function $-2\sin 2x$ is -2*sin(2*x). The functional code is input argumented using the single inverted comma hence we conduct the following at the command prompt:

```
>>ezplot('-2*sin(2*x)') ↵
```

Figure 1.2(c) presents the outcome from above execution. The window in which the graph is plotted is called the MATLAB figure window. Any graphics is plotted in the figure window, which has its own menu (such as File, Edit, etc) as shown in the figure 1.2(c).

1.4 Some queries about MATLAB environment

Users need to know the answers to some questions when they start working in MATLAB. Some MATLAB environment related queries are presented as follows:

How can I change the numeric format?

When you perform any computation at the command prompt, the output is returned up to the four decimal display due to the short numeric format which is the default one. There are other numeric formats also. To reach the numeric format dialog box, the clicking operation sequence is MATLAB command window ⇒ File ⇒ Preferences ⇒ Command Window ⇒ Numeric Format under Text Display ⇒ popup menu for different options available.

How can I change the font or background color settings?

One might be interested to change the background color or font color while working in the command window. The clicking sequence is MATLAB command window ⇒ File ⇒ Preferences ⇒ Fonts or Colors.

How can I delete some/all variables from the workspace?

In order to delete all variables present in the workspace, the clicking sequence is MATLAB command window ⇒ Edit ⇒ Clear Workspace (figure 1.1(c)). If you want to delete a particular workspace variable, select the concern variable in the workspace browser (assuming it is open like the figure 1.2(d)) using the mouse pointer and then rightclick ⇒ delete.

How can I clear workspace but not the variables?

Once you conduct some sessions at the command prompt, monitor screen keeps all interactive sessions. You can clear the screen contents without removing the variables present in the workspace by the command clc or performing the clicking operation MATLAB command window ⇒ Edit ⇒ Clear Command Window (figure 1.1(c)).

How can I know the current path?

In the upper portion of the figure 1.1(a), the current directory bar is located which indicates in which path the command prompt is in or execute cd (abbreviation for the current directory) at the command prompt.

How can I see different variables in the workspace?

There are two ways of viewing this – either use the command who or look at the workspace browser (like figure 1.2(d)) which exhibits information about workspace variables for example R is the name of the variable which holds some values and their data class is double precision. One can view, change, or edit the contents of a variable by doubleclicking the concern variables situated in the workspace browser as conducted in Microsoft Excel.

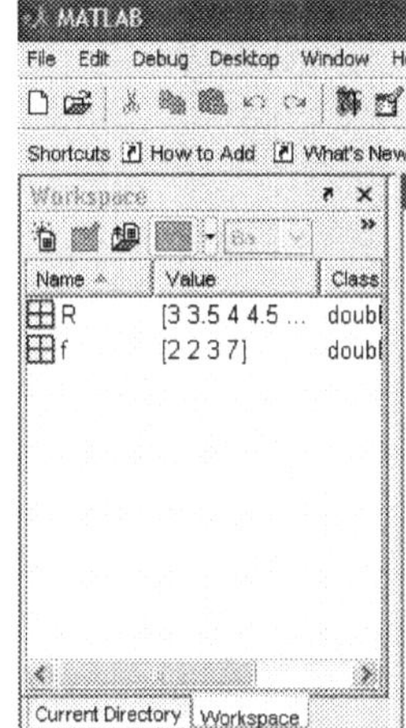

Figure 1.2(d) Workspace browser displays the variable information

How can I enter a long command line?

MATLAB statements can be too long to fit in one line. Giving a break in the middle of a statement is accomplished by the ellipsis (three dots are called ellipsis). We show that considering the entering of the vector x=[1:3:10]; as follows:

```
>>x=[1:3: ... ↵
          10] ↵
x =
          1    4    7    10
```

Typing takes place in two lines and there is one space gap before the ellipsis.

Editing at the command prompt

This is advantageous specially for them who work frequently in the command window without opening an M-file. Keyboard has different arrow keys marked by ← ↑ → ↓. One may type a misspelled command at the command prompt causing error message to appear. Instead of retyping the entire line, press uparrow (for previous line) or downarrow (for next line) to edit the MATLAB statement. Or you can reuse any past statement this way. For example, we generate a row vector 1 to 10 with increment 2 and assign the vector to x. The necessary command is x=1:2:10. Mistakenly you typed x+1:2:10. The response is as follows:

```
>>x+1:2:10 ↵
??? Undefined function or variable 'x'.
```

You discovered the mistake and want to correct that. Press ↑ key to see,

```
>>x+1:2:10
```

Edit the command going to the + sign using the left arrow key or mouse pointer. At the prompt, if you type x and press ↑ again and again, you see the used commands that start with x.

Saving and loading data

User can save workspace variables or data in a binary file having the extension .mat. Suppose you have the matrix A= $\begin{bmatrix} 3 & 4 & 8 \\ 0 & 2 & 1 \end{bmatrix}$ and wish to save A in a file by the name data.mat. Let us carry out the following:

>>A=[3 4 8;0 2 1]; ↵ ← Assigning the A to A

Now move on to the workspace browser (figure 1.2(d)) and you see the variable A including its information located in the subwindow. Bring the mouse pointer on the A, rightclick the mouse, and click the Save As. The Save dialog window appears and type only data (not the data.mat) in the slot of File name. If it is necessary, you can save all workspace variables using the same action but clicking File ⇒ Save Workspace As (figure 1.1(b)). One can retrieve the data file by clicking the menu File ⇒ Import Data (figure 1.1(b)). Another option is use the command load data at the command prompt.

How can I delete a file from the command prompt?

Let us delete just mentioned data.mat executing the command delete data.mat at the command prompt.

How can I see the data held in a variable?

Figure 1.2(d) presents some variable information in which you find A. Doubleclick A in the workspace browser and you find the matrix contents of A in a data sheet.

1.5 How to get help?

Help facilities in MATLAB are plentiful. One can access to information about a function file or topic in a variety of ways. Command **help** finds the help of a particular function file. You are familiar with the function **sin(x)** from earlier discussion and can have the MATLAB online help regarding **sin(x)** as follows:

```
>>help sin ↵

SIN   Sine.
        SIN(X) is the sine of the elements of X.

        See also asin, sind.

        Overloaded functions or methods (ones with the same name in other directories)
        help sym/sin.m

        Reference page in Help browser
        doc sin
```

One disadvantage of this method is that the user has to know the exact file name of a function. For a novice, this facility may not be appreciative. Casually we know a partial name of a function or try to check whether a function exists by that name. Suppose we intend to see whether any function by the name **eye** exists. We execute the following by the intermediacy of the command **lookfor** (no space gap between **look** and **for**) to see all possible functions bearing the file name **eye** or having the file name **eye** partly:

```
>>lookfor  eye ↵
 EYE Identity matrix.
 SPEYE  Sparse identity matrix.
 EYEDIAGRAM Generate an eye diagram.
      ⋮
```

The return is having all possible matches of functions containing the word **eye**. Now the command **help** can be conducted to go through a particular one for example the first one is **EYE** and we execute **help EYE** at the command prompt.

In order to have Window form help, click different windows of the pulldown menu of the figure 1.1(g). Make sure you have the full Help CD installed in your system. Any help item preceded by a bullet can be clicked to go inside the item. This help form is better when one navigates MATLAB's capability not looking for a particular function.

MATLAB has its own **Start** button (located at the lower left corner of the command window) like the Microsoft Windows. To reach to the academic discipline based toolbox help, the clicking sequence is **Start** ⇒ **Toolboxes** ⇒ **Name of the toolbox**.

If you just execute **help** at the command prompt, you find the names of dozens of libraries implanted in MATLAB as follows:

```
>>help ↵
HELP topics

matlab\general        - General purpose commands.
matlab\ops            - Operators and special characters.
matlab\lang           - Programming language constructs.
matlab\elmat          - Elementary matrices and matrix manipulation.
matlab\elfun          - Elementary math function
                ⋮
```

MATLAB exhibits a long list of libraries in which we find one by the name **elmat**. In order to know about the functions hidden under **elmat**, we execute **help elmat** at the command prompt to see the following:

```
>>help elmat  ↵
Elementary matrices and matrix manipulation.

Elementary matrices.
zeros       - Zeros array.
ones        - Ones array.
eye         - Identity matrix.
            ⋮
```

There is a function by the name **eye** in the displayed list so we execute **help eye** to know about it.

Hidden algorithm or mathematical expression is often necessary which we can have from MathWorks Website through the search option provided that our PC is connected to the Internet (figure 1.1(g)).

However we close the introductory discussion on MATLAB with this.

Chapter 2

This chapter illustrates simple computational operations on matrices. Matrices are nothing but the rectangular arrays of numbers which can be real, integer, complex, or symbolic variables set out in rows and columns. In MATLAB a matrix is a variable on which all manipulations, computations, and visualizations are conducted. In order to have manipulative skill, the reader is supplied with numerical examples on each type of matrix – row, column, and rectangular. Despite a row and a column matrices are the special case of a rectangular matrix, implementations of row and column matrices may require different or simpler form of functional representations. Usefulness of these simple operations is realized when one writes an M-file program describing a practical problem. Matrix size does not affect the concept or procedure, only it does the amount of computing that is involved. However we have tried to outline the following:

- Matrix addition, subtraction, and multiplication along with simple matrix arithmetic
- Different types of data flipping and power operations on matrix elements
- Indexing and coloning of arrays which are extremely vital to MATLAB context
- Appending, deleting, and modifying matrix elements on a variety of situations
- Summing, producting, maximum or minimum finding, etc on matrix elements

2.1 Matrix addition and subtraction

Matrix addition or subtraction is the basic arithmetic of matrices in MATLAB. The addition or subtraction happens for identical size matrices. Let us say the element by element additions of two row matrices $A=[1 \quad 2 \quad 3]$ and $B=[9 \quad 3 \quad -7]$ is $C=A+B=[10 \quad 5 \quad -4]$, two column matrices $A=\begin{bmatrix} x \\ 9 \\ 10 \end{bmatrix}$ and $B=\begin{bmatrix} 5 \\ 3 \\ 8 \end{bmatrix}$ is $C=A+B=\begin{bmatrix} x+5 \\ 12 \\ 18 \end{bmatrix}$, and two rectangular matrices $A=\begin{bmatrix} 7 & 4 & 2 \\ 9 & 0 & 1 \\ 10 & 9 & 3 \end{bmatrix}$ and $B=\begin{bmatrix} 5 & 7 & 9 \\ 3 & 1 & 0 \\ 8 & 3 & 0 \end{bmatrix}$ is $C=A+B=\begin{bmatrix} 12 & 11 & 11 \\ 12 & 1 & 1 \\ 18 & 12 & 3 \end{bmatrix}$. We perform the said additions as follows:

for the addition of row matrices,

```
>>A=[1 2 3]; ↵
>>B=[9 3 -7]; ↵
>>C=A+B ↵

C=
        10    5   -4
```

for the column matrices,

```
>>syms x ↵
>>A=[x;9;10]; B=[5;3;8]; ↵
>>C=A+B ↵

C =

 x+5
  12
  18
```

for the rectangular matrices,

```
>>A=[7 4 2;9 0 1;10 9 3]; ↵
>>B=[5 7 9;3 1 0;8 3 0]; ↵
>>C=A+B ↵

C =

  12   11   11
  12    1    1
  18   12    3
```

In each case first we assign the matrix to be added (which are A and B) to workspace A and B respectively and then the addition is performed by the operator + and the result is assigned to workspace C. If the matrix sizes are not identical, MATLAB prints an error message. The elements in the matrix can be integer, fractional, or even complex numbers. In the row and rectangular matrices, the elements are all numeric. But the column matrix B contains a symbolic element x which is rather an object than a number. For this kind of matrix data, we declare the symbolic variable x before entering the data writing the command syms x. Functions which are in symbolic toolbox and maple (execute help symbolic or maple to learn more about them) work on symbolic variables. If there were two symbolic data variables such as x and y, we would write syms x y before the assignment to A or B.

What if we have the matrix elements that are rational numbers and output matrix data intended to be in rational form too for example $A = \begin{bmatrix} \frac{3}{4} & \frac{4}{5} & -\frac{2}{3} \\ \frac{1}{7} & \frac{9}{5} & \frac{5}{9} \end{bmatrix}$ and $B = \begin{bmatrix} \frac{4}{7} & \frac{8}{3} & \frac{2}{3} \\ \frac{3}{4} & \frac{9}{7} & -\frac{1}{9} \end{bmatrix}$ from which $C = A + B = \begin{bmatrix} \frac{37}{28} & \frac{52}{15} & 0 \\ \frac{25}{28} & \frac{108}{35} & \frac{4}{9} \end{bmatrix}$ (implementation is shown above).

```
>>A=sym([3/4 4/5 -2/3;1/7 9/5 5/9]); ↵ ← Assigning the matrix data of A to A
>>B=sym([4/7 8/3 2/3;3/4 9/7 -1/9]); ↵ ← Assigning the matrix data of B to B
>>C=A+B ↵

C =

[ 37/28,   52/15,      0]
[ 25/28,  108/35,    4/9]
```

Any decimal or integer numeric matrix data can be turned to a symbolic object matrix data using the command sym. Actually x=sym('x') is equivalent to syms x – a shortcut way of declaring symbolic objects or independent variable in an expression or matrix. Also the sym turns a decimal data to rational form for example sym(4.2) returns the rational number 21/5.

♦♦ Matrix subtraction

Element by element subtraction of identical size matrices is similar to that of the addition. The subtraction of earlier mentioned B from A should provide us [–8 –1 10], $\begin{bmatrix} x-5 \\ 6 \\ 2 \end{bmatrix}$, and $\begin{bmatrix} 2 & -3 & -7 \\ 6 & -1 & 1 \\ 2 & 6 & 3 \end{bmatrix}$ for the row, column, and rectangular matrices respectively. The operator - performs the subtraction therefore the command needs to be exercised for each of the three cases is C=A-B. The subtraction of the rational number matrices is also implementable in a similar fashion.

2.2 Matrix multiplication

Two matrix or array multiplications, namely scalar and vector, are commonly practiced in MATLAB whose discussions follow next.

♦♦ Scalar multiplication of two identical size matrices

Scalar multiplication is important in the sense that major multiplicative data handling in MATLAB happens in scalar form. The scalar multiplication of two identical size matrices is performed by the operator .* which essentially computes the element by element multiplication on the like positional elements of both matrices.

Let us say we have two row matrices A =[1 2 3] and B =[9 3 –7] whose scalar multiplication is C =[9 6 –21]. Again the scalar multiplications of two column matrices $A = \begin{bmatrix} x \\ 2y \\ 10 \end{bmatrix}$ and $B = \begin{bmatrix} 5 \\ 3 \\ 8 \end{bmatrix}$ is $C = \begin{bmatrix} 5x \\ 6y \\ 80 \end{bmatrix}$ and two rectangular matrices $A = \begin{bmatrix} 7 & 4 & 2 \\ 9 & 0 & 1 \\ 10 & 9 & 3 \end{bmatrix}$ and $B = \begin{bmatrix} 5 & 7 & 9 \\ 3 & 1 & 0 \\ 8 & 3 & 0 \end{bmatrix}$ is $C = \begin{bmatrix} 35 & 28 & 18 \\ 27 & 0 & 0 \\ 80 & 27 & 0 \end{bmatrix}$.

The placement order for A and B is immaterial that is A.*B or B.*A would produce the same result. The operator works even if the matrix elements are all rational numbers and the multiplied output is wanted in rational number for example scalar multiplication of $A=\begin{bmatrix}\frac{3}{4} & \frac{4}{5} & -\frac{2}{3}\\ \frac{1}{7} & \frac{9}{5} & \frac{5}{9}\end{bmatrix}$ and $B=\begin{bmatrix}\frac{4}{7} & \frac{8}{3} & \frac{2}{3}\\ \frac{3}{4} & \frac{9}{7} & -\frac{1}{9}\end{bmatrix}$ provides $C=\begin{bmatrix}\frac{3}{7} & \frac{32}{15} & -\frac{4}{9}\\ \frac{3}{28} & \frac{81}{35} & -\frac{5}{81}\end{bmatrix}$. MATLAB executions for all scalar multiplications are attached on the right. Font equivalence is maintained using the same letter for example A⇔ A.

All scalar multiplications:

for the column matrices,

```
>>syms x y ↵
>>A=[x;2*y;10]; ↵
>>B=[5;3;8]; ↵
>>C=A.*B ↵

C =

 5*x
 6*y
  80
```

for the rectangular matrices,

```
>>A=[7 4 2;9 0 1;10 9 3]; ↵
>>B=[5 7 9;3 1 0;8 3 0]; ↵
>>C=A.*B ↵

C =
      35   28   18
      27    0    0
      80   27    0
```

for the row matrices,

```
>>A=[1 2 3]; B=[9 3 -7]; ↵
>>C=A.*B ↵

C =
      9    6  -21
```

for the rational form rectangular matrices:

```
>>A=sym([3/4 4/5 -2/3;1/7 9/5 5/9]); ↵
>>B=sym([4/7 8/3 2/3;3/4 9/7 -1/9]); ↵
>>C=A.*B ↵

C =

[  3/7,   32/15,   -4/9 ]
[ 3/28,   81/35,  -5/81 ]
```

⬍⬍ Vector multiplication of two matrices

In general a matrix A of order $m \times n$ can be multiplied with another matrix B of order $n \times p$. In MATLAB the vector multiplication is defined by the operator *. If the vector multiplication of A and B is C, the order of C must be $m \times p$.

A row matrix $A=[2\quad -9\quad 7\quad -3]$ of order 1×4 can only be multiplied with B with exactly 4 rows (but any number of columns) for example $B=\begin{bmatrix}-1 & 1 & -1\\ -3 & 2 & 0\\ 7 & 3 & 2\\ 0 & 4 & 0\end{bmatrix}$ whose vector multiplication is given by $A\times B=[2\quad -9\quad 7\quad -3]\times\begin{bmatrix}-1 & 1 & -1\\ -3 & 2 & 0\\ 7 & 3 & 2\\ 0 & 4 & 0\end{bmatrix}=[74\quad -7\quad 12]$ where $m=1$, $n=4$, and $p=3$. Some other examples are in the following:

first matrix: column matrix $A=\begin{bmatrix}-1\\ -3\\ 7\end{bmatrix}$, second matrix: $B=[-x\quad 2]$, and $A\times B=\begin{bmatrix}x & -2\\ 3x & -6\\ -7x & 14\end{bmatrix}$,

first matrix $A=\begin{bmatrix}7 & 4 & 9\\ 9 & 0 & 2\end{bmatrix}$, second matrix $B=\begin{bmatrix}5 & 7\\ 3 & 1\\ 2 & 0\end{bmatrix}$, and $A\times B=\begin{bmatrix}65 & 53\\ 49 & 63\end{bmatrix}$, and

first matrix $A=\begin{bmatrix}\frac{3}{4} & \frac{4}{5}\\ \frac{1}{7} & \frac{9}{5}\end{bmatrix}$, second matrix $B=\begin{bmatrix}\frac{4}{7} & \frac{8}{3}\\ \frac{3}{4} & \frac{9}{7}\end{bmatrix}$, and $A\times B=\begin{bmatrix}\frac{36}{35} & \frac{106}{35}\\ \frac{1403}{980} & \frac{283}{105}\end{bmatrix}$.

All vector multiplications conducted in MATLAB are shown below (font equivalence is maintained using the same letter for example A⇔ A):

for vector multiplication of row matrix (first matrix),

```
>>A=[2 -9 7 -3]; ↵
>>B=[-1 1 -1;-3 2 0;7 3 2;0 4 0]; ↵
>>C=A*B ↵

C=
      74  -7  12
```

for rational number rectangular matrices,

```
>>A=sym([3/4 4/5;1/7 9/5]); ↵
>>B=sym([4/7 8/3;3/4 9/7]); ↵
>>C=A*B ↵

C=

[     36/35,     106/35  ]
```

for column matrix (first matrix),

```
>>syms x ↵
>>A=[-1 -3 7]'; ↵
>>B=[-x 2]; ↵
>>C=A*B ↵

C=

[     x,     -2]
[   3*x,     -6]
[  -7*x,     14]
```

for both rectangular matrices,

```
>>A=[7 4 9;9 0 2]; ↵
>>B=[5 7;3 1;2 0]; ↵
>>C=A*B ↵
```

[1403/980, 283/105]

C=

65 53
49 63

2.3 Simple matrix arithmetic

The reader is referred to the section 14.2 for the arithmetic operator reference. We address matrix based simple arithmetic in the following on the fact that the basic computational element in MATLAB is a matrix.

♦♦ Adding a scalar to each element in a matrix

Assume that 4, $-x$, and 8 are to be added with all elements of the row matrix $R=[2 \quad -9 \quad 1 \quad 4 \quad 8]$, column matrix $C=\begin{bmatrix}-3\\14\\15\end{bmatrix}$, and rectangular matrix $A=\begin{bmatrix}-3 & 1\\14 & 3\\15 & 1\end{bmatrix}$ respectively. Following the addition, the matrices are going to be [6 –5 5 8 12], $\begin{bmatrix}-3-x\\14-x\\15-x\end{bmatrix}$, and $\begin{bmatrix}5 & 9\\22 & 11\\23 & 9\end{bmatrix}$ for R, C, and A respectively whose implementations are the following (font equivalence is maintained using the same letter for example A⇔A and all addition is assigned to V):

for the row matrix,	for the column matrix,	for the rectangular matrix,
>>R=[2 -9 1 4 8]; ↵ >>V=R+4 ↵ V = 6 -5 5 8 12	>>C=[-3 14 15]'; ↵ >>syms x ↵ ←section 2.1 for syms >>V=C-x ↵ V = -3-x 14-x 15-x	>>A=[-3 1;14 3;15 1]; ↵ >>V=A+8 ↵ V = 5 9 22 11 23 9

Suppose we intend to add $\frac{2}{3}$ to each element in A and store the data in rational form for which the command we need is V=sym(A+2/3).

♦♦ Multiplying a scalar to each element in a matrix

Just mentioned R, C, and A matrix elements are to be multiplied by the single scalars –2, $-3x$, and 9 in order to obtain [–4 18 –2 –8 –16], $\begin{bmatrix}9x\\-42x\\-45x\end{bmatrix}$, and $\begin{bmatrix}-27 & 9\\126 & 27\\135 & 9\end{bmatrix}$ for which the commands we need are -2*R, -3*x*C, and 9*A respectively. For the rational scalar (for example A is to be multiplied by $\frac{2}{3}$) and rational output, the command for the A should have been 2*sym(A)/3.

♦♦ Dividing every element in a matrix by a scalar

All elements of ongoing matrices R, C, and A are to be divided by the single scalars –2, $-3x$, and 9 so that we obtain [–1 4.5 –0.5 –2 –4], $\begin{bmatrix}\frac{1}{x}\\\frac{-14}{3x}\\\frac{-5}{x}\end{bmatrix}$, and $\begin{bmatrix}-\frac{1}{3} & \frac{1}{9}\\\frac{14}{9} & \frac{1}{3}\\\frac{5}{3} & \frac{1}{9}\end{bmatrix}$ and the required commands are R/(-2), C/(-3)/x, and A/9 respectively. In the case of rational scalar (for example A is to be divided by 9) and rational output, we exercise the command sym(A)/9.

♦♦ Taking reciprocal of all elements in a matrix

Reciprocal of all elements in a matrix is taken by the operator ./. There should not be any 0 element in the matrix for the reciprocal operation. For example we should have $[\frac{1}{2} \quad -\frac{1}{9} \quad 1 \quad \frac{1}{4} \quad \frac{1}{8}]$, $\begin{bmatrix}-\frac{1}{3}\\\frac{1}{14}\\\frac{1}{15}\end{bmatrix}$, and $\begin{bmatrix}-\frac{1}{3} & 1\\\frac{1}{14} & \frac{1}{3}\\\frac{1}{15} & 1\end{bmatrix}$ following the reciprocal operation and whose commands are 1./R, 1./C, and 1./A for ongoing R, C, and A respectively. For the rational form output and for the R, we exercise the command 1./sym(R). If we execute 3./R, we basically compute $[\frac{3}{2} \quad -\frac{1}{3} \quad 3 \quad \frac{3}{4} \quad \frac{3}{8}]$.

♦♦ Mathematical operations on all elements in a matrix

One niche about MATLAB is most functions work on all elements in a matrix when the matrix is its input argument. In section 1.3, we addressed the sine function. Suppose $A=\begin{bmatrix}\frac{\pi}{2} & 0\\-\frac{\pi}{2} & \frac{\pi}{4}\end{bmatrix}$, taking sine on all elements in the matrix should return $\begin{bmatrix} \sin(\frac{\pi}{2}) & \sin 0 \\ \sin(-\frac{\pi}{2}) & \sin(\frac{\pi}{6}) \end{bmatrix} = \begin{bmatrix} 1 & 0 \\ -1 & 0.5 \end{bmatrix}$ which is implemented as follows:

```
>>A=[pi/2 0;-pi/2 pi/6]; ↵    ← Matrix A is assigned to the workspace variable A
>>B=sin(A) ↵                  ← sine computation is conducted and the result is assigned to workspace B

B =
        1.0000         0
       -1.0000    0.5000
```

This sort of computation takes place on all trigonometric, hyperbolic, and other mathematical functions presented in the table 14.A.

2.4 Matrix data flipping

By and large we perform three kinds of matrix data flipping in MATLAB as presented in the following (font equivalence is maintained using the same letter for example A⇔ A and the flipped data is assigned to workspace F).

⬍⬍ Flipping from the left to right

Flipping from the left to right of a row or rectangular matrix is performed by the function **fliplr** (abbreviation for flipping from left to right). Suppose we have the row matrix R=[2 4 3 –4 6 9 3 7 10]. If you flip the elements of R from left to right, the resulting matrix should be [10 7 3 9 6 –4 3 4 2]. For a rectangular matrix, the flipping operation from left to right takes place over each column that is turning the first column to the last, the second column to the second from the last, and so on. Considering $A = \begin{bmatrix} 4 & 23 & 85 & 34 \\ 5 & 43 & 41 & 87 \\ 8 & 65 & 76 & 71 \end{bmatrix}$, just mentioned flipping should return $\begin{bmatrix} 34 & 85 & 23 & 4 \\ 87 & 41 & 43 & 5 \\ 71 & 76 & 65 & 8 \end{bmatrix}$. Both implementations are exercised as follows:

Left to right flipping of the row matrix,

```
>>R=[2 4 3 -4 6 9 3 7 10]; ↵
>>F=fliplr(R) ↵

F =
     10    7    3    9    6   -4    3    4    2
```

Left to right flipping of rectangular matrix,

```
>>A=[4 23 85 34;5 43 41 87;8 65 76 71]; ↵
>>F=fliplr(A) ↵

F =
        34   85   23    4
        87   41   43    5
        71   76   65    8
```

Since a column matrix has only one column, no change to the column matrix is brought about by the **fliplr**.

⬍⬍ Flipping from up to down

The function **flipud** (abbreviation for flipping from up to down) flips the elements of a column or rectangular matrix from up to down. Flipping the column matrix $C = \begin{bmatrix} 4 \\ 7 \\ 8 \\ 3 \\ 1 \end{bmatrix}$ from up to down results the matrix $\begin{bmatrix} 1 \\ 3 \\ 8 \\ 7 \\ 4 \end{bmatrix}$. Flipping from up to down to a rectangular matrix happens over each row for example $D = \begin{bmatrix} 4 & 23 & 85 \\ 5 & 43 & 41 \\ 8 & 65 & x \\ 3 & 12 & 13 \end{bmatrix}$ becomes $\begin{bmatrix} 3 & 12 & 13 \\ 8 & 65 & x \\ 5 & 43 & 41 \\ 4 & 23 & 85 \end{bmatrix}$ due to the flipping. No change occurs to a row matrix when the **flipud** is applied on it. Both examples are implemented as follows:

Up to down flipping of the column matrix,

```
>>C=[4 7 8 3 1]'; ↵
>>F=flipud(C) ↵

F =
      1
      3
      8
      7
      4
```

Up to down flipping of the rectangular matrix,

```
>>syms x ↵                     ← section 2.1 for syms
>>D=[4 23 85;5 43 41;8 65 x;3 12 13]; ↵
>>F=flipud(D) ↵

F =

[  3,  12,  13]
[  8,  65,   x]
[  5,  43,  41]
[  4,  23,  85]
```

◆◆ Flipping the row or column matrix data about the half index

Let us consider a finite one dimensional discrete function $f[n]$ whose integer index n varies from 0 to $N-1$ where N is the number of samples in the $f[n]$. To interpret graphically, we flip the function $f[n]$ about its half index $\frac{N}{2}$ as follows:

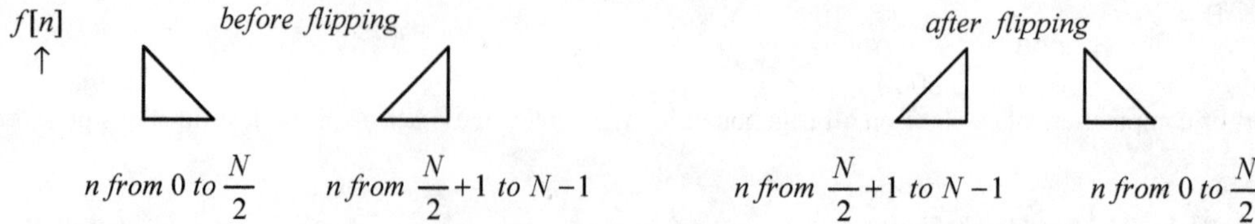

n *from* 0 *to* $\frac{N}{2}$ n *from* $\frac{N}{2}+1$ *to* $N-1$ n *from* $\frac{N}{2}+1$ *to* $N-1$ n *from* 0 *to* $\frac{N}{2}$

MATLAB function **fftshift** performs just mentioned half index flipping. Let us say we have the odd and even sample number discrete functions $x[n]$=[10 2 1 1 2] and $y[n]$=[10 2 1 1 2 10] respectively. Following the half index flipping, one should obtain the flipped functions as [1 2 10 2 1] and [1 2 10 10 2 1] for $x[n]$ and $y[n]$ respectively whose implementations are shown below:

Flipping for the odd number sample,

```
>>x=[10 2 1 1 2]; ↵
>>F=fftshift(x) ↵

F =

     1   2   10   2   1
```

Flipping for the even number sample,

```
>>y=[10 2 1 1 2 10]; ↵
>>F=fftshift(y) ↵

F =

     1   2   10   10   2   1
```

2.5 Power operations on matrix elements

There can be different instances regarding the power operations (all of which is conducted by the operator .^) on matrix elements.

◆◆ Raising the power on each element of a matrix by a scalar

Let us say the power of all elements in the matrix $A=\begin{bmatrix}-2 & -1\\ 0 & -5\\ 5 & 6\end{bmatrix}$ is to be raised by 4 so that we have $\begin{bmatrix}16 & 1\\ 0 & 625\\ 625 & 1296\end{bmatrix}$ after raising the power.

◆◆ Raising power of a scalar as the elements in a matrix

Suppose power of −3 is to be raised according to the matrix $R=\begin{bmatrix}2 & 3\\ 4 & -2\\ 1 & 0\end{bmatrix}$ which should provide $(-3)^{\begin{bmatrix}2 & 3\\ 4 & -2\\ 1 & 0\end{bmatrix}}=$ $\begin{bmatrix}9 & -27\\ 81 & 0.1111\\ -3 & 1\end{bmatrix}$.

◆◆ Raising element to element power of two matrices

Let us say two identical (identicalness is compulsory) size matrices are $C=\begin{bmatrix}3 & -1\\ -2 & 5\\ 4 & 7\end{bmatrix}$ and $F=\begin{bmatrix}x & -3\\ 3 & 0\\ y & 3\end{bmatrix}$.

Powering the elements of C as the like positional elements of F returns $\begin{bmatrix}3^x & (-1)^{-3}\\ (-2)^3 & 5^0\\ 4^y & 7^3\end{bmatrix}=\begin{bmatrix}3^x & -1\\ -8 & 1\\ 4^y & 343\end{bmatrix}$.

◆◆ Powering a square matrix

Power of a square matrix A (like A^2) happens using the vector multiplication as discussed in the section 2.2. When A is a square matrix, A^2 means the vector multiplication A*A.

◆◆ Implementations

All implementations are presented in the following (font equivalence is maintained using the same letter for example A⇔ A and the return is assigned to the workspace V where V is any user-given name):

Power 4 on A:	**R as power on -3:**	**elements of F as power on C:**
>>A=[-2 -1;0 -5;5 6]; ↵ >>V=A.^4 ↵ V = 16 1 0 625 625 1296	>>R=[2 3;4 -2;1 0]; ↵ >>V=(-3).^R ↵ V = 9.0000 -27.0000 81.0000 0.1111 -3.0000 1.0000 **for the rational form:** >>V=(-3).^sym(R); ↵	>>C=[3 -1;-2 5;4 7]; ↵ >>syms x y ↵ ← section 2.1 for syms >>F=[x -3;3 0;y 3]; ↵ >>V=C.^F ↵ V = [3^x, -1] [-8, 1] [4^y, 343]

The elements in A, R, C, and F can be real, complex, or symbolic elements. Each of the example matrices can be a row or column one.

2.6 Indexing and coloning of arrays or matrices

One can imagine that MATLAB is a practice world for data arrays. Once some data is stored in some workspace variable, control on the data element is frequently required. Knowledge of the array indexing enables the reader to maneuver the array elements. If A is a row or column array or matrix in MATLAB, then the A(1), A(2), A(3), etc represent the first, second, third, etc elements in the array respectively. Colon operator (:) renders the control in maneuvering the consecutive array elements. Let us proceed with the following (font equivalence is maintained using the same letter for example A⇔ A) tutorials by assigning the row matrix [2 4 3 −10 0 9 73 29 −31 50] to A:

```
>>A=[2 4 3 -10 0 9 73 29 -31 50]; ↵
```

Suppose we intend to form a row matrix B where B will be collected from the second, third, and ninth elements of A i.e. B=[4 3 −31]. Then a row matrix C is to be formed from the third through eighth elements of A i.e. C=[3 −10 0 9 73 29]. Their formations from A are presented in the following:

formation of matrix B,	**formation of matrix C,**	**Entering the matrix D,**
>>B=A([2 3 9]) ↵ B = 4 3 -31	>>C=A(3:8) ↵ C = 3 -10 0 9 73 29	>>syms x y a ↵ ← section 2.1 for syms >>D=[2 4 x -10 0 y 73 a -31 50].'; ↵

As executed, the required element indexes are placed as a row matrix through the first brace beside the A. For the consecutive index like 3 through 8 is written by 3:8. What if we have a column matrix $D=\begin{bmatrix} 2 \\ 4 \\ x \\ -10 \\ 0 \\ y \\ 73 \\ a \\ -31 \\ 50 \end{bmatrix}$ and the matrix is entered as shown above. Now we form a matrix E from the tenth and seventh elements of D i.e. $E=\begin{bmatrix} 50 \\ 73 \end{bmatrix}$ and F from the first five elements of D i.e. $F=\begin{bmatrix} 2 \\ 4 \\ x \\ -10 \\ 0 \end{bmatrix}$ whose implementations are as follows:

Forming the matrix E from D,	**Forming matrix F from D,**
>>E=D([10 7]) ↵ E = 50 73 **Entering the matrix G,** >>G=[8 64 27 56 98 43 4;-64 216 729 40 12 23 568;678 … ↵ -90 70 61 67 445 3;1 47 45 72 34 -5 -7;3 87 82 29 10 -16 -59]; ↵	>>F=D(1:5) ↵ F = 2 4 x -10 0

After that let us see how coloning of square or rectangular matrices can be accomplished. A rectangular matrix has two indexes – one for row and the other for column. For example $G=\begin{bmatrix} 8 & 64 & 27 & 56 & 98 & 43 & 4 \\ -64 & 216 & 729 & 40 & 12 & 23 & 568 \\ 678 & -90 & 70 & 61 & 67 & 445 & 3 \\ 1 & 47 & 45 & 72 & 34 & -5 & -7 \\ 3 & 87 & 82 & 29 & 10 & -16 & -59 \end{bmatrix}$ has the left uppermost, right uppermost, left lowermost, and right lowermost elements 8, 4, 3, and −59 whose row and column indexes are (1,1), (1,7), (5,1), and (5,7) respectively. In the second row the element 729 has the index coordinates (2,3) and so on. However we input the matrix G into the workspace using the lower line commands of the last page. Referring to the commands, the last word of the first line is 678. After typing 678, leave one space by pressing spacebar and type three dots (called ellipsis, section 1.4). Then press the enter key and type other matrix elements of the row which were interrupted. Anyhow matrix G is now in MATLAB workspace. We perform the coloning of G applying the operator both in the row and column index directions. For each case below, the required matrix elements are shown by elements inside the dotted box.

Matrix H is to be formed from the second and fourth columns of G:

$$\begin{bmatrix} 8 & 64 & 27 & 56 & 98 & 43 & 4 \\ -64 & 216 & 729 & 40 & 12 & 23 & 568 \\ 678 & -90 & 70 & 61 & 67 & 445 & 3 \\ 1 & 47 & 45 & 72 & 34 & -5 & -7 \\ 3 & 87 & 82 & 29 & 10 & -16 & -59 \end{bmatrix}$$

Matrix K is to be formed from the third and fifth rows of G:

$$\begin{bmatrix} 8 & 64 & 27 & 56 & 98 & 43 & 4 \\ -64 & 216 & 729 & 40 & 12 & 23 & 568 \\ 678 & -90 & 70 & 61 & 67 & 445 & 3 \\ 1 & 47 & 45 & 72 & 34 & -5 & -7 \\ 3 & 87 & 82 & 29 & 10 & -16 & -59 \end{bmatrix}$$

Matrix L is to be formed from the fourth through seventh columns of G:

$$\begin{bmatrix} 8 & 64 & 27 & 56 & 98 & 43 & 4 \\ -64 & 216 & 729 & 40 & 12 & 23 & 568 \\ 678 & -90 & 70 & 61 & 67 & 445 & 3 \\ 1 & 47 & 45 & 72 & 34 & -5 & -7 \\ 3 & 87 & 82 & 29 & 10 & -16 & -59 \end{bmatrix}$$

Matrix M is to be formed from the third through fifth rows of G:

$$\begin{bmatrix} 8 & 64 & 27 & 56 & 98 & 43 & 4 \\ -64 & 216 & 729 & 40 & 12 & 23 & 568 \\ 678 & -90 & 70 & 61 & 67 & 445 & 3 \\ 1 & 47 & 45 & 72 & 34 & -5 & -7 \\ 3 & 87 & 82 & 29 & 10 & -16 & -59 \end{bmatrix}$$

Finally, matrix N is to be formed from the intersection of the third through fifth rows and the fourth through seventh columns of G:

$$\begin{bmatrix} 8 & 64 & 27 & 56 & 98 & 43 & 4 \\ -64 & 216 & 729 & 40 & 12 & 23 & 568 \\ 678 & -90 & 70 & 61 & 67 & 445 & 3 \\ 1 & 47 & 45 & 72 & 34 & -5 & -7 \\ 3 & 87 & 82 & 29 & 10 & -16 & -59 \end{bmatrix}$$

All formations are presented on the right. Matrix elements can be real, complex, or symbolic variables. In a nutshell, in order to pick up

(a) rows, the command is matrix name(required row/rows,:),
(b) columns, the command is matrix name(:,required column/ columns),
(c) submatrices, the command is matrix name(required row/ rows, required column/columns).

forming H **from** G,

```
>>H=G(:,[2 4]) ↵

H =

    64   56
   216   40
   -90   61
    47   72
    87   29
```

forming K **from** G,

```
>>K=G([3 5],:) ↵

K =

   678  -90   70   61   67  445    3
     3   87   82   29   10  -16  -59
```

forming L **from** G,

```
>>L=G(:,4:7) ↵

L =

    56   98   43    4
    40   12   23  568
    61   67  445    3
    72   34   -5   -7
    29   10  -16  -59
```

forming M **from** G,

```
>>M=G(3:5,:) ↵

M =

   678  -90   70   61   67  445    3
     1   47   45   72   34   -5   -7
     3   87   82   29   10  -16  -59
```

forming N **from** G,

```
>>N=G(3:5,4:7) ↵

N =

    61   67  445    3
    72   34   -5   -7
    29   10  -16  -59
```

2.7 Appending, deleting, and editing matrix elements

Sometimes it is necessary that we perform the appending, deleting, and editing operations on an existing matrix in MATLAB workspace whose tutorials follow next (font equivalence is maintained using the same letter for example A⇔ A).

⬍⬍ Appending rows

Assume that $A=\begin{bmatrix}1&3&5\\2&6&8\\9&5&0\\4&7&8\end{bmatrix}$ is formed by appending two row matrices [9 5 0] and [4 7 8] with the matrix $B=\begin{bmatrix}1&3&5\\2&6&8\end{bmatrix}$. We first enter matrix B into MATLAB and append one row after another using the command shown below:

for entering B,	for appending the first row,	for appending the second row,
>>B=[1 3 5;2 6 8] ↵	>>B=[B;[9 5 0]] ↵	>>A=[B;[4 7 8]] ↵
B = 1 3 5 2 6 8	B = 1 3 5 2 6 8 9 5 0	A = 1 3 5 2 6 8 9 5 0 4 7 8

The command B=[B;[9 5 0]] tells that the row [9 5 0] is to be appended with the existing B (inside the third bracket) and that the result is again assigned to B. You can append as many rows as you want. The important point is the number of elements in each row that is to be appended must be equal to the number of columns in the matrix B.

⬍⬍ Appending columns

Suppose $C=\begin{bmatrix}1&3&5&9&3\\2&6&8&0&1\\9&5&0&1&9\end{bmatrix}$ is formed by appending two column matrices $\begin{bmatrix}9\\0\\1\end{bmatrix}$ and $\begin{bmatrix}3\\1\\9\end{bmatrix}$ with matrix $D=\begin{bmatrix}1&3&5\\2&6&8\\9&5&0\end{bmatrix}$. We get the matrix D into MATLAB and append one column after another as follows:

for entering D,	for appending the first column,	for appending the second column,
>>D=[1 3 5;2 6 8;9 5 0] ↵	>>D=[D [9 0 1]'] ↵	>>C=[D [3 1 9]'] ↵
D = 1 3 5 2 6 8 9 5 0	D = 1 3 5 9 2 6 8 0 9 5 0 1	C = 1 3 5 9 3 2 6 8 0 1 9 5 0 1 9

The column matrix [9 0 1]' and D has one space gap within the third brace. In the second of above implementation, the resultant matrix is again assigned to D. Append as many columns as you want just remember that the number of elements in each column that is to be appended must be equal to the number of rows in the matrix D.

⬍⬍ Deleting rows or columns from a matrix

Considering $A=\begin{bmatrix}4&2&0&4&-1\\7&5&2&6&0\\5&4&7&8&2\\1&3&4&1&3\end{bmatrix}$ from which the third row [5 4 7 8 2] is to be deleted. After the deletion of the third row, the matrix A should look like $\begin{bmatrix}4&2&0&4&-1\\7&5&2&6&0\\1&3&4&1&3\end{bmatrix}$. Again the second column of A which is $\begin{bmatrix}2\\5\\4\\3\end{bmatrix}$ is to be deleted from A. Once deletion is conducted, the matrix A becomes $\begin{bmatrix}4&0&4&-1\\7&2&6&0\\5&7&8&2\\1&4&1&3\end{bmatrix}$. Since we change matrix A on deletion of the third row, we need to reenter A. Both deletions are exercised as follows:

for deleting the third row from A,	for deleting the second column from A,
>>A=[4 2 0 4 -1;7 5 2 6 0;5 4 7 8 2;1 3 4 1 3]; ↵ >>A(3,:)=[ ] ↵	>>A=[4 2 0 4 -1;7 5 2 6 0;5 4 7 8 2;1 3 4 1 3]; ↵ >>A(:,2)=[ ] ↵
A = 4 2 0 4 -1 7 5 2 6 0 1 3 4 1 3	A = 4 0 4 -1 7 2 6 0 5 7 8 2 1 4 1 3

The commands A(3,:) and A(:,2) select the third row and second column from A respectively and the empty matrix [ ] is assigned to the selected row or column. This way you can delete a range of rows or columns for example the third and fourth columns of A can be deleted using the command A(:,3:4)=[ ].

◆◆ Replacing a row/column/submatrix by another

A row, column, or submatrix of a large rectangular matrix can be replaced by another matrix of identical order. Let us begin with the row replacement considering $A=\begin{bmatrix}1&2&3&4&5\\7&8&9&0&11\\13&9&2&2&1\\4&7&6&2&90\end{bmatrix}$. The second row of A which is [7 8 9 0 11] is to be replaced by a row matrix [2 2 2 2 2]. After replacement, the A should look like $\begin{bmatrix}1&2&3&4&5\\2&2&2&2&2\\13&9&2&2&1\\4&7&6&2&90\end{bmatrix}$. Then, the fourth column of A which is $\begin{bmatrix}4\\0\\2\\2\end{bmatrix}$ is to be replaced by $\begin{bmatrix}0\\0\\0\\0\end{bmatrix}$. The replacement results the new matrix as $\begin{bmatrix}1&2&3&0&5\\7&8&9&0&11\\13&9&2&0&1\\4&7&6&0&90\end{bmatrix}$. After that we proceed with the replacement of a submatrix. Let us say the elements of A inside the dotted marks which are shown by $\begin{bmatrix}1&2&3&4&5\\7&8&9&0&11\\13&9&2&2&1\\4&7&6&2&90\end{bmatrix}$ are to be replaced by a matrix $B=\begin{bmatrix}6&6\\3&3\\0&0\end{bmatrix}$. The resulting matrix should be $\begin{bmatrix}1&2&3&4&5\\7&8&6&6&11\\13&9&3&3&1\\4&7&0&0&90\end{bmatrix}$ in which the submatrix is the intersecting elements of the second through fourth rows and the third through fourth columns of A. Since the replacement changes the matrix A, we need to reenter the matrix A time and again (press uparrow key ↑ at the command prompt). All replacements are shown below:

for the row replacement,

```
>>A=[1 2 3 4 5;7 8 9 0 11;13 9 2 2 1;4 7 6 2 90]; ↵
>>A(2,:)=[2 2 2 2 2] ↵

A =
     1     2     3     4     5
     2     2     2     2     2
    13     9     2     2     1
     4     7     6     2    90
```

for the column replacement,

```
>>A=[1 2 3 4 5;7 8 9 0 11;13 9 2 2 1;4 7 6 2 90]; ↵
>>A(:,4)=[0 0 0 0]' ↵

A =
     1     2     3     0     5
     7     8     9     0    11
    13     9     2     0     1
     4     7     6     0    90
```

for the submatrix replacement,

```
>>A=[1 2 3 4 5;7 8 9 0 11;13 9 2 2 1;4 7 6 2 90]; ↵
>>B=[6 6;3 3;0 0]; ↵
>>A(2:4,3:4)=B ↵

A =
     1     2     3     4     5
     7     8     6     6    11
    13     9     3     3     1
     4     7     0     0    90
```

editing the element coordinated by (2,4),

```
>>A=[1 2 3 4 5;7 8 9 0 11;13 9 2 2 1;4 7 6 2 90]; ↵
>>A(2,4)=-100 ↵

A =
     1     2     3     4     5
     7     8     9  -100    11
    13     9     2     2     1
     4     7     6     2    90
```

◆◆ Editing elements in a matrix

Suppose the element (2,4) of ongoing matrix A (which is 0) is to be changed by −100 so that we have $\begin{bmatrix}1&2&3&4&5\\7&8&9&-100&11\\13&9&2&2&1\\4&7&6&2&90\end{bmatrix}$ following the editing (implementation is shown above). Again the first column of A is to be multiplied by 2 keeping the others unchanged which should provide $\begin{bmatrix} 2 & 2 & 3 & 4 & 5 \\ 14 & 8 & 9 & 0 & 11 \\ 26 & 9 & 2 & 2 & 1 \\ 8 & 7 & 6 & 2 & 90 \end{bmatrix}$. A row or column matrix does not need two indexes. For example the element −3 of R =[0 4 −3 5 2 2 1] which has the index 3 is to be replaced by −20 and we should have the edited matrix as [0 4 −20 5 2 2 1]. Again the last three elements of R which have the indexes 5, 6, and 7 respectively are to be set 0 so that we get [0 4 −3 5 0 0 0]. These implementations are presented in the following:

multiplying the first column of A by 2,

```
>>A=[1 2 3 4 5;7 8 9 0 11;13 9 2 2 1;4 7 6 2 90]; ↵
>>A(:,1)=2*A(:,1) ↵

A =
     2    2    3    4    5
    14    8    9    0   11
    26    9    2    2    1
     8    7    6    2   90
```

changing the third element of R by −20,

```
>>R=[0 4 -3 5 2 2 1]; R(3)=-20 ↵

R =
     0   4  -20   5   2   2   1
```

setting the last three elements of R to 0,

```
>>R=[0 4 -3 5 2 2 1]; R(5:7)=0 ↵

R =
     0   4  -3   5   0   0   0
```

♦♦ Building a large matrix from smaller matrices

Row and column matrix appending techniques discussed earlier facilitate to build a composite matrix from smaller matrices. Considering $A = \begin{bmatrix} 0 & -5 & 6 \\ 7 & 6 & 9 \end{bmatrix}$, $B = \begin{bmatrix} 1 & 7 \\ 9 & 1 \end{bmatrix}$, $C = \begin{bmatrix} 1 \\ 1 \end{bmatrix}$, and $D = \begin{bmatrix} -1 & 0 & 10 & 11 \\ 9 & 7 & 13 & 14 \end{bmatrix}$, a large matrix E is to be formed from the submatrices A, B, C, and D where E is required to be $\begin{bmatrix} A & B \\ C & D \end{bmatrix} = \begin{bmatrix} 0 & -5 & 6 & 1 & 7 \\ 7 & 6 & 9 & 9 & 1 \\ 1 & -1 & 0 & 10 & 11 \\ 1 & 9 & 7 & 13 & 14 \end{bmatrix}$. Its implementation

forming the large matrix:

```
>>A=[0 -5 6;7 6 9]; ↵
>>B=[1 7;9 1]; C=[1;1]; ↵
>>D=[-1 0 10 11;9 7 13 14]; ↵
>>E=[A B;C D] ↵

E =
     0   -5    6    1    7
     7    6    9    9    1
     1   -1    0   10   11
     1    9    7   13   14
```

is presented above on the right. The first three lines are just the matrix entering commands. In the fourth line, we have E=[A B;C D]. Using the command A B forms $\begin{bmatrix} 0 & -5 & 6 & 1 & 7 \\ 7 & 6 & 9 & 9 & 1 \end{bmatrix}$ (the numbers of rows of A and B have to be the same here it is 2). Again using the command C D merges the C and D and provides $\begin{bmatrix} 1 & -1 & 0 & 10 & 11 \\ 1 & 9 & 7 & 13 & 14 \end{bmatrix}$. Matrix formed by [A B] is placed on the top of the matrix formed by [C D] if the command [A B;C D] is used. The number of columns formed by [A B] (here it is 5) and the number of columns formed by [C D] (it is also 5) must be identical. Matrix E can again be merged with some other matrices to form another large dimension matrix.

2.8 Summing and producting matrix elements

MATLAB function sum adds all elements in a row, column, or rectangular matrix when the matrix is its input argument. Example matrices are R=[1 −2 3 9], $C = \begin{bmatrix} 23 \\ -20 \\ 30 \\ 8 \end{bmatrix}$, and $A = \begin{bmatrix} 2 & 4 & 7 \\ -2 & 7 & 9 \\ 3 & 8 & -8 \end{bmatrix}$ whose all element sums are 11, 41, and 30 for the R, C, and A respectively. We execute the summations as follows (font equivalence is maintained using the same letter for example A⇔ A):

Sum for the row matrix,

```
>>R=[1 -2 3 9]; ↵
>>sum(R) ↵

ans =
      11
```

Product for the row matrix,

```
>>prod(R) ↵

ans =
      -54
```

Sum for the column matrix,

```
>>C=[23 -20 30 8]'; ↵
>>sum(C) ↵

ans =
        41
```

Product for the column matrix,

```
>>prod(C) ↵

ans =
      -110400
```

Sum for the rectangular matrix,

```
>>A=[2 4 7;-2 7 9;3 8 -8]; ↵
>>sum(sum(A)) ↵

ans =
        30
```

Product for the rectangular matrix,

```
>>prod(prod(A)) ↵

ans =
        1354752
```

Product for the symbolic matrix,

```
>>syms x ↵   ← section 2.1
>>D=[x x^3 -2*x^3]; ↵
>>prod(D) ↵

ans =
        -2*x^7
```

For a rectangular matrix, two functions are required because the inner sum performs the summing over each column and the result is a row matrix. The outer sum provides the sum over the resulting row matrix.

We have similar function for the matrix elements' product finding. The product of all elements in just mentioned R, C, and A are −54, −110400, and 1354752 respectively. Both functions are operational for real, complex even for the symbolic variables. For instance the product of all elements of $D=[x \quad x^3 \quad -2x^3]$ is $-2x^7$. All product executions are also shown at the end of the last page.

2.9 Finding the maximum/minimum and data sorting

Given a matrix, one can find the maximum element from the matrix using the command max (min for the minimum). Section 2.8 mentioned R, C, and A are having the maxima 9, 30, and 9 (among all elements in the matrix) and the minima −2, −20, and −8 respectively. We assume that the three matrices are in the MATLAB workspace on that the maxima and minima findings in the three matrices happen as follows:

for the row matrix,	**for the column matrix,**	**for the rectangular matrix,**	**for index finding in R,**
>>max(R) ↵ ans = 9 >>min(R) ↵ ans = -2	>>max(C) ↵ ans = 30 >>min(C) ↵ ans = -20	>>max(max(A)) ↵ ans = 9 >>min(min(A)) ↵ ans = -8	>>[M,I]=max(R) ↵ M = 9 I = 4

If the matrix is a row or column one, we apply one max or min. For a rectangular matrix, the max or min operates on each column individually that is why two functions are required. The functions are equally applicable for decimal number elements.

♦♦ Minimum or maximum with index

In the row matrix R, the maximum 9 is occurring as the fourth element in the matrix. Suppose we also intend to find the position index (that is 4) of the maximum in the R. Now we need two output arguments – one for the maximum and the other for its index. Its implementation is shown above on the right in which the two output arguments M and I correspond to the maximum and its index respectively. The function min also keeps this type of index returning option.

♦♦ Sorting elements in a matrix

The function sort can sort the elements of a row or column matrix in ascending order. In the case of a rectangular matrix, the sorting operation will be over each column. Sorting the elements of section 2.8 mentioned R, C, and A in ascending order should provide us [−2 1 3 9], $\begin{bmatrix}-20\\8\\23\\30\end{bmatrix}$, and $\begin{bmatrix}-2 & 4 & -8\\2 & 7 & 7\\3 & 8 & 9\end{bmatrix}$ respectively whose implementations are presented below assuming that the three matrices are in the workspace:

for the row matrix,	**for the column matrix,**	**for the rectangular matrix,**	**for sorting with index in R,**
>>sort(R) ↵ ans = -2 1 3 9	>>sort(C) ↵ ans = -20 8 23 30	>>sort(A) ↵ ans = -2 4 -8 2 7 7 3 8 9	>>[S,I]=sort(R) ↵ S = -2 1 3 9 I = 2 1 3 4

Elements of the matrices can be decimal numbers as well. If you want to sort all elements in the A, first turn the whole matrix to a column one writing A(:) and then use the command sort(A(:)). The sorting so happened is in the ascending order. What if we want that to be in the descending order? The answer is first assign the sorted matrix to some matrix V writing V=sort(R); or V=sort(C); and then use the command fliplr(V) or flipud(V) (section 2.4) depending on the row or column matrix respectively.

Sorting with the index option is also included in the function. For instance the sorted elements −2, 1, 3, and 9 for the row matrix case are occupying the 2nd, 1st, 3rd, and 4th indexes in the R respectively so the indexes as a row matrix should be [2 1 3 4]. We require two output arguments now (one for the sorted vector and the other for the index vector) whose implementation is presented above on the right and in which the S and I (user-chosen variables) correspond to the sorted and index vectors, both returns are as a row matrix respectively.

2.10 Array or matrix manipulation

The user can change the array type applying proper MATLAB function from one to two or three dimension or vice versa. We address few array type conversions in the following (font equivalence is maintained using the same letter for example A⇔ A).

◆◆ Rectangular matrix to row or column matrix

The matrix $A = \begin{bmatrix} 1 & 3 & 5 \\ 2 & 6 & 8 \\ 9 & 5 & 0 \end{bmatrix}$ is converted to a column matrix $C = \begin{bmatrix} 1 \\ 2 \\ 9 \\ 3 \\ 6 \\ 5 \\ 5 \\ 8 \\ 0 \end{bmatrix}$ by placing one column after another using the colon command. Another matrix $R = [1 \quad 3 \quad 5 \quad 2 \quad 6 \quad 8 \quad 9 \quad 5 \quad 0]$ is to be formed from A by placing one row after another. Both manipulations are shown below:

for column conversion,

```
>>A=[1 3 5;2 6 8;9 5 0];↵
>>C=A(:) ↵

C =
     1
     2
     9
     3
     6
     5
     5
     8
     0
```

for row conversion,

```
>>B=A'; ↵
>>R=B(:)' ↵

R =
     1    3    5    2    6    8    9    5    0
```

from H to N conversion,

```
>>H=[3 14 -9 0 12 11 56 78 9 34 91 30]; ↵
>>N=reshape(H,3,4) ↵

N =
     3    0   56   34
    14   12   78   91
    -9   11    9   30
```

from H to M conversion,

```
>>M=reshape(H,4,3)' ↵

M =
     3   14   -9    0
    12   11   56   78
     9   34   91   30
```

from F to O conversion,

```
>>F=[5 7 -9 7 23 11 9 10]'; ↵
>>O=reshape(F,2,4) ↵

O =
     5   -9   23    9
     7    7   11   10
```

In the row conversion case we first transposed the A and assigned that to some B and then transposed the column matrix formed by B(:). The reason for doing so is the command A(:) always places the elements in A columnwise.

◆◆ Row or column matrix to rectangular matrix

A long row or column matrix can be converted to a rectangular matrix through the use of the function reshape whose general format is reshape (given matrix name, required number of rows, required number of columns). Let us consider the row matrix $H = [3 \quad 14 \quad -9 \quad 0 \quad 12 \quad 11 \quad 56 \quad 78 \quad 9 \quad 34 \quad 91 \quad 30]$ which has 12 elements. Whatever be the order of the reshaped matrix, the product of the order of the reshaped matrix must be 12. It is evident that we may have 3×4, 4×3, 6×2, or 2×6 matrices from H. When the elements of H are placed consecutively, they may be arranged either in column by column or in row by row.

Column by column:

From H, we wish to form a matrix N of order 3×4 in which the first column will be the first three elements of H, the second column will be the second three elements of H, and so will be the others i.e. H is reshaped as $N = \begin{bmatrix} 3 & 0 & 56 & 34 \\ 14 & 12 & 78 & 91 \\ -9 & 11 & 9 & 30 \end{bmatrix}$ (implementation is shown above).

Row by row:

The matrix M of order 3×4 is to be formed from H. In M, the first row will be the first four elements of H, the second row will be the second four elements of H, and so will be the others i.e. $M = \begin{bmatrix} 3 & 14 & -9 & 0 \\ 12 & 11 & 56 & 78 \\ 9 & 34 & 91 & 30 \end{bmatrix}$ (implementation is shown above). Since the function reshape always operates on column basis, the number of rows becomes the number of columns and vice versa and then transposition is conducted for the M formation.

Next we take the example of the column matrix $F = \begin{bmatrix} 5 \\ 7 \\ -9 \\ 7 \\ 23 \\ 11 \\ 9 \\ 10 \end{bmatrix}$ which has 8 elements therefore the product of the order of the reshaped matrix must be 8. Like the row one, there can be two possible reshaping.

for formation of P from F,

```
>>P=reshape(F,4,2)' ↵

P =
     5    7   -9    7
    23   11    9   10
```

Column by column:
We have two options to reshape F – either 2×4 or 4×2. Let us say the matrix O of order 2×4 is to be formed from F in which the columns are the consecutive elements of F that is $O=\begin{bmatrix} 5 & -9 & 23 & 9 \\ 7 & 7 & 11 & 10 \end{bmatrix}$ (implementation is shown on the upper right side of the last page).

Row by row:
Again a matrix P of order 2×4 is to be formed from F in which the rows are consecutive elements of F and it should look like $P=\begin{bmatrix} 5 & 7 & -9 & 7 \\ 23 & 11 & 9 & 10 \end{bmatrix}$. The numbers of columns and rows interchange when they are put as the input arguments in the reshape and the transposition takes place afterwards (execution is shown on the lower right corner of the last page).

♦♦ Rectangular matrix from the same row/column/rectangular matrix

Given a row, column, or rectangular matrix, a rectangular matrix can be formed employing the function repmat (abbreviation for the repetition of matrices) by placing the given matrix repetitively, which has the common syntax repmat (given row/column/rectangular matrix, the required number of repetitions along the row, the required number of repetitions along the column).

Matrix $D=\begin{bmatrix} 3 & -1 & 0 \\ 3 & -1 & 0 \\ 3 & -1 & 0 \end{bmatrix}$ is to be formed from $R=[3 \quad -1 \quad 0]$ by placing three Rs one over the other.

Then placing four column matrices $C=\begin{bmatrix} 4 \\ 10 \\ -7 \end{bmatrix}$ side by side forms $E=\begin{bmatrix} 4 & 4 & 4 & 4 \\ 10 & 10 & 10 & 10 \\ -7 & -7 & -7 & -7 \end{bmatrix}$. Taking $A=\begin{bmatrix} 4 & 10 \\ 7 & 0 \end{bmatrix}$, a large matrix F is to be formed from six As by placing 3 A up and 3 A down i.e. $F=\begin{bmatrix} A & A & A \\ A & A & A \end{bmatrix}=$ $\begin{bmatrix} 4 & 10 & 4 & 10 & 4 & 10 \\ 7 & 0 & 7 & 0 & 7 & 0 \\ 4 & 10 & 4 & 10 & 4 & 10 \\ 7 & 0 & 7 & 0 & 7 & 0 \end{bmatrix}$. All three repetitive formations are shown as follows:

for the D formation,
```
>>R=[3 -1 0]; ↵
>>D=repmat(R,3,1) ↵

D =

     3    -1     0
     3    -1     0
     3    -1     0
```

for the E formation,
```
>>C=[4 10 -7]'; ↵
>>E=repmat(C,1,4) ↵

E =

     4     4     4     4
    10    10    10    10
    -7    -7    -7    -7
```

for the F formation,
```
>>A=[4 10;7 0]; ↵
>>F=repmat(A,2,3) ↵

F =

     4    10     4    10     4    10
     7     0     7     0     7     0
     4    10     4    10     4    10
     7     0     7     0     7     0
```

2.11 Rounding, remainder after integer division, and factoring

As the title articulates we introduce the truncation or rounding of matrix elements, remainder after integer division of matrix elements, and factorization of integers in this section (font equivalence is maintained using the same letter for example R⇔ R).

♦♦ Truncating matrix elements

Function fix discards the fractional parts of a matrix elements regardless of the magnitude and returns the integer part on all elements in the matrix when the matrix is its input argument. Let us say we have the row matrix $R=[1.2578 \quad -9.3445 \quad -8.9999]$ which should return $[1 \quad -9 \quad -8]$ following the removal of the fractional parts and we carry out the implementation as follows:

```
>>R=[1.2578 -9.3445 -8.9999]; ↵   ← We assigned the row matrix to the workspace R
>>V=fix(R) ↵                      ← Truncated elements are assigned to V as a row matrix

V =

     1    -9    -8
```

If the R were a rectangular matrix, the command would be applied equally to all elements in the matrix.

for rounding the C elements:
```
>>C=[1.5001 -9.5000 -8.4999]; ↵
>>V=round(C) ↵

V =

     2   -10    -8
```

♦♦ Rounding matrix elements

Any fractional number can be rounded to its nearest integer using the function round which means if the fractional part of the number is greater than or equal to 0.5, it is taken as 1 and if it is less than 0.5, it is taken as 0. Referring to C=[1.5001 −9.5000 −8.4999], the rounding operation on all elements on the C should provide us [2 −10 −8] whose implementation is presented on the lower right corner of the last page and the rounded elements are held in V. The C can in general be a rectangular matrix.

♦♦ Remainder after integer division

When an integer is divided by another integer, there is no fractional part in the integer division for example the integers 3 and 2 provide the quotients $\frac{2}{3}=0$ and $\frac{3}{2}=1$. Remainder after integer division can be found by the function rem which basically computes integer−divider×quotient. When 2 is divided by 3, we should get 2−3×0=2 as the remainder after integer division. Similarly 3 by 2 should provide us 1. Again the same operation on all elements of $A = \begin{bmatrix} 2 & 9 \\ -56 & -5 \\ 6 & 76 \\ 3 & 2 \end{bmatrix}$ by −3 should return $\begin{bmatrix} 2 & 0 \\ -2 & -2 \\ 0 & 1 \\ 0 & 2 \end{bmatrix}$. Also the same operation for the like positional elements of dividend $D = \begin{bmatrix} 2 & 3 & 4 \\ 7 & 9 & 2 \end{bmatrix}$ and divider $B = \begin{bmatrix} 3 & 4 & 2 \\ -3 & 2 & 3 \end{bmatrix}$ should return us $\begin{bmatrix} 2 & 3 & 0 \\ 1 & 1 & 2 \end{bmatrix}$. All these are presented below (every result is assigned to V).

when 2 divided by 3,
```
>>V=rem(2,3) ↵

V =

     2
```
when 3 divided by 2,
```
>>V=rem(3,2) ↵

V =

     1
```

when A is divided by -3,
```
>>A=[2 9;-56 -5;6 76;3 2]; ↵
>>V=rem(A,-3) ↵

V =
     2     0
    -2    -2
     0     1
     0     2
```

like positional elements of D divided by B,
```
>>D=[2 3 4;7 9 2]; ↵
>>B=[3 4 2;-3 2 3]; ↵
>>V=rem(D,B) ↵

V =

     2     3     0
     1     1     2
```

for factoring an integer,
```
>>V=factor(84) ↵

V =
     2     2     3     7
```

♦♦ Prime factors of an integer

An integer can be factored using the command factor when the integer its input argument. The factor integers are returned as a row matrix. For example 84=2×2×3×7 is conducted above on the right.

2.12 Matrix element testing and dimension finding

Once a workspace variable holds a matrix, you may have some query about the data type. Some MATLAB functions can be helpful in this regard.

♦♦ Nonzero elements in a matrix

The number of nonzero elements in a matrix can be determined by the function nnz (abbreviation for number of non zero) when the matrix is its input argument. For example there are 5 nonzero elements in $A = \begin{bmatrix} 0 & 3 & 8 \\ 9 & 0 & 6 \\ 0 & 0 & 1 \end{bmatrix}$. The A can be a row or column matrix too.

The function nonzeros selects the nonzero elements from a matrix when the matrix is its input argument. The search is carried out according to columns. The output matrix is a column one regardless of the type of input matrix (row, column, or rectangular). For the example A, we should have the nonzero elements 3, 8, 9, 6, and 1 as a column matrix. Both implementations are shown above.

for the number of nonzero elements in A,
```
>>A=[0 3 8;9 0 6;0 0 1]; ↵
>>nnz(A) ↵

ans =

     5
```
for the length of R,
```
>>R=[1 2 0 3]; ↵
>>length(R) ↵

ans =

     4
```

for selecting nonzero elements from A,
```
>>nonzeros(A) ↵

ans =
     9
     3
     8
     6
     1
```
for matrix size of A,
```
>>size(A) ↵

ans =

     3     3
```

♦♦ Knowing the order/length of a matrix/vector

Command length finds the number of elements in a row or column matrix when the matrix is its input argument. We should obtain 4 for the row matrix R=[1 2 0 3] as the length of the matrix. Again the command size returns the size of any array or matrix present in the workspace. Just discussed A is in the workspace and we should see 3×3 as the matrix dimension. Both functions' implementation is shown above. The outcome of the size is a two element row matrix for a two dimensional array indicating the row and column numbers respectively. For a three dimensional array (subsection 14.4.1), the output of the size is a three element row matrix. Sometimes we do not intend to display the dimension of an array. One can assign the output of the size to some variable m writing m=size(A); and the row and column numbers in A can be picked up afterwards by the commands m(1) and m(2) respectively. We can also view the array size in the workspace browser (section 1.4).

◆◆ Determine whether all/any element (s) is/are nonzero

All elements in a matrix are nonzero – yes or no? This kind of logical decision taking can be conducted using the function all. If the answer is yes, the return is 1 otherwise 0. For a row or column matrix, one all function is enough but for a rectangular matrix we need two all functions because it works over each column in a rectangular matrix. For instance the answer of having all elements' nonzero should be 1, 0, and 0 for $R=[1 \quad -2 \quad 3]$, $C=\begin{bmatrix}0\\0\\0\end{bmatrix}$, and $A=\begin{bmatrix}4 & -2 & 9\\9 & 0 & 3\end{bmatrix}$ respectively whose implementations are presented below:

all elements nonzero in R?	**all elements nonzero in C?**	**all elements nonzero in A?**
>>R=[1 -2 3]; ↵ >>all(R) ↵ ans = 1	>>C=[0 0 0]'; ↵ >>all(C) ↵ ans = 0	>>A=[4 -2 9;9 0 3]; ↵ >>all(all(A)) ↵ ans = 0
any element nonzero in R? >>any(R) ↵ ans = 1	**any element nonzero in C?** >>any(C) ↵ ans = 0	**any element nonzero in A?** >>any(any(A)) ↵ ans = 1

Another logical situation whether any element of a matrix is nonzero may appear. We have similar function any which works in a like manner and whose implementations over ongoing R, C, and A are shown above. In the following section we discuss syntax about the conditional element query related to the index.

2.13 Position indexes of matrix elements with conditions

MATLAB function find looks for the position indexes of matrix elements subject to some logical condition whose general format is [R C]=find(condition) where the indexes R and C stand for the row and column directions respectively.

Let us consider $A=\begin{bmatrix}11 & 10 & 11 & 10\\12 & 10 & -2 & 0\\-7 & 17 & 1 & -1\end{bmatrix}$ which we enter by the following:

>>A=[11 10 11 10;12 10 -2 0;-7 17 1 -1]; ↵ $\leftarrow A$ is assigned to A

We would like to know what the position indexes of matrix elements where the elements are greater than 10 are. The elements of A being greater than 10 have the position indexes (1,1), (2,1), (3,2), and (1,3). MATLAB finds the required index in accordance with columns. Placing the row and column indexes vertically, we have $\begin{bmatrix}1\\2\\3\\1\end{bmatrix}$ and $\begin{bmatrix}1\\1\\2\\3\end{bmatrix}$ respectively. The output arguments R and C of the find receives these two column matrices respectively. The input argument of the find must be a logical statement, any element in A greater than 10 is written as $A>10$. However the position indexes are found as shown above.

where elements of A are greater than 10,
```
>>[R C]=find(A>10) ↵

R =
     1
     2
     3
     1
C =
     1
     1
     2
     3
```

where elements of A =10,	**where elements of $A \le 0$,**	**for the row matrix D,**
>>[R C]=find(A==10) ↵ R = 1 2 1 C = 2 2 4	>>[R C]=find(A<=0) ↵ R = 3 2 2 3 C = 1 3 4 4	>>D=[-10 34 1 2 8 4]; ↵ >>R=find(D>=8) ↵ R = 2 5 **for the column matrix E,** >>E=[-2 8 -2 7]'; ↵ >>C=find(E~=-2) ↵ C = 2 4

To work with more conditions, what are the position indexes in the matrix A where the elements are equal to 10? The answer is (1,2), (2,2), and (1,4). Again the position indexes where the elements are less than or equal to zero are (3,1), (2,3), (2,4), and (3,4) (section 14.3 for operator reference). So far we considered a rectangular matrix for demonstration of position index finding. Let us see how the **find** works for a row or column matrix. Let us take D =[−10 34 1 2 8 4] from which we find the position indexes of the elements where they are greater than or equal to 8. Obviously, they are the 2nd and 5th elements. Here we do not need two output arguments of the **find**. Again let us find the position indexes of the elements of the column matrix $E=\begin{bmatrix}-2\\8\\-2\\7\end{bmatrix}$ where the elements are not equal to −2. The 2nd and 4th elements are not equal to −2. The executions for all these conditional findings are presented at the end of the last page. The output of the function **find** is a row one for the row matrix input and a column one for the column matrix input.

2.14 Matrix of ones, zeroes, and constants

MATLAB commands **ones** and **zeros** implement user-defined matrix of ones and zeroes respectively. Each function conceives two input arguments, the first and second of which are the required numbers of rows and columns respectively. Let us say we intend to form the matrices $A=\begin{bmatrix}1&1&1\\1&1&1\\1&1&1\\1&1&1\end{bmatrix}$, $B=\begin{bmatrix}1&1&1\\1&1&1\\1&1&1\end{bmatrix}$, and $C=\begin{bmatrix}1&1&1&1\\1&1&1&1\end{bmatrix}$. Their orders are 4×3, 3×3, and 2×4 respectively and the implementations are as follows:

for A,
```
>>A=ones(4,3) ↵

A =
     1     1     1
     1     1     1
     1     1     1
     1     1     1
```

for B,
```
>>B=ones(3) ↵

B =
     1     1     1
     1     1     1
     1     1     1
```

for C,
```
>>C=ones(2,4) ↵

C =
     1     1     1     1
     1     1     1     1
```

Either the number of rows or columns will do if the matrix is a square. For the row and column matrices of ones for example of length 6, the commands would be **ones(1,6)** and **ones(6,1)** respectively.

Formation of the matrix of zeroes is quite similar to that of the matrix of ones. Replacing the function **ones** by **zeros** does the formation. Matrix of zeroes like $A=\begin{bmatrix}0&0&0\\0&0&0\\0&0&0\\0&0&0\end{bmatrix}$, $B=\begin{bmatrix}0&0&0\\0&0&0\\0&0&0\end{bmatrix}$, and $C=\begin{bmatrix}0&0&0&0\\0&0&0&0\end{bmatrix}$ whose orders are 4×3, 3×3, and 2×4 and which are formed by the commands **A=zeros(4,3)**, **B=zeros(3)**, and **C=zeros(2,4)** respectively. A row and a column matrices of 6 zeroes are formed by the commands **zeros(1,6)** and **zeros(6,1)** respectively.

A matrix of constants is obtained by first creating a matrix of ones of the required size and then multiplying by the constant number. For example the matrix $\begin{bmatrix}0.2&0.2&0.2\\0.2&0.2&0.2\\0.2&0.2&0.2\\0.2&0.2&0.2\end{bmatrix}$ can be generated by the command **0.2*ones(4,3)**.

2.15 Inner product, outer product, and array extension

By all means a row or column matrix represents a vector in MATLAB. In section 1.3 we addressed how the reader generates a row or column matrix using the colon operator or data entering. We intend to address two important matrix products namely inner and outer and matrix size extension in the following.

⬥⬥ Inner product of two vectors

By expression we define the matrix inner product $\langle X,Y\rangle$ of two identical size (where the size or the number of elements in each vector is N) vectors X and Y as $\langle X,Y\rangle=\sum_{j=1}^{N}X_jY_j$. For instance X =[7 8 4] and Y =[−2 3 2] provide the inner product as $\langle X,Y\rangle$ =18 which is just a scalar. In MATLAB first we enter the vectors X and Y but they must be as a row and a column matrices respectively. Then the matrix multiplication operator * is used to have the vector or inner product as follows:

```
>>X=[7 8 4]; Y=[-2 3 2]'; ↵   ← Assigning X and Y to X and Y as a row and a column matrices respectively
>>P=X*Y ↵                     ← Workspace P holds the inner product ⟨X,Y⟩

P =

    18
```

⬥⬥ Outer product of two vectors

The outer product of two dissimilar size row vectors X and Y (whose lengths are M and N respectively) is defined by the matrix product of the X as a column vector and Y as a row vector. Unlike the inner product the outer product is a matrix of order $M \times N$. For example X =[7 8 4] and Y =[−2 3] (where M =3 and N =2) provide us the outer product matrix as $\begin{bmatrix} -14 & 21 \\ -16 & 24 \\ -8 & 12 \end{bmatrix}$ whose implementation follows next:

```
>>X=[7 8 4]'; Y=[-2 3]; ↵     ← Assigning the X and Y as a column and a row matrices respectively
>>P=X*Y ↵                     ← Workspace P holds the outer product matrix of the size 3×2

P =

   -14   21
   -16   24
    -8   12
```

Symbolic element as well as the complex one can be the matrix elements (sections 2.1 and 10.2).

♦♦ Array extension by including some element

Given a matrix, one can extend the matrix size by appending some user-defined element using the function padarray. Suppose we have matrix $A = \begin{bmatrix} 6 & 5 \\ 9 & 2 \end{bmatrix}$ and intend to extend its size to 3×4 appending one row and two columns of 0 afterwards A so that at the end we have $B = \begin{bmatrix} 6 & 5 & 0 & 0 \\ 9 & 2 & 0 & 0 \\ 0 & 0 & 0 & 0 \end{bmatrix}$. Other possibilities might be placing the element 0 before and on either sides of A so that we have $C = \begin{bmatrix} 0 & 0 & 0 & 0 \\ 0 & 0 & 6 & 5 \\ 0 & 0 & 9 & 2 \end{bmatrix}$ and $D = \begin{bmatrix} 0 & 0 & 0 & 0 & 0 & 0 \\ 0 & 0 & 6 & 5 & 0 & 0 \\ 0 & 0 & 9 & 2 & 0 & 0 \\ 0 & 0 & 0 & 0 & 0 & 0 \end{bmatrix}$ respectively. The function padarray accepts three input arguments, the first, second, and third of which are the matrix name, required row and column numbers as a two element row matrix, and the reserve indicatory word under quote for the placement respectively. Here we need one row and two columns for the example A so the second input argument of the function should be [1 2]. The indicatory words are pre, post, and both for the three cases respectively, and each of which must be placed under quote. However the three formations are shown below:

for the formation of B,

```
>>A=[6 5;9 2]; ↵
>>B=padarray(A,[1 2],0,'post') ↵

B =

     6     5     0     0
     9     2     0     0
     0     0     0     0
```

for the formation of C,

```
>>C=padarray(A,[1 2],0,'pre') ↵

C =
     0     0     0     0
     0     0     6     5
     0     0     9     2
```

for the formation of D,

```
>>D=padarray(A,[1 2],0,'both') ↵

D =
     0     0     0     0     0     0
     0     0     6     5     0     0
     0     0     9     2     0     0
     0     0     0     0     0     0
```

The padding element does not have to be 0, you can place any other element for the extension. Elements in A can be real, complex, or symbolic.

With the discussion of the array product and extension, we bring an end to the chapter.

Chapter 3

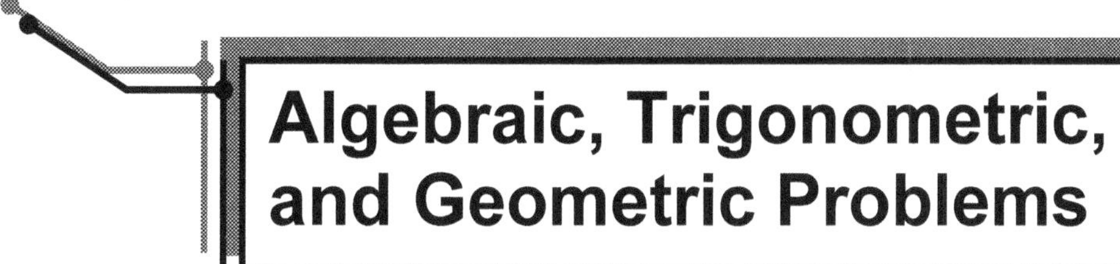

This chapter is devised to solving the problems that appear frequently in algebra, trigonometry, and geometry. Though the problems seem to be elementary, they are reasonably important for advanced scientific and engineering computations. Whereever possible, the symbolic as well as the numeric way to solve these problems is addressed in terms of mathematical symbolism. Since we pay attention to explanations based on implementational appeal rather than mathematics, we worked out the model problems in detail. A number of examples are devoted to lay out the following:

- Polynomial representation and polynomial based manipulations and computations
- Basic algebra problems such as partial fraction, expression based computation, etc
- Trigonometric problems and algebraic equation solving in symbolic and numeric approach
- Geometric object formation and computations based on the constructed geometric objects

3.1 Polynomial representation and its roots

A polynomial is represented by a row matrix using the polynomial coefficients in descending power. For a polynomial of order n, there must be $n+1$ coefficients in the polynomial or elements in the row matrix. For example the polynomial $p(x)=-17x^3+17x^2-7x+1$ has the coefficient row matrix $[-17 \quad 17 \quad -7 \quad 1]$ and we enter it as follows:

```
>>p=[-17 17 -7 1]; ↵
```
← Workspace p is holding the polynomial coefficients of $p(x)$ as a row matrix

Any missing term in the polynomial is set to 0 for example the $-17x^3-7x+1$ has the representation p=[-17 0 -7 1];. In order to see the polynomial as powers of x, one can use the command poly2str (abbreviation for polynomial to (2) string) as follows:

```
>>poly2str(p,'x') ↵
```
← 1st and 2nd input arguments of the function are the polynomial coefficients as a row matrix and user-required variable under quote respectively

```
ans =

        -17 x^3 + 17 x^2 - 7 x + 1
```

If you wanted to see the polynomial in terms of z, the command would be poly2str(p,'z'). There is another option for a polynomial entering called symbolic option. In this option we first need to declare the independent variable of the polynomial using syms (section 2.1) and then write the vector code (section 14.2) of the polynomial. The first example polynomial is entered as follows:

```
>>syms x ↵
>>p=-17*x^3+17*x^2-7*x+1; ↵        ← Workspace p is now holding the expression not the coefficients
```

There is a function called pretty which returns any functional expression as close as mathematical form provided that its input argument is the vector string or code. In vector string form, the x^3 is coded as x^3. When x^3 is the input argument of the pretty, the return of the pretty is x^3 provided that the independent variable x is defined using syms before. The pretty is applied only for the display reason whence computation is conducted on the scalar or vector code of an expression. Now we have the polynomial stored in the workspace p and let us display it as follows:

```
>>pretty(p) ↵
            3       2
      -17 x  + 17 x  - 7 x + 1
```

If you need to extract the polynomial coefficients from the expression stored in p, the command sym2poly (abbreviation for the symbolic to (2) polynomial coefficients) can be exercised on the assignee p as follows:

```
>>sym2poly(p) ↵                  ← It returns the polynomial coefficients as a row matrix

ans =

       -17    17    -7    1       ← These are the coefficients we entered to p before
```

♦♦ Roots of a polynomial from its equation

A polynomial equation of degree n has n roots. Depending on the coefficients of a polynomial, the roots can be real or complex. The polynomial equation $4x^2+4x+1=0$ has the roots −0.5 and −0.5 and we intend to find those. MATLAB function roots finds the roots of a polynomial equation when the polynomial coefficients in descending power of x as a row matrix is its input argument. If the equation were of higher degree than that of 2 for example $x^5+5.5x^4+7.5x^3-2.5x^2-8.5x-3=0$ and whose roots are given by $x=-3, -2, -1, -0.5$, and 1, it could also be solved by the function. Example of a polynomial equation bearing complex roots is $x^3+x^2+4x+4=0$ whose roots are -1, $2i$, and $-2i$. All root finding examples are shown below (in which the workspace A holds the polynomial coefficients as a row matrix and the roots are returned to workspace r as a column matrix in each case):

roots for $4x^2+4x+1=0$:	**roots for** $x^5+5.5x^4+7.5x^3-2.5x^2-8.5x-3=0$:	**roots for** $x^3+x^2+4x+4=0$:
>>A=[4 4 1]; ↵ >>r=roots(A) ↵ r = -0.5000 -0.5000	>>A=[1 5.5 7.5 -2.5 -8.5 -3]; ↵ >>r=roots(A) ↵ r = -3.0000 -2.0000 1.0000 -1.0000 -0.5000	>>A=[1 1 4 4]; ↵ >>r=roots(A) ↵ r = - 0.0000 + 2.0000i - 0.0000 - 2.0000i - 1.0000

♦♦ Forming a polynomial equation from its roots

This is the reverse problem to the one we stated just now. If the roots of a polynomial equation are given, the equation is formed by virtue of the function poly which accepts the roots of the polynomial as the input argument placed in a row matrix. From ongoing discussion, we should be having $4x^2+4x+1=0$, $x^5+5.5x^4+7.5x^3-2.5x^2-8.5x-3=0$, and $x^3+x^2+4x+4=0$ starting from their roots $\begin{Bmatrix}-0.5\\-0.5\end{Bmatrix}$, $\begin{Bmatrix}-3\\-2\\1\\-1\\-0.5\end{Bmatrix}$, and $\begin{Bmatrix}2i\\-2i\\-1\end{Bmatrix}$ respectively whose computations are attached on the right. In each case we assigned the roots as a row matrix and the return polynomial coefficients as descending power of x to the workspace variables R and p (user-chosen names) respectively. In order to display the polynomials as power of x, one can execute the command poly2str(p,'x') as we did earlier. Note that both sides of the first equation are divided by 4 which do not change the equation at all.

forming $4x^2+4x+1=0$ **from its roots:**

```
>>R=[-0.5 -0.5]; p=poly(R) ↵

p =
      1.0000    1.0000    0.2500
```

forming $x^5+5.5x^4+7.5x^3-2.5x^2-8.5x-3=0$:

```
>>R=[-3 -2 1 -1 -0.5]; p=poly(R) ↵

p =
    1.0000    5.5000  7.5000  -2.5000  -8.5000  -3.0000
```

forming $x^3+x^2+4x+4=0$ **from its roots:**

```
>>R=[2i -2i -1]; p=poly(R) ↵          ← Section 10.2 for i

p =
       1    1    4    4
```

3.2 Polynomial related computations

Numerous built-in functions are there to the context of polynomial computation in MATLAB. Some elementary computations are addressed in the following (font equivalence is maintained in all executions for example x⇔ x).

♦♦ Expansion of a powered polynomial or expression

The function **expand** expands powered polynomials containing binomial, trinomial, or higher terms. The independent variables in the polynomial or expression need to be declared as symbolic using the **syms** (section 2.1) and we employ the vector code (section 14.2) of the power polynomial. Following the expansion, the command **pretty** of last section can be exercised to view the computation in nice form. We are going to test out $p(x,y) = (2x-3y)^4 = 16x^4 - 96x^3y + 216x^2y^2 - 216xy^3 + 81y^4$ and $q(x) = (4-5x)(5+2x)\left(\frac{7}{9}-x\right) = \frac{140}{9} - \frac{299}{9}x + \frac{83}{9}x^2 + 10x^3$ as follows:

Expansion for $p(x,y)$:

```
>>syms x y ↵
>>p=expand((2*x-3*y)^4); ↵ ← p holds p(x,y)
>>pretty(p) ↵
    4        3         2  2         3        4
16 x  -  96 x  y + 216 x  y  - 216 x y  + 81 y
```

Expansion for $q(x)$:

```
>>syms x ↵
>>q=expand((4-5*x)*(5+2*x)*(7/9-x)); ↵   ←q⇔ q(x)
>>pretty(q) ↵
                           2      3
140/9 - 299/9 x + 83/9 x  + 10 x
```

♦♦ Factorization of a polynomial or expression

In order to factorize an expression, we declare the related variables in the expression using the **syms** and apply the command **factor** on the vector code of the expression. The return of the **factor** is also the vector code from the factorization. Once factorization is performed, the **pretty** of last section displays the readable form. For instance we wish to verify the functions $q(x) = 27x^3 - 189x^2 + 441x - 343 = (3x-7)^3$ and $p(x,y) = a^3\cos x + ya^2 - ay\cos x - y^2 = (a\cos x + y)(a^2 - y)$ as follows:

Factorization for $q(x)$:

```
>>syms x ↵
>>q=27*x^3-189*x^2+441*x-343; ↵
>>f=factor(q); ↵        ← f holds the factored q(x)
>>pretty(f) ↵
              3
     (3 x - 7)
```

Factorization for $p(x,y)$:

```
>>syms a x y ↵
>>p=a^3*cos(x)+y*a^2-a*y*cos(x)-y^2; ↵
>>f=factor(p); ↵    ← f holds the factored p(x,y)
>>pretty(f) ↵
       2
     (a  - y ) (cos(x) a + y)
```

♦♦ Value of a polynomial at some x

The function **polyval** (abbreviation for the polynomial value at) evaluates a polynomial of x at any x which accepts two input arguments. The first and second input arguments of the function take the polynomial coefficients in descending power of x as a row matrix and the value of x (where we are interested at) respectively. Suppose the polynomial $x^4 - 7x^3 + 21x^2 - 37x - 30$ has the value 540 at x =−3 which needs to be computed using the **polyval** and the implementation is as follows:

computation of $x^4 - 7x^3 + 21x^2 - 37x - 30$ at x =−3:

```
>>y=[1 -7 21 -37 -30]; ↵
>>polyval(y,-3) ↵

ans =
        540
```

multiplication of $p_1(x)$ and $p_2(x)$ in symbolic form:

```
>>syms x ↵
>>p1=2*x^2-3*x+1; ↵  ←p1 holds p1(x)
>>p2=3*x^2-4*x+1; ↵  ←p2 holds p2(x)
>>p=expand(p1*p2) ↵ ← p ⇔ p(x)

p =

6*x^4-17*x^3+17*x^2-7*x+1
```

multiplication of $p_1(x)$ and $p_2(x)$ in numeric form:

```
>>p1=[2 -3 1]; ↵ ← p1(x) coefficients
>>p2=[3 -4 1]; ↵ ← p2(x) coefficients
>>p=conv(p1,p2) ↵ ← p⇔ p(x)

p =
       6  -17   17   -7    1
```

We first assigned the polynomial coefficients as a row matrix to the workspace variable **y** (user-given name) and then applied the **polyval** on **y** as shown above on the left.

♦♦ Multiplication of polynomials

It is given that the polynomial $p(x) = 6x^4 - 17x^3 + 17x^2 - 7x + 1$ is the multiplication of the polynomials $p_1(x) = 2x^2 - 3x + 1$ and $p_2(x) = 3x^2 - 4x + 1$ and we intend to implement that. There are two approaches in the computation, the first and second of which are the symbolic and numeric respectively. In the symbolic form we first declare the independent variable of the polynomials using the **syms**, assign the vector code of the polynomial to some variable like **p1** or **p2**, and then conduct the polynomial multiplication using the * operator. The multiplied result is expanded by using the command **expand**. Its implementation is shown above in which the workspace **p** holds the multiplication result. While using the numeric form, we first enter the polynomial coefficients as the descending power of x to some assignees **p1** or **p2** as a row matrix and then apply the function **conv** (abbreviation for convolution) on the assignees for the polynomial multiplication. The return of **conv** is a row matrix indicating the coefficients of the multiplied polynomial. Its implementation is presented along with the symbolic one on the lower right corner of the last page (use poly2str for x related power form).

◆◆ Division of polynomials

Polynomial division can also be in symbolic and numeric sense. Suppose the polynomial $p(x) = x^4 - x + 1$ is to be divided by $s(x) = x^2 + x + 1$. Performing long division, one obtains the quotient and remainder polynomials as $q(x) = x^2 - x$ and $r(x)=1$ respectively which we intend to implement.

There is another package called maple associated in MATLAB which also performs the symbolic computation. Figure 3.1(a) presents the common hierarchy of toolboxes implanted in MATLAB. The maple package is invoked from MATLAB command prompt. Any maple executable statement is put under single inverted comma through the first brace beside the word maple. The symbolic quotient and remainder polynomials are implemented with the maple functions quo (abbreviation for quotient) and rem (abbreviation for remainder) respectively. When the two functions (one at a time) are executed in maple, there are four input arguments, the first, second, third, and fourth of which are the reserve word quo or rem under quote, vector code of $p(x)$, vector code of $s(x)$, and prime or independent variable of $p(x)$ or $s(x)$ respectively. The prime variable must be declared as symbolic using the syms prior to computation. However the execution is as follows:

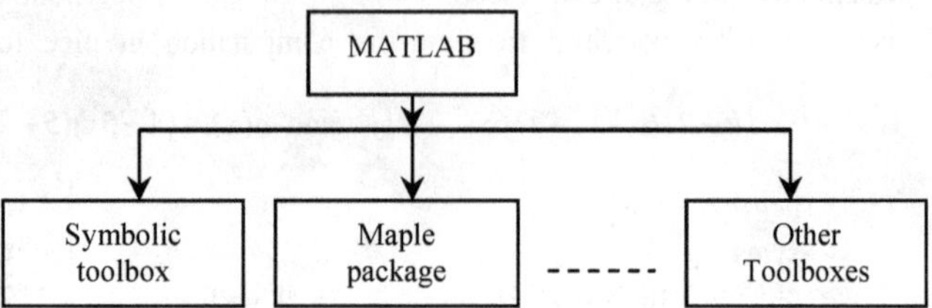

Figure 3.1(a) Hierarchy of MATLAB toolboxes

Symbolic division for the single variable case,

```
>>syms x ↵              ← Declare x as symbolic
>>p=x^4-x+1; ↵          ← Assign x^4 - x + 1 to p
>>s=x^2+x+1; ↵          ← Assign x^2 + x + 1 to s
>>q=maple('quo',p,s,x) ↵ ← apply quo for q(x)

q =

x^2-x                   ← q holds q(x)
>>r=maple('rem',p,s,x) ↵ ← apply rem for r(x)

r =

1                       ← r holds r(x)
```

Symbolic division for the two variable case,

```
>>syms x y ↵ ← Declare x and y as symbolic
>>p=3*x^4-8*y^4; ↵ ← Assign 3x^4 - 8y^4 to p
>>s=x-2*y; ↵       ← Assign x - 2y to s
>>q=maple('quo',p,s,x); ↵ ← q holds q(x,y)
>>pretty(q) ↵ ← Display readable q contents (last section)
     3        2          2         3
  3 x  + 6 y x  + 12 y  x  + 24 y
>>r=maple('rem',p,s,x); ↵ ← r holds r(x,y)
>>pretty(r) ↵ ← Display readable r contents
         4
     40 y
```

As another example, the dividend and divider polynomials are $p(x, y) = 3x^4 - 8y^4$ and $s(x, y) = x - 2y$ respectively. Long division yields the quotient and remainder polynomials as $q(x, y) = 3x^3 + 6x^2y + 12xy^2 + 24y^3$ and $r(x, y) = 40y^4$ respectively where x is the prime variable of the division. See its execution above on the right.

In the numeric division we exercise the division only through the polynomial coefficients and for a single independent variable using the function deconv (abbreviation for deconvolution) which has the common syntax [q r]=deconv(p,s). From above mentioned single variable case, the polynomials $s(x) = x^2 + x + 1$, $p(x) = x^4 - x + 1$, $q(x) = x^2 - x$, and $r(x)=1$ have the coefficient form (section 3.1) representations [1 1 1], [1 0 0 −1 1], [1 −1 0], and [1] for divider, dividend, quotient, and remainder polynomials respectively. The deconv accepts two input arguments – the dividend and divider polynomial coefficients and returns two output arguments – the quotient and remainder polynomials, all of which as a row matrix respectively. On having the coefficients, the readable form is seen using the poly2str of section 3.1. Let us carry out the said division as presented above on the right.

Polynomial division in numeric form:

```
>>p=[1 0 0 -1 1]; s=[1 1 1]; ↵
>>[q r]=deconv(p,s) ↵

q =
     1    -1     0
r =
     0     0     0     0     1
```

To display the $q(x)$ in readable form:

```
>>poly2str(q,'x') ↵

ans =
   x^2 - 1 x
```

3.3 Partial fraction in symbolic and coefficient forms

Any function $f(x)$ which is the division of two polynomials in x can be turned to partial fraction both in symbolic and numeric sense. Examples chosen for the partial fraction are the following.

First example: $\dfrac{x}{(3+2x)(x-1)} = \dfrac{3}{5(2x+3)} + \dfrac{1}{5(x-1)}$

Second example: $\frac{3x^5-x}{(3x-2)(2x-1)(-x+5)}=-\frac{x^2}{2}-\frac{37x}{12}-\frac{1147}{72}-\frac{22}{117(3x-2)}+\frac{13}{72(2x-1)}-\frac{9370}{117(x-5)}$

Third example: $\frac{-2x^7}{(x+1)^4}=-2x^3+8x^2-20x+40+\frac{2}{(x+1)^4}-\frac{14}{(x+1)^3}+\frac{42}{(x+1)^2}-\frac{70}{x+1}$

Fourth example: $\frac{1}{x^3+1}=\frac{1}{3(x+1)}-\frac{x-2}{3(x^2-x+1)}$ (avoiding complex factorization)

Symbolic form partial fraction

Symbolic form partial fraction is implementable using the maple toolbox (last section) function parfrac (abbreviation for the partial fraction) but the function is located in the convert library of maple. The common syntax for calling the function is maple('convert',f,'parfrac',x) in which the first and third input arguments of the function are the reserve words in MATLAB placed under quote. The second and fourth input arguments of the function are the vector functional code (section 14.2) and its independent variable respectively. Declaration of the independent variable as symbolic (section 2.1) prior to calling the function is compulsory. Following commands perform straightforward partial fractions on aforementioned examples (font equivalence is maintained in all executions for example x⇔ x):

symbolic partial fraction: example 1:

```
>>syms x ↵
>>N=x; D=(3+2*x)*(x-1); f=N/D; ↵
>>R=maple('convert',f,'parfrac',x); ↵
>>pretty(R) ↵
          1             1
  3/5 --------- + 1/5 ------
       3 + 2 x         x - 1
```

symbolic partial fraction: example 2:

```
>>syms x ↵
>>N=3*x^5-x; D=(3*x-2)*(2*x-1)*(-x+5); f=N/D; ↵
>>R=maple('convert',f,'parfrac',x); ↵
>>pretty(R) ↵
        2   37     1147   22      1      13    1        9370   1
 - 1/2 x  - --- x - ------- - ----- -------- + --- --------- - -------- -------
            12       72     117  3 x - 2   72  2 x - 1    117   x - 5
```

symbolic partial fraction: example 4:

```
>>syms x ↵
>>f=1/(x^3+1); ↵
>>R=maple('convert',f,'parfrac',x); ↵
>>pretty(R) ↵
          1           -2 + x
  1/3 ----- - 1/3 -----------
        x+1          2
                    x  - x + 1
```

symbolic partial fraction: example 3:

```
>>syms x ↵
>>N=-2*x^7; D=(x+1)^4; f=N/D; ↵
>>R=maple('convert',f,'parfrac',x); ↵
>>pretty(R) ↵
      3     2                  2        14        42      70
  -2 x  + 8 x  - 20 x + 40 + -------- - -------- + -------- - -----
                                 4         3          2      x+1
                             (x +1)     (x+1)      (x+1)
```

It is possible to assign the numerator and denominator of $f(x)$ separately to the workspace variables N and D respectively and the function $f(x)$ is formed afterwards from N/D which is assigned to f. In all four examples the return from maple is assigned to the workspace variable R and we utilized pretty of section 3.1 to display the readable form on R. The N, D, f, and R are user-chosen names.

Numeric form partial fraction

Numeric form partial fraction of $f(x)$ is conducted using the function residue (abbreviation for residual due to polynomial division) which accepts two input arguments – the first and second of which are the numerator and denominator polynomial coefficients of $f(x)$ in descending power of x and as a row matrix respectively. For the third example $\frac{-2x^7}{(x+1)^4}$, the numerator and denominator polynomial coefficients are [−2 0 0 0 0 0 0 0] and [1 4 6 4 1] (because $(x+1)^4=x^4+4x^3+6x^2+4x+1$) respectively. You can view or assign the coefficients of the denominator using the command syms x, sym2poly((x+1)^4) (sections 2.1 and 3.1). The first and second input arguments of the residue should be just mentioned numerator and denominator polynomial coefficients respectively. The number of the output arguments of the residue is three. The rational part $\frac{2}{(x+1)^4}-\frac{14}{(x+1)^3}+\frac{42}{(x+1)^2}-\frac{70}{x+1}$ of the third example has the residues −70, 42, −14, and 2 for the linear denominator factor $(x+1)$, $(x+1)^2$, $(x+1)^3$, and $(x+1)^4$ respectively which can be placed in a row matrix as [−70 42 −14 2] and which is the first return from the residue. The linear factor roots

for the first example (numeric partial fraction),

```
>>N=[1 0]; ↵
>>syms x ↵
>>D=sym2poly((3+2*x)*(x-1)); ↵
>>[R P K]=residue(N,D) ↵

R =
        0.3000
        0.2000
P =
       -1.5000
        1.0000
K =
       []
```

numeric partial fraction: second example:

```
>>syms x ↵
>>N=sym2poly(3*x^5-x); ↵
>>D=sym2poly((3*x-2)*(2*x-1)*(-x+5)); ↵
>>[R P K]=residue(N,D) ↵

R =
     -80.0855
      -0.0627
       0.0903
P =
       5.0000
       0.6667
       0.5000
K =
      -0.5000   -3.0833  -15.9306
```

of the denominator of the rational part of the example 3 are −1, −1, −1, and −1 for $(x+1)$, $(x+1)^2$, $(x+1)^3$, and $(x+1)^4$ respectively. These four roots can be placed as a row matrix as [−1 −1 −1 −1] which will be the second output argument of the **residue**. The nonrational part $-2x^3+8x^2-20x+40$ has the polynomial coefficients in descending power of x as [−2 8 −20 40] which becomes the third output argument of **residue**. Formal executions for the numeric partial fraction of the four examples are attached on the right (the first and second examples are in the last page). In all examples the input arguments N and D hold the numerator and denominator polynomial coefficients respectively. The output arguments R, P, and K are the rational component residuals, the linear denominator factor roots (also called poles), and the nonrational part polynomial coefficients respectively. For reader's convenience, we rewrite the partial fractions for the four examples in terms of decimal as follows:

numeric partial fraction: example 3:

```
>>N=[-2 0 0 0 0 0 0 0]; ↵
>>D=[1 4 6 4 1]; ↵
>>[R P K]=residue(N,D) ↵

R =
  -70.0000
   42.0000
  -14.0000
    2.0000
P =
   -1.0000
   -1.0000
   -1.0000
   -1.0000
K =
    -2    8   -20   40
```

numeric partial fraction: example 4:

```
>>syms x ↵
>>N=1; ↵
>>D=sym2poly(x^3+1); ↵
>>[R P K]=residue(N,D) ↵

R =
  -0.1667 - 0.2887i
  -0.1667 + 0.2887i
   0.3333
P =
   0.5000 + 0.8660i
   0.5000 - 0.8660i
  -1.0000
K =
   []
```

First example: $\dfrac{x}{(3+2x)(x-1)}=\dfrac{0.3}{x+1.5}+\dfrac{0.2}{x-1}$

Second example: $\dfrac{3x^5-x}{(3x-2)(2x-1)(-x+5)}=-0.5x^2-3.0833x-15.9306-\dfrac{0.0627}{x-0.6667}+\dfrac{0.0903}{x-0.5}-\dfrac{80.0855}{x-5}$

Third example: same as before

Fourth example: $\dfrac{1}{x^3+1}=\dfrac{0.3333}{x+1}-\dfrac{0.1667-j0.2887}{x-0.5+j0.866}-\dfrac{0.1667+j0.2887}{x-0.5-j0.866}$ (considering complex factorization)

The returns assigned to R and P are in column matrix form. If the nonrational part does not exist in the partial fraction, the return to K is an empty matrix [ ] (examples 1 and 4). Since the **residue** solely works on polynomial coefficients, we extracted the coefficients using **sym2poly** in the first, second, and fourth examples. The R and P returns are in order for example the first element of R corresponds to the first element of P. The **residue** functions on the linear denominator factor that is why complex factorization is performed in the fourth example.

3.4 Numerator and denominator from an expression

Given an algebraic expression, one can separate its numerator and denominator components using the function **numden** (abbreviation for numerator and denominator) which is conducted completely using the symbolic concept. We need to declare the independent variable using **syms** (section 2.1). The function has two output arguments – one for the numerator and the other for the denominator. The input argument of the function as well as its output argument exercises vector string form (section 14.2). For example, the expression $\dfrac{x^2}{y}+yx+\dfrac{5y}{7x}$ has the numerator and denominator $7x^3+7x^2y^2+5y^2$ and $7xy$ respectively. There are two independent variables in the expression – x and y. Again the trigonometric function $\dfrac{\cos A}{\cos A-5}-\dfrac{\sin A}{\sin A+3}$ has the numerator and denominator as $3\cos A+5\sin A$ and $(\cos A-5)(\sin A+3)$ respectively in which the single independent variable is A. Both implementations are presented below:

Numerator and denominator separation for the first expression:

```
>>syms x y ↵
>>[n d]=numden(x^2/y+y*x +5/7*y/x); ↵
>>pretty(n) ↵
          3       2  2       2
       7 x  + 7 y  x  + 5 y
>>pretty(d) ↵
       7 y x
```

Numerator and denominator separation for the second expression:

```
>>syms A ↵
>>f1=cos(A)/(cos(A)-5); f2=sin(A)/(sin(A)+3); ↵
>>[n d]=numden(f1-f2); ↵
>>pretty(n) ↵
       3 cos(A) + 5 sin(A)
>>pretty(d) ↵
       (cos(A) - 5) (sin(A) + 3)
```

Font equivalence is maintained in all executions for example x⇔x. The vector string of the output numerator and denominator are returned to the workplace n and d (can be any variable of your choice) respectively. Command **pretty** (section 3.1) just displays the strings in readable form. It is permissible that we enter long expression part by part. For example the first and second parts of the second expression are assigned to the workspace f1 and f2 (can be any name of your choice) respectively. The whole expression is composed of f1-f2 on which the **numden** is exercised.

3.5 LCM and GCD of integers and functions

Function lcm finds the least common multiplier (LCM) of integers which accepts two same size rectangular matrix of integers as its input arguments in general. For example the integers 27 and 84 have the LCM 756. Again the LCM of like positional elements of $A=\begin{bmatrix}34\\12\\10\end{bmatrix}$ and $B=\begin{bmatrix}2\\8\\3\end{bmatrix}$ is $C=\begin{bmatrix}34\\24\\30\end{bmatrix}$. The LCM of all elements in the matrix $A=\begin{bmatrix}10 & 2\\7 & 9\\18 & 3\end{bmatrix}$ is 630. All implementations are presented on the right (font equivalence is maintained for example A⇔ A). In the third case slight programming is required. The command A=A(:) turns the rectangular matrix to a column one and the return is assigned to A again. The N holds the number of elements in A which is 6 (section 2.12). The k-th element in A is selected by A(k). Using a for-loop (subsection 14.3.3) provides control on every element in A. Sequentially we find LCM between the element stored in L starting from the first one and A(k) using the command lcm(L,A(k)) and assign the result to L again using L=lcm(L,A(k)). Thus L holds the LCM of all elements in A at the end of the loop.

Expression based LCM finding is also possible through the use of the maple package (section 3.2). For example the LCM of the two expressions $f(x,y)=x^4-y^4$ and $h(x,y)=x^3-y^3$ is $(x^3+x^2y+xy^2+y^3)(x^3-y^3)$ whose implementation is also presented above. Independent variables of the expressions $f(x,y)$ and $h(x,y)$ are declared using the syms (section 2.1) prior to exercising the function. In above execution the vector codes (section 14.2) of $f(x,y)$ and $h(x,y)$ are assigned to workspace f and h respectively. The maple is taking three input arguments, the first, second, and third of which are the reserve word lcm for LCM (must be placed under quote), the vector code of $f(x,y)$, and the vector code $h(x,y)$ respectively. The return is assigned to L (user-chosen name) whose readable form is seen using the pretty (section 3.1).

LCM for two single integers,

```
>>lcm(27,84) ↵

ans =

       756
```

LCM for two column matrices,

```
>>A=[34 12 10]'; ↵
>>B=[2 8 3]'; ↵
>>C=lcm(A,B) ↵

C =

          34
          24
          30
```

LCM for all elements in a matrix,

```
>>A=[10 2;7 9;18 3]; ↵
>>A=A(:); N=length(A); L=A(1); ↵
>>for k=2:N, L=lcm(L,A(k)); end ↵
>>L ↵

L =

     630
```

LCM for two expressions,

```
>>syms x y ↵
>>f=x^4-y^4; h=x^3-y^3; ↵
>>L=maple('lcm',f,h); ↵
>>pretty(L) ↵
        3      2     2      3      3    3
     (x  + y x  + y  x + y  ) (x  - y  )
```

Finding the greatest common divider (GCD) is very similar to that of the LCM. All we need is replace the function lcm by the gcd in the continuing examples.

3.6 Algebraic substitution and variable elimination

Suppose we have the equation $3x-2y=3$ and function $e^{2x^2-3xy+5y^2}$. We intend to eliminate x from the $e^{2x^2-3xy+5y^2}$ where x is obtained from $3x-2y=3$ and following the substitution we should have $e^{\frac{35}{9}y^2-\frac{y}{3}+2}$. The function algsubs (abbreviation for algebraic substitution) which is located in maple (section 3.2) performs the algebraic substitution. Since the computation is symbolic, all related variables in the expression are declared using syms (section 2.1) prior to applying the function. Let us conduct the substitution as follows:

```
>>syms x y ↵                          ← Declaration of x and y as symbolic, x⇔x , y⇔y
>>e='3*x-2*y=3'; ↵                    ← Vector code(section 14.2) of 3x − 2y = 3 is assigned to workspace e
>>f='exp(2*x^2-3*x*y+5*y^2)'; ↵       ← Vector code of e^(2x^2−3xy+5y^2) is assigned to workspace f
>>R=maple('algsubs',e,f,x); ↵         ← Elimination of x from f and the result is assigned to workspace R
>>pretty(R) ↵                         ← Display the readable form of R using pretty (section 3.1)
                              2
        exp(- 1/3 y + 35/9 y  + 2)
```

There are four input arguments inside the maple, the first, second, third, and fourth of which are the function name placed under quote, two consecutive expressions, and the variable to be eliminated respectively. Step by step variable elimination is also possible. For instance we have three equations: $3x-2y-4z+u=3$, $4x+6y^2-6z+9u=9$, and $z-8u=7$ in which four unknown variables are related − x, y, z, and u. From the first two equations we intend to eliminate x so that the resulting equation becomes y, z, and u related (let us call it R_1). Again we intend to eliminate

z from the third equation and R_1 so that at the end we should be having y and u related $4y+\frac{7}{2}u+9y^2=\frac{29}{2}$ whose implementations follow next:

```
>>syms x y z u ↵                       ← Declaration of all related variables as symbolic, x⇔x , y⇔y , z⇔z , u⇔u
>>e1='3*x-2*y-4*z+u=3'; ↵              ← Vector code of the first equation is assigned to workspace e1
>>e2='4*x+6*y^2-6*z+9*u=9'; ↵          ← Vector code of the second equation is assigned to workspace e2
>>e3='z-8*u=7'; ↵                      ← Vector code of the third equation is assigned to workspace e3
>>R1=maple('algsubs',e1,e2,x); ↵       ← Elimiation of x from the first and second equations, R1⇔R1
>>R=maple('algsubs',R1,e3,z); ↵        ← Elimiation of z from the R1 and third equations, R holds the y
                                          and u related equation
>>pretty(R) ↵                          ← Display the readable form of R using the pretty
                           2
    4 y + 7/2 u - 15/2 + 9 y  = 7
```

Suppose we require to express u in terms of y which should be $u=-\frac{8}{7}y+\frac{29}{7}-\frac{18}{7}y^2$ and which means we need to solve (section 3.8) the equation stored in R for u as follows:

```
>>U=solve(R,u); ↵ ← Workspace U holds the expressed expression related to y , U is user-chosen name
>>pretty(U) ↵      ← Display the readable form of U using the pretty
                                2
    - 8/7 y + 29/7 - 18/7 y
```

3.7 Complete square from an expression

The expression $7x^2-24xy^2+9y^4$ turns to $7\left(x-\frac{12y^2}{7}\right)^2-\frac{81y^4}{7}$ following the complete square formation. There is a library in maple (section 3.2) called student which keeps this kind of complete square forming option through the function completesquare. Before using the function, one needs to declare all related variables in the expression as symbolic using the syms (section 2.1) and activate the student package using the with command of maple. Another example can be ax^2+bx+c = $a\left(x+\frac{b}{2a}\right)^2+c-\frac{b^2}{4a}$. Both implementations are presented above (font equivalence is maintained for example x⇔x). The first line is for the activation of the student package. Vector code (section 14.2) of each expression is assigned to the workspace e. The maple has three input arguments, the first, second, and third of which are the function name under quote, the expression assignee, and the prime variable on which the complete square is to be performed respectively. The return from the maple is assigned to R whose readable form is seen using the command pretty (section 3.1).

Complete square for the first example,

```
>>maple('with','student'); ↵
>>syms x y ↵
>>e=7*x^2-24*x*y^2+9*y^4; ↵
>>R=maple('completesquare',e,x); ↵
>>pretty(R) ↵
               2 2           4
    7 (x - 12/7 y  )  - 81/7 y
```

Complete square for the second example,

```
>>maple('with','student'); ↵
>>syms a b c x ↵
>>e=a*x^2+b*x+c; ↵
>>R=maple('completesquare',e,x); ↵
>>pretty(R) ↵
                                 2
                         2      b
    a (x + 1/2  b/a)  - 1/4 --- + c
                                a
```

3.8 Solving algebraic equations

By virtue of the function solve, we find the solution of a single or multiple algebraic equations when the equations are its input arguments. The notion of the solution is symbolic and a number of simultaneous linear, algebraic, or trigonometric equations can be handled this way. Associated variables in the equations are declared using the syms (section 2.1) before one applies the function. The common syntax of the implementation is solve (equation-1,equation-2,……so on in vector string form – section 14.2, unknowns separated by comma). The equations are assigned under quote while placing or assigning. In the following we assign the first equation to e1, the second equation to e2, and so on. Font equivalence is maintained for example x⇔x. The return from the function solve is in general a structure array (section 14.4). In order to view the solution, one needs to call the individual member of the array. If s is a structure array and u is one of its members, we call the member using the command s.u. One can assign the s.u to some other workspace variable and apply the command pretty (section 3.1) on the assignee to view the readable form of the solution. Again decimal form of the solution is achievable through the use of the command double. Let us see the following examples on algebraic equation solving.

Example 1

It is given that the simultaneous linear equatuion set $\begin{Bmatrix} x-y-3z+2u=-8 \\ 9x+8y-7z+u=5 \\ 9x+4y+2z=23 \\ -3x+y-6z+7u=-12 \end{Bmatrix}$ has the solution $\begin{bmatrix} x \\ y \\ z \\ u \end{bmatrix} = \begin{bmatrix} 1 \\ 2 \\ 3 \\ 1 \end{bmatrix}$ and we intend to obtain the solution. We attached the implementation above on the right in which the assignee s (any user-given name) holds the solution as a structure array. In order to see the solution corresponding to each variable, we exercise the following:

Equation solving for example 1:

```
>>syms x y z u ↵                          ← Declaration of associated variables
>>e1='x-y-3*z+2*u=-8'; ↵                  ← Assign the first equation to e1
>>e2='9*x+8*y-7*z+u=5'; ↵                 ← Assign the second equation to e2
>>e3='9*x+4*y+2*z=23'; ↵                  ← Assign the third equation to e3
>>e4='-3*x+y-6*z+7*u=-12';↵               ← Assign the fourth equation to e4
>>s=solve(e1,e2,e3,e4,x,y,z,u) ↵          ← solve on e1, e2, e3, and e4

s =                                       ← s holds the solution as a structure array
      u: [1x1 sym]                        ← u is a member of s
      x: [1x1 sym]                        ← x is a member of s
      y: [1x1 sym]                        ← y is a member of s
      z: [1x1 sym]                        ← z is a member of s
```

to see the value of x **:**	**value of** y **:**	**value of** z **:**	**value of** u **:**
>>s.x ↵	>>s.y ↵	>>s.z ↵	>>s.u ↵
ans =	ans =	ans =	ans =
1	2	3	1

Example 2

In example 1, all equations were having power 1 on the related variables. Equation involving power term more than 1 for instance $\begin{Bmatrix} x^2-y^2-z^2=a^2 \\ 2y+x=4 \\ z-x=2 \end{Bmatrix}$ is also solvable. Here the number of related variables is more than the number of equations therefore the solution will not be unique. Let us say we are looking for the solution for $\{x, y, z\}$ so that the solution becomes in terms of a and is given by $\{x,y,z\} = \left(\begin{bmatrix} -4+2\sqrt{-4-a^2} \\ -4-2\sqrt{-4-a^2} \end{bmatrix}, \begin{bmatrix} 4-\sqrt{-4-a^2} \\ 4+\sqrt{-4-a^2} \end{bmatrix}, \begin{bmatrix} -2+2\sqrt{-4-a^2} \\ -2-2\sqrt{-4-a^2} \end{bmatrix} \right)$ (two solutions for each determinate x, y, or z). Our objective is to obtain the solution using the symbology we mentioned. The implementation is shown above on the right. In order to view the output, we execute the following:

Equation solving for the example 2:

```
>>syms x y z a ↵          ← Declaration of associated variables
>>e1='x^2-y^2-z^2=a^2'; ↵ ← Assign the first equation to e1
>>e2='2*y+x=4'; ↵          ← Assign the second equation to e2
>>e3='z-x=2'; ↵            ← Assign the third equation to e3
>>s=solve(e1,e2,e3,x,y,z) ↵ ← solve on e1, e2, and e3

s =                        ← s holds the solution as a structure array
     x: [2x1 sym]          ← x is a member of s
     y: [2x1 sym]          ← y is a member of s
     z: [2x1 sym]          ← z is a member of s
```

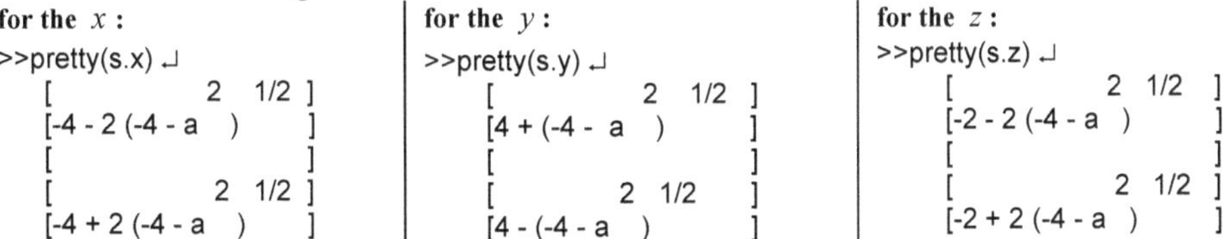

for the x **:**

```
>>pretty(s.x) ↵
   [               2  1/2 ]
   [-4 - 2 (-4 - a )      ]
   [                      ]
   [               2  1/2 ]
   [-4 + 2 (-4 - a )      ]
```

for the y **:**

```
>>pretty(s.y) ↵
   [              2  1/2 ]
   [4 + (-4 - a )        ]
   [                     ]
   [              2  1/2 ]
   [4 - (-4 - a )        ]
```

for the z **:**

```
>>pretty(s.z) ↵
   [               2  1/2 ]
   [-2 - 2 (-4 - a )      ]
   [                      ]
   [               2  1/2 ]
   [-2 + 2 (-4 - a )      ]
```

All members of the structure array are a two element column matrix and the solution is in order. For example the first element of each column matrix is one solution of the given equation set.

Example 3

The function solve first attempts to find the symbolic solution if it is possible otherwise provides numerical solution such an example is { $\cos(x+2)=y$ and $x=y^2$ }. It is given that the numerical solution of the set is { x =0.9713 and y =− 0.9855} which we intend to obtain. Employing alike symbology, we verify the solution as follows:

Equation solving for example 3:

```
>>syms x y ↵
>>e1='cos(x+2)=y'; ↵
>>e2='x=y^2'; ↵
>>s=solve(e1,e2,x,y) ↵

s =
    x: [1x1 sym]
    y: [1x1 sym]
```

```
>>s.x ↵

ans =

.97126945009862137236722172434639
>>s.y ↵

ans =

-.98553003510731288740261765261355
```

```
>>double(s.x) ↵

ans =

0.9713
>>double(s.y) ↵

ans =

-0.9855
```

The command **double** provides the decimal solution from **s.x** or **s.y** which is in symbolic form.

Example 4

Solving trigonometric equations through the **solve** is no exception. It is given that the trigonometric equations $\sec^2 x + 2\tan x = 0$ and $3\cos x + 2\sin x = 2$ have the solutions $x = \left\{ \frac{3\pi}{4} \text{ or } -\frac{\pi}{4} \right\}$ and $x = \left\{ -\tan^{-1}\frac{5}{12} \text{ or } \frac{\pi}{2} \right\}$ respectively whose implementations are attached on the right (similar symbology is maintained). Note that for a single variable case there is no need to declare the related variable and the solution return is not a structure array instead placed as a column matrix form. If you say I need the decimal form, use the command **double(s)**. Section 3.2 mentioned **maple** also possesses the **solve** function which solves the trigonometric equation in a similar fashion. The solution returned by **solve** for the first equation is the principal value. The general trigonometric solution for the first equation through the **solve** of **maple** is obtained as follows:

Example 4: for the first equation:

```
>>e='sec(x)^2+2*tan(x)=0'; ↵
>>s=solve(e) ↵

s =

 -1/4*pi
 3/4*pi
```

Example 4: for the second equation:

```
>>e='3*cos(x)+2*sin(x)=2'; ↵
>>s=solve(e) ↵

s =

          1/2*pi
 -atan(5/12)
```

```
>>maple('_EnvAllSolutions:=true:solve(sec(x)^2+2*tan(x)=0,x)') ↵

ans =

-1/4*pi+2*pi*_Z1, 3/4*pi+2*pi*_Z1
```

The function **solve** of **maple** accepts two input arguments, the first and second of which are the equation and the prime variable respectively. The word **_EnvAllSolutions** is reserve to **maple** indicating general solution requirement. The assignment operator in **maple** is :=. The reserve word **true** indicates that we are after the general solution. The **_Z1** means any integer. The line ending statement in MATLAB is ; whereas it is : in **maple**. From above execution, one reads off the general solution as $x = 2\pi n - \frac{\pi}{4}$ or $2\pi n + \frac{3\pi}{4}$ where n is any integer (_Z1$\Leftrightarrow n$).

Equation solving for the example 5:

```
>>e='x^3+x^2+4*x+4=0'; ↵
>>s=solve(e) ↵

s =
   -1
   2*i
  -2*i
```

Example 5

In section 3.1 we addressed the root finding in terms of polynomial coefficients. You can apply the **solve** to find the roots as well. Take the example $x^3 + x^2 + 4x + 4 = 0$ which has the roots -1, $2i$, and $-2i$ (complex roots) and whose implementation is attached on the upper right.

Example 6

Transcendental equation like $x\tan x = 2$ using the **solve** returns a single solution which is $x = -1.2646$. Since $\tan x$ has multiple roots, some engineering problem requires that we find all possible roots within a given interval (also called the eigenvalues of the equation). As an example, it is given that x =1.0750, 1.5750, 3.6450, and 4.7150 are the roots of the equation over $0 \le x \le 6$. Slight programming is necessary to solve the problem. Our written function file **mzero** finds the multiple roots from any functional values numerically. As a first step, type the codes of the M-file presented in the figure 3.1(b) in a new M-file (section 1.3) and save the file by the name **mzero** in your working path of MATLAB. Within the given interval of x, we choose some step size. The smaller is the step size, the better is the accuracy. For example choosing a step size 0.01 provides the roots as two decimal accurate. Once we decide the step size, the x values are generated as a row vector and the given function is computed using the scalar code (section 14.2) at the values of x vector. While writing the scalar code, the equation is arranged such that the right side of the equation is zero. The function **mzero** has two input arguments, the first and second of which are the x and functional values of the function both as a row matrix respectively. The return of the **mzero** is the roots as a row matrix. However we call the function from the command prompt as follows:

```
function mz=mzero(x,y)
s=sign(y);
v=abs(diff(s));
r=find(v==2);
if isempty(r)
  disp('No crossing')
else
  mz=(x(r)+x(r+1))/2;
end
```

Figure 3.1(b) M-file for finding multiple zeroes from a function

```
>>x=0:0.01:6; ↵
>>y=x.*tan(x)-2; ↵
>>s=mzero(x,y) ↵
```

←**x** is a row matrix over the given interval $0 \le x \le 6$ and choosing the step size 0.01

←**y** is the computed $x\tan x - 2$ values at the x points in the row vector **x**

←**s** holds the roots returned from **mzero** as a row matrix

```
s =

    1.0750    1.5750    3.6450    4.7150
```

If you select the step size 0.001, the roots so returned become 3 digit accurate. Example 4 or other mentioned equations can also be solved numerically this way.

3.9 Expansion of trigonometric functions

The trigonometric functions with multiple angles such as $\sin 3x$, $\cos 4x$, $\tan 3x$ ... etc can be expanded to smaller angles. The function **expand** is helpful in this regard which takes the vector code (section 14.2) of the trigonometric expression. Since the expansion is symbolic, the concern variable must be declared using the **syms** (section 2.1) prior to the expansion. Following the expansion, the command **pretty** (section 3.1) is used to see the readable form. You can assign the return from **expand** to some variable of your choice which holds the vector code of the expansion however several examples are attached below.

Trigonometric notation	Command we need for the expansion	Trigonometric notation	Command we need for the expansion
$\sin 2A =$ $2\sin A\cos A$	>>syms A ↵ >>pretty(expand(sin(2*A))) ↵ 2 sin(A) cos(A)	$\cos(4\sin^{-1}x) =$ $8x^4 - 8x^2 + 1$	>>syms x ↵ >>pretty(expand(cos(4*asin(x)))) ↵ 2 4 1 - 8 x + 8 x
$\tan 3A =$ $\dfrac{3\tan A - \tan^3 A}{1 - 3\tan^2 A}$	>>syms A ↵ >>pretty(expand(tan(3*A))) ↵ 3 3 tan(A) - tan(A) --------------------- 2 1 - 3 tan(A)	$\tan(5\tan^{-1}x) =$ $\dfrac{5x - 10x^3 + x^5}{1 - 10x^2 + 5x^4}$	>>syms x ↵ >>pretty(expand(tan(5*atan(x)))) ↵ 3 5 5 x - 10 x + x --------------------- 2 4 1 - 10 x + 5 x
$\sin 2A =$ $2\sin A\cos A$	>>syms A ↵ >>pretty(expand(sin(2*A))) ↵ 2 sin(A) cos(A)	$\cos 3A =$ $4\cos^3 A - 3\cos A$	>>syms A ↵ >>pretty(expand(cos(3*A))) ↵ 3 4 cos(A) - 3 cos(A)

3.10 Computations of expressions

MATLAB is a very powerful software for computation of expressions. Long and clumsy functions are easily computed in scalar or vector form on its user-friendly platform. Expressions that can be used as the token of complicated computations are exemplified below. In the subsequent discussions we maintain the font equivalence for instance A⇔ A.

3.10.1 Functions of one variable

Let us consider that the following one variable related expressions have to be evaluated for some x for instance for x =1, 1.5, 3, 3.5, 4, and 2.5.

$$A.\ e^x\cos x \quad B.\ \frac{\log_{10}x}{\cosh x} \quad C.\ \sin^2 x\cos^2 x \quad D.\ \frac{1}{\sqrt{\tan^2 x + 9x^3}} \quad E.\ \sum_x -9x^2\sqrt{\left|\ln\frac{x}{2}\right|} \quad F.\ \prod_x \frac{1+\frac{x}{2}}{1+\frac{x}{4}}$$

Computed values of above expressions are presented in tabular form in the following which we intend to accomplish in MATLAB.

	Expression A	Expression B	Expression C	Expression D	Expression E	Expression F
x	$e^x \cos x$	$\dfrac{\log_{10}x}{\cosh x}$	$\sin^2 x\cos^2 x$	$\dfrac{1}{\sqrt{\tan^2 x + 9x^3}}$	$-9x^2\sqrt{\left\|\ln\frac{x}{2}\right\|}$	$\prod_x \dfrac{1+\frac{x}{2}}{1+\frac{x}{4}}$
1	1.46869394	0	0.206705452	0.295843502	−298.8665 for all x	6.6462 for all x
1.5	0.317022143	0.074855696	0.004978714	0.066049413		
3	-19.88453084	0.047391465	0.019518255	0.064147347		
3.5	-31.01118644	0.032828926	0.107907847	0.05089765		
4	-35.68773248	0.02204683	0.244707435	0.041618264		
2.5	-9.759927258	0.064892567	0.229883941	0.084160582		

This kind of computation can best be conducted through the scalar code (code details in the section 14.2) of the functions. The trigonometric function's input argument is intended to be in radians. Computations for all examples are presented on the upper right side in the following page. The required x values must be in a row or column matrix and assigned to the workspace variable **x** prior to the computation. Referring to the expression A, the command **f=exp(x).*cos(x)** means we computed the $e^x\cos x$ for every single value stored in **x** and assigned the computation result to the workspace **f**. The variable name **x** or **f** is user-defined. The commands **cos(x)**, **exp(x)**, and **exp(x).*cos(x)** perform the operations

$$\begin{bmatrix} \cos 1 \\ \cos 1.5 \\ \cos 3 \\ \cos 3.5 \\ \cos 4 \\ \cos 2.5 \end{bmatrix}, \begin{bmatrix} e^1 \\ e^{1.5} \\ e^3 \\ e^{3.5} \\ e^4 \\ e^{2.5} \end{bmatrix}, \text{ and } \begin{bmatrix} e^1 \cos 1 \\ e^{1.5} \cos 1.5 \\ e^3 \cos 3 \\ e^{3.5} \cos 3.5 \\ e^4 \cos 4 \\ e^{2.5} \cos 2.5 \end{bmatrix}$$

respectively. This sort of interpretation follows for the other expressions as well. If the x is a row matrix, so is f again if the x is a column matrix, so is f. For the expressions E and F, two functions sum and prod are utilized respectively whose discussions are seen in section 2.8.

The x values we chose are discrete. Consecutive values are generated using the colon operator (section 1.3). For instance we intend to calculate each of the just cited expressions over $-1 \le x \le 5$ but with a step size 0.1 in that case the x as a row matrix would be created by the command x=-1:0.1:5;.

Subsection 3.10.1 mentioned computation for the expression A:

```
>>x=[1 1.5 3 3.5 4 2.5]; ↵
>>f=exp(x).*cos(x) ↵

f =
    1.4687    0.3170  -19.8845  -31.0112  -35.6877   -9.7599
```

Computation for the expression B:

```
>>f=log10(x)./cosh(x) ↵

f =
         0    0.0749    0.0474    0.0328    0.0220    0.0649
```

Computation for the expression C:

```
>>f=(sin(x).^2).*(cos(x).^2) ↵

f =
    0.2067    0.0050    0.0195    0.1079    0.2447    0.2299
```

Computation for the expression D:

```
>>f=1./sqrt((tan(x).^2)+9*(x.^3)) ↵

f =
    0.2958    0.0660    0.0641    0.0509    0.0416    0.0842
```

Computation for the expression E:

```
>>f=sum(-9*(x.^2).*sqrt(abs(log(x/2)))) ↵

f =
  -298.8665
```

Computation for expression F:

```
>>f=prod((1+x/2)./(1+x/4)) ↵

f =
    6.6462
```

3.10.2 Functions of two variables

Different cases are seen regarding the two variable function computation. We address some of them in the following.

For a single set of x and y values

Let us say the two variable function $f(x, y) = -7x^2 + 9y^x + e^{-y^2}$ is to be evaluated at $x = 0$ and $y = 1$ and which is $f(0, 1) = 9.3679$ – the problem statement. First we write the vector code (section 14.2) of the function and then assign it to some workspace variable f under quote. Assign the given x and y values to workspace x and y respectively and call the function eval on f for the evaluation. If you write the command V=eval(f), the result is assigned to V (implementation is shown above on the right).

For a single set of x and y:

```
>>f='-7*x^2+9*y^x+exp(-y^2)'; ↵
>>x=0; y=1; eval(f) ↵

ans =
    9.3679
```

For several sets of x and y values

We wish to compute just mentioned $f(x, y)$ for several sets of x and y values for instance $x = \begin{bmatrix} 0 \\ 2 \\ -1 \end{bmatrix}$ and $y = \begin{bmatrix} 1 \\ -1 \\ 2 \end{bmatrix}$ respectively so that the computation becomes $\begin{bmatrix} f(0, 1) \\ f(2, -1) \\ f(-1, 2) \end{bmatrix} = \begin{bmatrix} 9.3679 \\ -186321 \\ -2.4817 \end{bmatrix}$ – problem statement. The computation takes place through the use of the scalar code. First we assign the x and y data both as a row or column matrix (must be identical in size and must hold the elements in order of the sets) and then assign the scalar code to workspace f without quote. The f holds the computed values as attached on the right. It is important to cite that the computed f data follows the matrix size of x or y. The sets for the x and y values are discrete not consecutive here in this example. Suppose the sets of x and y change over $-3 \le x \le 1$ and $-2 \le y \le 2$ both with a step 0.5 and we intend to compute the ongoing $f(x, y)$ at those x and y values whose command would be x=-3:0.5:1; y=-2:0.5:2; f=-7*x.^2+9*y.^x+exp(-y.^2);. Previously mentioned single set value can also be computed this way.

For several sets of x and y:

```
>>x=[0 2 -1]'; y=[1 -1 2]'; ↵
>>f=-7*x.^2+9*y.^x+exp(-y.^2) ↵

f =
    9.3679
  -18.6321
   -2.4817
```

For rectangular x and y grid based computation

Most two dimensional scientific and engineering functions use this sort of grid based computation. One fact should be stressed that one dimensional functional values take the form of a row or column matrix on the other hand two dimensional functional values assume the shape of a rectangular matrix. If the row directed values of the rectangular matrix represent the x directed values of $f(x, y)$, for sure the columns of the rectangular matrix represent the y

directed values of the function. Examples are the best for understanding. Let us say $f(x, y)=x^2+xy+y^2$ is to be computed over the rectangular domain defined by $-1\le x\le 0.5$ with a x step 0.5 and $-4\le y\le 4$ with a y step 2. Figure 3.1(c) presents the nodes (indicated by the bold dots) at which we are interested to find the functional values. In other words we are looking for the functional values $\begin{bmatrix} f(-1,4) & & f(0.5,4) \\ \vdots & \cdot^{\cdot^{\cdot}} & \\ f(-1,-2) & & \\ f(-1,-4) & f(-0.5,-4) \cdots & f(0.5,-4) \end{bmatrix}$ as a rectangular matrix and which should be $\begin{bmatrix} 13 & 14.25 & 16 & 18.25 \\ 3 & 3.25 & 4 & 5.25 \\ 1 & 0.25 & 0 & 0.25 \\ 7 & 5.25 & 4 & 3.25 \\ 21 & 18.25 & 16 & 14.25 \end{bmatrix}$ following the computation. As a first step, we generate the coordinate points from the given domain description using the function **meshgrid**. The function has two input arguments which are the x and y variations with the given step size respectively but both are as a row matrix. The **meshgrid** can have two output arguments, all x and all y coordinates respectively but both as a rectangular matrix of identical size (whose elements correspond to the node points of the figure 3.1(c)).

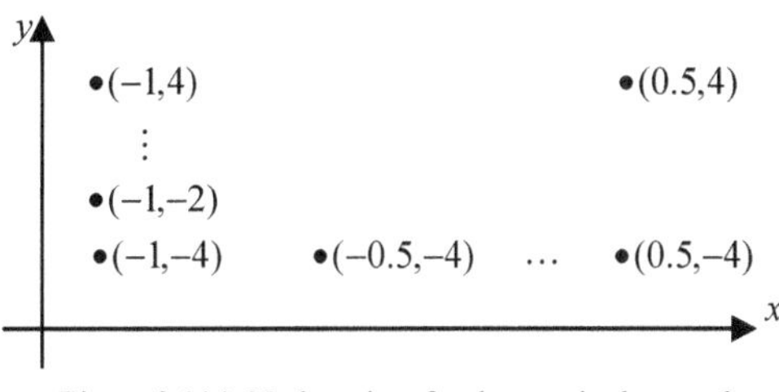

Figure 3.1(c) Node points for the required x and y domain over $-1\le x\le 0.5$ and $-4\le y\le 4$

While entering the input argument to the **meshgrid**, the y row matrix is created from more to less value that is 4 to −4 with the step −2 just to be consistent with the node order. The two output arguments of **meshgrid** for the example should return $\begin{bmatrix} -1 & -0.5 & 0 & 0.5 \\ -1 & -0.5 & 0 & 0.5 \\ -1 & -0.5 & 0 & 0.5 \\ -1 & -0.5 & 0 & 0.5 \\ -1 & -0.5 & 0 & 0.5 \end{bmatrix}$ and $\begin{bmatrix} 4 & 4 & 4 & 4 \\ 2 & 2 & 2 & 2 \\ 0 & 0 & 0 & 0 \\ -2 & -2 & -2 & -2 \\ -4 & -4 & -4 & -4 \end{bmatrix}$ demonstrating all x and all y coordinates respectively. Once the x and y coordinates are generated, the computation takes place writing the scalar code of the function as attached on the right. The workspace f holds the computed values in the rectangular matrix form. The f is just a matrix. There is no information regarding the x or y. It is the user who keeps a mark about the x or y variation.

For rectangular grid based computation:

```
>>[x,y]=meshgrid(-1:0.5:0.5,4:-2:-4); ↵
>>f=x.^2+x.*y+y.^2 ↵

f =

   13.0000   14.2500   16.0000   18.2500
    3.0000    3.2500    4.0000    5.2500
    1.0000    0.2500         0    0.2500
    7.0000    5.2500    4.0000    3.2500
   21.0000   18.2500   16.0000   14.2500
```

If we have to calculate a function like $\sum_y\sum_x f(x,y)$, first we generate the rectangular matrix f for given x and y domain description and then use two **sum** functions of the section 2.8 on f that is **sum(sum(f))**. As an example, let us calculate $\sum_{n=-2}^{3}\sum_{m=-1}^{4} m\cos\frac{2\pi n}{12}=33.5885$ where m and n vary intergerwise. Obviously the independent variables are now m and n in lieu of x and y respectively. The computation is shown on the right. If the increment is 1, we do not write the increment in the row vector generation (input argument of the **meshgrid**).

For the double sum computation:

```
>>[m,n]=meshgrid(-1:4,-2:3); ↵
>>f=m.*cos(2*pi*n/12); ↵
>>sum(sum(f)) ↵

ans =

   33.5885
```

3.11 Geometric problems

Referring to section 3.2, we discussed the hierarchy of the **maple** toolbox embedded in MATLAB. There are many libraries in **maple**, one of which is called **geometry** that helps us solve many well-known geometric problems. One needs to activate the library **geometry** exactly using the command **maple('with(geometry)')**; before solving the geometric problems at the command prompt. Let us go through the following geometric problems (font equivalence like A⇔ A is maintained in the subsequent sections).

3.11.1 Defining a geometric object

Point, line, triangle, square, circle, ellipse, or hyperbola can be the example of a geometric object. We define these objects using specific name reserved in the **maple** or its **geometry** library. A geometric object may be defined in several ways for instance a triangle is defined from three points, three sides, and two sides and angle inbetween. Since D is the differential operator in **maple**, do not use the D to assign some geometric object. We present the definition style of some familiar geometric objects in the following.

♦♦ Defining a point

A point has horizontal and vertical coordinates in two dimensional geometry. Let us say the point is A (0,4) and we enter this geometric object as follows:

```
>>maple('with(geometry)'); ↵        ← Activate the geometry package
```

>>maple('point(A,0,4)'); ↵ ← Define the point A where the word **point** is reserve in **maple**

There are three input arguments in **point**, the first, second, and third of which are the point name, x coordinate, and y coordinate respectively. Multiple points for example A (0,4), B (5,–6), and C (–8,4) are entered in one line as follows:

>>maple('point(A,0,4),point(B,5,-6),point(C,-8,4)'); ↵ ← Each point is separated by a comma

♦♦ Defining a line

A two dimensional line is defined from two given points or from its algebraic equation. Let us say we have two points whose coordinates are A (0,4) and B (4,–3). The straight line AB passing through A and B has the equation $7x+4y-16=0$ and is entered as follows:

>>maple('with(geometry),point(A,0,4),point(B,4,-3)'); ↵ ← **maple** statement is separated by a comma

>>maple('line(L,[A,B],[x,y])'); ↵ ← We defined line L which is AB from A and B (see defining a point)

The **maple** reserve word **line** defines a straight line which has three input arguments, the first, second, and third of which are the user-supplied line name, point names under third brace but separated by a comma, and user-supplied related variables of the line under the third brace but separated by a comma respectively. Here the related variables are x and y. We named the line AB as L in **maple**. If you say I need to see the line's equation, the **maple** function **Equation** extracts it from the object L as attached on the upper right. Starting from the algebraic equation, one defines the line object writing the command maple('line(L,7*x+4*y-16=0,[x,y])') in which the symbols have aforementioned meanings.

```
>>maple('Equation(L)') ↵

ans =

-16+7*x+4*y = 0
```

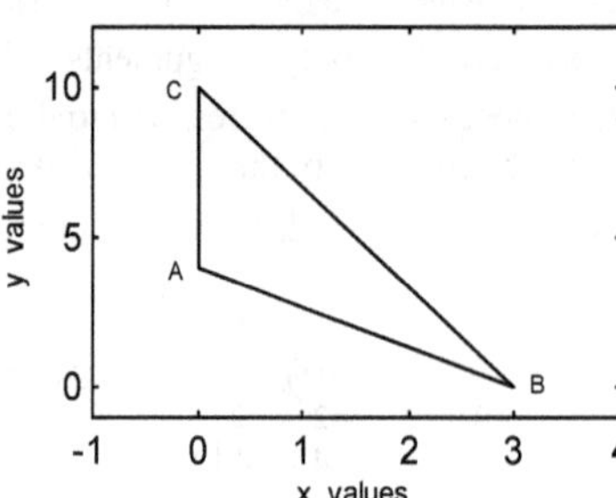

Figure 3.2(a) Triangle formed by the points A, B, and C

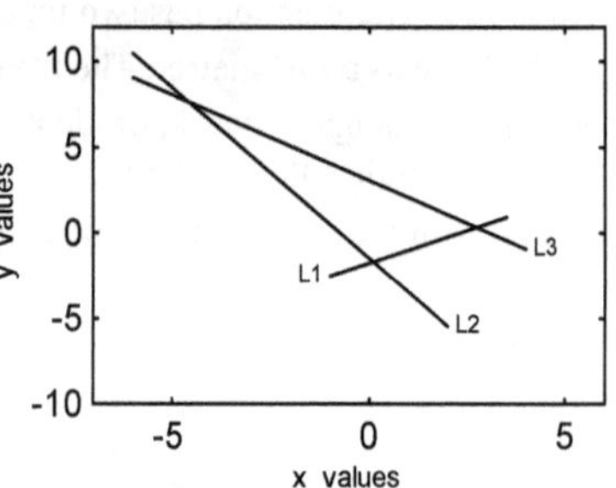

Figure 3.2(b) Triangle formed by the lines L1, L2, and L3

♦♦ Defining a triangle

A triangle is defined in different ways – from three given points, from three lines, from three sides, and two sides and angle inbetween. Two sides of the triangle meet at a point called vertex. We begin with three points A (0,4), B (3,0), and C (0,10) (figure 3.2(a)), call the triangle object ABC as T, and form it as follows:

>>maple('with(geometry)'); ↵

>>maple('point(A,0,4),point(B,3,0),point(C,0,10)'); ↵ ← Define all three points (see defining a point) of T

>>maple('triangle(T,[A,B,C])'); ↵ ← Defining the triangle T from the points A, B, and C

The function **triangle** has two input arguments, the first and second of which are the user-defined triangle name and point names under the third brace separated by a comma respectively. Then we have three equations of straight lines which are given by L1: $3x-4y=7$, L2: $4x+2y=-3$, and L3: $x+y=3$ and which forms the triangle of the figure 3.2(b) from their intersections (see defining a line). We construct the triangle T from the intersection of the three lines as follows:

>>maple('line(L1,3*x-4*y=7,[x,y]),line(L2,4*x+2*y=-3,[x,y]),line(L3,x+y=3,[x,y])'); ↵

>>maple('triangle(T,[L1,L2,L3],[x,y])'); ↵ ← Define the triangle T from the lines L1, L2, and L3

The lines are separated by a comma when they are placed inside the **maple**. Now the function **triangle** has three input arguments, the first, second, and third of which are the user-defined triangle name, line names under the third brace separated by a comma, and related variables under the third brace separated by a comma respectively. Next the three sides 3, 3, and 4 are given from which the triangle T is to be formed (figure 3.2(c)) and we do so as follows:

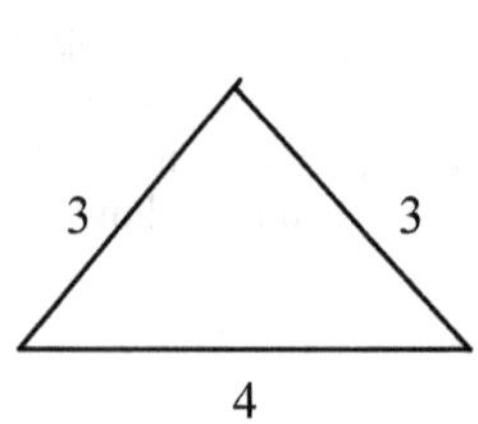

Figure 3.2(c) Triangle formed by sides

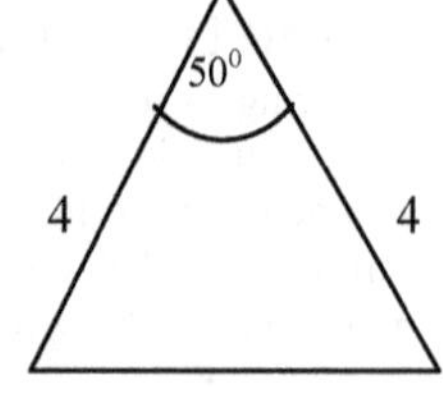

Figure 3.2(d) Triangle from two sides and angle between them

>>maple('triangle(T,[3,3,4])'); ↵ ← Triangle T from sides, first and second input arguments of the **triangle** are triangle name and side values under the third brace separated by a comma respectively

Finally we have two sides, each of which is equal to 4, and angle between them is 50^0 (figure 3.2(d)). We form the triangle as follows:

```
>>maple('triangle(T,[4,angle=50*pi/180,4])'); ↵
```
← First input argument of **triangle** is the triangle name

The second input argument of the **triangle** must be placed under the third brace but the brace holds three elements separated by commas, the first, second, and third of which are one side length, angle inbetween the sides in radians passed through the reserve word **angle=**, and the other side length respectively.

⬍⬍ Defining a square

A square is constructed from two opposite vertices of the diagonal, two adjacent vertices, and a vertex and center of the square. Corresponding **maple** function is **MakeSquare**. Let us start with two opposite vertices A (2,5) and C (9,0) (referring to figure 3.3(a)). Our objective is to construct the square $ABCD$ from these two vertices which lie in the two corners of diagonal of the square and which we carry out by the following:

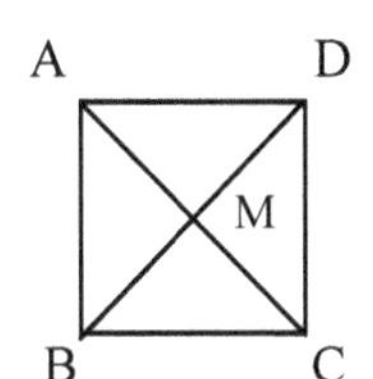

Figure 3.3(a) Square ABCD

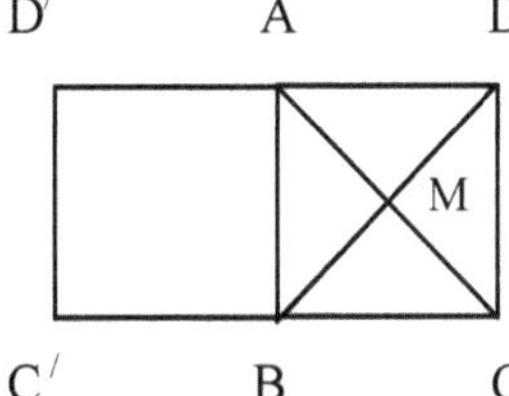

Figure 3.3(b) Two squares ABCD and ABC/D/ can be formed from two adjacent vertices A and B

```
>>maple('with(geometry),point(A,2,5),point(C,9,0)'); ↵
```
←See defining a point for point entering

```
>>maple('MakeSquare(S,[A,C,diagonal])'); ↵
```
←We named (user-chosen) the square object as **S**

The **MakeSquare** has two input arguments, the first of which is the square name. In the second input argument there are three elements separated by commas but placed in the third brace, the first, second, and third of which are the first vertex point name, second vertex point name, and the reserve word **diagonal** respectively. Now let us construct the square $ABCD$ starting from one vertex A (2,5) and the center $M\left(\frac{11}{2},\frac{5}{2}\right)$ as follows (symbols have their ongoing meanings):

```
>>maple('point(A,2,5),point(M,11/2,5/2),MakeSquare(S,[A,center=M])'); ↵
```

The **MakeSquare** has now two input arguments, the first of which is the square name. The second input argument has two elements placed in the third brace and separated by a comma – vertex point name and the center point name passed through the reserve word **center=** respectively. Yet again if two adjacent vertices A (2,5) and B (3,−1) of the square $ABCD$ are given, we construct the geometric object as follows (with ongoing symbol meanings):

```
>>maple('point(A,2,5),point(B,3,-1),MakeSquare(S,[A,B,adjacent])'); ↵
```

From above execution, the second input argument of the **MakeSquare** have three elements, the first, second, and third of which are the two point names and the reserve word **adjacent** placed in the third brace and separated by a comma respectively. From two adjacent points A and B, we can have two identical squares (figure 3.3(b)) labeled by ABCD and ABC/D/. MATLAB's geometric object construction is also consistent with that.

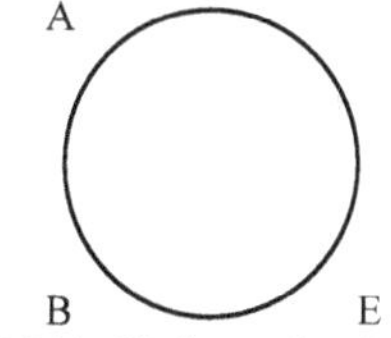

Figure 3.3(c) Circle passing through three points A, B, and E

⬍⬍ Defining a circle

A circle is defined from three points, from two end points of a diameter, from center and radius, and from an algebraic equation. Examples are presented for each case in which the **maple** function **circle** constructs the circle from user definition. In figure 3.3(c) a circle is formed from three points A (1,4), B (12,8), and E (2,8) which we construct as follows:

```
>>maple('with(geometry),point(A,1,4),point(B,12,8),point(E,2,8)'); ↵
```
← See defining a point for **point**

```
>>maple('circle(C,[A,B,E],[x,y])'); ↵
```
← We named the circle object as **C**

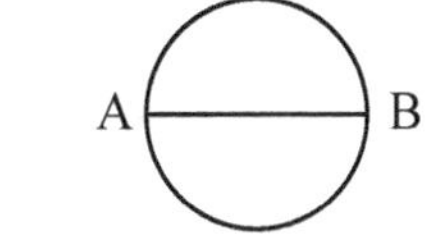

Figure 3.3(d) Circle from diameter AB

The function **circle** has three input arguments, the first, second, and third of which are the user-given circle name, the three point names under third brace but separated by a comma, and user-given related variables of the circle equation under the third brace but separated by a comma (must be 2, we assume that the circle equation is x and y related) respectively. Then, from the two end points A (1,4) and B (5,10) of the diameter of the circle like the figure 3.3(d), one constructs the circle object as follows:

```
>>maple('point(A,1,4),point(B,5,10),circle(C,[A,B],[x,y])'); ↵
```

Out of the three input arguments of the **circle**, the first, second, and third are the user-given circle name, the two end point names under the third brace but separated by a comma, and user-given related variables of the circle equation under the third brace but separated by a comma respectively. Next a circle is to be formed from center coordinates A (1,4) and radius $\sqrt{5}$ and which we form by the following bearing the usual meanings:

```
>>maple('point(A,1,4),circle(C,[A,sqrt(5)],[x,y])'); ↵
```

The second input argument of above **circle** contains the center point name and radius value (**sqrt(5)**⇔$\sqrt{5}$) respectively.

Finally taking the circle equation $3x^2+3y^2+6x-9y+1=0$, we construct the object as follows:

```
>>maple('circle(C,3*x^2+3*y^2+6*x-9*y+1=0,[x,y])'); ↵
```
← Second input argument of **circle** is the equation

♦♦ Defining a parabola

Figure 3.3(e) presents a parabola and its parameters concerning the equation $y^2 = 4ax$. The **maple** function **parabola** constructs the object but in general for the conic equation $ax^2 + by^2 + cxy + dx + fy + e = 0$. A parabola can be defined from five distinct points, from focus and vertex, from directrix and focus, and from an algebraic equation. Let us say we have the five distinct points $A\,(1{,}0)$, $B\,(0{,}1)$, $C\,(-20{,}3)$, $E\,(-4,-1)$, and $F\,(-64{,}5)$ and construct the parabolic object P by first entering the points (defining a point is presented previously) as follows:

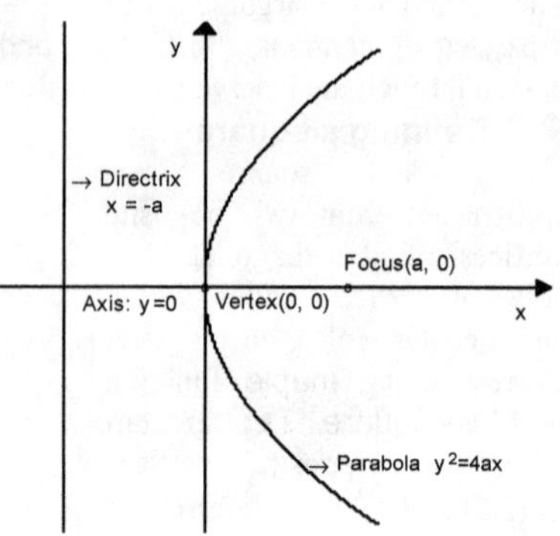

Figure 3.3(e) A parabola and its parameters

```
>>maple('with(geometry),point(A,1,0),point(B,0,1)'); ↵
>>maple('point(C,-20,3),point(E,-4,-1),point(F,-64,5)'); ↵
>>maple('parabola(P,[A,B,C,E,F],[x,y])'); ↵
```

The function **parabola** has three input arguments, the first, second, and third of which are the user-given parabola name, the five point names under the third brace but separated by a comma, and user-given related variables of the parabola equation under the third brace but separated by a comma (must be 2) respectively. Afterwards we proceed with the focus $F\,(1{,}2)$ and vertex $V\,(4{,}7)$ to form the parabola as follows:

```
>>maple('point(F,1,2),point(V,4,7),parabola(P,[focus=F,vertex=V],[x,y])'); ↵
```
← F, V entered first

Out of the three input arguments of the **parabola**, the first and third have previously mentioned meanings. The second input argument has two elements placed in the third brace and separated by a comma – focal point name and vertex point name passed through the reserve words **focus=** and **vertex=** respectively. Thirdly we form the parabola from the directrix equation DX: $3x + 5y - 81 = 0$ and focus $F\,(1,\,2)$ as presented in the following:

```
>>maple('point(F,1,2),line(DX,3*x+5*y-81=0,[x,y]),parabola(P,[directrix=DX,focus=F],[x,y])'); ↵
```

See the defining a point and a line for focus and directrix entering. Again out of the three input arguments of the **parabola**, the first and third have previously mentioned meanings. The second input argument has two elements placed in the third brace and separated by a comma – directrix line name and focus point name passed through the reserve words **directrix=** and **focus=** respectively. Finally we form a parabola entering its equation $x = 1 + 2y - 3y^2$ as follows:

```
>>maple('parabola(P,x=1+2*y-3*y^2,[x,y])'); ↵
```
← Usual meanings for the first and third input arguments

The second input argument of **parabola** is the vector code (section 14.2) of its equation. Anyhow we demonstrated the constructions of few geometric objects. In a similar fashion one can construct any other geometric object such as ellipse or hyperbola (execute **mhelp geometry[ellipse]** or **mhelp geometry[conic]** at the command prompt to learn more).

♦♦ Knowing about a geometric object

So far in this section we discussed only the geometric object construction. Once the geometric object is constructed, the reader might be interested to inspect other relevant properties of the object. For example we defined the triangular object T earlier from the intersection of the three lines. The **maple** function **detail** displays the relevant properties of a geometric object when the object is its input argument. Let us do so for the T (assuming that you executed aforementioned commands on the triangle) as follows:

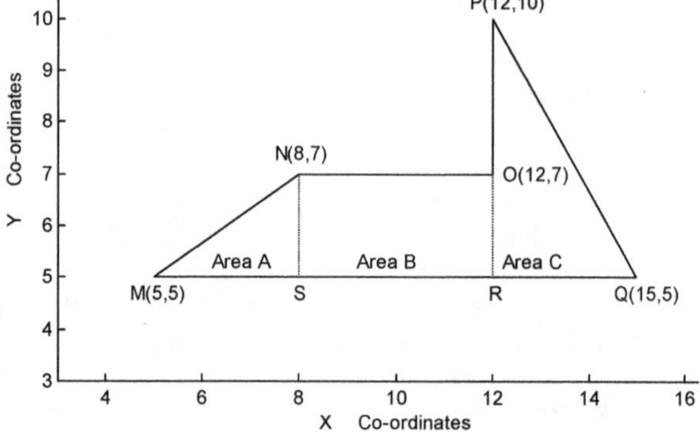

Figure 3.4(a) Polygon formed by points M, N, O, P, and Q

```
>>maple('detail(T)') ↵

ans =

`name of the object:  T\nform of the object:
triangle2d\nmethod to define the triangle:  points\nthe three vertices:  [[1/11, -37/22], [19/7, 2/7], [-9/2, 15/2]]`
```

As displayed, the triangle has the vetrtex points $\left(\frac{1}{11},-\frac{37}{22}\right)$, $\left(\frac{19}{7},\frac{2}{7}\right)$, and $\left(-\frac{9}{2},\frac{15}{2}\right)$ although our definition was from lines. For other geometric objects like line L, cicle C, or square S, you can also execute the **detail** to see the description of the object. In the definition of a line, we have shown how the command **Equation** displays the equation of a line. In fact one can apply the command **Equation** to view the equation of any other object for example parabola, ellipse, or other.

3.11.2 Area of a geometric object

Two dimensional closed geometric objects such as triangle, circle, or ellipse form an area. Area of a geometrical object is computed by the **maple** function **area** when the object is its input argument. Given that the triangle formed from three points A(0,4), B(3,10), and C(0,10) has the area 9 square unit which we wish to compute (see defining a triangle in the last subsection) as follows:

```
>>maple('with(geometry),point(A,0,4),point(B,3,10),point(C,0,10),triangle(T,[A,B,C])'); ↵
>>maple('area(T)') ↵

ans =

    9
```

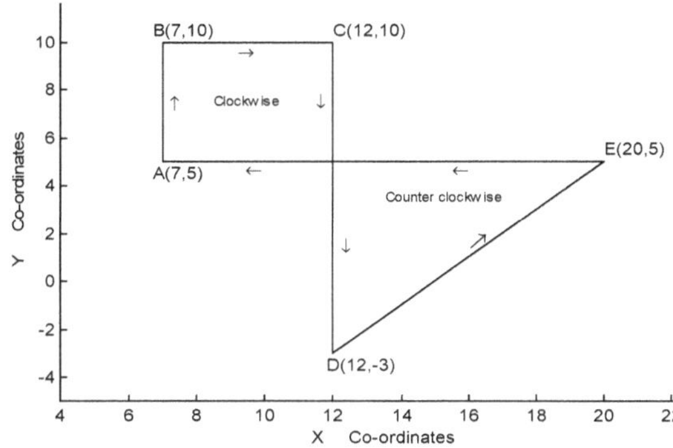

Figure 3.4(b) Polygon formed by points A, B, C, D, and E

We defined the triangle from three vertices. If the triangle were defined from three lines or other way, the **area** would also be applicable. Next example is a circle whose equation is given by $2x^2 + 2y^2 - x - y - a = 0$ and which has the area $\pi\frac{4a+1}{8}$ where a is a positive constant. There is a function called **assume** in **maple** which declares the logical condition of any variable related with the equation of a geometrical object. For example the a is a positive constant is fed writing the command **assume(a>0)**. Our objective is to obtain this area (see the circle definition in the last subsection) as follows:

```
>>maple('with(geometry):assume(a>0):circle(C,2*x^2+2*y^2-x-y-a=0,[x,y]):area(C)') ↵

ans =

pi*(1/8+1/2*a)
```

Note that the command : in **maple** indicates the suppression of execution of a command line. Similarly you can compute the area of an ellipse.

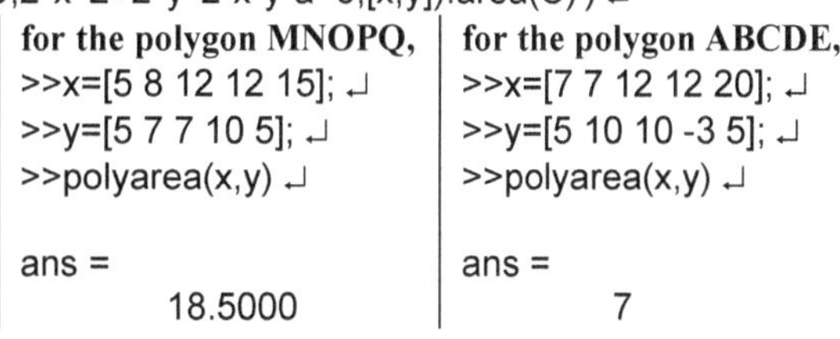

for the polygon MNOPQ,	for the polygon ABCDE,
>>x=[5 8 12 12 15]; ↵	>>x=[7 7 12 12 20]; ↵
>>y=[5 7 7 10 5]; ↵	>>y=[5 10 10 -3 5]; ↵
>>polyarea(x,y) ↵	>>polyarea(x,y) ↵
ans =	ans =
18.5000	7

So far area we found is geometric expression based and symbolic. An M-file called **polyarea** (abbreviation for the polygonal area) computes the numerical area of a polygon formed by the corner coordinates, which has the common syntax **polyarea**(x coordinates in row or column matrix, y coordinates in row or column matrix). For instance the points M(5,5), N(8,7), O(12,7), P(12,10), and Q(15,5) subtend the polygon of the figure 3.4(a), its area is given by 18.5 square unit, and we intend to compute that. Shown above on the right is its implementation. During the computation of the area, edges of the polygon must not intersect. If edge intersection is there, the return is the absolute difference between clockwise and counterclockwise encircled areas. Such an example is indicated by the points A(7,5), B(7,10), C(12,10), D(12,–3), and E(20,5) in the figure 3.4(b). From the figure 3.4(b), the net area is given by 7 square unit which we wish to calculate and whose implementation is also presented above on the right side in this page.

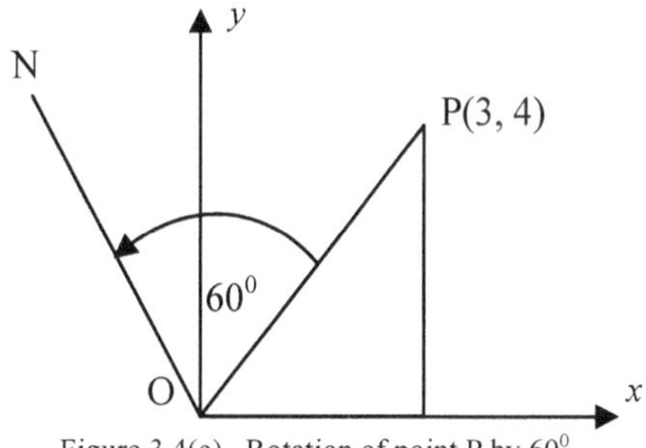

Figure 3.4(c) Rotation of point P by 60^0 counterclockwise about the origin

3.11.3 Rotation of a geometric object

A geometric object can be rotated in clockwise or counterclockwise direction about some point or line. The **maple** function **rotation** determines the equation or expression of the geometric object following the rotation. Let us start with the point $P(3,4)$. P is rotated by 60^0 counterclockwise about the origin O (figure 3.4(c)). The new location of P is N whose coordinates need to be calculated and which are given by $N\left(\frac{3}{2}-2\sqrt{3},\frac{3\sqrt{3}}{2}+2\right)$. Let us have it computed (subsection 3.11.1 for **point**) as follows:

```
>>maple('with(geometry),point(P,3,4)'); ↵
>>maple('rotation(N,P,pi/3,counterclockwise)'); ↵
>>maple('coordinates(N)') ↵

ans =
```

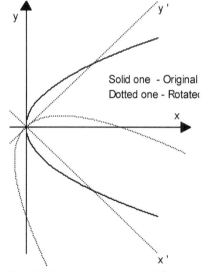

Figure 3.4(d) A parabola is rotated 45^0 clockwise about the origin

```
[3/2-2*3^(1/2), 2+3/2*3^(1/2)]
```

Referring to the implementation, the function **rotation** has four input arguments, the first, second, third, and fourth of which are the user-given new object name, object name which is to be rotated, angle of rotation in radians, and the reserve word **counterclockwise** respectively. Once the second line is executed, the new point object N is formed. As executed, the function **coordinates** within the **maple** extracts the x and y coordinates from the point object N when the object is its input argument. Our next example is the parabola $P: y^2 = 4x$. P is rotated about the origin by 45^0 clockwise. Figure 3.4(d) presents both parabolas – before and after the rotation. Our concern is to find the equation of the dotted parabola which is given by $\frac{x^2}{2} + xy + \frac{1}{2}y^2 - 2\sqrt{2}\,x + 2\sqrt{2}\,y = 0$. Let us find the new parabolic equation (call it N as well) as presented on the upper right (subsection 3.11.1 for the **parabola** and **Equation**). The **rotation** functions with the same type of input arguments as explained before. Only the point is for clockwise rotation we have the reserve word **clockwise** in the fourth input argument of the **rotation**. Thus you can apply the function to any other geometric object.

For the rotation of the parabola:

```
>>maple('with(geometry),parabola(P,y^2=4*x,[x,y])'); ↵
>>maple('rotation(N,P,pi/4,clockwise)'); ↵
>>maple('Equation(N)') ↵

ans =

1/2*x^2+x*y+1/2*y^2+2*y*2^(1/2)-2*x*2^(1/2) = 0
```

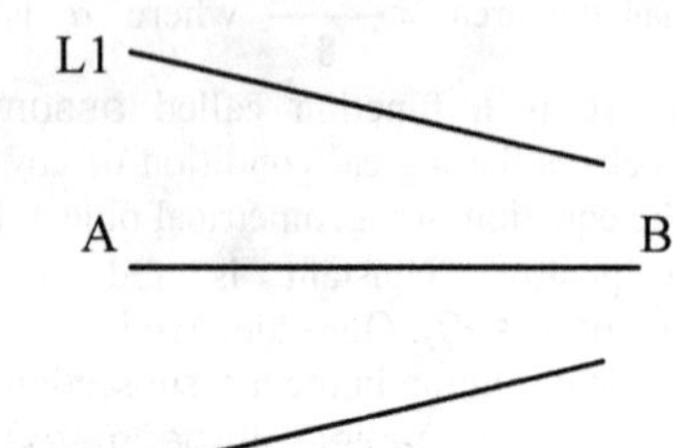

Figure 3.4(e) Line L1 is the reflection of L2 with respect to line AB

3.11.4 Reflection of a geometric object

Reflection of a geometric object is defined as the mirror image of that object with respect to some point or line. The **maple** function **reflection** finds the equation or representation of a geometric object following the reflection. Figure 3.4(e) depicts the reflection of the object line L1 with respect to line AB, which is labeled by the line L2. It is given that the object line L1: $x - y - 5 = 0$ and the reference line AB: $4x - 5y = 8$ provide the reflection line L2: $31x - 49y + 61 = 0$. Reflection of a point is another point for example the point R(4,–9) is the reflection point of P(2,5) with respect to the point O(3,–2). Again the reflection of a circle about a line is another circle for instance R: $x^2 + y^2 - \frac{93x}{10} + \frac{12y}{5} + \frac{45}{2} = 0$ is the reflection circle of the circle C: $2x^2 + 2y^2 - x - 4y + 1 = 0$ about the line L: $2x - y - 5 = 0$. Attached on the right is the implementation for all illustrations. The function **reflection** accepts three input arguments, the first, second, and third of which are the user-given reflection object name, object name which is to be reflected, and the reference point or line name respectively. In all executions we named the reflection object as R and font equivalence is maintained for other objects. We discussed the **line**, **point**, **circle**, **Equation**, and **coordinates** earlier.

for the line reflection about the line,

```
>>maple('with(geometry),line(L1,x-y-5=0,[x,y])'); ↵
>>maple('line(AB,4*x-5*y=8,[x,y])'); ↵
>>maple('reflection(L2,L1,AB)'); ↵
>>maple('Equation(L2)') ↵

ans =

-31/41*x+49/41*y-61/41 = 0
```

for the point reflection about another point,

```
>>maple('point(P,2,5),point(O,3,-2)'); ↵
>>maple('reflection(R,P,O)'); ↵
>>maple('coordinates(R)') ↵

ans =

[4, -9]
```

for the circle reflection about the line,

```
>>maple('line(L,2*x-y-5=0,[x,y])'); ↵
>>maple('circle(C,2*x^2+2*y^2-x-4*y+1=0,[x,y])'); ↵
>>maple('reflection(R,C,L)'); ↵
>>maple('Equation(R)') ↵

ans =

x^2-93/10*x+y^2+12/5*y+45/2 = 0
```

3.11.5 Miscellaneous geometric problems

If we start describing the whole **geometry** package, that requires writing another book. Apart from previously mentioned tutorials, there are many geometric problems that can be solved conveniently in the workspace. A number of tutorials are presented in the following.

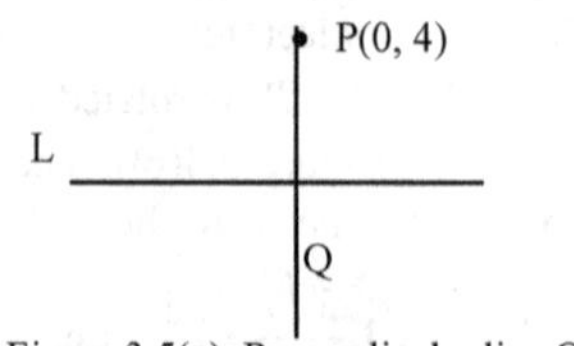

Figure 3.5(a) Perpendicular line Q to L through P

✦✦ Perpendicular line to a line passing through a point

We have a line L: $4x - 7y = 89$ and a point P(0,4). We wish to find the perpendicular line Q to L that passes through the P (figure 3.5(a)) and which should be $4y + 7x = 16$. The **maple** function **PerpendicularLine** finds the Q as follows:

```
>>maple('with(geometry),point(P,0,4),line(L,4*x-7*y=89,[x,y]),PerpendicularLine(Q,P,L)'); ↵
>>maple('Equation(Q)') ↵            ← In order to display the equation of Q
```

ans =

16-7*x-4*y = 0

The PerpendicularLine has three input arguments, the first, second, and third of which are the user-given perpendicular line name, the given point name, and the given line name respectively (subsection 3.11.1 for point, line, and Equation).

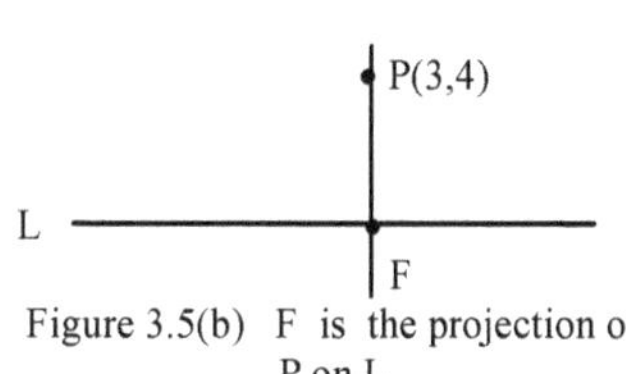

Figure 3.5(b) F is the projection of P on L

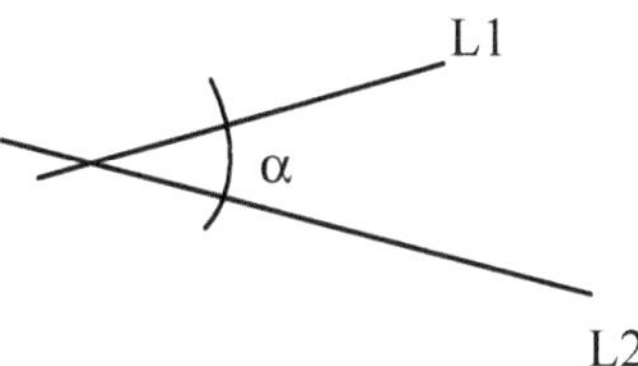

Figure 3.5(c) Angle between the two lines L1 and L2

⬍⬍ Projection of a point on a line

It is given that the point P(3,4) has the projection point $F\left(\frac{123}{13}, -\frac{95}{13}\right)$ on the line L: $4x - 7y = 89$ (figure 3.5(b)). The maple function projection finds the F starting from P and L as attached on the right (subsection 3.11.1 for point and line). Function coordinates finds the x and y coordinates from F. The projection has three input arguments, the first, second, and third of which are the user-given projection point name, given point name, and given line name respectively. The : is the statement ending command in maple.

For the projection of a point on a line:

```
>>maple('with(geometry),point(P,3,4)'); ↵
>>maple('line(L,4*x-7*y=89,[x,y])'); ↵
>>maple('projection(F,P,L):coordinates(F)') ↵

ans =

[123/13, -95/13]
```

⬍⬍ Finding the angle between two lines

Given that the angle between the two straight lines L1: $2x - 7y = 4$ and L2: $3x + 4y = 4$ is $\alpha = \tan^{-1}\frac{29}{22}$ (figure 3.5(c)) and we intend to find it. The maple function FindAngle determines the angle as attached on the right (subsection 3.11.1 for line). The FindAngle conceives two input arguments – the name of the two lines respectively.

For the angle between two lines:

```
>>maple('with(geometry)'); ↵
>>maple('line(L1,2*x-7*y=4,[x,y])'); ↵
>>maple('line(L2,3*x+4*y=4,[x,y])'); ↵
>>maple('FindAngle(L1,L2)') ↵

ans =
        atan(29/22)
```

⬍⬍ Are two triangles similar?

The command AreSimilar determines whether two triangles are similar. For example one triangle is defined from the three points – A(0,0), B(2,0), and C(2,3) and the other is from the points E(5,6), F(1,0), and G(2,–1). Given that the two triangles are not similar which we intend to verify and whose implementation is as follows (subsection 3.11.1 for the triangle definition from the three points):

```
>>maple('with(geometry)'); ↵
>>maple('triangle(T1,[point(A,0,0), point(B,2,0), point(C,2,3)])'); ↵ ← We named first triangle as T1
>>maple('triangle(T2,[point(E,5,6), point(F,1,0), point(G,2,-1)])'); ↵ ← We named second triangle as T2
>>maple('AreSimilar(T1,T2)') ↵ ← AreSimilar has two input arguments, the names of triangles respectively

ans =

false
```

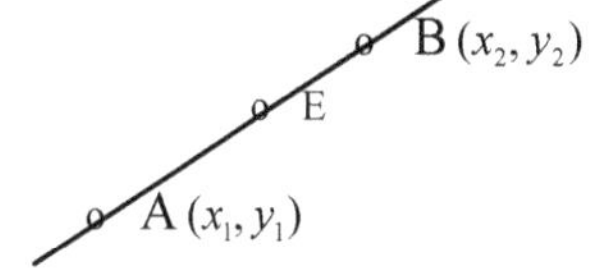

Figure 3.5(d) Point E divides AB internally by a ratio k

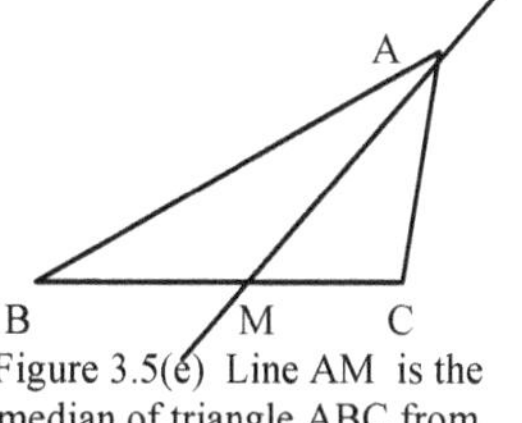

Figure 3.5(e) Line AM is the median of triangle ABC from vertex A

⬍⬍ Are three points collinear?

Three points are said to be collinear if they lie on a straight line. We illustrate that with A(0,0), B(2,0), and C(2,3) which are not collinear and is tested through the function AreCollinear as follows:

```
>>maple('with(geometry)'); ↵
>>maple('point(A,0,0),point(B,2,0),point(C,2,3)'); ↵ ← Subsection 3.11.1 for point
>>maple('AreCollinear(A,B,C)') ↵ ← AreCollinear has three input arguments, the names of the points respectively

ans =

false
```

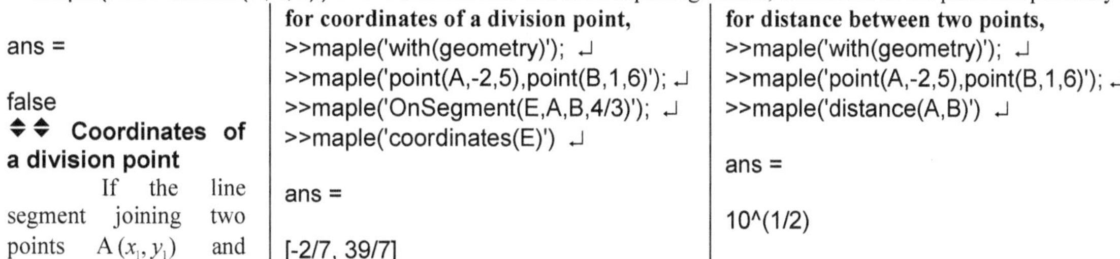

⬍⬍ Coordinates of a division point

If the line segment joining two points $A(x_1, y_1)$ and $B(x_2, y_2)$ are internally divided by a ratio k (that is AE:EB= k :1, figure 3.5(d)), the coordinates of the division point are

for coordinates of a division point,

```
>>maple('with(geometry)'); ↵
>>maple('point(A,-2,5),point(B,1,6)'); ↵
>>maple('OnSegment(E,A,B,4/3)'); ↵
>>maple('coordinates(E)') ↵

ans =

[-2/7, 39/7]
```

for distance between two points,

```
>>maple('with(geometry)'); ↵
>>maple('point(A,-2,5),point(B,1,6)'); ↵
>>maple('distance(A,B)') ↵

ans =

10^(1/2)
```

given by $\left(\frac{kx_2+x_1}{k+1}, \frac{ky_2+y_1}{k+1}\right)$. Example points are A(−2,5) and B(1,6) and we wish to find the coordinates of E for the ratio $\frac{4}{3}$ and which should be $\left(-\frac{2}{7}, \frac{39}{7}\right)$. We conduct the maple function OnSegment for the division point as attached at the end of the last page. The OnSegment has four input arguments, the first, second, third, and fourth of which are the user-given division point name, given first point name, given second point name, and the ration respectively. The command coordinates displays the x and y coordinates of a point when the point is its input argument.

♦♦ Distance between two points and between a point and a line

The function which is applicable for the distance computation is the distance. For instance the distance between two given points A(−2,5) and B(1,6) is $\sqrt{10}$. Again the distance from A to the line L: $2x-7y=71$ is $\frac{110}{\sqrt{53}}$. Point to point distance computation is presented at the end of the last page (subsection 3.11.1 for point and line). Point to line distance computation is attached on the right. The distance has two input arguments in each case, the names of the objects respectively.

For the distance of a point to a line:

```
>>maple('with(geometry)'); ↵
>>maple('point(A,-2,5)'); ↵
>>maple('line(L,2*x-7*y=71,[x,y])'); ↵
>>maple('distance(A,L)') ↵

ans =

110/53*53^(1/2)
```

♦♦ Is a point on a line or a circle?

Let us take the example point, line, and circle as A(1,0), L: $7x-9y-45=0$, and C: $2x^2+2y^2-4x+7y+2=0$ respectively. If A is on L or C, it must satisfy the equation of L or C. The maple functions IsOnLine and IsOnCircle allow us to check that respectively. For the examples at hand, A does not lie on L but does on C. Both implementations are attached on the right. See subsection 3.11.1 for the point, line, and circle. Both functions have two input arguments, the first and second of which are the point name and the line or circle name respectively. Sometimes it is necessary to know the condition on which a point is on a line or a circle. To illustrate this, we need to append one more input argument (called the reserve word cond) in IsOnLine or IsOnCircle. Let us say a point is given as A$\left(a, \frac{a}{4}\right)$. If A has to be on the line L, the condition we need is $\frac{19a}{4}-45=0$. Similarly if A has to be on the circle C, the condition we need is $\frac{17}{16}a^2-\frac{9}{8}a+1=0$. Following is the implementation with the added input argument (assuming that the L and C are there):

Is A on L?

```
>>maple('with(geometry)'); ↵
>>maple('point(A,1,0)'); ↵
>>maple('line(L,7*x-9*y-45=0,[x,y])'); ↵
>>maple('IsOnLine(A,L)') ↵

ans =

false
```

Is A on C?

```
>>maple('circle(C,2*x^2+2*y^2-4*x+7*y+2=0,[x,y])'); ↵
>>maple('IsOnCircle(A,C)') ↵

ans =

true
```

finding the condition for A to be on L,

```
>>maple('point(A,a,a/4)'); ↵
>>maple('IsOnLine(A,L,cond)') ↵

ans =

IsOnLine:   hint: unable to determine if -45+19/4*a is zeroFAIL
```

finding the condition for A to be on C,

```
>>maple('point(A,a,a/4)'); ↵
>>maple('IsOnCircle(A,C,cond)') ↵

ans =

IsOnCircle:   hint: unable to determine if 17/16*a^2+1-9/8*a is zeroFAIL
```

♦♦ Median, altitude, and angular bisector from a vertex to a triangle

Given that the three vertices of the triangle ABC (figure 3.5(e)) are A(2,7), B(−2,−2), and C(5,3). We intend to find the median, altitude, and angular bisector of the triangle from vertex A and whose equations are given as $13x-y-19=0$, $7x+5y-49=0$, and $4x\sqrt{97}+45x-20y+3y\sqrt{97}+50-29\sqrt{97}=0$ respectively. Employing the maple functions median, altitude, and bisector helps us find all these. Attached on the right is the execution for the median (subsection 3.11.1 for point, triangle, and Equation). The median has three input arguments, the first, second, and third of which are the user-chosen median name (call it AM), vertex point of the triangle, and the triangle name (call it T) respectively. The altitude and angular bisector implementation is presented on the right of the next

for the median,

```
>>maple('with(geometry),point(A,2,7)'); ↵
>>maple('point(B,-2,-2),point(C,5,3)'); ↵
>>maple('triangle(T,[A,B,C],[x,y])'); ↵
>>maple('median(AM,A,T)'); ↵
>>maple('Equation(AM)') ↵

ans =

-19/2+13/2*x-1/2*y = 0
```

page. The functions altitude and bisector follow similar input argument intaking to that of the median in which we named the two lines as AH and AS respectively. The command simplify in maple simplifies an equation when the equation is its input argument. Now one might need the coordinates of the end points for each of the aforementioned three lines. For example the coordinates of

for the altitude,

```
>>maple('altitude(AH,A,T)'); ↵
>>maple('Equation(AH)') ↵

ans =

-49+7*x+5*y = 0
```

for the angular bisector,

```
>>maple('bisector(AS,A,T)'); ↵
>>maple('simplify(Equation(AS))') ↵

ans =

4*x*97^(1/2)+45*x-20*y+3*y*97^(1/2)+50-29*97^(1/2) = 0
```

the end points of the line AM are (2,7) and $\left(\frac{3}{2},\frac{1}{2}\right)$ which we wish to obtain. Each of the three maple functions needs one more input argument as the fourth one but user-defined (let us call it M). On that we perform the following:

```
>>maple('median(AM,A,T,M)'); ↵
>>maple('map(coordinates,DefinedAs(AM))') ↵

ans =

[[2, 7], [3/2, 1/2]]
```

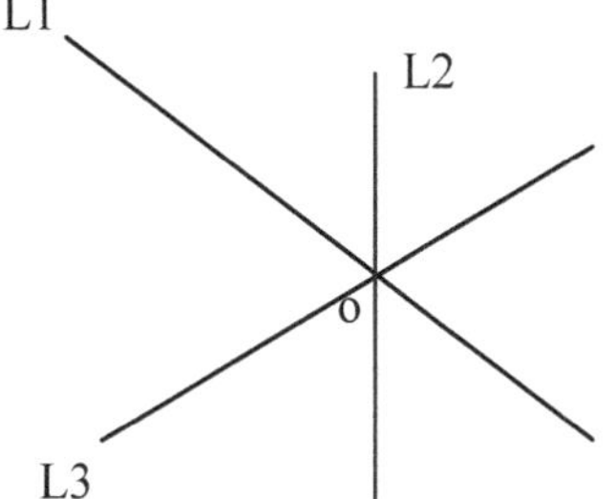

Figure 3.6(a) Three concurrent lines L1, L2, and L3 pass through a single point o

The function map of maple in above implementation determines the x and y coordinates of the object AM as defined previously which is passed through the command DefinedAs and whose input argument is the name of the object. This sort of end point finding is also possible for the altitude or angular bisector.

♦♦ Are three straight lines concurrent?

Three straight lines are said to be concurrent if they pass through a single point o as shown in figure 3.6(a). We perform the testing on the lines L1: $2x-7y=4$, L2: $3x+4y=4$, and L3: $4x-y=3$ and given that they are not concurrent. The function AreConcurrent ascertains this as shown below (subsection 3.11.1 for the line).

```
>>maple('with(geometry),line(L1,2*x-7*y=4,[x,y])'); ↵
>>maple('line(L2,3*x+4*y=4,[x,y]),line(L3,4*x-y=3,[x,y])'); ↵
>>maple('AreConcurrent(L1,L2,L3)') ↵

ans =

false
```

```
>>maple('line(L3,4*x-b*y=3,[x,y])'); ↵
>>maple('AreConcurrent(L1,L2,L3,cond)') ↵

ans =

AreConcurrent:   unble to determine if 89+4*b
is zeroFAIL
```

The AreConcurrent has three input arguments which are the names of the line objects. Suppose the third line equation is modified as L3: $4x-by=3$. Now to have the three lines concurrent, the condition we need is $4b+89=0$. The AreConcurrent now needs four input arguments in which the fourth one is the reserve word cond but of coarse the L3 equation needs to be entered first. Its implementation is also shown above on the right.

♦♦ Are four points concyclic?

Four points are said to be concyclic when they lie on a circle. Given that the four points A(2,8), B(3,7), C(0,9), and E(−1,5) are not concyclic and which we test through the function AreConcyclic (subsection 3.11.1 for the point entering). The function has four input arguments as presented above, the names of the four points. Suppose you have the flexibility to change the y coordinate of the point E and which is now E(−1,a). To have the four points concyclic, the condition is $-\frac{4(a^2-7a-20)}{166911(a^2+2)}=0$ which also needs to be determined. We find the condition adding one reserve word cond at the end of the function but first we enter the E. The command maple('cond') displays only the condition attained from previous geometric object as presented above.

Testing the four points to be concyclic:

```
>>maple('with(geometry)'); ↵
>>maple('point(A,2,8),point(B,3,7)'); ↵
>>maple('point(C,0,9),point(E,-1,5)'); ↵
>>maple('AreConcyclic(A,B,C,E)') ↵

ans =

false
```

Finding the condition for concyclic:

```
>>maple('point(E,-1,a)'); ↵
>>maple('AreConcyclic(A,B,C,E,cond)'); ↵
>>maple('cond') ↵

ans =

-4/166911*(-20+a^2-7*a)/(2+a^2) = 0
```

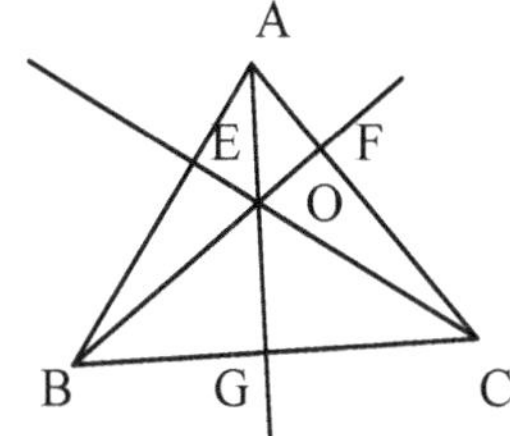

Figure 3.6(b) O is the orthocenter of triangle ABC

♦♦ Is a line tangent to a circle?

Given that the line L: $5x-8y=3$ is not a tangent to the circle C: $2x^2+2y^2-4x+7y+2=0$ which we intend to verify. The function AreTangent helps us test that. Attached on the right in next page is the implementation (subsection 3.11.1 for the line and circle). The function has two input arguments, the names of the line and circle respectively.

for tangent testing,

```
>>maple('with(geometry)'); ↵
>>maple('line(L,5*x-8*y=3,[x,y])'); ↵
>>maple('circle(C,2*x^2+2*y^2-4*x+7*y+2=0,[x,y])'); ↵
>>maple('AreTangent(L,C)') ↵

ans =

false
```

♦♦ Finding the orthocenter of a triangle

Perpendiculars drawn from the vertices to the opposite sides of a triangle are concurrent. That concurrent point is called the orthocenter of the triangle (figure 3.6(b)). It is given that $O\left(-\frac{1}{2},2\right)$ is the orthocenter of the triangle ABC constructed from the points A(8,2), B(2,–1), and C(2,–3) and we intend to determine that. The maple function orthocenter computes the orthocenter of a triangle as presented on the right (subsection 3.11.1 for point, triangle, and coordinates). The function orthocenter has two input arguments, the first and second of which are the user-given orthocenter name and triangle name respectively.

for the orthocenter finding,

```
>>maple('with(geometry)'); ↵
>>maple('point(A,8,2),point(B,2,-1),point(C,2,-3)'); ↵
>>maple('triangle(T,[A,B,C]),orthocenter(O,T)'); ↵
>>maple('coordinates(O)') ↵

ans =

[-1/2, 2]
```

♦♦ Are two circles orthogonal?

Two nonconcentric circles are said to be orthogonal if tangents drawn at the point of intersection of the two circles are right angle to each other. Anyhow the function AreOrthogonal of the maple determines the orthogonality of two given circles. It is given that the circles C1: $x^2+y^2-4x-4y-1=0$ and C2: $x^2+y^2+6x-4y-3=0$ are orthogonal and we make certain that as attached on the right (subsection 3.11.1 for circle). The function AreOrthogonal has two input arguments, the names of the circle objects.

for the orthogonality of two circles,

```
>>maple('with(geometry)'); ↵
>>maple('circle(C1,x^2+y^2-4*x-4*y-1=0,[x,y])'); ↵
>>maple('circle(C2,x^2+y^2+6*x-4*y-3=0,[x,y])'); ↵
>>maple('AreOrthogonal(C1,C2)') ↵

ans =

true
```

♦♦ Intersection of some geometric objects

Geometric objects can intersect. Coordinates of their intersection points are found by the function intersection. It is given that the point $P\left(\frac{17}{23},\frac{2}{23}\right)$ is the intersection of the lines with equations L1: $5x-8y=3$ and L2: $7x-2y=5$. Again the intersection points of the line L: $x-8y=3$ and circle C: $x^2+y^2-x-y-1=0$ are $M\left(\frac{3}{5}+\frac{4\sqrt{221}}{65},-\frac{3}{10}+\frac{\sqrt{221}}{130}\right)$ and $N\left(\frac{3}{5}-\frac{4\sqrt{221}}{65},-\frac{3}{10}-\frac{\sqrt{221}}{130}\right)$ and we intend to find them. We have them

for the intersection of two lines,

```
>>maple('with(geometry),line(L1,5*x-8*y=3,[x,y])'); ↵
>>maple('line(L2,7*x-2*y=5,[x,y])'); ↵
>>maple('intersection(P,L1,L2):coordinates(P)') ↵

ans =

[17/23, 2/23]
```

for the intersection of line and circle,

```
>>maple('line(L,x-8*y=3,[x,y])'); ↵
>>maple('circle(C,x^2+y^2-x-y-1=0,[x,y])'); ↵
>>maple('intersection(P,L,C,[M,N])'); ↵
>>maple('coordinates(M)') ↵

ans =

[3/5+4/65*221^(1/2), -3/10+1/130*221^(1/2)]
```

computed as attached above (subsection 3.11.1 for line, circle, and coordinates) on the right. In the first case the function intersection accepts three input arguments, the first, second, and third of which are the user-given intersection point name and geometric object names respectively. In the second case we apply the same order of input arguments but include one more at the end which contains two user-given point names separated by a comma and placed under the third brace. It is the user who decides about the number of intersection points. Between a line and a circle, the highest power of the equation terms is 2 so there are two intersection points. We displayed only the coordinates of the M for space reason. Execute maple('coordinates(N)') for the other coordinates. One may not appreciate the long string output. Carry out the pretty (section 3.1) to print output in symbolic form for example M=maple('coordinates(M)');pretty(sym(M)). Thus intersection of parabola, ellipse, hyperbola, or any other curves can be obtained.

♦♦ Circumcircle, incircle, and excircle of a triangle

Suppose a triangle is formed from three lines L1: $3x-4y-1=0$, L2: $4x-3y+5=0$, and L3: $8x+6y-9=0$. The circumcircle (circle passing through the three vertices), incircle (circle touching the three sides), and excircle (circle touching two extrapolated sides and the third sides, there are three such circles) of the triangle are given by C: $x^2+y^2+\frac{375}{112}x+\frac{95}{84}y-\frac{1375}{336}=0$, I: $x^2+y^2+\frac{x}{8}-\frac{57y}{56}-\frac{47871}{313600}=0$, and E: $\left\{x^2+y^2+\frac{91x}{6}-\frac{19y}{6}+\frac{85729}{3600}=0\right.$,

$x^2+y^2-\dfrac{85x}{42}-\dfrac{19y}{6}+\dfrac{492529}{176400}=0$, and $x^2+y^2+\dfrac{x}{8}+\dfrac{95y}{8}+\dfrac{95329}{6400}=0\}$ respectively and we wish to find them. The maple functions are also having the same names as the circles are. Following is the implementation of all these:

for the circumcircle,

```
>>maple('with(geometry)'); ↵
>>maple('line(L1,3*x-4*y-1=0,[x,y])'); ↵
>>maple('line(L2,4*x-3*y+5=0,[x,y])'); ↵
>>maple('line(L3,8*x+6*y-9=0,[x,y])'); ↵
>>maple('triangle(T,[L1,L2,L3])'); ↵
>>maple('circumcircle(C,T)'); ↵
>>maple('Equation(C)') ↵

ans =

x^2-1375/336+y^2+375/112*x+95/84*y = 0
```

for the incircle,

```
>>maple('incircle(I,T)'); ↵
>>maple('Equation(I)') ↵

ans =

x^2-47871/313600+y^2+1/8*x-
57/56*y = 0
```

for the excircle,

```
>>maple('excircle(E,T)'); ↵
>>maple('Equation(E[1])') ↵

ans =

x^2+492529/176400+y^2-85/42*x-
19/6*y = 0
```

The reader is referred to subsection 3.11.1 for the line, triangle, and Equation. Each of the three functions has two input arguments, the first and second of which are the user-given circle name and the triangle name respectively. For the excircle case, the three circles can be reached using the command E[1], E[2], and E[3] (may not be in our order). We have shown only the first one.

Figure 3.6(c) DEF is the medial triangle of the triangle ABC

♦♦ Determine the medial triangle of a triangle

Medial triangle is a triangle which is formed by joining the midpoints of the sides of the triangle. Concerning the figure 3.6(c), inner triangle DEF is the medial triangle of the larger triangle ABC. Considering the triangle formed from the three lines of just mentioned example, it is given that the vertices of the medial triangle are $\left(-\dfrac{375}{224},-\dfrac{95}{168}\right)$, $\left(\dfrac{311}{800},\dfrac{589}{600}\right)$, and $\left(-\dfrac{214}{175},-\dfrac{817}{700}\right)$ respectively. The function medial forms the medial triangle object from which one can pick up the coordiates as attached on the right (see the median discussion for the second line command). The medial has two input arguments, the first and second of which are the user-given medial triangle name (we called it M) and given triangle name respectively. For the readable form, one can apply the command O=maple('map(coordinates,DefinedAs(M))'); pretty(sym(O)).

```
>>maple('medial(M,T)'); ↵
>>maple('map(coordinates,DefinedAs(M))') ↵

ans =

[[-214/175, -817/700], [-375/224, -95/168], [311/800, 589/600]]
```

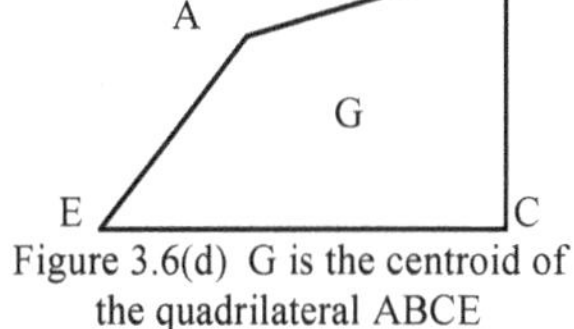

Figure 3.6(d) G is the centroid of the quadrilateral ABCE

♦♦ Centroid of a polygon

The function used for this purpose is the centroid. Let us say $\left(1,\dfrac{21}{4}+\dfrac{\cos t}{4}\right)$ are the centroid coordinates of the quadrilateral formed from the four vertices A(2, cos$t$), B(3,7), C(0,9), and E(−1,5) (see the figure 3.6(d)) and we intend to obtain that. That is what is attached on the right (subsection 3.11.1 for the point and earlier in this section for the coordinates). The centroid has two input arguments, the first and second of which are the user-given centroid name which we called G and the vertices of the polygon placed under the third brace and separated by a comma respectively.

for the centroid coordinates:

```
>>maple('with(geometry)'); ↵
>>maple('point(A,2,cos(t)),point(B,3,7)'); ↵
>>maple('point(C,0,9),point(E,-1,5)'); ↵
>>maple('centroid(G,[A,B,C,E])'); ↵
>>maple('coordinates(G)') ↵

ans =

[1, 1/4*cos(t)+21/4]
```

3.11.6 Help about the geometry package

Many more functions of the package are yet to be examined. You have seen just a flavor what geometry package can implement. We can explore the comprehensive help of the geometry package from the execution of the following:

```
>>mhelp geometry ↵
Help For: Introduction to the geometry package

Calling Sequence:
  function(args)
  geometry[function](args)

Description:
       ⋮
```

MATLAB displays a long list help about the available functions in the **geometry** package. Slide the vertical scroll bar with the help of the mouse to see different help paragraphs completely. From the displayed help topic, choose any **maple** function. Suppose we selected the **circle** from the last displayed list. To get the help about the **circle**, we execute the following:

```
>>mhelp circle ↵

Multiple matches found:
     plottools,circle
     geometry,circle
```

Above output indicates that by the name **circle** there are two **maple** functions – one is located in **plottools** package and the other is in the **geometry** package. Specifically, to display the help of the **circle** in the **geometry** package, we carry out the following:

```
>>mhelp geometry[circle] ↵
```

You will see another long list help regarding the **circle** as follows:

```
Function: geometry[circle] - define the circles

Calling Sequence:
  circle(c, [A, B, C], n, 'centername'=m )
  circle(c, [A, B], n, 'centername'=m )
  circle(c, [A, rad], n, 'centername'=m )
  circle(c, eqn, n, 'centername'=m )
      ⋮
```

In a similar fashion one can explore details of any other function of the **geometry** package. Table 3.A presents some functions found in the **geometry** package. We close the chapter following the presentation of the table.

Table 3.A Some **geometry** functions found in the **maple**

Name of the **maple** function	Purpose of the function
EulerLine	finds the Euler line of a given triangle
SimsonLine	finds the Simson line of a given triangle with respect to a given point on the circumcircle of the triangle
Appolonius	finds the Appolonius circles of three given circles
PedalTriangle	finds the pedal triangle of a point with respect to a triangle
RadicalCenter	finds the radical center of three given circles
RadicalAxis	finds the radical axis of two given circles
CircleOfSimilitude	finds the circle of similitude of two circles
TangentLine	finds the tangents of a point with respect to a circle
dsegment	defines a directed segment
AreConjugate	tests if two triangles are conjugate for a circle
convexhull	finds the convex hull enclosing the given points
similitude	finds the insimilitude and outsimilitude of two circles
stretch	finds the stretch of a geometric object
inversion	finds the inversion of a point, line, or circle with respect to a given circle
AreHarmonic	tests if a pair of points is harmonic conjugate to another pair of points
GlideReflection	finds the glide-reflection of a geometric object
SpiralRotation	finds the spiral-rotation of a geometric object
GergonnePoint	finds the Gergonne point of a given triangle
CrossProduct	computes the cross product of two directed segment
Pole	finds the pole of a given line with respect to a given conic or a given circle
IsEquilateral	tests if a given triangle is equilateral
IsRightTriangle	tests if a given triangle is a right triangle
NagelPoint	finds the Nagel point of a given triangle
powerpc	computes power of a given point with respect to a given circle
AreParallel	tests if two lines are parallel to each other

Chapter 4

Elements arranged in rectangular array are called a matrix. Elements can be symbols, integers, decimal numbers, or complex numbers. In MATLAB the word variable usually refers to a matrix. The primary objective of MATLAB's advent was to facilitate the computation of the matrix algebra. But nowadays its capability has reached far beyond the objective. Enhanced with the Maple package, MATLAB offers a great flexibility to matrix element oriented computing whether symbolic or numeric. Rapid use of newer techniques in physical science majors and engineering compels a real understanding and implementation of the matrix algebra. Although simple matrix manipulation and arithmetic are introduced in chapter 2, we wish to execute the matrix algebra specific problems in this chapter addressing the following:

- Formation of different matrix algebra termed matrices such as identity, diagonal, etc
- Fundamental algebra operations such as pivoting, Gaussian elimination, inversion, etc
- Matrix basis related techniques – eigenvalue-eigenvector, singular value decomposition, etc
- Matrix based measures such as rank, norm, determinant, condition number, etc
- Factorization of matrices whether triangular based, orthogonal based, or other

4.1 Formation of identity and diagonal matrices

An identity matrix is one whose diagonal elements are unity and off-diagonal elements are zeroes. According to matrix algebra, identity matrices are defined only for the square matrices but in MATLAB, we can have identity matrix through the use of function **eye** for a rectangular matrix too, which has the common syntax **eye**(required row number, required column number). If required matrix is square, there is no need to write both the column and row numbers only one will do. Examples of the identity matrices are $A=\begin{bmatrix}1 & 0 & 0\\0 & 1 & 0\\0 & 0 & 1\end{bmatrix}$, $B=\begin{bmatrix}1 & 0 & 0\\0 & 1 & 0\end{bmatrix}$, and $C=\begin{bmatrix}1 & 0 & 0\\0 & 1 & 0\\0 & 0 & 1\\0 & 0 & 0\end{bmatrix}$ whose orders are 3×3, 2×3, and 4×3 for A, B, and C respectively. How A, B, and C are formed is shown at the beginning on the right of the following page (font equivalence is maintained for example A⇔ A). In a diagonal matrix all elements are zeroes except the diagonal elements (not all the elements in the diagonal are zeroes, some elements in the diagonal can be zeroes). A diagonal matrix is generated by using the command **diag** whose input argument is the diagonal entered as a row matrix. For instance the diagonal matrix $D=\begin{bmatrix}2&0&0\\0&6&0\\0&0&7\end{bmatrix}$ has the diagonal as a row matrix [2 6 7] whose implementation is shown above on the right side.

for identity matrix A,	**for identity C,**	**for identity B,**	**for diagonal D,**
>>A=eye(3) ↵	>>C=eye(4,3) ↵	>>B=eye(2,3) ↵	>>A=[2 6 7]; ↵ >>D=diag(A) ↵
A = 1 0 0 0 1 0 0 0 1	C = 1 0 0 0 1 0 0 0 1 0 0 0	B = 1 0 0 0 1 0	D = 2 0 0 0 6 0 0 0 7

4.2 Reduced row echelon form of a matrix

Reduced row echelon form of a matrix is required to find the rank of a matrix or linear dependence of vectors. In order to obtain the reduced row echelon form of a matrix, we apply the command **rref** (abbreviation for reduced row echelon form) whose input argument is the matrix. It is given that the matrix $A=\begin{bmatrix}6&7&-8&8\\-1&-2&5&3\\-3&0&7&5\end{bmatrix}$ has the reduced row echelon form

$$B=\begin{bmatrix}1&0&0&\frac{41}{23}\\0&1&0&\frac{30}{23}\\0&0&1&\frac{34}{23}\end{bmatrix}=\begin{bmatrix}1&0&0&1.7826\\0&1&0&1.3043\\0&0&1&1.4783\end{bmatrix}$$

and we obtain that as attached above on the right (font equivalence is maintained for example A⇔ A). Rational form output is seen using the command **sym** (section 2.1) on the elements of A. In each case we assigned the return from the **rref** to the workspace B (can be any user-chosen name).

Reduced row echelon form in the numeric form,

```
>>A=[6 7 -8 8;-1 -2 5 3;-3 0 7 5]; ↵
>>B=rref(A) ↵

B =
    1.0000         0         0    1.7826
         0    1.0000         0    1.3043
         0         0    1.0000    1.4783
```

for the symbolic form,

```
>>B=rref(sym(A)) ↵

B =

[  1,   0,   0,  41/23]
[  0,   1,   0,  30/23]
[  0,   0,   1,  34/23]
```

4.3 Pivoting about an element and minor of a matrix

If A denotes a matrix, any element in the matrix is A_{ij} where i and j correspond to the row and column indexes respectively. When A_{ij} is not equal to zero, it is possible to make the lower and upper elements of A_{ij} zero applying the elementary transformations – this is called pivoting of the matrix A about the entry A_{ij}.

For example $B=\begin{bmatrix}\frac{18}{7}&\frac{33}{7}&0\\-1&-3&-7\\\frac{26}{7}&-\frac{34}{7}&0\end{bmatrix}$ is the pivoted matrix about $A_{23}=-7$ of $A=\begin{bmatrix}2&3&-4\\-1&-3&-7\\3&-7&-5\end{bmatrix}$ and we intend to implement that. The computation is merely symbolic (section 2.1) and carried out through the **pivot** function of the **maple** (section 3.2) as attached on the right. Inside the **maple**, there are four input arguments, the first, second, third, and fourth of which are the function name under quote, matrix name, row index for matrix pivoting, and column index for matrix pivoting respectively. If the decimal form is required, exercise the command **double(B)**.

For pivoting of the A:

```
>>A=sym([2 3 -4;-1 -3 -7;3 -7 -5]); ↵
>>B=maple('pivot',A,2,3) ↵

B =

[  18/7,   33/7,    0]
[    -1,     -3,   -7]
[  26/7,  -34/7,    0]
```

For the minor of A:

```
>>A=sym([3 4 2 9;0 7 6 7;0 1 5 9]); ↵
>>B=maple('minor',A,3,2) ↵

B =

[ 3,  2,  9]
[ 0,  6,  7]
```

Minor of a matrix A about the matrix element A_{ij} is defined as the matrix formed by removing the ith row and j^{th} column. To proceed with an example, let us take $A=\begin{bmatrix}3&4&2&9\\0&7&6&7\\0&1&5&9\end{bmatrix}$. The element 1 in A has the index i=3 and j=2 accordingly the minor about A_{32} is given by $B=\begin{bmatrix}3&2&9\\0&6&7\end{bmatrix}$ which we implement through the **maple** function minor as attached on the lower right corner of the last page. The first line in the command is the assignment of the matrix to A and the second line assigns the computed result to B. The maple holds four input arguments, the first, second, third, and fourth of which are the function name under quote, matrix name, row index for matrix minoring, and column index for matrix minoring respectively. The computation is purely symbolic and the decimal form is obtained by using the command double(B) if it is necessary.

4.4 Adjoint of a square matrix

Adjoint of a square matrix is defined as the transpose of the matrix formed by the cofactors of matrix elements. It is given that $B = \begin{bmatrix} 7x-30 & -4x+10 & 10 \\ 6 & 3x-2 & -18 \\ -7 & -11 & 21 \end{bmatrix}$ is the adjoint of the square matrix $A = \begin{bmatrix} 3 & 4 & 2 \\ 0 & 7 & 6 \\ 1 & 5 & x \end{bmatrix}$ which we implement through the maple (section 3.2) function adjoint or adj as attached on the right. The computation is completely symbolic (section 2.1) for this reason matrix variable like x needs to be declared using the command syms x. We assigned the maple output to the workspace B (font equivalence is maintained for example A⇔ A). If all elements in A are decimal, the adjoint computation takes place using the command A=sym(A); B=double(maple('adj',A)).

For the matrix adjoint:

```
>>syms x ↵
>>A=[3 4 2;0 7 6;1 5 x]; ↵
>>B=maple('adj',A) ↵

B =

[ 7*x-30,    -4*x+10,    10]
[      6,      3*x-2,   -18]
[     -7,        -11,    21]
```

4.5 Gaussian elimination of a matrix

Gaussian elimination means making the lower triangle of a matrix zero by performing the elementary row operations. It is given that the $B = \begin{bmatrix} x & 1 & 0 \\ 0 & \frac{3x-1}{x} & 5 \\ 0 & 0 & -\frac{14x^2-3x-10}{3x-1} \end{bmatrix}$ is derived from the matrix $A = \begin{bmatrix} x & 1 & 0 \\ 2 & x & -3x \\ 1 & 3 & 5 \end{bmatrix}$ following the Gaussian elimination and we intend to obtain that. The maple function gausselim (abbreviation for the gaussian elimination) helps us compute that. Shown on the right (font equivalence is maintained for example A⇔ A) is the implementation. We assigned the maple output to the workspace B on which the pretty (section 3.1) is conducted. There is another function called ffgausselim (abbreviation for the fraction free gaussian elimination) which returns fraction free matrix. The matrix following the Gaussian elimination turns to $\begin{bmatrix} x & 1 & 0 \\ 0 & 3x-1 & 5x \\ 0 & 0 & -14x^2+3x+10 \end{bmatrix}$ multiplying the second row with x and the third row with $3x-1$ whose execution is also shown above. If all elements in A are decimal, the elimination computation takes place using the command A=sym(A); B=double(maple('gausselim',A)).

for the Gaussian elimination,

```
>>syms x ↵
>>A=[x 1 0;2 x -3*x;1 3 5]; ↵
>>B=maple('gausselim',A); ↵
>>pretty(B) ↵
    [x          1                0          ]
    [                                       ]
    [        3 x - 1                        ]
    [0      ---------            5          ]
    [           x                           ]
    [                                       ]
    [                            2          ]
    [                       14 x  - 3 x - 10]
    [0          0        - -----------------]
    [                           3 x - 1     ]
```

for fraction free Gaussian elimination,

```
>>B=maple('ffgausselim',A); ↵
>>pretty(B) ↵
    [x      1          0       ]
    [                          ]
    [0   3 x - 1      5 x      ]
    [                          ]
    [                2         ]
    [0      0     -14 x  + 3 x + 10]
```

4.6 Rank of matrices

The number of the linearly independent rows or columns of a matrix A is called the rank of A. If A is of order $M \times N$, then the rank of $A \leq$ minimum(M , N). The command rank finds the rank of a matrix when the matrix is its input argument. It is given that the numeric matix $A = \begin{bmatrix} 1 & 2 & 4 & 3 \\ 3 & -1 & 2 & -2 \\ 5 & -4 & 0 & -7 \end{bmatrix}$ and the symbolic element matrix $B = \begin{bmatrix} x & x \\ 1 & 1 \end{bmatrix}$ have the ranks 2 and 1 respectively and we wish to obtain them. Both implementations are attached above (font equivalence is maintained for example A⇔ A , section 2.1 for the syms). A row or column matrix has the rank 1.

For the matrix rank:

```
>>A=[1 2 4 3;3 -1 2 -2; 5 -4 0 -7]; ↵
>>rank(A) ↵

ans =
     2

>>syms x ↵
>>B=[x x;1 1]; rank(B) ↵

ans =
     1
```

4.7 Determinant of a square matrix

Determinant of a matrix is possible if the matrix is square. It is given that 124 and $2x^2 - 2x - 4x^3 + 4xy$ are the determinant values for the square matrices $A = \begin{bmatrix} 2 & 4 & 3 \\ -4 & 6 & 9 \\ 3 & 7 & 10 \end{bmatrix}$ and $B = \begin{bmatrix} x & x^2 & y \\ 2x & x & 1 \\ 0 & 2 & 2 \end{bmatrix}$ respectively and we wish to compute them. We attached both computations on the right (font equivalence is maintained like A⇔ A, section 2.1 for the syms). In each case we assigned the computed value to the workspace C (can be any user-chosen name). For the second matrix, the pretty (section 3.1) is applied to see the readable form on the string stored in C.

For matrix determinant of A:

```
>>A=[2 4 3;-4 6 9;3 7 10]; ↵
>>C=det(A) ↵

C =

   124
>>syms x y ↵        ← for B
>>B=[x x^2 y;2*x x 1;0 2 2]; ↵
>>C=det(B); pretty(C) ↵
       2           3
   2 x  - 2 x - 4 x  + 4 x y
```

4.8 Power of a square matrix and matrix polynomial

Power of a square matrix is raised by the operator ^. Suppose we have the square matrix $A = \begin{bmatrix} 4 & 5 & 1 \\ 0 & 1 & 3 \\ 8 & 3 & 0 \end{bmatrix}$ on which

$$A^2 = \begin{bmatrix} 4 & 5 & 1 \\ 0 & 1 & 3 \\ 8 & 3 & 0 \end{bmatrix} \times \begin{bmatrix} 4 & 5 & 1 \\ 0 & 1 & 3 \\ 8 & 3 & 0 \end{bmatrix} = \begin{bmatrix} 4\times4+5\times0+1\times8 & 4\times5+5\times1+1\times3 & 4\times1+5\times3+1\times0 \\ 0\times4+1\times0+3\times8 & 0\times5+1\times1+3\times3 & 0\times1+1\times3+3\times0 \\ 8\times4+3\times0+0\times8 & 8\times5+3\times1+0\times3 & 8\times1+3\times3+0\times0 \end{bmatrix} =$$

$\begin{bmatrix} 24 & 28 & 19 \\ 24 & 10 & 3 \\ 32 & 43 & 17 \end{bmatrix}$. If the power is 4, we have $A^4 = \begin{bmatrix} 1856 & 1769 & 863 \\ 912 & 901 & 537 \\ 2344 & 2057 & 1026 \end{bmatrix}$. Again let us say $B = \begin{bmatrix} \frac{1}{3} & \frac{6}{7} \\ \frac{2}{9} & \frac{5}{7} \end{bmatrix}$ hence $B^2 = \begin{bmatrix} \frac{19}{63} & \frac{44}{49} \\ \frac{44}{189} & \frac{103}{147} \end{bmatrix}$. Matrix polynomial is similar to the algebraic polynomial with the exception that the variable is a square matrix. Let us evaluate the matrix polynomial $P = -3A^3 + 7A^2 + 9I$ for $A = \begin{bmatrix} 1 & 2 \\ 3 & -1 \end{bmatrix}$ which should be $\begin{bmatrix} 37 & -42 \\ -63 & 79 \end{bmatrix}$.

All computations are presented below (font equivalence is maintained for example A⇔ A, section 2.1 for the sym).

for A^2,

```
>>A=[4 5 1;0 1 3;8 3 0]; ↵
>>A^2 ↵

ans =
    24    28    19
    24    10     3
    32    43    17
```

for A^4,

```
>>A^4 ↵

ans =
    1856    1769     863
     912     901     537
    2344    2057    1026
```

for the rational number,

```
>>B=sym([1/3 6/7;2/9 5/7]); ↵
>>B^2 ↵

ans =

[   19/63,     44/49]
[  44/189,   103/147]
```

for the matrix polynomial,

```
>>A=[1 2;3 -1]; ↵
>>P=-3*A^3+7*A^2+9*eye(2)↵

P =
    37   -42
   -63    79
```

It is understood that the I is the identity matrix of the same order as that of A which is 2×2 (section 4.1).

4.9 Inverse of a square matrix

The function inv (abbreviation for the inverse) computes the inverse of a square matrix when the matrix is its input argument but on the condition that the determinant of the square matrix is not zero. Let us take the square matrix $A = \begin{bmatrix} 2 & 1 & 5 \\ 0 & 2 & 1 \\ 0 & 0 & 2 \end{bmatrix}$ as example whose inverse is given by $B = \begin{bmatrix} \frac{1}{2} & -\frac{1}{4} & -\frac{9}{8} \\ 0 & \frac{1}{2} & -\frac{1}{4} \\ 0 & 0 & \frac{1}{2} \end{bmatrix} = \begin{bmatrix} 0.5 & -0.25 & -1.125 \\ 0 & 0.5 & -0.25 \\ 0 & 0 & 0.5 \end{bmatrix}$. It may be required that the inverse be in rational form. Both the numeric and rational implementations are presented below:

for the inverse in numeric form,

```
>>A=[2 1 5;0 2 1;0 0 2]; ↵
>>B=inv(A) ↵

B =
    0.5000   -0.2500   -1.1250
         0    0.5000   -0.2500
         0         0    0.5000
```

for the inverse in rational form,

```
>>A=sym([2 1 5;0 2 1;0 0 2]); ↵
>>B=inv(A) ↵

B =

[  1/2,   -1/4,   -9/8]
[    0,    1/2,   -1/4]
[    0,      0,    1/2]
```

For the expression inverse:

```
>>syms x y ↵
>>A=[x y;x+y 1]; B=inv(A); pretty(B) ↵
[           1                       y           ]
[- ------------------    ------------------     ]
[          2                       2            ]
[   -x + x y + y           -x + x y + y         ]
[                                               ]
[      x + y                       x            ]
[ ------------------   - ------------------     ]
[          2                       2            ]
[ -x + x y + y             -x + x y + y         ]
```

Matrices of the symbolic variables are easy to deal with the **inv**. Given that the inverse of $A=\begin{bmatrix} x & y \\ x+y & 1 \end{bmatrix}$ is $B=$

$\begin{bmatrix} -\frac{1}{y^2+yx-x} & \frac{y}{y^2+yx-x} \\ \frac{x+y}{y^2+yx-x} & -\frac{x}{y^2+yx-x} \end{bmatrix}$ whose implementation is also attached at the end of the last page on the right along with the other two. We maintained the font equivalence like A⇔ A (sections 2.1 and 3.1 for the sym, syms, and pretty).

4.10 Characteristic polynomial and matrix of a square matrix

Characteristic polynomial of a square matrix A is defined by $|\lambda I - A|$ where I is the identity matrix of the same order as that of A, λ is the eigenvalue of A, and the modulus sign indicates the determinant of the square matrix. The command poly computes the characteristic polynomial of a square matrix when the matrix is its input argument. It is given that the $\lambda^3+6\lambda^2-23\lambda+9$ and $\lambda^2+6\lambda-7+x$ are the characteristic polynomials of square matrices on numeric $A=\begin{bmatrix} 1 & 2 & -1 \\ -1 & -7 & 2 \\ 0 & 9 & 0 \end{bmatrix}$ and symbolic $B=\begin{bmatrix} 1 & x \\ -1 & -7 \end{bmatrix}$ respectively which we intend to compute. Both implementations are attached on the right. In each case we assigned the matrix to corresponding variable and the output of the poly to the workspace P. As a return from the poly, we obtain the polynomial coefficients that is [1 6 –23 9] (section 3.1) for the numeric case. In the symbolic case, the related variables in the matrix are declared using the command syms (section 2.1) and the output is the whole polynomial in terms of t (symbol λ is unavailable in the workspace and default t⇔ λ). The matrix $C=\lambda I - A=\begin{bmatrix} \lambda-1 & -2 & 1 \\ 1 & \lambda+7 & -2 \\ 0 & -9 & \lambda \end{bmatrix}$ is called the characteristic matrix of A which we also intend to obtain.

Polynomial for the coefficient form,

```
>>A=[1 2 -1;-1 -7 2;0 9 0]; P=poly(A) ↵

P =

    1.0000   6.0000  -23.0000   9.0000
```

Polynomial for the symbolic variables,

```
>>syms x, B=[1 x;-1 -7]; P=poly(B) ↵

P=

t^2+6*t-7+x
```

for the characteristic matrix,

```
>>A=sym([1 2 -1;-1 -7 2;0 9 0]); ↵
>>C=maple('charmat',A,'L') ↵

C =

[ L-1,    -2,    1]
[   1,   L+7,   -2]
[   0,    -9,    L]
```

There is a maple (section 3.2) function called charmat (abbreviation for characteristic matrix) which finds the characteristic matrix from A but the computation is purely symbolic whose implementation is also presented above. The maple accepts three input arguments, the first, second, and third of which are the function name under quote, given matrix name, and user-given variable name (say L) for λ under quote respectively.

4.11 Eigenvalues and eigenvectors of a square matrix

For a square matrix of order $N \times N$, the characteristic equation $|\lambda I - A|=0$ is a polynomial of degree N and has N roots. These roots of the characteristic equation are called the eigenvalues of the matrix A. For each eigenvalue, there is a matrix X of order $N\times 1$ which satisfies the matrix equation $A\,X=\lambda X$. If the equation is satisfied by the vector X, then the X is called an eigenvector of the matrix A. Matrix multiplication of A and X results the order of $A\,X$ as $N\times 1$ again the order of the matrix λX is also $N\times 1$. For the N eigenvalues, we must have N eigenvectors. The eigenvalues are unique but the eigenvectors are not.

only for the eigenvalues,

```
>>A=[2 2 0;2 1 1;-7 2 -3]; ↵
>>E=eig(A) ↵

E =
   -4.0000
    3.0000
    1.0000
```

However it is given that the eigenvalues of $A=\begin{bmatrix} 2 & 2 & 0 \\ 2 & 1 & 1 \\ -7 & 2 & -3 \end{bmatrix}$ are -4, 1, and 3 and the eigenvectors are

$\begin{bmatrix} 0.0747 \\ -0.2242 \\ 0.9717 \end{bmatrix}$, $\begin{bmatrix} -0.4364 \\ 0.2182 \\ 0.8729 \end{bmatrix}$, and $\begin{bmatrix} -0.6667 \\ -0.3333 \\ 0.6667 \end{bmatrix}$ which we intend to obtain. The function eig (from the eigenvalue) helps us

for $\lambda=-4$ *for* $\lambda=1$ *for* $\lambda=3$

determine the eigenvalues of a square matrix taking the matrix as its input argument. Its implementation (font equivalence like A⇔ A is maintained) is presented above on the right in which the first line is the matrix entering. The eigenvalues of A as a column matrix are returned to the workspace variable E (user-chosen name) in the second line. The eig keeps the provision for returning the eigenvectors as well but with different number of output arguments (implementation is at the beginning of the next page on the right). The command [Y X]=eig(A) means that there are two output arguments for the eig (Y and X – both names are user-given). The Y and X correspond to the eigenvectors and eigenvalues respectively. The matrix returned to Y is formed by placing the eigenvectors side by side. The X is a diagonal matrix whose diagonal elements are the eigenvalues of A. The placement of the eigenvectors and eigenvalues is in order for example the first column in Y corresponds to the first diagonal element of the X or eigenvalue –4. Once executed, one might need to access the individual eigenvalue and eigenvetor. For example the second eigenvector can be picked up from the Y using the command Y(:,2) (section 2.6) and its eigenvalue from X(2,2). We picked up the second eigenvector and assigned that to T as attached on the right. Again as a column matrix we can store the eigenvalues to the workspace D (user-chosen) using the command diag as shown on the right.

Depending on the nature of A, the eigenvalues can be real or complex however the eig is suitable for handling the complex eigenvalues in general. Since eigenvectors are not unique, sometimes symbolic solution is appreciated. For example, the ongoing matrix A has the eigenvectors $\begin{bmatrix} 2 \\ 1 \\ -2 \end{bmatrix}$, $\begin{bmatrix} -2 \\ 1 \\ 4 \end{bmatrix}$, and $\begin{bmatrix} 1 \\ -3 \\ 13 \end{bmatrix}$ for 3, 1, and –4 respectively. It is implementable by declaring the elements of A as symbolic (section 2.1) in that case we need the command [Y X]=eig(sym(A)). Every numeric

for the eigenvalues and eigenvectors,

```
>>[Y X]=eig(A) ↵

Y =
    0.0747   -0.6667   -0.4364
   -0.2242   -0.3333    0.2182
    0.9717    0.6667    0.8729

X =
   -4.0000         0         0
         0    3.0000         0
         0         0    1.0000
```

only the second eigenvector,

```
>>T=Y(:,2) ↵

T =
   -0.6667
   -0.3333
    0.6667
```

only the eigenvalues from X,

```
>>D=diag(X) ↵

D =
   -4.0000
    3.0000
    1.0000
```

eigenvector returned by the eig is normalized for example the first eigenvector $\begin{bmatrix} 0.0747 \\ -0.2242 \\ 0.9717 \end{bmatrix}$ has the magnitude $\sqrt{0.0747^2 + (-0.2242)^2 + 0.9717^2} = 1$. The reader can verify that each eigenvalue-eigenvector set satisfy the matrix equation $A\ X = \lambda\ X$.

4.12 Basis and null space of some vectors

If S is a set of non-zero vectors such as $S = \{V_1, V_2, V_3, \ldots V_n\}$ spanning the vector space F, then a subset of S is a basis of F. To find the basis, we check the linear dependence of a subset of vectors. If any dependence is there, we exclude the dependent vector to make the subset linearly independent. This way we continue until the whole set of vectors is investigated. Let us say $S = \{V_1, V_2, V_3, V_4\}$ where $V_1 = \begin{bmatrix} 3 \\ 2 \\ 6 \end{bmatrix}$, $V_2 = \begin{bmatrix} 4 \\ 2 \\ 3 \end{bmatrix}$, $V_3 = \begin{bmatrix} 5 \\ 3 \\ 2 \end{bmatrix}$, and $V_4 = \begin{bmatrix} 4 \\ 2 \\ 1 \end{bmatrix}$. It is given that V_4 can be written as $a\ V_1 + b\ V_2 + c\ V_3$ where $a = -\frac{4}{11}$, $b = \frac{9}{11}$, and $c = \frac{4}{11}$. Since V_4 can be expressed in terms of V_1, V_2, and V_3, it can not be the basis of S. We say that $\{V_1, V_2, V_3\}$ is the basis of S – this is what we are supposed to find for the example vector set.

The function basis of the maple (section 3.2) helps us find symbolically the basis vectors from some given vector set. Any vector is written using the reserve word vector( ) and the vector elements are housed in order by the third braces but separated by a comma. Attached on the right is the implementation for the basis finding in which the first two lines are to assign the given four vectors within the maple to the workspace variables v1, v2, v3, and v4 (user-chosen names) respectively where := is the maple assignment operator. Also two line commands in maple are separated by the operator :. The third line in the implementation just calls the basis() to find the basis vectors. The input arguments of the basis are the vector assignee names separated by a comma but housed in the second braces.

basis finding for some vectors:

```
>>maple('v1:=vector([3,2,6]):v2:=vector([4,2,3]):'); ↵
>>maple('v3:=vector([5,3,2]):v4:=vector([4,2,1]):'); ↵
>>maple('basis({v1,v2,v3,v4})') ↵

ans =

{v1, v2, v3}
```

← It means the basis $\{V_1, V_2, V_3\}$

A basis vector Y for the null space of matrix A (does not have to be square) actually satisfies the matrix equation $AY = 0$. Nullity ν of a matrix A is defined as the difference between the number of columns of A and rank of A. If the order of A is $M \times N$ and nullity of A is ν, the basis matrix for the null space of A will be of order $N \times \nu$. We explicate the concept with $A = \begin{bmatrix} 2 & 3 & 1 & 2 & 3 & 1 \\ 8 & 8 & 8 & -3 & -3 & -3 \end{bmatrix}$. The rank of matrix A is 2 since rows are linearly independent. Nullity of A is ν =6–2=4 hence the null space of A has four basis vectors which form a matrix of order $N \times v$ =6×4. It is given that $Y = \begin{bmatrix} -2 & \frac{25}{8} & \frac{33}{8} & \frac{17}{8} \\ 1 & -\frac{11}{4} & -\frac{15}{4} & -\frac{7}{4} \\ 1 & 0 & 0 & 0 \\ 0 & 1 & 0 & 0 \\ 0 & 0 & 1 & 0 \\ 0 & 0 & 0 & 1 \end{bmatrix}$ is a null space basis for the matrix A (columns of A or Y are vectors) which we wish to compute – this is the problem statement. One can verify that $A \times Y = \begin{bmatrix} 0 & 0 & 0 & 0 \\ 0 & 0 & 0 & 0 \end{bmatrix}$ but the point is the Y is not unique. However attached on the right is the finding of the null space matrix by dint of the function null in which the first line is to assign the given matrix to workspace A. The sym (section 2.1) turns the numeric A elements to symbolic ones for rational null space. If you need the decimal output, use the command Y=null(A). We assigned the return from the null to Y which is Y. Note that the vectors in Y are not identical with those in our Y but $AY = 0$ is valid indeed.

for the null space of A:

```
>>A=[2 3 1 2 3 1;8 8 8 -3 -3 -3]; ↵
>>Y=null(sym(A)) ↵

Y =

[ -27/8,  -19/8,    -2,   -11/8]
[     0,      0,     1,       0]
[  15/4,   11/4,     1,     7/4]
[     0,      1,     0,       0]
[     1,      0,     0,       0]
[     0,      0,     0,       1]
```

4.13 Singular value decomposition and condition number

Definitions of the eigenvalues and eigenvectors hold true for square matrices. Spectral decomposition theorem helps any symmetric matrix be decomposed into the product of three matrices. Let A be a matrix of order $M \times N$, A can be expressed as $A = U \times D \times V^T$ where the multiplication sign indicates the matrix multiplication and V^T is the transpose of V. The U and V are called the unitary matrices and their determinant should be 1. Orders of U, D, and V are $M \times M$, $M \times N$, and $N \times N$ respectively. This decomposition is termed as the singular value decomposition of A. The decomposition exists for general matrices – square or rectangular. The D is a diagonal matrix (can be a rectangular one). Diagonal elements of D are called the singular values of A. Singular values are obtained by taking the positive square roots of the eigenvalues of $A \times A^T$ (A^T is the transpose of A). Matrix $A^T \times A$ or $A \times A^T$ is symmetric and their eigenvalues are nonnegative. Columns of U and V are the eigenvectors of $A \times A^T$ and $A^T \times A$ respectively.

The decomposition $A = U \times D \times V^T$ for $A = \begin{bmatrix} 4 & 1 & 0 & 9 \\ 5 & 7 & -1 & 0 \\ 6 & 9 & 4 & 2 \end{bmatrix}$ is given by $U = \begin{bmatrix} 0.4090 & 0.9062 & -0.1073 \\ 0.5168 & -0.3269 & -0.7912 \\ 0.7521 & -0.2682 & 0.6020 \end{bmatrix}$,

$D = \begin{bmatrix} 15.0297 & 0 & 0 & 0 \\ 0 & 8.5537 & 0 & 0 \\ 0 & 0 & 3.3079 & 0 \end{bmatrix}$, and $V = \begin{bmatrix} 0.5810 & -0.0445 & -0.2337 & -0.7783 \\ 0.7183 & 0.4438 & -0.0688 & 0.5314 \\ 0.1658 & 0.0872 & 0.9672 & -0.1717 \\ 0.3450 & -0.8908 & 0.0721 & 0.2869 \end{bmatrix}$. Our objective is to obtain U, D, and V matrices starting from A. The function svd (abbreviation for the singular value decomposition) performs the singular value decomposition of a matrix when the matrix is its input argument. Presented on the right is the decomposition we are seeking for in which the first line is to assign the given matrix data to workspace A. In the second line we call the svd for the decomposition with three output arguments – U, D, and V where U⇔U, D⇔D, and V⇔V. The U, D, or V can be any user-chosen names but in the shown order. We know that the eigenvectors are not unique. Multiplying an eigenvector by minus 1 does not alter the decomposition. This is obvious from the second column vector of the U and the return to U.

for the singular value decomposition:

```
>>A=[4 1 0 9;5 7 -1 0;6 9 4 2]; ↵
>>[U D V]=svd(A) ↵

U =
    0.4090  -0.9062  -0.1073
    0.5168   0.3269  -0.7912
    0.7521   0.2682   0.6020
D =
    15.0297        0        0    0
          0   8.5537        0    0
          0        0   3.3079    0
V =
    0.5810  -0.0445  -0.2337  -0.7783
    0.7183   0.4438  -0.0688   0.5314
    0.1658   0.0872   0.9672  -0.1717
    0.3450  -0.8908   0.0721   0.2869
```

for the condition number of A:

```
>>cond(A) ↵

ans =
    4.5436
```

The condition number of a matrix is defined as the ratio of its largest to smallest singular values. A large condition number indicates contiguous linear dependency among the columns of the matrix or in other words the matrix is nearly a singular one. Just now we computed the singular values of the aforementioned A. Its condition number shold be $\frac{15.0297}{3.3079}$=4.5436. The function cond (abbreviation for condition number) determines the condition number of a matrix when the matrix is its input argument. Its implementation is presented above too.

4.14 Matrix norms and trace

Determinant is defined only for the square matrices. Matrix norm is a way of measuring the magnitude of a rectangular matrix by a single number. There are several types of matrix norms such as Frobenius norm, 1-norm (L_1 norm), 2-norm (L_2 norm), ∝-norm (L_∞ norm), etc whose discussions are in the following.

Frobenius norm:

The Frobenius norm of any matrix A of order $M \times N$ is defined by $\|A\|_F = \sqrt{\sum_{j=1}^{M}\sum_{i=1}^{N} A_{ij}^2}$. In words, the Frobenius norm of a matrix is the positive square root of the sum of its squared elements. To compute the Frobenius norm of a matrix, we use the syntax norm(matrix name,'fro') where the fro is reserve to MATLAB. The Frobenius norm of the rectangular matrix $A = \begin{bmatrix} 6 & 7 & 8 \\ -1 & -2 & 5 \end{bmatrix}$ is $F = \sqrt{6^2 + 7^2 + 8^2 + (-1)^2 + (-2)^2 + 5^2} = 13.3791$ whose computation is shown on the right in which the first line is to assign the given matrix to workspace A and the second line is to call the function. The matrix input argument can be a row or column one as well.

for Frobenius norm:
```
>>A=[6 7 8;-1 -2 5]; ↵
>>F=norm(A,'fro') ↵

F =                    ← F⇔ F
   13.3791
```

L_1 norm:

The L_1 norm of a row or column matrix is given by the sum of absolute values of the elements in the matrix. For example the L_1 norms of row matrix $R = [1 \quad -3 \quad 7]$ and column matrix $C = \begin{bmatrix} 4 \\ -5 \\ -6 \end{bmatrix}$ are given by 11 and 15 respectively. The norm of a rectangular matrix is given by the largest column sum of the absolute values of elements in the rectangular matrix. For example $A = \begin{bmatrix} 6 & 7 & -8 \\ -1 & -2 & 5 \end{bmatrix}$ has the L_1 norm 13. To compute the L_1 norm of a matrix, we use the syntax norm(matrix name,1). The implementations of all three examples are presented above. In the first line implementation, we assigned the given matrices to like names like R to R and the second line is to call the function. In all three examples, the return from norm is assigned to N (can be any user-chosen name).

for row matrix,
```
>>R=[1 -3 7]; ↵
>>N=norm(R,1) ↵

N =
    11
```

for column matrix,
```
>>C=[4 -5 -6]'; ↵
>>N=norm(C,1) ↵

N =
    15
```

for rectangular matrix,
```
>>A=[6 7 -8;-1 -2 5]; ↵
>>N=norm(A,1) ↵

N =
    13
```

L_2 norm:

L_2 norm or 2-norm of a rectangular matrix A is defined as the largest singular value (section 4.13) of A. In order to compute L_2 norm, we apply the syntax norm(A ,2) or norm(A). For instance the $A = \begin{bmatrix} 6 & 7 & -8 & 0 \\ -1 & -2 & 5 & -4 \\ -3 & 5 & 4 & 5 \end{bmatrix}$ has the L_2 norm 13.3304 which we intend to compute and whose computation is shown on the right. The input argument of the function can be a row or column matrix as well.

for L_2 norm,
```
>>A=[6 7 -8 0;-1 -2 5 -4;-3 5 4 5]; ↵
>>N=norm(A,2) ↵      ← N⇔ L2

N =
    13.3304
```

L_∞ norm:

To compute L_∞ norm of a matrix, we use the command norm(matrix name, inf) where inf is the reserve word. The L_∞ norm of a row or column matrix is defined as the largest absolute value of the elements in the matrix. For example L_∞ norms of $R = [1 \quad -3 \quad -57 \quad 0]$ and $C = \begin{bmatrix} 14 \\ -50 \\ -62 \\ 13 \end{bmatrix}$ are 57 and 62 respectively. The norm of a rectangular matrix is the largest row sum of the absolute values of the elements in A for instance $A = \begin{bmatrix} 6 & 7 & -8 \\ -1 & -2 & 5 \\ -3 & 0 & 7 \\ 10 & 13 & 0 \end{bmatrix}$ has $L_\infty = 23$. Findings of the L_∞ norms for different matrices are presented above applying ongoing symbology.

for the row matrix,
```
>>R=[1 -3 -57 0]; ↵
>>N=norm(R,inf) ↵

N =
    57
```

for the column matrix,
```
>>C=[14 -50 -62 13]'; ↵
>>N=norm(C,inf) ↵

N =
    62
```

for the rectangular matrix,
```
>>A=[6 7 -8;-1 -2 5;-3 0 7;10 13 0]; ↵
>>N=norm(A,inf) ↵  ← N⇔ L∞

N =
    23
```

L_p norm of a vector:

By vector what we mean is a row or column matrix. The p - norm of a vector X, whose length is N, is $L_p = \left[\sum_{i=1}^{N} |X_i|^p\right]^{\frac{1}{p}}$. To compute the L_p norm of a vector, we apply the command norm(X , p). Let us test the 4-norm of R=[9 7 −10] which should be L_4=[|9|^4+|7|^4+|−10|^4]$^{1/4}$=11.7347 and whose computation is attached on the right applying ongoing function and symbology.

For the L_4 norm:

```
>>R=[9 7 -10]; ↵
>>N=norm(R,4) ↵

N =                ← N⇔ L4

    11.7347
```

$L_{-\infty}$ norm of a vector:

Minus infinity norm of a vector X is defined as the minimum of the absolute values of the elements in X . To compute $L_{-\infty}$ norm of a vector, we employ the command norm (matrix name,-inf) where -inf is reserve to MATLAB. Considering R=[1 −3 −57 0], the $L_{-\infty}$ of R is 0 whose execution is presented on the right applying ongoing function and symbology.

For the $L_{-\infty}$ norm:

```
>>R=[1 -3 -57 0]; ↵
>>N=norm(R,-inf) ↵

N =                ← N⇔ L-∞

     0
```

Trace of a matrix:

Trace of a matrix is defined as the sum of the diagonal elements of the matrix. To calculate the trace of a matrix, we use the syntax trace(matrix name). For instance the trace of the matrix $A=\begin{bmatrix}-2 & 7 & 0\\ 12 & 4 & 3\\ 15 & 2 & 0\end{bmatrix}$ is 2 whose straightforward execution is attached on the right. We assigned the return from the trace to T (any user-chosen name). Finding the trace of a row or column matrix in MATLAB returns the same row or column matrix but the returned matrix is a row one.

For the matrix trace:

```
>>A=[-2 7 0;12 4 3;15 2 0]; ↵
>>T=trace(A) ↵

T =

     2
```

4.15 Linearly and logarithmically spaced vectors and normalization

Linearly spaced vector elements form an arithmetic progression. If the first element in the vector is a and common difference of the progression is d, the vector becomes [a $a+d$ $a+2d$ .. $a+(N-1)d$] where N is the number of elements in the vector. Clearly d is equal to $\frac{Last\ element - First\ element}{N-1}$. The function linspace (abbreviation for the linear space) forms a linearly spaced vector for which the syntax is linspace(first element, last element, number of points from first to last) and whose output is a row matrix. Let us form a row vector R from 3 to 13 with 6 points therefore d=2 and R should be [3 5 7 9 11 13]. A column vector C is to be formed from −7 to 3 with 5 points so that $d=\frac{5}{2}$ and $C=\begin{bmatrix}-7\\ -\frac{9}{2}\\ -2\\ \frac{1}{2}\\ 3\end{bmatrix}$.

Both vectors are implemented on the right in which the return from the linspace is assigned to like names. The command sym (section 2.1) turns the fractional number to rational form. A row matrix is changed to column one using the transpose operator ' for the column vector case.

Linearly spaced row vector:

```
>>R=linspace(3,13,6) ↵

R =

     3   5   7   9   11   13
```

Linearly spaced column vector:

```
>>C=sym(linspace(-7,3,5))' ↵

C =

    -7
  -9/2
    -2
   1/2
     3
```

Logarithmically (base of the logarithm is 10) spaced vector elements form a geometric progression. If the first element in the vector with length N is a and the common ratio of the progression is r, the vector is given by [a ar ar^2.. ar^{N-1}]. The function logspace (abbreviation for logarithmically spaced) generates a logarithmically spaced vector with the syntax logspace(power of the first element, power of the last element, number of points from the first to last) and whose output is a row vector. Suppose we wish to form a logarithmically spaced vector where power of the elements will be from 3 to 4 and the number of elements will be 5 therefore $a=10^3$, N=5, and $r=10^{\frac{1}{4}}$ and which results the vector to be L=[10^3 $10^3 10^{\frac{1}{4}}$ $10^3 10^{\frac{2}{4}}$ $10^3 10^{\frac{3}{4}}$ $10^3 10^{\frac{4}{4}}$]=[1000 1778 3162 5623 10000] (neglecting the fractional parts). Attached above on the right is its implementation. If the power of 10 is higher, the return from the logspace will be of higher digits that is why the return is in exponential form. Concerning the execution, 1.0e+004 * means 1.0×10^4× and each of the return element is multiplied by 10^4. By putting a transpose operator, we turned the row vector to a column one and assigned that to L (any user-chosen name).

Logarithmically spaced vector:

```
>>L=logspace(3,4,5)' ↵

L =
   1.0e+004 *
         0.1000
         0.1778
         0.3162
         0.5623
         1.0000
```

Sometimes a vector needs normalization. Let us say we have the vector $A=[6\ \ 4\ \ 6]$. The magnitude of A is $2\sqrt{22}$ hence the normalized vector is $\begin{bmatrix} \frac{3}{\sqrt{22}} & \frac{1}{11\sqrt{22}} & \frac{3}{\sqrt{22}} \end{bmatrix}$=[0.6396 0.4264 0.6396]. You find the execution on the right in which the first line is to assign the given vector to workspace A. The A.^2 squares every element in A. The **sum** (section 2.8) adds all elements in the vector. With and without the use of **sym** (section 2.1) on A, you see the rational and numeric forms of the normalized vector respectively. The A can be a column matrix too. In both cases the workspace N holds the normalized vector. If you are interested to see the readable form, use **pretty(N)** for the symbolic case, section 3.1.

normalization of a vector: for symbolic form:

```
>>A=[6 4 6]; ↵
>>N=A/sqrt(sum(sym(A).^2)) ↵

N =

[ 3/22*22^(1/2), 1/11*22^(1/2), 3/22*22^(1/2)]
```

normalization in numeric form:

```
>>N=A/sqrt(sum(A.^2)) ↵

N=
     0.6396    0.4264    0.6396
```

What if the data elements are in a matrix for example $A=\begin{bmatrix} -2 & 7 & 0 \\ 12 & 4 & 3 \\ 15 & 2 & 0 \end{bmatrix}$? We intend to normalize the A along the row direction to get $A=\begin{bmatrix} -0.2747 & 0.9615 & 0 \\ 0.9231 & 0.3077 & 0.2308 \\ 0.9912 & 0.1322 & 0 \end{bmatrix}$. Its complete implementation is attached below on the right in which the first line is to assign the given matrix data to A. We assigned the A to N so that we do not change the A. In the second line we enter into a for-loop (subsection 14.3.3) whose counter index k controls the row number of the matrix N. The command N(k,:) means the k-th row in N. Following the normalizing computation on N(k,:) as we did before on a single vector, we assign the outcome to N(k,:) again. There are 3 rows that is why the end index in for-loop is 3. If there were 7 rows, the index would be 7. If you intend to normalize in column direction, the change you need is N(:,k)=N(:,k)/sqrt(sum(N(:,k).^2)); where N(:,k) means the k-th column in N.

normalization in the row direction:

```
>>A=[-2 7 0;12 4 3;15 2 0]; N=A; ↵
>>for k=1:3 N(k,:)=N(k,:)/sqrt(sum(N(k,:).^2)); end ↵
>>N ↵

N =
   -0.2747    0.9615         0
    0.9231    0.3077    0.2308
    0.9912    0.1322         0
```

4.16 Pseudoinverse of a rectangular matrix

A matrix G of order $N \times M$ is said to be the Moore-Penrose inverse or pseudoinverse of another given non-null rectangular matrix A (of order $M \times N$) if the properties $\begin{Bmatrix} AGA = A \\ GAG = G \\ GA\ is\ symmetric \\ AG\ is\ symmetric \end{Bmatrix}$ are satisfied. The matrix G is unique.

It is given that $G=\begin{bmatrix} -0.0055 & 0.0154 & 0.0077 \\ -0.0110 & 0.0308 & 0.0154 \\ -0.0165 & 0.0462 & 0.0231 \\ -0.1538 & 0.0308 & 0.0154 \end{bmatrix}$ is the pseudoinverse of the matrix $A=\begin{bmatrix} 1 & 2 & 3 & -7 \\ 4 & 8 & 12 & -2 \\ 2 & 4 & 6 & -1 \end{bmatrix}$ which we intend to compute. We can have the pseudoinverse of A computed by the agency of **pinv** (abbreviation for the <u>pseudoinv</u>erse) as shown above. Referring to the implementation, the first and second lines are to assign the given matrix to workspace A and to call the **pinv** with the A as its input argument respectively. The return from **pinv** is assigned to G (user-chosen) which is G.

for the pseudoinverse:

```
>>A=[1 2 3 -7;4 8 12 -2;2 4 6 -1]; ↵
>>G=pinv(A) ↵

G =
   -0.0055    0.0154    0.0077
   -0.0110    0.0308    0.0154
   -0.0165    0.0462    0.0231
   -0.1538    0.0308    0.0154
```

4.17 Bilinear and quadratic forms

If we define X and Y as row and column vectors of length M and N respectively and A is a matrix of order $M \times N$, then XAY is called a bilinear form. For example $X=[x_1\ \ x_2]$, $Y=\begin{bmatrix} y_1 \\ y_2 \\ y_3 \end{bmatrix}$, and $A=\begin{bmatrix} 8 & 3 & -2 \\ 9 & 7 & 5 \end{bmatrix}$ express XAY as $[x_1\ \ x_2]\begin{bmatrix} 8 & 3 & -2 \\ 9 & 7 & 5 \end{bmatrix}\begin{bmatrix} y_1 \\ y_2 \\ y_3 \end{bmatrix}=8x_1y_1+9y_1x_2+3y_2x_1+7y_2x_2-2x_1y_3+5x_2y_3$ – that is what the bilinear form is.

With the help of multiplication operator, we easily implement that as shown below on the right. All related independent variables are declared as symbolic (section 2.1) using the **syms** in the first line. In the second line, we assigned the given X, Y, and A matrices to the like names. Note that the X and Y are row and column matrices respectively. In the third line we multiplied the three matrices using X*A*Y and assigned the result to workspace O (the **expand** expands the multiplication result). The **pretty** (section 3.1) just shows the readable form on the code stored in O.

for the bilinear form:

```
>>syms x1 x2 y1 y2 y3 ↵   ← x1⇔ x_1 , x2⇔ x_2 , and so on
>>X=[x1 x2]; Y=[y1;y2;y3]; A=[8 3 -2;9 7 5]; ↵
>>O=expand(X*A*Y); ↵            ← O⇔ XAY
>>pretty(O) ↵
    8 y1 x1 + 9 y1 x2 + 3 y2 x1 + 7 y2 x2 - 2 y3 x1 + 5 y3 x2
```

If X is equal to Y and A is a square matrix, then XAX^T is called the quadratic form where T is the transposition operator. The quadratic form is actually the sum of squares, which can be written as $\sum_{i=1}^{M}(x_i - \bar{x})^2 = XAX^T$. For example $X = [x_1 \quad x_2 \quad x_3]$ and $A = \begin{bmatrix} 2 & 3 & -4 \\ 1 & 9 & 7 \\ 2 & 3 & -6 \end{bmatrix}$ provides $[x_1 \quad x_2 \quad x_3]\begin{bmatrix} 2 & 3 & -4 \\ 1 & 9 & 7 \\ 2 & 3 & -6 \end{bmatrix}\begin{bmatrix} x_1 \\ x_2 \\ x_3 \end{bmatrix} = 2x_1^2 + 9x_2^2 - 6x_3^2 + 4x_1x_2 - 2x_1x_3 + 10x_2x_3$ whose implementation is attached above applying bilinear form mentioned function and symbology. Since in general any symbolic variable is assumed to be complex in MATLAB, we did not use X' for the transposition of X instead we did X.' meaning transposition without the conjugate.

for the quadratic form:

```
>>syms x1 x2 x3 ↵
>>X=[x1 x2 x3]; A=[2 3 -4;1 9 7;2 3 -6]; ↵
>>O=expand(X*A*X.'); ↵
>>pretty(O) ↵
      2                             2                   2
  2 x1  + 4 x1 x2 - 2 x1 x3 + 9 x2  + 10 x2 x3 - 6 x3
```

4.18 Orthonormalization of a matrix

A matrix Q is said to be an orthonormal basis for the range of A if Q satisfies $Q^TQ = I$ where I is the identity matrix of order $r \times r$ and r is the rank of A. Let us consider $A = \begin{bmatrix} 2 & 2 & -3 \\ 2 & 2 & 2 \\ -2 & -2 & 0 \\ 0 & 0 & 2 \end{bmatrix}$ whose rank is 2. It is given that $Q = \begin{bmatrix} 0.7333 & 0.4714 \\ 0.4 & -0.7071 \\ -0.5333 & 0.2357 \\ -0.1333 & -0.4714 \end{bmatrix}$ is the orthonormal basis for A which we intend to find. The function **orth** (abbreviation for the orthonormalization) computes the orthonormal basis of a matrix when the matrix is its input argument. Attached on the right is the execution of the command in which the first and second lines are to assign the given matrix to workspace A and to call the function for the orthonormalization respectively. We assigned the return from the function to workspace Q (user-chosen) which is our Q. Since the orthonormalization is found using the eigenvector (section 4.11) and multiplying an eigenvector by -1 does not invalidate the definition, our mentioned Q and the found one differ in the first column. One can prove that Q^TQ or the command Q'*Q provides the identity matrix $\begin{bmatrix} 1 & 0 \\ 0 & 1 \end{bmatrix}$.

for the orthonormal basis of A:

```
>>A=[2 2 -3;2 2 2;-2 -2 0;0 0 2]; ↵
>>Q=orth(A) ↵

Q =
   -0.7333    0.4714
   -0.4000   -0.7071
    0.5333    0.2357
    0.1333   -0.4714
```

There is another variant in the symbolic context which is located in the **maple** package (section 3.2). A square matrix A is said to be orthogonal if it satisfies $AA^T = A^TA = I$ where A^T is the transpose of A and I is the identity matrix. The function **orthog** (taken from orthogonality, applicable for square matrix only) tests the orthogonality whose output is either true or false. Considering $A = \begin{bmatrix} \frac{2}{3} & -\frac{2}{3} & \frac{1}{3} \\ \frac{1}{3} & \frac{2}{3} & \frac{2}{3} \\ \frac{2}{3} & \frac{1}{3} & -\frac{2}{3} \end{bmatrix}$, one can verify that $A \times A^T = A^T \times A = \begin{bmatrix} 1 & 0 & 0 \\ 0 & 1 & 0 \\ 0 & 0 & 1 \end{bmatrix}$ whose implementation is shown above on the right. In the implementation, we assigned the given matrix to workspace A but symbolically (section 2.1). Within the **maple**, the command maple('orthog',A) means applying the **orthog** on A.

for the orthogonality check:

```
>>A=sym([2/3 -2/3 1/3;1/3 2/3 2/3;2/3 1/3 -2/3]); ↵
>>maple('orthog',A) ↵

ans =

true
```

4.19 Minimal polynomial and matrix exponential of a square matrix

Cayley-Hamilton theorem says that any square matrix A satisfies the characteristic polynomial $C(\lambda) = |\lambda I - A|$ where λ is a scalar and I is the identity matrix of the same order as that of A. The characteristic polynomial $C(\lambda)$ is not necessarily the polynomial of lowest degree such that $C(A)=0$. It is possible to have a polynomial $f(A)$ whose degree is less than that of the characteristic one such that $f(A)=0$. Thus the least degree polynomial satisfying $f(A)=0$ is termed as the minimal polynomial. For example $f(A)=A^2+A-2$ is the minimal polynomial for the square $A=\begin{bmatrix}1 & 0 & 0\\ -1 & 0 & 2\\ 1 & 1 & -1\end{bmatrix}$ which we wish to obtain. The maple (section 3.2) function minpoly (abbreviation for the minimal polynomial) determines the minimal polynomial symbolically. Presented on the right is execution of the command. In the execution, the first line is to assign the given matrix as symbolic using the sym (section 2.1). In the second line we called the minpoly within the maple. There are three input arguments inside the maple, the first, second, and third of which are the function name under quote, assignee square matrix name, and user-chosen independent variable name under quote (we chose A, could be any user-given name) respectively.

finding the minimal polynomial:

```
>>A=sym([1 0 0;-1 0 2;1 1 -1]); ↵
>>maple('minpoly',A,'A') ↵

ans =

-2+A+A^2
```

For every square matrix A, e^A can be expressed as $I+A+\frac{A^2}{2!}+\frac{A^3}{3!}+$ ...... Utilizing the characteristic or minimal polynomial of A, higher powers of e^A can be reduced to the lower ones thereby converging the series for e^A. The convergent series is called the matrix exponential of A. It is given that the $e^{At}=\begin{bmatrix}e^{4t} & 0 & 0\\ 1-e^{4t} & 1 & 0\\ e^{4t}-1 & e^{4t}-1 & e^{4t}\end{bmatrix}$ is the matrix exponential for $A=\begin{bmatrix}4 & 0 & 0\\ -4 & 0 & 0\\ 4 & 4 & 4\end{bmatrix}$ which we intend to compute. The function expm (abbreviation for the exponential of square matrix) computes e^{At} from given A. Shown above is the computation in which in the first line we declared the t as symbolic writing syms t and assigned the given matrix elements to workspace A (which is also symbolic). In the second line we called the expm and the return from it is put to y. If you wish to see the readable form, use the pretty(y). If e^A is needed, just we insert $t=1$. Again the numeric form can be exercised using A=[4 0 0;-4 0 0;4 4 4]; y=expm(A); in which the y holds the matrix exponential e^A values in decimal. If the square matrix is too long, the symbolic form finding may take longer or may not exist.

for the matrix exponential:

```
>>syms t; A=sym([4 0 0;-4 0 0;4 4 4]); ↵
>>y=expm(A*t) ↵            ← y⇔e^(At)

y =

[    exp(4*t),             0,            0]
[ -exp(4*t)+1,             1,            0]
[  exp(4*t)-1,    exp(4*t)-1,     exp(4*t)]
```

4.20 LU triangular factorization of a square matrix

In the LU triangular factorization, a square matrix is expressed as the product of two triangular matrices – a lower and an upper triangular matrices. Examples of the lower and upper triangular matrices are $\begin{bmatrix}1 & 0 & 0\\ 7 & 0 & 0\\ 2 & 0 & 5\end{bmatrix}$ (super diagonal elements are zeroes) and $\begin{bmatrix}1 & 2 & 3\\ 0 & 0 & 3\\ 0 & 0 & 5\end{bmatrix}$ (subdiagonal elements are zeroes) respectively. If A is a square matrix, A can be written as $A=L\times U$ where L and U correspond to the lower and upper triangular matrices respectively of the same order as that of A. The factorization is not a unique one. One may end up with different L and U but the product of L and U is A that is for sure. It is

for the symbolic LU factorization:

```
>>maple('A:=matrix(4,4,[2,3,4,7,2,0,1,3,9,1,3,7,1,8,2,4])'); ↵
>>maple('LUdecomp(A,L=L,U=U)'); ↵
>>L=sym(maple('print(L)')) ↵       ← L⇔L, L is user-chosen

L =

[    1,       0,       0,     0]
[    1,       1,       0,     0]
[  9/2,    25/6,       1,     0]
[  1/2,   -13/6,    13/5,     1]
>>U=sym(maple('print(U)')) ↵       ← U⇔U, U is user-chosen

U =

[    2,     3,      4,      7]
[    0,    -3,     -3,     -4]
[    0,     0,   -5/2,  -47/6]
[    0,     0,      0,   61/5]
```

given that $A=\begin{bmatrix}2&3&4&7\\2&0&1&3\\9&1&3&7\\1&8&2&4\end{bmatrix}$ can be factored as $L=\begin{bmatrix}1&0&0&0\\1&1&0&0\\\frac{9}{2}&\frac{25}{6}&1&0\\\frac{1}{2}&-\frac{13}{6}&\frac{13}{5}&1\end{bmatrix}$ and $U=\begin{bmatrix}2&3&4&7\\0&-3&-3&-4\\0&0&-\frac{5}{2}&-\frac{47}{6}\\0&0&-\frac{13}{2}&-\frac{49}{6}\end{bmatrix}$ which we intend to obtain. The function LUdecomp (abbreviation for the Lower and Upper decomposition) of the maple (section 3.2) performs the decomposition symbolically. In the last page on the lower right corner we have shown the execution in which the first line is to assign the given matrix A to A through the reserve word matrix within the maple. The matrix has three input arguments, the first, second, and third of which are row number of A, column number of A, and rowwise elements of A each separated by a comma but housed in the third brace respectively – matrix entering style in maple. Also the := is the assignment operator in maple. The function LUdecomp has three input arguments, the first, second, and third of which are the matrix assignee name, user-given lower triangular matrix name passed through L=, and user-given upper triangular matrix name passed through U= respectively. We chose the matrix names to be L and U respectively as well. If you wish the lower and upper triangular matrix return names to be X and Y, we would write L=X and U=Y in the second and third input arguments respectively. The command print(L) of maple displays the object content in L. The return from maple is turned to symbolic using sym and assigned to L for user's availability.

For the numeric computation there is another function called lu (abbreviation for the lower and upper) which is conducted as shown on the right. The first line in the implementation is the assignment of the given matrix to A without sym. The lu has one input (given matrix name) and two output arguments indicated by L and U respectively where L⇔L and U⇔U.

for the numeric LU factorization:

```
>>A=[2 3 4 7;2 0 1 3;9 1 3 7;1 8 2 4]; ↵
>>[L,U]=lu(A); ↵
```

4.21 QR decomposition of a matrix

The idea underlying the decomposition says that any non-zero vector or matrix A can be expressed as the product of two matrices i.e $A=Q\times R$ where Q is orthogonal (meaning $Q^TQ=I$) and R is upper triangular. The matrix Q is not unique but $A=Q\times R$ is observed. It is given that $A=\begin{bmatrix}3&3&3\\0&-3&-3\\0&-4&-4\\4&4&4\end{bmatrix}$ is QR decomposed as $Q=\begin{bmatrix}\frac{3}{5}&0&0&\frac{4}{5}\\0&-\frac{3}{5}&-\frac{4}{5}&0\\0&-\frac{4}{5}&\frac{3}{5}&0\\\frac{4}{5}&0&0&-\frac{3}{5}\end{bmatrix}$ and $R=\begin{bmatrix}5&5&5\\0&5&5\\0&0&0\\0&0&0\end{bmatrix}$. Our objective is to implement that.

For the symbolic Q-R decomposition:

```
>>maple('A:=matrix(4,3,[3,3,3,0,-3,-3,0,-4,-4,4,4,4])'); ↵
>>R=maple('QRdecomp(A,Q=Q)'); ↵
>>sym(maple('print(Q)')) ↵        ← To see Q

ans =

[ 3/5,    0,   4/5,    0]
[   0, -3/5,     0,  4/5]
[   0, -4/5,     0, -3/5]
[ 4/5,    0,  -3/5,    0]
>>sym(R) ↵                        ← To see R

ans =

[ 5, 5, 5]
[ 0, 5, 5]
[ 0, 0, 0]
[ 0, 0, 0]
```

For the numeric QR decomposition computation:

```
>>A=[3 3 3;0 -3 -3;0 -4 -4;4 4 4]; ↵
>>[Q,R]=qr(A); ↵
```

Placed on the right is the symbolic decomposition by dint of the maple (section 3.2) function QRdecomp (abbreviation for the Q and R decomposition). The explanation of the first line implementation is similar to that of the last section. In the second line the QRdecomp has two input arguments within the maple, the first and second of which are the matrix assignee name and user-given Q matrix name passed through Q= respectively. We chose the Q matrix name to be Q that is why Q=Q. The default return from the maple is the R matrix which we assigned to the workspace R in the second line. The maple command print displays the object Q contents but to make it available in MATLAB, we use the sym. Observe that our Q and the return Q are not identical but both satisfy $A=Q\times R$.

Again we discussed so far only the symbolic type computation. There is another function by the name qr which serves the purpose of the numeric computation and whose implementation is also shown above for the same A. Now we enter the given matrix to A in MATLAB style (section 1.3) in the first line. In the second line we called the function qr with the given matrix name as the input argument and the qr has two output arguments Q and R understandably Q⇔Q and R⇔R.

4.22 Jordan form decomposition of a square matrix

If the eigenvalues of a square matrix A are all distinct, the A has a diagonal representation with the eigenvalues on the diagonal. For repeated eigenvalues of a square matrix, it is not always possible to find a diagonal matrix representation however it is possible to find some basis vectors so that the new representation is almost a diagonal form called a Jordan canonical form or Jordan form. The form has the eigenvalues of A in the diagonal and either 0 or 1 in the superdiagonal or subdiagonal. For example if A has an eigenvalue λ with multiplicity 4, then Jordan form (assuming superdiagonal) takes one of the following forms – $\begin{bmatrix} \lambda & 0 & 0 & 0 \\ 0 & \lambda & 0 & 0 \\ 0 & 0 & \lambda & 0 \\ 0 & 0 & 0 & \lambda \end{bmatrix}$, $\begin{bmatrix} \lambda & 1 & 0 & 0 \\ 0 & \lambda & 0 & 0 \\ 0 & 0 & \lambda & 0 \\ 0 & 0 & 0 & \lambda \end{bmatrix}$, $\begin{bmatrix} \lambda & 1 & 0 & 0 \\ 0 & \lambda & 0 & 0 \\ 0 & 0 & \lambda & 1 \\ 0 & 0 & 0 & \lambda \end{bmatrix}$, $\begin{bmatrix} \lambda & 1 & 0 & 0 \\ 0 & \lambda & 1 & 0 \\ 0 & 0 & \lambda & 1 \\ 0 & 0 & 0 & \lambda \end{bmatrix}$, or $\begin{bmatrix} \lambda & 1 & 0 & 0 \\ 0 & \lambda & 1 & 0 \\ 0 & 0 & \lambda & 0 \\ 0 & 0 & 0 & \lambda \end{bmatrix}$. Which Jordan form the matrix A assumes depends on the nature of A. A square matrix of type $\begin{bmatrix} \lambda & 1 & 0 & 0 \\ 0 & \lambda & 1 & 0 \\ 0 & 0 & \lambda & 1 \\ 0 & 0 & 0 & \lambda \end{bmatrix}$ is called a Jordan block. We presented only the upper Jordan block, there can be lower Jordan form also for example $\begin{bmatrix} \lambda & 0 \\ 1 & \lambda \end{bmatrix}$ or $\begin{bmatrix} \lambda & 0 & 0 \\ 1 & \lambda & 0 \\ 0 & 1 & \lambda \end{bmatrix}$. Considering a square matrix A of order $N \times N$, one can write $Q^{-1}AQ = J$ where J is just mentioned Jordan canonical form consisted of the Jordan blocks. It is noteworthy that the matrix Q is not unique but the Jordan form is.

Let us consider the matrix $A = \begin{bmatrix} 3 & -1 & 1 & 1 & 0 & 0 \\ 1 & 1 & -1 & -1 & 0 & 0 \\ 0 & 0 & 2 & 0 & 1 & 1 \\ 0 & 0 & 0 & 2 & -2 & -1 \\ 0 & 0 & 0 & 0 & 2 & 2 \\ 0 & 0 & 0 & 0 & 2 & 2 \end{bmatrix}$ which has the eigenvalues 0, 2 (of multiplicity 4), and 4. It is given that a representation of

$$Q = \begin{bmatrix} 0 & -\frac{1}{4} & -1 & -\frac{1}{2} & 0 & \frac{1}{4} \\ \frac{1}{4} & 0 & -1 & \frac{1}{2} & 0 & \frac{1}{4} \\ 0 & \frac{1}{2} & 0 & 0 & -\frac{5}{2} & -\frac{3}{2} \\ \frac{1}{4} & -\frac{3}{4} & 0 & 0 & 2 & \frac{3}{2} \\ \frac{1}{2} & \frac{1}{2} & 0 & 0 & 0 & 0 \\ -\frac{1}{2} & \frac{1}{2} & 0 & 0 & 0 & 0 \end{bmatrix}$$

turns the given A to the Jordan form

$$Q^{-1}AQ = J = \begin{bmatrix} 0 & 0 & 0 & 0 & 0 & 0 \\ 0 & 4 & 0 & 0 & 0 & 0 \\ 0 & 0 & 2 & 1 & 0 & 0 \\ 0 & 0 & 0 & 2 & 1 & 0 \\ 0 & 0 & 0 & 0 & 2 & 0 \\ 0 & 0 & 0 & 0 & 0 & 2 \end{bmatrix}$$

. Our objective is to obtain the matrices for the Q and J starting from the A. Let us enter the given matrix A to workspace A as follows:

for the Jordan form:

```
>>[Q J]=jordan(sym(A)) ↵

Q =

[  0, -1/4,  -1, -1/2,   0,  1/4]
[ 1/4,   0,  -1,  1/2,   0,  1/4]
[  0,  1/2,   0,    0, -5/2, -3/2]
[ 1/4, -3/4,  0,    0,   2,  3/2]
[ 1/2,  1/2,  0,    0,   0,    0]
[-1/2,  1/2,  0,    0,   0,    0]

J =

[ 0, 0, 0, 0, 0, 0]
[ 0, 4, 0, 0, 0, 0]
[ 0, 0, 2, 1, 0, 0]
[ 0, 0, 0, 2, 1, 0]
[ 0, 0, 0, 0, 2, 0]
[ 0, 0, 0, 0, 0, 2]
```

```
>>A=[3 -1 1 1 0 0;1 1 -1 -1 0 0;0 0 2 0 1 1;0 0 0 2 -2 -1;0 0 0 0 2 2;0 0 0 0 2 2]; ↵
```

The function **jordan** determines the matrices Q and J when the A is its input argument. Both the symbolic and numeric findings are possible applying the **jordan**. Placed above on the right is the execution for the symbolic one. The input argument of the **jordan** is sym(A) which turns the elements of A to symbolic (section 2.1). There are two output arguments indicated by [Q J] obviously Q⇔Q and J⇔J (can be any user-given names). If you need the decimal or numeric form, execute [Q J]=jordan(A).

4.23 Cholesky decomposition of a square matrix

Any positive definite (as well as symmetric) matrix A can be decomposed as $A = C \times C^T$ where C is the lower triangular and has positive entries on the main diagonal and C^T represents the transpose of C. The C is termed as the Cholesky factor of A. It is given that $C=\begin{bmatrix}4&0&0&0\\1&3&0&0\\2&2&2&0\\1&1&3&1\end{bmatrix}$ is the Cholesky factor of $A=\begin{bmatrix}16&4&8&4\\4&10&8&4\\8&8&12&10\\4&4&10&12\end{bmatrix}$ which we wish to compute. We can have the factor symbolically using the **maple** (section 3.2) function **cholesky** as attached above in which the first line is to assign the given matrix to workspace A (can be any user-given name). In the second line we called the function for the factorization. The return is assigned to C (can be any user-given name).

for the Cholesky factor:

```
>>A=[16 4 8 4;4 10 8 4;8 8 12 10;4 4 10 12]; ↵
>>C=maple('cholesky',sym(A)) ↵   ← C⇔C

C =

[ 4,  0,  0,  0]
[ 1,  3,  0,  0]
[ 2,  2,  2,  0]
[ 1,  1,  3,  1]
```

4.24 Special matrices

MATLAB is a world of matrices, a number of matrices based on the linear algebra terms can be generated very easily. We mention some of them in the following.

♦♦ Hilbert matrix

A Hilbert matrix is one in which each entry of the matrix is formed by $\frac{1}{i+j-1}$ where i is the row index and j is the column index and the matrix is a symmetric one. Say a Hilbert matrix of order 4×4 is to be formed which should be $H_{4\times4}=$

$$\begin{bmatrix}\frac{1}{1+1-1}&\frac{1}{1+2-1}&\frac{1}{1+3-1}&\frac{1}{1+4-1}\\\frac{1}{2+1-1}&\frac{1}{2+2-1}&\frac{1}{2+3-1}&\frac{1}{2+4-1}\\\frac{1}{3+1-1}&\frac{1}{3+2-1}&\frac{1}{3+3-1}&\frac{1}{3+4-1}\\\frac{1}{4+1-1}&\frac{1}{4+2-1}&\frac{1}{4+3-1}&\frac{1}{4+4-1}\end{bmatrix}=\begin{bmatrix}1&\frac{1}{2}&\frac{1}{3}&\frac{1}{4}\\\frac{1}{2}&\frac{1}{3}&\frac{1}{4}&\frac{1}{5}\\\frac{1}{3}&\frac{1}{4}&\frac{1}{5}&\frac{1}{6}\\\frac{1}{4}&\frac{1}{5}&\frac{1}{6}&\frac{1}{7}\end{bmatrix}$$

$$=\begin{bmatrix}1&0.5&0.3333&0.25\\0.5&0.3333&0.25&0.2\\0.3333&0.25&0.2&0.1667\\0.25&0.2&0.1667&0.1429\end{bmatrix}$$

. Corresponding MATLAB function is **hilb** (abbreviation for Hilbert). To form a Hilbert matrix of order $N\times N$, we use the syntax **hilb(** N **)**. The matrix implementation is shown above. Rational form is seen using the **sym** (section 2.1). In both cases we assigned the return to workspace H which is our $H_{4\times4}$.

Hilbert matrix in numeric form:

```
>>H=hilb(4) ↵

H =

    1.0000    0.5000    0.3333    0.2500
    0.5000    0.3333    0.2500    0.2000
    0.3333    0.2500    0.2000    0.1667
    0.2500    0.2000    0.1667    0.1429
```

in rational form:

```
>>H=sym(hilb(4)) ↵

H =

[   1,  1/2,  1/3,  1/4]
[ 1/2,  1/3,  1/4,  1/5]
[ 1/3,  1/4,  1/5,  1/6]
[ 1/4,  1/5,  1/6,  1/7]
```

♦♦ Hadamard matrix

The number of rows or columns (say N) of a Hadamard matrix must be an integer 2^m where m =1, 2, 3…etc. The lowest order Hadamard matrix is of order 2×2 where N =2 and m =1 and is given by $H_{2\times2}=\begin{bmatrix}1&1\\1&-1\end{bmatrix}$. Advantage of recursive relationship is taken to form the Hadamard matrices of other orders. Letting H_N represent the Hadamard matrix of order $N\times N$, the recursive relationship is given by $H_N=\begin{bmatrix}H_{N/2}&H_{N/2}\\H_{N/2}&-H_{N/2}\end{bmatrix}$ so $H_{4\times4}=$

$$\begin{bmatrix}\begin{bmatrix}1&1\\1&-1\end{bmatrix}&\begin{bmatrix}1&1\\1&-1\end{bmatrix}\\\begin{bmatrix}1&1\\1&-1\end{bmatrix}&-\begin{bmatrix}1&1\\1&-1\end{bmatrix}\end{bmatrix}=\begin{bmatrix}1&1&1&1\\1&-1&1&-1\\1&1&-1&-1\\1&-1&-1&1\end{bmatrix}$$

. The function **hadamard** generates a Hadamard matrix of order $N\times N$ with the syntax **hadamard(** N **)**. Shown on the right is the implementation for the $H_{4\times4}$.

for Hadamard matrix:

```
>>H=hadamard(4) ↵

H =              ← H⇔H4x4

     1     1     1     1
     1    -1     1    -1
     1     1    -1    -1
     1    -1    -1     1
```

♦♦ Companion matrix of a polynomial

If λ is an eigenvalue of the square matrix A, the characteristic polynomial of A is $G(\lambda)=|\lambda I-A|=$ $\alpha_n\lambda^n+\alpha_{n-1}\lambda^{n-1}+\alpha_{n-2}\lambda^{n-2}+\alpha_{n-3}\lambda^{n-3}+\ .....+\alpha_1\lambda+\alpha_0$. If the order of the characteristic polynomial is n (or the matrix A is of order $n\times n$), there are $n+1$ polynomial coefficients in $G(\lambda)$. Given the polynomial coefficients of the characteristic polynomial $G(\lambda)$, the companion matrix is generated as $\begin{bmatrix} \frac{-\alpha_{n-1}}{\alpha_n} & \frac{-\alpha_{n-2}}{\alpha_n} & \cdots & \frac{-\alpha_1}{\alpha_n} & \frac{-\alpha_0}{\alpha_n} \\ 1 & 0 & \cdots & 0 & 0 \\ 0 & 1 & \cdots & 0 & 0 \\ \vdots & \vdots & \ddots & \vdots & \vdots \\ 0 & 0 & \cdots & 1 & 0 \end{bmatrix}$. To obtain a companion matrix from $G(\lambda)$, we employ the function **compan** with the syntax **compan**($G(\lambda)$ polynomial coefficients in descending power of λ as a row matrix). Let us consider the characteristic polynomial $G(\lambda) = -6\lambda^3 + 3\lambda^2 + \lambda + 7$ whose coefficient form is [–6 3 1 7]. The order of the polynomial is 3 and there are four polynomial coefficients, those can be written as α_3, α_2, α_1, and α_0. Comparing the polynomial coefficients, one obtains the companion matrix

as $\begin{bmatrix} \frac{-\alpha_2}{\alpha_3} & \frac{-\alpha_1}{\alpha_3} & \frac{-\alpha_0}{\alpha_3} \\ 1 & 0 & 0 \\ 0 & 1 & 0 \end{bmatrix} = \begin{bmatrix} \frac{1}{2} & \frac{1}{6} & \frac{7}{6} \\ 1 & 0 & 0 \\ 0 & 1 & 0 \end{bmatrix} = \begin{bmatrix} 0.5 & 0.1667 & 1.1667 \\ 1 & 0 & 0 \\ 0 & 1 & 0 \end{bmatrix}$ and our objective is to have it. Shown on the upper right is the implementation of the matrix in which the workspace P holds the $G(\lambda)$ coefficients. By dint of the **sym**, we can even view the rational form as presented.

Companion matrix in numeric form:

```
>>P=[-6 3 1 7]; ↵
>>compan(P) ↵

ans =
    0.5000    0.1667    1.1667
    1.0000         0         0
         0    1.0000         0
```

Companion matrix in symbolic form:

```
>>sym(compan(P)) ↵

ans =

[ 1/2, 1/6, 7/6]
[   1,   0,   0]
[   0,   1,   0]
```

♦♦ Vandermonde matrix of a column vector

The Vandermonde matrix is defined as $V = \begin{bmatrix} C_1^{N-1} & C_1^{N-2} & C_1^{N-3} & C_1^1 & & 1 \\ C_2^{N-1} & C_2^{N-2} & C_2^{N-3} & C_2^1 & \cdots & 1 \\ C_3^{N-1} & C_3^{N-2} & C_3^{N-3} & C_3^1 & & 1 \\ & & \vdots & & & \\ C_N^{N-1} & C_N^{N-2} & C_N^{N-3} & C_N^1 & & 1 \end{bmatrix}$ when $C = \begin{bmatrix} C_1 \\ C_2 \\ C_3 \\ \vdots \\ C_N \end{bmatrix}$. The function **vander** determines the matrix with the syntax **vander**(C) where C can be entered as a row or column matrix. For example the $C = \begin{bmatrix} 1 \\ 4 \\ 6 \end{bmatrix}$ should return us $\begin{bmatrix} 1^2 & 1 & 1 \\ 4^2 & 4 & 1 \\ 6^2 & 6 & 1 \end{bmatrix} = \begin{bmatrix} 1 & 1 & 1 \\ 16 & 4 & 1 \\ 36 & 6 & 1 \end{bmatrix}$ where N=3 and its straightforward implementation is on the right. The first and second lines of the implementation are to assign the column matrix to C and to call the function respectively. The return from the function we assigned to V which can be any user-given name.

for Vandermonde matrix:

```
>>C=[1 4 6]'; ↵
>>V=vander(C) ↵

V =
     1     1     1
    16     4     1
    36     6     1
```

♦♦ Toeplitz matrix

A Toeplitz matrix is one whose elements are constant along each diagonal and it is symmetric for a square one. The function **toeplitz** forms a Toeplitz matrix with the syntax **toeplitz**(constant elements as a row or column matrix) for the square Toeplitz or **toeplitz**(superdiagonal constant elements as a row matrix, subdiagonal constant elements as a row matrix) for the rectangular Toeplitz.

Let us generate a square Toeplitz from $C = \begin{bmatrix} 5 \\ 0 \\ -4 \\ 9 \\ 1 \end{bmatrix}$ which should be $T_{5\times5} = \begin{bmatrix} 5 & 0 & -4 & 9 & 1 \\ 0 & 5 & 0 & -4 & 9 \\ -4 & 0 & 5 & 0 & -4 \\ 9 & -4 & 0 & 5 & 0 \\ 1 & 9 & -4 & 0 & 5 \end{bmatrix}$. Again a rectangular Toeplitz of order 3×5 is to be formed where the subdiagonal elements are R=[10 –9 7] and the superdiagonal elements are C=[10 55 5 40 6] and the matrix should look like $\begin{bmatrix} 10 & 55 & 5 & 40 & 6 \\ -9 & 10 & 55 & 5 & 40 \\ 7 & -9 & 10 & 55 & 5 \end{bmatrix}$. Both examples are implemented on the upper right side of the following page in which we assigned the given constant element matrices to like names for example R to R. In both cases we assigned the return from the function to workspace T which can be any user-given name and which is our required Topilitz matrix. The first elements of R and C must be identical to be consistent with the definition when a rectangular Toeplitz is to be formed.

for 5×5 Toeplitz matrix,

```
>>C=[5 0 -4 9 1]'; ↵
>>T=toeplitz(C) ↵

T =

     5     0    -4     9     1
     0     5     0    -4     9
    -4     0     5     0    -4
     9    -4     0     5     0
     1     9    -4     0     5
```

for 3×5 Toeplitz matrix,

```
>>R=[10 -9 7]; ↵
>>C=[10 55 5 40 6]; ↵
>>T=toeplitz(R,C) ↵

T =

    10    55     5    40     6
    -9    10    55     5    40
     7    -9    10    55     5
```

♦♦ Hankel matrix

Hankel matrix can be square or rectangular. Elements in the square Hankel matrix are zeroes below the first anti-diagonal and the matrix is symmetric. For example the square Hankel matrix $\begin{bmatrix} 6 & -3 & 9 \\ -3 & 9 & 0 \\ 9 & 0 & 0 \end{bmatrix}$ is formed from $C = \begin{bmatrix} 6 \\ -3 \\ 9 \end{bmatrix}$. Again the rectangular Hankel $\begin{bmatrix} 6 & 7 & -1 & 9 \\ 7 & -1 & 9 & 2 \\ -1 & 9 & 2 & 4 \end{bmatrix}$ is formed from the super anti-diagonal $A=[6 \quad 7 \quad -1]$ and sub anti-diagonal $B=[-1 \quad 9 \quad 2 \quad 4]$ elements. The last element of A must be equal to the first element of B. The function hankel forms a Hankel matrix maintaining the syntax hankel(anti-diagonal elements as a row or column matrix) for the square or hankel (super anti-diagonal elements as a row or column matrix, sub anti-diagonal elements as a row or column matrix) for the rectangular matrix. The reader finds their formations as shown above. In above implementation we assigned the given matrices to like names for instance A to A and the return from hankel is assigned to H in both cases.

for the square Hankel,

```
>>C=[6 -3 9]'; ↵
>>H=hankel(C) ↵

H =

     6    -3     9
    -3     9     0
     9     0     0
```

for the rectangular Hankel,

```
>>A=[6 7 -1]; ↵
>>B=[-1 9 2 4]; ↵
>>H=hankel(A,B) ↵

H =

     6     7    -1     9
     7    -1     9     2
    -1     9     2     4
```

♦♦ Band matrix

Elements of a band matrix are zeroes everywhere except along a band or strip that runs diagonally through the martix usually but not necessarily about the principal diagonal. $B = \begin{bmatrix} 1 & 9 & 2 & 0 & 0 & 0 \\ -2 & 1 & 9 & 2 & 0 & 0 \\ a & -2 & 1 & 9 & 2 & 0 \\ 0 & a & -2 & 1 & 9 & 2 \\ 0 & 0 & a & -2 & 1 & 9 \\ 0 & 0 & 0 & a & -2 & 1 \end{bmatrix}$ is a band matrix in which the band elements are $[a \quad -2 \quad 1 \quad 9 \quad 2]$. The maple function (section 3.2) band generates a $N \times N$ band matrix in symbolic sense with the syntax band(band elements as a vector, N). The number of band elements must be an odd number and it must not be greater than $2N-1$ where $N \times N$ is the order of the band matrix. Placed on the right is the formation of the matrix. Concerning the implementation, we assigned the band elements to workspace A as a vector in the first line within the maple in which the := is the maple assignment operator and vector is a reserve word to maple for vector formation. The vector elements are housed by the third brace and separated by a comma. The maple return we assigned to B in the second line. To make B available from maple to MATLAB, we used sym(B).

For the band matrix generation:

```
>>maple('A:=vector([a,-2,1,9,2])'); ↵
>>B=maple('band(A,6)'); ↵
>>sym(B) ↵

ans =

[ 1,   9,   2,   0,   0,   0]
[-2,   1,   9,   2,   0,   0]
[ a,  -2,   1,   9,   2,   0]
[ 0,   a,  -2,   1,   9,   2]
[ 0,   0,   a,  -2,   1,   9]
[ 0,   0,   0,   a,  -2,   1]
```

Since a tridiagonal matrix is primarily a three element band one, it can be generated utilizing the band. The band vector contains three elements for a tridiagonal matrix.

4.25 Generating equations from coefficient matrices or vice versa

Suppose we have a coefficient matrix $A = \begin{bmatrix} 2 & 3 & -4 & 5 \\ -1 & -3 & -7 & 3 \\ 3 & -7 & 0 & 2 \end{bmatrix}$ and a column vector $C = \begin{bmatrix} a \\ b \\ 3 \end{bmatrix}$. Equations from A and C are to be formed in terms of variables x, y, z, and u and the equations are obtained from matrix equation $\begin{bmatrix} 2 & 3 & -4 & 5 \\ -1 & -3 & -7 & 3 \\ 3 & -7 & 0 & 2 \end{bmatrix} \begin{bmatrix} x \\ y \\ z \\ u \end{bmatrix} = \begin{bmatrix} a \\ b \\ 3 \end{bmatrix}$ which ultimately provides $\begin{Bmatrix} 2x+3y-4z+5u = a \\ -x-3y-7z+3u = b \\ 3x-7y+2u = 3 \end{Bmatrix}$. We wish to obtain the equations starting from the A and C – this is the problem statement.

The maple (section 3.2) function geneqns is used to generate the equations. You find the implementation on the right in this regard. The given A is assigned to A within the maple through the reserve word matrix. The rows and the whole matrix are housed by the third brace. Rows or elements in a row are separated by a comma. The := is the assignment operator in maple. In the second line we assigned the given C to C within the maple through the reserve word vector. Vector elements are also housed by the third brace and separated by a comma. In the third line of the implementation, we called the function geneqns with three input arguments, the first, second, and third of which are the coefficient matrix assignee name, independent variables of the equations placed in order in the third brace but separated by a comma, and the column vector assignee name respectively. The return is in vector code (section 14.2) form. If you wish to see the readable form, assign the third line return to some variable O and exercise pretty (section 3.1) followed by sym to see the equations as shown above.

forming equations from matrix:

```
>>maple('A:=matrix([[2,3,-4,5],[-1,-3,-7,3],[3,-7,0,2]])'); ↵
>>maple('C:=vector([a,b,3])'); ↵
>>maple('geneqns(A,[x,y,z,u],C)') ↵

ans =

{2*x+3*y-4*z+5*u = a, -x-3*y-7*z+3*u = b, 3*x-7*y+2*u = 3}
>>O=maple('geneqns(A,[x,y,z,u],C)'); ↵
>>pretty(sym(O)) ↵
{2 x + 3 y - 4 z + 5 u=a, -x - 3 y - 7 z +3 u=b, 3 x - 7 y+2 u=3}
```

The reverse operation that is from equations to matrix is performed by the maple function genmatrix (abbreviation for generation of matrix). Assume that the given equations are $x+2z=2.4-8y$, $3x-5y=6-z$, and $z=-x-5y+23$ from which we should have $\begin{bmatrix}1 & 8 & 2\\ 3 & -5 & 1\\ 1 & 5 & 1\end{bmatrix}\begin{bmatrix}x\\ y\\ z\end{bmatrix}=\begin{bmatrix}2.4\\ 6\\ 23\end{bmatrix}$. Our objective is to obtain the coefficient matrix $A=\begin{bmatrix}1 & 8 & 2\\ 3 & -5 & 1\\ 1 & 5 & 1\end{bmatrix}$ and column vector $C=\begin{bmatrix}2.4\\ 6\\ 23\end{bmatrix}$ starting from the given equations.

forming matrix from equations:

```
>>maple('eqns:={x+2*z=2.4-8*y,3*x-5*y=6-z,z=-x-5*y+23}'); ↵
>>A=maple('genmatrix(eqns,[x,y,z],C)'); ↵
>>sym(A) ↵

ans =

[ 1, 8, 2]
[ 3, -5, 1]
[ 1, 5, 1]
>>sym(maple('print(C)')) ↵

ans =

[ 2.4, 6, 23]
```

Shown on the right is the execution. In the implementation, we entered the vector code of all given equations within the maple. All equations are placed under the second brace and assigned to workspace eqns (can be any user-given name) as a set. Equations in the set are separated by a comma. In the second line we called the function genmatrix within the maple with three input arguments, the first, second, and third of which are the equation set name, independent variables of the equations placed in order in the third brace but separated by a comma, and user-chosen column matrix name (we chose C, can be any other assignee) respectively. The return from the maple is the coefficient matrix A which we assigned to A in MATLAB (can be user-chosen name) but in maple terminology. In order to make it available in MATLAB, we use sym(A). Again within the maple, the column vector C is stored in C. We make it available calling first in maple and then in MATLAB. If you say I need both to be in MATLAB, use the commands A=sym(A) and C=sym(maple('print(C)')). Note that the return to C is a row vector. To make it column one, just we use the transpose operator ' that is C=sym(maple('print(C)'))'. Usefulness of the function is understood when we have 6 or 7 variable equations.

We do not wish to include all features of the matrix theory due to the space reason. Readers can have online assistance about the other available functions executing help matfun and mhelp linalg at the command prompt. It is important to mention that searching assistance for M-file and maple functions starts with help and mhelp respectively. However we bring an end to the chapter.

Chapter 5

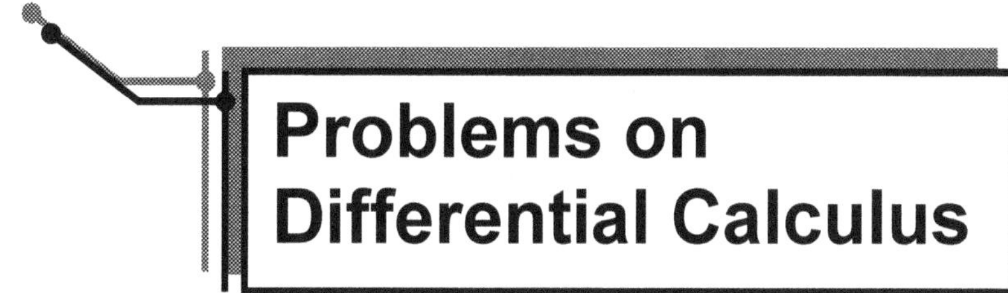

Differential calculus finds wide spectrum of uses in many branches of pure and applied mathematics. In a broad sense, problems pertaining to differentials are the contents of this chapter. Nowadays problems of differentials are having an articulate mixing up with those of other disciplines. Ordinary differentials are prevalently put to use in analytic geometry for example in curve tracing and polynomial approximation of some functions. Application of partial derivatives is implied in vector calculus problems. MATLAB's capability of maneuvering differential calculus problems in symbolic and numeric forms is awfully appreciative. Following specimen problems are provided to demonstrate the utility of MATLAB in this facilitation:

- Symbolic finding of functional limits and differential coefficients of various orders and types
- Numeric style of determining the derivatives based on polynomial coefficients
- Taylor series approximation of one and multi-dimensional functions accompanying their user friendly graphical-user-interface (GUI) tool
- Important vector calculus problems such as gradient, divergence, and curl of different fields
- The way to determine the curve properties like average, tangent, minima, and maxima

5.1 Limit of a function

The limit of a function is an elementary differential calculus problem which we calculate using the function limit. To determine the limit, we declare the related variables of the limit function as symbolic using the syms of section 2.1 and apply the command with the syntax limit (function as a vector string – section 14.2, variable of the limit, limiting value). Let us begin with the example $\underset{x \to 2}{Lt} \dfrac{10\sin^2(x-2)}{(x-2)^2}=10$ which we wish to comupute. The vector string representation of the limit function, related variable, and the limiting value are 10*sin(x-2)^2/(x-2)^2, x, and 2 respectively. Maintaining the font equivalence for example x⇔ x , we perform the computation as follows:

```
>>syms x ↵
>>L=limit(10*sin(x-2)^2/(x-2)^2,x,2) ↵   ← We assigned the return of limit to the workspace variable L
```

L =

10

The name L is user-given. It is given that the $8a^{\frac{7}{2}}$, $\frac{2}{3}$, 0, 8, and $\frac{MN}{\pi^2}$ are the computed values for the following functions (A through E respectively) and we intend to compute them.

$A.\ \underset{x \to a}{Lt} \frac{x^4 - a^4}{\sqrt{x} - \sqrt{a}}$ $B.\ \underset{x \to \infty}{Lt} \frac{2x^3 - x}{3x^3 - 7x - 8}$ $C.\ \underset{\theta \to 0}{Lt} \frac{\cos^2\left(\frac{\pi}{2}\cos\theta\right)}{\sin^2\theta}$

$D.\ \underset{k \to 2}{Lt}\ \underset{x \to k}{Lt} \frac{(k^2-4)\tan 2(x-k)}{(k-2)(x-k)}$ $E.\ \underset{n \to 0}{Lt}\ \underset{m \to 0}{Lt} \frac{(1-e^{\frac{Mm}{\pi}})(1-e^{\frac{Nn}{\pi}})}{(1-e^m)(1-e^n)}$

Employing the same symbology, implementation of the limits from A through E is presented as follows:

for the problem A,	for the problem B,	for the problem C,	for the problem D,
>>syms x a ↵ >>n=x^4-a^4; ↵ >>d=sqrt(x)-sqrt(a); ↵ >>L=limit(n/d,x,a) ↵	>>syms x ↵ >>n=2*x^3-x; ↵ >>d=3*x^3-7*x-8; ↵ >>L=limit(n/d,x,inf) ↵	>>syms t ↵ >>n=cos(pi/2*cos(t))^2; ↵ >>d=sin(t)^2; ↵ >>L=limit(n/d,t,0) ↵	>>syms k x ↵ >>n=(k^2-4)*tan(2*(x-k)); ↵ >>d=(k-2)*(x-k); f=n/d; ↵ >>f1=limit(f,x,k); L=limit(f1,k,2) ↵
L =	L =	L =	L =
8*a^(7/2)	2/3	0	8

For the problems A through D, we assigned the numerator and denominator of the limit function separately to the workspace variables n and d respectively (for the problem E, they are p and q respectively not to be mixed up with the same name). The complete function is composed of n/d or p/q on which the limit is applied. This type of function entering is convenient for a long expression. In the problem D and E, there are two limit functions. The inner limit is computed and assigned to the workspace varible f1 afterwards the outer limit is conducted on the f1. All computed values are assigned to the L. For the symbol infinity (∞), we write the reserve word inf. The limit also keeps the provision for finding the left and right limits. Considering the function $f(x) = \frac{1}{x(x-2)}$, it is given that the left limit at $x=0$ is $\underset{x \to 0_-}{Lt} f(x) = \infty$ and the right limit at $x=0$ is $\underset{x \to 0_+}{Lt} f(x) = -\infty$ which we wish to compute. Attached on the right is the implementation. Now there are four input arguments of the limit, the first three of which bear the same meanings as discussed before and the fourth of which is the reserve word left or right under quote for the left or right limit respectively.

for the problem E,

```
>>syms M N m n ↵
>>p=(1-exp(M*m/pi))*(1-exp(N*n/pi)); ↵
>>q=(1-exp(m))*(1-exp(n)); ↵
>>f1=limit(p/q,m,0); ↵
>>L=limit(f1,n,0) ↵

L =

N/pi^2*M
```

left limit at $x=0$,	right limit at $x=0$,
>>syms x ↵ >>f=1/x/(x-2); ↵ >>L=limit(f,x,0,'left') ↵	>>syms x ↵ >>f=1/x/(x-2); ↵ >>L=limit(f,x,0,'right') ↵
L =	L =
inf	-inf

5.2 Derivatives of polynomials using coefficients

Polynomials are represented by the coefficients (section 3.1). The function polyder (abbreviation for the polynomial derivative) computes derivative polynomial coefficients when the given polynomial coefficients as a row matrix is its input argument (polyder⇔$\frac{d}{dx}$). It is given that $\frac{d}{dx}[9x^5 - 8x^4 + 3x^3 - 2x + 7] = 45x^4 - 32x^3 + 9x^2 - 2$ which we intend to compute. In terms of coefficient we should obtain [45 −32 9 0 −2] from [9 −8 3 0 −2 7] whose implementation is attached on the right. We assigned the starting polynomial coefficients to A and the return of the polyder to workspace B which essentially holds the derivative coefficients. Section 3.1 mentioned poly2str is exercised on B to see the coefficients as powers of x. The second and third order derivatives require using the polyder two and three times respectively i.e. $\frac{d^2y}{dx^2}$⇔polyder(polyder(y)) and $\frac{d^3y}{dx^3}$⇔polyder(polyder(polyder(y))). Given that the second and third order derivatives of $-7x^5 + 2x^4 + 1$ are $-140x^3 + 24x^2$ and $-420x^2 + 48x$ respectively which we intend to compute. In coefficient form, they have the representations [−7 2 0 0 0 1], [−140 24

```
>>A=[9 -8 3 0 -2 7]; ↵
>>B=polyder(A) ↵

B =

    45   -32     9     0    -2

>>poly2str(B,'x') ↵

ans =

   45 x^4 - 32 x^3 + 9 x^2 - 2
```

0 0], and [–420 48 0] for the given polynomial, second order derivative, and third order derivative respectively. Employing the same symbology, the implementation of the second and third order derivatives is shown as follows:

for the second derivative coefficients,
```
>>A=[-7 2 0 0 0 1]; ↵
>>B=polyder(polyder(A)) ↵

B =
      -140   24   0   0
```

for the third derivative coefficients,
```
>>B=polyder(polyder(polyder(A))) ↵

B =
      -420   48   0
```

to display the third derivative as power of x,
```
>>poly2str(B,'x') ↵

ans =
      -420 x^2 + 48 x
```

The number of polyder is the same as the order of derivative. Repetitive writing of the polyder can be avoided by using a for-loop (subsection 14.3.3). To find the Nth order derivative from a polynomial A using the for-loop, one can use the command A=[-7 2 0 0 0 1]; B=A; for k=1:3, B=polyder(B); end for the third order case in which the last counter of the for-loop indicates the derivative order and B holds the resulting polynomial coefficients.

Executing with two input arguments, the polyder returns the derivative coefficients of the product polynomials. Given that $\frac{d}{dx}[(7x^2+2x-9)\times(3x^3+4x+1)] = 105x^4+24x^3+3x^2+30x-34$ which we wish to compute (implementation is attached on the right). The workspace variables p1 and p2 hold the first and second polynomial coefficients and which are the input arguments of the polyder now respectively.

Again the division of the two polynomials for example $\frac{d}{dx}\left[\frac{x^2+x+1}{x^3-x+1}\right] = \frac{-x^4-2x^3-4x^2+2x+2}{x^6-2x^4+2x^3+x^2-2x+1} = \frac{[-1\ \ -2\ \ -4\ \ 2\ \ 2]}{[1\ \ 0\ \ -2\ \ 2\ \ 1\ \ -2\ \ 1]}$ (in coefficient form and which will be the return from the polyder) is conducted exercising two output arguments as shown on the right. We assigned the numerator x^2+x+1 and denominator x^3-x+1 polynomial coefficients to the workspace N and D respectively. There are two output arguments of the polyder this time called NO and DO (user-given names) and which hold the computed numerator and denominator polynomial coefficients respectively.

Sometimes the value of the derivative at some x is required following the derivative taking for example given that the value of $\frac{d}{dx}\left[\frac{x^2+x+1}{x^3-x+1}\right]$ is $-\frac{18}{25}$=–0.72 at x=–2 which we wish to compute. Just now we computed the derivative and the numerator and denominator polynomial coefficients of the derivative are stored in the workspace NO and DO respectively. We exercise the command polyval of the section 3.2 to compute the value in decimal form whose symbolic form is achievable through the use of the sym of section 2.1. Both implementations are presented above on the right.

for the multiplication of two polynomials,
```
>>p1=[7 2 -9]; p2=[3 0 4 1]; ↵
>>B=polyder(p1,p2); poly2str(B,'x') ↵

ans =
      105 x^4 + 24 x^3 + 3 x^2 + 30 x – 34
```

for the division of two polynomials,
```
>>N=[1 1 1]; D=[1 0 -1 1]; ↵
>>[NO DO]=polyder(N,D) ↵

NO =
      -1   -2   -4   2   2
DO =
      1   0   -2   2   1   -2   1
>>poly2str(NO,'x') ↵ ← to see as power of x

ans =
      -1 x^4 - 2 x^3 - 4 x^2 + 2 x + 2
>>poly2str(DO,'x') ↵ ← to see as power of x

ans =
      x^6 - 2 x^4 + 2 x^3 + x^2 - 2 x + 1
```

for the evaluation at some x,
```
>>polyval(NO,-2)/polyval(DO,-2) ↵

ans =
      -0.7200
>>sym(polyval(NO,-2)/polyval(DO,-2)) ↵

ans =
      -18/25
```

5.3 Symbolic differentiation of functions

Most problems of the last section are associated with the coefficients of the polynomials. Symbolic differentiation of mathematical function conveniently takes place by means of the function diff (abbreviation for differentiation that is diff⇔$\frac{d}{dx}$) when the mathematical function is its input argument. The mathematical functions must be written in vector code (section 14.2) and the related variables in the function must be declared using the syms (section 2.1) prior to the computation. Considering $\sin^{-1}x$ from which $\frac{d}{dx}(\sin^{-1}x)=\frac{1}{\sqrt{1-x^2}}$, we intend to implement this. The vector codes for $\sin^{-1}x$ and $\frac{1}{\sqrt{1-x^2}}$ are asin(x) and 1/(1-x^2)^(1/2) respectively. The second code should be the return from the diff when the first is the input. One can assign the return to any user-given name for example d. The pretty of section 3.1 displays the readable form as shown on the right. You can even directly use the pretty like pretty(diff(asin(x))) to see the output. The pretty form is visually attractive but the mathematical maneuvering requires the vector code. Maintaining the same symbology and function, we present a number of examples in the table 5.A which shows the implementation of few standard functions.

For the symbolic differentiation:
```
>>syms x ↵
>>d=diff(asin(x)) ↵
>>pretty(d) ↵
            1
      -------------
              2 1/2
        (1 - x )
```

Table 5.A Differentiation of some standard functions

Calculus computation	MATLAB computation	Calculus computation	MATLAB computation
$\frac{d}{dx}(\sin x) = \cos x$	syms x, pretty(diff(sin(x))) ⇒ cos(x)	$\frac{d}{dx}(\cos x) = -\sin x$	syms x, pretty(diff(cos(x))) ⇒ -sin(x)
$\frac{d}{dx}(\tan x) = 1+\tan^2 x$	syms x, pretty(diff(tan(x)))⇒ 2 1 + tan(x)	$\frac{d}{dx}(\cot x) = -(1+\cot^2 x)$	syms x, pretty(diff(cot(x))) ⇒ 2 -1 - cot(x)
$\frac{d}{dx}(\sec x) = \sec x \tan x$	syms x,pretty(diff(sec(x))) ⇒ sec(x) tan(x)	$\frac{d}{dx}(\operatorname{cosec} x) = -\operatorname{cosec} x \cot x$	syms x,pretty(diff(csc(x))) ⇒ -csc(x) cot(x)
$\frac{d}{dx}(\cos^{-1} x) = -\frac{1}{\sqrt{1-x^2}}$	syms x,pretty(diff(acos(x))) ⇒ 1 - ------------- 2 1/2 (1 - x)	$\frac{d}{dx}(\tan^{-1} x) = \frac{1}{1+x^2}$	syms x,pretty(diff(atan(x))) ⇒ 1 -------- 2 1 + x
$\frac{d}{dx}(\operatorname{cosec}^{-1} x) =$ * $-\frac{1}{x\sqrt{x^2-1}}$	syms x,pretty(diff(acsc(x)))⇒ 1 - ------------------------- 2/ 1 \ 1/2 x | 1 - ------- | | 2 | \ x /	$\frac{d}{dx}(\operatorname{cosech}^{-1} x)$ * $= -\frac{1}{x\sqrt{1+x^2}}$	syms x,pretty(diff(acsch(x))) ⇒ 1 - --------------------- 2/ 1 \ 1/2 x | 1 + ------- | | 2 | \ x /
$\frac{d}{dx}(\sinh x) = \cosh x$	syms x,pretty(diff(sinh(x))) ⇒ cosh(x)	$\frac{d}{dx}(\log_e x) = \frac{1}{x}$	syms x,pretty(diff(log(x))) ⇒ 1/x
$\frac{d}{dx}(\tanh x) = 1-\tanh^2 x$	syms x,pretty(diff(tanh(x))) ⇒ 2 1 - tanh(x)	$\frac{d}{dx}(x^n) = nx^{n-1}$	syms x n,pretty(diff(x^n)) ⇒ n x n -------- x
$\frac{d}{dx}(\tanh^{-1} x) = \frac{1}{1-x^2}$	syms x,pretty(diff(atanh(x)))⇒ 1 ---------- 2 1 - x	$\frac{d}{dx}(\sinh^{-1} x) = \frac{1}{\sqrt{1+x^2}}$	syms x,pretty(diff(asinh(x)))⇒ 1 ------------ 2 1/2 (1 + x)
$\frac{d}{dx}(e^x) = e^x$	syms x,pretty(diff(exp(x))) ⇒ exp(x)	$\frac{d}{dx}(a^x) = a^x \ln a$	syms a x,pretty(diff(a^x)) ⇒ x a log(a)
* Some functions may need slight simplification to appear the return from the **diff** and calculus one same			

◆◆ Differentiating composite functions

The **diff** is also capable of differentiating composite functions. In the following, some functions and their derivatives are given side by side which we wish to compute in MATLAB.

A. function: $x^3\tan^3 x$ and its derivative is $3x^2\tan^3 x + 3x^3\tan^2 x(1+\tan^2 x)$

B. function: $(12x^4-4x+1)(9x^3-5)$ and its derivative is $(12x^4-4x+1)\ 27x^2 + (9x^3-5)(48x^3-4)$

C. function: $\frac{7x-3}{x^2\sqrt{2x^5-13}}$ and its derivative is $\frac{7}{x^2\sqrt{2x^5-13}} - \frac{2(7x-3)}{x^3\sqrt{2x^5-13}} - \frac{5(7x-3)x^2}{\sqrt{(2x^5-13)^3}}$

D. function: $\sqrt[4]{[3\sin^3(3x-1)+\ln x]^3}$ and its derivative is $\frac{3\{27\sin^2(3x-1)\cos(3x-1)+\frac{1}{x}\}}{4\{3\sin^3(3x-1)+\ln x\}^{\frac{1}{4}}}$

E. function: $x^4 J_3(x)$ and its derivative is $x^4\ [-\frac{3}{x}J_3(x) + J_2(x)] + J_3(x)\ 4x^3$

F. function: $\tan\left(\frac{u-5}{2u+5}\right)$ and its derivative is $\left[\frac{1}{2u+5} - \frac{2(u-5)}{(2u+5)^2}\right]\sec^2\left(\frac{u-5}{2u+5}\right)$

Exercising the ongoing symbols and functions, the derivative computations are attached below on the right and at the beginning of the next page. In all examples we assigned the return from **diff** to workspace **d** which holds vector string for each of the derivatives. In example B, the return polynomial is in multiplied form. If we intend to expand the polynomial, the command **expand** (section 3.2) helps us do so as follows:

```
>>pretty(expand(d)) ↵
        6       3          2
   756 x  - 384 x  + 20 + 27 x
```

Differentiation for the example A,

```
>>syms x,d=diff(x^3*tan(x)^3); pretty(d) ↵
   2       3        3       2            2
3 x  tan(x)  + 3 x  tan(x)  (1 + tan(x) )
```

Differentiation for the example B,

```
>>syms x,d=diff((12*x^4-4*x+1)*(9*x^3-5));pretty(d) ↵
      3          3                4          2
(48 x  - 4) (9 x  - 5) + 27 (12 x  - 4 x + 1) x
```

Differentiation for the example C,

```
>>syms x,d=diff((7*x-3)/(x^2*sqrt(2*x^5-13))); pretty(d) ↵
                                                              2
          7                   7 x - 3              (7 x - 3) x
 ------------------------ - 2------------------------ - 5------------------
  2      5       1/2        3      5       1/2        5       3/2
 x   (2 x   -  13)         x   (2 x   - 13)       (2 x   -  13)
```

Differentiation for the example D,

```
>>syms x ↵
>>d=diff((3*sin(3*x-1)^3+log(x))^(3/4));pretty(d) ↵
                               2
            27 sin(3 x - 1)   cos(3 x - 1) + 1/x
   3/4 -------------------------------------------
                            3              1/4
              ( 3 sin(3 x - 1)   +  log(x)  )
```

As the return says, the derivative of the example B is read off as $756x^6 - 384x^3 + 27x^2 + 20$. In the example E, the $J_3(x)$ is a special type of function which we call Bessel function of the first kind of order 3 (section 6.6 for different Bessel functions). The independent variable is u in the example F that is why the declaration using the **syms** is for **u**. The **pretty** displays the parenthesis ( ) for a bulk expression in terms of the characters |, /, and \.

Differentiation for the example E,

```
>>syms x,d=diff(x^4*besselj(3,x)); pretty(d) ↵
      3                      4 /                        besselj(3, x) \
   4 x   besselj(3, x) + x   | besselj(2, x) - 3 ---------------- |
                             \                          x         /
```

Differentiation for the example F,

```
>>syms u,d=diff(tan((u-5)/(2*u+5))); pretty(d) ↵
   /               u - 5     2  \   /       1                 u - 5      \
   | 1 + tan( ------------ )    |   |  ----------- - 2 --------------- |
   \             2 u + 5        /   |    2 u + 5                    2    |
                                    \                       (2 u + 5)    /
```

♦♦ Successive differentiation of functions

According to the calculus notation, $\frac{d^n y}{dx^n}$ is the n th order derivative of y which can also be found using the **diff** with different number of input arguments. Now the first and second input arguments of the **diff** accept the given function code and the order respectively.

For the successive diff. of cos:

```
>>syms x,d=diff(cos(2*x-5),5) ↵

d =
        -32*sin(2*x-5)
```

With $y = \cos(2x-5)$, $\frac{d^5 y}{dx^5} = -32\sin(2x-5)$ – which we intend to calculate (implementation is above on the right, **d** holds the result of the differentiation).

Let us compute $\frac{d^4}{dx^4}(1-7x+x^3)^3 = 3024\,x^5 - 17640x^3 + 1080x^2 + 17640x - 1008$ (execution on the right). The return from the **diff** is not in expanded form that is why we used the command **expand**.

For successive differentiation of the powered polynomial:

```
>>syms x,d=diff((1-7*x+x^3)^3,4); ↵
>>pretty(expand(d)) ↵
                    3          5          2
   17640 x - 17640 x  + 3024 x  + 1080 x  -  1008
```

For the composite-successive differentiation:

```
>>syms x ↵
>>y=exp(-2*x)*cos(3*x-4); d=7*diff(y,4)+diff(y,2)-20*y; ↵
>>pretty(d) ↵
     -858 exp(-2 x) cos(3 x - 4) - 828 exp(-2 x) sin(3 x - 4)
```

We wish to compute the composite derivative $7\frac{d^4 y}{dx^4} + \frac{d^2 y}{dx^2} - 20y$ for $y = e^{-2x}\cos(3x-4)$ which should be $-858e^{-2x}\cos(3x-4) - 828e^{-2x}\sin(3x-4)$ (execution is shown above). We assigned first the function to the workspace **y** and then carried out various differentiations based on the **y**. The function $7\frac{d^4 y}{dx^4}$ is coded as **7*diff(y,4)**, so is others.

♦♦ Derivative evaluation

We intend to evaluate $\frac{d^4}{dx^4}[(1-7x+x^3)^3]$ at $x = -1$ which should be -2952. From previous discussion, we know that the workspace variable **d** holds the string for the successive derivative. The substitution of $x = -1$ takes place in the **d** through the use of the function **eval** whose input argument is the code of the function requiring be evaluated but the assignment of 1 to **x** is carried out first. However the complete computation is attached on the right.

Derivative evaluation at $x = -1$:

```
>>syms x ↵
>>d=diff((1-7*x+x^3)^3,4); ↵
>>x=-1; eval(d) ↵

ans =
        -2952
```

Let us evaluate $7\frac{d^4 y}{dx^4} + \frac{d^2 y}{dx^2} - 20y$ at $x = \pi$ for $y = e^{-2x}\cos(3x-4)$ and which should be 0.1229. Attached on the right is the computation.

Derivative evaluation at $x = \pi$:

```
>>syms x ↵
>>y=exp(-2*x)*cos(3*x-4); ↵
>>d=7*diff(y,4)+diff(y,2)-20*y; ↵
>>x=pi; eval(d) ↵

ans =
        0.1229
```

Not all functions have the independent variable x. Let us compute $\frac{d^2}{dz^2}\left[\frac{z-4}{z+3}\right]$ at $z = -5$ and which should return us the value $\frac{7}{4}$ in rational form. We presented its implementation on the right. Even though we have different independent variable, the **diff** automatically perceives that. Only the use of the **eval** returns the decimal form on the contrary section 2.1 mentioned **sym** over the **eval** provides the necessary rational form (i.e. **sym(eval(d))** returns **7/4**).

Derivative evaluation at $z = -5$:

```
>>syms z ↵
>>y=(z-4)/(z+3); d=diff(y,2); ↵
>>z=-5; eval(d) ↵

ans =
        1.7500
```

5.4 Partial differentiation of functions

To find out the partial derivative of a function of several variables, one variable is taken as the variable and the rest are assumed to be constant. The total number of partial derivatives is equal to the number of independent variables. Last section exercised **diff** also computes the partial derivative of a multivariable function. The partial derivative of f with respect to x is denoted by $\frac{\partial f}{\partial x}$. In MATLAB terminology, $\frac{\partial f}{\partial x}$ is equivalent to **diff(f,x)** considering the font equivalence like **x**$\Leftrightarrow x$. Note that the second input argument of the **diff** is the independent variable unlike the previous section which is the order of differentiation – an integer. Since the computation is purely symbolic, we declare all related variables of f using the command **syms** (section 2.1).

Example of a two variable function is $U = f(x,y) = x^2 + y^3 - 7x^2y^5$. Several partial derivatives of U are $\frac{\partial U}{\partial x} = 2x - 14xy^5$, $\frac{\partial U}{\partial y} = 3y^2 - 35x^2y^4$, $\frac{\partial^2 U}{\partial y \partial x} = -70xy^4$, $\frac{\partial^2 U}{\partial y^2} = 6y - 140x^2y^3$, and $\frac{\partial^3 U}{\partial y^3} = 6 - 420x^2y^2$. Implementations of all these are shown below:

for $\frac{\partial U}{\partial x}$,
```
>>syms x y ↵
>>U=x^2+y^3-7*x^2*y^5; ↵
>>Ux=diff(U,x) ↵

Ux =
     2*x-14*x*y^5
```

for $\frac{\partial U}{\partial y}$,
```
>>Uy=diff(U,y) ↵

Uy =
     3*y^2-35*x^2*y^4
```

for $\frac{\partial^2 U}{\partial y \partial x}$,
```
>>Uyx=diff(diff(U,y),x) ↵

Uyx =
     -70*x*y^4
```

for $\frac{\partial^2 U}{\partial y^2}$,
```
>>Uyy=diff(U,y,2) ↵

Uyy =
     6*y-140*x^2*y^3
```

Referring to above leftmost implementation, there are two independent variables in U which are x and y and declared by the **syms**. The second line is just the assignment of the function to **U**. We assigned different partial derivatives $\frac{\partial U}{\partial x}$, $\frac{\partial U}{\partial y}$, $\frac{\partial^2 U}{\partial y \partial x}$, $\frac{\partial^2 U}{\partial y^2}$, and $\frac{\partial^3 U}{\partial y^3}$ to user-given names **Ux**, **Uy**, **Uyx**, **Uyy**, and **Uyyy** respectively. For **Ux**, first type the capital **U** and then do small **x** from the keyboard. For **Uyx**, we first find $\frac{\partial U}{\partial y}$ (conducted by **diff(U,y)**) and then differentiate **diff(U,y)** with respect to **x** (conducted by **diff(diff(U,y),x)**). The **diff** also keeps the provision to accept three input arguments, the first, second, and third of which are the functional code, independent variable, and the order of the differentiation respectively (for successive differentiation like $\frac{\partial^3 U}{\partial y^3}$). The example presented is a two-variable one, it can be a function of any number of variables more than 2. One can view the readable form using **pretty(diff(U,y,3))** for **Uyyy**. What if we need to evaluate $\frac{\partial^3 U}{\partial y^3}$ at $x=1$ and $y=3$ and which should be -3774. Its evaluation is also shown above on the right side applying the function **eval** of the last section.

for $\frac{\partial^3 U}{\partial y^3}$,
```
>>Uyyy=diff(U,y,3) ↵

Uyyy =
     6-420*x^2*y^2
```
for evaluation of the third order derivative,
```
>>x=1; y=3; ↵
>>eval(Uyyy) ↵

ans =
   -3774
```

5.5 Derivatives of parametric and implicit equations

Although there is no option for finding the derivative of the parametric equation in previous section (5.3 and 5.4) mentioned **diff**, slight computation can help us do so. Given that $\frac{dy}{dx} = \frac{-3\sin t \cos t}{3\cos^2 t - 2}$ is the derivative of the parametric equations { $x = \sin t \cos^2 t$, $y = \cos^3 t$ } which we intend to compute. The computation is attached on the right. Both x and y are the functions of the parameter t – this becomes our independent variable. We take the advantage of the relationship $\frac{dy}{dx} = \frac{dy}{dt} \Big/ \frac{dx}{dt}$ in the computation. The second and third lines in the implementation are the assignment of the vector code (section 14.2) of the expressions to the workspace **x** and **y** respectively. The $\frac{dy}{dt}$ and $\frac{dx}{dt}$ are conducted by the commands **diff(y,t)** and **diff(x,t)** respectively. The workspace **d** holds the vector code of the straightforward division of $\frac{dy}{dt}$ by $\frac{dx}{dt}$. The return is not in simplified form that is why we simplified the contents of the **d** using the command **simplify(d)** prior to applying the **pretty** (section 3.1) on the **d**.

Parametric derivative:
```
>>syms t ↵
>>x=sin(t)*cos(t)^2; ↵
>>y=cos(t)^3; ↵
>>d=diff(y,t)/diff(x,t); ↵
>>pretty(simplify(d)) ↵
          sin(t) cos(t)
     -3 ---------------
                  2
           3 cos(t)  - 2
```

What if we require the $\frac{d^2y}{dx^2}$ for the same parametric expressions. It is given that $\frac{d^2y}{dx^2}$ = $\frac{3(\cos^2 t-2)}{\cos t(27\cos^6 t-54\cos^4 t+36\cos^2 t-8)}$ and we intend to implement that. Remembering the fact $\frac{d^2y}{dx^2}=\frac{d}{dt}\left(\frac{dy}{dx}\right)\Big/\frac{dx}{dt}$, it is attached on the right (assuming that aforementioned **x** and **y** are in the workspace and **d** is holding the $\frac{dy}{dx}$ string). We assigned the $\frac{d^2y}{dx^2}$ computation result to the workspace **d2** (of coarse it is in terms of the **t** and we simplified the return using the **simplify**). In a similar fashion the third order derivative $\frac{d^3y}{dx^3}$ is computed from $\frac{d}{dt}\left(\frac{d^2y}{dx^2}\right)\Big/\frac{dx}{dt}$. Evaluation of a derivative may be necessary for specific parameter. Suppose we wish to find $\frac{d^2y}{dx^2}$ at $t=\pi$ and which should be 3. The assignee **d2** holds the expression for $\frac{d^2y}{dx^2}$ in terms of t. We substitute $t=\pi$ in **d2** using previously mentioned **eval** as attached on the upper right side.

Second order parametric derivative:

```
>>d2=diff(d,t)/diff(x,t); pretty(simplify(d2)) ↵
                          2
                    cos(t)  - 2
  3 ----------------------------------------------------------
                    6              4              2
    cos(t) (27 cos(t)  - 54 cos(t)  + 36 cos(t)  - 8 )
```

for evaluation:

```
>>t=pi; ↵
>>eval(d2) ↵

ans =
        3
```

An equation can be a function of both the independent and dependent variables which is termed as the implicit function for instance $y^2+2xy=0$ where $y=f(x)$ and x and y are the independent and dependent variables respectively. Starting from the implicit equation, it is given that $\frac{dy}{dx}=-\frac{y}{x+y}$ and we wish to obtain that. The **maple** (section 3.2) function **implicitdiff** (abbreviation for implicit differentiation) computes the derivative from the equation as attached on the right. The first line is the assignment of the vector code (section 14.2) of the given equation to the variable **e** (user-given) inside the **maple** under the quote where := is the **maple** assignment operator. The **implicitdiff** has three input arguments, the first, second, and third of which are the equation name, dependent variable name, and independent variable name respectively. The return from the **maple** is assigned to the workspace **d** which holds the vector string of the derivative. The third line is to display the readable form of the string stored in **d**. The second order derivative $\frac{d^2y}{dx^2}$ can also be computed from $y^2+2xy=0$ and which should be $\frac{d^2y}{dx^2}=\frac{y^2+2xy}{x^3+3x^2y+3xy^2+y^3}$ (implementation is attached above on the right side). Different order derivative equivalence is as follows: **implicitdiff(e,y,x)**⇔$\frac{dy}{dx}$, **implicitdiff(e,y,x,x)**⇔$\frac{d^2y}{dx^2}$, **implicitdiff(e,y,x,x,x)**⇔$\frac{d^3y}{dx^3}$, and so on.

Derivative from implicit function:
for the first order derivative,

```
>>maple('e:=y^2+2*y*x=0'); ↵
>>d=maple('implicitdiff(e,y,x)'); ↵
>>pretty(sym(d)) ↵
          y
   - ----------
        y + x
```

for the second order derivative,

```
>>d=maple('implicitdiff(e,y,x,x)'); ↵
>>pretty(sym(d)) ↵
            y (y + 2 x)
  ---------------------------------
      3       2           2     3
     y  + 3 y  x + 3 y x  + x
```

5.6 Taylor series expansion of a function

Taylor series approximates a function by a polynomial utilizing the derivatives of the function. If any function $f(x)$ and its derivatives are differentiable, then Taylor series expansion of $f(x)$ is given by $f(x)=f(0)+xf'(0)+\frac{x^2}{2!}f''(0)+\frac{x^3}{3!}f'''(0)+\frac{x^4}{4!}f^{iv}(0)+\frac{x^5}{5!}f^{v}(0)+$...etc. The higher is the number of terms of the polynomial, the better is the approximation of $f(x)$. To obtain the Taylor series approximation of a function, we use the syntax **taylor**(function as a vector string–section 14.2). But the related variable of given function needs to be declared using the **syms** (section 2.1) before the computation. Given that $x-\frac{x^3}{6}+\frac{x^5}{120}$ is the Taylor series approximation of $\sin x$ and we intend to compute that. Attached on the right is the implementation (**x**⇔x). The return of the **taylor** is assigned to the workspace **S** which holds the vector string of the polynomial. Section 3.1 mentioned **pretty** displays the readable form on **S**.

Taylor series of sine:

```
>>syms x, S=taylor(sin(x)) ↵

S =
        x-1/6*x^3+1/120*x^5
>>pretty(S) ↵
              3          5
     x - 1/6 x  + 1/120 x
```

Some Taylor series (examples A through D) is furnished in the following. We verify MATLAB validity of the series employing same function and symbology attached on the right in next page.

A. $e^{-x}=1-x+\frac{x^2}{2}-\frac{x^3}{6}+\frac{x^4}{24}-\frac{x^5}{120}+\cdots$

B. $\ln(1-x)=-x-\frac{x^2}{2}-\frac{x^3}{3}-\frac{x^4}{4}-\frac{x^5}{5}-\frac{x^6}{6}-\cdots$

C. $\ln x$, does not exist

D. $\sin x\cos x=x-\frac{2}{3}x^3+\frac{2}{15}x^5-\frac{4}{315}x^7\ldots$

The function taylor attempts to expand a function up to the fifth order that is the default order. User-defined order more than 5 occurs using the syntax taylor(function string, $n+1$) where n is the required order in the approximation. Considering the example of $\sin x$ and up to the 8th order, the expansion of $\sin x$ is $x-\frac{x^3}{6}+\frac{x^5}{120}-\frac{x^7}{5040}$ (execution attached on the right).

Again Taylor series of $f(x)$ about certain point is also obtainable from the function. For instance $1-\frac{(x-\frac{\pi}{2})^2}{2}+\frac{(x-\frac{\pi}{2})^4}{24}$ is the approximation of $\sin x$ about $x=\frac{\pi}{2}$ up to the 4th order and which needs the syntax taylor(function string, $n+1$,point about). Computation is shown on the right as well.

Expansion based on variable for example $\sin x$ about variable u up to the second order which is $\sin u+(x-u)\cos u-\frac{1}{2}\sin u(x-u)^2$ is also accomplished in a similar fashion (attached on the right).

As an example of computation after series expansion, $\sin x\big|_{about\ x=\frac{\pi}{2}}$ up to the 4-th order is to be evaluated at $x=\frac{3\pi}{4}$

Taylor series for the example A,

```
>>syms x,S=taylor(exp(-x)); pretty(S) ↵
                2         3          4          5
       1 - x + 1/2 x  - 1/6 x  + 1/24 x  - 1/120 x
```

Taylor series for the example B,

```
>>syms x, S=taylor(log(1-x)); pretty(S) ↵
             2         3         4         5
       -x - 1/2 x  - 1/3 x  - 1/4 x  - 1/5 x
```

Taylor series for the example C,

```
>>syms x, S=taylor(log(x)) ↵
??? Error using ==> sym.taylor
Error, does not have a taylor expansion, try series()
```

Taylor series for the example D,

```
>>syms x, S=taylor(sin(x)*cos(x)); pretty(S) ↵
                   3         5
            x - 2/3 x  + 2/15 x
```

up to the 8th order $\sin x$ approximation,

```
>>syms x, S=taylor(sin(x),9); pretty(S) ↵
                  3          5           7
          x - 1/6 x  + 1/120 x  - 1/5040 x
```

for $\sin x$ about $x=\frac{\pi}{2}$ up to the 4th order,

```
>>syms x, S=taylor(sin(x),5,pi/2); pretty(S) ↵
                         2                  4
   1 - 1/2 (x - 1/2 pi)  + 1/24 (x - 1/2 pi)
```

for $\sin x$ about $x=u$ up to the 2nd order,

```
>>syms x u, S=taylor(sin(x),3,u); pretty(S) ↵
                                              2
      sin(u) + cos(u) (x - u) - 1/2 sin(u) (x - u)
```

for the computation following the expansion,

```
>>syms x pi, S=taylor(sin(x),5,pi/2); ↵
>>x=3*pi/4; pretty(eval(S)) ↵
                 2            4
    1 - 1/32 pi  + 1/6144 pi
>>double(eval(S)) ↵

ans =
      0.7074
```

which should return $1-\frac{\pi^2}{32}+\frac{\pi^4}{6144}$ or 0.7074. We have the computation by dint of the eval as presented above. For the decimal conversion from rational or symbolic form, one uses the command double.

Shown illustrations so far dealt only with the functions of one variable. Another nice feature of the taylor is that it is well adapted to the case when a function is described by two or more independent variables. General expansion of Taylor series of a multivariable function $f(x_1,x_2,x_3,\ldots\ldots,x_m)$ at $x_m=a$ up to the nth order is given by $f(x_1,x_2,x_3,\ldots\ldots,x_m=a)+\frac{(x_m-a)}{1!}\frac{\partial f}{\partial x_m}\Big|_{x_m=a}+\frac{(x_m-a)^2}{2!}\frac{\partial^2 f}{\partial x^2_m}\Big|_{x_m=a}+\frac{(x_m-a)^3}{3!}\frac{\partial^3 f}{\partial x^3_m}\Big|_{x_m=a}+$.. so on. To obtain the Taylor series of a multivariable function up to the order n about some point a , the syntax is taylor(function string,independent variable for variation, $n+1$, a). For example $e^{3y^2-7z+8v+8}+8(x-2)e^{3y^2-7z+8v+8}+34(x-2)^2e^{3y^2-7z+8v+8}+\frac{304}{3}(x-2)^3e^{3y^2-7z+8v+8}$ is the series of $e^{2x^2+3y^2-7z+8v}$ about $x=2$ up to the 3rd order which we intend to obtain. Related variables are $x_1=x$, $x_2=y$, $x_3=z$, and $x_4=v$. Applying ongoing functions and symbology, the execution is presented above in which the substring %1 indicates the long expression like $e^{3y^2-7z+8v+8}$.

for the multivariable function,

```
>>syms x y z v, S=taylor(exp(2*x^2+3*y^2-7*z+8*v),x,4,2); ↵
>>pretty(S) ↵
                                          2                  3
   %1 + 8 %1 (x - 2) + 34 %1 (x - 2)  + 304/3 %1 (x - 2)
                                     2
             %1 := exp(8 + 8 v + 3 y  - 7 z)
```

◆◆ Interactive tool for the Taylor series approximation

By now it is obvious that the Taylor series approximates some function using a polynomial. But it is important to know that how close the approximation is. Some function may not be properly approximated using lower order but may be close using the higher order polynomials. MATLAB keeps the provision for a graphical tool by the name tayortool which interactively renders the closeness in the approximation. In order to activate the graphical interface, let us execute the following:

>>taylortool ↵

Figure 5.1(a) shows the response in which you find the function f(x) as x*cos(x) that means $f(x) = x\cos x$. In the slot of $T_N(x)$ there is x-1/2 x^3 +1/24 x^5 -1/720 x^7 ⇔ $x - \frac{x^3}{2} + \frac{x^5}{24} - \frac{x^7}{720}$. The N=7 means the approximation is up to 7th order. The a=0 means the series is about x=0. The -2*pi <x 2*pi means the approximation over $-2\pi \le x \le 2\pi$. In the graph there are two plots – one solid line (the plot of $x\cos x$) and the other dotted line (plot of $x - \frac{x^3}{2} + \frac{x^5}{24} - \frac{x^7}{720}$). When the dotted line is close to the solid line, the approximation is proper. User can define his own f(x), a, N, and the interval. In the figure 5.1(a), the approximation is not proper. We started increasing the N and found the proper approximation at N=17. The moment you change the Taylor series parameters, the graphical interface updates automatically.

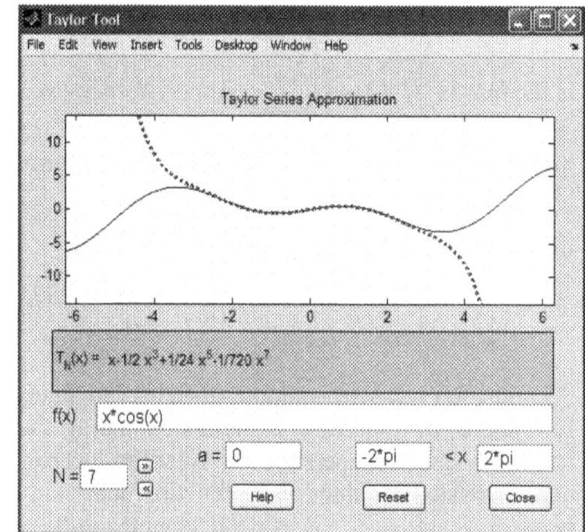

Figure 5.1(a) Graphical user interface for the Taylor series approximation

5.7 Jacobian and Hessian matrices of some function

Suppose a vector function F is formed from m functions and given by $F = [f_1 \ f_2 \ f_3 \ \cdots f_m]$ in which each function is the function of n variables like x_1, x_2, x_3, ... x_n. A matrix of the partial derivatives can be formed as

$$\begin{bmatrix} \frac{\partial f_1}{\partial x_1} & \frac{\partial f_1}{\partial x_2} & \frac{\partial f_1}{\partial x_3} & \cdots & \frac{\partial f_1}{\partial x_n} \\ \frac{\partial f_2}{\partial x_1} & \frac{\partial f_2}{\partial x_2} & \frac{\partial f_2}{\partial x_3} & \cdots & \frac{\partial f_2}{\partial x_n} \\ \frac{\partial f_3}{\partial x_1} & \frac{\partial f_3}{\partial x_2} & \frac{\partial f_3}{\partial x_3} & \cdots & \frac{\partial f_3}{\partial x_n} \\ & & \vdots & & \\ \frac{\partial f_m}{\partial x_1} & \frac{\partial f_m}{\partial x_2} & \frac{\partial f_m}{\partial x_3} & \cdots & \frac{\partial f_m}{\partial x_n} \end{bmatrix}$$

which is known as the Jacobian matrix of F and mathematically denoted by $J_F(X)$ where X is the vector formed by the independent variables. Considering $F(x,y) = \begin{bmatrix} x^3 + y^2 x \\ e^{xy} \\ \sin(2x-3y) \end{bmatrix}$ (assuming column oriented vector function), it is given that $J_F(x,y) = \begin{bmatrix} 3x^2 + y^2 & 2xy \\ ye^{xy} & xe^{xy} \\ 2\cos(2x-3y) & -3\cos(2x-3y) \end{bmatrix}$ which we intend to compute. There are two independent variables in $J_F(x,y)$. To obtain the Jacobian of a vector function, we first declare the independent variables using the syms (section 2.1) and then use the function jacobian with the syntax jacobian (section 14.2 cited vector code of F as a column matrix, independent variables in the vector function as a row matrix). The Jacobian computation is placed above on the right side in which the workspace F and J hold the vector function and Jacobian matrix code respectively. The pretty (section 3.1) displays the readable form. We may need to compute the Jacobian at some point for example at $x = \frac{\pi}{2}$ and $y = 0$ i.e. $J_F\left(\frac{\pi}{2}, 0\right) = \begin{bmatrix} \frac{3\pi^2}{4} & 0 \\ 0 & \frac{\pi}{2} \\ -2 & 3 \end{bmatrix} = \begin{bmatrix} 7.4022 & 0 \\ 0 & 1.5708 \\ -2 & 3 \end{bmatrix}$. The workspace J of the last implementation contains the Jacobian code in which we substitute the x and y values using the function subs as shown on the right side. Since the function jacobian works symbolically, it is better that the variables are inserted in symbolic form that is why we used the command sym. For the decimal computation, one applies the command double(subs(J)).

for the Jacobian computation symbolically,

```
>>syms x y, F=[x^3+y^2*x;exp(x*y);sin(2*x-3*y)]; ↵
>>J=jacobian(F,[x y]); ↵
>>pretty(J) ↵
        [      2    2                          ]
        [   3 x  + y             2 x y         ]
        [                                      ]
        [  y exp(x y)           x exp(x y)     ]
        [                                      ]
        [2 cos(2 x - 3 y)   -3 cos(2 x - 3 y) ]
```

for the Jacobian evaluation,

```
>>x=sym(pi/2); y=sym(0); ↵
>>subs(J) ↵

ans =

[ 3/4*pi^2,        0]
[        0,   1/2*pi]
[       -2,        3]
```

for the Hessian matrix,

```
>>maple('f:=x^3*y+z^4'); ↵
>>H=maple('hessian(f,[x,y,z])'); ↵
>>pretty(sym(H)) ↵
      [            2          ]
      [6 x y    3 x       0   ]
      [                       ]
      [   2                   ]
      [3 x       0        0   ]
      [                       ]
      [                      2]
      [ 0        0      12 z  ]
```

Let f be a scalar function of n variables denoted by x_1, x_2, x_3, ... x_n. Hessian of f (denoted by $H_f(X)$) is the matrix $H_f(X)=\frac{\partial^2 f}{\partial x_i \partial x_j}$ where $X=[x_1, x_2, x_3, \ldots x_n]$ and i, j vary from 1 to n. Hessian is associated with the quadratic form of a matrix. We illustrate the formation of the Hessian matrix considering the function $f=x^3y+z^4$ and which should be $H_f(x,y,z)=\begin{bmatrix} \frac{\partial^2 f}{\partial x^2} & \frac{\partial^2 f}{\partial x\partial y} & \frac{\partial^2 f}{\partial x\partial z} \\ \frac{\partial^2 f}{\partial y\partial x} & \frac{\partial^2 f}{\partial y^2} & \frac{\partial^2 f}{\partial y\partial z} \\ \frac{\partial^2 f}{\partial z\partial x} & \frac{\partial^2 f}{\partial z\partial y} & \frac{\partial^2 f}{\partial z^2} \end{bmatrix} = \begin{bmatrix} 6xy & 3x^2 & 0 \\ 3x^2 & 0 & 0 \\ 0 & 0 & 12z^2 \end{bmatrix}$ following the computation. The maple (section 3.2) function hessian computes the Hessian matrix symbolically as shown on the lower right corner of the last page. The first line of the command is the assignment of the vector code of the given function to the workspace f where := is the maple assignment operator. The hessian has two input arguments, the first and second of which are the function name and the related variables of the function under the third brace but separated by a comma respectively. The return from the hessian is assigned to workspace H which indicates $H_f(X)$. The pretty just displays the codes in H in readable form.

5.8 Gradient, divergence, and curl of different fields

Problems related to the gradient of scalar fields and the divergence and curl of vector fields are seen in vector calculus. The maple package (section 3.2) has the facility to implement these three operations. The gradient, divergence, and curl expressions are dependent on the coordinate system. All these computations are in symbolic sense. Any point in 3D space is described by (x,y,z), (ρ,φ,z), and (r,θ,φ) for the rectangular, cylindrical, and spherical coordinate systems respectively. The symbolic variables are not available in the text mode programming that is why we write r for ρ and r, t for θ, and p for φ in the following.

♦♦ Gradient of a scalar field

Gradient of any scalar field S is denoted by ∇S and given by $\nabla S=\frac{\partial S}{\partial x}\overline{a}_x+\frac{\partial S}{\partial y}\overline{a}_y+\frac{\partial S}{\partial z}\overline{a}_z$, $\nabla S=\frac{\partial S}{\partial \rho}\overline{a}_\rho+\frac{1}{\rho}\frac{\partial S}{\partial \varphi}\overline{a}_\varphi+\frac{\partial S}{\partial z}\overline{a}_z$, and $\nabla S=\frac{\partial S}{\partial r}\overline{a}_r+\frac{1}{r}\frac{\partial S}{\partial \theta}\overline{a}_\theta+\frac{1}{r\sin\theta}\frac{\partial S}{\partial \varphi}\overline{a}_\varphi$ for the rectangular, cylindrical, and spherical coordinate systems respectively. It is given that the scalar fields $S=(x^2+2y)z^2$, $S=(\rho+2)^2 z\cos 3\varphi$, and $S=3r^2\sin\varphi\cos\theta$ have the gradient expressions $\nabla S=2xz^2\overline{a}_x+2z^2\overline{a}_y+2z(x^2+2y)\overline{a}_z$, $\nabla S=2(\rho+2)z\cos 3\varphi\,\overline{a}_\rho-\frac{3(\rho+2)^2 z\sin 3\varphi}{\rho}\overline{a}_\varphi+(\rho+2)^2\cos 3\varphi\,\overline{a}_z$, and $\nabla S=6r\sin\varphi\cos\theta\,\overline{a}_r-3r\sin\varphi\sin\theta\,\overline{a}_\theta+\frac{3r\cos\varphi\cos\theta}{\sin\theta}\overline{a}_\varphi$ for the three coordinate systems respectively and we wish to compute them. The maple function grad performs the computation of the gradient of any scalar field as attached on the right.

Gradient of a scalar field: for the rectangular field,

```
>>maple('S:=(x^2+2*y)*z^2'); g=maple('grad(S,[x,y,z])'); ↵
>>pretty(sym(g)) ↵
        [    2        2          2          ]
        [2 x z     2 z      2 (x  + 2 y) z  ]
```

for the cylindrical field,

```
>>maple('S:=(r+2)^2*z*cos(3*p)'); ↵
>>g=maple('grad(S,[r,p,z], coords=cylindrical)'); ↵
>>pretty(sym(g)) ↵
[                                   2                          ]
[                        (r + 2) z sin(3 p)          2         ]
[2 (r + 2)z cos(3p)  -3 -------------------   (r + 2) cos(3 p) ]
[                                r                             ]
```

for the spherical field,

```
>>maple('S:=3*r^2*sin(p)*cos(t)'); ↵
>>g=maple('grad(S,[r,t,p],coords=spherical)'); ↵
>>pretty(sym(g)) ↵
[                                              r cos(p) cos(t) ]
[6 r sin(p) cos(t)    -3 r sin(p) sin(t)     3 ----------------]
[                                                  sin(t)      ]
```

The vector code (section 14.2) of the scalar field S is assigned to the workspace S in maple using the maple assignment operator := in each case. The grad has three input arguments, the first, second, and third of which are the field name, independent variables under the third brace but separated by a comma, the indicatory reserve word for coordinate system passed through coords= (default is rectangular, cylindrical and spherical for the other two coordinate systems) respectively. In each case we assigned the maple output to the MATLAB assignee g which holds the gradient code. The independent variables as well as the gradient components (returned as a three element row matrix) are in order for example $x \to y \to z$ for the rectangular case. The pretty just shows the readable form.

♦♦ Divergence of a vector field

Divergence of a vector field $\overline{A}$ is symbolized by $\nabla\bullet\overline{A}$ which is a scalar. Divergence expressions for different coordinate systems are as follows: $\nabla\bullet\overline{A}=\frac{\partial A_x}{\partial x}+\frac{\partial A_y}{\partial y}+\frac{\partial A_z}{\partial z}$, $\nabla\bullet\overline{A}=\frac{1}{\rho}\frac{\partial(\rho A_\rho)}{\partial\rho}+\frac{1}{\rho}\frac{\partial A_\varphi}{\partial\varphi}+\frac{\partial A_z}{\partial z}$, and $\nabla\bullet\overline{A}=$

$\frac{1}{r^2}\frac{\partial(r^2 A_r)}{\partial r}+\frac{1}{r\sin\theta}\frac{\partial(A_\theta \sin\theta)}{\partial\theta}+\frac{1}{r\sin\theta}\frac{\partial A_\varphi}{\partial\varphi}$ for the rectangular, cylindrical, and spherical coordinate systems respectively. Given that $\frac{1}{x+y}-\sin y+7e^{7z}$, $\frac{3\rho^2 z+\cos\varphi+\rho^2\cos\varphi}{\rho}$, and $\frac{4r^2\sin\theta+2\cos\theta\sin\theta\cos\varphi-r\sin\varphi}{r\sin\theta}$ are the divergence for the vectors $\overline{A}=\ln(x+y)\overline{a}_x+\cos y\,\overline{a}_y+e^{7z}\,\overline{a}_z$, $\overline{A}=\rho^2 z\overline{a}_\rho+\sin\varphi\overline{a}_\varphi+\rho z\cos\varphi\overline{a}_z$, and $\overline{A}=r^2\overline{a}_r+\sin\theta\cos\varphi\overline{a}_\theta+r\cos\varphi\overline{a}_\varphi$ in the rectangular, cylindrical, and spherical coordinate systems respectively and our objective is to compute them. The vector $\overline{A}$ is entered as a three element row matrix and in order for example $x\rightarrow y\rightarrow z$ for the rectangular case. The vector code represents each component of the vector $\overline{A}$. The components of $\overline{A}$ are placed inside the third brace but separated by a comma (A$\Leftrightarrow\overline{A}$). The corresponding maple function is diverge which is what we applied as shown on the right. In each case the output of the diverge from the maple is assigned to the workspace d in MATLAB (not in maple). All gradient mentioned symbols and functions apply here.

Divergence of a vector field: for the rectangular field,

```
>>maple('A:=[log(x+y),cos(y),exp(7*z)]'); ↵
>>d=maple('diverge(A,[x,y,z])'); ↵
>>pretty(sym(d)) ↵
            1
        ---------  -  sin(y)  +  7 exp(7 z)
          x + y
```

for the cylindrical field,

```
>>maple('A:=[r^2*z,sin(p),r*z*cos(p)]'); ↵
>>d=maple('diverge(A,[r,p,z],coords=cylindrical)'); ↵
>>pretty(sym(d)) ↵
            2              2
        3 r  z + cos(p) + r  cos(p)
        -----------------------------
                      r
```

for the spherical field,

```
>>maple('A:=[r^2,sin(t)*cos(p),r*cos(p)]'); ↵
>>d=maple('diverge(A,[r,t,p],coords=spherical)'); ↵
>>pretty(sym(d)) ↵
          2
       4 r  sin(t) + 2 cos(p) cos(t) sin(t) - r sin(p)
       -----------------------------------------------
                          r sin(t)
```

♦♦ Curl of a vector field

Symbolic notation for the curl of a vector field $\overline{A}$ is $\nabla\times\overline{A}$ which is a vector. The name of the maple counterpart is also curl. Style of the implementation of the curl is similar to that of the divergence. Different curl expressions are presented as $\begin{vmatrix}\overline{a}_x & \overline{a}_y & \overline{a}_z\\ \frac{\partial}{\partial x} & \frac{\partial}{\partial y} & \frac{\partial}{\partial z}\\ A_x & A_y & A_z\end{vmatrix}$,

$\frac{1}{\rho}\begin{vmatrix}\overline{a}_\rho & \rho\overline{a}_\varphi & \overline{a}_z\\ \frac{\partial}{\partial\rho} & \frac{\partial}{\partial\varphi} & \frac{\partial}{\partial z}\\ A_\rho & \rho A_\varphi & A_z\end{vmatrix}$, and $\frac{1}{r^2\sin\theta}\begin{vmatrix}\overline{a}_r & r\overline{a}_\theta & r\sin\theta\,\overline{a}_\varphi\\ \frac{\partial}{\partial r} & \frac{\partial}{\partial\theta} & \frac{\partial}{\partial\varphi}\\ A_r & rA_\theta & r\sin\theta\,A_\varphi\end{vmatrix}$

for the rectangular, cylindrical, and spherical coordinate systems respectively. Vectors employed for the illustration of divergence are used for finding the curls too. It is given that $-\frac{\overline{a}_z}{x+y}$, $-z\sin\varphi\overline{a}_\rho+(\rho^2-z\cos\varphi)\overline{a}_\varphi+\frac{\sin\varphi}{\rho}\overline{a}_z$, and

Curl of a vector field: for the rectangular field,

```
>>c=maple('curl(A,[x,y,z])'); ↵
>>pretty(sym(c)) ↵
          [                1  ]
          [  0     0  ---------]
          [              x + y ]
```

for the cylindrical field,

```
>>c=maple('curl(A,[r,p,z],coords=cylindrical)'); ↵
>>pretty(sym(c)) ↵
        [                  2                sin(p) ]
        [-z sin(p)        r  - z cos(p)     -------]
        [                                      r   ]
```

for the spherical field,

```
>>c=maple('curl(A,[r,t,p],coords=spherical)'); ↵
>>pretty(sym(c)) ↵
[  2                                                            ]
[ r  cos(t) cos(p) + r sin(t) sin(p)                sin(t) cos(p) ]
[-----------------------------------   -2 cos(p)   -------------- ]
[              2                                        r        ]
[             r  sin(t)                                          ]
```

$\frac{r\cos\theta\cos\varphi+\sin\theta\sin\varphi}{r\sin\theta}\overline{a}_r\;-2\cos\varphi\overline{a}_\theta+\frac{\sin\theta\cos\varphi}{r}\overline{a}_\varphi$ are the curls for the vectors mentioned in the divergence in the rectangular, cylindrical, and spherical coordinate systems respectively. We aim at receiving them from the maple whose implementation is attached above on the right side. In each case we assigned the return from the maple to the workspace c. The return is a three element row matrix whose elements are the curl vector components in order for example $x\rightarrow y\rightarrow z$ for the rectangular case. The input arguments of the curl are similar to those of the diverge.

♦♦ Composite manipulation involving gradient, divergence, and curl

There are instances when scalar or vector manipulations like $\nabla\bullet(\overline{A}\times\overline{B})$, $\nabla\bullet(\nabla\times\overline{A})$, $\nabla\times(\nabla\times\overline{A})$, etc are necessary. This is merely the extension of the functions we discussed just now. Few examples are cited concerning the composite manipulation involving the gradient, divergence, and curl in the following.

Example of $\nabla\times(\nabla\times\overline{A})$:

Compute $\nabla\times(\nabla\times\overline{A})$ for $\overline{A}=\rho^2 z\overline{a}_\rho+\sin\varphi\overline{a}_\varphi+\rho z\cos\varphi\overline{a}_z$ in cylindrical system. Implementation is at next page on the right. $\nabla\times\overline{A}$ is assigned to B and maple final return is assigned to O. Execute pretty(simplify(sy m(O))) to see $\nabla\times(\nabla\times\overline{A})=\dfrac{1+\rho^2}{\rho^2}\cos\varphi\,\overline{a}_\rho+\dfrac{1-\rho^2}{\rho^2}\sin\varphi\,\overline{a}_\varphi+3\rho\,\overline{a}_z$.

Example of $\nabla\times(\overline{A}\times\overline{B})$:

If $\overline{A}=x^2\overline{a}_x+y\overline{a}_y+(x+z)\overline{a}_z$ and $\overline{B}=zx\overline{a}_x+z^3\overline{a}_z$, find $\nabla\times(\overline{A}\times\overline{B})$. Its computation is also presented on the right in which the : is the execution suppression (it means the line will be executed but not displayed on the screen) command in maple. The maple function crossprod finds the cross product of two vectors symbolically when the vectors are its input arguments respectively. $\overline{A}\times\overline{B}$ is assigned to C and maple final return is assigned to O. Execute pretty(simplify(sym(O))) to see $\nabla\times(\overline{A}\times\overline{B})=(3z^2x^2-x^2-3zx)\overline{a}_x+(3yz^2+yz)\overline{a}_y+(2zx+z^2-2xz^3-z^3)\overline{a}_z$.

Composite manipulations: for $\nabla\times(\nabla\times\overline{A})$:

```
>>maple('A:=[r^2*z,sin(p),r*z*cos(p)]'); ↵
>>maple('B:=curl(A,[r,p,z],coords=cylindrical)'); ↵
>>O=maple('curl(B,[r,p,z],coords=cylindrical)'); ↵
```

for $\nabla\times(\overline{A}\times\overline{B})$:

```
>>maple('A:=[x^2,y,x+z]:B:=[z*x,0,z^3]'); ↵
>>maple('C:=crossprod(A,B)'); ↵
>>O=maple('curl(C,[x,y,z])'); ↵
```

for $\nabla\bullet(\overline{A}\times\overline{B})$:

```
>>maple('A:=[r^2*z,0,r*z]:B:=[sin(p),z,0]'); ↵
>>maple('C:=crossprod(A,B)'); ↵
>>O=maple('diverge(C,[r,p,z],coords=cylindrical)'); ↵
>>pretty(sym(O)) ↵
                               2
     z (-2 z + cos(p) + 2 r  )
```

Example of $\nabla\bullet(\overline{A}\times\overline{B})$:

Choosing $\overline{A}$ and $\overline{B}$ from the cylindrical system where $\overline{A}=\rho^2z\overline{a}_\rho+\rho z\,\overline{a}_z$ and $\overline{B}=z\overline{a}_\varphi+\sin\varphi\,\overline{a}_\rho$, let us find $\nabla\bullet(\overline{A}\times\overline{B})$ and which should be $\nabla\bullet(\overline{A}\times\overline{B})=z(-2z+\cos\varphi+2\rho^2)$. Shown above is the execution in which the C holds the cross product of the two vectors (applying ongoing functions and variables).

5.9 Laplacian of a scalar field

Laplacian (it is also coordinate system dependent) of a scalar function V is denoted by ∇^2V which has the maple (section 3.2) cognate laplacian and functions symbolically. Expressions for the laplacians in various coordinate systems are $\nabla^2V=\dfrac{\partial^2V}{\partial x^2}+\dfrac{\partial^2V}{\partial y^2}+\dfrac{\partial^2V}{\partial z^2}$, $\nabla^2V=\dfrac{1}{\rho}\dfrac{\partial}{\partial\rho}\left(\rho\dfrac{\partial V}{\partial\rho}\right)+\dfrac{1}{\rho^2}\dfrac{\partial^2V}{\partial\varphi^2}+\dfrac{\partial^2V}{\partial z^2}$, and $\nabla^2V=\dfrac{1}{r^2}\dfrac{\partial}{\partial r}\left(r^2\dfrac{\partial V}{\partial r}\right)+\dfrac{1}{r^2\sin\theta}\dfrac{\partial}{\partial\theta}\left(\sin\theta\dfrac{\partial V}{\partial\theta}\right)+\dfrac{1}{r^2\sin^2\theta}\dfrac{\partial^2V}{\partial\varphi^2}$ for the rectangular, cylindrical, and spherical systems respectively. Starting from the scalar functions $V=\dfrac{x^2y^3}{z}$, $V=z\rho\cos^2\varphi$, and $V=r\sin\theta\cos^2\varphi$, one ends up with $\nabla^2V=\dfrac{2y^3}{z}+\dfrac{6yx^2}{z}+\dfrac{2x^2y^3}{z^3}$, $\nabla^2V=\dfrac{-z\cos^2\varphi+2z\sin^2\varphi}{\rho}$, and $\nabla^2V=\dfrac{2-3\cos^2\varphi}{r\sin\theta}$ for the three coordinate systems respectively and we intend to implement them. Implementation of all three examples is attached on the right in which the maple assignee V holds the vector code (section 14.2) of the scalar field in each case (:= is the maple assignment operator). The function laplacian has three input arguments, the first, second, and third of which are the field name, independent variables under the third brace but separated by a comma, the indicatory reserve word for the coordinate system passed through coords= (default is rectangular, cylindrical and spherical for the other two coordinate systems) respectively. Unavailabilty of the symbols in the workspace makes us use r for ρ and r, t for θ, and p for φ. In each case, the return from the maple is assigned to the workspace L which holds the code of ∇^2V. The pretty(sym(L)) displays the readable form (sections 2.1 and 3.1).

Laplacian of a scalar field: for the rectangular system,

```
>>maple('V:=x^2*y^3/z'); ↵
>>L=maple('laplacian(V,[x,y,z])'); ↵
>>pretty(sym(L)) ↵
          3          2        2  3
         y         x  y      x  y
     2 ----- + 6 ------- + 2 ---------
         z          z          3
                              z
```

for the cylindrical system,

```
>>maple('V:=z*r*cos(p)^2'); ↵
>>L=maple('laplacian(V,[r,p,z],coords=cylindrical)'); ↵
>>pretty(sym(L)) ↵
                  2             2
         -z cos(p)  + 2 z sin(p)
         ---------------------------
                      r
```

for the spherical system,

```
>>maple('V:=r*sin(t)*cos(p)^2'); ↵
>>L=maple('laplacian(V,[r,t,p],coords=spherical)'); ↵
>>pretty(simplify(sym(L))) ↵
                   2
          3 cos(p)   - 2
        - ------------------
              r sin(t)
```

5.10 Average, arc length, and tangent of a curve

If a curve $y=f(x)$ is given, its functional average, arc length, and tangent are computed by the maple (section 3.2) functions FunctionAverage, ArcLength, and Tangent respectively. The functional average and arc length are computed from $x=a$ and $x=b$ and applying the expressions $\frac{1}{b-a}\int_{x=a}^{x=b} f(x)dx$ and $\int_{x=a}^{x=b}\sqrt{1+(\frac{dy}{dx})^2}dx$ respectively. All three functions reside in the Student library of maple down the Calculus1. We invoke the library writing with(Student [Calculus1]). We know that $\sin x$ has 0 functional average from $x=0$ and $x=2\pi$ whose computation is attached on the right. The FunctionAverage has two input arguments, the first and second of which are the vector code (section 14.2) of the given function and x variation respectively. There are two dots between the begining and ending of the x interval which is passed by x=. If the independent variable were u, it would be u=. However we assigned the maple output to the workspace A.

for the functional average,

```
>>maple('with(Student[Calculus1])'); ↵
>>A=maple('FunctionAverage(sin(x),x=0..2*pi)') ↵

A =

0
```

Next it is given that $\sqrt{17}-\frac{1}{4}\ln(\sqrt{17}-4)$ =4.6468 is the arc length of the curve $y=x^2$ between the points $x=0$ and $x=2$ and we wish to compute it (implementation on the right). The ArcLength has two input arguments, the first and second of which are the given function vector code and interval description respectively. We assigned the return to the workspace L which holds the code of the arc length. For readable and decimal forms, we use the commands pretty(sym(L)) and double(sym(L)) respectively.

for the arc length,

```
>>maple('with(Student[Calculus1])'); ↵
>>L=maple('ArcLength(x^2,x=0..2)') ↵

L =

17^(1/2)-1/4*log(-4+17^(1/2))
>>pretty(sym(L)) ↵          ← For symbolic display
      1/2                1/2
    17   - 1/4 log(-4 + 17   )
>>double(sym(L)) ↵          ← For decimal display

ans =
      4.6468
```

It is given that $y=x+1$ is the tangent to the curve x^2-3x+5 at $x=2$ which we wish to compute. Its implementation is also shown on the right in which the Tangent has two input arguments, the first and second of which are the given function vetor code and given x point respectively. We assigned the return from the maple to the workspace y which is a user-supplied name.

for the tangent,

```
>>maple('with(Student[Calculus1])'); ↵
>>y=maple('Tangent(x^2-3*x+5,x=2)') ↵

y =

x+1
```

5.11 Minimum and maximum from a function

The minimum or maximum finding can be one and two dimensional. The finding can be in symbolic or numeric, both of which are addressed in the following.

♦♦ Minimum or maximum symbolically

The maple (section 3.2) functions maximize and minimize determine the maximum and minimum from a given expression respectively. It is given that the function $f(x)=-2x^2+5x-9$ has the maximum at $x=\frac{5}{4}$ over $-2\le x\le 6$ and the functional value of $f(x)$ is $-\frac{47}{8}$ at $x=\frac{5}{4}$ which we are interested to find. Attached above on the right is the implementation.

for the maximum of the polynomial,

```
>>maple('maximize(-2*x^2+5*x-9,x=-2..6,location)') ↵

ans =

-47/8, {[{x = 5/4}, -47/8]}
```

for the minimum of $\sin x$**,**

```
>>maple('minimize(sin(x),x=0..2*pi,location)') ↵

ans =

-1, {[{x = 3/2*pi}, -1]}
```

The maximize has three input arguments, the first, second, and third of which are the given function vector code (section 14.2), x interval variation, and the reserve word location for the x point finding respectively. In the interval description, the beginning and ending interval is placed before and after two dots respectively and passed through x=. Not all functions have maximum it is better if we check the graph of the function using ezplot (subsection 13.1.1). If no maximum is found, the value of the function is returned at the end point of the interval where it is greater. The maple returns two output arguments, the first and second of which are the functional value at the maximum (-47/8) and the point taking place at that is the return {[{x = 5/4}, -47/8]} means $f(x)$=-47/8 at x=5/4.

As another example, $5te^{-4t}$ has the maximum $\frac{5}{4}e^{-1}$ over $0\le t\le 6$ which occurs at $t=\frac{1}{4}$ and whose verification needs the command maple('maximize(5*t*exp(-4*t),t=0..6,location)'). This sort of maximum finding is all right if the function possesses one maximum. What if the function holds several maxima or local maxima? For instance the function $\sin x\cos x$ has the maximum value $\frac{1}{2}$ occuring at $x=-\frac{3\pi}{4}$, $\frac{\pi}{4}$, $\frac{5\pi}{4}$, $\frac{9\pi}{4}$, and $\frac{13\pi}{4}$ over $-\pi\le x\le 4\pi$ which we determine as shown below:

```
>>maple('_EnvAllSolutions:=true:maximize(sin(x)*cos(x),x=-pi..4*pi,location)') ↵
```

ans =

1/2, {[{x = 13/4*pi}, 1/2], [{x = -3/4*pi}, 1/2], [{x = 1/4*pi}, 1/2], [{x = 5/4*pi}, 1/2], [{x = 9/4*pi}, 1/2]}

The **maple** reserve word **_EnvAllSolutions** decides to find all solutions within the given interval which we activate by assigning the reserve word **true** through the assignment operator **:=**. The colon (:) is the execution suppression in **maple**.

The minimum finding follows the procedure similar to that of the maximum finding only do we apply the function **minimize**. For example the $\sin x$ has the minimum value -1 over $0 \le x \le 2\pi$ and it happens at $x = \frac{3\pi}{2}$ (implementation is attached on the middle right side of the last page).

We have shown the implementation on the minimum or maximum finding for one dimensional function. The reader is referred to subsection 11.1.2 for two or three dimensional functions.

♦♦ One minimum or maximum numerically

The function **fminbnd** (abbreviation for functional minimum with bound) determines the location of the minimum of a composite function. For instance the function $h(x) = \frac{e^{-2(x-1)}\cos^3(x-1)}{x} + (x-1)^2$ when plotted over $1 \le x \le 2$ using the **ezplot** shows one minimum (the $h(x)$ value at the minimum is 0.4069) at x =1.4392 – our objective is to find that. Placed on the right is its computation in which the first line is to assign the vector code (section 14.2) of $h(x)$ under quote to workspace **h** (any user-chosen name) and second line is to call the function. The function has three input arguments, the first, second, and third of which are the function assignee name, lower bound of the interval $1 \le x \le 2$, and upper bound of the interval respectively. We assigned the return from the function to **m** which is the x value corresponding to the minimum. The function **subs** substitutes the value of **m** (second input argument) to **h** (first input argument) to calculate the functional value corresponding to the minimum.

```
>>h='exp(-2*(x-1))*cos(x-1)^3/x+(x-1)^2'; ↵
>>m=fminbnd(h,1,2) ↵

m =
      1.4392      ← Value of x at minimum
>>subs(h,m) ↵

ans =
      0.4069   ← h(x) value at minimum
```

If a function holds a maximum multiplying the function by -1 turns that to a minimum and the **fminbnd** can then be applied on the function because it is designed to be for the minimum.

♦♦ Data based minimum or maximum

In section 2.9, we addressed the functions **min** and **max** for a given set of data which can be used for finding the minimum and maximum of a function respectively. While using the functions, we select some step size, generate a row or column vector for the independent variable, calculate the function using the scalar code (section 14.2), and apply the function **min** or **max** on that. Let us choose just mentioned $h(x)$ with the step size 0.0001 whose computation is presented on the right abiding by the notion and symbology of the section 2.9. In a similar fashion one can determine the maximum as well.

```
>>x=1:0.0001:2; ↵
>>h=exp(-2*(x-1)).*cos(x-1).^3./x+(x-1).^2; ↵
>>[M,I]=min(h) ↵

M =
      0.4069   ← h(x) value at minimum
I =
      4393     ← Integer index at minimum
>>x(I) ↵

ans =
      1.4392     ← Value of x at minimum
```

♦♦ Multiple minimum or maximum numerically

So far we solely focused on one minimum or maximum. Our written function files **mmax** and **mmin** (figures 5.1(b) and 5.1(c)) find multiple maxima and minima respectively. Type the given codes in two new M-files and save the files by the names **mmax** and **mmin** respectively. It is given that the function $y(t) = 3 + \sin^2 t$ has two maxima at t = 1.5707 and t =4.7124 over $0 \le t \le 2\pi$ which we intend to find. Our function file works on step size (smaller – better, say 0.0001) selection. As a first step we create a row vector on the chosen step size writing **t=0:0.0001:2*pi;**. Then we calculate the functional values using the scalar code which becomes **y=3+sin(t).^2;**. After that we call the **mmax** as attached on the right. The **mmax** has two input arguments, the first and second of which are the independent variable and functional values respectively both as a row matrix. The multiple maxima values are returned as a row matrix. There are two maxima that is why it is a two element row matrix. For three maxima, it would be three element row matrix. In a similar fashion we can call the **mmin** for multiple minima.

```
function mm=mmax(x,y)
s=sign(diff(y));
a=diff(s);
r=find(a==-2);
if isempty(r)
  disp('No maximum')
else
  mm=(x(r)+x(r+1))/2;
end
```

Figure 5.1(b) Function file for multiple maxima

```
function mm=mmin(x,y)
s=sign(diff(y));
a=diff(s);
r=find(a==2);
if isempty(r)
  disp('No minimum')
else
  mm=(x(r)+x(r+1))/2;
end
```

Figure 5.1(c) Function file for multiple minima

For multiple maxima:

```
>>mmax(t,y) ↵

ans =
      1.5707    4.7124
```

However we close the chapter along with the discussion of the maximum and minimum.

Chapter 6

Problems of integral calculus are the subject matter of this chapter. Integration is the reverse process of the differentiation. With precision, integration enables us to calculate analytically/numerically areas, volumes, surface areas, and centroids enclosed by the curved lines or surfaces and many other quantities which it is necessary to find in both pure and applied mathematics. It will be appreciative to the reader that simpler commands turn out the clumsy and tedious integration problems to be easily performed in MATLAB. Anyhow our comprehensive discussion on the integral calculus covers the following:

- Symbolic integration of the standard functions along with the composite ones
- Clear presentation of both the definite and indefinite integrals
- Multiple integration considering both the symbolic and numeric options with many examples
- Series summation, curve property computation, and few integral calculus related functions

6.1 Symbolic integration of functions

In this section at the beginning, we concentrate on the standard indefinite integral computation in MATLAB environment. The computation is purely symbolic for which we utilize the function int (abbreviation for the integration). One can say the int of MATLAB is equivalent to the integration symbol $\int \ldots.\ dx$ of calculus. Indefinite integration of a function is accompanied by a constant which is not returned by the int. The independent variable of the integrand is declared using the syms (section 2.1) before any integration is conducted. The syntax we use for the integration is int(function or integrand as a vector string – section 14.2). All through in this section we are going to maintain the font equivalence like x⇔ x . Known is $\int \cos x dx = \sin x$ and we wish to compute it. The $\cos x$ has the independent variable x and code cos(x). We carry out the integration as follows:

```
>>syms x, I=int(cos(x)) ↵
```

```
I =

sin(x)
```

We use a comma for the separation between two MATLAB statements. The integration is conducted and the return is assigned to the workspace I which is any user-given name. The return is also the vector code of the resulting computation. Section 3.1 mentioned **pretty** displays the readable form if it is necessary. Anyhow applying the same symbology and function, several standard integration computations are presented in the table 6.A without the use of the **pretty**.

Table 6.A Integrations of some standard functions and their MATLAB counterparts

Mathematical computation	MATLAB computation	Mathematical computation	MATLAB computation
$\int \sin x dx = -\cos x$	syms x,int(sin(x)) ⇒ -cos(x)	$\int e^x dx = e^x$	syms x,int(exp(x)) ⇒ exp(x)
$\int \tan x dx = -\ln \cos x$	syms x,int(tan(x)) ⇒ -log(cos(x))	$\int a^x dx = \dfrac{a^x}{\ln a}$	syms a x,int(a^x) ⇒ 1/log(a)*a^x
$\int \sin^{-1} x dx = x \sin^{-1} x + \sqrt{1-x^2}$	syms x,int(asin(x)) ⇒ x*asin(x)+(1-x^2)^(1/2)	$\int \sinh x dx = \cosh x$	syms x,int(sinh(x)) ⇒ cosh(x)
$\int \cos^{-1} x dx = x \cos^{-1} x - \sqrt{1-x^2}$	syms x,int(acos(x)) ⇒ x*acos(x)-(1-x^2)^(1/2)	$\int \cosh x dx = \sinh x$	syms x,int(cosh(x)) ⇒ sinh(x)
$\int x^n dx = \dfrac{x^n+1}{n+1}$	syms x n, int(x^n) ⇒ x^(n+1)/(n+1)	$\int \sinh^{-1} x dx = x \sinh^{-1} x - \sqrt{1+x^2}$	syms x,int(asinh(x)) ⇒ x*asinh(x)-(1+x^2)^(1/2)

Let us consider the $\sin^{-1} x$ integration of table 6.A and display its readable form (first the return is assigned to I) as follows:

```
>>syms x,I=int(asin(x)); ↵
>>pretty(I) ↵
                    2  1/2
   x asin(x) + (1 - x   )
```

One can even use the **pretty** directly without assignment for example **pretty(int(asin(x)))**. This sort of symbolic display is possible for all other integrations in the table 6.A.

6.1.1 Single indefinite integration

Earlier examples illustrated only the standard functions now we intend to execute some single indefinite integration regarding composite functions. In the following we include several single indefinite integration alongside its final integration result which we wish to compute.

$A.\ \int \frac{(\ln x)^4}{x} dx = \frac{1}{5}(\ln x)^5$

$B.\ \int \frac{1}{x(x^2+1)^2} dx = \ln x - \frac{1}{2}\ln(x^2+1) + \frac{1}{2(x^2+1)}$

$C.\ \int \sin^3 x \cos^3 x dx = -\frac{1}{6}\sin^2 x \cos^4 x - \frac{1}{12}\cos^4 x$

$D.\ \int \frac{1}{\sqrt{3u^2-3u+1}} du = \frac{1}{\sqrt{3}} \sinh^{-1}\left\{2\sqrt{3}\left(u-\frac{1}{2}\right)\right\}$

$E.\ \int e^{-7x}\cos(3x-34)dx = -\frac{7}{58}e^{-7x}\cos(3x-34) + \frac{3}{58}e^{-7x}\sin(3x-34)$

Attached on the middle right side of this page is their implementation maintaining the same symbology and function. In all examples we assigned the return code to the workspace I. In the example D, the independent variable is u that is why **syms u** is used.

for the single indefinite integration: example A,

```
>>syms x, I=int((log(x)^4)/x); pretty(I) ↵
              5
     1/5 log(x)
```

single indefinite integration: for example B,

```
>>syms x,I=int(1/x/(x^2+1)^2); pretty(I) ↵
                       2                   1
   log(x) - 1/2 log(x   + 1) + 1/2  ---------
                                       2
                                      x  + 1
```

single indefinite integration: for example C,

```
>>syms x,I=int(sin(x)^3*cos(x)^3); pretty(I) ↵
                2       4                 4
     - 1/6  sin(x)   cos(x)  -  1/12 cos(x)
```

single indefinite integration: for example D,

```
>>syms u,I=int(1/sqrt(3*u^2-3*u+1)); pretty(I) ↵
            1/2            1/2
     1/3   3      asinh(2  3      (u - 1/2))
```

single indefinite integration: for example E,

```
>>syms x,I=int(exp(-7*x)*cos(3*x-34)); pretty(I) ↵
- 7/58exp(-7x)cos(3x-34) + 3/58 exp(-7x)sin(3x- 34)
```

6.1.2 Double indefinite integration

Two **int** functions are adopted to determine the double integration of a composite function of two independent variables. The general form of a double indefinite integration is $\iint f(x,y)dxdy$. There are two independent variables, x and y. Prior to the

for the double indefinite integration: example A,

```
>>syms x y, I=int(int(x*y*exp(x^2+y^2),x),y); pretty(I) ↵
                 2     2
     1/4 exp( x  +  y  )
```

for example B:

```
>>syms u v,I=int(int(1/(u+v^2),u),v); pretty(I) ↵
               2                1/2          v
   v log( u + v  )  -  2 v  + 2 u     atan(-------)
                                             1/2
                                            u
```

for example C,

```
>>syms r t,I=int(int(r^2*sin(t)^2*cos(t),r),t); pretty(I) ↵
                   3   3
          1/9  sin(t)   r
```

integration, we declare them using syms like the single counterpart. The syntax we apply is int(int(vector code of the given function, inner independent variable), outer independent variable). Let us evaluate the following double indefinite integrals whose computed results are also attached beside.

$A.\ \iint xye^{x^2+y^2}dxdy = \frac{1}{4}e^{x^2+y^2}$ $\qquad B.\ \iint \frac{dudv}{u+v^2} = v\ln(u+v^2) - 2v + 2\sqrt{u}\tan^{-1}\frac{v}{\sqrt{u}}$

$C.\ \iint r^2\sin^2\theta\cos\theta\, drd\theta = \frac{1}{9}r^3\sin^3\theta$

The reader is referred to the lower right corner of the last page for the computations of above integrals. In every example, we assigned the computed result to the workspace I and the pretty just shows the readable form on the vector code stored in I. Since mathematical symbols are not available in the workspace, we wrote t for θ other than this font equivalence is maintained. In the example B, the two independent variables are u and v for this reason we wrote syms u v. Note that there is one space gap among syms, u, and v.

for the triple indefinite integration: example A,

```
>>syms x y z,I=int(int(int((z^3-1)*x*y*exp(x^2+y^2),x),y),z); ↵
>>pretty(I) ↵
                2    2          4
      1/4 exp(x  + y  ) (1/4 z  - z)
```

triple indefinite integration: for example B,

```
>>syms u v w, I=int(int(int(log(u)*v/(w+1),u),v),w); ↵
>>pretty(I) ↵
                          2                                2
      1/2  log(w + 1) v   u log(u)  -  1/2  log(w + 1) v   u
```

triple indefinite integration: for example C,

```
>>syms r t p,I=int(int(int(r^(3/2)*sin(t)*cos(p)^2,r),t),p); ↵
>>pretty(I) ↵
                                                     5/2
  - 2/5 (1/2 cos(p) sin(p) + 1/2 p) cos(t) r
```

6.1.3 Triple indefinite integration

In triple integration, just we need to employ ongoing int three times nestedly. However the syntax is int(int(int(vector code of the given function, innermost independent variable), middle independent variable), outermost independent variable). Of coarse the associated variables need to be declared as we did before. We wish to evaluate the following triple indefinite integrals whose computed values are also placed side by side:

$A.\ \iiint (z^3-1)xye^{x^2+y^2}dxdydz = \frac{1}{4}e^{x^2+y^2}\left(\frac{1}{4}z^4 - z\right)$ $\qquad B.\ \iiint \frac{v}{w+1}\ln u\, dudvdw = \frac{1}{2}u\ln u\ v^2\ln(w+1) - \frac{1}{2}uv^2\ \ln(w+1)$

$C.\ \iiint r^{\frac{3}{2}}\sin\theta\cos^2\varphi\, dr\, d\theta\, d\varphi = -\frac{2}{5}\cos\theta\ r^{\frac{5}{2}}\left(\frac{\varphi}{2} + \frac{\sin\varphi\cos\varphi}{2}\right)$

Placed on the upper right is the implementation of above. The independent variables are separated by one space gap. The workspace I holds the computed result (i.e. the vector code) for the integration in all examples (the t and p are used instead of θ and φ respectively).

6.2 Symbolic definite integration

Definite integrals include lower and upper limits to the indefinite integrals. Different definite integrals are addressed in the following. Aforementioned int is also applicable here but with different number of input arguments which accounts for the lower and upper limits of the integration.

6.2.1 Single definite integration

To evaluate a single definite integral of the form $\int_{x=a}^{x=b} f(x)\,dx$, we use the command int(vector code of $f(x)$, x, a, b).

for the single definite integration: example A,

```
>>syms x,I=int(log(x)^4/x,1,4); pretty(I) ↵
                  5
     32/5  log(2)
```

single definite integration: for example B,

```
>>syms x,I=int(1/x/(x^2+1)^2,3,9); ↵
>>pretty(I) ↵
     log(3) - 1/2 log(41) - 9/205 + 1/2 log(5)
```

single definite integration: for example C,

```
>>syms x,I=int(sin(x)^3*cos(x)^3,-pi/2,pi/2); ↵
>>pretty(I) ↵
     0
```

Writing the independent variable inside the int is optional. If the lower and upper limits have symbolic constants, those symbolic constants can not be the independent variables of the function string. Let us consider following definite integrals whose computed values are also given and which we intend to compute.

$A.\ \int_{x=1}^{x=4}\frac{(\ln x)^4}{x}dx = \frac{32}{5}(\ln 2)^5$ $\qquad B.\ \int_{x=3}^{x=9}\frac{1}{x(x^2+1)^2}dx = \ln 3 - \frac{1}{2}\ln\frac{41}{5} - \frac{9}{205}$ $\qquad C.\ \int_{x=-\frac{\pi}{2}}^{x=\frac{\pi}{2}}\sin^3 x\cos^3 x dx = 0$

$D.\ \int_{x=0}^{x=3\pi} e^{-7x}\cos(3x-34)dx = e^{-21\pi}\left[\frac{7}{58}\cos(34) + \frac{3}{58}\sin(34)\right] + \frac{7}{58}\cos(34) + \frac{3}{58}\sin(34)$

$E.\ \int_{u=0}^{u=4}\frac{1}{\sqrt{3u^2-3u+1}}du = \frac{1}{\sqrt{3}}\ln\left(7\sqrt{3}+2\sqrt{37}\right) - \frac{1}{\sqrt{3}}\ \ln(2-\sqrt{3})$

Presented on the upper right side is the execution for the examples A through C and at the beginning of the next page on the upper right side is that for the examples D and E. In all examples we assigned the computed values to the workspace I which holds the vector code of the computation. The pretty just shows the readable form.

Some return might seem bizarre for instance $e^{-21\pi}\cos(34)$ can be written as $\dfrac{\cos 34}{(e^{\pi})^{21}}$ which is a part of the return from the example D. The command **simple** in the examples D and E simplifies the code stored in the I. One might be interested about the decimal value of the integral following the computation for example $\frac{32}{5}(\ln 2)^5=1.024$ in the example A. We use the command **double(I)** for that.

single definite integration: for example D,

```
>>syms x,I=int(exp(-7*x)*cos(3*x-34),0,3*pi);pretty(simple(I)) ↵
        cos(34)           sin(34)
   7/58 ---------- + 3/58 ---------- + 7/58 cos(34) + 3/58 sin(34)
            21                21
        exp(pi)           exp(pi)
```

single definite integration: for example E,

```
>>syms u,I=int(1/sqrt(3*u^2-3*u+1),0,4); pretty(simple(I)) ↵
                              1/2        1/2
                     1/2   -7 3    - 2 37
                 1/3 3    log(-------------------)
                                        1/2
                                  -2 + 3
```

6.2.2 Double definite integration

To perform a double definite integral of the form $\int_{y=c}^{y=d}\int_{x=a}^{x=b} f(x,y)\,dxdy$, we apply the command **int(int(**vector code of $f(x,y)$, x , a , b), y , c , d). All related variables are declared using the **syms**. Let us evaluate following double definite integrals:

$$A.\ \int_{v=3}^{v=6}\int_{u=0}^{u=v}\frac{dudv}{u^2+v^2}=\frac{\pi}{4}\ln 2 \qquad B.\ \int_{y=1}^{y=2}\int_{x=0}^{x=1} xye^{x^2+y^2}dxdy=\frac{1}{4}(e^5-e^2)-\frac{1}{4}(e^4-e) \qquad C.\ \int_{\theta=\frac{\pi}{6}}^{\theta=\frac{\pi}{4}}\int_{r=0}^{r=4\sin 2\theta} r\sin\theta\cos\theta\,drd\theta=\frac{11}{12}$$

$$D.\ \int_{z=2}^{z=4}\int_{x=-\infty}^{x=\infty}\frac{3zdxdz}{x^2+z^4}=3\pi\ln 2$$

We attached all computations on the right. All integration results are assigned to the workspace **I** which holds the vector code of the computation. The symbol ∞ is passed to the **int** using the reserve word **inf**. Due to unavailability, t is used instead of θ. In the example A, the upper limit of the inner integration is a function of the second independent variable. Similar situation is also seen in the example C. The reader is referred to table 14.A for functional equivalence. If you need decimal form for any of the four examples, just use the command **double(I)**.

for double definite integral: example A,

```
>>syms u v,I=int(int(1/(u^2+v^2),u,0,v),v,3,6);pretty(I) ↵
          1/4 pi log(2)
```

for double definite integral: for example B,

```
>>syms x y,I=int(int(x*y*exp(x^2+y^2),x,0,1),y,1,2);pretty(I) ↵
    1/4 exp(5) - 1/4 exp(4) - 1/4 exp(2) + 1/4 exp(1)
```

for double definite integral: for example C,

```
>>syms r t,I=int(int(r*sin(t)*cos(t),r,0,4*sin(2*t)),t,pi/6,pi/4); ↵
>>pretty(I) ↵
          11
          ---
          12
```

for double definite integral: for example D,

```
>>syms x z, I=int(int(3*z/(x^2+z^4),x,-inf,inf),z,2,4); ↵
>>pretty(I) ↵
        3 pi log(2)
```

6.2.3 Triple definite integration

It is obvious from the last two subsections that evaluation of a triple definite integral of the form $\int_{z=e}^{z=f}\int_{y=c}^{y=d}\int_{x=a}^{x=b} f(x,y,z)\,dxdydz$ requires writing the command **int(int(int(**vector code of $f(x,y,z)$, x , a , b), y , c , d), z , e , f) whose straightforward implementation is conducted considering the following examples:

$$A.\ \int_{x=0}^{x=a^2}\int_{y=0}^{y=x}\int_{z=0}^{z=y} x^2y^2z\,dzdydx=\frac{a^{16}}{80} \qquad B.\ \int_{\varphi=0}^{\varphi=\pi}\int_{\theta=0}^{\theta=\frac{\pi}{2}}\int_{r=0}^{r=2\cos\varphi} r^2\sin\theta\sin\varphi\,dr\,d\theta\,d\varphi=0$$

$$C.\ \int_{u=0}^{u=\sqrt{5}}\int_{v=0}^{v=\sqrt{9-u^2}}\int_{w=0}^{w=\sqrt[3]{(9-u^2-v^2)^2}} u\,\sqrt[3]{9-u^2-v^2}\,dw\,dv\,du=\frac{422}{15}$$

We have shown the integration calculation on the right. In the example A, the independent variables are x, y, and z but there is one constant a present in the integration that is not known to the **int**. Therefore we declare a using the **syms** as well. All computations are assigned to the workspace **I** on which **pretty** is applied to view the readable form. Once again, the **t** and **p** are used for θ and φ respectively. If you need decimal value, use the command **double(I)**. You may feel cumbersome to write the long string for multiple integration. Let us perform the

for the triple definite integral: example A,

```
>>syms x y z a, I=int(int(int(x^2*y^2*z,z,0,y),y,0,x),x,0,a^2); pretty(I) ↵
             16
        1/80 a
```

for the triple definite integral: for example B,

```
>>syms r t p,I=int(int(int(r^2*sin(t)*sin(p),r,0,2*cos(p)),t,0,pi/2),p,0,pi); pretty(I) ↵
        0
```

for the triple definite integral: for example C,

```
>>syms u v w ↵
>>I=int(int(int(u*(9-u^2-v^2)^(1/3),w,0,(9-u^2-v^2)^(2/3)),v,0,(9-u^2)^(1/2)),u,0,sqrt(5)); ↵
>>pretty(I) ↵
        422
        -----
        15
```

integration C step by step. The inner integration is first performed and then stored the result in the variable y1 by the following command: syms u v w,y1=int(u*(9-u^2-v^2)^(1/3),w,0,(9-u^2-v^2)^(2/3));. Now the middle integration is conducted and assigned the result to y2 using y2=int(y1,v,0,(9-u^2)^(1/2));. The outermost integration takes place using int(y2,u,0,sqrt(5)).

6.3 Numerical integration

All types of integrands do not have the close form integration under which the numerical methods are applied. Unlike the symbolic computation, there are several functions that integrate different types of integrand numerically. We describe some implementation of the numerical integration in the following.

6.3.1 Single integration

Numerically we compute the definite integration of the type $\int_{x=a}^{x=b} f(x)\,dx$ employing the function quad (abbreviation for the quadrature integration). First one needs to define the integrand using scalar code (section 14.2). Mentioning the independent variable of the integration is compulsory but through the function inline. The inline has two input arguments, the first and second of which are the integrand scalar code and independent variable respectively but both under quote. Then one assigns the inline defined function to some user-given workspace variable. In order to evaluate the integral, we call the function quad with three input arguments, the first, second, and third of which are the inline defined workspace variable name, lower limit of the integration, and upper limit of the integration respectively. Let us compute the following integrals numerically whose computed values are also given.

$A.\ \int_{x=-\frac{\pi}{3}}^{x=\frac{\pi}{2}} \sin^3 x\cos^3 x dx = 0.013$ $\quad B.\ \int_{x=3}^{x=9} \frac{1}{x(x^2+1)^2} dx = 0.0026$ $\quad C.\ \int_{x=0}^{x=3\pi} e^{-7x}\cos(3x-34)dx = -0.0750$

for the numerical single integration: for example A,

```
>>f=inline('sin(x).^3.*cos(x).^3','x'); ↵
>>quad(f,-pi/3,pi/2) ↵

ans =
        0.0130
```

numerical integration: for example B,

```
>>f=inline('1./(x.*(x.^2+1).^2)','x'); ↵
>>quad(f,3,9) ↵

ans =
        0.0026
```

numerical integration: for example C,

```
>>f=inline('exp(-7*x).*cos(3*x-34)','x'); ↵
>>quad(f,0,3*pi) ↵

ans =
        -0.0750
```

Attached on the upper right is the implementation for above examples. In all three examples we assigned the inline defined function to the workspace f. The quad uses some default tolerance for the numeric computation. If one wishes to insert the relative error, the necessary syntax is quad(f,lower limit,upper limit,relative error). For instance the example A needs the command quad(f,-pi/3,pi/2,0.0001) for a tolerance 10^{-4}. There is other function for the single definite numerical integration called quadl, execute help quadl for details at the command prompt.

6.3.2 Double integration

Numerical double integration is implementable through the use of the function dblquad (abbreviation for the double quadrature integration). In order to evaluate an integration of the type $\int_{y=c}^{y=d}\int_{x=a}^{x=b} f(x,y)\,dxdy$ using the dblquad, we have to define the given integrand using the scalar code (section 14.2) and last subsection mentioned inline. Afterwards we call the dblquad using the syntax dblquad (f,lower limit of x ,upper limit of x ,lower limit of y ,upper limit of y) where f is the inline defined function. Let us evaluate the following double integrals numerically using the dblquad:

$$A.\ \int_{v=-5}^{v=3}\int_{u=3}^{u=7} (u^2+v)\sqrt{u}\,dudv = 1896.3148$$

$$B.\ \int_{\theta=-\frac{\pi}{3}}^{\theta=\frac{\pi}{2}}\int_{r=2}^{r=5} r^3(\cos^2\theta+\sin^4\theta)\,dr\,d\theta = 344.6455$$

$$C.\ \int_{z=-4}^{z=6}\int_{w=1}^{w=2} \frac{z^3}{w^2+z^4}\,dw\,dz = 0.4036$$

$$D.\ \int_{y=0}^{y=\pi}\int_{x=0}^{x=\frac{\pi}{2}} x\cos(x^2+y)\,dxdy = -1.7812$$

for numerical double integration: example A,

```
>>f=inline('(u.^2+v).*sqrt(u)','u','v'); ↵
>>dblquad(f,3,7,-5,3) ↵

ans =
        1.8963e+003
```

numerical double integration: for example B,

```
>>f=inline('r.^3.*(cos(t).^2+sin(t).^4)','r','t'); ↵
>>dblquad(f,2,5,-pi/3,pi/2) ↵

ans =
        344.6455
```

numerical double integration: for example C,

```
>>f=inline('z.^3./(w.^2+z.^4)','w','z'); ↵
>>dblquad(f,1,2,-4,6) ↵

ans =
        0.4036
```

numerical double integration: for example D,

```
>>f=inline('x.*cos(x.^2+y)','x','y'); ↵
>>dblquad(f,0,pi/2,0,pi) ↵

ans =
        -1.7812
```

Attached on the right is the implementation of all above examples. We assigned the inline defined function to the workspace f in all examples. Unlike the single counterpart, the inline now accepts three input arguments, the first, second, and third of which are the scalar code of the integrand under quote, inner independent variable of the integration under quote, and outer independent variable of the integration under quote respectively. We used t for θ in the example B. In the example A, the return e+003 indicates 10^3. If the reader wishes to apply other relative error than the default one, the required syntax is dblquad (f,lower limit of x ,upper limit of x ,lower limit of y ,upper limit of y ,relative error) for example we could have used the command dblquad(f,0,pi/2,0,pi,0.0001) for the last example with a relative error 0.0001.

6.3.3 Triple integration

The numerical integration of the triple integral $\int_{z=e}^{z=f}\int_{y=c}^{y=d}\int_{x=a}^{x=b} f(x, y, z)\,dx\,dy\,dz$ is conducted employing the function triplequad which has the common syntax triplequad(f,lower limit of x ,upper limit of x ,lower limit of y ,upper limit of y ,lower limit of z ,upper limit of z) where f is the inline defined function for the integrand as we did in the last two subsections. As usual, we proceed with the numerical computation of the following examples:

$$A.\ \int_{z=0}^{z=\pi}\int_{y=\frac{\pi}{2}}^{y=\pi}\int_{x=0}^{x=\frac{\pi}{2}} \sin(2x-3y-z)\ dxdydz = -0.6667$$

$$B.\ \int_{z=2}^{z=4}\int_{y=1}^{y=2}\int_{x=0}^{x=1} zx\ln(x^2+y)\ dxdydz = 2.0135$$

$$C.\ \int_{\varphi=0}^{\varphi=2\pi}\int_{\theta=-\frac{\pi}{2}}^{\theta=\frac{\pi}{2}}\int_{r=0}^{r=2} r^2(\cos^2\theta+\cos^2\varphi)\,dr\,d\theta d\varphi = 52.6379$$

for numerical triple integration: example A,

```
>>f=inline('sin(2*x-3*y-z)','x','y','z'); ↵
>>triplequad(f,0,pi/2,pi/2,pi,0,pi) ↵

ans =
   -0.6667
```

numerical triple integration: for example B,

```
>>f=inline('z.*x.*log(x.^2+y)','x','y','z'); ↵
>>triplequad(f,0,1,1,2,2,4) ↵

ans =
    2.0135
```

numerical triple integration: for example C,

```
>>f=inline('r.^2.*(cos(t).^2+cos(p).^2)','r','t','p'); ↵
>>triplequad(f,0,2,-pi/2,pi/2,0,2*pi) ↵

ans =
   52.6379
```

Shown on the upper right side is the implementation of the three examples. In all three examples we assigned the inline defined function using the scalar code to the workspace f. The inline now has four input arguments, the first and second through fourth of which are the functional code and the independent variables in order respectively. We used t and p for θ and φ respectively in the example C.

6.4 Summation of a series

The MATLAB function symsum (abbreviation for the symbolic sum) computes the summation of a series symbolically provided that we are able to detect the common term in the series. Both the finite and infinite series are handled using the function. Let us consider the finite series 3+7+11+.. +23 which has the sum 78 and which we wish to compute. The common difference in the series is 4 therefore the common term in the series is given by 3+(n −1)4 or $4n-1$ where n changes from 1 to 6. In summation form one writes the series as $\sum_{n=1}^{n=6}(4n-1)$. The symsum accepts three input arguments, the first, second, and third of which are the vector code (section 14.2) of the common term, lower limit of the summation, and upper limit of the summation respectively assuming that the increment is 1. Prior to computation we declare the related variable in the common term using the syms (section 2.1). Attached on the right is the implementation of the series. Let us determine the summation of the following series whose final results are also provided:

Series summation:

```
>>syms n ↵
>>symsum(4*n-1,1,6) ↵

ans =

78
```

$$A.\ \frac{1}{1^2}+\frac{1}{2^2}+\frac{1}{3^2}+\frac{1}{4^2}+\frac{1}{5^2}+........=\frac{\pi^2}{6}$$

$$B.\ \frac{1}{2.4}+\frac{1}{3.5}+\frac{1}{4.6}+\frac{1}{5.7}+\frac{1}{6.8}+\frac{1}{7.9}+\frac{1}{8.10}=\frac{14}{45}$$

$$C.\ \frac{100}{6+3^2}+\frac{100}{6+5^2}+\frac{100}{6+7^2}+\frac{100}{6+9^2}=\frac{381520}{29667}$$

$$D.\ \frac{3}{2!}+\frac{3}{3!}+\frac{3}{4!}+\frac{3}{5!}+\frac{3}{6!}+\frac{3}{7!}+............+\infty=3e-6$$

$$E.\ \sum_{n=1,3,}^{n=11}\frac{1}{2n}=\frac{3254}{3465}$$

F .Generate $1+2\cos 2x+3\cos 4x+4\cos 6x+5\cos 8x+6\cos 10x+7\cos 12x$

By inspection the series A through D have the common terms $\frac{1}{n^2}$, $\frac{1}{(n+1)(n+3)}$, $\frac{100}{6+(2n-1)^2}$, and $\frac{3}{(n+1)!}$ whose vector codes are 1/n^2, 1/(n+1)/(n+3), 100/(6+(2*n-1)^2), and 3/sym('(n+1)!') respectively. The summations of the series are presented as follows (font equivalence like n⇔ n is maintained):

for the series A,

```
>>syms n ↵
>>symsum(1/n^2,1,inf) ↵

ans =

1/6*pi^2
```

for the series B,

```
>>syms n ↵
>>symsum(1/(n+1)/(n+3),1,7) ↵

ans =

14/45
```

for the series C,

```
>>syms n ↵
>>symsum(100/(6+(2*n-1)^2),2,5) ↵

ans =

381520/29667
```

The common term n variations for the series A through D are 1 to ∞, 1 to 7, 2 to 5, and 1 to ∞ respectively. The infinity symbol ∞ has the MATLAB synonym inf. The factorial term $(n+1)!$ has the code sym('(n+1)!'). In the example E, the series is already given in summation form but the problem is n increment is not 1 so we manipulate the expression until its increment becomes 1. Changing the n by $2p-1$ provides $\sum_{n=1,3,}^{n=11}\frac{1}{2n}=\sum_{p=1}^{p=6}\frac{1}{2(2p-1)}$ whose execution is attached above on the right. Sometimes the symsum helps us generate the long expression for instance the example F and we do so noticing the common term $(n+1)\cos 2nx$ (n changes from 0 to 6, execution is shown above) for which the workspace E holds the generated expression.

for the series D,

```
>>syms n ↵
>>symsum(3/sym('(n+1)!'),1,inf) ↵

ans =

3*exp(1)-6
```

for the series E,

```
>>syms p ↵
>>symsum(1/2/(2*p-1),1,6) ↵

ans =

3254/3465
```

for the series F,

```
>>syms x n, E=symsum((n+1)*cos(2*n*x),n,0,6) ↵

E =

1+2*cos(2*x)+3*cos(4*x)+4*cos(6*x)+5*cos(8*x)+6*cos(10*x)+7*cos(12*x)
```

6.5 Volume of a solid and surface of revolution

If the area bounded by the single valued curve $y=f(x)$ from $x=a$ to $x=b$ is rotated about x axis, the volume of the solid formed is given by $V=\pi\int_{x=a}^{x=b}[f(x)]^2dx$ or if the area bounded by the single valued curve $x=f(y)$ from $y=a$ to $y=b$ is rotated about y axis, the volume of the solid formed is given by $V=\pi\int_{y=a}^{y=b}[f(y)]^2dy$. The maple (section 3.2) function VolumeOfRevolution helps us compute the volume but in association with the library Student[Calculus1]. For example $\frac{512\pi}{15}$ is the volume of revolution when $y=4x-x^2$ is rotated about the x axis from x=0 to x=4 and we wish to compute that. Attached on the right is the computation in which the first line of the command is to activate the library and second line is to call the function. The VolumeOfRevolution has three input arguments, the first, second, and third of which are the given function vector code – section 14.2, x limits passed through x= .., and the reserve word horizontal for the x axis of the rotation but passed to axis= respectively. If the volume of revolution is formed from the rotation about the y axis, we use the command axis=vertical. The computed result is assigned to V on which the decimal form is seen by double(sym(V)).

Computation for the volume of revolution,

```
>>maple('with(Student[Calculus1])'); ↵
>>V=maple('VolumeOfRevolution(4*x-x^2,x=0..4,axis=horizontal)') ↵

V =

512/15*pi
```

Computation for the surface of revolution,

```
>>maple('with(Student[Calculus1])'); ↵
>>S=maple('SurfaceOfRevolution(4*x-x^2,x=0..4,axis=horizontal)') ↵

S =

31/4*pi*17^(1/2)-65/16*pi*log(-4+17^(1/2))
>>pretty(sym(S)) ↵
                  1/2   65                   1/2
        31/4 pi 17    - ---- pi log(-4 + 17    )
                        16
```

Surface of revolution due to the rotation about x axis is given by $S_x=2\pi\int_{x=a}^{x=b}y\sqrt{1+\left(\frac{dy}{dx}\right)^2}\,dx$ where $y=f(x)$ and the same for the rotation about y axis is given by $S_y=2\pi\int_{y=a}^{y=b}y\sqrt{1+\left(\frac{dx}{dy}\right)^2}\,dy$ where $x=f(y)$. We consider the example function used for the volume of revolution and it is given that the surface of revolution due to the rotation of the curve $y=4x-x^2$ from x=0 to x=4 about the x axis is $S_x=\frac{31\pi\sqrt{17}}{4}-\frac{65\pi\ln(\sqrt{17}-4)}{16}$ which we intend to calculate. In the same maple library, there is another function called SurfaceOfRevolution which computes the S_x or S_y. Its input argumentation follows the same description as aforementioned VolumeOfRevolution does. However the computation is attached on the upper right side in which we assigned the computed surface area to the workspace S that is S=S_x. Readable form on the code stored in S is displayed using the pretty (section 3.1) followed by sym. If you need the decimal data, use the command double(sym(S)).

6.6 Some integral calculus functions

Different kinds of integral calculus functions are available in MATLAB. The functions may be handled numerically or symbolically. We present some of them in the table 6.B.

Table 6.B Some integral calculus functions and their MATLAB synonyms

Function name and definition	MATLAB synonym	Wanted computation	MATLAB command
Error function $erf(x)=\frac{2}{\sqrt{\pi}}\int_0^x e^{-t^2}dt$, $-\infty\le x\le\infty$, $-1\le erf(x)\le 1$	erf(x) where x can be a scalar or rectangular matrix in general	$erf(2)=0.9953$	>>erf(2) ↵ ans = 0.9953
Complementary error function $erfc(x)=\frac{2}{\sqrt{\pi}}\int_x^\infty e^{-t^2}dt$, $-\infty\le x\le\infty$, $0\le erfc(x)\le 2$	erfc(x) where x can be a scalar or rectangular matrix in general	$erfc(1)=0.1573$	>>erfc(1) ↵ ans = 0.1573
Gamma function $\Gamma x=\int_{t=0}^{t=\infty} t^{x-1}e^{-t}dt$, $x\neq 0$	gamma(x) where x can be a scalar or rectangular matrix in general	$\Gamma 4=6$	>>gamma(4) ↵ ans = 6
Beta function $B(z,w)=\int_{t=0}^{t=1} t^{z-1}(1-t)^{w-1}dt$, $0< z$, $w<\infty$	beta(z,w) where both the z and w can be a scalar or identical size rectangular matrix in general	$B(2,3)=0.0833$	>>beta(2,3) ↵ ans = 0.0833
Sine integral $Si(x)=\int_{t=0}^{t=x}\frac{\sin t}{t}dt$	sinint(x) where x can be a scalar or rectangular matrix in general	$Si(2.1)=1.6487$	>>sinint(2.1) ↵ ans = 1.6487
Cosine integral $Ci(x)=\int_{t=\infty}^{t=x}\frac{\cos t}{t}dt$	cosint(x) where x can be a scalar or rectangular matrix in general	$Ci(4)=-0.1410$	>>cosint(4) ↵ ans = -0.1410
Exponential integral $Ei(x)=\int_{t=x}^{t=\infty}\frac{e^{-t}}{t}dt$	expint(x) where x can be a scalar or rectangular matrix in general	$Ei(3.2)=0.0101$	>>expint(3.2) ↵ ans = 0.0101

In above table we presented the computation for a single scalar. Let us say $x=\begin{bmatrix}0.1 & 0.2\\ 0 & 0.3\end{bmatrix}$. If we take error function on all elements in x, we should have $\begin{bmatrix}erf(0.1) & erf(0.2)\\ erf(0) & erf(0.3)\end{bmatrix}=\begin{bmatrix}0.1125 & 0.2227\\ 0 & 0.3286\end{bmatrix}$. Its computation is attached on the right in which we assigned the rectangular matrix to x, computed the error function on all elements in x using erf(x), and assigned the result to y. This sort of computation is possible for all functions placed in the table 6.B. One can graph any function in the table 6.B by first creating a row matrix which holds the x variation. For instance we intend to graph the $erf(x)$ over $0\le x\le 3$. The user needs to select some step size say 0.2. The row matrix becomes x=0:0.2:3; (section 1.3) and the functional values of $erf(x)$ we have from y=erf(x). Afterwards we graph the function taking the help of the plot (execute plot(x,y)) from the section 13.2.

```
>>x=[0.1 0.2;0 0.3]; ↵
>>y=erf(x) ↵

y =
    0.1125    0.2227
         0    0.3286
```

While using the input argument to any function, the knowledge of the input variable is important. Without proper knowledge of variable variation, computed data may hamper subsequent computation. For example the cosine integral of a negative number like –2.2 is complex which is verified executing cosint(-2.2).

Some integral function also keeps the provision for symbolic computation. For instance $Si(x)$ in the table 6.B has the derivative $\frac{d}{dx}[Si(x)]=\frac{\sin x}{x}$ which we compute employing the syms and diff (sections 2.1 and 5.3 respectively) as attached on the right. We assigned the computed derivative to the workspace d.

Sine integral differentiation:

```
>>syms x, d=diff(sinint(x)) ↵

d =

sin(x)/x
```

◆◆ Bessel's equation and function

The differential equation $x^2\frac{d^2y}{dx^2}+x\frac{dy}{dx}+(x^2-\alpha^2)y=0$ is called Bessel's equation of the order α where α≥0. One of the power series solutions of the equation is the Bessel's function $J_\alpha(x)$ where $J_\alpha(x)=$

$\sum_{n=0}^{\infty}\frac{(-1)^n}{2^{2n+\alpha}\Gamma(n+1)\Gamma(n+\alpha+1)}x^{2n+\alpha}$. $J_\alpha(x)$ is called Bessel function of the first kind of order α. To evaluate Bessel function of the first kind $J_\alpha(x)$, we use the syntax **besselj**(order α, x value). Let us say the value of the Bessel function of the first kind of order 1 at x =3 (that is $J_1(3)$ =0.3389) is required. We have the computation as shown below on the right side.

for $J_1(3)$:

```
>>besselj(1,3) ↵
ans =
       0.3391
```

The arguments of the **besselj** can be the like positional elements of two matrices. What we mean is if A=$\begin{bmatrix}0 & 1\\ 2 & 3\end{bmatrix}$ and B=$\begin{bmatrix}0 & 5.5\\ 2 & 1\end{bmatrix}$, the command **besselj(A,B)** returns $\begin{bmatrix}J_0(0) & J_1(5.5)\\ J_2(2) & J_3(1)\end{bmatrix}$. Symbolic differentiation and integration of Bessel function can be carried out too. We know that $\frac{d}{dx}[J_n(x)]=\frac{n}{x}J_n(x)-J_{n+1}(x)$ and $\int x^{n+1}J_n(x)dx=x^{n+1}J_{n+1}(x)$ where n is used for the order instead of α and verify them in MATLAB as presented on the right side. There are two associated variables (n and x) in $J_n(x)$, both of which need declaration using **syms**. The workspace **y** and **d** hold the codes for $J_n(x)$ and $\frac{d}{dx}[J_n(x)]$ respectively. Section 6.1 discussed **int** computes $\int x^{n+1}J_n(x)dx$ and assigns the result to workspace **I**. The **pretty** of section 3.1 just displays the readable form.

for differentiation of Bessel function,

```
>>syms x n, y=besselj(n,x); ↵
>>d=diff(y); pretty(d) ↵
                          n besselj(n,x)
  - besselj(n + 1,x) + ------------------
                                x
```

for integration of Bessel function,

```
>>I=int(x^(n+1)*y); pretty(I) ↵
      (n + 1)
     x        besselj(n + 1,x)
```

When α of $J_\alpha(x)$ is positive or negative odd multiple of $\frac{1}{2}$, one can express the $J_\alpha(x)$ in terms of the sine and cosine functions. To show an example, we present the implementation of $J_{-\frac{3}{2}}(x)=\sqrt{\frac{2}{x\pi}}\left[-\sin x-\frac{\cos x}{x}\right]$ for which one needs the **maple** (section 3.2) library **convert** as shown on the right side. The **convert** has two input arguments, the first and second of which are the functional code of $J_{-\frac{3}{2}}(x)$ and the reserve word **sincos** for the sine and cosine conversion respectively. We assigned the **maple** return to the workspace variable **y**. The contents of **y** are converted to symbolic variable to display the output in symbolic form by making the use of the command **pretty**.

for the sine and cosine conversion,

```
>>y=maple('convert(besselj(-3/2,x),sincos)'); ↵
>>pretty(sym(y)) ↵
        1/2
       2    (sin(x) x + cos(x))
    - -----------------------------
               1/2  3/2
             pi    x
```

Suppose we intend to graph $J_\alpha(x)$ for α=1.2 and over $0\le x\le 10$ choosing the x step as 0.2. The command we need is **x=0:0.2:10; y=besselj(1.2,x); plot(x,y)** where the **y** holds the computed values of $J_\alpha(x)$ at the x points stored in **x**, graph is not shown.

The second family of the Bessel's function is given by $Y_\alpha(x)=\frac{J_\alpha(x)\cos(\alpha\pi)-J_{-\alpha}(x)}{\sin(\alpha\pi)}$ where $Y_\alpha(x)$ is called the Bessel's function of the second kind of order α. $Y_\alpha(x)$ is a linear combination of $J_\alpha(x)$ and $J_{-\alpha}(x)$. However to evaluate the Bessel function of the second kind, we use the command **bessely**(order α, x value). Let us compute the $Y_{\frac{3}{2}}(4)$ =0.3671 as shown above on the right side.

for the computation of $Y_{\frac{3}{2}}(4)$,

```
>>bessely(3/2,4) ↵

ans =

0.3671
```

The argument of Bessel's function mentioned so far is a real number. There are circumstances when it is indispensable to use complex number arguments. Then $J_\alpha(x)$ becomes $J_\alpha(ix)$ which is denoted by $I_\alpha(x)$ and called the modified Bessel function of the first kind of order α for which the MATLAB generic is **besseli**. We encounter another function with complex argument for $Y_\alpha(x)$ which we call the modified Bessel function of the second kind of order α (denoted by $K_\alpha(x)$). The resembling MATLAB function is

Table 6.C Bessel functions and their MATLAB counterparts

Name	Symbolic notation	MATLAB counterpart
Bessel function of the first kind of order α	$J_\alpha(x)$	besselj(α , x)
Bessel function of the second kind of order α	$Y_\alpha(x)$	bessely(α , x)
Modified Bessel function of the first kind of order α	$I_\alpha(x)$	besseli(α , x)
Modified Bessel function of the second kind of order α	$K_\alpha(x)$	besselk(α , x)
Hankel function of the first kind of order α	$H_\alpha^1(x)$	besselh(α ,1, x)
Hankel function of the second kind of order α	$H_\alpha^2(x)$	besselh(α ,2, x)

besselk. Writing the input arguments of **besseli** and **besselk** follows the same style as does the **besselj** and **bessely**. That is not all. The last family of the Bessel function is the third kind which has other acronym – Hankel's function. Hankel function is of two types – the first kind [$H_\alpha^1(x)$] and the second kind [$H_\alpha^2(x)$] and they are defined by $H_\alpha^1(x) = J_\alpha(x) + jY_\alpha(x)$ and $H_\alpha^2(x) = J_\alpha(x) - jY_\alpha(x)$ respectively. Corresponding MATLAB functions are **besselh(**α **,1,** x **)** and **besselh(**α **,2,** x **)** respectively. We summarize all Bessel functions in table 6.C before closing the chapter.

Chapter 7

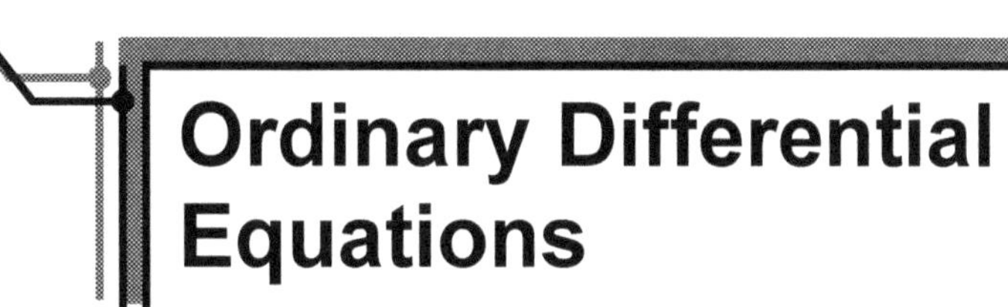

This chapter highlights the implementation of ordinary differential equation (ODE) problems. Differential equations are equations that comprise from the derivatives of some unknown functions. Very often the differential equations come into view in mathematical models that endeavor to describe the real-life problems. Broadly speaking, solving differential equations falls into two categories – one is the analytical or symbolic solution and the other is the numerical solution. Pedagogically analytical one is preferable on the contrary major simulation enigma demands the numerical solution. However we attempt to explain the following very briefly:

- Ordinary differential equation and its general form
- Symbolic solution of differential equations presenting many examples
- Numeric solution of the differential equations employing easy-to-use built-in functions
- Different order and types of differential equations commonly seen in pure mathematics

7.1 Ordinary differential equations

To forecast the behavior of a physical system, we construct mathematical models. We know that the derivatives measure the rates of change of a system. Frequently derivatives constitute the mathematical model of a system. The mathematical models or algebraic equations involving the derivatives are called differential equations. When we have one dependent and one independent variables, the differential equation is termed as the ordinary differential equation. For instance $\frac{dy}{dx}+y=9$ and $\frac{d^4y}{dx^4}+y=9$ are the ordinary differential equations, where y is the dependent and x is the independent variables. Order of a differential equation is the highest order of derivatives present in the equation. A first order ordinary differential equation has the form $f\left(x, y, \frac{dy}{dx}\right)$=0, a second order ordinary differential equation has the form $f\left(x, y, \frac{dy}{dx}, \frac{d^2y}{dx^2}\right)$=0…so forth. The solution of an ordinary differential equation is the function that satisfies the differential equation over some interval of the independent variable. Method of finding the solution of an ordinary differential equation can be symbolic or numeric, both of which are addressed in the following two sections.

7.2 Symbolic solution of ordinary differential equations

The master function dsolve (abbreviation for differential equation solve) finds almost all widely practiced ordinary differential equation's analytical solution in close mathematical form if it really exists. The input of or output from the function is symbolic. The vector code (section 14.2) of the given differential equation is written for finding the solution. Unless description of the independent variable is inserted, t is understood as the independent variable to the dsolve. The code of the equation, initial condition, and independent variable all are written under quote but separated by a comma. We maintain font equivalence in all computations onwards (like x⇔ x). The return from the dsolve can be assigned to some user-given name say S which essentially holds the vector code of the solution. The pretty of the section 3.1 is applied on the S to view the readable form. But to acquire more experience and mastery of techniques, we touch various differential equations in the following as seen in the ODE text.

7.2.1 First order ordinary differential equations

We address some examples of the differential equations with and without the initial conditions in the following. In order to feed the first order derivative, the operator D is used which indicates the $\frac{d}{dt}$ or $\frac{d}{dx}$ of calculus on which the $\frac{dy}{dt}$ is written as Dy. If the dependent variable is u , we write Du for the derivative. Regardless of the independent variable, Dy or Du represents the first order derivative. Some first order differential equations accompanying their final solutions are provided in the following which we intend to compute.

A. $\frac{dy}{dx}=4x^4y^2$ has the solution $y=\frac{-5}{4x^5+5C}$

B. $\frac{dy}{dx}=4x^4y^2$ with the initial condition $y(0)=2$ has the solution $y=\frac{-10}{8x^5-5}$

C. $2x\frac{dy}{dx}=\frac{y^2}{x}+4y$ has the solution $y=\frac{2x^2}{C-x}$

D. Bernoulli equation $x^3y'+xy=y^2$ has the solution $y=\frac{x}{1-x+Cxe^{-\frac{1}{x}}}$

E. Riccati equation $\frac{dy}{dt}=\frac{y^2}{t}+\frac{y}{t}-\frac{2}{t}$ with the initial condition $y(1)=2$ has the solution $y=\frac{2t^3+4}{4-t^3}$

Attached on the right side is the implementation of all examples. In example A, the equation has the vector code Dy=4*x^4*y^2 and independent variable x which become the input arguments to the dsolve respectively. The - C1 means the arbitrary constant C. In example B, there is one initial condition $y(0)=2$ which is written as y(0)=2. When the initial condition is present, the dsolve has three input arguments, the first, second, and third of which are the equation code, initial condition, and independent variable respectively. The return might need rearranging to be identical with the given expression (for instance examples B and E). The arbitrary constant C in the examples C and D are equivalent to 2 C1 and C1 respectively. In the example E, the independent variable is t which is the default one so there is no necessity to write about it. Actually the workspace S holds the code for the solution of y in all examples. For some differential equation the output might seem bizarre. Let us try to find the solution of the differential equation $\frac{dy}{dx}+y\sin x=x$ applying the same function and symbology as follows:

```
>>S=dsolve('Dy+sin(x)*y=x','x'); pretty(S) ↵
                  /
                 |
 exp(cos(x))     | x exp(-cos(x)) dx + exp(cos(x)) C1
                 |
                /
```

First order ODE: for example A,

```
>>S=dsolve('Dy=4*x^4*y^2','x'); ↵
>>pretty(S) ↵
         5
  - --------------
          5
     4 x  - 5 C1
```

First order ODE: for example B,

```
>>S=dsolve('Dy=4*x^4*y^2','y(0)=2','x'); ↵
>>pretty(S) ↵
          5
  - ----------
          5
     4 x  - 5/2
```

First order ODE: for example C,

```
>>S=dsolve('2*x*Dy=y^2/x+4*y','x'); ↵
>>pretty(S) ↵
           2
          x
   -2 ----------
        x - 2 C1
```

First order ODE: for example D,

```
>>S=dsolve('x^3*Dy+x*y=y^2','x'); ↵
>>pretty(S) ↵
              x
  ----------------------------
   1 - x + exp(- 1/x) C1 x
```

First order ODE: for example E,

```
>>S=dsolve('Dy=y^2/t+y/t-2/t,y(1)=2'); ↵
>>pretty(S) ↵
            3
    - 1/2 t  - 1
    --------------
              3
     -1 + 1/4 t
```

As the return says, the solution of the equation is $y = e^{\cos x}\int xe^{-\cos x}dx + Ce^{\cos x}$ that means the close form solution is possible through some integration.

7.2.2 Second order ordinary differential equations

A second order ordinary differential equation has the form $f\left(x, y, \frac{dy}{dx}, \frac{d^2y}{dx^2}\right)$=0. The second order derivative like $\frac{d^2y}{dt^2}$ or $\frac{d^2u}{dt^2}$ is represented by D2y or D2u respectively where D2 is the second order derivative operator irrespective of the independent variable. There must be two initial values in the second order equation if the initial values are given. We follow the same function and workspace variable as we did for the first order in the last subsection. Also we apply the vector code to write the equation. We are going to verify the following second order differential equations whose solutions are also given beside.

A. $\frac{d^2y}{dt^2} - 2\frac{dy}{dt} - 15y = 0$ has the solution $y(t) = C_1e^{5t} + C_2e^{-3t}$ where C_1 and C_2 are two arbitrary constants

B. $u'' + u' + u = 0$ with $u(0) = 1$ and $u'(0) = \sqrt{3}$ has the solution $u(t) = e^{-\frac{t}{2}}\cos\frac{\sqrt{3}}{2}t + e^{-\frac{t}{2}}\left(2 + \frac{1}{\sqrt{3}}\right)\sin\frac{\sqrt{3}}{2}t$

C. $y'' + 4y' + 4y = e^x + e^{-2x}$ has the solution $y = e^{-2x}(C_1 + C_2x) + \frac{e^x}{9} + \frac{x^2e^{-2x}}{2}$

D. Euler equation $2t^2\frac{d^2y}{dt^2} - 3t\frac{dy}{dt} - 3y = 0$ has the solution $y(t) = \frac{C_1 + C_2t^{\frac{7}{2}}}{t^{\frac{1}{2}}}$

Second order ODE: for example A,

```
>>S=dsolve('D2y-2*Dy-15*y=0'); ↵
>>pretty(S) ↵
     C1 exp(5 t) + C2 exp(-3 t)
```

Second order ODE: for example B,

```
>>S=dsolve('D2u+Du+u=0','u(0)=1,Du(0)=sqrt(3)'); ↵
>>pretty(S) ↵
         1/2                          1/2                           1/2
   (1/3 3    + 2) exp(- 1/2 t) sin(1/2 3    t) + exp(- 1/2 t) cos(1/2 3    t)
```

Shown above is the implementation of the examples A and B. In example A, the equation has the code D2y-2*Dy-15*y=0 whose default variable is t. The C1 and C2 indicate the arbitrary constants C_1 and C_2 respectively. In example B, the dependent variable is u on that D2u⇔$\frac{d^2u}{dt^2} = u''$ and Du⇔$\frac{du}{dt} = u'$. The initial conditions $u(0) = 1$ and $u'(0) = \sqrt{3}$ are passed by writing u(0)=1 and Du(0)=sqrt(3) respectively. The dsolve has two input arguments, the first and second of which are the equation code and initial condition set respectively. All initial conditions as a set are put under the quote but each one is separated by a comma. In the example C, the independent variable is x so the default t does not work any more. Information of the independent variable has to be passed on through the second input argument of the dsolve (solution is shown on the right). The solution of the example D (attached on the right) needs rearrangement to have identical expression. In all examples workspace S holds the code of the solution.

Second order ODE: for example C,

```
>>S=dsolve('D2y+4*Dy+4*y=exp(x)+exp(-2*x)','x'); ↵
>>pretty(S) ↵
                                                          2
 exp(-2 x) C2 + exp(-2 x) x C1 + 1/18 (2 exp(3 x) + 9 x  ) exp(-2 x)
```

Second order ODE: for example D,

```
>>S=dsolve('2*t^2*D2y-3*t*Dy-3*y=0'); ↵
>>pretty(S) ↵
       C1         3
      ------ + C2 t
       1/2
      t
```

7.2.3 Higher order ordinary differential equations

The methodology so described in the last two subsections is just extended to handle the higher order ordinary differential equations. Applying the symbol, function, and input argument style of the last two subsections, we carry out the computation of the following higher order differential equations whose final solutions are also provided beside.

A. $y''' + y' - 2y = 0$ has the solution $y(x) = C_1e^x + e^{-\frac{x}{2}}\left[C_2\cos\frac{\sqrt{7}x}{2} + C_3\sin\frac{\sqrt{7}x}{2}\right]$ where C_1, C_2, and C_3 are the arbitrary constants

Higher order ODE: for example A,

```
>>S=dsolve('D3y+Dy-2*y=0','x'); ↵
>>pretty(S) ↵
                                                  1/2
 C1 exp(x) + C2 exp(- 1/2 x) sin(1/2 7    x)

                                                  1/2
      + C3 exp(- 1/2 x) cos(1/2 7    x)
```

B. $y''' - y'' = 0$ with the initial conditions $y(1) = 1$, $y'(0) = 3$, and $y''(-1) = -1$ and the independent variable u has the solution $y(u) = e^2 - e - 2 + (3 + e)u - e^{u+1}$

Higher order ODE: for example B,

```
>>S=dsolve('D3y-D2y=0','Dy(0)=3,D2y(-1)=-1,y(1)=1','u'); ↵
>>pretty(simplify(S)) ↵
     -exp(1) - 2 + exp(2) + u exp(1) + 3 u - exp(1 + u)
```

for example B: entering input arguments separately,

```
>>E='D3y-D2y=0'; ↵
>>I='Dy(0)=3,D2y(-1)=-1,y(1)=1'; ↵
>>S=dsolve(E,I,'u'); pretty(simplify(S)) ↵
     -exp(1) - 2 + exp(2) + u exp(1) + 3 u - exp(1 + u)
```

The solution of the example A is presented on the lower right corner of the last page in which the third order derivative y''' has the code D3y where D3 is the derivative operator regardless of the independent variable. The C1, C2, and C3 indicate the three arbitrary constants C_1, C_2, and C_3 respectively. The solution of the example B is placed above. The three initial conditions $y(1)=1$, $y'(0)=3$, and $y''(-1)=-1$ are passed on writing y(1)=1, Dy(0)=3, and D2y(-1)=-1 respectively. In both examples, the return is assigned to the workspace S which holds the code for $y(x)$ or $y(u)$. In the example B, we utilized the command simplify to simplify the return stored in S. If a differential equation is long, we can enter first the equation or the initial conditions and call the dsolve then. We presented the implementation above for the example B again in which the first and second lines are to assign the differential equation and the conditions to the workspace variables E and I (any user-given name) respectively, both of which are under the quote. In the dsolve, we do not use the quote again but maintain the same input argument order as done previously.

7.2.4 System of differential equations

A system of differential equations is given by $\begin{Bmatrix} \dfrac{dy_1}{dt} = f_1(t, y_1, y_2, \ldots\ldots, y_n) \\ \dfrac{dy_2}{dt} = f_2(t, y_1, y_2, \ldots\ldots, y_n) \\ \vdots \\ \dfrac{dy_n}{dt} = f_n(t, y_1, y_2, \ldots\ldots, y_n) \end{Bmatrix}$ where y_1, y_2, …., and y_n are the n dependent variables and t is the independent variable. Our intention is to find the functions y_1, y_2, …., and y_n satisfying simultaneously the differential equations of the system. Ongoing function dsolve is so versatile that it can find the solution of the system of differential equations as well. The common syntax is dsolve(equation 1, equation 2, etc, initial condition set, independent variable). The coding of the equations or initial conditions follows the same style as conducted in the previous subsections. There is some exception regarding the return from the dsolve which is now a structure array (section 14.4).

It is given that $\begin{bmatrix} y_1 \\ y_2 \end{bmatrix} = \begin{bmatrix} -\dfrac{3}{5}e^t + \dfrac{8}{5}e^{6t} \\ \dfrac{6}{5}e^t + \dfrac{4}{5}e^{6t} \end{bmatrix}$ is the solution of the system $\begin{Bmatrix} \dfrac{dy_1}{dt} = 5y_1 + 2y_2 \\ \dfrac{dy_2}{dt} = 2y_1 + 2y_2 \end{Bmatrix}$ contingent to the initial conditions $\begin{Bmatrix} y_1(0) = 1 \\ y_2(0) = 2 \end{Bmatrix}$ which we wish to compute. The dependent variables y_1 and y_2, the derivatives $\dfrac{dy_1}{dt}$ and $\dfrac{dy_2}{dt}$, and the initial conditions $y_1(0)=1$ and $y_2(0)=2$ are written as y1 and y2, Dy1 and Dy2, and y1(0)=1 and y2(0)=2 respectively. Attached on the right side is the computation of the solution. The first two lines are to assign the vector codes of the equations to the workspace e1 and e2 (can be any user-given names) respectively. The third line is to assign the given initial conditions to the workspace I (can any name of your choice). Note that the equations are under a quote but the initial condition set is under the quote. The fourth line calls the dsolve for the solution and assigns the outcome to the user-given S. The dsolve has three input arguments, the first, second, and third of which are the given first equation, given second equation, and the given initial condition set respectively. If the independent variable were x instead of default t, the command would be S=dsolve(e1,e2,I,'x') in which the fourth input argument is the independent variable indicatory letter under a quote. Without the presence of the initial conditions, the command would be S=dsolve(e1,e2,'x'). The contents of S say that the solution of the system is returned as a structured array which has two members y1 and y2, obviously they are the dependent variables. In order to pick up the member y1 from the structure S, we use the command S.y1. Similar explanation also follows for the y2. We assigned the members of the array to the workspace p1 and p2 (can be any other user-given names) which essentially hold the code for the solution of y_1 and y_2 respectively from what the pretty just displays the nice form.

Solving system of ODE:

```
>>e1='Dy1=5*y1+2*y2'; ↵
>>e2='Dy2=2*y1+2*y2'; ↵
>>I='y1(0)=1,y2(0)=2'; ↵
>>S=dsolve(e1,e2,I) ↵

S =
     y1: [1x1 sym]
     y2: [1x1 sym]
>>p1=S.y1; p2=S.y2; ↵
>>pretty(p1) ↵
     8/5 exp(6 t) - 3/5 exp(t)
>>pretty(p2) ↵
     4/5 exp(6 t) + 6/5 exp(t)
```

Let us compute the solution of the nonhomogeneous system $\left\{\begin{array}{l} \dfrac{dx}{dt}=31x-21y+9z-e^{-3t} \\ \dfrac{dy}{dt}=44x-30y+12z+2t \\ \dfrac{dz}{dt}=-22x+14y-8z+\sin t \end{array}\right\}$ satisfying the initial conditions $\left\{\begin{array}{c} x(0)=-2 \\ y(0)=1 \\ z(0)=0 \end{array}\right\}$ which is given by $\begin{bmatrix} x \\ y \\ z \end{bmatrix}=\begin{bmatrix} (33t+\frac{3743}{30})e^{-3t}-\frac{1317}{10}e^{-2t}-7t+\frac{35}{6}-\frac{9}{10}\cos t+\frac{9}{10}\sin t \\ (44t+\frac{7426}{45})e^{-3t}-\frac{1701}{10}e^{-2t}-\frac{25}{3}t+\frac{131}{18}-\frac{6}{5}\cos t+\frac{6}{5}\sin t \\ (-22t-\frac{3713}{45})e^{-3t}+86e^{-2t}+\frac{2}{5}\cos t-\frac{1}{5}\sin t+\frac{14}{3}t-\frac{35}{9} \end{bmatrix}$. Following the symbology and functions from ongoing discussion, we find the solution of the system below on the right side. The first two lines are to assign the three differential equations and the initial condition set to the workspace e1, e2, e3, and I respectively. The third line calls the function **dsolve** for the solution which returns a structure holding three members x, y, and z representing $x(t)$, $y(t)$, and $z(t)$ respectively. We picked up the $x(t)$, $y(t)$, and $z(t)$ from the S in the fourth line command and assigned them to the workspace p1, p2, and p3 respectively. So to say, the last three variables hold the codes for the $x(t)$, $y(t)$, and $z(t)$ respectively we are looking for. Just to view the solution for $x(t)$, we executed the last line command. In a similar fashion you can verify the symbolic solution for the $y(t)$ and $z(t)$ executing pretty(p2) and pretty(p3) respectively.

Solving the nonhomogeneous system of ODEs:

```
>>e1='Dx=31*x-21*y+9*z-exp(-3*t)'; e2='Dy=44*x-30*y+12*z+2*t'; ↵
>>e3='Dz=-22*x+14*y-8*z+sin(t)'; I='x(0)=-2,y(0)=1,z(0)=0'; ↵
>>S=dsolve(e1,e2,e3,I) ↵

S =
        x: [1x1 sym]
        y: [1x1 sym]
        z: [1x1 sym]
>>p1=S.x; p2=S.y; p3=S.z; ↵     ← p1⇔ x(t), p2⇔ y(t), p3⇔ z(t)
>>pretty(p1) ↵
                  3743
 -7 t + 35/6 + ------ exp(-3 t) - 9/10 cos(t) + 9/10 sin(t) + 33 t exp(-3 t)
                   30

      1317
    - ------ exp(-2 t)
       10
```

7.2.5 Nonlinear differential equations

Previously mentioned equations are mostly linear differential equations. Mathematical formulations of many systems exhibit nonlinear differential equations. Nevertheless the **dsolve** keeps the provision for finding the solution of scores of well-defined nonlinear differential equations. We use the same input argumentation to the **dsolve** as done before. In writing the code for the nonlinear differential equation, we may need the code for $\left(\frac{dy}{dx}\right)^2$ which is written as Dy^2 similarly $\left(\frac{dy}{dx}\right)^3$ ⇔Dy^3, $\left(\frac{d^2y}{dx^2}\right)^2$ ⇔D2y^2, etc. It is important to cite that insertion of the initial condition is not accepted to the **dsolve** in finding the solution of the nonlinear equations. Because several values of an arbitrary constant are possible for a particular x and y or its derivatives thereby giving a family of solutions.

Let us consider the nonlinear equation $x^2\left(\frac{dy}{dx}\right)^2+xy\left(\frac{dy}{dx}\right)-6y^2=0$ which has the general solution $\left(y-\frac{C_1}{x^3}\right)$ ($y-C_1x^2$)=0 and our objective is to have the solution. Placed above on the right side is the execution of the problem. The workspace S holds the code of the solution for y but as a two element column matrix. In the general solution, one takes the roots of the two y as $\frac{C_1}{x^3}$ and C_1x^2 and places them as column matrix $\begin{bmatrix} \frac{C_1}{x^3} \\ C_1x^2 \end{bmatrix}$ that is what the return is (C1⇔ C_1 and C2⇔ C_2).

Solving the nonlinear ODE:

```
>>S=dsolve('x^2*Dy^2+x*y*Dy-6*y^2=0','x'); ↵
>>pretty(S) ↵

                    [C1   ]
                    [------ ]
                    [  3  ]
                    [x    ]
                    [     ]
                    [    2]
                    [C1 x ]
```

Not to be confined with the first order equations, let us consider the second order nonlinear equation $\frac{d^2y}{dx^2}+2\left(\frac{dy}{dx}\right)^3$=0 whose solution is $(y-\sqrt{x+C_1}-C_2)(y+\sqrt{x+C_1}-C_2)=0$ and which we wish to compute. Placed on the right side is the solution of the equation in which the roots of the y in the general solution is placed as a two element column matrix too. One can reach the individual string in the two element column matrix **S** using the commands **S(1)** and **S(2)** respectively.

Solving the second nonlinear ODE:

```
>>S=dsolve('D2y+2*Dy^3=0','x'); ↵
>>pretty(S) ↵
              [        1/2       ]
              [(x + C1)    + C2 ]
              [                  ]
              [         1/2      ]
              [-(x + C1)    + C2]
```

7.3 Numerical solution of ordinary differential equations

We have already discussed the finding of the analytical solution of various order ordinary differential equations (ODEs). In most previous cases it was possible to have a close form solution for the differential equations. Yet a lot of differential equations do not have the close form solution. Analytically unsolvable differential equations are solved numerically by the Taylor series approximation of the dependent variable up to certain order. In reality simple linear differential equations may not occur but an understanding of it paves the way for the understanding of more complicated and practical systems that it would follow.

In the subsequent sections we present the exact (analytical) and numerical solutions of various kinds of differential equations. Since the numerical as well as the exact solution has been found, one gains some insight of the accuracy of the numerical methods. There are several methods to find the numerical solutions of differential equations such as Euler method, modified Euler method, Runge-Kutta methods, predictor-corrector methods...etc. All the while our approach is computationally objectiveness for that reason we will not go through the theory of these methods. MATLAB is rich in having differential equation solvers. Unlike the symbolic solver **dsolve**, there are many differential equation solvers for the numerical solution. Table 7.A presents descriptions of some ODE solvers found in MATLAB. However following steps should be observed before executing a particular ODE solver:

Table 7.A Acronyms and descriptions of some ODE solver functions

Name of the ODE solver	Description of the ODE solver
ode23	Can solve nonstiff differential equations using low order method [uses Runge-Kutta (2,3) formula]
ode45	Can solve nonstiff differential equations using medium order method [uses Runge-Kutta (4,5) formula]
ode113	Can solve nonstiff differential equations using variable order method
ode23s	Can solve stiff differential equations using low order method
ode15s	Can solve stiff differential equations using variable order method
ode23t	Can solve moderately stiff differential equations using trapezoidal rule
ode23tb	Can solve stiff differential equations using low order method
ode15i	Can solve implicit differential equations using variable order method

Steps to be observed for finding the numerical solution of a differential equation

Step A

How an M-file is opened and executed (section 1.3) and how a function file works (section 14.5)

Step B

An M-file by the name **f** (as we will be exercising in the subsequent sections, file name **f** can be any user-chosen name) must contain the code of the differential equation (s)

Step C

Differential equation (s) must be rewritten in proper style [for example $\frac{dy}{dx}=f(x,y)$ for the first order, $\frac{d^2y}{dx^2}=f\left(x,y,\frac{dy}{dx}\right)$ for the second order, and so on] so that the highest order derivative is on the left side of the equation

Step D

User's working path in MATLAB and the path or folder containing the M-file **f** must be identical

Step E

An ODE solver is chosen based on the polynomial approximation order, stiffness of the dependent variable, and accuracy required which are to be acquainted by the user

Step F

Relative and absolute errors must be considered if the control on error is needed

Step G

The initial values of the dependent variable (s) and the derivative (s) at a particular independent variable must be known $\left[\text{ for instance } y \text{ or } \frac{dy}{dx} \text{ at } x=0 \right]$, both of which must be at the same x

Step H

In general the arguments of the M-file **f** are column vectors because the solutions are usually column vectors due to the discrete nature

Along with different options, changing the solver properties and having graphical plots of numerical outputs are also possible. Readers can have online help executing **help ode23**, **help odeget**, **help odeset**, **help odeplot**, etc.

7.3.1 First order differential equations

Referring to the subsection 7.2.1, we solved the differential equation $\frac{dy}{dx}=4x^4y^2$ with the initial condition $y=2$ when $x=0$. Its particular solution was found as $y=\frac{-10}{8x^5-5}$. Let us compute the solution y from x =0 to x =0.5 with the step size 0.1. Attached on the upper right side is the computed value for the y under the heading analytical solution. Our objective is to obtain the identical numerical solution while employing the ODE solver.

The numerical solution of the differential equation is also attached on the right side under the heading numerical first order ODE solving. We attempt to solve the differential equation utilizing the ODE solver **ode23** which uses the Runge-Katta 2 and 3 order method. To make the solver operational, the given differential equation must be written as $\frac{dy}{dx}=f(x, y)$, step C from the beginning discussion. Fortunately the given equation is in that form. Type the two line code as presented on the right in a new M-file (step A) and save the file by the name **f** in your working path. The derivative term $\frac{dy}{dx}$ is assumed to be any user-given

Analytical solution:

at x	value of $y=\frac{-10}{8x^5-5}$
0	2
0.1	2
0.2	2.001
0.3	2.0078
0.4	2.0333
0.5	2.1053

Numerical first order ODE solving:

M-file for $\frac{dy}{dx}=4x^4y^2$ **:**

```
function dy=f(x,y)
dy=4*x^4*y^2;
```

Calling the ODE solver for the numerical solution:

```
>>[x y]=ode23('f',[0:0.1:0.5],2); ↵
>>[x y] ↵

ans =

        0   2.0000
   0.1000   2.0000
   0.2000   2.0010
   0.3000   2.0078
   0.4000   2.0333
   0.5000   2.1052
     ↑        ↑
```

values of x values of y

name **dy** and the functional return also happens to the same **dy** which is placed after the reserve word **function** (one space gap before **dy**). The function **f** has two input arguments in the M-file, the first and second of which correspond to the independent and dependent variables in the given differential equation respectively. We write the vector code (section 14.2) of the right side of the rearranged differential equation. However we call the solver **ode23** as shown above on the right side. The **ode23** has three input arguments, the first, second, and third of which are the function file name under a quote, required independent variable variation as a row matrix (section 1.3, here it is the x values we are interested at), and the value of y at x =0 respectively (step G). There are two output arguments in the **ode23** indicated by **[x y]** (can be any user-given name for example **[u v]**), the first and second of which are the x and y values of the given equation we are interested at but both returns are as a column matrix of identical size. From x =0 to x =0.5 with the step size 0.1, there are 6 points so the length of the column matrix **x** or **y** is 6. We called **[x y]** just to see the contents in the following line.

As the return says the analytical and the numerical solutions are identical at least up to 3 decimal places. As far as the fourth digit is concern, slight discrepancy is seen. Let us not expect too much from a machine. Nevertheless one can obtain the exact solution by changing the default relative error. However from this comparison, the numerical computational power of the **ode23** is easily understood.

Solve the following first order differential equations numerically applying ongoing function and symbology:

A. $\frac{du}{dt}=\frac{-t^2+e^t}{u}$ from $t=1$ to $t=1.5$ with step size 0.1 subject to $u(1)=-3$

B. $(x^2+y^3)\frac{dy}{dx}=x+\sinh y$ from $x=0$ to $x=0.3$ with step size 0.05 subject to $y(0)=5$

Problem A

The independent and dependent variables are t and u respectively. It is given that the analytical solution of the equation is $u=-\sqrt{-\frac{2t^3}{3}+2e^t+\frac{29}{3}-2e}$. Upon the insertion of various t values, we end up with the u values as presented in the next page table on the upper left side. The equation is already in rearranged form. We write the code for the right side of the equation as (-t^2+exp(t))/u along with du for $\frac{du}{dt}$. The complete code of the M-file is also presented in the table on the lower left corner. Type the code in a new M-file, save the file by the name f, and call the ode23 as shown in the table. The second input argument of the ode23 now indicates the t variation from 1 to 1.5 with a step 0.1. The third input argument of the solver is the initial value of u at t =1.

Analytical solution for the problem A:		Numerical solution for problem A: Calling the ODE solver for the numerical solution:	Numerical solution for problem B: M-file for the problem B:

at t	value of $u = -\sqrt{-\frac{2t^3}{3}+2e^t+\frac{29}{3}-2e}$	`>>[t u]=ode23('f',[1:0.1:1.5],-3); ↵`
		`>>[t u] ↵`
			`function dy=f(x,y)`
			`dy=(x+sinh(y))/(x^2+y^3);`
			Calling the ODE solver:
			`>>[x y]=ode23('f',[0:.05:0.3],5); ↵`
			`>>[x y] ↵`

1 1.1 1.2 1.3 1.4 1.5	-3 −3.058 −3.1174 −3.1787 −3.2421 −3.3081	ans = 1.0000 -3.0000 1.1000 -3.0580 1.2000 -3.1174 1.3000 -3.1787 1.4000 -3.2421 1.5000 -3.3081 ↑ ↑ values of t values of u	ans = 0 5.0000 0.0500 5.0299 0.1000 5.0601 0.1500 5.0908 0.2000 5.1218 0.2500 5.1533 0.3000 5.1852 ↑ ↑ values of x values of y

M-file for $\frac{du}{dt}=\frac{-t^2+e^t}{u}$:
`function du=f(t,u)`
`du=(-t^2+exp(t))/u;`			

Problem B

Not all first order differential equations have the close form analytical solution. $(x^2+y^3)\frac{dy}{dx}=x+\sinh y$ is such an example. Having gone through the ongoing examples, we extrapolate our concept to seek the numerical solution of the ODE for which we need the rearranged form $\frac{dy}{dx}=\frac{x+\sinh y}{x^2+y^3}$ and whose M-file code and solver calling are also placed in above table on the right side. The execution steps for the implementation are similar to those of the other two. It goes without saying that the numerical solution is possible despite the unavailability of the analytical solution. The only thing is we can not compare the output with the exact value. Having verified the other two equations, we have the reason to rely on the ode23.

7.3.2 Second order differential equations

To elucidate the numerical computation of a second order ordinary differential equation, let us consider the second order nonhomogeneous equation $2\frac{d^2y}{dx^2}-5\frac{dy}{dx}+2y=x$ subject to the initial conditions $\begin{Bmatrix} y(0)=2 \\ y'(0)=-3 \end{Bmatrix}$ whose analytical solution is found to be $y(x)=\frac{5}{4}+\frac{x}{2}-\frac{31}{12}e^{2x}+\frac{10}{3}e^{\frac{x}{2}}$ and $\frac{dy(x)}{dx}=\frac{1}{2}-\frac{31}{6}e^{2x}+\frac{5}{3}e^{\frac{x}{2}}$. We intend to have the numerical solution from $x=0$ to $x=0.5$ with the step size 0.1. Attached on the right side is the computed data for the solution which we are supposed to get from MATLAB.

Analytical solution of $2\frac{d^2y}{dx^2}-5\frac{dy}{dx}+2y=x$:		
Value of x	Value of $y(x)$	Value of $\frac{dy}{dx}$
0	2	−3
0.1	1.6489	−4.0585
0.2	1.18	−5.3658
0.3	0.5656	−6.9779
0.4	−0.228	−8.963
0.5	−1.2421	−11.4044

The solver ode23 also numerically solves a second order ordinary differential equation of the form $\frac{d^2y}{dx^2}=f\left(x,\ y,\ \frac{dy}{dx}\right)$ but some mathematical juggling is associated with the M-file description of the differential equation. The differential equation must hold the second order term on the left and others on the right. The bottom line is whatever be the order, we first transform the given differential equation to a set of first order linear equations taking some substitution and then seek for the solution. For the second order, there should be two linear equations (three equations for the third order, and so on). The number of dependent variables must be equal to the order of the given equation and in the transformed set there should not be any derivative, only must exist the dependent variables considered for the substitution. The substitution starts by writing the given dependent variable as the first variable in the transformed set of the first orders from what $y_1=y$ and $\frac{dy_1}{dx}=\frac{dy}{dx}=y_2$. We rewrite the given equation as $\frac{d^2y}{dx^2}=\frac{5}{2}\frac{dy}{dx}-y+\frac{x}{2}$ on that we have the transformed two equation set as $\begin{Bmatrix} \frac{dy_1}{dx} = y_2 \\ \frac{dy_2}{dx} = \frac{5}{2}y_2 - y_1 + \frac{x}{2} \end{Bmatrix}$. Note that all first order derivatives are on the left and others are on the right but no derivative is on the right of the set. Attached on the right side is the M-file as well as the numerical solution for the differential equation. The dy (any user-given name) corresponds to the two first order derivatives in the transformed set but as a two element row matrix (for the third order differential equation it becomes three element, and so on) whose consistency is dy(1)$\Leftrightarrow \frac{dy_1}{dx}$ and dy(2)$\Leftrightarrow \frac{dy_2}{dx}$. Not only the derivatives, the new dependent variables in the first order set also observe the following: y(1)$\Leftrightarrow y_1$ and y(2)$\Leftrightarrow y_2$ where y is a two element row matrix (for the third order differential equation it becomes three element that is y(3)$\Leftrightarrow y_3$, and so on). The input arguments in the f(x,y) correspond to the independent and dependent variables respectively. Referring to the last line of the function file, we write dy=dy'; because ode23 needs column vector to be executable since initially we form the dy as a row matrix (just to transpose the row matrix to a column one). Anyhow type the codes in a new M-file, save the file by the name f, and call the solver as shown on the right. The second input argument of the ode23 is the required x variation as a row matrix. The third input argument of the ode23 holds the two initial conditions as a two element row matrix but in order that is first $y(0)=2$ and then $y'(0)=-3$. The ode23 is also capable of returning the numerical $\frac{dy}{dx}$ for the same interval of x when solving a second order equation. The output argument x holds the x values as a column matrix whereas the y holds the $y(x)$ and $\frac{dy}{dx}$ values as two columns respectively. The commands y(:,1) and y(:,2) provide the $y(x)$ and $\frac{dy}{dx}$ values separately but both as a column matrix. Once again the initial values of $y(x)$ and $\frac{dy}{dx}$ must correspond to the first element of the second input argument [0:0.1:0.5].

Numerical solution for the ODE:

M-file for $2\frac{d^2y}{dx^2} - 5\frac{dy}{dx} + 2y = x$ **:**

```
function dy=f(x,y)
dy(1)=y(2);
dy(2)=5/2*y(2)-y(1)+x/2;
dy=dy';
```

Calling the ODE solver for the numerical solution:

```
>>[x y]=ode23('f',[0:0.1:0.5],[2 -3]); ↵
>>[x y] ↵

ans =
        0    2.0000   -3.0000
   0.1000    1.6490   -4.0584
   0.2000    1.1801   -5.3657
   0.3000    0.5657   -6.9777
   0.4000   -0.2278   -8.9626
   0.5000   -1.2419  -11.4039
     ↑         ↑         ↑
```

values of x values of y values of $\frac{dy}{dx}$

7.3.3 Higher order differential equations

The concept, function, and symbology illustrated in the last subsection can easily be extended to the higher order equations. We demonstrate that taking the third order Euler differential equation $6t^3\frac{d^3u}{dt^3} - 7t^2\frac{d^2u}{dt^2} + 9t\frac{du}{dt} - 4u = 3t - 3$ under the initial conditions $\begin{Bmatrix} u''(1)=1 \\ u'(1)=3 \\ u(1)=0 \end{Bmatrix}$ from $t=1$ to $t=1.25$ with the step 0.05. It is given that $u(t) = \left(\frac{1017}{484} - \frac{27}{22}\ln t\right)t^2 + \frac{3}{5}t - \frac{2088}{605}t^{\frac{1}{6}} + \frac{3}{4}$, $\frac{du(t)}{dt} = \left(\frac{360}{121} - \frac{27}{11}\ln t\right)t + \frac{3}{5} - \frac{348}{605}t^{-\frac{5}{6}}$ and $\frac{d^2u(t)}{dt^2} = \frac{63}{121} + \frac{58}{121}t^{-\frac{11}{6}} - \frac{27}{11}\ln t$ is the close form solution of the equation. At the indicated points we computed the values of $u(t)$, $\frac{du(t)}{dt}$, and $\frac{d^2u(t)}{dt^2}$ and placed them on the right table what we are supposed to obtain.

Analytical solution of $6t^3\frac{d^3u}{dt^3} - 7t^2\frac{d^2u}{dt^2} + 9t\frac{du}{dt} - 4u = 3t - 3$ **:**

Value of t	Value of $u(t)$	Value of $\frac{du(t)}{dt}$	Value of $\frac{d^2u(t)}{dt^2}$
1	0	3	1
1.05	0.1512	3.0459	0.8392
1.1	0.3045	3.0841	0.6892
1.15	0.4595	3.115	0.5486
1.2	0.6159	3.1391	0.4163
1.25	0.7733	3.1568	0.2913

Let us pay attention to the numerical solution notifying that the dependent and independent variables are u and t respectively. As indicated in the last subsection, we perform some substitutions like $u_1 = u$, $u_2 = \frac{du}{dt}$, and $u_3 = \frac{d^2u}{dt^2}$ in order to transform the given equation to a set of three first order linear equations on that $\frac{du_1}{dt} = \frac{du}{dt} = u_2$ and $\frac{du_2}{dt} = \frac{d^2u}{dt^2} = u_3$.

We rewrite the given equation to have $\frac{d^3u}{dt^3} =$

$$\frac{3t - 3 + 7t^2 \frac{d^2u}{dt^2} - 9t\frac{du}{dt} + 4u}{6t^3} = \frac{3t - 3 + 7t^2u_3 - 9tu_2 + 4u_1}{6t^3}$$

thereby providing the system of differential equations pertaining to the u_1, u_2, and u_3 as $\left\{\begin{array}{l} \frac{du_1}{dt} = u_2 \\ \frac{du_2}{dt} = u_3 \\ \frac{du_3}{dt} = \frac{3t - 3 + 7t^2u_3 - 9tu_2 + 4u_1}{6t^3} \end{array}\right\}$.

Now is the time to give the MATLAB codes to the system. The new dependent variables u_1, u_2, and u_3 and the new derivatives $\frac{du_1}{dt}$, $\frac{du_2}{dt}$, and $\frac{du_3}{dt}$ are inserted by u(1), u(2), and u(3) and du(1), du(2), and du(3) respectively. The expression $\frac{3t - 3 + 7t^2u_3 - 9tu_2 + 4u_1}{6t^3}$ in the third equation is stringed as (3*t-3+7*t^2*u(3)-9*t*u(2)+4*u(1))/t^3/6. Shown above on the right side is the computation conducted numerically using the ode23. On comparison of the analytical with the numerical solutions, it is understandable that the accuracy of numerical computation is greatly appreciated.

Numerical solution for the ODE:

M-file for $6t^3\frac{d^3u}{dt^3} - 7t^2\frac{d^2u}{dt^2} + 9t\frac{du}{dt} - 4u = 3t - 3$:

```
function du=f(t,u)
du(1)=u(2);
du(2)=u(3);
du(3)=(3*t-3+7*t^2*u(3)-9*t*u(2)+4*u(1))/t^3/6;
du=du';
```

Calling the ODE solver for the numerical solution:

```
>>[t u]=ode23('f',[1:0.05:1.25],[0 3 1]); ↵
>>[t u] ↵

ans =

    1.0000         0    3.0000    1.0000
    1.0500    0.1512    3.0459    0.8392
    1.1000    0.3045    3.0841    0.6892
    1.1500    0.4595    3.1150    0.5486
    1.2000    0.6159    3.1391    0.4163
    1.2500    0.7733    3.1568    0.2913
      ↑         ↑         ↑         ↑
```

values of t u $\frac{du}{dt}$ $\frac{d^2u}{dt^2}$

The procedure we applied with the ode23 solver equally applies to any other solver placed in the table 7.A.

7.3.4 System of differential equations

Actually the system of differential equations should have been treated first because of its proximity in the M-file code writing of the differential equation solver. In the subsection 7.2.4, we illustrated that $\begin{bmatrix} y_1 \\ y_2 \end{bmatrix} = \begin{bmatrix} -\frac{3}{5}e^t + \frac{8}{5}e^{6t} \\ \frac{6}{5}e^t + \frac{4}{5}e^{6t} \end{bmatrix}$ is the solution of the system $\left\{\begin{array}{l} \frac{dy_1}{dt} = 5y_1 + 2y_2 \\ \frac{dy_2}{dt} = 2y_1 + 2y_2 \end{array}\right\}$ contingent to the initial conditions $\left\{\begin{array}{l} y_1(0) = 1 \\ y_2(0) = 2 \end{array}\right\}$. Let us consider that the solution is required from t =0 to 0.5 with a step 0.1. Using the expressions for the y_1 and y_2, we calculated the values of the dependent variables and placed them on the right side. Our objective is to obtain the solution.

In the numerical solution of the system of differential equations, we apply the same solver, each equation in the system must be of the first order, and the given system must be rearranged so that all first order derivatives are on the left and others on the right. Fortunately the given equation is so. On having the rearranged set, we follow the technique in the M-file code writing according to the last two subsections. Also attached on the right side is the numerical solution of the system. The code correspondence is dy(1)⇔$\frac{dy_1}{dt}$, dy(2)⇔$\frac{dy_2}{dt}$, y(1)⇔y_1, and y(2)⇔y_2. The third input argument of the ode23 is the initial conditions for the two dependent variables in the system respectively. Now the return

Analytical solution of the system:

Value of t	Value of y_1	Value of y_2
0	1.0000	2.0000
0.1	2.2523	2.7839
0.2	4.5793	4.1218
0.3	8.8695	6.4595
0.4	16.7420	10.6087
0.5	31.1476	18.0469

Numerical solution for the system:

M-file for the system:

```
function dy=f(t,y)
dy(1)=5*y(1)+2*y(2);
dy(2)=2*y(1)+2*y(2);
dy=dy';
```

Calling the ODE solver for the numerical solution:

```
>>[t y]=ode23('f',[0:0.1:0.5],[1 2]); ↵
>>[t y] ↵

ans =

         0    1.0000    2.0000
    0.1000    2.2514    2.7835
    0.2000    4.5755    4.1198
    0.3000    8.8580    6.4538
    0.4000   16.7126   10.5940
    0.5000   31.0830   18.0146
      ↑         ↑         ↑
```

values of t y_1 y_2

to the **y** is solution of the dependent variables as the column matrix for the y_1 and y_2 respectively (unlike the previous cases). In order to have the values for the y_1 and y_2 separated, one can use the commands y(:,1) and y(:,2) respectively.

As another example, we present only the numerical solution of the system $\begin{cases} \frac{dx}{dt} = 31x - 21y + 9z - e^{-3t} \\ \frac{dy}{dt} = 44x - 30y + 12z + 2t \\ \frac{dz}{dt} = -22x + 14y - 8z + \sin t \end{cases}$ satisfying the initial conditions $\begin{cases} x(0) = -2 \\ y(0) = 1 \\ z(0) = 0 \end{cases}$ presented in the subsection 7.2.4. We wish to compute the solution for t =0 to 0.25 with a step 0.05.

Attached on the right side is the solution in which the related variable or its derivative consistency is as follows: dy(1)⇔ $\frac{dx}{dt}$, dy(2)⇔ $\frac{dy}{dt}$, dy(3)⇔ $\frac{dz}{dt}$, y(1)⇔ x, y(2)⇔ y, and y(3)⇔ z. Now the return to the y is a three column matrix, the three dependent variables respectively. Individual solution can be picked up by writing y(:,1), y(:,2), and y(:,3) for the x, y, and z respectively.

Numerical solution for the second system:
M-file for the system:

```
function dy=f(t,y)
dy(1)=31*y(1)-21*y(2)+9*y(3)-exp(-3*t);
dy(2)=44*y(1)-30*y(2)+12*y(3)+2*t;
dy(3)=-22*y(1)+14*y(2)-8*y(3)+sin(t);
dy=dy';
```

Calling the ODE solver for numerical solution:

```
>>[t y]=ode23('f',[0:0.05:0.25],[-2 1 0]); ↵
>>[t y] ↵

ans =
        0   -2.0000    1.0000         0
   0.0500   -5.7299   -4.2609    2.5853
   0.1000   -8.6252   -8.3851    4.6113
   0.1500  -10.8271  -11.5618    6.1717
   0.2000  -12.4558  -13.9528    7.3467
   0.2500  -13.6138  -15.6957    8.2042
     ↑          ↑         ↑         ↑
 values of t    x         y         z
```

Since we have the y as the dependent variable, we could have employed any other variable not to be mixed up but that is not a problem to a machine which is obvious from above implementation.

7.3.5 Some factors to be considered for the ODE solution

Inserting the input and obtaining the output for all ODE functions presented in table 7.A are executed in the same way as executed for the ode23 in the preceding sections. Of coarse the higher order approximation of the dependent variable would give the result that is close to the exact. From ODE theory we know that the Runge-Kutta 4-5 order (whose MATLAB counterpart is ode45) is more accurate than the Runge-Kutta 2-3 (ode23). Computationally we wish to prove that here. Let us pick up the example of the subsection 7.3.2. We exercised both the ode23 and ode45 on the M-file written for the differential equation. The comprehensive outcome is the following:

Exact solution:			Numerical solution with ode23:	Numerical solution with ode45:
x	y	$\frac{dy}{dx}$	>>[x y]=ode23('f',[0:0.1:0.5],[2 -3]); ↵ >>[x y] ↵	>>[x y]=ode45('f',[0:0.1:0.5],[2 -3]); ↵ >>[x y] ↵
0 0.1 0.2 0.3 0.4 0.5	2 1.6489 1.18 0.5656 −0.228 −1.2421	−3 −4.0585 −5.3658 −6.9779 −8.963 −11.4044	ans = 0 2.0000 -3.0000 0.1000 1.6490 -4.0584 0.2000 1.1801 -5.3657 0.3000 0.5657 -6.9777 0.4000 -0.2278 -8.9626 0.5000 -1.2419 -11.4039 ↑ ↑ ↑ x y $\frac{dy}{dx}$	ans = 0 2.0000 -3.0000 0.1000 1.6489 -4.0585 0.2000 1.1800 -5.3658 0.3000 0.5656 -6.9779 0.4000 -0.2280 -8.9630 0.5000 -1.2421 -11.4044 ↑ ↑ ↑ x y $\frac{dy}{dx}$

One can inspect that the numerical output making the use of the ode45 (higher order) becomes exact.

This might not be true always because the choice of the relative or absolute error in the numerical computation is a factor of the accuracy too. The default relative error of the ode23 is 10^{-3}. What if one tries to find the solution of the ongoing ODE with the relative error 10^{-6} ? To argument the relative error, another function called odeset is used. The relative error is a property of the differential equation solver, which is notified by the reserve word RelTol (abbreviation for the Relative Tolerance). The execution is presented on the right side in which the user option is assigned to some workspace variable O (can be any user-given name). The odeset has two input arguments, the first and second of which are the reserve word under quote and the specified relative error respectively (10^{-6} ⇔1e-6). When we call the solver, the O becomes the last input argument of the ode23. As the return says, reducing the relative error from 10^{-3} to 10^{-6} makes the solution exact.

Calling ode23 using specific relative tolerance:

```
>>O=odeset('RelTol',1e-6); ↵
>>[x y]=ode23('f',[0:0.1:0.5],[2 -3],O); ↵
>>[x y] ↵

ans =
        0    2.0000   -3.0000
   0.1000    1.6489   -4.0585
   0.2000    1.1800   -5.3658
   0.3000    0.5656   -6.9779
   0.4000   -0.2280   -8.9630
   0.5000   -1.2421  -11.4044
```

Either increasing the approximation order or reducing the relative error yields better solution.

◆◆ **Critical cases**

There are instances when the numerical method would fail. Referring to subsection 7.3.1, we solved $\frac{dy}{dx}=4x^4y^2$ from interval $x=0$ to $x=0.5$. Let us try to solve the equation from $x=0$ to $x=1.5$ with the same step size as follows:

```
>>[x y]=ode23('f',[0:0.1:1.5],2); ↵

Warning: Failure at t=9.105613e-001. Unable to meet integration tolerances without reducing the step size below
the smallest value allowed (1.776357e-015) at time t.
> In ode23 at 346
```

What went wrong? We know that the analytical solution is $y=\frac{-10}{8x^5-5}$. Setting the denominator $8x^5-5$ to 0 provides $x=\sqrt[5]{\frac{5}{8}}=0.9103$. At $x=\sqrt[5]{\frac{5}{8}}$, y becomes undefined that is why above warning message is appearing. Over the required interval of x, there must not be any x at which the y is undefined or infinite. Under these circumstances, analytical solution might be possible but not the numerical one.

7.3.6 Graphing the ODE solution

Graphing the ODE solution means graphing the dependent or its derivative against the independent variable. Graphing the solution appears as two situations – symbolic and numerical. We address both of them in the following.

Recall that the symbolic differential equation solver dsolve returns the close form expression as a string and which we assigned in the workspace variable S in all symbolic solutions. For a single graph, the ezplot of the subsection 13.1.1 is the best option.

Graphing the symbolic solution:

```
>>S=dsolve('Dy=4*x^4*y^2','y(0)=2','x'); ↵
>>ezplot(S,[0 5]) ↵
```

Let us say the solution of the example B of subsection 7.2.1 is to be graphed (that is y versus x graph) over $0\le x\le 5$ for which we exercise above right side attached commands. We did not show the graph for space reason but MATLAB will not disappoint you. The workspace S is holding the solution string for the $y=\frac{-10}{8x^5-5}$. If you say I need to calculate the solution over $0\le x\le 0.5$ with a step 0.1 from S, we first generate the x vector with given step size and then calculate the functional value of y at every x point (which is stored in x) using the function subs as shown below.

Again let us say we have to calculate the derivative $\frac{dy}{dx}$ over the same x interval. We find the derivative using the diff of section 5.3, assign that to some variable d, and calculate the derivative values using the subs as attached on the right side. The commands plot(x,y) and plot(x,d1) show y versus x and $\frac{dy}{dx}$ versus x graphs from the computed data respectively (section 13.2 for the plot, graph is not shown for the space reason). If the graph of y and $\frac{dy}{dx}$ on common x needs to be plotted, we exercise the command plot(x,y,x,d1). In a similar fashion one can graph the higher order derivatives as well.

Calculation of the solution or its derivatives:

```
>>x=0:0.1:0.5; y=subs(S) ↵ ← y holds y values

y =

    2.0000    2.0000    2.0010    2.0078    2.0333    2.1053

>>d=diff(S); ↵        ← d holds the string for dy/dx

>>d1=subs(d) ↵        ← d1 holds the computed values of dy/dx

d1 =

     0    0.0016    0.0256    0.1306    0.4234    1.1080
```

As you see, the function plot is a plotter from the numerical data. The return from the numerical solver ode23 is already in numerical data form and we employ the plot to graph the solution in the order just mentioned. As an example, let us graph the solution of the subsection 7.3.2. From the implementation we know that the first two columns of the y are holding the solutions for the y and $\frac{dy}{dx}$ respectively. Having the solution available, the command plot(x,y(:,1),x,y(:,2)) graphs the y and $\frac{dy}{dx}$ on common x values.

Anyhow we desist the session of the ordinary differential equations with this. We hope that the simplest problems outlined as they happen to be in pure mathematics would substantiate the reader in applying the ordinary differential equations in applied sciences and engineering.

Chapter 8

This chapter elucidates the implementation of most common continuous and discrete transforms. Functional analysis through Fourier or Laplace domain is very common in scientific and engineering problems. The transform terminology always follows one common notion that is the forward-inverse or in other words the analysis-synthesis approach. Explicitly direct implementation of the transform is presented but efficient computational algorithm might be inherent to the terminology which is not discussed at all. Our implementations outline the following:

- Fourier analysis strategy and various series expansions of the continuous periodic functions
- Forward and inverse Fourier transforms applied to the nonperiodic functions
- Discrete Fourier transform for discrete functions in the forward and inverse domains
- Laplace transform of continuous functions both in forward and inverse domains
- Z transform for the discrete functions in the forward and inverse domains

8.1 What is Fourier analysis?

Fourier analysis is fundamentally the decomposition of any function in terms of the sinusoidal functions. The reason for the analysis is that the sine function has well-defined functional characteristics such as frequency, time period, etc. The selection of the Fourier method depends on the nature and properties of a function. Again the sine function has different forms of representation for example the cosine function is a shifted sine function. The complex exponential is also a sine function with appropriate translation, rotation, or scaling. In a broad context the functions that enfold the Fourier analysis are $\begin{Bmatrix} periodic \\ nonperiodic \end{Bmatrix}$ and $\begin{Bmatrix} continuous \\ discrete \end{Bmatrix}$. In the subsequent sections very briefly we highlight how one utilizes MATLAB to implement different classes of Fourier terminology to different functions. All Fourier analysis has the transform domain expression and its inverse. The transform domain expression can be real or complex. The inversion of the transform is just turning to the domain of the function we start with.

8.2 Fourier series of continuous periodic functions

Fourier series of a periodic function $f(t)$ with a period T expresses the function in terms of the discrete sinusoidal functions. Figure 8.1(a) presents the basic concept behind the Fourier series analysis. Theoretically the continuous function $f(t)$ is the sum of infinite continuous sinusoidal functions. The sinusoidal functions appear either in real or complex form however brief descriptions of various form Fourier series are as follows:

Real form 1: $f(t)=\frac{A_0}{2}+\sum_{n=1}^{\infty}\left(A_n\cos\frac{2\pi nt}{T}+B_n\sin\frac{2\pi nt}{T}\right)$ where the coefficients A_n and B_n are given by $A_n=\frac{2}{T}\int_T f(t)\cos\frac{2\pi nt}{T}dt$ and $B_n=\frac{2}{T}\int_T f(t)\sin\frac{2\pi nt}{T}dt$. Component sinusoidal function frequencies are related with the n whose variations are n=0, 1, 2, ...etc for A_n and n=1, 2, ...etc for B_n. For each value of n, we have one sine function and the function is called a harmonic. The symbol $\int_T$ indicates the integration over one period T as the function $f(t)$ is defined. The term $\frac{A_0}{2}$ in the expansion is called the average value of the periodic function $f(t)$.

Real form 2: $f(t)=\frac{A_0}{2}+\sum_{n=1}^{\infty}C_n\cos\left(\frac{2\pi nt}{T}-\varphi_n\right)$ where $C_n=\sqrt{A_n^2+B_n^2}$ and $\varphi_n=\tan^{-1}\frac{B_n}{A_n}$. The meanings of the symbols are identical with those of the real form 1.

Complex form: $f(t)=\sum_{n=-\infty}^{\infty}C_n\, e^{j\frac{2\pi nt}{T}}$ where the coefficients are given by $C_n=\frac{1}{T}\int_T f(t)e^{-j\frac{2\pi nt}{T}}dt$ and the other symbols in the expression have the real form mentioned meanings (section 10.2 for j).

The term $\frac{2\pi}{T}$ is the angular frequency ω in radian/sec if T is in second. From the function description, one period of the function may appear from $-\frac{T}{2}$ to $\frac{T}{2}$, 0 to T, or other and the limits of the integration are set accordingly. We maintain the font equivalence like n⇔n in the following discussions.

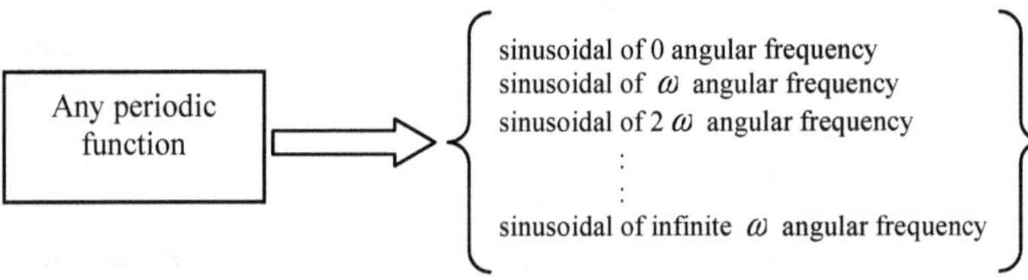

Figure 8.1(a) The basic idea behind the Fourier series

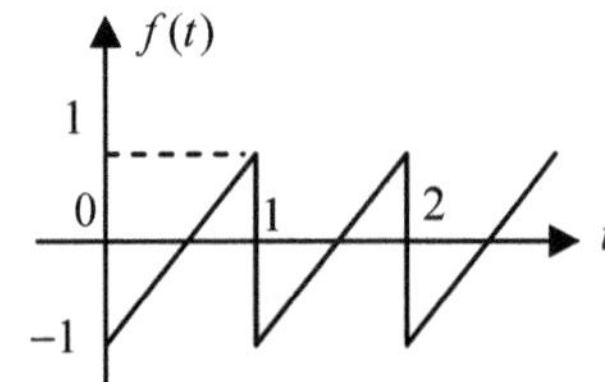

Figure 8.1(b) A sawtooth function

8.2.1 Symbolic Fourier series coefficients

Finding Fourier series means finding the discrete coefficients A_n, B_n, C_n, and φ_n from the given continuous periodic function $f(t)$. We employ the **int** function (section 6.2) to obtain the integration for various coefficients since no built-in function is available for the series computation to date. In symbolic computation, we do not use decimal or exponential data form for example 0.2 is written as $\frac{2}{10}$. Also the exponential form 10^{-3} is written as $\frac{1}{1000}$. Prior to the integration, we declare the integrand variables using the command **syms** (section 2.1). Let us go through the following examples regarding the symbolic coefficient finding.

Example 1

Let us find the real form 1 Fourier series coefficients for the function of the figure 8.1(b). The function has the period T=1 and the equation $f(t)=2t-1$ starting from t=0. The coefficients should be $A_n=2\int_0^1(2t-1)\cos 2\pi nt\,dt=0$ and $B_n=2\int_0^1(2t-1)\sin 2\pi nt\,dt=-\frac{2}{\pi n}$. Attached on the upper right side in the next page is the computation for the coefficients. There are two independent variables in each integrand – n and t which need to be declared using the **syms** in the first command line. The vector codes (section 14.2) for the integrands $(2t-1)\cos 2\pi nt$ and $(2t-1)\sin 2\pi nt$ are (2*t-1)* cos(2*pi*n*t) and (2*t-1)*sin(2*pi*n*t) respectively. Concerning the second line of the execution, we performed the integration using the **int** and assigned the result to the workspace An (can be any user-given name). At this point the An holds the vector code of the return from the **int**. The command **simple** finds the simplified form of the code stored in An and **pretty** (section 3.1) displays the readable form on that. The A_n which is held in An is supposed to be 0 but that is not the result. This is all because of the integer n. MATLAB does not possess any information about the variable n. We utilize the **assume** function of the **maple** (section 3.2) to pass the information that n is an integer. The **assume** has two input arguments, the first and second of which are the variable name (which is n) and the reserve word integer in maple respectively. The maple also has simplifying function by the name simplify. The command maple('simplify',An) performs simplification on the codes stored in An whose outcome we again assigned to An but in MATLAB confirming that A_n=0. The computation of the B_n is very similar to that of the A_n which is also presented after the execution of A_n. Once the integer condition is declared in maple, it remains active. If you intend to remove the integer condition from the maple, exercise the command clear maplemex at the command prompt.

Fourier series: Example 1: execution for A_n:

```
>>syms n t ↵
>>An=2*int((2*t-1)*cos(2*pi*n*t),t,0,1) ↵

An =

2*(cos(pi*n)^2-1+pi*n*sin(pi*n)*cos(pi*n))/pi^2/n^2
>>pretty(simple(An)) ↵
         cos(2 pi n) - 1 + pi n sin(2 pi n)
         ----------------------------------
                        2  2
                      pi  n
>>maple('assume(n,integer)'); ↵
>>An=maple('simplify',An) ↵

An =

0
```

Execution for B_n:

```
>>Bn=2*int((2*t-1)*sin(2*pi*n*t),t,0,1); ↵
>>Bn=maple('simplify',Bn) ↵

Bn =

-2/pi/n
```

Example 2

Example 1 demonstrates the finding of the Fourier series coefficients for the real form 1. In this example we intend to find the real form 2 Fourier series coefficients (that is C_n and φ_n) for the periodic function mentioned in the example 1. The computation provides us $C_n = \frac{2}{n\pi}$ and $\varphi_n = \frac{\pi}{2}$. The workspace variables An and Bn of the example 1 hold the codes for the coefficients A_n and B_n respectively. The C_n and φ_n just need writing the vector codes of $\sqrt{A_n^2 + B_n^2}$ and $\tan^{-1}\frac{B_n}{A_n}$ which are sqrt(An^2+Bn^2) and atan(Bn/An) respectively and whose implementations are shown on the right side. We assigned the returns to the workspace Cn and Phin (can be any user-chosen name) which refer to C_n and φ_n respectively. The simplification on Cn is further conducted by using the command Cn= maple('simplify',Cn) which should return the code for $\frac{2}{n\pi}$.

Coefficient for the example 2:

```
>>Cn=sqrt(An^2+Bn^2) ↵ ← Cn⇔ C_n

Cn =

2/pi*(1/n^2)^(1/2)
>>Phin=atan(Bn/An) ↵     ← Phin⇔ φ_n

Phin =

1/2*pi
```

Coefficient for the example 3:

```
>>syms n t ↵
>>Cn=int((2*t-1)*exp(-j*2*pi*n*t),t,0,1) ↵

Cn =

i/pi/n
```

Example 3

In this example we wish to find the complex Fourier series coefficient for the periodic function of the example 1. Plugging the periodic function parameters, one obtains $C_n = \int_0^1 (2t-1)e^{-j2\pi nt} dt = \frac{j}{\pi n}$ with integer n. Applying ongoing functions and symbology, we carry out the execution as shown above. The function int in general works for the complex functions. In the implementation the vector code for $(2t-1)e^{-j2\pi nt}$ is (2*t-1)*exp(-j*2*pi*n*t) where j or i is the imaginary number in MATLAB. We assigned the return to the workspace Cn which is our complex C_n.

Example 4

In the last three examples we elaborately implemented the findings of Fourier series coefficients for all three forms for a single periodic function. We wish to find the same for the periodic function of the figure 8.1(c). The function in one period is defined by $\begin{Bmatrix} f(t) = 3t & for\ 0 \le t \le 1 \\ f(t) = 3 - 3t & for\ 1 \le t \le 2 \end{Bmatrix}$. Subsection 3.11.1 mentioned maple function line helps us find the equation of a straight line passing through two points. In the period T=2 starting from 0 in the figure 8.1(c), there are two linear functions and there should be two integrations for every Fourier series coefficient.

Figure 8.1(c) A triangular function

Computed Fourier series coefficients are as follows: $A_n = \int_0^1 3t\cos\pi nt\, dt + \int_1^2 (3-3t)\cos\pi nt\, dt = 6\frac{(-1)^n - 1}{n^2\pi^2}$ and $B_n = \int_0^1 3t\sin\pi nt\, dt + \int_1^2 (3-3t)\sin\pi nt\, dt = -3\frac{(-1)^n - 1}{\pi n}$ for the real form 1, $C_n = \frac{-3((-1)^n - 1)\sqrt{4 + n^2\pi^2}}{n^2\pi^2}$ and $\varphi_n =$

$-\tan^{-1}\left(\frac{n\pi}{2}\right)$ for the real form 2, and $C_n=\frac{1}{2}\left(\int_0^1 3te^{-jn\pi t}dt+\int_1^2 (3-3t)e^{-jn\pi t}dt\right)=\frac{3[-\pi nj-2+2(-1)^n+(-1)^n\pi nj]}{2n^2\pi^2}$ for the complex form. Our objective is to have these coefficients.

Attached on the right is the computation of all three form coefficients. We have applied the functions and symbology of the last three examples. Various code equivalences are as follows: 3*t*cos(pi*n*t) ⇔ $3t\cos\pi nt$, (3-3*t)*cos(pi*n*t) ⇔ $(3-3t)\cos\pi nt$, n ⇔ n, t⇔ t, An⇔ A_n, Bn⇔ B_n, Cn ⇔ C_n, 3*t*exp(-j*pi*n*t)⇔ $3te^{-jn\pi t}$, (3-3*t)*exp(-j*pi*n*t) ⇔ $(3-3t)e^{-jn\pi t}$, and Phin⇔ φ_n. We applied simplify command of the maple for the simplification, but the command usually works for the complex numbers. The n~ means the real part of n where n is integer so n~ is equivalent to n in the executed coefficients. In maple the imaginary number is I (identical with the i or j of MATLAB) for this reason the return in the complex form is in terms of I.

Coefficient for the example 4: for the real form 1:

```
>>syms n t ↵
>>An=int(3*t*cos(pi*n*t),t,0,1)+int((3-3*t)*cos(pi*n*t),t,1,2); ↵
>>maple('assume(n,integer)'); An=maple('simplify',An); ↵
>>pretty(An) ↵
             n~
         (-1)   - 1
       6 ------------
              2   2
            pi  n~
>>Bn=int(3*t*sin(pi*n*t),t,0,1)+int((3-3*t)*sin(pi*n*t),t,1,2); ↵
>>Bn=maple('simplify',Bn); pretty(Bn) ↵
             n~
         (-1)   - 1
      -3 ----------
            pi n~
```

Coefficient for the example 4: for the real form 2:

```
>>Cn=sqrt(An^2+Bn^2); ↵
>>pretty(simple(Cn)) ↵
               n~          2   2 1/2
          ((-1)   - 1) (4 + pi  n~ )
       -3 ---------------------------
                      2   2
                    pi  n~
>>Phin=atan(Bn/An) ↵

Phin =

-atan(1/2*pi*n)
```

Coefficient for the example 4: for the complex form:

```
>>Cn=1/2*(int(3*t*exp(-j*pi*n*t),t,0,1)+int((3-3*t)*exp(-j*pi*n*t),t,1,2)); ↵
>>Cn=maple('simplify',Cn); pretty(Cn) ↵
                            n~         n~
           -pi n~ I - 2 + 2 (-1)   + (-1)   pi n~ I
       3/2 -----------------------------------------
                           2   2
                         pi  n~
```

8.2.2 Numeric Fourier series coefficients

In subsection 8.2.1 the implementation mainly highlights the symbolic or analytical form of the computation for any n or harmonic. Here we introduce the computational tactics for numeric harmonics. Fourier series coefficient expressions for the A_n, B_n, C_n, or φ_n must be available in the workspace of MATLAB before the numeric value finding. The command subs (abbreviation for the substitution) can be helpful in this regard. Let us consider the example 1 of the last subsection in which we have $B_n=-\frac{2}{n\pi}$ and the n can vary from 1 to infinity. The n =1 should provide us $B_1=-\frac{2}{\pi}=-0.6366$ and we find so as shown on the right side. We assume that the code for the B_n is available to Bn in the workspace from example 1 of the last subsection. The subs has two input arguments, the first and second of which are the name of the assignee holding the code and the value of the n we are interested at respectively (for symbolic output we used the sym, section 2.1). The return from the subs is assigned to B1 (can be any user-given name). If you wish to see the decimal value, exercise the command double on B1 which is also presented.

Again let us say we intend to find the values of B_n for n =1, 2, 3, and 4 and which should be $\left[-\frac{2}{\pi}\quad -\frac{1}{\pi}\quad -\frac{2}{3\pi}\quad -\frac{1}{2\pi}\right]$ and is conducted on the right side as well. The four values of n are written as the four element row matrix and over the matrix the sym is applied. If it is necessary, executing double(B) yields the four values in decimal form as a row matrix. The n values do not have to be consecutive for example writing the second argument as [4 2 3 1] returns the B_n value for n =4 first. The four n values could have been written as 1:4 according to MATLAB notation and the command would have been B=subs(Bn,sym(1:4)). Now we present three more examples on numerical Fourier series in the following.

Numeric coefficient: for a single n:

```
>>B1=subs(Bn,sym(1)) ↵

B1 =

-2/pi
>>double(B1) ↵

ans =
     -0.6366
```

Numeric coefficient: for multiple n:

```
>>B=subs(Bn,sym([1 2 3 4])) ↵

B =

[ -2/pi,  -1/pi, -2/3/pi, -1/2/pi]
```

Example 1

Let us find the average value (which should be zero looking at the graph) of the periodic function from A_n in the example 4 of the last subsection. The average value $\frac{A_0}{2}$ is obtained by setting n =0 in A_n. Since $A_n = 6\frac{(-1)^n - 1}{n^2\pi^2}$, setting n =0 results a form which is indeterminate (in this case $\frac{0}{0}$). The machine can not handle undefined expression. If we use **subs** for n =0, we see the return as **NaN** indicating not a number. We need to redo the computation for A_n. Start pressing the up-arrow key one at a time from the keyboard and you find the expression for **An**. Replace **n** by **0** and execute the command for **An** again. After that **An/2** provides the average value of the function. The limit taking might work for some indeterminate coefficients (section 5.1).

Example 2

Example 4 of last subsection also presents the finding of the real form 2 Fourier series coefficients. We wish to find the 3rd harmonic of the Fourier series expansion which are $C_3 = \frac{2\sqrt{4+9\pi^2}}{3\pi^2}$ and $\varphi_3 = -\tan^{-1}\left(\frac{3\pi}{2}\right)$ from setting n =3 in the respective expressions. We know that the workspace variables **Cn** and **Phin** hold the codes for the C_n and φ_n respectively. Right attached commands are conducted afterwards applying ongoing functions and symbology. The **C3** and **Phi3** (can be any user-given names) refer to C_3 and φ_3 respectively. If the reader is interested in finding the 3rd, 5th, and 7th harmonics, the command **subs(Cn,sym([3 5 7]))** can be exercised in which the required harmonics are placed as a three element row matrix as the second input argument of the **subs**. The decimal form of the coefficient is exhibited by using the command **double(subs(Cn,sym([3 5 7])))**. Similar computational style applies to the phase angle φ_n as well.

Numeric coefficient: example 2:

```
>>C3=subs(Cn,sym(3)); ↵
>>pretty(simple(C3)) ↵
                 2 1/2
        (4 + 9 pi  )
  2/3 ---------------
              2
            pi
>>Phi3=subs(Phin,sym(3)); ↵
>>pretty(Phi3) ↵
        -atan(3/2 pi)
```

Example 3

The complex form coefficient C_n cited in the example 4 of the last subsection is stored in the workspace variable **Cn**. Now we have only the complex coefficient C_n (redo the implementation). We intend to find the 3rd harmonic from the expression of C_n and which should be $C_3 = \frac{-4-6j\pi}{6\pi^2}$ setting n =3 in C_n. The implementation is included on the right side applying ongoing function and symbology (C3 $\Leftrightarrow C_3$). A set of harmonics can also be found as we did in previous examples but all coefficients will be complex. The command **double** for decimal finding equally applies here. The real, imaginary, magnitude, and phase angle separations from the complex coefficients take place using the commands **real**, **imag**, **abs**, and **angle** on C3 respectively.

Example 3:

```
>>C3=subs(Cn,sym(3)); ↵
>>pretty(C3) ↵
          -6 I pi - 4
     1/6 -------------
               2
             pi
```

8.2.3 Graphing Fourier series coefficients

Graphing the Fourier series coefficient means graphing the coefficients A_n, B_n, C_n, or φ_n against n as a discrete plot. Concerning their expressions as presented earlier, the values of the A_n, B_n, C_n, and φ_n are discrete and different for different n. MATLAB function **stem** (subsection 13.2.9) is the best option for discrete plotting of the Fourier series coefficients. From the expression of the coefficient, we first obtain the numerical value applying the functions of subsection 8.2.2 and then employ the function **stem**. The beginning example of last subsection presents that the workspace variable **B** holds the four harmonics as $\begin{bmatrix} -\frac{2}{\pi} & -\frac{1}{\pi} & -\frac{2}{3\pi} & -\frac{1}{2\pi} \end{bmatrix}$ for n =1, 2, 3, and 4 respectively (redo the implementation). We wish to plot these four coefficients against the four harmonics. Right included commands are conducted after previous implementation. The function **stem** accepts the decimal value not the symbolic one so we turn the symbolic values stored in **B** to decimal using the command **double**. Execution of the **stem** command displays the plot of the figure 8.2(a). The horizontal and vertical axes refer to n and Fourier series coefficient values respectively. For the addition of the graphical properties, see section 13.3. One more example is presented in the following for coefficient plotting.

Figure 8.2(a) Plot of the four Fourier series coefficients

for graphing the four Fourier series coefficients:

```
>>B=double(B); ↵   ← Converted decimal values again assigned to workspace B
>>n=[1 2 3 4]; ↵   ← The four harmonics are assigned to n as a four element row matrix
>>stem(n,B) ↵
```

Example

Referring to the example 4 of subsection 8.2.1, the real form 2 magnitude and phase coefficients C_n and φ_n are stored in the workspace variables **Cn** and **Phin** respectively (redo the implementation). We intend to plot these two coefficients for 10 harmonics ranging from $n=1$ to $n=10$ for which we conduct the following:

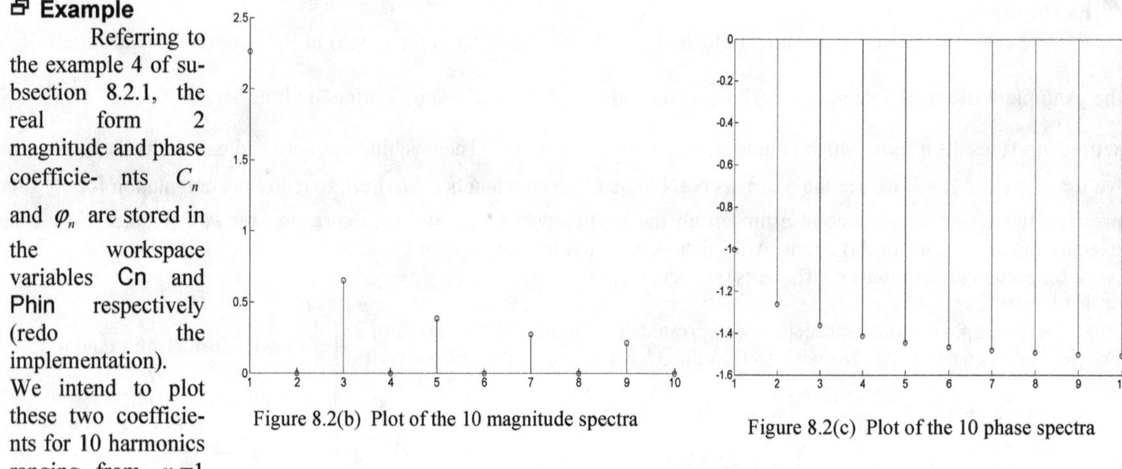

Figure 8.2(b) Plot of the 10 magnitude spectra

Figure 8.2(c) Plot of the 10 phase spectra

```
>>n=1:10; ↵                      ← n holds the 10 integers as a row matrix, section 1.3
>>C10=subs(Cn,sym(1:10)); ↵ ← C10 holds the 10 magnitude spectrum values as a row matrix
                                   followed by the substitution, last subsection for substitution
>>stem(n,double(C10)) ↵   ← Graphing the spectrum turning the symbolic values stored in C10 to decimal
```

Figure 8.2(b) displays the spectra of the 10 magnitude coefficients. The figure says that the nature of the function does not allow the even harmonics to exist. However the phase spectrum is obtained as follows (**C10** and **Phi10** are user-given names):

```
>>Phi10=subs(Phin,sym(1:10)); ↵   ← Phi10 holds the 10 phase spectra values as a row matrix
                                       followed by the substitution
>>stem(n,double(Phi10)) ↵         ← Graphing the phase spectra like the figure 8.2(c)
```

Critical situation:

Occasionally there is complicity while computing some spectrum without simplification for example ongoing φ_n. The φ_n could possess denominator like $(-1)^n-1$ and turn to zero for even harmonics thereby resulting an undefined expression. One can overcome this sort of difficulty taking the limiting value at those harmonics. MATLAB function **limit** (section 5.1) finds the limit of some expression symbolically. But the limit finding must take place one at a time. For the same phase spectra, for-loop programming (subsection 14.3.3) is applied as shown on the right side. The for-loop counter **k** changes from 1 to 10 which simulates the n variation. The function **limit** has two input arguments, the first and second of which are the expressional code (here it is the string code for the **Phin**) and the limit value (here it is $n=1,2,..,10$ but one at a time taken care of by the **k**) respectively. The **sym(k)** turns the number **k** to symbolic **k**. Each time the output of the **limit** is assigned to the **k**th element of the new workspace variable **Phi10** using the command **Phi10(k)** so that at end of the for-loop the **Phi10** is also a row matrix.

Use of for-loop for finding the limiting values:

```
>>for k=1:10 Phi10(k)=limit(Phin,sym(k)); end ↵
>>stem(n,double(Phi10)) ↵  ← Graphs the figure 8.2(c)
```

8.2.4 Reconstruction from Fourier series coefficients

In this section our objective is to sum some harmonics so that we reconstruct approximately the original shape of the periodic function $f(t)$. Theoretically speaking we must sum the Fourier series harmonics up to the infinity in order to reconstruct the function perfectly but the machine can not perform infinite sums or the harmonics might become insignificant after some value of n.

Considering the example 1 of the subsection 8.2.1, the periodic function of the figure 8.1(b) is expressed as $f(t)=\sum_{n=1}^{\infty}-\frac{2}{n\pi}\sin 2n\pi t$. We choose some finite integer instead of infinity say 5 and compute the sum $f_5(t)=\sum_{n=1}^{5}-\frac{2}{n\pi}\sin 2n\pi t$ where $f_5(t)$ indicates the construction of $f(t)$ from 5 harmonics or terms. There are 3 cycles in the function of the figure 8.1(b). Let us concentrate on two cycles just to have less computational burden from what reason the t variation should be $0\le t\le 2$. We focus only on the sample point of t on the given continuous function as far as a computer performs discrete computation. The calculation or reconstruction takes place on the sample points on t as well. That necessitates some user-chosen step size on the t within the range $0\le t\le 2$ and let it be 0.01.

For the computation we generate a row matrix considering the time interval and step size writing the command **[0:0.01:2]**. It means we are focusing on the t points at 0, 0.01, 0.02, ,2. Any particular harmonic n can be controlled by using a for-loop (subsection 14.3.3). For each n, we compute the expression $-\frac{2}{n\pi}\sin 2n\pi t$ on all t points using the scalar code (section 14.2) and which is -2/n/pi*sin(2*n*pi*t). However the complete code for the computation is as follows:

>>t=[0:0.01:2]; ↵ ← The t variation as a row matrix is assigned to the workspace variable t

>>f5=0; ↵ ← Assigning 0 outside the for-loop to workspace variable f5, f5⇔ $f_5(t)$, f5 is user-chosen name

>>for n=1:5 f5=f5-2/n/pi*sin(2*n*pi*t); end ↵

A programming artifice is used here. Initially f5=0, the computed values of the function are added with the f5 for n=1. When n=2, the f5 holds the values for the n=1. The looping is continued until n=5 therefore f5 holds the sum for all harmonics at the end. Or in other words, two identical size row matrices are being added element by element in each harmonic or n. Consequently the workspace variable f5 holds the reconstructed function $f_5(t)$ as a row matrix by summing the 5 harmonics at those specific t points.

The reconstruction needs to be checked with the original shape of the figure 8.1(b). In the example 6 of section 10.13, how this periodic function can be generated is addressed in detail. The t vector existing in the workspace is equally applicable for the original function meaning those specific t points. We provide the code for the two cycle generation of the $f(t)$ in figure 8.1(b) as follows:

>>f=sawtooth(2*pi*t); ↵ ← f holds two cycle $f(t)$ in figure 8.1(b) as a row matrix at those specific t points

In order to plot the original and the reconstructed one together (subsection 13.2.2), we exercise the following:

>>plot(t,f,t,f5) ↵

The reconstructed function as well as the original one is presented in the figure 8.2(d).

Understandably the reconstruction is not exact. The reason is we have chosen only 5 terms in lieu of infinite terms. To see the effect on 10 terms, the change we need is in the last counter index of the for-loop. Also we need to assign 0 to some other workspace variable say f10 to store the reconstruction data so we carry out the following:

>>f10=0; ↵

Start pressing the up-arrow key from the keyboard and modify the for-loop as follows:

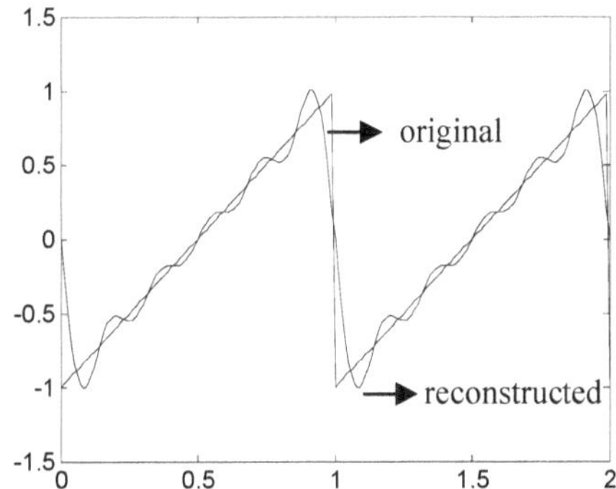

Figure 8.2(d) Reconstruction from Fourier series coefficients

>>for n=1:10 f10=f10-2/n/pi*sin(2*n*pi*t); end ↵ ← f10 holds reconstruction from 10 harmonics

If you say I intend to plot all three cases together, the command you need is plot(t,f,t,f5,t,f10), graph is not shown. In order to differentiate the three plots, you can execute the command legend('Original','5-terms','10-terms'). Thus the reader can explore the reconstruction on the Fourier series of any other function from different number harmonics.

Mean square error from reconstruction

Mean square error (mse) often provides a deterministic measure of deviation of the reconstruction from that of the actual one which is defined as mse= $\frac{1}{t\ span}\int_t [f(t)-f_5(t)]^2\,dt$ considering the 5-term. In the case of the discrete computation, the integration turns to summation however we calculate the mse for the 5-term as follows:

>>e=f-f5; ↵ ← e holds the error in reconstruction, e⇔ $f(t)-f_5(t)$, e is any user-given name

>>mean(e.^2) ↵ ← e.^2⇔ $[f(t)-f_5(t)]^2$

ans =

0.0423 ← mse from the 5-term reconstruction

The command e.^2 squares every element in the row matrix e and the mean finds the average of all elements in the row matrix e.^2. In order to see the mse for the 10 terms, all we need is execute e=f-f10; mean(e.^2) which should return 0.0256.

8.3 Fourier transform of nonperiodic functions

Fourier transform is applicable for a continuous and nonperiodic finite function $f(t)$. One can say that the Fourier transform is a Fourier series in which the period of the function is infinity. The transform has two forms – forward and inverse. The forward transform is the analysis phase which turns the function $f(t)$ from t or time domain to ω or angular frequency domain (let us call $F(\omega)$). On the contrary the inverse counterpart recovers the time domain

$$f(t)\xrightarrow{\text{forward Fourier transform}}F(\omega)\xrightarrow{\text{inverse Fourier transform}}f(t)$$

Figure 8.3(a) The concept behind the Fourier transform

function $f(t)$ from the $F(\omega)$ in angular frequency domain which is also called the synthesis process. The finiteness of $f(t)$ is assured if the value of $\int_{t=-\infty}^{t=\infty} |f(t)|\,dt$ is finite. That is why the periodic function does not have a Fourier transform. Also the function like t^t or e^{t^2} which increases continuously with t does not have the Fourier transform. Figure 8.3(a) presents the concept behind the Fourier transform. In the next two subsections we explain how the forward and inverse Fourier transforms of nonperiodic functions can be symbolically computed in MATLAB.

8.3.1 Forward Fourier transform

The forward Fourier transform converts a nonperiodic and continuous function $f(t)$ to $F(\omega)$ through the formula $F(\omega)= \int_{t=-\infty}^{t=\infty} e^{-j\omega t} f(t)\,dt$. The transform $F(\omega)$ is a complex function of ω (omega) and continuous as well. MATLAB function that computes the forward Fourier transform is **fourier**. The common syntax of the function is **fourier** (given function $f(t)$ in vector string form – section 14.2, independent variable of $f(t)$, wanted transform variable) but also works with the first input argument. The default return from the **fourier** is in terms of **w** (corresponds to the frequency variable ω) and in vector string form. The independent variable of $f(t)$ must be declared symbolically using the command **syms** prior to the computation (section 2.1). The readable form of the forward transform string can be viewed through the use of the command **pretty** (section 3.1).

Let us see the Fourier transform of $f(t)=e^{-|t|}$ which should be $F(\omega)= \int_{t=-\infty}^{t=\infty} e^{-j\omega t} f(t)\,dt = \int_{t=-\infty}^{t=\infty} e^{-j\omega t} e^{-|t|}\,dt = \frac{2}{1+\omega^2}$.

The vector code of the function $e^{-|t|}$ is **exp(–abs(t))** and we compute the transform as follows:

```
>>syms t ↵                    ← Declaring the independent t of e^-|t| as symbolic, t⇔t
>>F=fourier(exp(-abs(t))) ↵   ← Forward Fourier transform is assigned to workspace variable F, F⇔F(ω),
                                F is user-chosen name
F =

2/(1+w^2)                     ← Vector code of F(ω), w⇔ω
>>pretty(F) ↵                 ← Displaying the transform string stored in F in readable form
           2
      ----------
            2
       1 + w
```

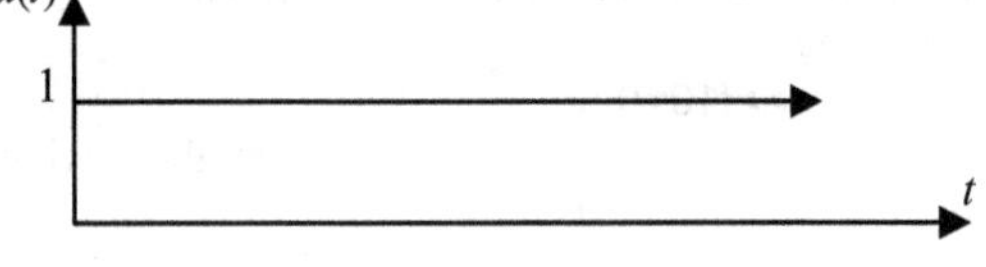

Figure 8.3(b) Plot of unit step function, $u(t)$

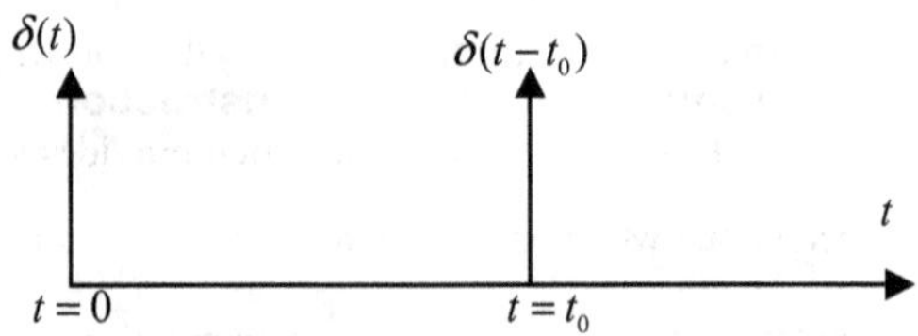

Figure 8.3(c) Plot of impulse function

If the independent variable of the given function were x (use **syms x** before) i.e. $f(x)=e^{-|x|}$, the command would be **F=fourier(exp(-abs(x)))** and still the transform return is in terms of **w**. When the transform variable is required from **w** to **z**, one uses the command **F=fourier(exp(-abs(x)),x,z)** for which **syms z** should be conducted before.

For a function which does not have the transform for example e^{t^2} and whose code is **exp(t^2)**, the response of the **fourier** is as follows:

```
>>F=fourier(exp(t^2)) ↵

F =

fourier(exp(t^2),t,w)
```

Above output indicates no close form results and just the definition of the transform.

The unit step and impulse (or Dirac delta) functions are important functions to the context of Fourier transform. Figure 8.3(b) shows the plot of the unit step function, which is denoted by $u(t)$ and whose MATLAB counterpart is **heaviside(t)**. Forward Fourier transform of the unit step function is $F(\omega)=\pi\delta(\omega)-\frac{i}{\omega}$ where $\delta(\omega)$ is the Dirac delta or impulse function (figure 8.3(c)) as regards to ω and is obtained as follows applying ongoing function and symbology:

```
>>syms t, F=fourier(heaviside(t)) ↵

F =

pi*dirac(w)-i/w      ← Vector string of πδ(ω) − i/ω is held in F
```

Regarding the output, **dirac(w)** corresponds to $\delta(\omega)$. The unit step function can be shifted to the left or right for example $u(t)$ shifted to the right at t =2 is denoted by $u(t-2)$ and has the transform $F[u(t-2)]=e^{-2i\omega}(\pi\delta(\omega)-\frac{i}{\omega})$ is obtained as follows (F is the Fourier transform operator):

```
>>F=fourier(heaviside(t-2)) ↵        ← F⇔F[u(t − 2)]⇔F(ω)

F =
```

exp(-2*i*w)*(pi*dirac(w)-i/w) ← Vector code of $e^{-2i\omega}(\pi\delta(\omega)-\frac{i}{\omega})$

Dirac delta or impulse function located at $t=t_0$ on t axis is denoted by $\delta(t-t_0)$ (figure 8.3(c)) and has the Fourier transform $F(\omega)=e^{-i\omega t_0}$ for example $F\,[\delta(t-2)]=e^{-i2\omega}$. MATLAB representation for the $\delta(t)$ is dirac(t) and we find the transform for $\delta(t-2)$ as follows:

```
>>fourier(dirac(t-2)) ↵

ans =

exp(-2*i*w)
```
← Code of $e^{-i2\omega}$

We close the subsection presenting few examples on the forward Fourier transform and their MATLAB commands in addition (the notations and symbols have the aforementioned meanings) in table 8.A. In the example 4 the i means imaginary number j. In the subsection 8.2.1, we addressed the assume facility in the light of the maple package. Ongoing function fourier belongs to the symbolic toolbox but the maple package also has the same name function with the identical input argumentation (example 3 in the table). Two different line commands are separated by a comma (example 4).

Table 8.A Fourier transform and its MATLAB counterpart for some functions

Example 1 $f(t)=e^{-t^2}$ $F(\omega)=\sqrt{\pi}\,e^{-\frac{1}{4}\omega^2}$	**Command for the example 1:** >>syms t, F=fourier(exp(-t^2)); ↵ >>pretty(F) ↵ 1/2 2 pi exp(- 1/4 w)
Example 2 $f(t)=\frac{1}{1+t^2}$, $F(\omega)=$ $\pi[e^{\omega}u(-\omega)+e^{-\omega}u(\omega)]$	**Command for the example 2:** >>syms t ↵ >>F=fourier(1/(1+t^2)); ↵ >>pretty(F) ↵ exp(w) pi heaviside(-w)+exp(-w) pi heaviside(w)
Example 3 $f(t)=e^{-\lvert at\rvert}$ $F(\omega)=F[f(t)]=\frac{2a}{a^2+\omega^2}$ where $a>0$	**Command for the example 3:** >>maple('assume(a>0)'); ↵ >>F=maple('fourier(exp(-abs(a*t)),t,w)') ↵ F = 2*a/(a^2+w^2)
Example 4 $f(t)=\lvert 5t+7\rvert$ $F(\omega)=-\frac{10e^{j\frac{7}{5}\omega}}{\omega^2}$	**Command for the example 4:** >>syms t, F=fourier(abs(5*t+7)) ↵ F = -10*exp(7/5*i*w)/w^2

8.3.2 Inverse Fourier transform

Given a complex frequency function $F(\omega)$, its inverse Fourier transform is defined as $f(t)=F^{-1}[F(\omega)]=\frac{1}{2\pi}\int_{\omega=-\infty}^{\omega=\infty}F(\omega)e^{i\omega t}dt$ where F^{-1} is the inverse Fourier transform operator. MATLAB counterpart of F^{-1} is ifourier (abbreviation for the inverse fourier). To have the inverse Fourier transform of $F(\omega)$, the command we conduct is ifourier($F(\omega)$ in vector string form – section 14.2, frequency variable ω, inverse transform variable t). Prior to applying the ifourier, declaration of the related variables in $F(\omega)$ as symbolic employing the command syms (section 2.1) is mandatory. The default return from the ifourier is in terms of x.

Computational example is best for the concept. It is given that $F(\omega)=\frac{10}{6+5i\omega-\omega^2}$ is the Fourier transform of $f(t)=10[e^{-2t}-e^{-3t}]u(t)$. Our objective is to find the $f(t)$ from the expression of $F(\omega)$ using the ifourier as follows:

```
>>syms w t ↵
>>F=10/(6+5*i*w-w^2); ↵
>>f=ifourier(F,w,t); ↵
>>pretty(f) ↵
     10 heaviside(t) (exp(-2 t) - exp(-3 t))
```
- >>syms w t ← Defining ω and t as symbolic, t⇔t and w⇔ω, wanted output in t
- >>F=10/(6+5*i*w-w^2); ← Vector code of $F(\omega)$ is assigned to F, F⇔$F(\omega)$, F is user-chosen name
- >>f=ifourier(F,w,t); ← Inverse transform of $F(\omega)$ is assigned to f, f⇔$f(t)$, f is user-chosen name
- >>pretty(f) ← Display the readable form of f, section 3.1 for pretty
- 10 heaviside(t) (exp(-2 t) - exp(-3 t)) ← It indicates $10[e^{-2t}-e^{-3t}]u(t)$

In the following we have some forward transform frequency functions. The upper and lower case assignees represent the forward and inverse Fourier transforms respectively (for instance $X(\omega)$ ⇔forward Fourier transform and $x(t)$ ⇔inverse Fourier transform). One can easily implement the inverse Fourier transforms of these frequency functions as follows:

Example 1

Angular frequency function: $X(\omega)=\frac{5e^{i(2\omega-8)}}{6-(4-\omega)i}$ and inverse transform: $x(t)=5\,e^{-6t-12+4it}u(t+2)$

Vector code representation of $X(\omega)$: 5*exp(i*(2*w-8))/(6-(4-w)*i)

Command:

```
>>syms w t ↵
>>X=5*exp(i*(2*w-8))/(6-(4-w)*i); ↵
>>x=ifourier(X,w,t); ↵
```
- >>syms w t ← Defining ω and t as symbolic
- >>X=5*exp(i*(2*w-8))/(6-(4-w)*i); ← Assigning the code of $X(\omega)$ to workspace X
- >>x=ifourier(X,w,t); ← Inverse transform of $X(\omega)$ is assigned to workspace x

```
>>pretty(x) ↵                          ← Display the readable form of x
            5 heaviside(t + 2) exp(-12 - 6 t + 4 I t)        ← I means imaginary number
```

Example 2

Angular frequency function: $H(\omega)=\dfrac{\sin\omega}{\omega}$ and inverse transform: $h(t)=\dfrac{1}{2}[u(t+1)-u(t-1)]$

Vector code representation of $H(\omega)$: sin(w)/w

Command:

```
>>syms w t ↵
>>h=ifourier(sin(w)/w,w,t); ↵  ← Inverse transform of H(ω) is assigned to workspace h, h⇔ h(t)
>>pretty(h) ↵                  ← Display the readable form of h
            - 1/2 heaviside(t - 1) + 1/2 heaviside(t + 1)
```

Example 3

Angular frequency function: $Y(\omega)=\dfrac{15\sin(4\omega-12)}{\omega-3}$ and inverse transform: $y(t)=\dfrac{15}{2}e^{i3t}[u(t+4)-u(t-4)]$

Vector string representation of $Y(\omega)$:15*sin(4*w-12)/(w-3)

Command:

```
>>syms w t ↵
>>Y=15*sin(4*w-12)/(w-3); ↵  ← Assigning the code of Y(ω) to workspace Y
>>y=ifourier(Y,w,t); ↵       ← Inverse transform of Y(ω) is assigned to workspace y, y⇔ y(t)
>>pretty(simple(y)) ↵        ← Display the readable form of y following simplification using the
                                                                        command simple
            15/2 exp(3 I t) (heaviside(t + 4) - heaviside(t - 4))
```

Example 4

$H(\omega)=\begin{cases}1 & if\ \omega>0\\ -1 & if\ \omega<0\end{cases}$ is an example when the frequency function is given in graphical form (figure 8.3(d)).

Employing the unit step function, one can write $H(\omega)=u(\omega)-u(-\omega)$ whose inverse Fourier transform is $\dfrac{i}{t\pi}$ and following is the implementation:

```
>>syms w t ↵
>>H=heaviside(w)-heaviside(-w); ↵  ← H⇔ H(ω)
>>h=ifourier(H,w,t); ↵             ← h⇔ h(t)
>>pretty(h) ↵          ← Display the readable form of h, I⇔ i
     I
    -----
    t pi
```

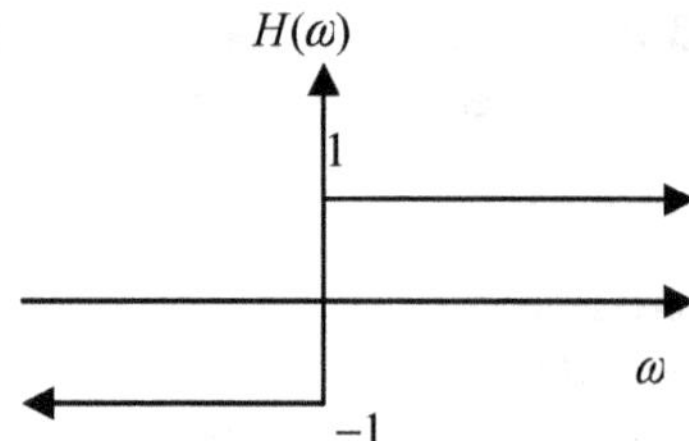

Figure 8.3(d) Plot of $H(\omega)$ vs ω

8.3.3 Graphing the Fourier transform

The forward Fourier transform $F(\omega)$ is a continuous and complex function of ω. It possesses four components – real, imaginary, magnitude, and phase. The variation of these components with respect to ω is termed as the spectrum. As an example let us find the four spectra of the transform $F(\omega)=\dfrac{10}{6+5i\omega-\omega^2}$ for $-10\le\omega\le10$. It is important to mention that although the frequency ω is continuous, we choose substantial discrete points in the given ω domain to graph the $F(\omega)$ in continuous sense. There are two styles for graphing the transform – symbolic and numeric. We address both of which separately in the following.

Symbolic style:

In this approach we do not choose the step size. MATLAB automatically chooses the step size. The function that graphs the spectrum is the ezplot (subsection 13.1.1). The $F(\omega)$ has the vector code 10/(6+5*i*w-w^2). Symbolically the real, imaginary, magnitude, and phase spectra are written as $\mathrm{Re}\{F(\omega)\}$, $\mathrm{Im}\{F(\omega)\}$, $|F(\omega)|$, and $\angle F(\omega)$ and their MATLAB counterparts are real, imag, abs, and angle respectively on that we graph these spectra as follows:

```
>>ezplot('real(10/(6+5*i*w-w^2))',[-10,10]) ↵   ← For graphing Re{F(ω)} like figure 8.4(a)
>>ezplot('imag(10/(6+5*i*w-w^2))',[-10,10]) ↵   ← For graphing Im{F(ω)} like figure 8.4(b)
>>ezplot('abs(10/(6+5*i*w-w^2))',[-10,10]) ↵    ← For graphing | F(ω) | like figure 8.4(c)
```

```
>>ezplot('angle(10/(6+5*i*w-w^2))',[-10,10]) ↵
```
← For graphing $\angle F(\omega)$ like figure 8.4(d)

For addition of graphical features, please see section 13.3. This style is better for quick plotting of a single spectrum.

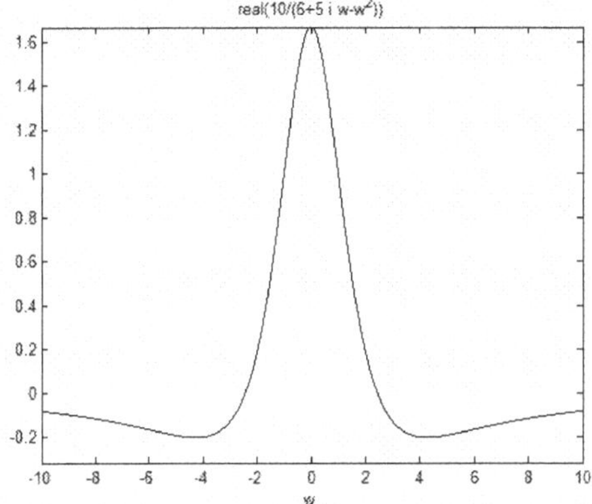

Figure 8.4(a) Plot of $\text{Re}\{F(\omega)\}$ vs ω

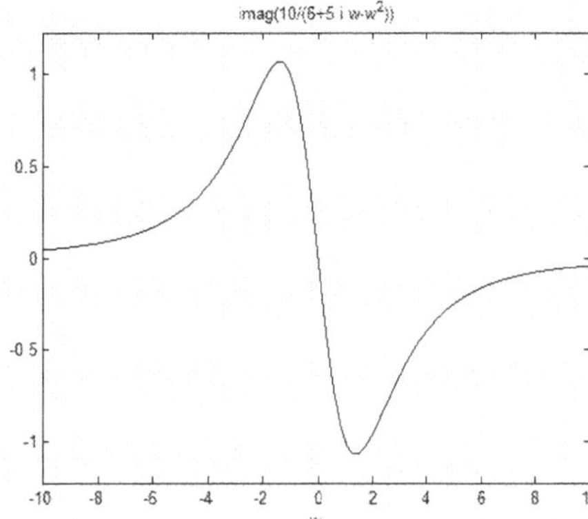

Figure 8.4(b) Plot of $\text{Im}\{F(\omega)\}$ vs ω

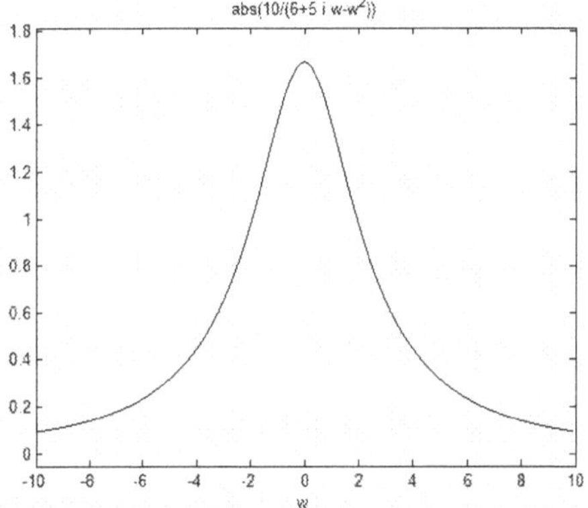

Figure 8.4(c) Plot of $|F(\omega)|$ vs ω

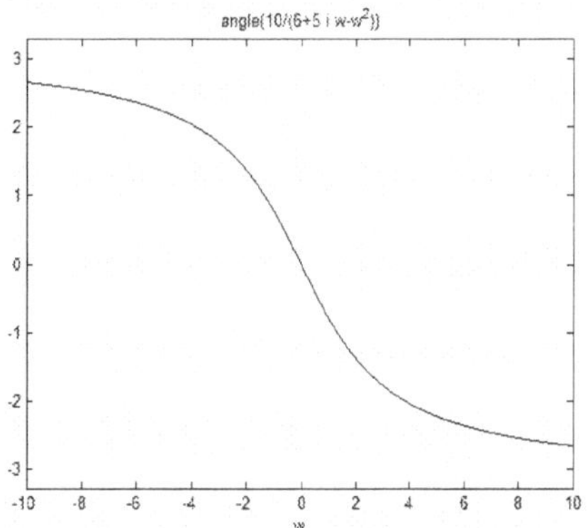

Figure 8.4(d) Plot of $\angle F(\omega)$ vs ω

Numeric style:

The numerical approach needs the scalar code writing of the $F(\omega)$ (section 14.2) and the graphing function is the plot (subsection 13.2.1). Also another important point is the user has to decide the step size or sample point of the ω variation. As a first step we generate a row or column vector data from the user-given ω sample point and range and then calculate $F(\omega)$ or other spectrum on those ω points. If the ω vector is a row or column matrix, so is the calculated spectrum (of identical length). However the graphings of the four spectra for the example transform are shown below:

>>w=-10:0.01:10; ↵ ← We chose the step size 0.01 for ω and w is a row matrix (section 1.3)

>>F=10./(6+5*i*w-w.^2); ↵ ← Scalar code of $F(\omega)$ is assigned to F and F holds the complex value of $F(\omega)$ as a row matrix for each element in w, F is user-chosen name

>>R=real(F); I=imag(F); A=abs(F); P=angle(F); ↵ ← Picking up the four components from $F(\omega)$ where the assignees are the following: R⇔ $\text{Re}\{F(\omega)\}$, I⇔ $\text{Im}\{F(\omega)\}$, A⇔ $|F(\omega)|$, and P⇔ $\angle F(\omega)$ but all of them is row matrix of the same size as that of w, assignee names are user-chosen

>>plot(w,R) ↵ ← Plotting the real spectrum $\text{Re}\{F(\omega)\}$ like figure 8.4(a), figure not shown for space reason

In a similar fashion the other three spectra can be plotted by using the commands plot(w,I), plot(w,A), and plot(w,P) respectively. The default phase angle return from the angle is from $-\pi$ to π. If the phase spectrum $\angle F(\omega)$ needs to be in degrees, the command P=180/pi*angle(F); can be exercised.

In the spectrum analysis sometimes we plot the magnitude spectrum $|F(\omega)|$ in decibel (dB) scale which is defined as $20\log_{10}|F(\omega)|$ or $10\log_{10}|F(\omega)|$ depending on $f(t)$ borne information. The decibel needs a reference value. Usually for the magnitude spectrum, it is the maximum value of the $|F(\omega)|$. The workspace variable A is holding the $|F(\omega)|$ values. For sure the values stored in A are positive. Dividing the $|F(\omega)|$ by the maximum $|F(\omega)|$ normalizes the spectrum between 0 and 1. Theoretically speaking we implement $20\log_{10}\frac{|F(\omega)|}{|F(\omega)|_{max}}$ to obtain the decibel plot on the spectrum. However we find the maximum value in A applying the command **max** (section 2.9) as follows:

>>M=max(A); ↵ ← Workspace M holds the maximum value of $|F(\omega)|$, M⇔$|F(\omega)|_{max}$, M is user-chosen

>>D=20*log10(A/M); ↵ ←D holds normalized dB values of $|F(\omega)|$, D⇔ $20\log_{10}\frac{|F(\omega)|}{|F(\omega)|_{max}}$, D is user-chosen

>>plot(w,D) ↵ ← graphing the decibel plot of $|F(\omega)|$ for $-10 \le \omega \le 10$

Figure 8.4(e) depicts the decibel magnitude spectrum without any labeling (section 13.3 for the graphical properties). The vertical axis of the graph now represents the decibel values for example 0 dB corresponds to the maximum value 1 in the normalized spectrum or the maximum in the magnitude spectrum of the figure 8.4(c). As you see, the spectrum spreads about the maximum due to the logarithmic scale.

When the decibel value becomes too much negative, it indicates the $|F(\omega)|$ is very small or close to 0. At exactly $|F(\omega)|=0$, the decibel value is minus infinity. For practical calculations we sometimes clip the unnecessary negative values. For example in the graph 8.4(e), the dB values are between 0 and –25. Let us say any dB value less than –20 should be clipped to –20. We know that the dB values are stored in D as a row matrix. We find the integer position indexes of such values in D through **find** function (section 2.13) as follows:

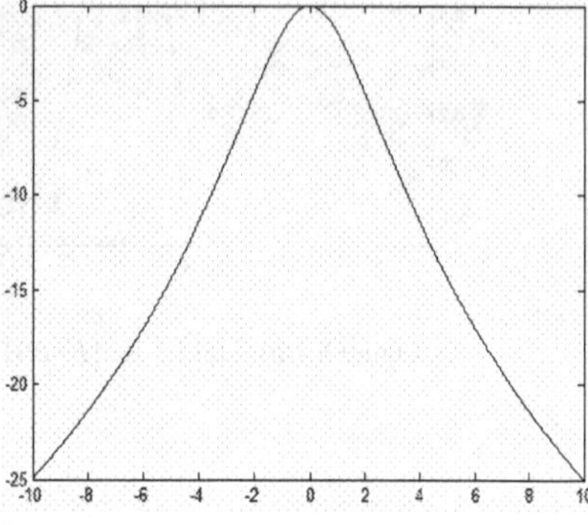

Figure 8.4(e) dB plot of the $|F(\omega)|$

>>p=find(D<=-20); D(p)=-20; ↵

The integer indexes of less than or equal to –20 dB in D are found and assigned to workspace p (user-chosen name). Those index elements are set to –20 using the command D(p)=-20;. Verify the calculation exercising plot(w,D).

8.4 Discrete Fourier transform of discrete functions

The discrete Fourier transform (DFT) is merely relevant to a discrete function or sequence $f[n]$. The independent variable n is integer only. The values of $f[n]$ are the samples of a function but the $f[n]$ does not hold any sampling information. For different values of n, the $f[n]$ is just a row or column matrix. The forward discrete Fourier transform $F[k]$ of the discrete function $f[n]$ is defined as $F[k]=\sum_{n=1}^{N} f[n]e^{-j2\pi(k-1)\frac{(n-1)}{N}}$ where N is the number of samples in $f[n]$. The transform $F[k]$ is discrete and possesses N samples as well. The discrete frequency variable k is integer. The recovery of $f[n]$ from $F[k]$ takes place through the inverse discrete Fourier transform (IDFT) which is defined as $f[n]=\frac{1}{N}\sum_{n=1}^{N} f[n]e^{j2\pi(k-1)\frac{(n-1)}{N}}$ where the symbols have just mentioned meanings. The index n or k can vary from 1 to N in the presented expressions. But they can vary from 0 to $N-1$ (most textbook follows this convention) in that instant the modified expressions become $F[k]=\sum_{n=0}^{N-1} f[n]e^{-j2\pi k\frac{n}{N}}$ and $f[n]=\frac{1}{N}\sum_{n=0}^{N-1} f[n]e^{j2\pi k\frac{n}{N}}$ for DFT and IDFT respectively. Use of either expression does not change the function or its transform contents at all. The $F[k]$ is in general complex. Figure 8.5(a) presents the concept behind the discrete Fourier transform. When we handle the $f[n]$ only for the length of N being the power of 2, the transform is called the fast Fourier transform. In MATLAB the DFT and IDFT are simulated using the functions **fft** (abbreviation for the fast Fourier transform but also handles the sequence whose length is other than power of 2) and **ifft** (abbreviation for the inverse fast Fourier transform) respectively.

$$f[n] \xrightarrow{\text{forward discrete Fourier transform}} F[k] \xrightarrow{\text{inverse discrete Fourier transform}} f[n]$$

Figure 8.5(a) The concept behind the discrete Fourier transform

Let us consider the discrete function $f[n]=[1\ \ 2\ \ 7\ \ -5\ \ -6\ \ 8]$. There are 6 samples in the $f[n]$. The choice of index n is the user's. Let us say n varies from 1 to 6, so does k. The expression $F[k]=\sum_{n=1}^{N} f[n]e^{-j2\pi(k-1)\frac{(n-1)}{N}}$ returns the computation of $F[k]$ as [7 $10.5-j6.0622$ $-9.5+j16.4545$ -3 $-9.5-j16.4545$ $10.5+j6.0622$]. Our objective is to obtain the complex sequence $F[k]$ from $f[n]$ and we do so as follows:

>>f=[1 2 7 -5 -6 8]; ↵ ← $f[n]$ is assigned to the workspace f as a row matrix, f is user-chosen name

>>F=fft(f) ↵ ← DFT on $f[n]$ is taken and assigned to the workspace F, F⇔ $F[k]$, F is user-chosen name

F =

7.0000 10.5000 - 6.0622i -9.5000 +16.4545i -3.0000 -9.5000 -16.4545i 10.5000 + 6.0622i

Starting from the computed values of $F[k]$, the expression $f[n]=\frac{1}{N}\sum_{n=0}^{N-1} f[n]e^{j2\pi k\frac{n}{N}}$ returns the function $f[n]$ we started with. Having the discrete forward transform values available in the workspace F, one can verify that as follows:

>>f=ifft(F) ↵ ← IDFT on $F[k]$ is taken and assigned to the workspace f, f⇔ $f[n]$, f is user-chosen name

f =

1.0000 2.0000 7.0000 -5.0000 -6.0000 8.0000

The plot of the discrete $F[k]$ versus discrete integer k is termed as the discrete Fourier spectrum. Since the $F[k]$ is complex, there are four discrete component spectra namely real, imaginary, magnitude, and phase whose symbolic representations are $\text{Re}\{F[k]\}$, $\text{Im}\{F[k]\}$, $|F[k]|$, and $\angle F[k]$ and whose MATLAB counterparts are **real**, **imag**, **abs**, and **angle** respectively. For instance the discrete phase angle spectrum (in radians) $\angle F[k]$ can be picked up from $F[k]$ employing the command angle(F). Let us see two more examples on DFT computation in the following.

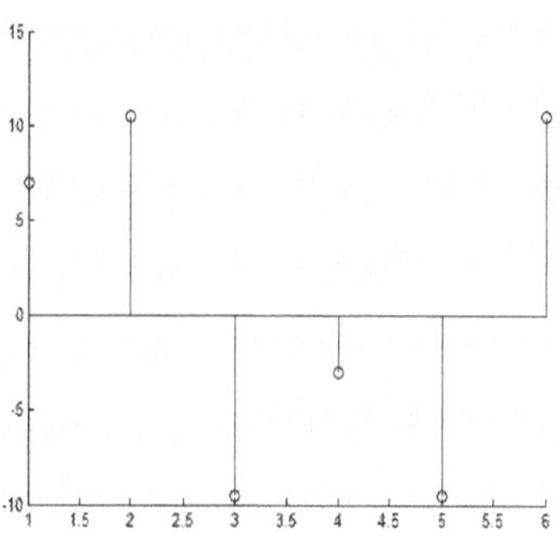

Figure 8.5(b) Plot of the discrete real spectrum $\text{Re}\{F[k]\}$ versus k

Example 1

The beginning example presents the $f[n]$ to be formed from some observational data. A discrete function may follow some functional pattern for example sine. Let us say the discrete sine function is $f[n]=5\sin\frac{2\pi n}{5}$ where n is integer and n exists from 0 to 5 thus making $f[n]$ discrete. We intend to find the discrete magnitude and phase spectra of the finite duration discrete sine function. Applying the $F[k]=\sum_{n=0}^{N-1} f[n]e^{-j2\pi k\frac{n}{N}}$, one obtains $|F[k]|$=[0 12.4495 5.0904 3.6327 5.0904 12.4495] and $\angle F[k]$=[180^0 -60^0 150^0 180^0 -150^0 60^0] for which the implementation is as follows:

>>n=0:5; ↵ ← Placing the index n as a row matrix to the workspace n, n is user-chosen assignee

>>f=5*sin(2*pi*n/5); ↵ ← Scalar code (section 14.2) of $5\sin\frac{2\pi n}{5}$ is assigned to f, f⇔ discrete $f[n]$

>>F=fft(f); ↵ ← DFT on $f[n]$ is taken and workspace F holds $F[k]$

>>A=abs(F) ↵ ← A holds $|F[k]|$ as a row matrix, A is user-chosen assignee

A =

0.0000 12.4495 5.0904 3.6327 5.0904 12.4495

>>P=180/pi*angle(F) ↵ ← P holds $\angle F[k]$ in degrees, default return of **angle** is in radian from $-\pi$ to π, P is user-chosen assignee

P =

180.0000 -60.0000 150.0000 180.0000 -150.0000 60.0000

Example 2

Suppose we wish to find the same discrete spectra as in example 1 but for the discrete function $f[n]=2^{-n}$ on the same n duration. Only change in previous commands do we need is in the scalar code of $f[n]$ which is 2.^(-n).

8.4.1 Graphing the discrete Fourier transform

Graphing the discrete Fourier transform happens through the use of the discrete function plotter **stem** (subsection 13.2.9). Referring to the beginning example of $F[k]$ computation, the workspace variable F holds the $F[k]$ for the data based $f[n]$. We wish to plot $\text{Re}\{F[k]\}$ versus k for this $f[n]$. Let us obtain the discrete real spectrum from the complex values stored in F as follows:

>>R=real(F) ↵ ← R holds $\text{Re}\{F[k]\}$, R is user-chosen assignee

R =

7.0000 10.5000 -9.5000 -3.0000 -9.5000 10.5000

In order to plot the real spectrum, knowledge about the integer index k needs to be known. The k changes from 1 to 6 therefore the graphing is as follows:

>>k=1:6; ↵ ← k holds the index integers as a row matrix

>>stem(k,R) ↵ ← first and second input arguments are index and real spectrum both as a row matrix

Above execution results the figure 8.5(b). One can execute the commands **stem(k,imag(F))**, **stem(k,abs(F))**, and **stem(k,angle(F))** for the discrete spectra $\text{Im}\{F[k]\}$, $|F[k]|$, and $\angle F[k]$ respectively.

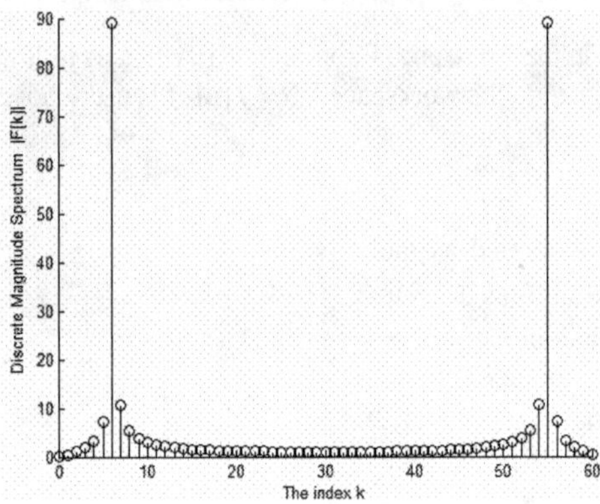

Figure 8.5(c) Discrete magnitude spectrum of a pure discrete sine wave

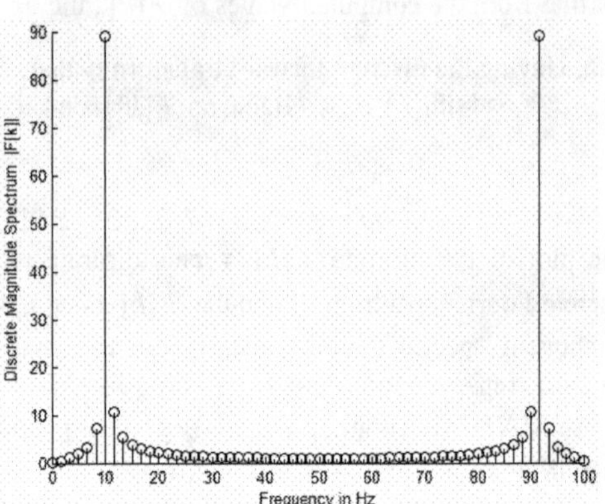

Figure 8.5(d) Discrete magnitude spectrum of the pure discrete sine wave plotted against frequency

8.4.2 DFT implications on discrete sine function

The sine function is the most addressed one in the scientific and engineering transform-based systems because of its widespread involvement. In discrete analysis, always we are focused on the sample. Behind the discrete terminology, a practical physical system is often continuous. Recall that $f[n]$ is just the samples taken at different index or integer n. Samples do not reveal actual system until we relate them with the practicalities. We know that the discrete function $f[n]$ is generated after sampling the function $f(t)$ with a specific frequency, called sampling frequency f_S. Or in other words the function $f(t)$ is sampled with a step size T_s where $T_s = \frac{1}{f_s}$. Now we demonstrate what allied implication holds the sampling frequency regarding the discrete Fourier transform.

Let us consider a single frequency sine function of $\begin{Bmatrix} amplitude\ \pm 3 \\ frequency\ 10Hz \end{Bmatrix}$ when t is in second and which has the continuous expression $x(t) = 3\sin 2\pi 10t$ and exists over $0 \le t \le 0.6\text{sec}$. The user has to decide the sampling frequency to discretize this continuous function. Let us say the sampling frequency is f_S=100 Hz with that the sampling period or the step size must be $T_s = \frac{1}{f_s}$=0.01sec which implies that we must choose the t step as 0.01sec while discretizing the $x(t)$. The moment we choose the t step size, we take the samples of the continuous function. Let us conduct the following:

>>t=0:0.01:0.6; ↵ ← **t** holds a row matrix whose elements are points on t at which the samples to be taken

>>x=3*sin(2*pi*10*t); ↵ ← **x** holds the discrete sine wave as a row matrix in which t information is lost

The **x** corresponds to the DFT theory mentioned $f[n]$. In order to decide the N, the number of elements in **x** is to be found as follows:

>>numel(x) ↵ ← The function **numel** finds the number of elements in the matrix **x**

```
ans =
        61
```

It indicates that we must take N=61 in the DFT computation thereby changing the index n or k from 0 to 60. An interesting fact is revealed from the following implementation. Let us graph (last subsection) the discrete magnitude spectrum $|F[k]|$ against the index k as follows:

>>k=0:60; ↵ ← **k** holds the DFT mentioned indexes from 0 to 60 as a row matrix

>>A=abs(fft(x)); ↵ ← **A** holds the discrete magnitude spectrum $|F[k]|$ for ongoing discrete sine function

>>stem(k,A) ↵ ← Graphing the magnitude spectrum

Figure 8.5(c) presents the discrete magnitude spectrum for the sine wave. The DFT has the half index symmetry that is $|F[k]|$ is symmetric about $\frac{N-1}{2}$ or k =30. For k =0 to 30, there is only one strong discrete peak which corresponds to the frequency of the continuous sine function $x(t)$ we started with.

Knowing the sampling frequency, it is also convenient to display the discrete magnitude plot in terms of the discrete frequency f (not $f[n]$) rather than the sample index k. The relationship is given by $f = \frac{f_S}{N-1}k$. For ongoing example, we have $\begin{Bmatrix} f_S = 100Hz \\ N = 61 \\ k = 0 \; to \; 60 \end{Bmatrix}$ thereby providing $f = \frac{100}{60}k$ hence the f changes from 0 to 100 Hz with a step $\frac{100}{60}$ Hz. Now we plot the horizontal axis of the figure 8.5(c) in terms of the discrete frequency as follows:

```
>>f=0:100/60:100; ↵        ← f holds the discrete frequencies as a row matrix
>>stem(f,A) ↵              ← The first input argument of the stem is now the discrete frequency row matrix
```

Above execution results the graph of the figure 8.5(d) in which you see the horizontal axis in terms of frequency in Hertz. In the plot exactly at f =10 does the peak magnitude appear – which is the function frequency of $x(t)$ we started with.

♦♦ Inference from the study

Suppose we do not have any information about the sinusoidal frequency present in a given discrete function. We can start with some sampling frequency and look for the strongest peak as done in the figure 8.5(d). If it does not appear, we can try with another sampling frequency. Thus the hidden frequency present in a discrete function can be detected.

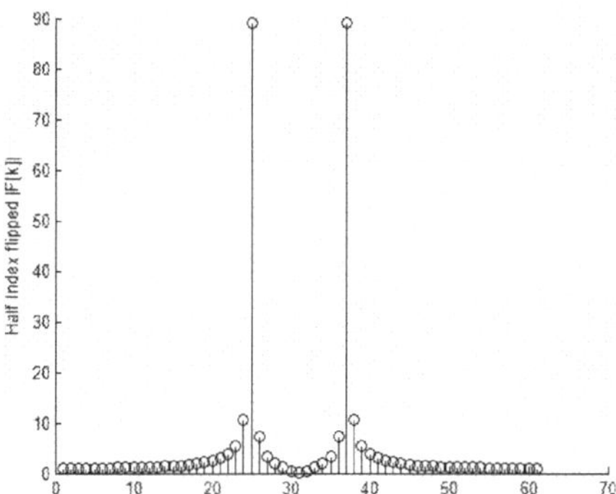

Figure 8.5(e) Half indexedly flipped discrete magnitude spectrum of a pure discrete sine wave

8.4.3 Half index flipping of the DFT

The discrete magnitude spectrum $|F[k]|$ of $f[n]$ is related with information content in the continuous counterpart $f(t)$ that is why it receives ample attention in the Fourier literature. From ongoing discussion, the $|F[k]|$ has half index symmetry and the total number of samples in it is N. Not only the magnitude one but the other spectra may also have even or odd symmetry about the half index. It means the first and second halves of the spectrum correspond to k values from 0 to $\frac{N}{2}-1$ and from $\frac{N}{2}$ to $N-1$ respectively assuming the k variation from 0 to $N-1$. If a function is composed of many frequencies, the significant frequency components of $|F[k]|$ are located at the smaller and larger values of k (for example k =0, 1, 2,... and $k = N-1$, $N-2$,...). Flipping the $|F[k]|$ about the half index gathers significant frequencies in the middle of the k axis which exhibits more perceptibleness in frequency in the $|F[k]|$ versus k.

♦♦ Importance of MATLAB fftshift function on the half index flipping

We know that any discrete one dimensional function takes the form of a row or column matrix. Working on a row or column matrix in a sense is working on the discrete function. MATLAB function **fftshift** performs the half index flipping which we addressed in the section 2.4. Concerning the **fftshift** if the number of samples in a discrete function is odd, the half index flipping happens about the index $k = \frac{N-1}{2}$ assuming k changes from 0 to $N-1$. Elements whose indexes are from $k = \frac{N+1}{2}$ to $k = N-1$ are placed in front of the other half. If N is even, elements whose indexes are from $k = \frac{N}{2}$ to $k = N-1$ are placed in front of the other. Two times half index flipping brings back the discrete function we start with provided that the number of samples in the function is even. That is to say, the **fftshift(fftshift(y))** returns **y**.

From the last subsection, the workspace variable **A** holds the discrete magnitude spectrum for the single frequency sine function whose plot is presented in the figure 8.5(c) and in which you find the two strong peaks are located close to k =0 and k =60. The half index flipping operation should bring these two peaks in the middle of the k axis for which we conduct the following:

```
>>AF=fftshift(A); stem(AF) ↵        ← Graphs the figure 8.5(e)
```

The workspace **AF** (can be any user-given name) holds the half indexedly flipped $|F[k]|$. As the figure 8.5(e) displays, the two strong peaks are brought in the middle. Note that we used only the flipped spectrum as the input argument of the **stem**. The **fftshift** does not hold the k information. It is the user who keeps the information about the index k. By default the **stem** numbers the horizontal indexes from 1 to the number of samples present in **AF** (which is here 61). If the information about the k is necessary, use **fftshift** on **k** and assign the **fftshift(k)** to some workspace variable.

Table 8.B A list of continuous functions and their Laplace transforms implemented in MATLAB

Mathematical form	MATLAB commands	Mathematical form	MATLAB commands
$L[\sin bt] = \frac{b}{s^2+b^2}$	>>syms b t ↵ >>F=laplace(sin(b*t)); ↵ >>pretty(F) ↵ b ----------- 2 2 s + b	$L[\cos bt] = \frac{s}{s^2+b^2}$	>>syms b t ↵ >>F=laplace(cos(b*t)); ↵ >>pretty(F) ↵ s ----------- 2 2 s + b
$L[\sinh bt] = \frac{b}{s^2-b^2}$	>>syms b t ↵ >>F=laplace(sinh(b*t)); ↵ >>pretty(F) ↵ b ----------- 2 2 s - b	$L[\cosh bt] = \frac{s}{s^2-b^2}$	>>syms b t ↵ >>F=laplace(cosh(b*t)); ↵ >>pretty(F) ↵ s ----------- 2 2 s - b
$L[e^{at}\cos bt] = \frac{s-a}{(s-a)^2+b^2}$	>>syms a b t ↵ >>F=laplace(exp(a*t)*cos(b*t)); ↵ >>pretty(F) ↵ s - a ---------------- 2 2 (s - a) + b	$L[e^{at}\sin bt] = \frac{b}{(s-a)^2+b^2}$	>>syms a b t ↵ >>F=laplace(exp(a*t)*sin(b*t)); ↵ >>pretty(F) ↵ b ---------------- 2 2 (s - a) + b
$L[u(t)] = \frac{1}{s}$	>>syms t ↵ >>F=laplace(heaviside(t)); ↵ >>pretty(F) ↵ 1/s	$L[\delta(t)] = 1$	>>syms t ↵ >>F=laplace(dirac(t)); ↵ >>pretty(F) ↵ 1
$L\left[\frac{1}{\sqrt{\pi(t+a)}}\right] = \frac{e^{as}erfc(\sqrt{as})}{\sqrt{s}}$ where $erfc(x)$ is complementary error function	>>syms a t ↵ >>F=laplace(1/sqrt(pi*(t+a))); ↵ >>pretty(F) ↵ 1/2 exp(a s) erfc((a s)) ----------------------------- 1/2 s	$L[J_0(at)] = \frac{1}{\sqrt{s^2+a^2}}$ where $J_0(x)$ is the Bessel function of the first kind of order 0	>>syms a t ↵ >>F=laplace(besselj(0,a*t)); ↵ >>pretty(F) ↵ 1 ------------------- 2 2 1/2 (s + a)
$L[-7+2t+t^4] = \frac{-7s^4+2s^3+24}{s^5}$	>>syms t ↵ >>F=laplace(-7+2*t+t^4); ↵ >>pretty(simplify(F)) ↵ 4 3 7 s - 2 s - 24 - ----------------- 5 s	$L[t\sin at] = \frac{2sa}{(s^2+a^2)^2}$	>>syms a t ↵ >>F=laplace(t*sin(a*t)); ↵ >>pretty(F) ↵ s a 2 -------------- 2 2 2 (s + a)
$L\left[\frac{\sinh mt}{t}\right] = \frac{1}{2}\ln\frac{s+m}{s-m}$	>>syms m t ↵ >>F=laplace(sinh(m*t)/t); ↵ >>pretty(F) ↵ s + m 1/2 log(---------) s - m	$L[t^{\frac{3}{2}}e^{t-1}] = \frac{3e^{-1}\sqrt{\pi}}{4(s-1)^{\frac{5}{2}}}$	>>syms t ↵ >>F=laplace(t^(3/2)*exp(t-1)); ↵ >>pretty(F) ↵ 1/2 exp(-1) pi 3/4 --------------- 5/2 (s - 1)
$L[Si(t)] = \frac{1}{s}\cot^{-1}s$ where $Si(t) = \int_{x=0}^{x=t}\frac{\sin x}{x}dx$ is the sine integral	>>syms t ↵ >>F=laplace(sinint(t)); ↵ >>pretty(F) ↵ acot(s) --------- s	$L[Ci(t)] = -\frac{\ln(s^2+1)}{2s}$ where $Ci(t) = \int_{x=\infty}^{x=t}\frac{\cos x}{x}dx$ is the cosine integral	>>syms t ↵ >>F=laplace(cosint(t)); ↵ >>pretty(F) ↵ 2 log(s + 1) - 1/2 ------------- s

8.5 Laplace transform

Laplace transform is also integral transform like the Fourier transform. The finiteness condition of the Fourier transform imposes the limitation that the function must converge as the t increases in the positive and negative directions thereby not making it suitable for all functions. If the $f(t)$ is not convergent, multiplying the function by the factor e^{-st} forces the function to be convergent yet not all. However Laplace transform also has the forward and inverse counterparts. Figure 8.6(a) depicts the analysis – synthesis notion behind the transform.

$$continuous\ f(t) \xrightarrow{forward\ Laplace\ transform} F(s) \xrightarrow{inverse\ Laplace\ transform} f(t)$$
$$and\ t \geq 0$$

Figure 8.6(a) The concept behind the Laplace transform

8.5.1 Forward Laplace transform of continuous functions

Forward Laplace transform $F(s)$ of the continuous $f(t)$ is defined as $L\,[f(t)] = F(s) = \int_{t=0}^{t=\infty} f(t)e^{-st}dt$ where $t > 0$, L is the forward transform operator, and s is the transform variable. MATLAB function that computes the transform is **laplace**. The common syntax of the function is **laplace(** $f(t)$ in vector string form – section 14.2, independent variable t, wanted transform variable s). Since the computation happens through symbolic toolbox, declaration of the related variables as symbolic using the **syms** (section 2.1) is compulsory before applying the function. The default return from the **laplace** is a function of **s**. Readable form from the return of the **laplace** can be seen using the command **pretty** (section 3.1).

Let us begin with the forward Laplace transform of e^{at} where $t > 0$ so we have $L\,[e^{at}] = F(s) = \int_{t=0}^{t=\infty} e^{at}\,e^{-st}dt = \dfrac{1}{s-a}$. Our objective is to obtain $\dfrac{1}{s-a}$ from e^{at} for which we conduct the following:

```
>>syms a t ↵              ← Declaring the related variables a and t of e^at as symbolic, a⇔a and t⇔t
>>F=laplace(exp(a*t)) ↵   ← Vector code of e^at is exp(a*t) and F holds the code of F(s),
                            F is any user-chosen assignee
F =

1/(s-a)
>>pretty(F) ↵             ← Display the readable form stored in F
    1
  ------
  s - a
```

The transform by making specific choice of independent variable (x) and transform variable (z) can be implemented by using the commands first **syms a x z** and then **laplace(exp(a*x),x,z)** which returns $\dfrac{1}{z-a}$.

Employing the same functions, symbols, and notations, we presented the Laplace transforms for a number of continuous functions in the table 8.B. Function like e^{2t^2} or t^t does not provide a close form function of s therefore the return becomes **laplace(exp(2*t^2),t,s)** meaning just the definition of the transform. Sometimes a mathematical expression may exist in different forms in that case the command **simplify** can be applied to simplify the expression as we did for the t polynomial in the table. Shifted unit step and Dirac delta functions are addressed in the subsection 8.3.1, their Laplace transforms can be found in a similar fashion for example $L\,[u(t-2)] = \dfrac{e^{-2s}}{s}$ or $L\,[\delta(t-2)] = e^{-2s}$. The transform on other situations is addressed in the following.

◆◆ Laplace transform of differential coefficients and equations

Laplace transforms of different derivatives of a continuous function $y(t)$ are given as follows: $L\left(\dfrac{dy}{dt}\right) = sY(s) - y(0)$, $L\left(\dfrac{d^2y}{dt^2}\right) = s^2Y(s) - sy(0) - y'(0) = s[sY(s) - y(0)] - y'(0)$, $L\left(\dfrac{d^3y}{dt^3}\right) = s^3Y(s) - s^2y(0) - sy'(0) - y''(0) = s[s[sY(s) - y(0)] - y'(0)] - y''(0)$ in general $L\left(\dfrac{d^ny}{dt^n}\right) = s^nY(s) - s^{n-1}y(0) - s^{n-2}y'(0) - \ldots\ldots\ldots\ldots - sy^{n-2}(0) - y^{n-1}(0)$ where

$Y(s)$ is the Laplace transform of $y(t)$. $Y(s)$ is equivalent to **laplace(y(t),t,s)** in MATLAB terminology. The dependent variable y is a function of t and is entered by writing the command **y=sym('y(t)')**. The nth derivative of y that is $\frac{d^n y(t)}{dt^n}$ is written as **diff(y,n)** where the command **diff** is the differential operator $\frac{d}{dt}$ and in which the first and second input arguments of **diff** are the dependent variable and order of the derivative respectively. To exemplify the computation, Laplace transform of the 4th order derivative is given by $L\left[\frac{d^4 y(t)}{dt^4}\right] = s[s[s[sY(s) - y(0)] - y'(0)] - y''(0)] - y'''(0)$ and we implement that as follows:

```
>>y=sym('y(t)'); ↵                ← y holds y(t)
>>F=laplace(diff(y,4)) ↵          ← Workspace F holds the whole string for the transform of the derivative,
                                    F is any user-supplied assignee
F =

s*(s*(s*(s*laplace(y(t),t,s)-y(0))-D(y)(0))-@@(D,2)(y)(0))-@@(D,3)(y)(0)
```

By virtue of the commands **simplify** and **pretty**, you can even view the readable form on execution of **pretty(simplify(F))** at the command prompt. We did not describe the entering syntax of the initial conditions so far. Their MATLAB analogue strings are $y(t)\Big|_{t=0} = y(0)$ ⇔y(0), $\frac{dy(t)}{dt}\Big|_{t=0} = y'(0)$ ⇔D(y)(0), $\frac{d^2y(t)}{dt^2}\Big|_{t=0} = y''(0)$ ⇔\`@@\`(D,2)(y)(0), $\frac{d^3y(t)}{dt^3}\Big|_{t=0} = y'''(0)$ ⇔\`@@\`(D,3)(y)(0), and so are the other order derivatives. The characters in the string of any particular derivative are consecutive, there is no blank space between the characters. Note that the higher order derivatives more than one hold \`@@\` in which the \` is a character from the keyboard and is different from the transpose operator. In the string of F, the character \` is not displayed but it must be present when the user wants to access the derivative string.

Let us find the Laplace transform of $7\frac{d^3y}{dt^3} - 5\frac{dy}{dt} + 3y$ when $y(0) = 9$, $y'(0) = 3$, and $y''(0) = 2$. Following the substitution and simplification, one should get $L\left(7\frac{d^3y}{dt^3} - 5\frac{dy}{dt} + 3y\right) = [7s^3 - 5s + 3]Y(s) - 63s^2 - 21s + 31$. We intend to obtain this in MATLAB and the implementation is as follows:

```
>>y=sym('y(t)'); ↵                ← y holds the dependent variable of the derivatives, y(t)
>>F=laplace(7*diff(y,3)-5*diff(y,1)+3*y); ↵ ← F holds the whole string for the transform of the derivative
>>syms Y ↵
>>S=subs(F,{'laplace(y(t),t,s)','y(0)','D(y)(0)','`@@`(D,2)(y)(0)'},{Y,9,3,2}) ↵

S =

7*s*(s*(s*Y-9)-3)+31-5*s*Y+3*Y          ← rearranged [7s^3 - 5s + 3]Y(s) - 63s^2 - 21s + 31 we are after
```

The derivative $7\frac{d^3y}{dt^3}$ is coded by **7*diff(y,3)**, so is the others. From earlier discussion we know that the string **laplace(y(t),t,s)** is equivalent to $Y(s)$ and is a part of the string stored in **F**. We intend to replace the string (because it is too long) by single **Y** but again we are dealing with the symbolic toolbox functions so the **Y** needs to be mentioned as symbolic that is why the third line of above command is used. The **subs** used for substitution inherits different options. Now the **subs** exercises three input arguments – the first, second, and third of which are the string to be substituted which is here the transform string **F**, parts of the string which are to be replaced under single inverted comma, and the new values of the various parts in the string respectively. The second and third input arguments of the **subs** are placed within the second brace {.. }. Inside the second brace, individual string components are separated by commas. The placement of the strings in the second and third input arguments must take place in order. For example here the order we have is

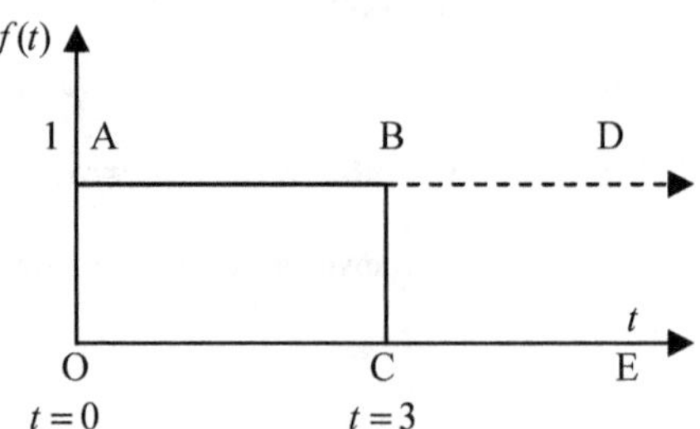

Figure 8.6(b) A rectangular pulse

$Y(s) \to y(0) \to y'(0) \to y''(0)$ both in the second and the third input arguments of the **subs**. However the workspace **S** holds the transform string following the initial value substitution.

Occasionally setting the transformed derivative expression to zero, only the $Y(s)$ as a function of the transform variable s is needed. For example $7\frac{d^3y}{dt^3} - 5\frac{dy}{dt} + 3y = 0$ in turns $[7s^3 - 5s + 3]Y(s) - 63s^2 - 21s + 31 = 0$ provides $Y(s) = \frac{63s^2 + 21s - 31}{7s^3 - 5s + 3}$. That is to say, we solve the expression stored in **S** for **Y** with the aid of the function **solve** (section 3.8) as follows:

```
>>T=solve(S,Y); ↵              ← T holds the string for the solution, T is any user-chosen name
>>pretty(T) ↵                  ← Display the readable form of the string stored in T
          2
      63 s  + 21 s - 31
      --------------------
          3
       7 s  - 5 s + 3
```

The first and second input arguments of the **solve** are the equation expression and the variable for which it is to be solved respectively.

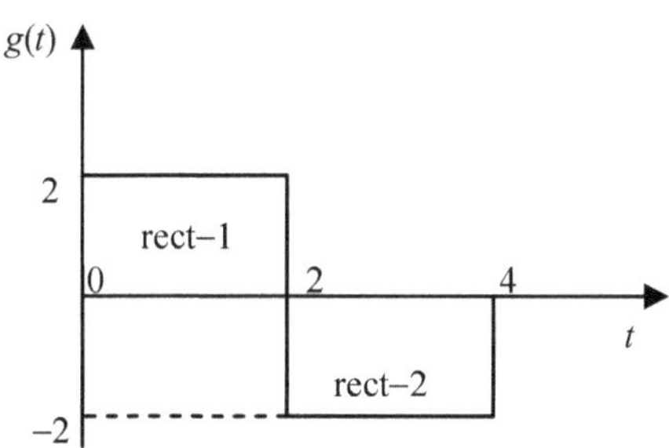

Figure 8.6(c) A square pulse

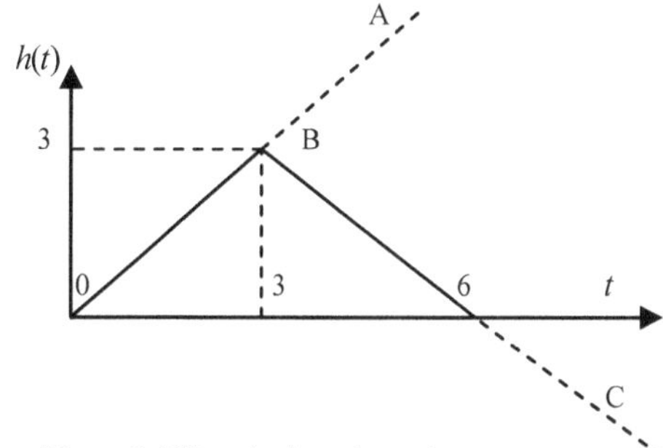

Figure 8.6(d) A triangular pulse

⬥⬥ Laplace transform of integrals

Laplace transform of the integral for example $L\left[\int_{x=0}^{x=t} f(x)\,dx\right] = \frac{F(s)}{s}$ is also obtainable where $F(s)$ is the Laplace transform of $f(t)$ and the implementation is as follows:

```
>>syms x t ↵                   ← Declaring the x and t as symbolic, x⇔x and t⇔t
>>f=sym('f(x)'); ↵             ← Declaring the f(x) as symbolic, f⇔f(x)
>>L=laplace(int(f,x,0,t)) ↵    ← Workspace L holds the L[∫_{x=0}^{x=t} f(x) dx], section 6.1 for the int

Warning: Explicit integral could not be found.
> In sym.int at 58
L =

laplace(f(t),t,s)/s
```

A warning message appears because no function is assigned to $f(x)$ which can be ignored. Anyhow the output is **laplace(f(t),t,s)/s**. With the definition $F(s)$ ⇔**laplace(f(t),t,s)**, the transform is $\frac{F(s)}{s}$.

⬥⬥ Laplace transform of graphical functions

The graphical functions can be represented in terms of the unit step function. For instance the rectangular pulse $f(t)$ =OABC shown in figure 8.6(b) can be constructed from OADE [which is the unit step function $u(t)$] and ECBD [which is the unit step function but shifted to the right at $t = 3$] that is $f(t)$ =OADE−ECBD= $u(t) - u(t-3)$ therefore the Laplace transform of $f(t)$ is $F(s) = \frac{1}{s} - \frac{e^{-3s}}{s}$ and the implementation is shown below:

```
>>syms t ↵                               ← Declaring the independent variable t as symbolic, t⇔t
>>f=heaviside(t)-heaviside(t-3); ↵       ← Workspace f holds f(t) = u(t) − u(t − 3), subsection 8.3.1
>>F=laplace(f) ↵                         ← Workspace F holds the string of F(s)
```

```
F =

1/s-exp(-3*s)/s
```

Next we have the finite square pulse $g(t)$ composed of rect−1 and rect−2 as labeled in the figure 8.6(c) and $g(t)$=rect−1+ rect−2= $2[u(t)-u(t-2)]-2[u(t-2)-u(t-4)]=2u(t)-4u(t-2)+2u(t-4)$ by expression. The transform of $g(t)$ is $G(s)$ $=\frac{2}{s}-\frac{4e^{-2s}}{s}+\frac{2e^{-4s}}{s}$ which can be obtained by exercising the following commands:

>>g=2*heaviside(t)-4*heaviside(t-2)+2*heaviside(t-4); ↵ ← Workspace g holds $g(t)$ assuming t is there
>>G=laplace(g); ↵ ← Workspace G holds the string of $G(s)$, g and G are user chosen
>>pretty(G) ↵ ← Displaying the readable form of G

```
              exp(-2 s)       exp(-4 s)
   2/s - 4 ------------ + 2 ------------
                 s               s
```

The finite triangular pulse $h(t)$ as depicted in figure 8.6(d) is constructed as $h(t)$=lower triangle 0B3+triangle 3B6. Equations of the straight lines 0BA and B6C are $h(t)=t$ and $h(t)=-t+6$ respectively. The triangles 0B3 and 3B6 are formed by $t[u(t)-u(t-3)]$ and $(6-t)[u(t-3)-u(t-6)]$ respectively so $h(t)=t\,u(t)+(6-2t)u(t-3)-(6-t)u(t-6)$ whose transform is $H(s)=\frac{1}{s^2}-\frac{2e^{-3s}}{s^2}+\frac{e^{-6s}}{s^2}$ and the commands we need are **h=t*heaviside(t)+(6-2*t)*heaviside(t-3)-(6-t)*heaviside(t-6); H=laplace(h);** where the H holds the string for $H(s)$. These techniques can be applied to the finite duration function of different types for instance sinusoidal, exponential, or other.

8.5.2 Inverse Laplace transform

If $F(s)$ is a function of Laplace transform variable s, the inverse Laplace transform of $F(s)$ is defined as $f(t)=L^{-1}[F(s)]=\frac{1}{2\pi i}\int_{s=c-i\infty}^{s=c+i\infty} e^{st}F(s)\,ds$ where L^{-1} is the inverse transform operator and c is a real number. The number c is selected in such a way that all singularities of $F(s)$ are to the left of the line $s=c$ in the s plane. This is the formal definition of the inverse Laplace transform but as a working convenience, $F(s)$ is maneuvered to take the form of commonly known functions whose inverse Laplace transforms are known. MATLAB function that performs the inverse Laplace transform is **ilaplace**. To take the inverse Laplace transform of $F(s)$, we use the command **ilaplace**(code of $F(s)$ in vector string form – section 14.2, independent variable of $F(s)$, return variable for the inverse transform $f(t)$). Also we declare the related variable using the **syms** before applying the **ilaplace**. Readable form of the inverse string is seen using the **pretty**. Let us see the implementation for $F(s)=\frac{1}{s^2+1}$. From the table 8.B, we read $f(t)=L^{-1}\left[\frac{1}{s^2+1}\right]=$ $\sin t$ for which implementation we carry out the following:

>>syms s t ↵ ← Independent variables of $F(s)$ and $f(t)$ are declared as symbolic, t⇔t and s⇔s
>>F=1/(s^2+1); ↵ ← Vector code of $F(s)$ is assigned to workspace F, F⇔$F(s)$, F is any user-chosen name
>>f=ilaplace(F,s,t) ↵ ← Inverse Laplace transform is returned to workspace f, f⇔$f(t)$, f is user-chosen name

```
f =

sin(t)
```
← Code for the $\sin t$

Since the default return of the **ilaplace** is also in terns of t, the command **ilaplace(1/(s^2+1))** would bring about the same outcome. Maintaining the symbology just discussed, three more examples are illustrated in the following.

◆◆ Example A

A polynomial of s for example $F(s)=3s-7s^2$ has the inverse transform $f(t)=3\frac{d[\delta(t)]}{dt}-7\frac{d^2[\delta(t)]}{dt^2}$:

>>syms s, F=3*s-7*s^2; ↵ ← code of $3s-7s^2$ is assigned to F
>>f=ilaplace(F) ↵ ← f holds the $f(t)$

```
f =

3*dirac(1,t)-7*dirac(2,t)
```

The dirac(2,t) in the return indicates $\frac{d^2[\delta(t)]}{dt^2}$ where $\delta(t)$ is the Dirac delta function (subsection 8.3.1) and the first input argument of the dirac is the derivative order.

Example B

Rational form function $F(s)=\frac{2s^3+3}{s^4-6s^3+32s}$ has the inverse $f(t)=\frac{3}{32}+\frac{13}{72}e^{-2t}+\frac{497}{288}e^{4t}+\frac{131}{24}te^{4t}$:

```
>>syms s, F=(2*s^3+3)/(s^4-6*s^3+32*s); ↵ ← Code of F(s) is assigned to the workspace F
>>f=ilaplace(F); ↵                   ← f contains the inverse transform string for f(t)
>>pretty(f) ↵                        ← Displaying the readable form of the string stored in f
                  /131     497\             13
          3/32 + |----- t + -----| exp(4 t) + --- exp(-2 t)        ← Rearranged f(t)
                  \ 24     288/             72
```

Example C

$F(s)=e^{-3s}\frac{s+2}{s^2+2s+5}$ has the inverse transform $f(t)=u(t-3)\,[\,e^{-t+3}\cos(2t-6)+\frac{1}{2}e^{-t+3}\sin(2t-6)\,]$:

```
>>syms s, F=exp(-3*s)*(s+2)/(s^2+2*s+5); ↵ ← Code of F(s) is assigned to the workspace F
>>f=ilaplace(F); ↵  ← f contains the inverse transform string for f(t)
>>pretty(f) ↵       ← Displaying the readable form of the string stored in f
   (exp(-t + 3) cos(2 t - 6) + 1/2 exp(-t + 3) sin(2 t - 6)) heaviside(t - 3)   ← Subsection 8.3.1 for u(t)
```

8.5.3 Integrodifferential equations using Laplace transform

An integrodifferential equation is composed of both the differential $\frac{d}{dt}$ and integral $\int .... dt$ operators. Subsection 8.5.1 illustrates the implementation of Laplace transform on the differential and integral operators. We combine these two techniques to solve an integrodifferential equation in the following two examples. To solve the integrodifferential equation, the equation is rearranged in two parts – the first is the integral part and the other is the rest of the equation so that the right side of the equation is zero for instance the integrodifferential equation $y'+\int_{x=0}^{x=t} y(x)dx = 2u(t)$ is written as $[y'-2u(t)]+\int_{x=0}^{x=t} y(x)dx = 0$. Laplace transforms of the two parts are taken separately and then added to form the complete integrodifferential equation.

Example A

Solve the equation $y'+\int_{x=0}^{x=t} y(x)dx = 2u(t)$ subject to $y(0)=4$. Taking Laplace transform on both sides of the equation and applying the initial condition, one obtains $Y(s)=\frac{2(2s+1)}{s^2+1}$ from which the inverse transform is $y(t)=4\cos t+2\sin t$. Our objective is to obtain the $Y(s)$ and $y(t)$ starting from the integrodifferential equation. The nonintegral and integral parts of the equation are separated as $[y'-2u(t)]+\int_{x=0}^{x=t} y(x)dx = 0$ on that account following is the implementation:

```
>>syms t ↵                  ← Declaration of independent variable t in the part [y' − 2u(t)] as symbolic
>>y=sym('y(t)'); ↵          ← Declaration of the dependent y(t) in the part [y' − 2u(t)] as symbolic
>>P1=laplace(diff(y)-2*heaviside(t)); ↵   ← Workspace P1 holds the transform on the [y' − 2u(t)]
>>y=sym('y(x)'); syms x ↵ ← Defining y(x) as function of x for the integral part as well as x as symbolic
>>P2=laplace(int(y,x,0,t)); ↵ ← Workspace P2 holds the transform of the integral part ignoring the warning
>>E=P1+P2; ↵ ← The complete integrodifferential equation is formed from P1+P2 and assigned to E
>>E=subs(E,{'y(0)'},{4}); ↵ ← Initial condition y(0)=4 is inserted in the string of E and assigned to E again
>>syms Y ↵              ← Declaring Y as symbolic for replacing the string laplace(y(t),t,s) stored in E by Y
>>E=subs(E,{'laplace(y(t),t,s)'},{Y}); ↵ ← String laplace(y(t),t,s) is replaced by Y and again assigned to E
>>Y=solve(E,Y); ↵           ← Y(s) is obtained forming an equation E=0 and assigned to Y, Y⇔Y(s)
>>pretty(Y) ↵               ← Displaying the readable form of Y from its string
          2 s + 1
      2 ------------
            2
           s  + 1
```

```
>>y=ilaplace(Y); ↵          ← Taking inverse Laplace transform, y⇔ L^-1 [ Y(s) ]⇔ y(t)
>>pretty(y) ↵               ← Displaying the readable form of y(t) stored in y
        4 cos(t) + 2 sin(t)
```

Example B

Let us solve the integrodifferential equation $8y''+12y'+6y+\int_{x=0}^{x=t} y(x)dx = 2\delta(t-2)$ with $y(0)=0$ and $y'(0)=3$ to obtain $Y(s)=\frac{2s(12+e^{-2s})}{8s^3+12s^2+6s+1}$ and $y(t)=3te^{-\frac{t}{2}}-\frac{3t^2e^{-\frac{t}{2}}}{4}-\frac{1}{16}t^2e^{1-\frac{t}{2}}u(t-2)+\frac{1}{2}te^{1-\frac{t}{2}}u(t-2)-\frac{3}{4}e^{1-\frac{t}{2}}u(t-2)$ for which the rearranged equation is $[8y''+12y'+6y-2\delta(t-2)]+[\int_{x=0}^{x=t} y(x)dx]=0$ and we implement that as follows:

```
>>syms t ↵ ← Declaration of independent variable t in the part [8y''+12y'+6y-2δ(t-2)] as symbolic
>>y=sym('y(t)'); ↵ ← Declaration of the dependent y(t) in the part [8y''+12y'+6y-2δ(t-2)] as symbolic
>>P1=laplace(8*diff(y,2)+12*diff(y)+6*y-2*dirac(t-2)); ↵ ← Workspace P1 holds the transform on
                                                            [8y''+12y'+6y-2δ(t-2)]
>>y=sym('y(x)'); syms x ↵ ← Defining y(x) as function of x for the integral part as well as x as symbolic
>>P2=laplace(int(y,x,0,t)); ↵ ← Workspace P2 holds the transform of the integral part ignoring the warning
>>E=P1+P2; ↵ ← The complete integrodifferential equation is formed from P1+P2 and assigned to E
>>E=subs(E,{'y(0)','D(y)(0)'},{0,3}); ↵ ← Initial conditions y(0) = 0 and y'(0) = 3 =4 are inserted in the
                                          string of E and assigned to E again
>>syms Y ↵          ← Declaring Y as symbolic for replacing the string laplace(y(t),t,s) stored in E by Y
>>E=subs(E,{'laplace(y(t),t,s)'},{Y}); ↵ ← String laplace(y(t),t,s) is replaced by Y and again assigned to E
>>Y=solve(E,Y); ↵           ← Y(s) is obtained forming an equation E=0 and assigned to Y, Y⇔ Y(s)
>>pretty(Y) ↵               ← Displaying the readable form of Y from its string
         s (12 + exp(-2 s) )
      2 ---------------------------
            3       2
         8 s  + 12 s  + 6 s + 1
>>y=ilaplace(Y); ↵          ← Taking inverse Laplace transform, y⇔ L^-1 [ Y(s) ]⇔ y(t)
>>pretty(y) ↵               ← Displaying the readable form of y(t) stored in y

                                        2
     (- 1/16 heaviside(t - 2) t  + 1/2 heaviside(t - 2) t - 3/4 heaviside(t - 2))

                                        2
          exp(- 1/2 t + 1) + (- 3/4 t  + 3 t) exp(- 1/2 t)
```

8.6 Z transform

Z transform is applicable for the discrete functions. Like the Fourier and Laplace transforms, the Z transform also shares the strategy of the forward-inverse as shown in the figure 8.7(a). The function $f[n]$ is discrete but the transform $F(z)$ is continuous. Depending on the integer index n variation, the Z transform can be bilateral or unilateral. In the former the n changes from minus infinity to plus infinity whereas the n changes from 0 to plus infinity in the latter. In MATLAB we implement the unilateral one as addressed in the following.

$$discrete\ f[n] \xrightarrow{forward\ Z\ transform} F(z) \xrightarrow{inverse\ Z\ transform} f[n]$$

Figure 8.7(a) The concept behind the Z transform

8.6.1 Forward Z transform of discrete functions

Unilateral forward Z transform $F(z)$ of the discrete function $f[n]$ is defined as $Z\ \{f[n]\}=F(z)=\sum_{n=0}^{n=\infty} f[n]z^{-n}$ where $n\geq 0$ and n is integer, and Z is the forward transform operator. MATLAB function **ztrans** (abbreviation for the Z transform) provides many symbolically known forward transforms. To have the unilateral Z transform of the discrete function $f[n]$ (assuming that the envelope of $f[n]$ follows some functional variation), we employ the command **ztrans**(vector code of $f[n]$ – section 14.2, independent variable of $f[n]$, wanted transform variable). Since the computation is merely symbolic, declaration of the associated variables using the **syms** (section 2.1) is mandatory.

Let us implement the transform with $f[n]=e^{na}$. Its unilateral Z transform is $F(z)=Z\{[e^{an}]\}=\sum_{n=0}^{n=\infty} e^{an}z^{-n}=$ $(1-e^az^{-1})^{-1}=\frac{z}{z-e^a}$. Starting from e^{na}, we intend to obtain $\frac{z}{z-e^a}$ – that is the problem statement for which we conduct the following:

```
>>syms n a z ↵ ← Declaring related and wanted transform variables as symbolic, a⇔a , n⇔n , z⇔z
>>F=ztrans(exp(n*a),n,z); ↵ ← F holds the Z transform on the vector code of e^na , F⇔F(z) , F user-chosen
>>pretty(simple(F)) ↵       ← Displaying the readable form of the string for F(z) stored in F,
       z                      simple for simplification, section 3.1 for pretty
 -------------
  z - exp(a)
```

The command **ztrans(exp(n*a))** also brings about the same result because of the default return. If the independent and transform variables were **p** and **w** respectively, the command would be **ztrans(exp(p*a),p,w)**. Discrete function like $f[n]=e^{-n^2}$ does not have Z transform, we see then **ztrans(exp(-n^2),n,z)** as the return which is the code for the definition $Z\{[e^{-n^2}]\}$. Applying the same symbols and functions, shown table 8.C presents the mathematical and MATLAB correspondence of some unilateral Z transforms.

Table 8.C Unilateral Z transforms of some discrete functions

Mathematical form	MATLAB commands	Mathematical form	MATLAB commands
$Z\{\sin[na]\}=\frac{z\sin a}{z^2-2z\cos a+1}$	>>syms a n ↵ >>F=ztrans(sin(n*a)); ↵ >>pretty(F) ↵ sin(a) z --------------------------- 2 - 2 z cos(a) + z + 1	$Z\{\cos[na]\}=\frac{z(z-\cos a)}{z^2-2z\cos a+1}$	>>syms a n ↵ >>F=ztrans(cos(n*a)); ↵ >>pretty(F) ↵ z (-cos(a) + z) -------------------------- 2 - 2 z cos(a) + z + 1
$Z\{[a^n]\}=\frac{z}{z-a}$	>>syms a n ↵ >>F=ztrans(a^n); ↵ >>pretty(simple(F)) ↵ z - ---------- -z + a	$Z\{u[n]\}=\frac{z}{z-1}$	>>syms n ↵ >>F=ztrans(heaviside(n)); ↵ >>pretty(F) ↵ z ------- z - 1
$Z\{\delta[n]\}=1$	>>d=sym('charfcn[0](n)'); ↵ >>F=ztrans(d); ↵ ← d⇔ $\delta[n]$ >>pretty(F) ↵ 1 The $\delta[n]$ is represented by sym('charfcn[0](n)') not by dirac(n)	$Z\{[r^n\sin na]\}=\frac{rz\sin a}{z^2-2zr\cos a+r^2}$	>>syms a n r ↵ >>F=ztrans(r^n*sin(n*a)); ↵ >>pretty(simple(F)) ↵ r sin(a) z ------------------------------ 2 2 -2 z r cos(a) + z + r
$Z\{[n^2a^n]\}=\frac{za(z+a)}{(z-a)^3}$	>>syms a n ↵ >>F=ztrans(n^2*a^n); ↵ >>pretty(F) ↵ z a (z + a) - ------------- 3 (-z + a)	$Z\{a^{n-3}u[n-3]\}=\frac{1}{z^2(z-a)}$	>>syms a n ↵ >>F=ztrans(a^(n-3)*heaviside(n-3)); ↵ >>pretty(simple(F)) ↵ 1 ------------ 2 (z - a) z

♦♦ Z transform of finite sequences

Most examples of $f[n]$ set in the table 8.C conceive n in the range $0\le n\le\infty$. Discrete functions may exist only for few values of n then $f[n]$ is called a finite sequence. We present two examples on the finite sequence transform in the following.

Let us consider the first finite sequence $f[n]=\begin{cases}2^{-\frac{n}{4}} & for\ 0\le n\le 8\\ 0 & elsewhere\end{cases}$. By dint of the unit step sequence $u[n]$ (discrete version of $u(t)$), the $f[n]$ is expressed as $f[n]=[2^{-\frac{n}{4}}]\{u[n]-u[n-8]\}$ on that $F(z)=Z\{f[n]\}=$

$Z\{[2^{-\frac{n}{4}}]u[n]\} - Z\{[2^{-\frac{n}{4}}]u[n-8]\} = \frac{2^{\frac{1}{4}}z}{2^{\frac{1}{4}}z-1} - \frac{1}{4}\frac{2^{\frac{1}{4}}}{(2^{\frac{1}{4}}z-1)z^7} = \frac{1}{4z^7}\left[4z^7 + 2\times2^{\frac{3}{4}}z^6 + 2\times2^{\frac{1}{2}}z^5 + 2\times2^{\frac{1}{4}}z^4 + 2z^3 + 2^{\frac{3}{4}}z^2 + 2^{\frac{1}{2}}z + 2^{\frac{1}{4}}\right]$ and we execute that as follows:

```
>>syms n ↵
>>f=2^(-n/4)*(heaviside(n)-heaviside(n-8)); ↵ ← Vector code of f[n] is assigned to f, f⇔ f[n]
>>F=ztrans(f); ↵                              ← F holds the transform on f[n], F⇔ F(z)
>>pretty(simple(F)) ↵ ← Displaying readable form of F(z) following simplification on the string stored in F
           7      3/4  6      1/2  5      1/4  4        3    3/4  2    1/2      1/4
  1/4 (4 z  + 2 2    z  + 2 2    z  + 2 2    z  + 2 z  + 2    z  + 2    z + 2   

                                          /  7
                                        ) / z
                                         /
```

The next illustrative finite sequence is $\begin{Bmatrix} f[n] & \rightarrow & 6 & -4 & 3 & 0 & 2 & 6 & 8 & 2 \\ n & \rightarrow & 3 & 4 & 5 & 6 & 7 & 8 & 9 & 10 \end{Bmatrix}$ which tells us that $f[n]$ does not follow any specific function and that $f[n]$ exists for $3 \le n \le 10$. At $n=3$, $f[n]=6$ can be represented as $f[3] = 6\delta[n-3]$. As a functional form, we can write $f[n] = 6\delta[n-3] - 4\delta[n-4] + 3\delta[n-5] + 0\delta[n-6] + 2\delta[n-7] + 6\delta[n-8] + 8\delta[n-9] + 2\delta[n-10]$. Applying $Z\{\delta[n-n_0]\} = \frac{1}{z^{n_0}}$ makes us get $F(z) = \frac{6z^7 - 4z^6 + 3z^5 + 2z^3 + 6z^2 + 8z + 2}{z^{10}}$ which we intend to implement as follows:

```
>>y=sym([6 -4 3 0 2 6 8 2]); ↵  ← Declare f[n] values as symbolic and put to a row matrix y
>>d=sym('charfcn[m](n)'); ↵     ← Define the general delta function δ[n – m] as symbolic, d⇔ δ[n – m]
>>syms m ↵                      ← Define m as symbolic for the use of δ[n – m]
>>f=[ ]; ↵ ← Assigning empty matrix to f for accumulation of delta functions as a row matrix (section 14.3.3)
>>for k=3:10 f=[f subs(d,m,k)]; end ↵ ← Create all delta functions from δ[n – 3] to δ[n – 10] and
                                        assign those to f, where f is a row matrix. For-loop counter
                                        k gives the control on the location of the delta functions
>>f=y.*f; ↵   ← f[n] for different n is formed from the scalar product (section 14.2) of y and
                f (this f contains only delta functions) and again assigned to f (assignee f contains f[n] at
                different n as a row matrix element)
>>f=sum(f); ↵  ← Summing (section 2.8) all delta functions in f to form function f[n], assignee f⇔ f[n]
>>F=ztrans(f); ↵ ← F⇔ F(z)
>>pretty(simplify(F)) ↵ ←Displaying readable form of F(z) following simplification on the string stored in F
        7      6      5      3      2
     6 z  - 4 z  + 3 z  + 2 z  + 6 z  + 8 z + 2
     -----------------------------------------
                        10
                       z
```

The function charfcn[m](n) is equivalent to discrete $\delta[n-m]$ in which the m and n are under the third and first braces respectively.

8.6.2 Inverse Z transforms

Given a Z transform function $F(z)$, its inverse Z transform (by operator Z^{-1}) is obtained in terms of the contour integral as $f[n] = \frac{1}{2\pi i}\oint_C F(z)z^{n-1}\,dz$ where C is a counterclockwise closed contour in the region of the convergence of $F(z)$ and the contour encircles the origin of the z-plane. MATLAB counterpart for the inverse Z transform is **iztrans** (abbreviation for the inverse z transform). To perform inverse Z transform on $F(z)$, we use the command iztrans(vector string of the transform $F(z)$ – section 14.2, transform variable, inverse transform variable). We declare the related variables of $F(z)$ using the **syms** before applying the **iztrans**. It is understood that the return function is discrete. From the table 8.C, we have $Z\{[a^n]\} = F(z) = \frac{z}{z-a}$ so the inverse Z transform is $Z^{-1}[\frac{z}{z-a}] = [a^n] = f[n]$

which happens through the following:

>>syms z a n ↵ ← Defining variables of $F(z)$ and return variable as symbolic, z⇔ z , a⇔ a , and n⇔ n

>>F=z/(z-a); ↵ ← Assigning vector code of $F(z)$ to F, F⇔ $F(z)$, F is user-chosen name

>>f=iztrans(F,z,n); ↵ ← Assigning inverse transform on F to f, f⇔ $f[n]$, f is user-chosen name

>>pretty(f) ↵ ← Displaying the readable form of the string stored in f

```
      n
     a
```

The command iztrans(F) also executes above result because of the default definition. If the F were in w and the return were required in terms of x, the command would be iztrans(F,w,x). Following the same functions and symbology, few more examples are illustrated in the following.

Example A

$X(z)=\dfrac{z^2}{(z-a)(z-c)}$ has the inverse transform $x[n]=\dfrac{a^{n+1}-c^{n+1}}{a-c}$ and is implemented as follows:

>>syms z a c n ↵ ←Defining variables of $X(z)$ and return variable as symbolic, z⇔ z ,a⇔ a ,n⇔ n ,c⇔ c

>>X=z^2/(z-a)/(z-c); ↵ ← Assigning vector code of $X(z)$ to X, X⇔ $X(z)$

>>x=iztrans(X,z,n); ↵ ← Assigning inverse transform on X to x, x⇔ $x[n]$

>>pretty(x) ↵ ← Displaying the readable form of the string stored in x

```
       n    n
    a a  - c c
    ------------
      - c + a
```

Example B

Given that the inverse transform of $F(z)=\dfrac{z^{-1}+z^{-2}}{\left(1-\frac{1}{2}z^{-1}\right)\left(1+\frac{1}{3}z^{-1}\right)}$ is $f[n]=-6\delta[n]+\dfrac{18}{5}\left(\dfrac{1}{2}\right)^n+\dfrac{12}{5}\left(-\dfrac{1}{3}\right)^n$. It is permissible that we assign the numerator and denominator of $F(z)$ separately and combine afterwards so that less mistakes can happen in typing or coding. Let us carry out the following:

>>syms z ↵ ←Defining variables of $F(z)$ as symbolic, z⇔ z

>>N=1/z+1/z^2; ↵ ← Assigning only the numerator code of $F(z)$ to workspace N

>>D=(1-1/2/z)*(1+1/3/z); ↵ ← Assigning only the denominator code of $F(z)$ to workspace D

>>f=iztrans(N/D); ↵ ← $F(z)$ is formed by N/D, f holds the inverse transform, f⇔ $f[n]$

>>pretty(f) ↵ ← Displaying the readable form of the string stored in f

```
                                      n              n
     -6 charfcn[0](n) + 18/5 (1/2)  + 12/5 (-1/3)
```

← charfcn[0](n)⇔ $\delta[n]$

Example C

Transform look-up table of MATLAB does not contain the inverse of the function like $F(z)=\ln(1-4z)$ therefore the response would be iztrans(log(1-4*z),z,n) while applying the function.

Example D

The transform function $F(z)=\dfrac{3}{(2-\frac{2}{3}z^{-1})^2(2-3z^{-1})(1-4z^{-1})}$ has the inverse counterpart $f[n]=\dfrac{195}{5929}3^{-n}+\dfrac{3}{308}n3^{-n}-\dfrac{729}{1960}\left(\dfrac{3}{2}\right)^n+\dfrac{432\times 4^n}{605}$. It is better if we assign the numerator and denominator strings separately and combine them latter as follows:

>>syms z ↵ ← Defining variables of $F(z)$ as symbolic, z⇔ z

>>N=3; ↵ ← Assigning only the numerator string of $F(z)$ to workspace N

>>D=(2-2/3/z)^2*(2-3/z)*(1-4/z); ↵ ← Assigning only the denominator string of $F(z)$ to workspace D

>>f=iztrans(N/D); ↵ ← Z^{-1} on $F(z)$ formed by N/D, f holds the string of $f[n]$

>>pretty(f) ↵ ← Displaying the readable form of the string stored in f

```
   195         n                  n        729        n    432    n
  ------- (1/3)  + 3/308 (1/3)  n -  ------- (3/2)  + ------ 4
   5929                                1960              605
```

8.6.3 Z transform on difference equations

In subsection 8.5.1 we discussed the Laplace transform on the differential coefficients. Similar implementation follows on the difference coefficients and difference equations. The difference coefficients always involve dependent variable terms like y_k, y_{k+1}, y_{k+2}, ... etc or $y[k]$, $y[k+1]$, $y[k+2]$, ... etc (another representation) where $y[k]$ is the discrete function and function of integer index k. They have equivalent MATLAB style of symbolic writing as sym('y(k)'), sym('y(k+1)'), sym('y(k+2)'), ... etc respectively. From the theory of unilateral Z transform we know that $F(z)=Z\{\,y[k+3]\,\}=z^3Y(z)-y[0]z^3-y[1]z^2-y[2]z$ where $Y(z)$ is the Z transform of $y[k]$ and implement that as follows:

```
>>y3=sym('y(k+3)'); ↵ ← Workspace variable y3 holds the code of y[k+3], y3⇔ y[k+3], y3 user-chosen
>>F=ztrans(y3) ↵      ← Workspace variable F holds the Z transform on y[k+3], F⇔ F(z), F user-chosen

F =

z^3*ztrans(y(k),k,z)-y(0)*z^3-y(1)*z^2-y(2)*z      ← Vector code (section 14.2) of the string for F(z)
```

In above string the equivalence is ztrans(y(k),k,z)⇔ $Y(z)$, y(0)⇔ $y[0]$, y(1)⇔ $y[1]$, and y(2)⇔ $y[2]$ (the last three obviously the initial conditions). The ztrans equally applies for the negative indices for example $F(z)=Z\{\,y[k-3]\,\}=\frac{1}{z^3}Y(z)$ is implemented by using the commands y3=sym('y(k-3)'); and F=ztrans(y3).

The difference equation $y_{k+2}+4y_{k+1}+4y_k=0$ along with the initial conditions $y_0=1$ and $y_1=2$ has the $Y(z)=\frac{z^2+6z}{(z+2)^2}$ and $y[k]=(-2)^k-2(-2)^k k$ – we intend to obtain it from MATLAB whose implementation is presented below (applying similar variable, function, and symbology to those of the section 8.5):

```
>>E=sym('y(k+2)+4*y(k+1)+4*y(k)'); ↵     ← Forming only the left side of the equation which is
                                            y_{k+2} + 4y_{k+1} + 4y_k and assign that to workspace E
>>T=ztrans(E); ↵              ← Z transform on E and assign that to workspace T, T is any user-chosen name
>>syms Y ↵                    ← Defining Y as symbolic, where Y⇔ Y(z) ⇔ztrans(y(k),k,z)
>>T=subs(T,{'ztrans(y(k),k,z)','y(0)','y(1)'},{Y,1,2}); ↵ ← Replacing ztrans(y(k),k,z), y(0), and y(1) from
                                the string held in T by Y, 1, and 2 respectively
>>Y=solve(T,Y); ↵             ← Finding Y(z) by forming an equation T=0 and output assigned to Y again
>>pretty(Y) ↵                 ← Displaying the readable form of the string for the Y(z) stored in Y
          z (z + 6)
        ---------------
          2
         z  + 4 z + 4
>>y=iztrans(Y,sym('k')); ↵ ← y holds inverse Z transform on string for Y and adding 2nd argument
                             sym('k'), we ask MATLAB to return the output in terms of k, y⇔ y[k]
>>pretty(y) ↵                 ← Displaying the readable form of the string for the y[k] stored in y
             k         k
      -2 (-2)  k + (-2)
```

With this example we bring an end to the chapter.

Chapter 9

Before we commence our exploration on the functions of statistics, it might be helpful to give a detail of the importance of such study. Statistics and probability are becoming increasingly important in natural science and in social science as well. To be illustrative, the fields of statistics compass communications engineering, computer communications, networking theory, artificial intelligence, robotics, growth-yield treatment in agriculture and plant science, demographic prediction, meteorological prediction…etc. The problems selected for this chapter cover the level of a first course in engineering and scientific statistics. There is a dedicated toolbox for the statistics in MATLAB. Out of numerous features in the toolbox, few introductory statistical functions are addressed as far as short context is concern. However we underscore the following:

- A substantial number of the built-in random number generators for singly or i.i.d. generation
- Frequency table preparation and various types of means such as geometric, harmonic, etc
- Important data statistics such as variance, standard deviation, median, moment, etc
- Probability density and cumulative distribution functions for random variables
- Least square data fitting, regression analysis, and principal component analysis

9.1 Random number generators

Generating random numbers is the first step of many statistical analyses. There are a number of programmed random number generators such as **unifrnd**, **randint**, **normrnd**, **randsrc**,…etc found in MATLAB for which the following discussions are presented. Each random number generator produces scalar or matrix depending on the type of input argument or arguments. Both the continuous and discrete random variables can be generated with specific functions. When we generate a particular random number in a matrix, the numbers in the matrix are called independently identical distributed or i.i.d. according to the statistical literature. Let us perform the following random variable generation in which the font equivalence like X⇔ X is maintained.

Uniformly distributed continuous random variable

The function unifrnd (abbreviation for uniformly fractional random) generates uniformly distributed continuous random variable X from user-defined range $A \le X \le B$ where $B > A$. One of the common syntaxes of the function is unifrnd(A , B) for example any fractional value in $-4 \le X \le 5$ can be generated using the command unifrnd(-4,5). The random numbers in row, column, or rectangular matrix can be generated by four input arguments with the syntax unifrnd(A , B , user-required row number, user-required column number). Attached on the right side is the implementation in which the bold heading describes the random numbers need to be generated. When you execute the commands, these output numbers may not appear in the command window due to the randomness of the generation but the numbers will be between the defined range that is for sure. In all cases we assigned the output of the function to the workspace X which can be any user-given name. A row and a column matrix of length 4 has the rectangular matrix dimension 1×4 and 4×1 which we used in the generation of the random numbers in the row and column matrices respectively. The fractional value means the generation is in the continuous sense. The term uniform means any value between –4 and 5 is equally likely.

Generation of a single random number X between –4 and 5,

```
>>X=unifrnd(-4,5) ↵

X =

   -2.2373
```

Generation of a column matrix X of length 4 in which every element is inbetween -4 and 5,

```
>>X=unifrnd(-4,5,4,1) ↵

X =

    4.0428
   -3.4790
   -0.8242
    1.3456
```

Generation of a row matrix X of length 4 in which every element is inbetween -4 and 5,

```
>>X=unifrnd(-4,5,1,4) ↵

X =

   -0.3486  4.4192  4.2521  -0.3076
```

Generation of a rectangular matrix X of order 2x3 in which every element is inbetween -4 and 5,

```
>>X=unifrnd(-4,5,2,3) ↵

X =

    3.3185  -2.7500  -2.2115
   -3.9112  -2.1751   1.4341
```

◆◆ Uniformly distributed random integers

The command randint (abbreviation for random integers) generates random integers based on user-requirement. The function has the syntax randint(user-required row number, user-required column number, integer range as a two element row matrix but first the lower bound and then the upper bound). Attached on the right side is the implementation of the random number generation subject to different input arguments. The bold headings describe the integers need to be generated. A single scalar has the rectangular matrix dimension 1×1. In all cases we assigned the return from the function randint to the workspace X.

One can use the function to generate the binary numbers 0 and 1. For example a single random binary number is generated by the command X=randint(1,1,[0 1]). A row matrix of 10 binary numbers is generated by X=randint(1,10,[0 1]).

Generation of a single random integer X between -3 and 5,

```
>>X=randint(1,1,[-3 5]) ↵

X =

     4
```

Generation of a column matrix X of length 3 in which each element is in between -3 and 5,

```
>>X=randint(3,1,[-3 5]) ↵

X =

     5
    -3
     0
```

Generation of a row matrix X of length 4 in which each element is in between -3 and 5,

```
>>X=randint(1,4,[-3 5]) ↵

X =

     5  3  -2  0
```

Generation of a rectangular matrix X of order 3x3 in which each element is in between -3 and 5,

```
>>X=randint(3,3,[-3,5]) ↵

X =

     4  -2  -1
    -3  -2  -2
    -2   2  -3
```

◆◆ Other random numbers

In many scientific problems, one needs to generate the Gaussian random number from user-supplied mean μ and standard deviation σ which we implement by the function normrnd (abbreviation for normal random number). The function in general provides matrix based Gaussian random numbers for which the common syntax is normrnd (μ , σ ,user-required row number, user-required column number). It should be noted that the random number might appear from $-\infty$ to $+\infty$ theoretically but with more likelihood towards the user-given mean. However on the right side is the execution of the random numbers. The bold headings mention the type of the number required. In all cases we assigned the return from the function to the workspace X (can be any user-chosen name). The generation is in continuous sense. A normal random number has μ =0 and σ =1 which is just a special case of the Gausssian random number.

Generation of a single Gaussian number X of mean μ =2 and standard deviation σ =4,

```
>>X=normrnd(2,4,1,1) ↵

X =

    6.2671
```

Generation of a column matrix X of length 3 in which every element is a Gaussian random number with μ =2 and σ =4,

```
>>X=normrnd(2,4,3,1) ↵

X =

    7.1610
    4.6744
    6.7634
```

Generation of a row matrix X of length 4 in which every element is a Gaussian random number with μ =2 and σ =4,

```
>>X=normrnd(2,4,1,4) ↵

X =

   -3.3447  4.8573  8.4942  -0.7671
```

Generation of a rectangular matrix X of order 3x3 in which every element is a Gaussian random number with μ =2 and σ =4,

```
>>X=normrnd(2,4,3,3) ↵

X =

    5.4320  -3.7639  4.7600
    7.0160   4.2846  5.2625
   -4.3749   0.4005  4.8476
```

Not only do we see Gaussian number in the statistics literature. More than a dozen random numbers are seen in the literature. We illustrated just three generators. This sort of generation is possible for the other random numbers which are presented in the table 9.A.

⬍⬍ Random numbers from a set

Suppose some random numbers are given in a set. Randomly we intend to select the members from the set. This sort of set based random number generation takes place using the function randsrc which has the common syntax randsrc(user-required row number, user-required column number, integer or fractional numbers in the set as a row matrix). As an example, let us say we intend to generate a single random number X from the set of −1 and 1 whose execution is the following:

```
>>X=randsrc(1,1,[-1 1]) ↵

X =
     -1
```

Again we wish to form a matrix of size 2×2 in which every element is from the integers 7, 3, and 98 for which we execute the following:

```
>>X=randsrc(2,2,[7 3 98]) ↵

X =
     7   98
     7    3
```

Table 9.A Random number generators and their MATLAB counterparts

Name of the random number	MATLAB generator	Executable form
Beta random numbers with parameters α and β	betarnd	A=betarnd(α , β , M , N) for matrix S=betarnd(α , β) for single number
Binomial random numbers with parameters N and p	binornd	A=binornd(N , p , M , N) for matrix S=binornd(N , p) for single number
Chi square random numbers with parameter n	chi2rnd	A=chi2rnd(n , M , N) for matrix S=chi2rnd(n) for single number
F random numbers with parameters n_1 and n_2	frnd	A=frnd(n_1 , n_2 , M , N) for matrix S=frnd(n_1 , n_2) for single number
Gamma random numbers with parameters α and β	gamrnd	A=gamrnd(α , β , M , N) for matrix S=gamrnd(α , β) for single number
Poisson random numbers with parameter λ	poissrnd	A=poissrnd(λ , M , N) for matrix S=poissrnd(λ) for single number
T random numbers with parameter n	trnd	A=trnd(n , M , N) for matrix S=trnd(n) for single number

Some other generators:

Name	Counterpart
Exponential random numbers……………………………	exprnd
Geometric random numbers………………………………	geornd
Hypergeometric random numbers………………………	hygernd
Lognormal random numbers………………………………	lognrnd
Multivariate normal random numbers…………………	mvnrnd
Negative binomial random numbers……………………	nbinrnd
Noncentral F random numbers……………………………	ncfrnd
Noncentral t random numbers……………………………	nctrnd
Noncentral Chi-square random numbers………………	ncx2rnd
Rayleigh random numbers…………………………………	raylrnd
Weibull random numbers …………………………………	weibrnd

* Argument M means the number of rows required to form matrix A
* Argument N means the number of columns required to form matrix A
* A is a matrix of random numbers and S is a single random number

9.2 Frequency table from positive integers

If we have a row or column matrix V of positive integers (0 is not a positive integer), the frequency table is found by the command tabulate. Frequency means the number of occurrences of each element in V. Let us say a row matrix is given as V=[2 4 2 3 3 5 6 2 4 8]. In V, the number 2 is appearing three times so its frequency is 3. There are 10 elements in V as a percentage the 2 occurs 30% of V. We presented the implementation on the right side. The first line is to assign the matrix elements to workspace V. The second line is to apply the function on V and assign the outcome to T. There are three columns in T in which the first, second, and third are the positive integers present in V up to the maximum, the frequency of each positive integer, and the percentage occurrence of the integer in V respectively. We have shown the tabulation using a left arrow indication for the 2 in the implementation. Any missing integer is set for 0 frequency. If you want to pick up the three as column matrix from T, use the command T(:,1), T(:,2), and T(:,3) respectively. If your data is in a rectangular matrix, first use the command V(:) and then apply the tabulate.

for frequency table:

```
>>V=[2 4 2 3 3 5 6 2 4 8]; ↵
>>T=tabulate(V) ↵

T =
     1    0    0
     2    3   30   ← for 2
     3    2   20
     4    2   20
     5    1   10
     6    1   10
     7    0    0
     8    1   10
```

9.3 Mean, geometric mean, and harmonic mean of a sample

Mean is the average on all observations of a random variable X which is given as $\frac{1}{N}\sum_{n=1}^{N} X_n$ where N is the number of observations on X. In MATLAB a random variable is entered as a matrix – row, column, or rectangular. To compute the mean of a random variable, we use the syntax **mean** (matrix name) for a row or column and **mean2**(matrix name) for a rectangular matrix. Font equivalence like X⇔ X is maintained in this section.

Suppose the X observation data is given as row matrix $R=[21 \quad 12 \quad 13 \quad 7 \quad 6 \quad 3 \quad 17]$, column matrix $C=\begin{bmatrix}5\\6\\-1\\0\\2\\8\end{bmatrix}$, and rectangular matrix $A=\begin{bmatrix}4 & 0 & 8\\6 & 5 & 2\\6 & 0 & 1\\2 & 1 & 6\end{bmatrix}$ whose means are 11.2857, 3.3333, and 3.4167 for R, C, and A respectively and our objective is to compute them. Placed on the right side is the computation for all three matrices. All means are assigned to the workspace M (can be any user-given name). Sometimes rational mean might be necessary for which we first use the command sym (section 2.1) on the matrix elements and then apply the mean. It is given that the rational mean of the elements on R is $\frac{79}{7}$ which we wish to obtain. One needs to execute mean(sym(R)) for that.

for the mean:
for the row matrix:

```
>>R=[21 12 13 7 6 3 17]; ↵
>>M=mean(R) ↵

M =
        11.2857
```

for the column matrix:

```
>>C=[5 6 -1 0 2 8]'; ↵
>>M=mean(C) ↵

M =
      3.3333
```

for the rectangular matrix:

```
>>A=[4 0 8;6 5 2;6 0 1; 2 1 6]; ↵
>>M=mean2(A) ↵

M =
            3.4167
```

Geometric mean of a sample is defined as $\sqrt[N]{\prod_{i=1}^{N} X_i}$ where X is the random variable and N is the number of elements in the sample. The function geomean (abbreviation for the geometric mean) computes the geometric mean from a sample for which we use the command geomean (row or column matrix name) or geomean(geomean(rectangular matrix name)). It is given that the geometric mean of the observations of X as a row matrix is $R=[21 \quad 12 \quad 13 \quad 7 \quad 6 \quad 3 \quad 17]$ whose geometric mean is $\sqrt[7]{21\times12\times13\times7\times6\times3\times17}=9.5066$. We wish to compute that. Attached on the right side is its implementation. The matrix elements must be positive numbers and can be fractional numbers too.

for the geometric mean:

```
>>R=[21 12 13 7 6 3 17]; ↵
>>M=geomean(R) ↵

M =
      9.5066
```

Definition of the harmonic mean is given by $H=\frac{N}{\sum_{i=1}^{N}\frac{1}{X_i}}$ where X and N have their usual meanings. Its corresponding function is harmmean (abbreviation for harmonic mean). To calculate the harmonic mean of a sample, we use the command harmmean (matrix name for a row/column one) or harmmean(harmmean(matrix name for a rectangular one)). The harmonic mean of all elements of $A=\begin{bmatrix}4 & 5 & 8\\6 & 5 & 2\\6 & -4 & 1\end{bmatrix}$ is given by $\frac{3}{\frac{7}{36}+\frac{1}{20}+\frac{13}{24}}=\frac{1080}{283}=$ 3.8163 which we intend to compute. Presented on the right side is its computation. You can see the rational result through the use of M=harmmean(harmmean(sym(A))). The mean, geomean, or harmmean functions over the columns of a rectangular matrix and the result is a row matrix that is why two functions are needed in each mean finding.

for the harmonic mean:

```
>>A=[4 5 8;6 5 2;6 -4 1]; ↵
>>M=harmmean(harmmean(A)) ↵

M=
      3.8163
```

for the range finding:

```
>>A=[4 -6 0;3 -3 -1;5 0 1;-7 3 2]; ↵
>>R=range(A(:)) ↵

R =
      12
```

9.4 Range, variance, and standard deviation of a sample

The range of a sample is the difference between the maximum and minimum values of a random variable. The function range finds the range of the data in a sample whose syntax is range (row or column matrix name) or range (rectangular matrix name (:)). It is given that the range of the sample data in the $A=\begin{bmatrix}4 & -6 & 0\\3 & -3 & -1\\5 & 0 & 1\\-7 & 3 & 2\end{bmatrix}$ is 12 (maximum and minimum are 5 and –7 respectively) – which we intend to obtain. Placed above on the right side is its implementation in which the first and second lines are to assign the matrix data to A and to call the function respectively. The command A(:) turns the rectangular A to a column matrix. We assigned the return from the range to workspace R (user-chosen).

If the mean of the random variable X is m, the variance of X is defined as $V(X)=\frac{1}{N-1}\sum_{i=1}^{N}(X_i-m)^2$ where $m=\frac{1}{N}\sum_{i=1}^{N}X_i$ and N is the number of observations on X. The command **var** finds the variance of some random variable observations when they are placed in a matrix for which the syntax is **var**(row or column matrix name) or **var**(rectangular matrix name(:)). For instance the observation data is given as $C=\begin{bmatrix}-2\\-8\\3\\-14\end{bmatrix}$ which has the variance 54.25 and which we intend to compute. The mean and variance of the data are calculated as m=–5.25 and $V(X)$= $\frac{(-2+5.25)^2+(-8+5.25)^2+(3+5.25)^2+(-14+5.25)^2}{4-1}=\frac{217}{4}$ =54.25 respectively. Attached on the right side is its implementation. The rational form computation is obtainable through the use of the command **sym** (section 2.1) which is also shown on the right side. In statistics literature the $V(X)$ is defined as $V(X)=\frac{1}{N}\sum_{i=1}^{N}(X_i-m)^2$ and which is calculated as $\frac{651}{16}$ =40.6875 and is obtainable using the command **V=var(C,1)** or **V=var(sym(C),1)** in which the second input argument 1 of **var** is reserve to MATLAB.

for the variance of the elements in C:

```
>>C=[-2 -8 3 -14]'; ↵
>>V=var(C) ↵

V =
        54.2500
```

for the rational variance:

```
>>V=var(sym(C)) ↵

V =

217/4
```

for the standard deviation of the elements in C:

```
>>S=std(C) ↵

S =
        7.3655
>>S=std(sym(C)) ↵

S =

1/2*217^(1/2)
```

Standard deviation of a random variable is defined as the positive square root of the variance and which is given by $\sigma(X)=\sqrt{\frac{1}{N-1}\sum_{i=1}^{N}(X_i-m)^2}$ where the symbols have just mentioned meanings and $\sigma(X)$ is the standard deviation of X. Its MATLAB counterpart is **std** (abbreviation for the standard deviation). The $\sigma(X)$ should be $\sqrt{54.25}$ =7.3655 for the elements in C which we have shown above on the right side. The input argument of the **std** follows the one as done in the **var**. We assigned the variance and standard deviation to the workspace **V** and **S** respectively (user-chosen names). Like the variance in the statistics literature, we also use the normalization by N i.e. $\sigma(X)=\sqrt{\frac{1}{N}\sum_{i=1}^{N}(X_i-m)^2}$ which we compute exercising **S=std(C,1)** or **S=std(sym(C),1)**, the rational standard deviation is also shown above on the right side.

9.5 Mean absolute deviation, median, and moment of a sample

Computation of mean absolute deviation of a random variable X is obtained from $\frac{1}{N}\sum_{i=1}^{N}|X_i-m|$ where m is the mean of X and its MATLAB counterpart is **mad** (abbreviation for the mean absolute deviation). In order to have the mean absolute deviation, we use the syntax **mad** (row or column matrix name) or **mad** (rectangular matrix name(:)). It is given that the data in the matrix $A=\begin{bmatrix}4&-4&-2\\5&0&6\end{bmatrix}$ has the mean absolute deviation $\frac{|4-1.5|+|-4-1.5|+|-2-1.5|+|5-1.5|+|0-1.5|+|6-1.5|}{6}$ =3.5 and we intend to compute that. Attached on the right side is its computation which we assigned to workspace **M**. The first and second lines are to assign the matrix to workspace **A** and to call the function **mad** respectively.

for the mean absolute deviation computation:

```
>>A=[4 -4 -2;5 0 6]; ↵
>>M=mad(A(:)) ↵

M =
        3.5000
```

For median computation:

```
>>X=[4 7 5 -5 0 1 9]; ↵
>>M=median(X) ↵

M =
        4
```

for moment computation:

```
>>X=[-1 2 90 34]; ↵
>>M=moment(X,4) ↵

M =
        3.4318e+006
>>M=moment(sym(X),4) ↵

M =

878531717/256
```

In the ascending order, the middle element of some observations of a random variable X is called the median. Assume that there are N sorted elements in a sample, the median is the $\left(\frac{N+1}{2}\right)^{th}$ element if the number of elements is odd or the average of the $\left(\frac{N}{2}\right)^{th}$ and $\left(\frac{N}{2}+1\right)^{th}$ elements if the number of elements is even. To obtain the median from observational data matrix, we use the command **median** (row or column matrix name) or **median** (rectangular matrix name(:)). It is given that the data in X =[4 7 5 −5 0 1 9] has the median 4 and we intend to obtain that. Placed on the right side is its implementation in which the first and second lines are to assign the given matrix to workspace A and to call the function **median** respectively. We assigned the return to the workspace M.

The Pth moment of a random variable X is defined as $M_X^P = \frac{1}{N}\sum_{i=1}^{N}(X-m)^P$ where the symbols have ongoing meanings and the integer P is the order of the moment. The function **moment** computes P^{th} moment with syntax **moment**(matrix name, P) for a row or column or **moment** (matrix name(:), P) for a rectangular matrix observational data. Let us compute the 4th moment of X =[−1 2 90 34] which is given by 3431764.52 – our objective is to find that. Relevant calculations are $m = \frac{-1+2+90+34}{4}$ =31.25 and $M_R^4 = \frac{(-1-31.25)^4+(2-31.25)^4+(90-31.25)^4+(34-31.25)^4}{4} = \frac{878531717}{256}$ =3431764.52. Attached on the lower right corner of the last page is its implementation in which the first and second lines are to assign the matrix to workspace X and to call the function **moment** respectively. We assigned the return to the workspace M. The return **e+006** means 10^6 so **3.4318e+006** is read off as 3.4318×10^6 because of the higher number digits. The rational output is seen by virtue of the **sym** which we presented too.

9.6 Covariance and correlation of random variables

In a rectangular matrix usually the columns represent the observations on the random variables. The number of columns can be taken as the number of random variables. Mean, median, or variance of a random variable describes the information about the variable itself. If we have two or more random variables placed in a rectangular matrix, covariance provides a relationship between the random variables or about their tendency to vary together rather than independently.

The covariance of a matrix is another matrix. Elements of the covariance matrix $V = \begin{bmatrix} V_{11} & V_{12} & \cdots & V_{1N} \\ V_{21} & V_{22} & \cdots & V_{2N} \\ \vdots & \vdots & \ddots & \vdots \\ V_{N1} & V_{N2} & \cdots & V_{NN} \end{bmatrix}$ of a matrix $A = \begin{bmatrix} A_{11} & A_{12} & \cdots & A_{1N} \\ A_{21} & A_{22} & \cdots & A_{2N} \\ \vdots & \vdots & \ddots & \vdots \\ A_{M1} & A_{M2} & \cdots & A_{MN} \end{bmatrix}$ is defined as $V_{ij} = \frac{\sum_{k=1}^{M}(A_{ki}-\overline{A_i})(A_{kj}-\overline{A_j})}{M-1}$ where $A_1 = \begin{bmatrix} A_{11} \\ A_{21} \\ \vdots \\ A_{M1} \end{bmatrix}$, $A_2 = \begin{bmatrix} A_{12} \\ A_{22} \\ \vdots \\ A_{M2} \end{bmatrix}$ ……, and $A_N = \begin{bmatrix} A_{1N} \\ A_{2N} \\ \vdots \\ A_{MN} \end{bmatrix}$ and $\overline{A_j}$ is the mean of the jth column of A. The diagonal elements of V are the variances and the off-diagonal elements are the covariances that is why V is called the variance-covariance matrix. Another name of V is dispersion matrix and it is a symmetric matrix. Orders of A and V are $M \times N$ and $N \times N$ respectively. To evaluate the covariance of a matrix, we use the command **cov**(matrix name) – (abbreviation for the <u>cov</u>ariance).

Let us consider $A = \begin{bmatrix} -2 & 6 & 6 \\ 4 & 30 & 1 \\ 1 & -4 & -4 \\ 5 & 0 & 5 \end{bmatrix}$ for elucidation where M =4 and N =3. The order of V must be 3×3 and V prescribes the matrix form $\begin{bmatrix} V_{11} & V_{12} & V_{13} \\ V_{21} & V_{22} & V_{23} \\ V_{31} & V_{32} & V_{33} \end{bmatrix}$. Since V is a symmetric matrix, we have $V_{12}=V_{21}$, $V_{13}=V_{31}$, and $V_{23}=V_{32}$. The means are $\overline{A_1}$=2, $\overline{A_2}$=8, and $\overline{A_3}$=2. Some intermediate computations are $V_{11} = \frac{\sum_{k=1}^{4}(A_{k1}-\overline{A_1})^2}{4-1} = \frac{(-2-2)^2+(4-2)^2+(1-2)^2+(5-2)^2}{4-1}$=10, $V_{22} = \frac{\sum_{k=1}^{4}(A_{k2}-\overline{A_2})^2}{4-1} = \frac{(6-8)^2+(30-8)^2+(-4-8)^2+(0-8)^2}{4-1} = \frac{696}{3}$=232, $V_{21}=V_{12}= \frac{\sum_{k=1}^{4}(A_{k1}-\overline{A_1})(A_{k2}-\overline{A_2})}{4-1} = \frac{(-2-2)(6-8)+(4-2)(30-8)+(1-2)(-4-8)+(5-2)(0-8)}{4-1} = \frac{40}{3}$=13.3333, $V_{31}=V_{13}= \frac{\sum_{k=1}^{4}(A_{k1}-\overline{A_1})(A_{k3}-\overline{A_3})}{4-1} = \frac{(-2-2)(6-2)+(4-2)(1-2)+(1-2)(-4-2)+(5-2)(5-2)}{4-1}$=−1, and eventually $V = \begin{bmatrix} 10 & 40/3 & -1 \\ 40/3 & 232 & 6 \\ -1 & 6 & 62/3 \end{bmatrix} = \begin{bmatrix} 10 & 13.3333 & -1 \\ 13.3333 & 232 & 6 \\ -1 & 6 & 20.6667 \end{bmatrix}$ which is what we intend to find. The implementation is shown at the beginning of the next page on the right side in which the first and second lines are to assign the matrix data to A and to call the function **cov** respectively. The return from the function **cov** is assigned to workspace V (user-given name). The rational form output is also achievable through the use of the function sym (section 2.1) which we also presented alongside the numeric computation. If the V_{ij} division takes place by M i.e. $V_{ij} = \frac{1}{M}\sum_{k=1}^{M}(A_{ki} - \overline{A_i})(A_{kj} - \overline{A_j})$, we use the command V=cov(A,1) where the second input argument 1 of cov is reserve and indicates the division by the M.

for the covariance in the numeric form:

```
>>A=[-2 6 6;4 30 1;1 -4 -4;5 0 5]; ↵
>>V=cov(A) ↵

V =

   10.0000   13.3333   -1.0000
   13.3333  232.0000    6.0000
   -1.0000    6.0000   20.6667
```

covariance in rational form:

```
>>V=cov(sym(A)) ↵

V =

[  10,   40/3,    -1]
[ 40/3,   232,     6]
[  -1,     6,  62/3]
```

The cov is designed for handling many random variables. In the statistics literature, the random variable observations are given separately. For instance the two observations are given as X =[−2 4 1 5] and Y =[6 30 −4 0] contrarily the covariance is defined as $c = \frac{1}{N}\sum_{k=1}^{N}(X_k - \overline{X})(Y_k - \overline{Y})$ where c is the covariance between the random variables X and Y and $\overline{X}$ and $\overline{Y}$ are their means respectively. For the given X and Y observation data, we should obtain c =10. Attached on the right side is its implementation. In the implementation the first two lines are to assign the given X and Y data to the workspace X and Y respectively. In the third line there are three input arguments to the cov now, the given two vector assignees and division indicatory number respectively – another option implanted in cov. Therefore the outcome is a 2×2 matrix (because of two random variables) from which we pick up only the element indexed by (1,2) and which is assigned to c as far as our requirement is concern.

Obtaining the literature like result:

```
>>X=[-2 4 1 5]; ↵
>>Y=[6 30 -4 0]; ↵
>>V=cov(X,Y,1); ↵
>>c=V(1,2) ↵

c =

    10
```

Correlation coefficient gives a measure of the linear association between two random variables. Correlation of the matrix formed by placing the random variables in columns is a matrix and is called the correlation matrix R. In general, it is applicable for more than two random variables and can be expressed in terms of the variance-covariance matrix V (as defined earlier). The correlation matrix R of the rectangular matrix A is defined as $R = D \times V \times D$ where × indicates the multiplication of matrices. From A, the diagonal matrix D is obtained by taking the reciprocals of standard deviations of the columns. Relating the variance-covariance matrix V, the diagonal matrix is given by $D = \begin{bmatrix} \frac{1}{\sqrt{V_{11}}} & 0 & 0 & 0 \\ 0 & \frac{1}{\sqrt{V_{22}}} & 0 & 0 \\ \vdots & \vdots & \vdots \ \ddots & \vdots \\ 0 & 0 & 0 & \frac{1}{\sqrt{V_{NN}}} \end{bmatrix}$. The diagonal elements of R are unity because a variable is perfectly correlated with itself. Each element of R satisfies $-1 \le R_{ij} \le 1$ where R_{ij} is any element in R. The order of R is $N \times N$ where A is of order $M \times N$ and V is of order $N \times N$. R is a symmetric matrix too. To obtain the correlation matrix of a matrix, we use the command corrcoef(matrix name) – (abbreviation for the correlation coefficient).

Let us choose the beginning A from what the reciprocals of the standard deviations of the first, second, and third columns of A are $\frac{1}{\sqrt{10}}$, $\frac{1}{\sqrt{232}}$, and $\frac{1}{\sqrt{62/3}}$ respectively. The diagonal matrix is formed as $D = \begin{bmatrix} \frac{1}{\sqrt{10}} & 0 & 0 \\ 0 & \frac{1}{\sqrt{232}} & 0 \\ 0 & 0 & \frac{1}{\sqrt{62/3}} \end{bmatrix}$. The R is computed as $\begin{bmatrix} 1 & \frac{2\sqrt{145}}{87} & -\frac{\sqrt{465}}{310} \\ \frac{2\sqrt{145}}{87} & 1 & \frac{3\sqrt{2697}}{1798} \\ -\frac{\sqrt{465}}{310} & \frac{3\sqrt{2697}}{1798} & 1 \end{bmatrix} = \begin{bmatrix} 1 & 0.2768 & -0.0696 \\ 0.2768 & 1 & 0.0867 \\ -0.0696 & 0.0867 & 1 \end{bmatrix}$ which we intend to determine. Attached on the right side is the computation of the correlation matrix. The first and second lines in the implementation are to assign the given matrix to the workspace A and to call the function corrcoef respectively. Exercising the sym and pretty (section 3.1) helps us view the rational form as well which we placed above too.

for correlation matrix in the numeric form:

```
>>A=[-2 6 6;4 30 1;1 -4 -4;5 0 5]; ↵
>>R=corrcoef(A) ↵   ← R⇔ R

R =

    1.0000    0.2768   -0.0696
    0.2768    1.0000    0.0867
   -0.0696    0.0867    1.0000
```

for correlation matrix in the rational form:

```
>>R=corrcoef(sym(A)); pretty(R) ↵
[                          1/2                 1/2 ]
[       1           2/87 145       - 1/310 465     ]
[                                                  ]
[              1/2                             1/2 ]
[  2/87  145               1         3/1798 2697   ]
[                                                  ]
[               1/2               1/2              ]
[- 1/310  465       3/1798 2697           1        ]
```

Again in the statistics literature the correlation coefficient of two random variables X and Y is found as $\rho=\frac{c}{\sigma(X)\sigma(Y)}=\frac{\frac{1}{N}\sum_{k=1}^{N}(X_k-\overline{X})(Y_k-\overline{Y})}{\sqrt{\frac{1}{N}\sum_{i=1}^{N}(X_i-\overline{X})^2}\sqrt{\frac{1}{N}\sum_{i=1}^{N}(Y_i-\overline{Y})^2}}$ for which the function **corrcoef** is still operational. Let us consider the two random variable observations as $X=[-2\ \ 4\ \ 1\ \ 5]$ and $Y=[6\ \ 30\ \ -4\ \ 0]$ on which the computed ρ should be 0.2768 and we find it as placed on the right side. In the implementation, the first two lines are to assign the given observations to workspace X and Y respectively. In the third line we call the corrcoef with two input arguments (the given two vectors as a row matrix respectively, another option provided in the corrcoef) and assign its outcome to R which should be 2×2 matrix because two vectors are there. The element with coordinates (1,2) or (2,1) in the R is the theory-mentioned ρ which we assigned to r (user-chosen name).

for ρ computation:

```
>>X=[-2 4 1 5]; ↵
>>Y=[6 30 -4 0]; ↵
>>R=corrcoef(X,Y); ↵
>>r=R(1,2) ↵ ← r⇔ ρ

r =
    0.2768
```

Table 9.B Different probability density functions (pdfs) and their MATLAB counterparts

Exponential distribution with parameter θ: $f(x)=\begin{cases}\frac{1}{\theta}e^{-\frac{x}{\theta}} & for\ \ x>0\\ 0 & elsewhere\end{cases}$, Type: Continuous, Executable form: **exppdf**(x , θ) where θ or x can be a scalar or matrix	Normal distribution with parameter μ an σ: $f(x)=\frac{1}{\sigma\sqrt{2\pi}}e^{-\frac{(x-\mu)^2}{2\sigma^2}}\quad for\ -\infty<x<\infty$ Type: Continuous, Executable form: **normpdf**(x , μ , σ) where x , μ , or σ can be a scalar or matrix
Discrete uniform distribution with parameter N (N is any positive integer): $f[x]=\begin{cases}\frac{1}{N} & for\ \ 1\le x\le N\\ 0 & elsewhere\end{cases}$ Type: Discrete, Executable form: **unidpdf**(x , N) where x (integer) and N can be scalar or matrix	Binomial distribution with parameter N and p: $f[x]={}^{N}C_x\, p^x q^{N-x}$ where x =0, 1, 2, 3... and N, $0<p<1$, and $q=1-p$ Type: Discrete, Executable form: **binopdf**(x , N , p) where x , N , or p can be scalar or matrix
Chi-square distribution with n degrees of freedom: $f(x)=\begin{cases}\frac{x^{\frac{n-2}{2}}e^{-\frac{x}{2}}}{2^{\frac{n}{2}}\Gamma\left(\frac{n}{2}\right)} & for\ \ x>0\\ 0 & elsewhere\end{cases}$ Type: Continuous, Executable form: **chi2pdf**(x , n) where x and n can be scalar or matrix	t distribution with n degrees of freedom: $f(x)=\frac{\Gamma\left(\frac{n+1}{2}\right)\left(1+\frac{x^2}{n}\right)^{-\frac{n+1}{2}}}{\sqrt{\pi n}\ \Gamma\left(\frac{n}{2}\right)}\quad for\ -\infty<t<\infty$ Type: Continuous Executable form: **tpdf**(x , n) where x and n can be scalar or matrix and n is an integer
F distribution with parameters n_1 and n_2 (n_1 and n_2 are called the degrees of freedom): $f(x)=\begin{cases}\frac{\Gamma\left(\frac{n_1+n_2}{2}\right)}{\Gamma\left(\frac{n_1}{2}\right)\Gamma\left(\frac{n_2}{2}\right)}\left(\frac{n_1}{n_2}\right)^{\frac{n_1}{2}}x^{\frac{n_1}{2}-1}\left(1+\frac{n_1}{n_2}x\right)^{-\frac{n_1+n_2}{2}} & for\, x>0\\ 0 & elsewhere\end{cases}$ Type: Continuous, Executable form: **fpdf**(x , n_1 , n_2) where arguments can be scalar or matrix	Beta distribution with parameters α and β: $f(x)=\begin{cases}\frac{\Gamma(\alpha+\beta)}{\Gamma(\alpha)\Gamma(\beta)}x^{\alpha-1}(1-x)^{\beta-1}\ \ for\ \ 0<x<1 \\ 0 \quad elsewhere\end{cases}$ where α >0, β >0 Type: Continuous, Executable form: **betapdf**(x , α , β)
Poisson distribution with parameter λ: $f[x]=\frac{\lambda^x e^{-\lambda}}{x!}$ for $\lambda>0$ and x =0, 1, 2, 3, 4, ... Type: Discrete, Executable form: **poisspdf**(x , λ)	Log normal distribution with parameters μ and σ: $f(x)=\frac{e^{-\frac{(\ln x-\mu)^2}{2\sigma^2}}}{x\sigma\sqrt{2\pi}}$ for x >0 Type: Continuous, Executable form: **lognpdf**(x , μ , σ)
Other probability density functions that are available in the statistical toolbox: Gamma – **gampdf**, Geometric – **geopdf**, Hypergeometric – **hygepdf**, Noncentral t – **nctpdf**, Non central chi square – **ncx2pdf**, Negative binomial – **nbinpdf**, Noncentral F – **ncfpdf**, Rayleigh – **raylpdf**, and Weibull - **weibpdf**	

9.7 Probability density functions

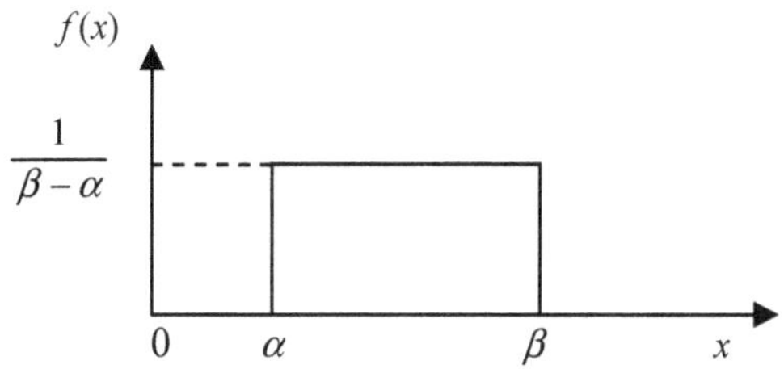

Figure 9.1(a) Probability density function of the continuous uniform random variable

Probability density function (often abbreviated as pdf) $f(x)$ is related with the frequency of occurrence of a random variable. Let us concentrate on the probability density function of the continuous uniform random variable. A random variable X is said to have a continuous uniform distribution with parameters α and β if its probability density function is given by $f(x)=\begin{cases}\frac{1}{\beta-\alpha} & for \quad \alpha<x<\beta \\ 0 & elsewhere\end{cases}$ where $\beta>\alpha$. The pdf is depicted in figure 9.1(a). Occurrence of any value of X from α to β is equally likely because $f(x)$ is constant. MATLAB has the pdf function by the name **unifpdf** (abbreviation for the uniform fractional probability density function). The function has the syntax **unifpdf**(value of x in general as a matrix, α, β). What **unifpdf** does is it returns the functional value of $f(x)$ at any x. Let us consider the pdf with the parameters α =3 and β=5 on that $f(4.1)$ and $f(5.5)$ should be 0.5 and 0 respectively. Again to show the matrix input argument, let us consider $A=\begin{bmatrix}3 & 5\\ 4 & -1\end{bmatrix}$ and our output should be $\begin{bmatrix}f(3) & f(5)\\ f(4) & f(-1)\end{bmatrix}$ = $\begin{bmatrix}0.5 & 0.5\\ 0.5 & 0\end{bmatrix}$. We conduct all executions as presented above. In all three examples we assigned the return from the **unifpdf** to the workspace **f** (can be any user-chosen name).

for the $f(4.1)$,	**for the $f(5.5)$,**	**for the matrix input,**

`>>f=unifpdf(4.1,3,5) ↵`
 	
`f =`
 	
`    0.5000`
	`>>f=unifpdf(5.5,3,5) ↵`
	
	`f =`
	
	`    0`
		`>>A=[3 5;4 -1]; ↵`
		`>>f=unifpdf(A,3,5) ↵`
		
		`f =`
		
		`    0.5000    0.5000`
		`    0.5000         0`

Sometimes the reader might need to plot the pdf for some x. For instance the pdf $f(x)$ of the continuous uniform random variable over $0\le x\le 9$ with the parameters α =3 and β=5 needs to be graphed. Under this type of circumstance we select some step size over the x interval and generate a row matrix on that. Let us choose 0.1 step size for x so the row vector we get using **x=0:0.1:9;**. After that the pdf functional values are obtained by the command **f=unifpdf(x,3,5);**. For the graphing, we employ the function **plot** of the section 13.2 and which should be **plot(x,f)**. The graph is very similar to the one in the figure 9.1(a) and not attached for the space reason.

At this point every pdf function has some parameters. Knowledge of these parameters is important before executing any pdf function in MATLAB. More than a dozen pdfs are available in the Statistical Toolbox. We present a brief list of them accompanying the definition in the table 9.B. To know more about any pdf distribution, execute **help** acronym for instance **help unifpdf** at the command prompt.

9.8 Statistics from a given distribution

Finding the statistics of a random variable means finding the mean and variance of the variable from a given probability density function. The mean m and variance V of a continuous random variable whose probability density function is $f(x)$ are given by $m=\int_{x=-\infty}^{x=\infty} x\,f(x)\,dx$ and $V=\int_{x=-\infty}^{x=\infty}(x-m)^2 f(x)\,dx$ respectively. On the contrary the mean and variance of a discrete counterpart (discrete probability density function is $f[x]$) are obtained from $m=\sum_{x=-\infty}^{x=\infty} x f[x]$ and $V=\sum_{x=-\infty}^{x=\infty}(x-m)^2 f[x]$ respectively. We present one example for each. For the continuous case, let us take beta distribution's probability density function $f(x)=\begin{cases}\frac{\Gamma(\alpha+\beta)}{\Gamma(\alpha)\Gamma(\beta)}x^{\alpha-1}(1-x)^{\beta-1} & for \quad 0<x<1 \\ 0 & elsewhere\end{cases}$ where α>0, β>0, and α and β are called the parameters of the beta distribution. Let us calculate the beta statistics for α =3 and β =4. Some computations are the following: m =

Table 9.C Other available functions to find the statistics

Name of the statistics	MATLAB counterpart
Uniform discrete	unidstat
Uniform continuous	unifstat
Binomial	binostat
Normal	normstat
Exponential	expstat
Gamma	gamstat
Chi square	chi2stat
t	tstat
F	fstat
Geometric	geostat
Hypergeometric	hygestat
Lognormal	lognstat
Negative binomial	nbinstat
Noncentral F	ncfstat
Noncentral t	nctstat
Non central chi square	ncx2stat
Rayleigh	raylstat
Weibull	weibstat

$\int_{x=0}^{x=1} x \frac{\Gamma 7}{\Gamma 3 \Gamma 4} x^2(1-x)^3\, dx$ =0.4286 and $V = \int_{x=0}^{x=1} \left(x - \frac{3}{7}\right)^2 \frac{\Gamma 7}{\Gamma 3 \Gamma 4} x^2(1-x)^3\, dx$ =0.0306. Our expectation is to find these m and V values starting from α and β of the distribution. The MATLAB function that finds the beta statistics is **betastat** (abbreviation for the beta statistics), which applies the syntax [m,V]=betastat(α , β) where m⇔ m and V⇔ V . Attached on the right side is its implementation.

for the beta statistics:

```
>>[m,V]=betastat(3,4) ↵

m =

    0.4286

V =

    0.0306
```

for the Poisson statistics:

```
>>[m,v]=poisstat(3) ↵

m =

     3

V =

     3
```

The next example is the discrete one for which we chose the Poisson distribution. Its probability density function with the parameter λ is given by $f[x] = \frac{\lambda^x e^{-\lambda}}{x!}$ where λ >0 and x =0, 1, 2, 3, etc. The mean and variance of the distribution are calculated by $m = \sum_{x=0}^{x=\infty} x \frac{\lambda^x e^{-\lambda}}{x\,!} = \lambda$ and $V = \sum_{x=0}^{x=\infty} (x-\lambda)^2 \frac{\lambda^x e^{-\lambda}}{x!} = \lambda$ respectively. The corresponding MATLAB function is **poisstat** (abbreviation for the Poisson statistics) with the syntax [m,V]=poisstat(λ) where m⇔ m and V⇔ V . As an example, the output from **poisstat** should be m =3 and V =3 for the parameter λ =3 that is what is shown on the upper right side.

We believe that the last two examples of computing the statistics for continuous and discrete random variables make the reader familiar with the style how one can find the statistics of some distribution in MATLAB. Table 9.C provides some other known distributions including their MATLAB counterparts.

Table 9.D Other available cumulative distribution functions

Cumulative distribution function	MATLAB counterpart
Beta	betacdf
Chi square	chi2cdf
F	fcdf
Gamma	gamcdf
Geometric	geocdf
Hypergeometric	hygecdf
Lognormal	logncdf
Negative binomial	nbincdf
Noncentral F	ncfcdf
Noncentral t	nctcdf
Noncentral Chi-square	ncx2cdf
Normal (Gaussian)	normcdf
Poisson	poisscdf
Rayleigh	raylcdf
T	tcdf
Discrete uniform	unidcdf
Uniform	unifcdf
Weibull	weibcdf

9.9 Cumulative distribution functions

The formal definition of cumulative distribution function (cdf) of a random variable X is given by $F(x) = \int_{v=-\infty}^{x} f(v)\,dv$ if the variable is continuous or $F[x] = \sum_{v=-\infty}^{v=x} f[v]$ if the variable is discrete where $f(x)$ and $f[x]$ are the probability density functions for the continuous and discrete cases respectively. Two examples one for each are presented. For the computation of a cumulative distribution function, the parameters of the probability density function must be available.

As an example of the continuous distribution, we choose the exponential one which is parameterized by θ . Its probability density function is given by $f(x) = \begin{cases} \frac{1}{\theta} e^{-\frac{x}{\theta}} & for\ \ x>0 \\ 0 & elsewhere \end{cases}$. The cdf of this distribution is $F(x) = \int_{v=0}^{x} \frac{1}{\theta} e^{-\frac{v}{\theta}}\, dv = 1 - e^{-\frac{x}{\theta}}$. Let us compute $F(3)$ for θ =2, which should be $F(3) = 1 - e^{-\frac{3}{2}}$ =0.7769. MATLAB counterpart of the cdf is **expcdf** (abbreviation for the exponential cumulative distribution function) which has two input arguments – x and θ respectively and the return is the $F(x)$ value. Attached on the right side is its computation in which F⇔ $F(3)$.

for the exponential cdf:

```
>>F=expcdf(3,2) ↵

F =

    0.7769
```

for the binomial cdf:

```
>>F=binocdf(3,5,0.4) ↵

F =

    0.9130
```

For the discrete example, let us choose the binomial distribution (table 9.B). Its cumulative distribution function is given by $F[x] = \sum_{v=0}^{v=x} {}^N C_v\, p^v q^{N-v}$. We calculate $F[3]$ in relation to the parameters N =5 and p =0.4 which becomes $F[3] = \sum_{v=0}^{v=3} {}^5 C_v\, (0.4)^v (0.6)^{5-v}$ =0.9130. MATLAB counterpart for the cdf is **binocdf** (abbreviation for the binomial cumulative distribution function) whose executable form is binocdf(x , N , p). The $F[3]$ computation is shown above on the right side in which F⇔ $F[3]$. Similar problems for the other distributions can be solved by the functions such as the ones that reside in the table 9.D.

Sometimes cumulative sum based on the data is required. Let us consider a random variable observation data as X =[9 6 3 −23 6]. If we take cumulative sum of the elements in the X, we find the cumulative sum matrix [9 9+6 9+6+3 9+6+3−23 9+6+3−23+6]=[9 15 18 −5 1]. This type of computation is performed by using the function **cumsum** (abbreviation for the cumulative sum). Attached on the right side is its computation in which the first and second lines are to assign the data to workspace X and to call the **cumsum** on X respectively. The return from the **cumsum** is assigned to S (can be any user-given name). If X is a row or column matrix, so is S. For a rectangular matrix, the function operates over each column.

for the cumulative sum:

```
>>X=[9 6 3 -23 6]; ↵
>>S=cumsum(X) ↵

S =

     9    15    18    -5     1
```

9.10 Inverse cumulative distribution functions or critical values

In the last heading we computed the cumulative distribution function $F(x)$ of a random variable starting from x along with the distribution parameters. Now $F(x)$ is given, the variable x is to be computed for a particular distribution. The reverse computation is called the inverse cumulative distribution function or finding the critical value. In the last section for the exponential distribution with the parameter θ=2, we had $F(3)$=0.7769. Now we provide $F(x)$=0.7769 to get x=3. The MATLAB function **expinv** (abbreviation for exponential distribution's inverse) helps us compute the inverse value, which has the syntax **expinv(** $F(x)$, θ **)** and whose return is the x value. However formal implementation of the problem is as follows:

```
>>x=expinv(0.7769,2) ↵      ← x⇔x

x =
         3.0003    ← Output is not 3 due to round off error
```

We considered 0.7769 as $F(x)$ but there is some fractional part after 4 decimal which we ignored that is why the discrepancy appears. This sort of computation is obtainable from the distributions placed in the table 9.E. Attention should be given to the numeric format and output as well when one has to deal with the discrete inverse cdfs (section 1.4).

Table 9.E Other available inverse cumulative distribution functions

Name of the cumulative distribution	MATLAB counterpart
Beta	betainv
Chi square	chi2inv
F	finv
Gamma	gaminv
Geometric	geoinv
Hypergeometric	hygeinv
Lognormal	logninv
Negative binomial	nbininv
Noncentral F	ncfinv
Noncentral t	nctinv
Noncentral Chi-square	ncx2inv
Normal (Gaussian)	norminv
Poisson	poissinv
Rayleigh	raylinv
T	tinv
Discrete uniform	unidinv
Uniform	unifinv
Weibull	weibinv

9.11 Best-fit straight line/curve of higher degree

Given a set of x and y data in the x - y plane, the best fit straight line or curve of higher degree from these points is obtained by employing the function **polyfit** (abbreviation for the polynomial fitting). In general we look for the polynomial coefficients from the given x and y data. The function has the common syntax **p=polyfit**(given x data as a row matrix, given y data as a row matrix, user-selected degree of the curve). The return to the **p** (a user-given name) is a row matrix holding the best fit polynomial coefficients in descending power of x. Two examples are mentioned – one for the straight line and the other for the curve of degree 2, which is a parabola. We maintain the font equivalence like x⇔x in the following.

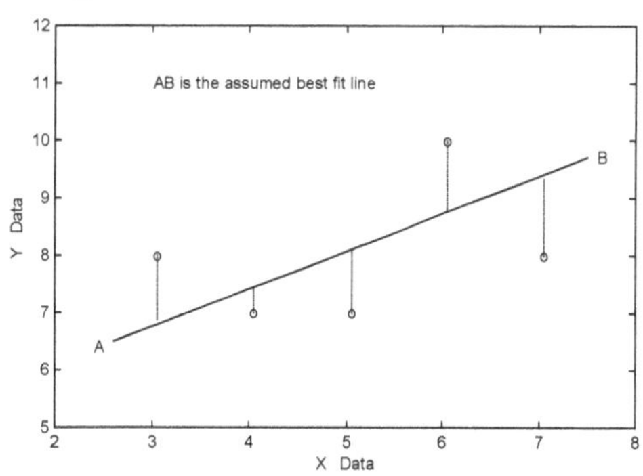

Figure 9.1(b) Plot of x and y data and the best fit line

♦♦ Example 1

Suppose we have five distinct points given as (3,8), (4,7), (5,7), (6,10), and (7,8). Shown o marks in the figure 9.1(b) are the plots of the given points. The line AB of the figure 9.1(b) is assumed to be the best-fit straight line passing through these points whose equation is $y = ax + b$ and the coefficients { a , b } need to be found. From the statistical theory, we know that the coefficients are given by $a = \frac{\Sigma x \Sigma y - N \Sigma xy}{(\Sigma x)^2 - N \Sigma x^2}$ and $b = \frac{\Sigma x \Sigma xy - \Sigma y \Sigma x^2}{(\Sigma x)^2 - N \Sigma x^2}$ where N is the number of points. From the given coordinates, we calculate different sums as follows: Σx=25, Σy=40, Σxy=203, Σx^2=135, and N=5 from which { a=0.3, b=6.5} and the equation of the best-fit line is $y = 0.3x + 6.5$ – this is what we are supposed to find.

for the example 1: the best-fit line in the coefficient form:

```
>>x=[3 4 5 6 7]; ↵
>>y=[8 7 7 10 8]; ↵
>>p=polyfit(x,y,1) ↵

p =

    0.3000    6.5000
```

the best-fit line in the polynomial of x form:

```
>>poly2str(p,'x') ↵

ans =

    0.3 x + 6.5
```

Attached on the lower right corner of the last page is the implementation of the problem in which only x and only y data of the five points are assigned to the workspace variables **x** and **y** respectively but both as a row matrix and in order. After that we call the **polyfit** with the three input arguments. A straight line has the degree 1 for this reason the third input argument in the **polyfit** is 1. Section 3.1 mentioned **poly2str** shows the line as a function of **x** (also shown).

♦♦ Example 2

This example exercise is for the best-fit curve of degree 2 or parabola. The best-fit parabola has the equation $y = ax^2 + bx + c$ and whose polynomial coefficients are obtained from $\begin{bmatrix} a \\ b \\ c \end{bmatrix} = \begin{bmatrix} \sum x^2 & \sum x & N \\ \sum x^3 & \sum x^2 & \sum x \\ \sum x^4 & \sum x^3 & \sum x^2 \end{bmatrix}^{-1} \begin{bmatrix} \sum y \\ \sum xy \\ \sum x^2 y \end{bmatrix}$. Let us consider the distinct points (−3,20), (−2,15), (−1,3), (0,6), (1,7), (2,7), (3,15), and (4,26) to find the best-fit parabola coefficients. Figure 9.1(c) depicts the plot of the given points by cross mark and assumed best-fit parabola ABC passing through them. Based on the given points, various sums are $\sum x$ =4, $\sum y$ =99, $\sum x^2$ =44, $\sum xy$ =77, $\sum x^2 y$ =829, $\sum x^3$ =64, $\sum x^4$ =452, and N=8 from which the calculated coefficients are $\begin{bmatrix} a \\ b \\ c \end{bmatrix} = \begin{bmatrix} -\frac{5}{168} & -\frac{1}{168} & \frac{1}{168} \\ \frac{1}{56} & \frac{5}{168} & -\frac{1}{168} \\ \frac{47}{168} & \frac{1}{56} & -\frac{5}{168} \end{bmatrix} \begin{bmatrix} 99 \\ 77 \\ 829 \end{bmatrix} = \begin{bmatrix} 1.5298 \\ -0.875 \\ 4.3988 \end{bmatrix}$ and the equation of the best-fit parabola is $y = 1.5298x^2 - 0.875x + 4.3988$. Our aim is to find the polynomial coefficients or the polynomial from the given data. Its computation is presented on the right applying the example 1 mentioned function and symbology.

```
for the example 2:
for the coefficient form,
>>x=[-3 -2 -1 0 1 2 3 4]; ↵
>>y=[20 15 3 6 7 7 15 26]; ↵
>>p=polyfit(x,y,2) ↵

p =
      1.5298   -0.8750    4.3988
to display as a polynomial of x,
>>poly2str(p,'x') ↵

ans =
      1.5298 x^2 - 0.875 x + 4.3988
```

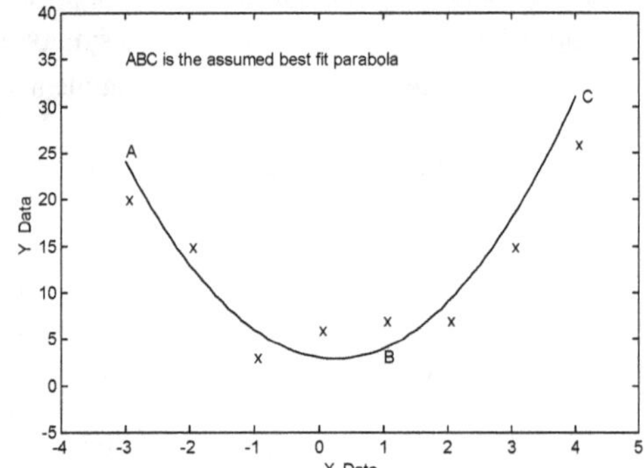

Figure 9.1(c) Plot of x and y data and the assumed best-fit parabola

Since the parabola is a curve of degree 2 that is why the third input argument of the **polyfit** is 2.

In a similar fashion, one can find the best fit curve of the degree 3 or higher in least mean square error sense using the **polyfit** just by changing the third input argument of the function. Notice that for the degree 2 curve, the number of unknowns is 3 (which are the polynomial coefficients), for the degree 3 curve, the number of unknowns is 4, and so on.

♦♦ Power law fitting

Sometimes data might follow specific pattern rather than a polynomial. It is given that the data in table 9.F follows the power law function $y = ab^{-x}$. In least square sense we intend to find the coefficients a and b. Still we can use the **polyfit** to determine these coefficients but some transformation is needed. Taking the natural logarithm (base e) on $y = ab^{-x}$ and setting $Y = \ln y$, $A = -\ln b$, and $B = \ln a$, one obtains $Y = B + Ax$ which is a linear variation like the example 1.

Table 9.F x and y data for $y = ab^{-x}$ curve fitting

x	y
0.1	1.4734
0.6	1.9021
1.1	2.4556
1.6	3.1702
2.1	4.0927
2.6	5.2837

```
for the y = ab^-x fitting:
>>x=[0.1 0.6 1.1 1.6 2.1 2.6]; ↵
>>y=[1.4734 1.9021 2.4556 3.1702 4.0927 5.2837]; ↵
>>Y=log(y); p=polyfit(x,Y,1) ↵

p =
      0.5108    0.3365
        ↑          ↑
        A          B
>>A=p(1); B=p(2); ↵
>>a=exp(B) ↵                         >>b=exp(-A) ↵

a =                                   b =
      1.4000                                0.6000
```

We presented its complete implementation above on the right side in which the first two lines are to assign the given data both as a row matrix to the workspace **x** and **y** respectively. On all data in **y**, natural logarithm is taken and assigned to **Y** using **Y=log(y);** in the third line because $Y = \ln y$. The **Y** becomes the second input argument of the **polyfit** like the example 1 because $Y = B + Ax$ and the return from the **polyfit** is a two element row matrix **p** corresponding to A and B which we picked up and assigned to like names in the fourth command line respectively. Since $a = e^B$ and $b = e^{-A}$ (table 14.A), we executed the last command line to find the required coefficients a and b whence $y = 1.4 \times 0.6^{-x}$ the equation we are looking for.

Depending on the given equation, different transformation may be necessary. For example the equation $y = ax^b$ becomes $Y = B + AX$ through $X = \ln x$, $Y = \ln y$, $B = \ln a$, and $A = b$ therefore we need to take natural logarithm on both the given x and y data. After entering the given x and y data to **x** and **y** respectively, the commands we need are the following: X=log(x);Y=log(y);p=polyfit(X,Y,1);A=p(1);B=p(2);a=exp(B);b=A;. Again natural number based functions like $y = ae^{bx}$ turns to $Y = B + Ax$ on $Y = \ln y$, $A = b$, and $B = \ln a$ for which we need the following: Y=log(y);p=polyfit(x,Y,1);A=p(1);B=p(2);a=exp(B);b=A;. While taking the logarithm, we make sure that there is no 0 in the given data because logarithm of 0 is undefined or infinity which machine can not handle.

9.12 Regression analysis

Suppose we have m dependent variables which are given in matrix form as $Y = \begin{bmatrix} y_1 \\ y_2 \\ \vdots \\ y_m \end{bmatrix}$, and each of which is a function of n independent variables $x_1, x_2, x_3, \ldots\ldots\ldots, x_n$. Also we assume that observational data for the independent variables is available as follows: $X = \begin{bmatrix} x_{11} & x_{12} & x_{13} & & x_{1n} \\ x_{21} & x_{22} & x_{23} & & x_{2n} \\ & & \vdots & & \\ x_{m1} & x_{m2} & x_{m3} & & x_{mn} \end{bmatrix}$, first row of X is the observation of y_1, second row of X is the observation of y_2, and so on. Having the X and Y data available, it is possible to find a linear relationship $Y = X\beta + \varepsilon$ in the least square sense where $\beta = \begin{bmatrix} \beta_1 \\ \beta_2 \\ \vdots \\ \beta_n \end{bmatrix}$ and $\varepsilon = \begin{bmatrix} \varepsilon_1 \\ \varepsilon_2 \\ \vdots \\ \varepsilon_m \end{bmatrix}$. The coefficients $\beta_1, \beta_2, \beta_3, \ldots\ldots\ldots\ldots, \beta_n$ are termed as the regression coefficients and the ε is called an error due to the regression analysis. Objective of the regression analysis is to estimate the regression coefficients β and error ε starting from X and Y which are given by $\beta = (X^T X)^{-1} X^T Y$ and $\varepsilon = Y - X\beta$. It is important to mention that the orders of Y, X, β, and ε are $m\times 1$, $m\times n$, $n\times 1$, and $m\times 1$ respectively. In order to perform the regression analysis, we employ the function **regress** with the syntax **regress** (Y data as column vector, X data in rectangular matrix form).

To exemplify this, let us take $X = \begin{bmatrix} 5 & 1 & 2 \\ 4 & -2 & 1 \\ -1 & 3 & -1 \\ 0 & 2 & -3 \end{bmatrix}$ and $Y = \begin{bmatrix} 7 \\ -2 \\ 8 \\ 0 \end{bmatrix}$. The regression coefficients are calculated as $\beta = \begin{bmatrix} \beta_1 \\ \beta_2 \\ \beta_3 \end{bmatrix} = (X^T X)^{-1} X^T Y = \begin{bmatrix} \frac{7}{184} & -\frac{5}{552} & -\frac{1}{23} \\ -\frac{5}{552} & \frac{15}{184} & \frac{4}{69} \\ -\frac{1}{23} & \frac{4}{69} & \frac{10}{69} \end{bmatrix} \begin{bmatrix} 5 & 4 & -1 & 0 \\ 1 & -2 & 3 & 2 \\ 2 & 1 & -1 & -3 \end{bmatrix} \begin{bmatrix} 7 \\ -2 \\ 8 \\ 0 \end{bmatrix} = \begin{bmatrix} 0.2319 \\ 2.9130 \\ 1.7826 \end{bmatrix}$ and error due to the regression is $\varepsilon = \begin{bmatrix} -0.6377 \\ 1.1159 \\ 1.2754 \\ -0.4783 \end{bmatrix}$. Our objective is to compute them for which we carry out the commands on the right. In the implementation, the first and second lines are to assign the Y and X matrices to the workspace **y** and **x** respectively. The retrum from **regress** is assigned to **b** (can be any user-given name) which holds the regression coefficients. Error is computed using the matrix code of $Y - X\beta$ which we assigned to the workspace **e** (can be any user-given name).

for the regression analysis:

```
>>y=[7 -2 8 0]'; ↵
>>x=[5 1 2;4 -2 1;-1 3 -1;0 2 -3]; ↵
>>b=regress(y,x) ↵   ← b ⇔ β

b =
        0.2319
        2.9130
        1.7826
>>e=y-x*b ↵              ← e⇔ ε

e =
       -0.6377
        1.1159
        1.2754
       -0.4783
```

9.13 Principal component analysis

If N random variables form a data matrix A of order $M \times N$ (whose rows represent M observations on each variable), the matrix A can be transformed to N orthogonal random variables. The first few transformed variables (say

P out of N) will carry nearly all the information possessed by the given N variables. The P transformed variables are termed as the principal components of A. Since $P<N$, the analysis is a dimension reduction approach. In most cases the given N random variables are correlated but the principal components hold orthogonality or uncorrelatedness. The first step of the analysis is to have the variance-covariance matrix V from A. The second step is to decompose V as $E \times D \times E^T$ where D is a diagonal matrix containing the ordered eigenvalues of V and $E=[E_1\ E_2\ E_3\ \ldots\ E_N]$. The E_1, E_2, E_3, ... E_N are the normalized column eigenvectors of V. The function **princomp** (abbreviation for the principal component) decomposes the given matrix data A to $E \times D \times E^T$ which is required from the analysis.

Let us consider $A=\begin{bmatrix}21 & 5\\18 & 7\\25 & 9\\20 & 5\\22 & 7\end{bmatrix}$ where M =5 and N =2. Applying the technique of section 9.6, we obtain $V=\begin{bmatrix}\frac{67}{10} & \frac{13}{5}\\ \frac{13}{5} & \frac{14}{5}\end{bmatrix}$. Concerning the section 4.11, we have the eigenvalues and normalized eigenvectors of V as $\frac{3}{2}$, 8 and $\begin{bmatrix}\frac{1}{\sqrt{5}}\\ -\frac{2}{\sqrt{5}}\end{bmatrix}$, $\begin{bmatrix}\frac{2}{\sqrt{5}}\\ \frac{1}{\sqrt{5}}\end{bmatrix}$ respectively. Having known the eigenvalues and eigenvectors, one writes $D=\begin{bmatrix}8 & 0\\0 & \frac{3}{2}\end{bmatrix}=\begin{bmatrix}8 & 0\\0 & 1.5\end{bmatrix}$ and $E=\begin{bmatrix}\frac{2}{\sqrt{5}} & \frac{1}{\sqrt{5}}\\ \frac{1}{\sqrt{5}} & -\frac{2}{\sqrt{5}}\end{bmatrix}=\begin{bmatrix}0.8944 & 0.4472\\0.4472 & -0.8944\end{bmatrix}$ hence the required decomposition is brought about. Its implementation is attached above on the right side. Concerning the implementation, the first line is to assign the matrix data to the workspace A. In the second line, the princomp decomposes the A which is its input argument. The function has four output arguments indicated by [E Q D S]. The second (Q) and fourth (S) outputs are called the component scores and Hotelling's T^2 respectively. We excluded their descriptions. The first (E) and third (D) outputs correspond to the theory-mentioned E and D respectively.

for principal component analysis:

```
>>A=[21 5;18 7;25 9;20 5;22 7]; ↵
>>[E Q D S]=princomp(A); ↵
>>E ↵              ← E⇔ E

E =
       0.8944  -0.4472
       0.4472   0.8944
         ↑        ↑
         E1       E2

>>D ↵              ← D⇔ D

D =
       8.0000         ← P =1
       1.5000         ← P =2
```

Note that the eigenvectors are not unique. Multiplying an eigenvector with a negative sign does not make any difference. The variance is a measure of the information content of a random variable. Since the diagonal elements of D are the variances of the columns of A, it can be said that $\frac{8}{8+1.5}$ =84.21% of the information contained in A is retained due to the transformation even if the second component is ignored (means setting 1.5 to 0).

9.14 Mahalanobis distance

Mahalanobis distance is given by $d^2(Y_i, \overline{X})=(Y_i-\overline{X})^T V^{-1}(Y_i-\overline{X})$ where Y_i is any k dimensional vector (that is the order of matrix Y_i is $m \times k$), V is the variance-covariance matrix as defined in section 9.6 (obtained from another k dimensional vector X and which is the reference for the computation), and $\overline{X}$ is the mean vector of the reference vector X. It gives a measure of distance between Y_i and $\overline{X}$ with respect to the variance-covariance matrix formed by X. The equation $(X-\overline{X})^T V^{-1}(X-\overline{X})=d^2$ represents a k dimensional ellipsoid in a k dimensional space where $\overline{X}$ is the mean of X and $\overline{X}$ is called the center of the ellipsoid. All points lying on the surface of the ellipsoid $(X-\overline{X})^T V^{-1}(X-\overline{X})=d^2$ are having the equal distances from $\overline{X}$. V is a positive definite matrix that means V has positive eigenvalues and it is symmetric and that d is a constant. An ellipse is nothing but a two dimensional ellipsoid. One important application of the distance is to analyze the multivariate data locally.

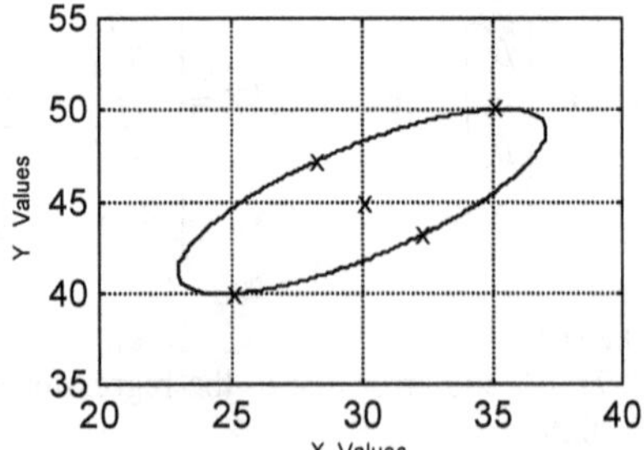

Figure 9.2(a) Ellipse formed by variance-covariance matrix V

We describe the concept taking 5 points in the $x-y$ plane which are given by A (28,47), B (32,43), C (25,40), D (35,50), and E (30,45). Shown x marks of figure 9.2(a) indicate the locations of these points. We have 2 dimensions x and y so k =2 that means X must have two columns. The given data can be arranged as $x = \begin{bmatrix} 28 \\ 32 \\ 25 \\ 35 \\ 30 \end{bmatrix}$ and $y = \begin{bmatrix} 47 \\ 43 \\ 40 \\ 50 \\ 45 \end{bmatrix}$ and the vector X is formed as $X = [x \quad y] = \begin{bmatrix} 28 & 47 \\ 32 & 43 \\ 25 & 40 \\ 35 & 50 \\ 30 & 45 \end{bmatrix}$. Sections 9.6 and 4.9 reveal that the variance-covariance matrix V of X is $V = \begin{bmatrix} \frac{29}{2} & \frac{21}{2} \\ \frac{21}{2} & \frac{29}{2} \end{bmatrix}$ and $V^{-1} = \begin{bmatrix} \frac{29}{200} & -\frac{21}{200} \\ -\frac{21}{200} & \frac{29}{200} \end{bmatrix}$. The means of x and y are 30 and 45 respectively from which $\overline{X} = \begin{bmatrix} 30 \\ 45 \end{bmatrix}$. Y_i can be any arbitrary point including the given A, B, C, D, or E. For the point A, we have $Y_1 = \begin{bmatrix} 28 \\ 47 \end{bmatrix}$, $Y_1 - \overline{X} = \begin{bmatrix} -2 \\ 2 \end{bmatrix}$, and the Mahalanobis distance is given by $d^2(Y_1, \overline{X}) = (Y_1 - \overline{X})^T V^{-1} (Y_1 - \overline{X}) = \begin{bmatrix} -2 \\ 2 \end{bmatrix}^T \times \begin{bmatrix} \frac{29}{200} & -\frac{21}{200} \\ -\frac{21}{200} & \frac{29}{200} \end{bmatrix} \times \begin{bmatrix} -2 \\ 2 \end{bmatrix}$ =2. In a similar fashion, we get 2, 2, 2, and 0 for the points B, C, D, and E respectively. The points A, B, C, and D are providing the same distance 2 from $\overline{X}$ relative to the matrix V therefore they are located on an ellipse, and the ellipse is graphed in the figure 9.2(a). The point E is not on the ellipse instead coincides with $\overline{X}$. The function adopted for the distance computation is **mahal** (abbreviation for Mahalanobis). To have the distance, we apply the syntax **mahal**(arbitrary vector Y_i, given reference vector X for the computation of the V).

For the example at hand, the first input argument is any coordinates (*x*, *y*) and the second input argument is the reference $X = \begin{bmatrix} 28 & 47 \\ 32 & 43 \\ 25 & 40 \\ 35 & 50 \\ 30 & 45 \end{bmatrix}$. To find the distance for the point A (28,47), our output must be 2 as computed before – this is the problem statement whose solution is attached on the right side. In the first line of the implementation we assigned the reference vector data to workspace **X**. The point A coordinates are assigned to workspace **Y** but as a two element row matrix. Again let us calculate the distances for the points A, C, and E and which should be 2, 2, and 0 respectively – this is the problem statement. Its computation is also shown on the right side. For the three points, we form the arbitrary matrix Y as $\begin{bmatrix} 28 & 47 \\ 25 & 40 \\ 30 & 45 \end{bmatrix}$ (from the given coordinates in order, A in the first row, C in the second row, and E in the third row). In both implementations we assigned the return from **mahal** to the workspace **d** which in general is the Mahalanobis distance as a column vector. We computed the distance considering A as a column vector but in MATLAB, the insersion style is a row one.

only for the point A:

```
>>X=[28 47;32 43;25 40;35 50;30 45]; ↵
>>Y=[28 47]; ↵          ← Y⇔Y
>>d=mahal(Y,X) ↵        ←d⇔d²(Y1,X̄)

d =

    2.0000
```

for the points A, C, and E:

```
>>Y=[28 47;25 40;30 45]; ↵
>>d=mahal(Y,X) ↵

d =

    2.0000   ← for A
    2.0000   ← for C
         0   ← for E
```

9.15 Crosscorrelation of random processes

The variation of a random variable versus some other independent variable like time is termed as a random process (can be said random function). The variance or correlation applies to random variables whereas crosscorrelation does to the random processes. We consider only the discrete processes for the computation. The function that is dedicated for the crosscorrelational computation is **xcorr** (abbreviation for the cross (x) correlation) which employs the syntax **xcorr** (process 1 as a row matrix, process 2 as a row matrix, type of the crosscorrelation).

The crosscorrelation $C_{xy}[m]$ of two discrete random processes $x[n]$ and $y[n]$ is defined as $C_{xy}[m] = E\{x[n]y[n-m]\}$ where E is the expectation operator. Let us see how the expression for $C_{xy}[m]$ is calculated.

for $m=0$, $C_{xy}[0]$ is the sum of the product of $x[n]$ and $y[n]$ divided by the number of observations,

for $m=1$, $C_{xy}[1]$ is the sum of the product of $x[n]$ and $y[n-1]$ divided by the number of observations that is slide the sequence $y[n]$ to the right by one element and take the product,

for $m=-1$, $C_{xy}[-1]$ is the sum of the product of $x[n]$ and $y[n+1]$ divided by the number of observations that is slide the sequence $y[n]$ to the left by one element and take the product, and so on for other m 's.

We compute the crosscorrelation for two example random processes $x[n]$ and $y[n]$ as presented below on the right table. For each $C_{xy}[m]$, we compute only the product of the dotted elements and consider only the number of observations inside the dotted mark as presented below:

Example processes for the computation:

n	−2	−1	0	1
$x[n]$	−1	6	−4	−5
$y[n]$	9	3	−10	8

Central:

$$\begin{array}{cccccl} \vdots -1 & 6 & -4 & -5 \vdots & & \leftarrow x[n] \\ \vdots\ 9 & 3 & -10 & 8\ \vdots & & \leftarrow y[n] \end{array}$$

$$x[n]\times y[n] = -9 \quad 18 \quad 40 \quad -40 \qquad \Sigma=9 \qquad C_{xy}[0]=\frac{9}{4}=2.25$$

Left shifts:

$$\begin{array}{ccccc l} & \vdots -1 & 6 & -4 \vdots & -5 & \leftarrow x[n] \\ 9 & \vdots\ 3 & -10 & 8\ \vdots & & \leftarrow y[n+1] \end{array}$$

$$x[n]\times y[n+1] = -3 \quad -60 \quad -32 \qquad \Sigma=-95 \qquad C_{xy}[-1]=-\frac{95}{3}=-31.6667$$

$$\begin{array}{cccccl} & & \vdots -1 & 6 \vdots & -4 \quad -5 & \leftarrow x[n] \\ 9 & 3 & \vdots -10 & 8 \vdots & & \leftarrow y[n+2] \end{array}$$

$$x[n]\times y[n+2] = 10 \quad 48 \qquad \Sigma=58 \qquad C_{xy}[-2]=\frac{58}{2}=29$$

$$\begin{array}{ccccccl} & & & \vdots -1 \vdots & 6 & -4 \quad -5 & \leftarrow x[n] \\ 9 & 3 & -10 & \vdots\ 8\ \vdots & & & \leftarrow y[n+3] \end{array}$$

$$x[n]\times y[n+3] = -8 \qquad \Sigma=-8 \qquad C_{xy}[-3]=-\frac{8}{1}=-8$$

In a similar fashion one can compute the right shifted values of $C_{xy}[m]$. However collecting all $C_{xy}[m]$ s, we have the computed crosscorrelation coefficients in tabular form as attached on the right side. The implementation is also shown on the right side in which we assigned the $x[n]$ and $y[n]$ both as a row matrix to x and y respectively.

Computed values from the crosscorrelation:

m	−3	−2	−1	0	1	2	3
$C_{xy}[m]$	−8	29	−31.6667	2.25	30.6667	−25.5	−45

Command we need:

```
>>x=[-1 6 -4 -5]; y=[9 3 -10 8]; C=xcorr(x,y,'unbiased') ↵

C =
    -8.0000  29.0000 -31.6667   2.2500  30.6667 -25.5000 -45.0000
```

The crosscorrelation so computed is termed as unbiased crosscorrelation, and which is indicated by the reserve word unbiased as the third input argument of the xcorr under quote. The user-given variable C holds the computed $C_{xy}[m]$ return as a row matrix. The crosscorrelation becomes autocorrelation when one uses $x[n]=y[n]$, which needs the syntax xcorr(x,'unbiased'). Execute help xcorr to learn more about the other variants of the function at the command prompt.

9.16 Help about other statistical functions

Our objective is not to explain the whole statistical toolbox functions. Comprehensive help inventory of the toolbox functions is seen by executing the following:

```
>>help stats ↵
  Statistics Toolbox
  Version 5.0 (R14) 05-May-2004
  Distributions.
       Parameter estimation.
       betafit   - Beta parameter estimation.
       binofit   - Binomial parameter estimation.
                 ⋮
```

From the displayed list, select any function and execute help function name to learn the details of the function at the command prompt e.g. help betafit.

Chapter 10

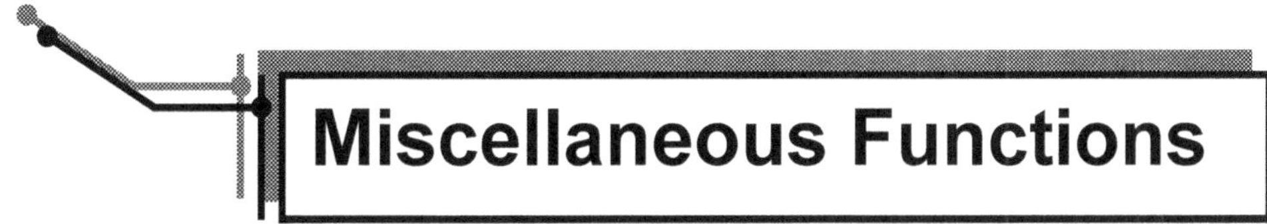

Although the chapters already discussed are focused on the title specific problems, it is sometimes necessary to perform computations in some other disciplines. We have chosen miscellaneous functions sampled from thousands just to show the computational capability of MATLAB in various disciplines in this chapter. Even though we are not going to address the complete function list, at least the reader will have some guidelines to carry on:

- A library of the classical functions and their computational techniques
- Complex number basics and computations, set theory functions, orthogonal polynomials, etc
- Conversion of numbers in various systems, vector products, and functional inverse
- Functional data generation for various functions both to the nonperiodic and periodic contexts

10.1 Some classical functions

There are some functions which are not frequently used but these functions are useful in specialized disciplines. For example Fresnel sine and cosine integrals are used in antenna engineering. Some special classical functions are located in the mfun library. There are over fifty functions found in the mfun library. In order to view the names of the functions included in the library, we perform the following:

```
>>help mfunlist ↵

MFUNLIST Special functions for MFUN.
        The following special functions are listed in alphabetical order
        according to the third column. n denotes an integer argument,
        x denotes a real argument, and z denotes a complex argument. For
        more detailed descriptions of the functions, including any
        argument restrictions, see the Reference Manual, or use MHELP.
```

```
bernoulli          n            Bernoulli Numbers
bernoulli          n,z          Bernoulli Polynomials
Bessell            x1,x         Bessel Function of the First Kind

                   ⋮

L                  n,x1,x       Generalized Laguerre
P                  n,x          Legendre
See also MFUN, MHELP.
```

MATLAB displays a number of functions available in the mfun library. The number and type of input arguments to a function are also displayed beside the function name. The common syntax for calling any function from the list is mfun(function name under quote, 1st input argument of the function, 2nd input argument of the function, etc). Along with examples some special functions and their MATLAB counterparts are addressed in the following but maintaining the font equivalence like m⇔ m .

Binomial coefficients ^mC_n

The binomial coefficients are defined as $^mC_n = \frac{m!}{n!(m-n)!}$ where m and n are integers and $m>n$. In the displayed mfunlist, we find the function by the name binomial whose executable form is mfun('binomial',m,n). For example $^5C_3 = \frac{5!}{3!(5-3)!} = 10$ is to be computed. Again a set of binomial coefficients can also be found such as $[^8C_2 \quad ^8C_0 \quad ^8C_1 \quad ^8C_4]$=[28 1 8 70]. In the binomial set, we have m =8 and n =[2 0 1 4]. Both implementations are attached on the right side. The n can be a scalar or matrix. The return from the mfun follows the n that is if n is a column matrix, so is the return. In each case we assigned the return to the workspace c which can be any user-given name.

for binomial coefficient $^5C_3$,

```
>>c=mfun('binomial',5,3) ↵

c =

    10
```

for a set of binomial coefficients,

```
>>m=8; ↵
>>n=[2 0 1 4]; ↵
>>c=mfun('binomial',m,n) ↵

ans =

    28    1    8    70
```

Fresnel sine and cosine integrals

The definition of Fresnel sine integral $S(x)$ is $\int_{t=0}^{t=x} \sin\left(\frac{\pi}{2}t^2\right) dt$ where x can be any real/complex numbers whose mfun function name is FresnelS and which has the executable form mfun('FresnelS',x) where x can be a scalar or matrix. For example we wish to find the Fresnel sine integral for each element of the row matrix R=[0 1.5 −2 4] and the output should be O=[$\int_{t=0}^{t=0} \sin\left(\frac{\pi}{2}t^2\right) dt \quad \int_{t=0}^{t=1.5} \sin\left(\frac{\pi}{2}t^2\right) dt \quad \int_{t=0}^{t=-2} \sin\left(\frac{\pi}{2}t^2\right) dt \quad \int_{t=0}^{t=4} \sin\left(\frac{\pi}{2}t^2\right) dt$]=[0 0.6974 −0.3436 0.4222]. The computation is presented above on the right side. Again let us say we intend to graph $S(x)$ for $0 \le x \le 2$. In this regard we assume some step size (say 0.2) for x, generate a row vector x writing x=[0:0.2:2]; (section 1.3), obtain the functional values of $S(x)$ at those x points stored in x writing O=mfun('FresnelS',x);, and apply the function plot of subsection 13.2.1 writing plot(x,O) to see the graph. If you reduce the step size of x, the execution might take longer because for every point a numerical integration needs to be performed.

for the Fresnel sine integral:

```
>>R=[0 1.5 -2 4]; ↵
>>O=mfun('FresnelS',R) ↵

O =

    0   0.6975   -0.3434   0.4205
```

Like the sine integral, there is Fresnel cosine integral with the definition $C(x) = \int_{t=0}^{t=x} \cos\left(\frac{\pi}{2}t^2\right) dt$ and whose mfun counterpart FresnelC works similarly as the FresnelS does.

Help for other mfun functions

We made you acquaint with three mfun functions still there are so many. In the earlier displayed mfun function list, you find the function names for different classical functions. Should you need help for any of them, use the command mhelp(function name under quote) at the command prompt. The called function appears before you in details. Just to give an example, the first function in the list is bernoulli and we execute the following to know about it:

```
>>mhelp('bernoulli') ↵

bernoulli - compute Bernoulli numbers and polynomials

Calling Sequence
   bernoulli(n, x)


Parameters
```

n - non-negative integer

x - (optional) expression

⋮

See Also

euler, inifcns

Following functions are not in the **mfun** list. You call them from the command window.

Inverse error function

The error function is defined as $erf(x)=\frac{2}{\sqrt{\pi}}\int_{t=0}^{t=x} e^{-t^2}dt$. If x is given, $erf(x)$ can be computed. What if $erf(x)$ is given, x is to be calculated? The function **erfinv(x)** (abbreviation for the error function's inverse) returns the inverse error function values where **x** can be a scalar or matrix. We know that $erf(0)=0$, $erf(\infty)=1$, and $erf(x)$ is not greater than 1. If we provide [0 1 3] as the input argument of the **erfinv**, we should get [0 ∞ undefined] whose computation is attached above. The workspace **x** holds the three values as a row matrix and the functional return is assigned to **y** which can be any user-given name. The infinity and undefined situations are returned as **Inf** and **NaN** (indicating not a number) respectively.

for the inverse error function:

```
>>x=[0 1 3]; ↵
>>y=erfinv(x) ↵

y =
      0   Inf   NaN
```

for the factorial function:

```
>>y=factorial(6) ↵

y =
      720
```

Factorial function

The function **factorial** finds the factorial of an integer n with the syntax **factorial(** n **)**. For example 6! =720 is found and assigned to the workspace **y** (can be any user-given name) as presented above on the right side.

10.2 Complex number basics

Arithmetic of complex numbers can be different from that of the real numbers arising from the fact that a real number is a scalar whereas a complex number is a vector. We discuss the very basics of the complex numbers in the following (font equivalence like A⇔ A is maintained).

Representation of complex numbers

Symbolically the imaginary unit of a complex number is denoted by i, j, or $\sqrt{-1}$ whose MATLAB representation is i, j, or **sqrt(-1)**. As an example the complex number $4+5i$ is entered into MATLAB by any of the following expressions **4+5i**, **4+5*i**, **4+i*5**, **4+5*j**, or **4+5*sqrt(-1)**.

Entering matrices of complex numbers

Matrix of complex numbers follows similar entering style to that of the integer or real number with little difference in conjugateness (section 1.3). Let us enter the complex number matrices $R=[3-i\ \ 4i\ \ -4]$, $C=\begin{bmatrix}7i\\-4+5i\\8i\end{bmatrix}$, and $A=\begin{bmatrix}2 & 5-i & 9i\\7i & 2+i & 11i\end{bmatrix}$ into MATLAB as shown on the right side. The operators .' and ' mean transpose without and with conjugate respectively. In the column matrix case if we use the operator ' at the end, we would assign $\begin{bmatrix}-7i\\-4-5i\\-8i\end{bmatrix}$ to **C**. In order to enter the matrix of rational numbers, we use the command **sym** of section 2.1 for example the complex row matrix $D=\begin{bmatrix}2+i\frac{3}{7} & \frac{5}{8}i\end{bmatrix}$ is entered to **D** as shown on the right side.

entering matrices of complex numbers: for R,

```
>>R=[3-i  4i  -4] ↵

R =
    3.0000 - 1.0000i      0 + 4.0000i   -4.0000
```

for C,

```
>>C=[7i  -4+5i  8i].' ↵

C =
        0 + 7.0000i
  -4.0000 + 5.0000i
        0 + 8.0000i
```

for A,

```
>>A=[2 5-i 9i;7i 2+i 11i] ↵

A =
    2.0000                5.0000 - 1.0000i      0 + 9.0000i
         0 + 7.0000i      2.0000 + 1.0000i      0 +11.0000i
```

for the rational complex number:

```
>>D=sym([2+i*3/7  5*i/8]) ↵

D =

[ (2)+(3/7)*i, (0)+(5/8)*i]
```

Modulus, argument, real part, imaginary part, and conjugate of a complex number

Modulus or absolute value of a complex number $A+iB$ is given by $\sqrt{A^2+B^2}$. To take the modulus of a complex number, we use the command **abs** (abbreviation for absolute value) with the syntax

modulus for the single complex number,

```
>>A=abs(4+3i) ↵

A =
      5
```

argument for the single complex number:

```
>>angle(4+3i) ↵

P =
      0.6435
```

modulus for the complex row matrix elements in R,

```
>>R=[12+5i -4-3i -8+6i]; ↵
>>A=abs(R) ↵

A =
      13    5    10
```

argument for the complex row matrix elements in R,

```
>>P=angle(R) ↵

P =
    0.3948   -2.4981    2.4981
```

abs(complex scalar or matrix). For example the modulus of $4+i3$ and elements in $R=[12+i5 \quad -4-i3 \quad -8+i6]$ are 5 and [13 5 10] respectively which we computed using the lower right corner attached command of the last page. In both cases we assigned the return to workspace A which can be any user-given name.

Argument of a complex number $A+iB$ is given by $\tan^{-1}\frac{B}{A}$. To find the argument, we use the function **angle** with the syntax **angle** (complex scalar or matrix name). The function returns any value from $-\pi$ to π. For instance the arguments of $4+i3$ and each element in $R=[12+i5 \quad -4-i3 \quad -8+i6]$ are $\tan^{-1}\frac{3}{4}$=0.6435^c and [0.3948^c −2.4981^c 2.4981^c] respectively which we implemented applying the lower right corner attached command of the last page. In both cases we assigned the return to the workspace P which can be any user-given name.

The conjugate of a complex number $A+iB$ is given by $A-iB$. To find the conjugate of a complex number, we apply the function **conj** with the syntax **conj**(complex scalar or matrix name). As an example the conjugate of $4+i3$ and all elements in $R=[12+i5 \quad -4-i3 \quad -8+i6]$ are $4-i3$ and $[12-i5 \quad -4+i3 \quad -8-i6]$ respectively. Both implementations are shown on the right side and assigned to the workspace C (user-given name).

conjugate for the single complex number,

```
>>C=conj(4+3i) ↵

C =

   4.0000 - 3.0000i
```

conjugate of the elements in the row matrix R,

```
>>R=[12+5i -4-3i -8+6i]; ↵
>>C=conj(R) ↵

C =

   12.0000-5.0000i -4.0000+3.0000i -8.0000- 6.0000i
>>real(R) ↵              ← for the real elements in R

ans =

   12   -4   -8
>>imag(R) ↵              ← for the imaginary elements in R

ans =

   5   -3   6
```

A complex number $A+iB$ has the real part A and the imaginary part B. To find the real and imaginary parts from complex number(s), we apply the functions **real** and **imag** with the syntax **real** (complex scalar or matrix name) and **imag** (complex scalar or matrix name) respectively. The real and imaginary parts for the elements in $R=[12+i5 \quad -4-i3 \quad -8+i6]$ are [12 −4 −8] and [5 −3 6] respectively whose findings are also attached above on the right side. The returns could have been assigned to some user-supplied names.

10.3 Complex number based computations

A lot of complex number specific manipulations can be conducted without too much programming in MATLAB. Let us go through the followings.

✦✦ Addition/subtraction of complex numbers

Two matrices of complex numbers $A=\begin{bmatrix}1+2i & 4+3i\\ 7-5i & 5+9i\end{bmatrix}$ and $B=\begin{bmatrix}6i & -4\\ 2+77i & 2-8i\end{bmatrix}$ are added to get $C=A+B=\begin{bmatrix}1+8i & 3i\\ 9+72i & 7+i\end{bmatrix}$. We have it computed as shown on the right side. For the same matrices, the subtraction is performed by A-B.

for the addition of two complex matrices:

```
>>A=[1+2i 4+3i;7-5i 5+9i]; B=[6i -4;2+77i 2-8i]; ↵
>>C=A+B ↵

C =

   1.0000 + 8.0000i        0 + 3.0000i
   9.0000 +72.0000i   7.0000 + 1.0000i
```

✦✦ Multiplication of complex numbers

Like the real numbers (section 2.2), multiplication of complex numbers can also be of two types – scalar and vector. The scalar multiplication (like positional element multiplication) of $A=\begin{bmatrix}\frac{9}{2}-\frac{4}{5}i\\ -\frac{6}{7}+7i\end{bmatrix}$ and $B=\begin{bmatrix}\frac{19}{9}-\frac{4}{25}i\\ \frac{1}{4}+5i\end{bmatrix}$ is $\begin{bmatrix}(\frac{9}{2}-\frac{4}{5}i)(\frac{19}{9}-\frac{4}{25}i)\\ (-\frac{6}{7}+7i)(\frac{1}{4}+5i)\end{bmatrix}=\begin{bmatrix}\frac{2343}{250}-\frac{542}{225}i\\ -\frac{493}{14}-\frac{71}{28}i\end{bmatrix}$ which needs the scalar operator .* (section 14.2) and the **sym** (section 2.1) for the rational numbers as shown on the right. Taking $A=\begin{bmatrix}1+i & 2-i & 7+i\\ i & 2i & -3i\end{bmatrix}$ and $B=\begin{bmatrix}7i\\ 9-i\\ 3i\end{bmatrix}$, the vector multiplication of A with B is $\begin{bmatrix}(1+i)7i+(2-i)(9-i)+(7+i)3i\\ i(7i)+2i(9-i)-3i(3i)\end{bmatrix}=$

for the scalar multiplication of complex numbers:

```
>>A=sym([9/2-4/5*i -6/7+7i].'); ↵
>>B=sym([19/9-4/25*i 1/4+5i].'); ↵
>>A.*B ↵

ans =

[ 2343/250-542/225*i]
[     -493/14-71/28*i]
```

for the vector multiplication of complex numbers:

```
>>A=[1+i 2-i 7+i;i 2i -3i]; ↵
>>B=[7i 9-i 3i].'; ↵
>>A*B ↵

ans =

   7.0000 +17.0000i
   4.0000 +18.0000i
```

$\begin{bmatrix} 7+17i \\ 4+18i \end{bmatrix}$ which we also implemented at the lower right corner of the last page.

Division of complex numbers

The general form of division of two complex numbers is $\frac{c+id}{a+ib} = \frac{ca+bd+ida-ibc}{a^2+b^2}$. Considering $A=3+4i$ and $B=7-8i$, the division of A by B is $\frac{A}{B} = \frac{-11+i52}{113}$ =–0.0973+ i 0.4602 which we carry out as presented on the right. The rational form return is also achievable through the use of the **sym** as shown on the right. We could assign the return to some variable. Use the command **pretty** on the symbolic return to see the mathematically readable form i.e. pretty(sym(A)/sym(B)). If A and B were identical size complex matrix, element by element division of the complex numbers would take place through the scalar code A./B.

division for the two single complex numbers,

```
>>A=3+4i; B=7-8i; ↵
>>A/B ↵

ans =
        -0.0973 + 0.4602i
```

division in rational form,

```
>>sym(A)/sym(B) ↵

ans =

-11/113+52/113*i
```

Logarithm of a complex number

Logarithm of a complex number is another complex number. Considering the complex number $A+iB$, the natural logarithim is given by $\ln(A+iB) = \frac{1}{2}\ln(A^2+B^2) + i\tan^{-1}\frac{B}{A}$ for example $\ln(5+i4) = 1.8568 + j0.6747$. Similarly the common logarithm is $\log_{10}(A+iB) = \frac{1}{2}\log_{10}(A^2+B^2) + i\tan^{-1}\frac{B}{A}\log_{10}e$ on that $\log_{10}(5+i4) = 0.8064 + i0.2930$. We included both logarithmic computations (table 14.A for the logarithmic functions) on the right which we assigned to the workspace L. In the case of a complex matrix input argument, the logarithmic function works on all elements as happens in MATLAB.

for the natural logarithm,

```
>>A=5+4i; ↵
>>L=log(A) ↵

L =
     1.8568 + 0.6747i
```

for the common logarithm,

```
>>L=log10(A) ↵

L =
     0.8064 + 0.2930i
```

A complex number with complex power

The general form of a complex number with complex power is $(A+iB)^{C+iD}$. Little manipulation separates the $(A+iB)^{C+iD}$ into the real and imaginary parts as $\left(\sqrt{A^2+B^2}\right)^C e^{-D\tan^{-1}\frac{B}{A}} \times \cos\left(C\tan^{-1}\frac{B}{A} + D\ln\sqrt{A^2+B^2}\right)$ and $\left(\sqrt{A^2+B^2}\right)^C e^{-D\tan^{-1}\frac{B}{A}} \sin\left(C\tan^{-1}\frac{B}{A} + D\ln\sqrt{A^2+B^2}\right)$ respectively. For a numerical example, let us say $(2-i4)^{3+i5}$ is to be calculated and whose real and imaginary parts should be -11749.3230 and -19402.1141 respectively which we implement using the right side attached command. Regarding the return from the implementation, the **e+004** means 10^4 therefore -1.1749e+004⇔–1.1749×10^4.

for the complex number with complex power,

```
>>(2-4i)^(3+5i) ↵

ans =

 -1.1749e+004 -1.9402e+004i
```

Rectangular to polar conversion or vice versa

Given a complex number in rectangular form $A+iB$, the polar or exponential form of the number is $re^{i\theta}$ where $r=\sqrt{A^2+B^2}$ and $\theta = \tan^{-1}\frac{B}{A}$. Its MATLAB counterpart is **cart2pol** (abbreviation for the <u>Cart</u>esian to (<u>2</u>) <u>pol</u>ar) and we use the syntax [θ , r]=cart2pol(A , B) where θ is in radians. Again given the polar form of a complex number is $re^{i\theta}$, the reverse conversion is $A=r\cos\theta$ and $B=r\sin\theta$ and the resembling MATLAB function is **pol2cart** (abbreviation for the <u>pol</u>ar to (<u>2</u>) <u>Cart</u>esian) with the syntax [A , B]=pol2cart (θ in radians, r). Unavailability of θ makes us write t instead of θ. The rectangular form number $5+i4$ has the polar form (r, θ) =(6.4031,0.6747^c) which we intend to obtain and vice versa. We see both implementations on the right side. Slight discrepancy is seen in the implementation, instead of 5 we are getting 5.0001. When we write 0.6747 as θ, we ignore the fifth digit and whatsoafter. The use of [A B]=pol2cart(t,r) returns the perfect result because t holds the complete data from the computation. Anyhow the input arguments of both functions can be matrix as well and output arguments are so.

from rectangular to polar conversion,

```
>>[t r]=cart2pol(5,4) ↵

t =
    0.6747
r =
    6.4031
```

from polar to rectangular conversion,

```
>>[A B]=pol2cart(0.6747,6.4031) ↵

A =
    5.0001
B =
    3.9998
```

♦♦ The nth root of a complex number

The problem statement here is to find the nth root of a complex number $A+iB$. If the nth root is x, then we have $x=\sqrt[n]{A+iB}$, or $x^n=A+iB$, or $x^n-A-iB=0$. Basically finding the nth root of $A+iB$ is nothing but solving $x^n-A-iB=0$ and it is easily solved by the function **solve** (section 3.8). Let us find the 4th root of $(4+3i)^2$. It is given that the four roots are $\left[\frac{3}{\sqrt{2}}-i\frac{1}{\sqrt{2}} \quad -\frac{1}{\sqrt{2}}+i\frac{3}{\sqrt{2}} \quad \frac{3}{\sqrt{2}}+i\frac{1}{\sqrt{2}} \quad -\frac{3}{\sqrt{2}}-i\frac{1}{\sqrt{2}}\right]$=[0.7071 $-i$2.1213 $-0.7071+i2.1213$ $2.1213+i0.7071$ $-2.1213-i0.7071$] which we wish to obtain. Our concern is to solve $x^4-(4+3i)^2=0$ whose solution is attached on the right side. The vector code of $x^4-(4+3i)^2$ is x^4-(4+3*i)^2. The return from the **solve** is assigned to the workspace S which can be any user-provided name. Mathematics readable form is seen through the use of **pretty** (section 3.1, here I⇔i). If you are interested in decimal form, the command **double** can make that happen which is also presented on the right side. Note that the return is a four element column matrix.

for the symbolic solution of the 4th root:

```
>>S=solve('x^4-(4+3*i)^2'); ↵
>>pretty(S) ↵
[       1/2          1/2 ]
[ 1/2 2    - 3/2 I 2     ]
[                        ]
[       1/2          1/2 ]
[- 1/2 2    + 3/2 I 2    ]
[                        ]
[       1/2          1/2 ]
[ 3/2 2    + 1/2 I 2     ]
[                        ]
[       1/2          1/2 ]
[- 3/2 2    - 1/2 I 2    ]
```

for the numeric solution of the 4th root:

```
>>double(S) ↵

ans =
   0.7071 - 2.1213i
  -0.7071 + 2.1213i
   2.1213 + 0.7071i
  -2.1213 - 0.7071i
```

♦♦ Real data to complex number

Suppose we have two identical size row matrices x=[5 6 7] and y=[8 9 −9] and we wish to form the complex matrix A=[$5+i8$ $6+i9$ $7-i9$] which needs to exercise the commands **x=[5 6 7]; y=[8 9 -9]; A=x+i*y;**. Again say we have some polar or exponential form data like r=[6 4 3] and θ=[$\frac{\pi}{3}$ $-\frac{\pi}{7}$ $\frac{\pi}{2}$] and we intend to form A=[$6e^{i\frac{\pi}{3}}$ $4e^{-i\frac{\pi}{7}}$ $3e^{i\frac{\pi}{2}}$] which requires to execute the following: **r=[6 4 3]; t=[pi/3 -pi/7 pi/2]; A=r.*exp(i*t);** where **t** for θ and we use the scalar code .* for the multiplication (section 14.2). If **t** were in degrees, the command would be **A=r.*exp(i*t*pi/180);**.

♦♦ Determinant of a complex square matrix

A square matrix may have complex elements, which can be numeric or symbolic. The determinant of $A=\begin{bmatrix}2+i & i\\ -i & 3i\end{bmatrix}$ is $-4+6i$. Again the determinant of symbolic $A=\begin{bmatrix}\cos x+iy & x+iy\\ x-iy & 4i\end{bmatrix}$ is $4i\cos x-4y-x^2-y^2$.

We apply the function **det** (section 4.7) to compute both determinants as shown on the right side. Note that the return from **det** is I for i.

for the determinant of the numeric A:

```
>>A=[2+i i;-i 3i]; ↵
>>det(A) ↵

ans =

-4.0000 + 6.0000i
```

for the determinant of the symbolic A:

```
>>syms x y ↵
>>A=[cos(x)+i*y x+i*y;x-i*y 4*i]; ↵
>>pretty(det(A)) ↵
                      2    2
  4 I cos(x) - 4 y - x  - y
```

♦♦ Inverse of a complex square matrix

It is given that the inverses of the matrices $A=\begin{bmatrix}1+4i & 4i\\ 7-5i & 3+2i\end{bmatrix}$ and $B=\begin{bmatrix}a+ic & b\\ c+i & d\end{bmatrix}$ are $C=\begin{bmatrix}-\frac{103}{821}-\frac{8i}{821} & \frac{56}{821}+\frac{100i}{821}\\ \frac{105}{821}-\frac{223i}{821} & -\frac{81}{821}-\frac{86i}{821}\end{bmatrix}$ and $D=\begin{bmatrix}\frac{d}{ad-bc+i(cd-b)} & \frac{-b}{ad-bc+i(cd-b)}\\ -\frac{c+i}{ad-bc+i(cd-b)} & \frac{a+ic}{ad-bc+i(cd-b)}\end{bmatrix}$ respectively and we intend to compute them. Responses of MATLAB on the execution of the **inv** (section 4.9) are attached on the right side. The **C** and **D** (user-given names) hold the inverses for the A and B respectively. The imaginary number i remains as i in **C** but the use of **pretty** shows it to be **I**. The subexpression **%1** which appears as the denominator in the inverse is equivalent to $ad+idc-bc-ib$ (indicated by %1 := d a + I d c - b c - I b). The := is the **maple** (section 3.2) assignment operator.

for the inverse of A:

```
>>A=sym([1+4i 4i;7-5i 3+2i]); ↵
>>C=inv(A); ↵
>>pretty(C) ↵
[  103                 56     100   ]
[- ----- - 8/821 I    ------ + ------ I ]
[  821                821    821    ]
[                                   ]
[ 105    223           81     86    ]
[ ----- - ------ I   - ----- - ------ I ]
[ 821    821           821    821   ]
```

for the inverse of B:

```
>>syms a b c d ↵
>>B=[a+i*c b;c+i d]; ↵
>>D=inv(B); ↵
>>pretty(D) ↵
[   d           b    ]
[ ------    - ------- ]
[  %1          %1    ]
[                    ]
[  c + I      a + I c ]
[- --------  ---------- ]
[   %1         %1    ]

%1 := d a + I d c - b c - I b
```

10.4 Complex expression computation

Perhaps MATLAB is the best tool to compute and manipulate the complex expressions. We present some expression based computations in the following.

♦♦ Complex expression expansion

We know that $\sin(x+iy)=\sin x\cosh y+i\cos x\sinh y$ and $(2x+iy)^3=8x^3+i12x^2y-6xy^2-iy^3$ which we easily perform through the function **expand** (section 3.2). The expansion is purely symbolic so we declare the related independent variables using the **syms** (section 2.1) before the expansion. We see both implementations on the right side.

for the expansion of $\sin(x+iy)$,

```
>>syms x y ↵
>>expand(sin(x+i*y)) ↵

ans =

sin(x)*cosh(y)+i*cos(x)*sinh(y)
```

for the expansion of $(2x+iy)^3$,

```
>>syms x y ↵
>>expand((2*x+i*y)^3) ↵

ans =

8*x^3+12*i*x^2*y-6*x*y^2-i*y^3
```

♦♦ Complex expression computation

Depending on the user-requirement, we need different approach to compute the complex expression. Let us go through the following examples on complex expression computation.

Example 1

Compute $\sin(x+iy)$ for $-1\le x\le 1$ with step 0.5 and $-0.3\le y\le 0.3$ with step 0.15. It is provided that we are supposed to have $\begin{bmatrix} -0.8796-i0.1645 & \cdots & \\ -0.8510-i0.0813 & \cdots & \\ & \vdots & \\ & & 0.8796+i0.1645 \end{bmatrix}$ at the indicated points in the $x-y$ domain. For example the values $-0.8796-i0.1645$ and $0.8796+i0.1645$ correspond to points $(-1,-0.3)$ and $(1,0.3)$ respectively. In section 3.10 we addressed the function **meshgrid** which is useful in this type of computation as shown below:

```
>>[x,y]=meshgrid(-1:.5:1,-.3:.15:.3); ↵   ← Generating grid points x and y from the given domain descriptions
>>f=sin(x+i*y) ↵                          ← Scalar code of sin(x+iy) is assigned to f, f user-chosen variable

f =

      Columns 1 through 4
      -0.8796 - 0.1645i   -0.5012 - 0.2672i   0 - 0.3045i    0.5012 - 0.2672i
      -0.8510 - 0.0813i   -0.4848 - 0.1321i   0 - 0.1506i    0.4848 - 0.1321i
      -0.8415             -0.4794             0              0.4794
      -0.8510 + 0.0813i   -0.4848 + 0.1321i   0 + 0.1506i    0.4848 + 0.1321i
      -0.8796 + 0.1645i   -0.5012 + 0.2672i   0 + 0.3045i    0.5012 + 0.2672i

      Column 5
       0.8796 - 0.1645i
       0.8510 - 0.0813i
       0.8415
       0.8510 + 0.0813i
       0.8796 + 0.1645i
```

The workspace **f** holds the data for $\sin(x+iy)$ at the indicated grid points. If you need to separate various parts (such as real or imaginary) from the computed data, use section 10.2 mentioned functions on the **f**. For example the real part data of $\sin(x+iy)$ is picked up by using the command **real(f)**.

Example 2

Compute the $f(z)=z^2+zi$ where z is complex and obviously given by $z=x+iy$ over $-1\le x\le 1$ with step 0.5 and $-0.3\le y\le 0.3$ with step 0.15. In the example 1, we generated the grid points and stored to the **x** and **y**. We do so here. After that we write **z=x+i*y;** because **x** and **y** data are real. Finally we use **f=z.^2+z*i;** (scalar code of $f(z)$) where **f** holds the $f(z)$ values as a complex rectangular matrix.

Example 3

In the last two examples the grids are rectangular domain based. The function **cplxgrid** by default generates polar grid over the rectangular domain $-1\le x\le 1$ and $1\le y\le 1$ but restricted on $|r|\le 1$ (because any complex number can be written as $re^{i\theta}$). The input argument of **cplxgrid** is a user-defined positive integer m, which returns a rectangular complex matrix grid of the size (m+1)×(2m+1). Actually this matrix is assumed to be the complex variable z in the function $f(z)$. For the computation we use the scalar code for example $f(z)=z^2+zi$ is computed on the polar grid using the scalar code **f=z.^2+z*i**.

10.5 Conversion of numbers from one base to other

The most common and widely used number system is decimal. The base of the decimal number is 10. In this system, any number is consisted of the integers 0 1 2 3 4 5 6 7 8 9. Let us say a number in decimal is 789 so $789=7\times10^2+8\times10^1+9\times10^0$. The number upon which the power is appearing is 10 that is why the base of the decimal number is 10. In a binary number, the base is 2. Any number in the binary system is consisted of 0 and 1. The number 42 of decimal in the binary system is written as 101010 which derives from $42=1\times2^5+0\times2^4+1\times2^3+0\times2^2+1\times2^1+0\times2^0$. In the hexadecimal system, the constituent numbers are 0 1 2 3 4 5 6 7 8 9 A B C D E F, where A, B, C, D, E, and F correspond to 10, 11, 12, 13, 14, and 15 of the decimal respectively. If the base of a number system is N, the number of that system is formed from the integers 0 to $N-1$. There are several functions that convert a number from one base to the other namely

- dec2bin – for conversion from decimal to (2) binary,
- bin2dec – for conversion from binary to (2) decimal,
- hex2dec – for conversion from hexa decimal to (2) decimal,
- dec2hex – for conversion from decimal to (2) hexadecimal,
- dec2base – for conversion from decimal to (2) any other base, and
- base2dec – for conversion from any other base to (2) decimal.

The number 42 conversion from the decimal to the binary (along with the reverse conversion) is implemented on the right side. Numbers other than decimal must be in string form (subsection 14.3.10) or under quote when they are put as the input arguments to the conversion functions. As different example, say the decimal number 85043 is to be converted in hexadecimal system which should be 14C33 $(1\times16^4+4\times16^3+(12)\times16^2+3\times16^1+\ 3\times16^0=85043)$. Its conversion is also attached on the right side.

If the input argument of any conversion function is a row matrix of integers, the return is a rectangular array of characters indicating the numbers in the system and in which each row represents a single number in the row matrix. For example we intend to convert each integer number in the row matrix N=[7 13 197 333] to its binary equivalent whose execution is presented on the right side. The 7 has the binary representation 111 which occupies the first row in the rectangular character array and so on. The converted numbers are preceded by the zero/zeroes up to the maximum number of digits. Any return from aforementioned execution can be assigned to the user-given workspace variable.

from decimal number 42 to binary,

```
>>dec2bin(42) ↵

ans =

101010
```

the reverse conversion of binary 101010 to decimal,

```
>>bin2dec('101010') ↵

ans =
    42
```

the conversion of decimal number 85043 to hexadecimal,

```
>>dec2hex(85043) ↵

ans =

14C33
```

the reverse conversion of hexadecimal to decimal,

```
>>hex2dec('14C33') ↵

ans =

85043
```

for the row matrix of integers,

```
>>N=[7 13 197 333]; ↵
>>dec2bin(N) ↵

ans =

000000111
000001101
011000101
101001101
```

10.6 Dot and cross products of vectors

The functions dot and cross find the dot and cross products of two vectors $\overline{A}$ and $\overline{B}$ with the syntax dot($\overline{A}$, $\overline{B}$) and cross($\overline{A}$, $\overline{B}$) respectively. For example the vectors $\overline{A}=-3i+2j+9k$ and $\overline{B}=i-7j+2k$ have the dot product $\overline{A}\circ\overline{B}=1$ and cross product $\overline{A}\times\overline{B}=67i+15j+19k$ which we wish to compute. Each vector is represented by a three element row matrix in which the vector components are elements in order for example $\overline{A}$=[−3 2 9]. However placed on the right is the computation of the two products in which the first two lines are to assign the two vectors to workspace A and B respectively then in the subsequent lines we call the two functions. The returns are assigned to workspace D and C (can be any user-given names) respectively.

As another example, three vectors are given by $\overline{P}=5a_x+9a_y+2a_z$, $\overline{Q}=-3a_x-7a_y+a_z$, and $\overline{R}=a_x-6a_y-8a_z$. We intend to determine the composite product $\dfrac{\overline{P}\circ[(\overline{P}-\overline{Q})\times(\overline{P}-\overline{R})]}{\left|(\overline{P}-\overline{Q})\times(\overline{P}-\overline{R})\right|}$=0.8843 (which is the shortest distance to the origin from the plane formed by the three points $\overline{P}$, $\overline{Q}$, and $\overline{R}$). On the right side is also its implementation in which the first three lines are to assign the vectors $\overline{P}$, $\overline{Q}$, and $\overline{R}$ to workspace P, Q, and R respectively. The vector subtraction $\overline{P}-\overline{Q}$ occurs just through

for the dot product,

```
>>A=[-3 2 9]; ↵
>>B=[1 -7 2]; ↵
>>D=dot(A,B) ↵

D =
     1
```

for the cross product,

```
>>C=cross(A,B) ↵

C =
    67    15    19
```

for the composite product,

```
>>P=[5 9 2]; ↵
>>Q=[-3 -7 1]; ↵
>>R=[1 -6 -8]; ↵
>>C=cross(P-Q,P-R); ↵
>>D=sqrt(sum(C.^2)); ↵
>>N=dot(P,C); ↵
>>N/D ↵

ans =
          0.8843
```

the row matrix subtraction P-Q on that cross(P-Q,P-R)⇔$(\overline{P}-\overline{Q})\times(\overline{P}-\overline{R})$ which we assigned to C (can be any user-given name). In the denominator of the given vector expression we need to calculate the vector magnitude which happens through the square root of the sum of square of each vector components in $(\overline{P}-\overline{Q})\times(\overline{P}-\overline{R})$. We did so using sqrt(sum(C.^2)) (sections 2.8 and 14.2) and assigned that to D. The dot product of the numerator vectors is carried out using dot(P,C) and assigned that to workspace N (can be any user-given name). Execution of N/D returns the whole computation.

So far we congested only the numerical dot and cross products. We can enjoy the facility of the symbolic dot and cross products as well. To exemplify, the cross product of $\overline{A}=(x+y)\overline{a}_x+zx\overline{a}_y$ and $\overline{B}=x\overline{a}_x-\cos x\overline{a}_y+e^x\overline{a}_z$ is $\overline{A}\times\overline{B}=+zxe^x\overline{a}_x-(x+y)e^x\overline{a}_y+[-(x+y)\cos x-zx^2]\overline{a}_z$ which we intend to compute. Declaring the associated variables using the syms (section 2.1), we conduct the right attached commands. In entering the vector components as a three element row matrix, we write the vector code (section 14.2) of each component and the cross product return is so.

for the symbolic cross product:

```
>>syms x y z ↵                     ← Declaring the x, y, z
>>A=[x+y z*x 0]; ↵                 ← Assigning the A to A
>>B=[x -cos(x) exp(x)]; ↵          ← Assigning the B to B
>>C=cross(A,B) ↵                   ← C⇔ A×B, C user-chosen

C =

[ z*x*exp(x),  -(x+y)*exp(x),  -(x+y)*cos(x)-z*x^2]
```

10.7 Inverse of a function

If a function $f(x)$ is given, its inverse function $f^{-1}(x)$ is obtained by exercising the function finverse whose input argument is the vector code (section 14.2) of the given function. The computation is symbolic so declaration of the related variables in the given function using the syms (section 2.1) is compulsory. It is provided that $f^{-1}(x)=\frac{5(x+2)}{4}$ is the inverse function of $f(x)=\frac{4}{5}x-2$ which we intend to compute. As a matter of fact, the $f(x)$ and $f^{-1}(x)$ are the image of each other about the line $y=x$. However the execution is seen on the right side in which the y and I hold the $f(x)$ and $f^{-1}(x)$ codes respectively and they can be any user-given names.

functional inverse for the linear function:

```
>>syms x ↵      ← Declare variable of f(x) as symbolic
>>y=4/5*x-2; ↵          ← Assigning code of f(x) to y
>>I=finverse(y) ↵     ← f^-1(x) is assigned to I

I =

5/2+5/4*x
```

for the quadratic function:

```
>>y=x^2-3*x-7; ↵      ← y⇔ f(x)
>>I=finverse(y); ↵    ← I⇔ f^-1(x)
Warning: finverse(x^2-3*x-7) is not unique.
> In sym.finverse at 43
>>pretty(I) ↵
                        1/2
     3/2 + 1/2 (37 + 4 x)
```

There are some functions which do not have the unique inverse for example the quadratic $f(x)=x^2-3x-7$ (because of the square root). Its inverse is given by $f^{-1}(x)=\frac{3\pm\sqrt{37+4x}}{2}$ which we also obtain from above attached commands applying ongoing function and symbology. It is evident that only one inverse is returned and we simply ignore the warning. Section 3.1 said pretty shows the readable form of the $f^{-1}(x)$ stored in I.

10.8 Polynomial interpolation

We know that a polynomial of degree n is written as $y=a_0+a_1x+a_2x^2+.....+a_{n-1}x^{n-1}+a_nx^n$. There are $n+1$ coefficients in the polynomial. Polynomial interpolation means finding the polynomial of degree n passing through $n+1$ distinct points.

Let us find the polynomial equation passing through the points (0,1), (1,2), (2,–3), (3,–4), and (4,5). We have 5 points so the degree of the interpolation polynomial should be 5–1=4. It is given that $y=1+\frac{25}{3}x-\frac{59}{6}x^2+\frac{8}{3}x^3-\frac{1}{6}x^4$ is the interpolated polynomial which we intend to obtain. We see its execution on the right side. For this purpose,

for the polynomial interpolation,

```
>>maple('A:=[0,1,2,3,4]'); ↵
>>maple('B:=[1,2,-3,-4,5]'); ↵
>>y=maple('interp(A,B,x)'); ↵
>>pretty(sym(y)) ↵
          4         3          2
  - 1/6 x  + 8/3 x  - 59/6 x  + 25/3 x + 1
```

we employ the maple (section 3.2) function interp (abbreviation for the interpolation) with the syntax interp(all x coordinates as a row matrix, all y coordinates as a row matrix, user-provided polynomial variable). Therefore we arrange the given x and y coordinate values in order to have $A=[0\quad 1\quad 2\quad 3\quad 4]$ and $B=[1\quad 2\quad -3\quad -4\quad 5]$ respectively. Concerning the implementation, the first and second lines are to assign the given x and y coordinates to workspace A and B respectively within the maple. In the maple, the := is the assignment operator and the row matrix elements are separated by a comma but housed inside the third brace. In the third line, the maple return is assigned to y in MATLAB. The A, B, x, and y are all user-given names. Sections 3.1 and 2.1 mentioned pretty and sym display the readable form of the interpolated polynomial. If previously worked out maple commands hold A or other names, you might see some error message. In order to clear previous maple actions, we execute clear maplemex at the command prompt. For simplicity we illustrated the interpolation taking integer points, you can input decimal number as the coordinates as well.

10.9 Orthogonal polynomials

We find the orthogonal polynomials in the maple (section 3.2) library orthopoly (abbreviation for the orthogonal polynomials). The orthopoly needs to be activated before any orthogonal polynomial related computations, which takes place by exactly executing maple('with(orthopoly)');. Available orthogonal polynomials are Chebyshev first and second kinds, Hermite, Laguerre, Legendre, and Jacobi. Inherent perspicuity of the orthogonal polynomials is that they are the solution of the linear differential equations. Let us go through the following in this regard.

Chebyshev polynomial of the first kind

The polynomial is defined by the recursive formula $T_n(x) = 2xT_{n-1}(x) - T_{n-2}(x)$ with $T_0(x) = 1$ and $T_1(x) = x$ where $n > 1$, n is the order of the polynomial, and n should be nonnegative integer. Polynomials of different orders are shown on the right side. The polynomials are orthogonal on the interval $[-1,1]$ with respect to the weight function $w(x) = \frac{1}{\sqrt{1-x^2}}$ that is the integration $\int_{x=-1}^{x=1} w(x)T_n(x)T_m(x)dx$ is equal to 0 for $m \neq n$. Anyhow the function T (comes from the earlier style of writing Chebyshev, which is Tchebyshev) returns the Chebyshev polynomial of different orders. The function T has two input arguments, the first and second of which are the order and polynomial variable respectively. Attached on the right side is the execution for obtaining $T_0(x)$ and $T_5(x)$ from the library. In each case we assigned the return to the workspace y which can be any user-given name. We chose the variable of the polynomial to be x which can be other as well. If you wish to see the mathematics readable form, execute pretty(sym(y)), sections 3.1 and 2.1.

Chebyshev polynomial of the first kind,

$T_0(x) = 1$

$T_1(x) = x$

$T_2(x) = 2x^2 - 1$

$T_3(x) = 4x^3 - 3x$

$T_4(x) = 8x^4 - 8x^2 + 1$

$T_5(x) = 16x^5 - 20x^3 + 5x$

.......so on.

Calling the T for $T_0(x)$:

```
>>maple('with(orthopoly)'); ↵
>>y=maple('T(0,x)') ↵

y =

1
```

Calling the T for $T_5(x)$:

```
>>y=maple('T(5,x)') ↵

y =

16*x^5-20*x^3+5*x
```

Other orthogonal polynomials such as Chebyshev of the second kind, Legendre, Hermite, Laguerre, and Gegenbauer have the function names U, L, H, L, and G respectively. If we intend to see further help on the disucussed T, we execute mhelp orthopoly[T] at the command prompt. Similarly you can explore other orthogonal polynomial implementational style just changing the function name (for example from T to G).

10.10 Piecewise continuous function

It is possible to define a piecewise continuous function through the maple (section 3.2) function piecewise. In maple terminology, "$f(x)$ is a function of x" is written as f:=x–> where := is the maple assignment operator. If the function were $g(c)$, we would write g:=c–>. As an example, we intend to define the piecewise continuous function $f(x) = \begin{cases} x & x \le -2 \\ 3x & -2 < x < 6 \\ x^2 & otherwise \end{cases}$ for which we execute the command maple('f:=x->piecewise(x<=-2,x,x<6,3*x,x^2)'); at the command prompt. In order to argument the function, first the interval description of the function appears and then does the piece function over the interval inside the piecewise. The interval (for example $x \le -2$) and function piece (for example x) are separated by a comma. We write the vector code (section 14.2) of each piece function. Operator reference is seen in subsection 14.3.1. It is assumed that the x in all intervals is increasing. For the second interval $-2 < x < 6$, the insertion of $x < 6$ is enough because the x is increasing so there is no need to write $-2 < x$. Again the value of the function at the knot for example at x =2 is taken from the first piece function not from the second piece one. The interval description is not necessary for "otherwise" inside the piecewise that is why the last piece is written as x^2 without interval. However we assigned the piecewise continuous function to workspace f but within the maple.

Next we may need to call f for the functional value return. The command maple('f',x) means "return the value of f at x from the maple workspace function f" or you can say we get f(x) in mathematics term. For instance $f(-2) = -2$ we get using the right attached command.

The functional return from the f as a row matrix might be necessary for subsequent computation. Let us say we intend to have the functional values of the

A single return from the piecewise continuous function,

```
>>maple('f',-2) ↵

ans =

-2          ← f(-2)
```

piecewise function over $-1 \le x \le 7$ with a step 0.1 whose computation is conducted as follows: y=[ ]; for x=-1:0.1:7,y=[y double(sym(maple('f',x)))]; end. There are several programming techniques are hidden here. You need the concept of data accumulation using the for-loop (subsection 14.3.3). For-loop index x provides a single x which becomes the input argument of the maple function f. The maple return is as character code so the sym turns the single f(x) value to symbolic. The double turns the symbolic single data to decimal. However the computed data for the piecewise continuous function $f(x)$ remains as a row matrix in the y which is a user-chosen name.

That is not all about the function. A variety of computations in respect to the piecewise continuous functions are supported through the maple package. For example the integration of $f(x)$ is found as $\int f(x)dx$ =

For integration of the piecewise continuous function:

```
>>I=maple('int(f(x),x)'); ↵
>>pretty(sym(I)) ↵
    {          2
    {  1/2 x              x <= -2
    {
    {       2
    { 3/2 x  - 4          x <= 6
    {
    {       3
    { 1/3 x  - 22         6 < x
```

$$\begin{Bmatrix} \int x dx & x \le -2 \\ \int_{x=-2}^{x=x} 3x dx + \text{functional value of } \int f(x)dx \text{ at } x=-2 & -2 < x < 6 \\ \int_{x=6}^{x=x} x^2 dx + \text{functional value of } \int f(x)dx \text{ at } x=6 & \text{otherwise} \end{Bmatrix} = \begin{Bmatrix} \frac{x^2}{2} & x \le -2 \\ \frac{3x^2}{2} - 4 & -2 < x < 6 \\ \frac{x^3}{3} - 22 & \text{otherwise} \end{Bmatrix}$$ which we wish to see.

The assignee f(x) is having the function within the maple. We carry out the integration of $f(x)$ as shown above in which int(f(x),x) means $\int f(x)dx$ and the I is any user-given name. The pretty (section 3.1) just shows the mathematics readable form.

10.11 Set theory functions

Any set is represented by a matrix – row, column, or rectangular in MATLAB. The set numbers can be integers, decimal numbers, characters, etc. Several set based functions are supplied in MATLAB whose discussions follow next.

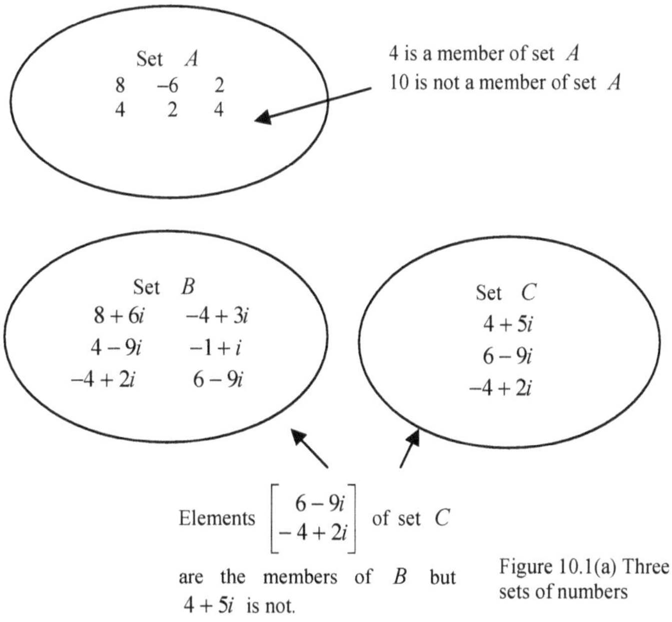

Set A
8 −6 2
4 2 4

4 is a member of set A
10 is not a member of set A

Set B
$8+6i$ $-4+3i$
$4-9i$ $-1+i$
$-4+2i$ $6-9i$

Set C
$4+5i$
$6-9i$
$-4+2i$

Elements $\begin{bmatrix} 6-9i \\ -4+2i \end{bmatrix}$ of set C are the members of B but $4+5i$ is not.

Figure 10.1(a) Three sets of numbers

Is an element the member of a set?

Suppose a set is given, an element may or may not be in that set. To determine whether an element is in a set, we use the function ismember with the syntax ismember (testing element(s), given set as row, column, or rectangular matrix). The return from the function is 1 or 0 depending on the presence or absence of the element under inspection. In the figure 10.1(a), 4 is a member of set A but 10 is not. Checking of one set elements with those of the other can occur as shown for the sets B and C in the figure 10.1(a). The ismember does not operate on columns instead on the whole matrix. We see both implementations on the right side in which we entered all elements of A, B, and C as rectangular, rectangular, and row matrices to workspace A, B, and C respectively. After that the ismember is invoked to verify the checking. As you see, the return 1 or 0 indicates the presence or absence of the element. For multiple elements like C, the reurn is also a row matrix in which every 0 or 1 corresponds to the like positional elements in C.

checking 10 as a member of set A,

```
>>A=[8 -6 2;4 2 4]; ↵
>>ismember(10,A) ↵

ans =
     0
```

checking the elements of set C as the members of B,

```
>>B=[8+6i -4+3i;4-9i -1+i;-4+2i 6-9i]; ↵
>>C=[4+5i 6-9i -4+2i]; ↵
>>ismember(C,B) ↵

ans =
     0   1   1
```

Union of two sets A and B

The function union finds the union of two sets A and B with the syntax union(A , B) symbolically $A \cup B$ ⇔union(A , B). Figure 10.1(b) shows the union of the set elements in A and B which we intend to implement. We first enter the members of A and B as a row matrix and then call the function union as follows:

```
>>A=[29 -30 29 479 72 34]; ↵
>>B=[29 -30 31 479 70 34]; ↵
>>union(A,B) ↵

ans =
      -30   29   31   34   70   72  479
```

The return is a row matrix as well indicating the union $A \cup B$. The function is also operational on the character sets (subsection 14.3.10).

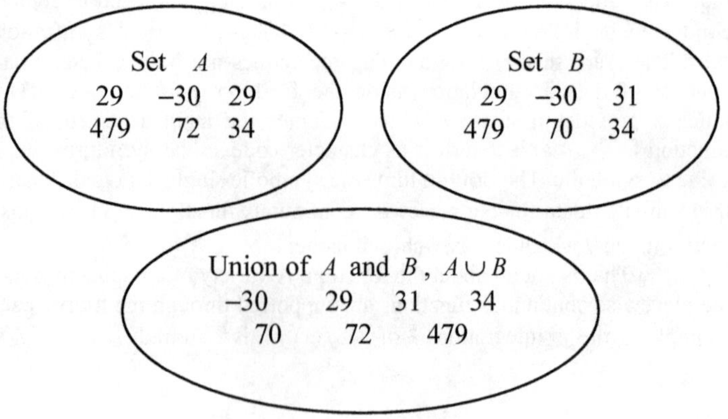

Figure 10.1(b) Union of two sets A and B

Intersection of two sets A and B

The function intersect finds the intersection of two sets A and B with the syntax intersect(A , B) i.e. $A \cap B$ ⇔intersect(A , B). Figure 10.1(b) mentioned sets A and B have the intersection $A \cap B =$ [−30 29 34 479] which we wish to compute. On having the sets available to A and B from the union execution, we conduct the right attached command.

for the intersection of sets A and B ,

```
>>intersect(A,B) ↵

ans =
      -30   29   34  479
```

Determining the unique elements in a set

In a given set, there may be repetition of some members. The function unique finds the uniquely occurred elements in the set when the set is its input argument. Our test matrix set is $A = \begin{bmatrix} 2 & 4 & 5 & 6 \\ 4 & 4 & 6 & 9 \\ 0 & 9 & 2 & 4 \end{bmatrix}$.

In A , the element 4 is occurring 4 times and 9 and 6 are occurring twice. The unique elements in A are [0 2 4 5 6 9] which we wish to determine. Attached on the right side is its implementation in which the first line is to assign the given matrix set to A and the second one is to call the function. The return from the function is a column matrix which could have been assigned to some user-given name. The function equally works on the character sets or strings.

determining the unique elements,

```
>>A=[2 4 5 6;4 4 6 9;0 9 2 4]; ↵
>>unique(A) ↵

ans =
     0
     2
     4
     5
     6
     9
```

Finding the difference between two sets

If two sets A and B have some identical elements, $A-B$ means the elements of A which are not in B except the common elements of A and B . The function setdiff (abbreviation for the set difference) performs the set difference $A-B$ with the syntax setdiff(A , B) where each matrix input argument is supposed to be row or column matrix not rectangular matrix. Let us say the test sets are the rectangular matrices $A = \begin{bmatrix} 2 & 4 \\ 5 & 6 \end{bmatrix}$ and $B = \begin{bmatrix} 4 & 5 \\ 0 & -1 \end{bmatrix}$. The common elements of A and B are 4 and 5. Then the $A-B$ should be [2 6]. Right attached commands help us implement that. In the implementation, the first two lines are to assign the given matrices to workspace A and B. In the third line we just call the function. The command A(:) turns the rectangular A to a column one, so does the other input argument. Return from setdiff is a column matrix holding the set difference elements.

for the set difference,

```
>>A=[2 4;5 6]; ↵
>>B=[4 5;0 -1]; ↵
>>setdiff(A(:),B(:)) ↵

ans =
     2
     6
```

for the complement of the intersection of two sets,

```
>>setxor(A,B) ↵

ans =
     31   70   72
```

Finding the complement set of the intersection of two sets

The complement set of two sets means all elements except the common elements of the two sets. Referring to the sets in the figure 10.1(b), we have 72 from A and 31 and 70 from B . In ascending order, the complement set is [31 70 72] symbolically which is $(A \cap B)^c$ and the MATLAB function setxor performs the operation with the syntax setxor(A , B) as shown above on the right side assuming that the two sets are existing in the workspace from previous execution.

10.12 Nonperiodic continuous functional data generation

Nonperiodic functions do not have repetitions over specific period. Their definitions emanate from the mathematical expressions, graphical representations, and data based generations. Generating the functional data is completely numeric and discrete. The user must define the interval over which the function exists. Within the given interval, we take sufficient samples or points on the function so that it acts like a continuous function. Nonperiodic function generation is addressed in the following (maintaining font equivalence like t⇔t throughout the whole section).

10.12.1 Functions from mathematical expressions

When the functions are given in terms of mathematical expressions over some given interval, we write the scalar code (section 14.2) of the functions for their generations like the following examples.

Example 1

Generate the function $f(t)=2$ for the interval $0 \le t \le 3$. Within the given interval the reader has to decide how many points on the t axis are required to represent the function. Let us say we increase the t from 0 to 3 with a step size 0.2 that means t assumes the values 0, 0.2, 0.4, ..3. At each of these values, $f(t)$ must be 2. For different t values, $f(t)$ becomes a row or column matrix. We generate the t as a row vector writing the code t=0:0.2:3; (section 1.3). Let MATLAB find the number of elements in the vector t by the command length(t). We generate the number of ones equal to the number of elements in t and multiply each element by 2 using the command 2*ones(1,length(t)) (section 2.14 for ones). However the formal procedure is as follows:

>>t=0:0.2:3; ↵ ← t holds the t variation as a row matrix, t is user-given name

>>f=2*ones(1,length(t)); ↵ ← Workspace variable f holds the function as a row matrix, f is user-given name

Example 2

Let us generate the ramp function $f(t)=t$ over the interval $0 \le t \le 3$ with a step size 0.1 as follows:

>>t=0:0.1:3; ↵ ← t holds the t variation as a row matrix

>>f=t; ↵ ← Workspace variable f holds the function as a row matrix

Now we do not need to generate ones like the example 1. In example 1 when t changes, one can not connect this change in terms of the functional relationship between $f(t)$ and t. In this example a definitive equation exists between $f(t)$ and t and we use the relationship to compute the function at different points on the t axis. If we had the shifted and scaled ramp function like $f(t)=\frac{4}{3}t-6$, the command would be f=4/3*t-6.

Table 10.A Nonperiodic functional data generation and its equivalent command

Function to be generated	Command we need
$f(t)=5e^{-t}$ for $0 \le t \le 0.1$ with a step 0.001	>>t=0:0.001:0.1; ↵ >>f=5*exp(-t); ↵
$f(t)=10(1-e^{-3t})$ for $0 \le t \le 0.1$ with a step 0.001	>>t=0:0.001:0.1; ↵ >>f=10*(1-exp(-3*t)); ↵
$f(t)=\|t\|$ for $-2 \le t \le 2$ with a step 0.1	>>t=-2:0.1:2; ↵ >>f=abs(t); ↵
$f(t)=\frac{3-\|t\|}{6}$ for $-2 \le t \le 2$ with a step 0.1	>>t=-2:0.1:2; ↵ >>f=(3-abs(t))/6; ↵
$f(t)=e^{-t^2}$ for $-2 \le t \le 2$ with a step 0.1 (called Gaussian)	>>t=-2:0.1:2; ↵ >>f=exp(-t.^2); ↵
$f(t)=\frac{1}{\sqrt{2\pi}}e^{-\left(\frac{t-4}{3}\right)^2}$ for $-2 \le t \le 2$ with a step 0.1 (Gaussian with different mean and scale)	>>t=-2:0.1:2; ↵ >>f=exp(-((t-4)/3).^2)/sqrt(2*pi); ↵
$f(t)=\frac{\sin \pi t}{\pi t}$ for $-2 \le t \le 2$ with a step 0.1 (called sinc function)	>>t=-2:0.1:2; ↵ >>f=sinc(t); ↵ (sinc is MATLAB built-in with the same definition)
$f(t)=\frac{\sin t}{t}$ for $-2 \le t \le 2$ with a step 0.1 (also called sinc function, different text defines differently)	>>t=-2:0.1:2; ↵ >>f=sinc(t/pi); ↵ (Using MATLAB built-in sinc)
$f(t)=3e^{-t}\sin 5t$ for $0 \le t \le 5$ with a step 0.1 (called damped sine function)	>>t=0:0.1:5; ↵ >>f=3*exp(-t).*sin(5*t); ↵
$f(t)=\begin{cases} 1 & for\ x>0 \\ -1 & for\ x<0 \end{cases}$ for $-2 \le t \le 2$ with a step 0.1 (called signum function)	>>t=-2:0.1:2; ↵ >>f=sign(t); ↵ (sign is MATLAB built-in with the given functional definition)

Example 3

Let us generate the parabolic function $f(t)=1-\frac{2}{5}t+t^2$ over interval $0 \le t \le 3$ with a step size 0.1 as follows:

>>t=0:0.1:3; ↵ ← t holds the t variation as a row matrix

>>f=1-2/5*t+t.^2; ↵ ← Workspace variable f holds the functional data as a row matrix

It is compulsory that we write the scalar code of a function related to t during the code writing (not the vector code, as discussed in section 14.2) on account of that the 1-2/5*t+t^.2 is the scalar code of the function $1-\frac{2}{5}t+t^2$.

Example 4

Let us generate the sinusoidal function $v(t)=0.3\sin 2\pi ft$ for the interval 0 to 20 millisecond where the frequency f=50 Hz and t represents time in second. Let us choose the time step as 0.1 millisecond and the last time point 20 millisecond is written as 20×10^{-3}sec whose MATLAB code is 20e-3 (1e-3 is equivalent to 10^{-3} not the natural number). The function $0.3\sin 2\pi ft$ is coded as 0.3*sin(2*pi*50*t) and the implementation is as follows:

```
>>t=0:0.1e-3:20e-3; ↵        ← t holds the t variation as a row matrix employing the chosen step size
>>v=0.3*sin(2*pi*t*50); ↵    ← Workspace variable v holds the function v(t) as a row matrix
```

If the sinusoidal function had some phase for example $v(t)=0.3\sin(2\pi ft-60^0)$, the command would be v= 0.3*sin(2*pi*t*50-pi/3); because the sine input argument must be in radians.

Miscellaneous examples

In the last four examples we introduced the idea behind the discrete functional data generation for several continuous functions. We presented few more examples in the table 10.A maintaining same function and symbology.

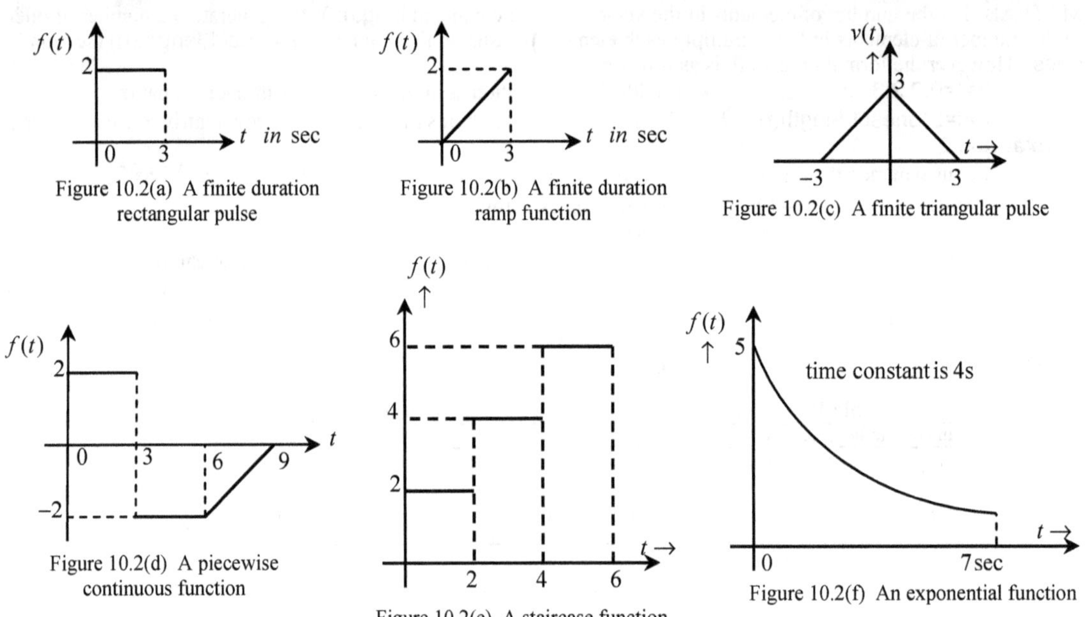

Figure 10.2(a) A finite duration rectangular pulse

Figure 10.2(b) A finite duration ramp function

Figure 10.2(c) A finite triangular pulse

Figure 10.2(d) A piecewise continuous function

Figure 10.2(e) A staircase function

Figure 10.2(f) An exponential function

10.12.2 Functions from graphical representations

Given the graphical representation, we can generate a function from its functional properties. Even though the graph is available, we need to write the mathematical expression of the graph for the computation or code writing reason. Let us proceed with the following examples.

Example 1

Generate the finite duration rectangular pulse of the figure 10.2(a). We solved the problem in example 1 of last subsection.

Example 2

The finite duration ramp pulse of the figure 10.2(b) is to be generated. The function passes through two points whose coordinates are (0,0) and (3,2) and the equation of the finite ramp pulse is $f(t)=\frac{2}{3}t$. Choosing a step size 0.1 sec within the interval $0\le t\le 3$ sec, we generate the function as follows:

```
>>t=0:0.1:3; ↵     ← t holds the t variation as a row matrix
>>f=2/3*t; ↵       ← Workspace variable f holds the function as a row matrix (code of 2/3 t is 2/3*t)
```

Example 3

We intend to generate the symmetric triangular function $v(t)$ of the figure 10.2(c) taking a t step size 0.1. The function is composed of two ramp or straight line functions. The left and right straight lines pass through the points $\begin{Bmatrix}(-3,0)\\(0,3)\end{Bmatrix}$ and $\begin{Bmatrix}(3,0)\\(0,3)\end{Bmatrix}$ and their equations are found using the function line of section 3.11 as $v(t)=t+3$ for $-3\le t<0$ and $v(t)=3-t$ for $0\le t\le 3$ respectively. Since there are two equations for two segments, writing one code for the whole function can not be performed. Let us generate the complete t vector with the given step size as follows:

```
>>t=-3:0.1:3; ↵        ← t holds the whole t variation as a row matrix (step size 0.1)
```

There are several approaches to generate the function. One approach is we generate ones exactly the number of elements in t and replace the ones by the functional values of $v(t)$ as follows:

>>v=ones(1,length(t)); ↵ ← v is a row matrix whose all elements are 1 (section 2.14), length finds the number of ones in t

Using the function find (section 2.13), we determine the integer index exactly corresponding to the interval occurring in t as shown below:

>>r1=find(-3<=t&t<0); ↵ ← r1 holds only the integer position indexes of t at which $-3 \le t < 0$ is satisfied

>>v(r1)=t(r1)+3; ↵

>>r2=find(0<=t&t<=3); ↵ ← r2 holds only the integer position indexes of t at which $0 \le t \le 3$ is satisfied

>>v(r2)=3-t(r2); ↵

The r1 or r2 is any user-given name. The logical condition $-3 \le t < 0$ is split in two parts, $-3 \le t$ and $t < 0$, for programming reason (subsection 14.3.1). The two logical expressions are connected by the AND operator. The command v(r1)=t(r1)+3; implements $v(t) = t + 3$. We applied t(r1) not t. If we had t+3, 3 would be added to all elements in t which is not how the function is defined. Again the assignment took place only to the indexes of the first interval by writing v(r1). Similar explanation can be cited for the other interval. However the whole function $v(t)$ is stored in the workspace variable v. The junction point of the two intervals should be properly defined. For example, the intervals $-3 \le t < 0$ and $0 \le t \le 3$ have the junction point $t = 0$ which is considered in the second interval not in the first one. Operator writing also needs proper attention. If we implement $0 \le t$ instead of $0 < t$, we end up with erroneous functional data.

Example 4

Let us generate the piecewise function of the figure 10.2(d) on an interval $0 \le t \le 9$ and using a step size 0.1. There are three segments in the function whose descriptions are $f(t) = \begin{cases} 2 & for \quad 0 \le t < 3 \\ -2 & for \quad 3 \le t < 6 \\ \frac{2}{3}t - 6 & for \quad 6 \le t < 9 \end{cases}$. Drawing the idea and functions of the last examples, we implement the following:

>>t=0:0.1:9; ↵ ← t holds the whole t variation $0 \le t \le 9$ as a row matrix with the step 0.1

>>f=ones(1,length(t)); ↵ ← f is a row matrix whose all elements are 1, the number of ones is exactly equal to the number of elements in t

>>r1=find(0<=t&t<3); ↵ ← r1 holds only the integer position indexes of t at which $0 \le t < 3$ is satisfied

>>f(r1)=2; ↵ ← assigns 2 only to the integer position indexes stored in r1 corresponding to $0 \le t < 3$

>>r2=find(3<=t&t<6); ↵ ← r2 holds only the integer position indexes of t at which $3 \le t < 6$ is satisfied

>>f(r2)=-2; ↵ ← assigns −2 only to the position indexes stored in r2 corresponding to $3 \le t < 6$

>>r3=find(6<=t&t<=9); ↵ ← r3 holds only the integer position indexes of t at which $6 \le t \le 9$ is satisfied

>>f(r3)=2/3*t(r3)-6; ↵ ← assigns $\frac{2}{3}t - 6$ values only to the position indexes stored in r3 corresponding to $6 \le t \le 9$

The workspace variable f holds the whole function as a row matrix.

Example 5

The staircase function of the figure 10.2(e) needs to be generated. Reading off the function from the graph and writing as a function, we have $f(t) = \begin{cases} 2 & for \quad 0 \le t < 2 \\ 4 & for \quad 2 \le t < 4 \\ 6 & for \quad 4 \le t < 6 \end{cases}$. Referring to the example 1 of last subsection, the function needs multiple constant generation on different intervals. In last two examples we illustrated how the multiple intervals are handled. The complete code of the function is as follows:

>>t=0:0.1:6; ↵ ← t holds the whole t variation $0 \le t \le 6$ as a row matrix choosing a step 0.1

>>f=ones(1,length(t)); ↵ ← f is a row matrix whose all elements are 1, the number of ones is exactly equal to the number of elements in t

>>r1=find(0<=t&t<2); ↵ ← r1 holds only the integer position indexes of t at which $0 \le t < 2$ is satisfied

>>f(r1)=2; ↵ ← assigns 2 only to the position indexes stored in r1 corresponding to $0 \le t < 2$

>>r2=find(2<=t&t<4); ↵ ← r2 holds only the integer position indexes of t at which $2 \le t < 4$ is satisfied

>>f(r2)=4; ↵ ← assigns 4 only to the position indexes stored in r2 corresponding to $2 \le t < 4$

>>r3=find(4<=t&t<=6); ↵ ← r3 holds only the integer position indexes of t at which $4 \le t < 6$ is satisfied

>>f(r3)=6; ↵ ← assigns 6 only to the position indexes stored in r3 corresponding to $4 \le t < 6$

When we graph the function using the plot(t,f) of subsection 13.2.1, we find the transition lines slightly deviated from a perfect vertical line. Reducing the step size from 0.1 to 0.05 or less solves the problem. In the last interval, mathematically we say $4 \le t < 6$ but for the closing point we write $t \le 6$. If we do not do so, the last value of f is taken as 1 (because we assigned before). Anyhow the workspace variable f holds the whole functional data as a row matrix.

Example 6

The exponential function of the figure 10.2(f) is to be generated. If the initial value (value at $t = 0$) and the time constant of an exponential function are A and t_c respectively, the function is given by the expression $f(t) = A\,e^{-\frac{t}{t_c}}$. With the given specification, the functional expression is going to be $f(t) = 5\,e^{-\frac{t}{4}}$. We generate the function considering a step size 0.1 as follows:

```
>>t=0:0.1:7; ↵
```
← t holds the whole t variation $0 \le t \le 7$ as a row matrix choosing a step 0.1 sec

```
>>f=5*exp(-t/4); ↵
```
← Workspace variable f holds the function as a row matrix (code of $5e^{-\frac{t}{4}}$ is 5*exp(-t/4))

10.12.3 Functions applying M-file descriptions

The reader is referred to sections 1.3 and 14.5 for the M-file and function file details. Examples illustrated so far in this section are implemented at the command prompt. If a function is piecewise continuous like the figure 10.2(e), code writing for each segment of the function might be lengthy specially for a function with multiple pieces. A MATLAB function file is better in this regard for which the following two examples are provided.

Example 1

Our objective is to write a function file that generates the piecewise continuous functional data of the figure 10.2(d) whose piecewise definition is given in the example 4 of the last subsection. There are two approaches on the M-file writing. The first approach assumes the input argument to the function file to be a single scalar (a single t value) and the other approach assumes the input argument to be the whole t vector. We address both in the following:

```
function y=f(t)
   if 0<=t&t<3
      y=2;
   elseif 3<=t&t<6
      y=-2;
   elseif 6<=t&t<9
      y=2/3*t-6;
   else
      y=0;
   end
```

Figure 10.3(a) Function file describing the function of the figure 10.2(d) assuming the t is a single scalar

Approach 1: Input is a single t value

In this approach we check the single t value using **if-else-end** statement (subsection 14.3.4) to which interval it belongs. The interval appears as the logical expression of the **if-else-end** statement. We split the interval $0 \le t < 3$ into $0 \le t$ and $t < 3$ and connect them by the AND operator (subsection 14.3.1). We assign the functional value to some variable (for example **y**) corresponding to the interval followed by **elseif** or **else**. The return data from the function file is accumulated outside the function file and the accumulation happens in another M-file or in the command window. The first step is to write the piecewise definition as shown in the figure 10.3(a) in a new M-file and save the file by the name **f** (can be user-given name) in your working path of MATLAB. We would like to verify that $f(t)=-2$ at $t=4$ for which we execute the following at the command prompt:

```
>>f(4) ↵
```
← calling the function for $t=4$

```
ans =
         -2
```
← single input provides single output

The next is to generate the complete function over the whole interval. Again one needs to decide the step size say 0.1 on that we exercise the following:

```
>>s=[ ]; for t=0:0.1:9 s=[s f(t)]; end ↵
```

The workspace variable **s** (can be any user-given name) holds the functional data of the figure 10.2(d) as a row matrix over the whole interval. Data accumulation and for-loop reference is seen in subsection 14.3.3.

```
function v=f(t)
v=[ ];
for k=1:length(t)
   if 0<=t(k)&t(k)<3
      y=2;
   elseif 3<=t(k)&t(k)<6
      y=-2;
   elseif 6<=t(k)&t(k)<9
      y=2/3*t(k)-6;
   else
      y=0;
   end
   v=[v y];
end
```

Figure 10.3(b) Function file describing the function of the figure 10.2(d) assuming the t is the whole t vector

```
function y=f(t)
   if 0<=t&t<2
      y=2;
   elseif 2<=t&t<4
      y=4;
   elseif 4<=t&t<=6
      y=6;
   else
      y=0;
   end
```

Figure 10.3(c) Function file describing the function of the figure 10.2(e) assuming the t is a single scalar

```
function v=f(t)
v=[ ];
for k=1:length(t)
   if 0<=t(k)&t(k)<2
      y=2;
   elseif 2<=t(k)&t(k)<4
      y=4;
   elseif 4<=t(k)&t(k)<=6
      y=6;
   else
      y=0;
   end
   v=[v y];
end
```

Figure 10.3(d) Function file describing the function of the figure 10.2(e) assuming the t is the whole t vector

Approach 2: Input is the whole t vector

Now we assume that the input to the function file is the whole t vector not a single scalar. The necessary code for this approach is presented in the figure 10.3(b). Write the codes in a new M-file editor and save the file by the **f** (you can choose your own file name, for simplicity we used again the same name **f** to be consistent with $f(t)$) in your working path. From the figure 10.2(d), the functional values at $t=1$, 4, and 9 are 2, –2, and 0 respectively. Let us verify those as follows:

```
>>t=[1 4 9]; ↵
```
← Assigning the t values as a row matrix

>>f(t) ↵ ← Calling the function for vector **t**

ans =

2 -2 0 ← The returns are the functional values of $f(t)$ respectively, multiple outputs

You can even call the **f(t)** from another M-file as long as they are in the same working path. The single scalar **t** in the figure 10.3(a) is now replaced by the **t(k)** beside the logical expression considering the **k**-th element in the time vector **t** in the figure 10.3(b). The for-loop of the figure 10.3(b) has the last counter as **length(t)** that makes the continuation until the total number of elements in **t** is taken care of. For every **k**, the content of **y** of the figure 10.3(b) is a scalar and we accumulate this **y** to **v** side by side. The t vector is a row matrix, so is the return of **f(t)**. Suppose we intend to generate the function from 0 to 9 with a step 0.1 and do so by the following:

>>t=0:0.1:9; ↵ ← **t** holds the whole t variation $0 \le t \le 9$ as a row matrix with the step 0.1

>>s=f(t); ↵ ← The workspace variable **s** holds the whole functional data as a row matrix

Example 2

We assume that the reader has gone through the example 1. Drawing the idea and notation of the example 1, we generate the function of the figure 10.2(e) using both approaches as follows:

Approach 1: Input is a single t value

The functional definition of the function can be seen in the example 5 of the last subsection. Figure 10.3(c) presents the code of the function. Type the codes in a new M-file editor and save the file by the name **f**. We call the function file for the generation of the function over the interval $0 \le t \le 6$ with a step size 0.1 as follows:

>>s=[ ]; for t=0:0.1:6 s=[s f(t)]; end ↵ ← Variable **s** holds the functional values as a row matrix

Approach 2: Input is the whole t vector

Figure 10.3(d) holds the necessary codes for the generation. Type the codes and save the file by the name **f**. The generation of the function over the interval $0 \le t \le 6$ with a step size 0.1 takes place as follows:

>>t=0:0.1:6; ↵ ← **t** holds the whole t variation $0 \le t \le 6$ as a row matrix with the step 0.1

>>s=f(t); ↵ ← The workspace variable **s** holds the functional data as a row matrix

Whether example 1 or 2, the generation is verified looking into the graph by using the **plot(t,s)** of subsection 13.2.1.

10.13 Some periodic functional data generation

A periodic function repeats its shape every after a period of the function. If the function $v(t)$ is periodic over a period T, the relationship $v(t)=v(t+T)$ exists at every t and the function has the frequency $f=\frac{1}{T}$. When the t is in second or meter, the f is in Hertz or per meter respectively. To generate a periodic function, the definition of the function in one period is enough. Like the nonperiodic functions of previous section, the definition or description of a periodic function can be expression, graphical representation, or M-file based. We address few periodic functions employing the built-in generators in the following.

Example 1

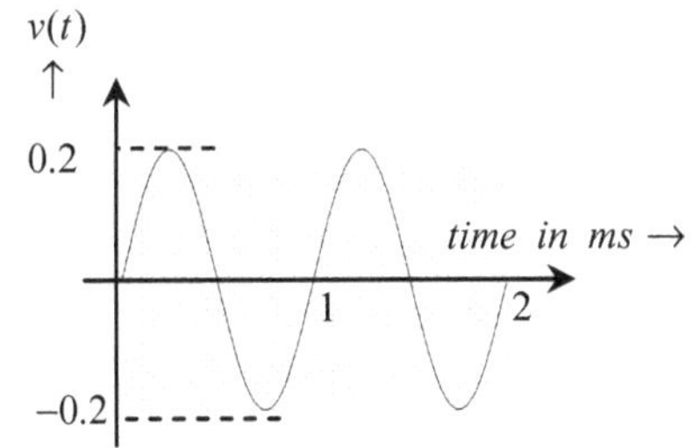

Figure 10.4(a) Plot of a two cycle sine wave

Figure 10.4(c) Half wave rectified sine wave

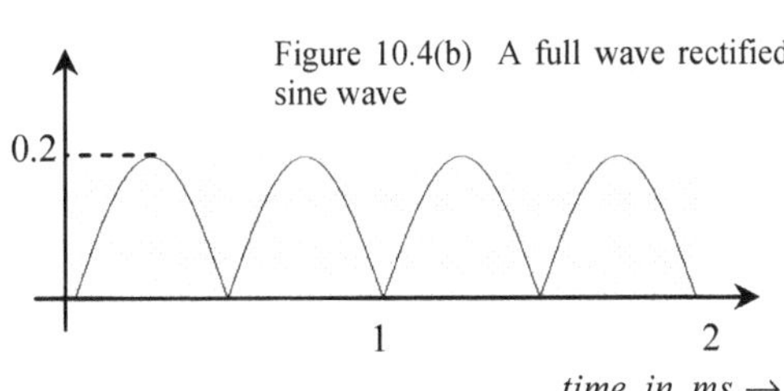

Figure 10.4(b) A full wave rectified sine wave

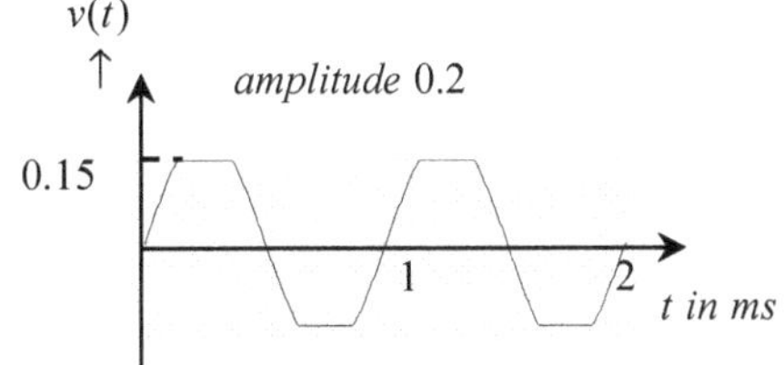

Figure 10.4(d) The sine wave of the figure 10.4(a) is clipped at ±0.15

Let us generate the wave of the figure 10.4(a). Our ability to pick up the information from a given graph is important. Referring to the figure, the time period and amplitude of the wave are T =1 msec and 0.2 respectively. The frequency of the sine wave is then $f=\frac{1}{T}$=1000 Hertz hence the equation of the wave is $v(t)=0.2\sin 2\pi 1000t$. To generate the two cycle wave choosing a step 0.01 msec, we exercise the following commands:

>>t=0:0.01e-3:2e-3; ↵ ← **t** holds t variation $0 \le t \le 2$ msec as a row matrix with a step 0.01 msec

```
>>v=0.2*sin(2*pi*1000*t); ↵
```
← The code of $0.2\sin 2\pi 1000t$ is 0.2*sin(2*pi*1000*t)

Two cycles mean 2 msec wave existence. The period 1 msec is equal to 10^{-3} sec whose code is **1e-3**. Workspace variable **v** (any user-given name) holds the functional data as a row matrix.

Example 2

Generate the full wave rectified sine wave of the figure 10.4(b). It is exactly the wave of the figure 10.4(a) but the negative halves are turned to positive. The command **abs** turns the negative value to a positive one. In example 1, we need to write **v=abs(0.2*sin(2*pi*1000*t));** to generate the wave assuming the same step size.

Example 3

The half wave rectified sine wave of the figure 10.4(c) is to be generated. This wave is also derived from the wave of the figure 10.4(a) from which the negative part of the wave is turned to zero (execute the two line commands of the example 1 first). In order to generate the function, we generate the function of the figure 10.4(a), find the integer indexes of the **t** vector at which the function is less than zero using the **find** (section 2.13), and set the functional values corresponding to those integer indexes to zero as follows:

```
>>r=find(v<0); ↵   ← r holds the integer indexes as a row matrix at which the function has negative values
>>v(r)=0; ↵        ← setting the negative v elements to 0, v holds the functional data as a row matrix
```

Example 4

We intend to generate the clipped sine wave of the figure 10.4(d). This wave is also derived (execute the two line commands of the example 1 first) from the wave of the figure 10.4(a). Once the wave data is generated, we check the value of the function at every point. If $v(t)>0.15$, we set $v(t)=0.15$ and if $v(t)<-0.15$, we set $v(t)=-0.15$ that is how the clipping can be implemented:

```
>>r1=find(v>0.15); ↵     ← r1 holds the integer t indexes at which the functional value > 0.15
>>v(r1)=0.15; ↵          ← 0.15 is assigned only to the r1 index values of the function vector v
>>r2=find(v<-0.15); ↵    ← r2 holds the integer t indexes at which the functional value < −0.15
>>v(r2)=-0.15; ↵         ← −0.15 is assigned only to the r2 index values of the function vector v
```

The clipped functional data of the figure 10.4(d) is now available in the workspace variable **v** in the form of a row matrix.

Example 5

In one period T, a square wave $v(t)$ is defined as $v(t)=\begin{Bmatrix} A & for & 0\le t\le D \\ -A & for & D<t\le T\end{Bmatrix}$ where D is the duty cycle of the wave as a percentage of T. Figure 10.4(e) depicts the plot of one cycle square wave in which the duty cycle varies from 0 to 100%. MATLAB format for the generation of the wave is **square(** $2\pi ft$, D **)** where $f=\frac{1}{T}$ is the frequency of the square wave in Hertz (when t is in second) and t is the desired time interval as a row vector over which we intend to see the square wave.

Figure 10.4(e) One cycle of a square wave

Let us generate a 10 Hertz square wave with amplitude variation ± 1, with duty cycle 50%, and over the interval $-0.3\le t\le 0.3$ sec. Again the selection of the step size is mandatory and let it be 0.01 sec. The wave generation is as follows:

```
>>t=-0.3:0.01:0.3; ↵                 ← t holds t variation −0.3≤t≤0.3 sec as a row matrix with a step 0.01 sec
>>v=square(2*pi*10*t,50); ↵          ← Workspace variable v (any name) holds the wave data as a row matrix
```

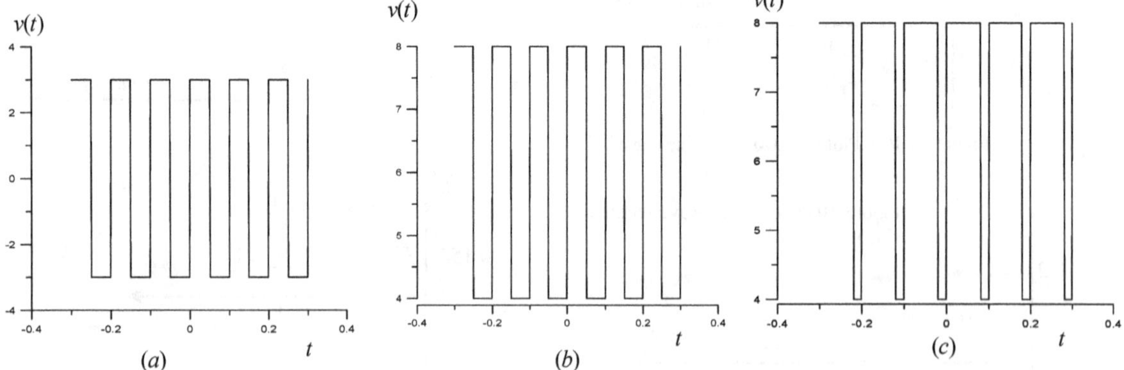

Figure 10.5(a)-(c) Different kinds of square waves: (a) amplitude ±3, frequency 10 Hz, duty cycle 50%, (b) amplitude swing 4 to 8, frequency 10 Hz, duty cycle 50%, and (c) amplitude swing 4 to 8, frequency 10 Hz, duty cycle 80%

Figures 10.5(a)-(c) show the square waves of different characteristics. Each of the waves has the time period (duration of one cycle) $T=0.1$ sec therefore frequency $f=\frac{1}{T}=10$ Hertz and exists over the interval $-0.3\le t\le 0.3$ sec. Choosing a step size 0.01 sec, the commands for the generation of the square waves are presented as follows:

```
>>t=-0.3:0.01:0.3; ↵        ← t holds t variation −0.3≤t≤0.3 as a row matrix with a step 0.01 sec
```

```
>>v=3*square(2*pi*10*t,50); ↵          ← Command for the figure 10.5(a)
>>v=6+2*square(2*pi*10*t,50); ↵        ← Command for the figure 10.5(b)
>>v=6+2*square(2*pi*10*t,80); ↵        ← Command for the figure 10.5(c)
```

In each case, the workspace variable **v** holds the functional data as a row matrix. The default swing of the **square** is ±1 so just multiplying by 3 can achieve the required swing of the wave in the figure 10.5(a). In figure 10.5(b), a linear mapping $y = mx + c$ is necessary to make the function **square** able to sweep from 4 to 8 where x and y correspond to the former and latter function values respectively. The related parameters m and c are to be found from the specification of the given function. When the value of **square** is -1 (means $x = -1$), the functional value of the figure 10.5(b) should be 4 (means y=4) so 4= $-m+c$. Again if the value of the **square** is 1 (means $x=1$), the functional value of the figure 10.5(b) should be 8 (means y=8) on that 8= $m+c$. Solving the two equations, one obtains $m=2$ and $c=6$. Treating the **square** as x, the equation of the wave of the figure 10.5(b) should be $y=2x+6$ or **v=6+ 2*square(2*pi*10*t,50)** – that is how we wrote the above command. This kind of linear transformation is applicable for the same type of wave shape for instance square to square, triangular to triangular, sine to sine, Gaussian to Gaussian, etc. In the periodic wave generation, the notions of the cycle and period must be transparent. With the time period 0.1 sec and duration 0.6 sec for each wave, there must be $\frac{0.6}{0.1}$=6 cycles in the generated wave.

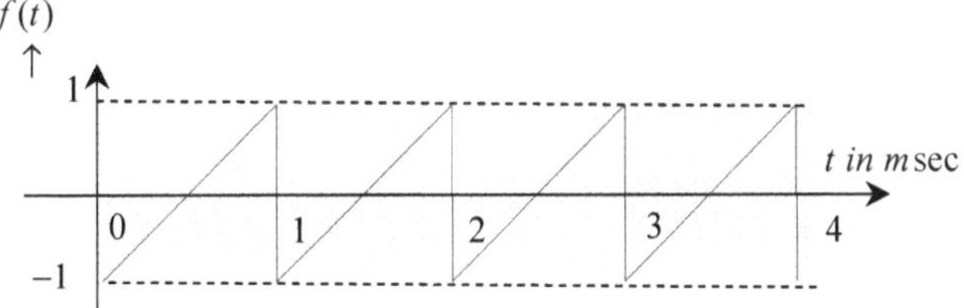

Figure 10.5(d) A sawtooth wave

🗗 Example 6

A sawtooth or periodic triangular wave is generated by using the function **sawtooth**. General format for the wave generation is **sawtooth(** $2\pi ft$ **)** where T is the time period of the sawtooth wave, $f=\frac{1}{T}$ is the frequency of the wave, and t is the desired time interval as a row vector over which we intend to see the wave. The default swing of the wave generated by the **sawtooth** is from -1 to 1. We intend to generate the sawtooth wave of the figure 10.5(d). Looking into the figure, the time period T of the wave is 1 msec therefore frequency f=1000 Hz. The wave exists for an interval $0 \le t \le 4$ msec. The step size selection comes from the user and let us say it is 0.001 msec on that the implementation is as follows:

```
>>t=0:0.001e-3:4e-3; ↵
```

Above **t** holds the t variation $0 \le t \le 4$ msec as a row matrix with the step 0.001 msec. Let us call the function as shown below:

```
>>f=sawtooth(2*pi*1000*t); ↵
```

Above workspace variable **f** (can be any name) holds the functional values of the figure 10.5(d) as a row matrix.

🗗 Example 7

The wave of the figure 10.6(a) is a variant of the wave in the figure 10.5(d). In the figure 10.5(d), the maximum 1 of the triangular wave is occurring at the 100% of the period point on the t axis (for example at 1 msec, 2msec, etc) on the contrary the maximum 1 of the figure 10.6(a) is occurring at 20% period of

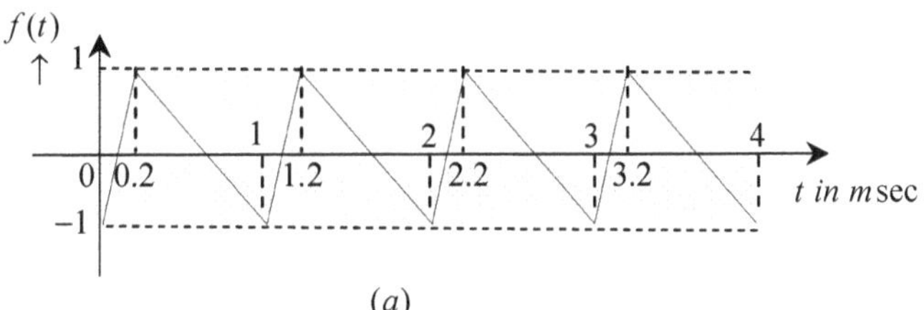

(a)

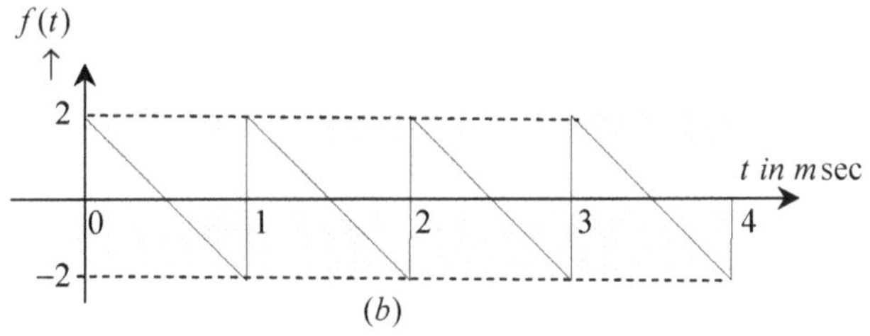

(b)

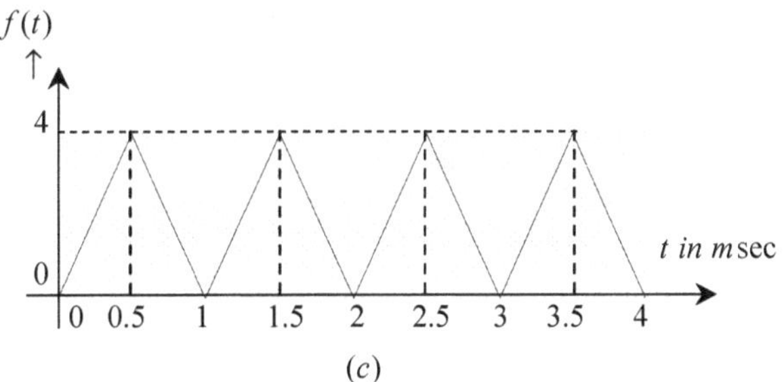

(c)

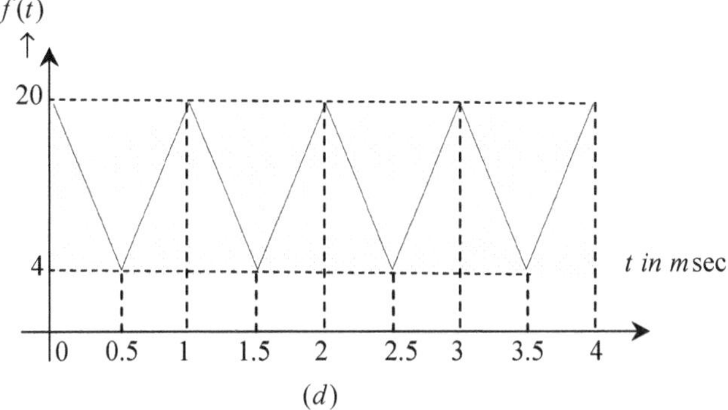

(d)

Figure 10.6(a)-(d) Periodic triangular waves of different characteristics the wave for example at 0.2 msec, 1.2 msec, etc. The function **sawtooth** is still effective to generate the wave of the figure 10.6(a) as follows (assuming the same step size):

>>t=0:0.001e-3:4e-3; ↵ ← t holds variation $0 \le t \le 4$ msec as a row matrix with the step 0.001 msec

>>f=sawtooth(2*pi*1000*t,0.2); ↵ ← Workspace variable f (any name) holds the wave data as a row matrix

Now there are two input arguments in the function **sawtooth**, the first and second of which are the $2\pi ft$ description and the peak point occurrence point in terms of 0-1 of the period respectively.

Example 8

The wave of the figure 10.6(b) is another variant of the wave in the figure 10.5(d). This time the peak value 2 is occurring at the 0% point on the period of the wave but the amplitude swing is ±2 instead of ±1. Multiplying the function **sawtooth** by 2 can achieve the change. However using the same step size, the wave generation is as follows:

```
>>t=0:0.001e-3:4e-3; ↵
>>f=2*sawtooth(2*pi*1000*t,0); ↵
```

Example 9

The wave in the figure 10.6(c) is also a variant of the wave in the figure 10.5(d). The maximum value 4 in the wave is taking place at the 50% of the period point. The amplitude swing is from 0 to 4 instead of –1 to 1. Referring to the example 5, a linear mapping is required to decide the functional relationship from the **sawtooth** to the one in the figure 10.6(c). We have the necessary equations $\begin{Bmatrix} 4 = m + c \\ 0 = -m + c \end{Bmatrix}$ and whose solution is $\begin{Bmatrix} m = 2 \\ c = 2 \end{Bmatrix}$ (treating the **sawtooth** as example 5 mentioned x). Therefore we have the required equation $y = 2x + 2$. Anyhow the formal implementation (using the same step size) is as follows:

```
>>t=0:0.001e-3:4e-3; ↵
>>f=2*sawtooth(2*pi*1000*t,0.5)+2; ↵
```

Example 10

Figure 10.6(d) presented wave is also a variant of the wave in the figure 10.5(d). It should be pointed out that the linear mapping is associated only with the amplitude swing not with the t information. As the graph says the swing of the wave in figure 10.6(d) is from 4 to 20 (in lieu of –1 to 1) therefore requiring to solve the equation $\begin{Bmatrix} 20 = m + c \\ 4 = -m + c \end{Bmatrix}$ according to the example 5 on that the solution is $\begin{Bmatrix} m = 8 \\ c = 12 \end{Bmatrix}$ and the equation we need is $y = 8x + 12$. The t information should be read out from the given graph. The first cycle of the graph exists from 0 to 1 msec. If we want to fit the given wave using the **sawtooth** of example 9, the first cycle of the wave had better be stated from 0.5 msec to 1.5 msec making the sense that the maximum is occurring at the 50% period of the wave (means the second input argument of the **sawtooth** should be 0.5). To be consistent with the given graph, we can say that the wave so mentioned is shifted by 0.5 msec on the t axis and the shifting is accounted for considering **sawtooth**($2\pi f(t - 0.5m\text{sec})$) instead of **sawtooth**($2\pi ft$). Anyhow the complete code of the generation using the same step is as follows:

>>t=0:0.001e-3:4e-3; ↵ ← t holds t variation $0 \le t \le 4$ msec as a row matrix with the step 0.001 msec

>>f=8*sawtooth(2*pi*1000*(t-0.5e-3),0.5)+12; ↵ ← Workspace variable f holds the wave data as a row matrix

Graphing the periodic waves

In all these periodic wave examples we just generated the functional data which we stored in the workspace **f** or **v**. You can verify the wave shape on plotting the data by dint of **plot(t,v)** or **plot(t,f)** (subsection 13.2.1).

We close the miscellaneous problem discussion with the periodic functional data generation.

Chapter 11

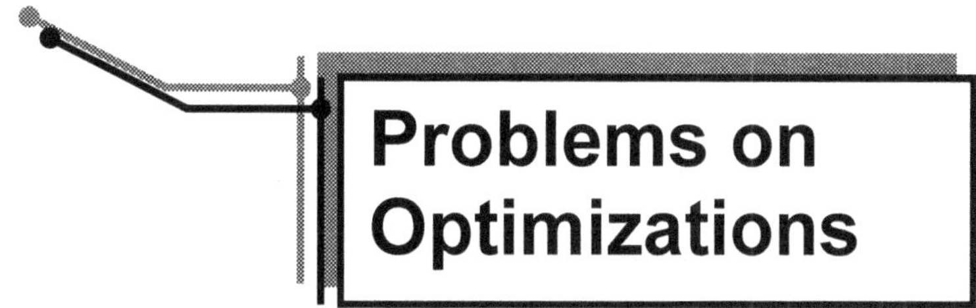

Problems on Optimizations

Man's longing to achieve the most or reject the worst gave birth to the theory of optimization. Optimization techniques have obvious applications in engineering process control, economics, social sciences, industrial production of commodities, operation managements, and in many other fields. Also the optimization is of paramount importance in the design and decision making of any physical or economic system. Knowing the quantitative measure of the system parameters and applying the optimum system parameters through the well-established theory improve the system effectiveness and performance for which we address the following in accordance with the contemporary optimization texts and literatures:

- ⬍⬍ Optimization in symbolic sense for different types of objective and constraint functions
- ⬍⬍ Two academically exercised optimizations called linear and quadratic programmings
- ⬍⬍ M-file based optimizations subject to both the linear and nonlinear constraints
- ⬍⬍ Optimizations based on multiple objective functions with goal attainment and minimax

11.1 Optimization in symbolic sense

In order to obtain the symbolic solution of the optimization problems, we apply the maple (section 3.2) package supplied functions. Finding the maximum and minimum both fall in the category of the optimization problems. The master functions maximize and minimize of the maple find the symbolic solution for the maximum and minimum of one, two, or three variable functions. In the optimization problems, we give prime importance on two types of functions namely objective function and constraint. The common syntax of the two optimizing functions are maximize(objective function,constraint) or minimize(objective function, constraint). The objective function needs the vector code (section 14.2) writing. Usually the elementary constraints are put through some intervals for instance $0 \le x \le 23$ means the x is changing from 0 to 23. We pass it writing x=0..23 (through the = and .. operators). If we need the location of the independent variable, the common syntax is maximize(objective function,

for the maximization of $x+4$:

```
>>maple('C:=x=0..23'); ↵
>>maple('F:=x+4'); ↵
```

without the location of x :

```
>>maple('maximize(F,C)') ↵

ans =

27
```

with the location of x :

```
>>maple('maximize(F,C,location)') ↵

ans =

27, {[{x = 23}, 27]}
```

constraint,location) where the location is the reserve word to the maple. Similar syntax follows for the minimize. We maintain the font equivalence like x⇔x in the subsequent sections. Several optimization problems are addressed in the following.

for the minimization of $x+4$:

without the location of x :

```
>>maple('minimize(F,C)') ↵

ans =

4
```

with the location of x :

```
>>maple('minimize(F,C,location)') ↵

ans =

4, {[{x = 0}, 4]}
```

11.1.1 Linear objective functions

Given objective function is said to be linear if the related variables in the function have power one for example $f(x)=x+4$ which has to be maximized over the interval $0 \le x \le 23$. Clearly the maximum 27 of $f(x)$ occurs at $x=23$ and the minimum 4 of $f(x)$ occurs at $x=0$. We wish to determine that – this is the problem statement.

At the lower right corner of the last page we attached the implementation only for the maximum, the first line of which is to assign the c-onstrint $0 \le x \le 23$ to the workspace variable C (can be any user-given name) within the maple where := is the maple assignment operator. The second line is to assign the vector code of the objective function $f(x)$ to workspace F (can be any user-given name) within the maple. The third line just calls the maximize to determine the maximum value. The fourth line implements the value of x at which the maximum occurs. The return 27, {[{x = 23}, 27]} means the maximum value is 27 (before comma) and the 27 occurs at $x=23$ indicated by {[{x = 23}, 27]}. Similar explanation follows for the minimum finding as attached on the upper right side in this page. Let us go through the following examples.

Linear function: for the example 1:

```
>>maple('C:=x=-5..5,y=-3..3'); ↵
>>maple('F:=x+3*y+8'); ↵
>>maple('maximize(F,C,location)') ↵

ans =

22, {[{x = 5, y = 3}, 22]}
```

◆◆ Example 1

Maximize the two variable linear objective function $f(x,y)= x+3y+8$ under the constraints $-5 \le x \le 5$ and $-3 \le y \le 3$. It is given that the maximum 22 of the $f(x,y)$ occurs at $x=5$ and $y=3$ which needs to be found. This problem becomes the extension of the methodology mentioned just now. Attached on the right side is the complete code of the implementation. Now there are two constraints $-5 \le x \le 5$ and $-3 \le y \le 3$ which we write using x=-5..5 and y=-3..3 respectively. The two constraints are separated by a comma but still we assign those to the same workspace variable C as done before. The F holds the vector code for $f(x,y)$. The return {[{x=5,y=3},22]} means the maximum 22 occurs at $x=5$ and $y=3$.

Linear function: for the example 2:

```
>>maple('C:=u=0..15,v=0..7,w=-5..3'); ↵
>>maple('G:=3*u/7+5*v-9*w+82'); ↵
>>maple('minimize(G,C,location)') ↵

ans =

55, {[{u = 0, v = 0, w = 3}, 55]}
```

◆◆ Example 2

Having gone through the last examples, three variable extension of the optimization has been very facilely. We intend to minimize the three variable linear function $g(u,v,w)=\frac{3u}{7}+5v-9w+82$ subject to $0 \le u \le 15$, $0 \le v \le 7$, and $-5 \le w \le 3$. It is given that the minimum value 55 of the $g(u,v,w)$ occurs at $u=0$, $v=0$, and $w=3$ and our objective is to obtain that. Shown above on the right side is the implementation in which G holds the vector code for $\frac{3u}{7}+5v-9w+82$. The independent variables are now u, v, and w and the code writing and the return happen accordingly. The return {[{u=0,v=0,w=3},55]} means the minimum 55 occurs at $u=0$, $v=0$, and $w=3$.

11.1.2 Other objective functions

for other objective functions: example 1:

```
>>maple('C:=x=0..3*pi'); ↵
>>maple('F:=sin(3*x)+cos(2*x)'); ↵
>>maple('minimize(F,C,location)') ↵

ans =

-2, {[{x = 1/2*pi}, -2], [{x = 5/2*pi}, -2]}
```

for other objective functions: example 2:

```
>>maple('C:=x=0..4, y=-4..0'); ↵
>>maple('F:=6*x^2-3*x+y^2+7*y+3'); ↵
>>maple('minimize(F,C,location)') ↵

ans =

-77/8, {[{x = 1/4, y = -7/2}, -77/8]}
```

We assume that the reader has gone through the last subsection mentioned linear objective functions because here we intend to extrapolate the maple functions and symbology for presenting other types of objective functions.

◆◆ Example 1

Let us minimize the objective function $f(x)=\sin 3x+\cos 2x$ subject to constraint $0 \le x \le 3\pi$. It is given that the minimum -2 of the $f(x)$ takes place at $x=\frac{\pi}{2}$ and $x=\frac{5\pi}{2}$ which we intend to compute. Attached on the right side is the presentation of the computation. The code equivalences are as follows: pi⇔π, sin(3*x)+cos(2*x)⇔$\sin 3x+\cos 2x$, C⇔$0 \le x \le 3\pi$, and F⇔$f(x)$. Now the return has two locations for the x points placed in the outer second brace but each one under the third brace and separated by a comma i.e. the return {[{x = 1/2*pi}, -2], [{x = 5/2*pi}, -2]} means the two minima of value -2 at the two indicated points.

♦♦ **Example 2**

The function $f(x,y)=6x^2-3x+y^2+7y+3$ needs to be minimized over the constraints $0\le x\le 4$ and $-4\le y\le 0$. Given that the minimum is $-\frac{77}{8}$ and occurs at $x=\frac{1}{4}$ and $y=-\frac{7}{2}$ which we intend to find. Obviously this is a two variable function. The computation on $f(x,y)$ is presented at the lower right corner of the last page applying ongoing function and symbology. The code equivalences are as follows: x=0..4⇔ $0\le x\le 4$, y=-4..0⇔ $-4\le y\le 0$, 6*x^2-3*x+y^2+7*y+3⇔ $6x^2-3x+y^2+7y+3$, and F⇔ $f(x,y)$. One would get the same result if all commands are put at a time like maple('minimize(6*x^2-3*x+y^2+7*y+3, x=0..4, y=-4..0,location)').

♦♦ **Example 3**

The three variable nonlinear objective function is no exception for instance we wish to maximize $f(x,y,z)=\cos^2 x+y^2+z^2+7yz$ over the constraints $0\le x\le 2\pi$, $0\le y\le 1$, and $-3\le z\le 2$. It is provided that the maximum 20 of the objective function occurs at three different points – $\begin{Bmatrix}x=0\\y=1\\z=2\end{Bmatrix}$, $\begin{Bmatrix}x=2\pi\\y=1\\z=2\end{Bmatrix}$, and $\begin{Bmatrix}x=\pi\\y=1\\z=2\end{Bmatrix}$ which we wish to obtain. Let us have the solution using ongoing terminology just by one line command (see the example 2) as follows:

```
>>maple('maximize(cos(x)^2+y^2+z^2+7*y*z,x=0..2*pi,y=0..1,z=-3..2,location)') ↵

ans =

20, {[{x = 0, z = 2, y = 1}, 20], [{z = 2, y = 1, x = 2*pi}, 20], [{z = 2, y = 1, x = pi}, 20]}
              ↑                          ↑                              ↑
           1st point                 2nd point                      3rd point
```

The code equivalences are as follows: x=0..2*pi⇔ $0\le x\le 2\pi$, y=0..1⇔ $0\le y\le 1$, z=-3..2⇔ $-3\le z\le 2$, and cos(x)^2+y^2+z^2+7*y*z⇔ $\cos^2 x+y^2+z^2+7yz$.

♦♦ **Exceptions**

Even though the minimize or maximize optimizes a lot of objective functions yet some problems may not be solvable or MATLAB may remain busy for a longer period of time without providing solution. Optimization solution is primarily function dependent. Some objective function may have minimum but if you ask for maximum, you may encounter infinity (indicated by Inf) as the output.

for linear programming: example 1:

```
>>C=[-5;9]; A=[1 1;-4 -5]; B=[2;-9]; ↵
>>[O,V]=linprog(C,A,B) ↵

O =

    1.0000    ← Value of x1
    1.0000    ← Value of x2

V =

    4.0000    ← Value of f(x1,x2)
                without constant
```

11.2 Optimization in numeric sense

In previous section we discussed the elementary optimization problems in symbolic sense. Most practical optimization problems are numerical computation based. We are going to address several optimization problems in this section, which are commonly solved through numerical algorithms. We explicitly utilize the functions and do not intend to discuss the hidden algorithms. Also the font equivalence like x⇔ x is maintained throughout the whole section. The optimization concerns the finding of minimum or maximum which we did not check at all.

11.2.1 Linear programming

The objective function f concerns the variables related in it as the power 1 in the linear programming. But the related independent variables can be many in numbers. The linear inequality constraints are arranged in the form $AX\le B$. By the optimization literature term, we define the problem writing $\underset{X}{\min}\ C^TX$ or $\underset{X}{\max}\ C^TX$ such that $AX\le B$. All related variables are arranged in matrices and the T indicates the transposition operator. The function we need for the optimization is linprog (abbreviation for linear programming) with the syntax [O,V]=linprog(C, A, B). From given f and $AX\le B$, we look for A (rectangular), B (column), C (column), and X (column) and determine the value of X where f is maximum or minimum. There are two output arguments in the linprog – O and V (user-chosen names), the first and second of which are the X values as a column matrix for the optimized solution and the functional value of f at the optimized point respectively. Let us see the following examples on the linear programming.

♦♦ **Example 1**

Optimize the function $f(x_1,x_2)=-5x_1+9x_2+87$ on the constraint $\begin{Bmatrix}x_1+x_2\le 2\\-4x_1-5x_2\le -9\end{Bmatrix}$. It is provided that the $f(x_1,x_2)$ has the optimum value 91 at $x_1=1$ and $x_2=1$ which we intend to compute. The constant in $f(x_1,x_2)$ has no role in the algorithm other than shifting up or down the function and we put it aside. The coefficients of $-5x_1+9x_2$ provide $C=\begin{bmatrix}-5\\9\end{bmatrix}$ and $X=\begin{bmatrix}x_1\\x_2\end{bmatrix}$. Arranging the inequalities in matrix form provides us $\begin{bmatrix}1 & 1\\-4 & -5\end{bmatrix}\begin{bmatrix}x_1\\x_2\end{bmatrix}\le\begin{bmatrix}2\\-9\end{bmatrix}$ wherefrom $A=\begin{bmatrix}1 & 1\\-4 & -5\end{bmatrix}$ and $B=\begin{bmatrix}2\\-9\end{bmatrix}$. We presented its implementation in the middle of the last page on the right side in which the first line is to assign all matrices to the like name variables and the second line is to call the function for the solution. Actual optimum value of $f(x_1,x_2)$ is obtained from V+87.

for linear programming: example 2:

```
>>C=[-5;69;-80]; B=[20;9;0]; ↵
>>A=[9 -27 60;-54 -5 10;11 -18 -6]; ↵
>>[O,V]=linprog(C,A,B) ↵

O =
   -0.1007   ← Value of x
   -0.1545   ← Value of y
    0.2789   ← Value of z
V =
  -32.4706   ← Value of f(x,y,z)
               without the constant
```

◆◆ Example 2

Let us optimize the function $f(x,y,z)=-5x+69y-80z-58$ subject to the constraint $\begin{cases}9x-27y+60z\le 20\\-54x-5y+10z\le 9\\11x-18y-6z\le 0\end{cases}$. It is given that the optimum value of $f(x,y,z)$ is –90.4706 and it occurs at x=–0.1007, y=–0.1545, and z=0.2789 which we intend to compute.

Applying the symbol and concept of the example 1, we have the following: $C=\begin{bmatrix}-5\\69\\-80\end{bmatrix}$ (excluding the constant –58 from $f(x,y,z)$), $X=\begin{bmatrix}x\\y\\z\end{bmatrix}$, $A=\begin{bmatrix}9 & -27 & 60\\-54 & -5 & 10\\11 & -18 & -6\end{bmatrix}$, and $B=\begin{bmatrix}20\\9\\0\end{bmatrix}$ on which the implementation is placed above. The actual optimum value is obtained from –58+V.

11.2.2 Quadratic programming

In quadratic programming the given objective function f has the maximum power 2 with respect to the concern variables but the related variable numbers in f can be 1, 2, 3, or more. We define the quadratic programming writing $\underset{X}{\min}\left(\frac{1}{2}X^T HX+C^T X\right)$ or $\underset{X}{\max}\left(\frac{1}{2}X^T HX+C^T X\right)$ such that $AX\le B$. The function we need for the optimization is **quadprog** (abbreviation for the quadratic programming). The common syntax of the function is [O,V]= quadprog(H, C, A, B) where all related variables have the subsection 11.2.1 mentioned meanings. Only do we have different matrix H from the linear programming which is called Hessian matrix and obtained from the section 5.7 mentioned technique for multi-variable f functions. From the given f and $AX\le B$, we look for A, B, C, H, and X and determine the value of X where f is maximum or minimum. Let us see the following examples.

◆◆ Example 1

It is given that $f(x)=3x^2-5x+9$ has the minimum value 6.9167 at x=0.8333 within $-2\le x\le 4$ or in other words optimize $\underset{x}{\min} f(x)$ such that $x\le 4$ (ignoring the lower bound). As return from the function **quadprog**, we should expect O=0.8333 and V=6.9167 (previously mentioned).

for quadratic programming: example 1:

```
>>H=6; C=-5; A=1; B=4; ↵
>>[O,V]=quadprog(H,C,A,B) ↵

O =
   0.8333  ← Value of x
V =
  -2.0833  ← Value of f(x)
             without constant
```

We put aside the constant in $f(x)$ like we did in the linear programming and rearrange $3x^2-5x$ to have the form $\frac{1}{2}X^T HX+C^T X$ therefore $f(x)=\frac{1}{2}[x^T]\times 6\times[x]+[-5]^T[x]$, H=6, $C=-5$, and $X=x$. From $x\le 4$, we have A=1 and B=4 and the execution is placed above on the right side. The first line is to assign the matrix values to the corresponding names and the second line is to call the function. The **quadprog** is devised for a large number of variables so you may see some warnings which can be ignored. In order to get the actual minimum value, we just need V+9.

♦♦ Example 2

Optimize the function $f(x_1,x_2)=\frac{1}{3}x_1^2+7x_2^2-9x_1x_2-12x_1-6x_2+89$ subject to $\begin{Bmatrix} x_1+x_2\le 2 \\ -x_1+2x_2\le 2 \\ 2x_1+x_2\le 3\end{Bmatrix}$. It is given that $f(x_1,x_2)$ has the optimum value 67.5198 at x_1=1.1978 and x_2=0.6043 and we wish to compute that. As done in the example 1, we keep aside the constant 89 and rearrange the $f(x_1,x_2)$ as $\frac{1}{2}[x_1\ \ x_2]\begin{bmatrix}\frac{2}{3} & -9\\ -9 & 14\end{bmatrix}\begin{bmatrix}x_1\\x_2\end{bmatrix}+[-12\ \ -6]\begin{bmatrix}x_1\\x_2\end{bmatrix}$ where $H=\begin{bmatrix}\frac{2}{3} & -9\\ -9 & 14\end{bmatrix}$, $C=\begin{bmatrix}-12\\-6\end{bmatrix}$ (the coefficients of the nonhomogeneous part $-12x_1-6x_2$ of $f(x_1,x_2)$ as a column matrix), and $X=\begin{bmatrix}x_1\\x_2\end{bmatrix}$. The Hessian matrix H is obtained from the homogeneous part $\frac{1}{3}x_1^2+7x_2^2-9x_1x_2$ of $f(x_1,x_2)$ through the partial differentiations, section 5.7. The given inequalities take the matrix form $\begin{bmatrix}1 & 1\\ -1 & 2\\ 2 & 1\end{bmatrix}\begin{bmatrix}x_1\\x_2\end{bmatrix}\le\begin{bmatrix}2\\2\\3\end{bmatrix}$ therefore $A=\begin{bmatrix}1 & 1\\ -1 & 2\\ 2 & 1\end{bmatrix}$ and $B=\begin{bmatrix}2\\2\\3\end{bmatrix}$. Attached on the right side is the complete solution. In the first two lines, we just assigned the four matrices to like variables. In the third line we called the quadprog, the O is having the solution for x_1 and x_2 as a two element column matrix. Actual optimum value of $f(x_1,x_2)$ is obtained from V+89.

for quadratic programming: the example 2:

```
>>H=[2/3 -9;-9 14]; C=[-12;-6]; ↵
>>A=[1 1;-1 2;2 1]; B=[2;2;3]; ↵
>>[O,V]=quadprog(H,C,A,B) ↵

O =

    1.1978 ← Value of x1
    0.6043 ← Value of x2
V =

   -21.4802 ← Value of f(x1,x2)
              without constant
```

The function $f(x,y)=\frac{1}{3}x^2+7y^2-9xy-12x-6y+89$ and constraint $\begin{Bmatrix} x+y\le 2 \\ -x+2y\le 2 \\ 2x+y\le 3\end{Bmatrix}$ would produce the same result. Making the independent variables different does not change the hidden algorithm at all.

♦♦ Example 3

Let us try to optimize the three variable function $f(x,y,z)$ $=9x^2+7y^2-2z^2-9xy-12xz+8yz+5y+z$ subject to the constraint $\begin{Bmatrix} x+z\le -2 \\ -x+2y\le -2 \\ 2z+y\le 30\end{Bmatrix}$. Applying ongoing concept and variables, we have $H=\begin{bmatrix}18 & -9 & -12\\ -9 & 14 & 8\\ -12 & 8 & -4\end{bmatrix}$, $C=\begin{bmatrix}0\\5\\1\end{bmatrix}$, $X=\begin{bmatrix}x\\y\\z\end{bmatrix}$, $A=\begin{bmatrix}1 & 0 & 1\\ -1 & 2 & 0\\ 0 & 1 & 2\end{bmatrix}$, and $B=\begin{bmatrix}-2\\-2\\30\end{bmatrix}$. Attached on the right side is the implementation of the problem. The x is having the value 1.0e+016×(-0.64) that means –0.64×10^{16} obviously a large number. Within the finiteness of the computer we can assume that as negative infinity. Similar explanation follows for the y and z values. Also the functional value is extremely large in the range of 10^{32}. This sort of value indicates that convergence of the algorithm is not achieved from the optimization.

for quadratic programming: example 3:

```
>>H=[18 -9 -12;-9 14 8;-12 8 -4]; C=[0;5;1]; ↵
>>A=[1 0 1;-1 2 0;0 1 2]; B=[-2;-2;30]; ↵
>>[O,V]=quadprog(H,C,A,B) ↵
Warning: Large-scale method does not
currently solve this problem formulation,
switching to medium-scale method.
> In quadprog at 236
Exiting: the solution is unbounded and at
infinity;
 the constraints are not restrictive enough.
O =
   1.0e+016 *

    -0.6400 ← Value of x
    -0.3200 ← Value of y
    -1.0000 ← Value of z
V =
    -4.5600e+032  ← Value of f(x,y,z)
```

11.2.3 M-file based optimization without constraint

In this type of optimization, we first write the M-file (section 1.3) code for the given objective function in a function file (function file has some input and some output, section 14.5) and then call particular built-in optimization function to have the solution. The independent variables of the objective function are written as x(1), x(2), x(3), etc. In optimization term, we look for $\min\limits_{X} f$ or $\max\limits_{X} f$. Even though there is no constraint, we need to provide an initial guess of the independent variables to commence with the computation. The function we apply for the unconstraint optimization is fminunc (abbreviation for function minimization unconstraint) which has the syntax [O,V]=fminunc(objective function file name under quote,initial guess of the independent variables as a row matrix). The output arguments O and V have the subsection 11.2.1 mentioned meanings. The fminunc optimizes irrespective of linear and nonlinear objective functions. We write the vector code (section 14.2) of the objective function pertaining to its independent variables. Let us perform the following examples.

M-file based optimization without constraint: Example 1:
Function file needed:

```
function y=f(x)
y=3*x^2-5*x+9;
```

Calling the optimizing function:

```
>>[O,V]=fminunc('f',0) ↵

O =
    0.8333  ← Value of x
V =
    6.9167  ← Value of f(x)
```

Optimization without constraint: example 2:
Function file needed:

```
function y=f(x)
y=exp(-x(1)-x(2))*(-3*x(1)^2-7*x(2)^2+12*x(1)*x(2)+2*x(1)-6*x(2)+88);
```

Calling the optimizing function:

```
>>[O,V]=fminunc('f',[20 25]) ↵

O =
    20.0000     25.0000
       ↑           ↑
       x1          x2
V =
    1.1536e-017  ← Value of f(x1,x2)
```

Optimization without constraint: example 3:
Function file needed:

```
function y=f(x)
y=(-x(3)^2+x(3))*(sin(x(1)-x(2)));
```

Calling the optimizing function:

```
>>[O,V]=fminunc('f',[1 1 0.2]) ↵

O =
    0.2146   1.7854   0.5000
      ↑        ↑        ↑
      x        y        z
V =
    -0.2500   ← Value of f(x,y,z)
```

❖❖ Example 1

The objective function $f(x)=3x^2-5x+9$ has the minimum value 6.9167 at x=0.8333. Let us find that using the M-file approach taking an initial guess x=0, execution is attached above on the right side. There is only one independent variable x so no need to write x(1) just x is enough. As a procedural step, type the codes of the function file in a new M-file in your working directory and save the file by the name f (can be any user-given name). We used the variable y (can be any user-given name) for the functional return. Then call the function fminunc from the command prompt as attached on the upper right side. Following the execution, you may see some warning message, we ignore the warnings.

❖❖ Example 2

Optimize the function $f(x_1,x_2)=e^{-x_1-x_2}(3x_1^2-7x_2^2+12x_1x_2+2x_1-6x_2+88)$ taking an initial guess x_1=20 and x_2=25. It is given that $f(x_1,x_2)$ has negligible optimum value at x_1=20 and x_2=25 and we wish to obtain that. The implementation is attached on the right side. The two initial guesses 20 and 25 are the second input argument (as a two element row matrix in order) of the fminunc. Now we write x(1)⇔ x_1 and x(2)⇔ x_2 where x is a row matrix. With this, the vector code of the objective function is exp(-x(1)-x(2))*(-3*x(1)^2-7*x(2)^2+12* x(1)*x(2)+2*x(1)-6*x(2)+88) and which is assigned to the return variable y as done in the example 1. Type the function file codes in a new M-file, save the file by the name f, and call the optimizing function fminunc as attached on the upper right side. Note that the independent variable values are returned as a row matrix in order. The functional value 1.1536e-017 means 1.1536×10^{-17} which is very very small in magnitude and assumed to be zero (let us ignore the warnings for the time being).

❖❖ Example 3

Let us optimize the function $f(x,y,z)=(-z^2+z)\sin(x-y)$ considering the initial guess x=1, y=1, and z=0.2. It is provided that the optimum value –0.25 of $f(x,y,z)$ occurs at x=0.2146, y=1.7854, and z=0.5 and our objective is to obtain that. Assuming that the reader has gone through the last two examples, the solution to the problem is attached above on the right side. The equivalences are as follows: x(1)⇔ x, x(2)⇔ y, x(3)⇔ z, and (-x(3)^2+ x(3))*(sin(x(1)-x(2)))⇔ $(-z^2+z)\sin(x-y)$. The three initial guesses enter as a three element row matrix in the second input argument to the fminunc. Now the return to O is a three element row matrix referring to the three independent variables respectively.

M-file based optimization: Linear constraints: Example 1:
Function file needed:

```
function y=f(x)
y=3*x^2-5*x+9;
```

Calling the optimizing function:

```
>>[O,V]=fmincon('f',-2,1,4) ↵

O =
    0.8333  ← Value of x
V =
    6.9167  ← Value of f(x)
```

11.2.4 M-file based optimization with constraint

In this type of optimization we include the constraints in addition to the problems mentioned in the last subsection. By the literature term, we seek for $\min\limits_{X} f$ or $\max\limits_{X} f$ where f is the objective function of many variables in general and for which we apply the function fmincon (abbreviation for the function minimization on constraint). The fmincon conceives both the linear and nonlinear objective functions. The coding to the given objective function and constraints takes place in a special way based on the given constraints. The given constraints can again be linear and nonlinear. Moreover each of the two constraints subdivides as the inequality and equality terms. Let us see some constraint cases in the following.

◆◆ Linear constraints

When the constraints are all linear and of the form $AX \le B$, we use the syntax [O,V]=fmincon(objective function file name under quote, initial guess of the independent variables as a row matrix in order, A, B) where A is a rectangular matrix in general and B is a column one. The output arguments O and V have the subsection 11.2.1 mentioned meanings.

Example 1:

Let us optimize the function $f(x)=3x^2-5x+9$ subject to $-2 \le x \le 4$. It is given that the minimum value 6.9167 of $f(x)$ occurs at x =0.8333 and we wish to obtain that. The interval $-2 \le x \le 4$ can be stated as the linear inequality constraint $x \le 4$ with the initial guess x =–2 wherefrom A =1 and B =4. Its implementation is presented at the lower right corner of the last page maintaining ongoing function and symbology (subsection 11.2.1, ignore the warnings).

Example 2:

Optimize the function $f(x_1,x_2)=3x_1^2-7x_2^2+12x_1x_2+2x_1-6x_2+88$ subject to $x_1+3x_2 \le 4$ and $3x_1-x_2 \ge -8$ with the initial guess x_1=0.5 and x_2=4. It is given that $f(x_1,x_2)$ has the optimum value 8 at x_1=–2 and x_2=2 and we wish to obtain that. The given inequalities are of mixed type – greater and less both. We multiply both sides of the second inequality by minus 1 to have $-3x_1+x_2 \le 8$ therefore $X=\begin{bmatrix}x_1\\x_2\end{bmatrix}$ and the two inequalities in matrix form are written as $\begin{bmatrix}1 & 3\\-3 & 1\end{bmatrix}\begin{bmatrix}x_1\\x_2\end{bmatrix} \le \begin{bmatrix}4\\8\end{bmatrix}$ and $A=\begin{bmatrix}1 & 3\\-3 & 1\end{bmatrix}$ and $B=\begin{bmatrix}4\\8\end{bmatrix}$. There are two independent variables and we write them as x(1)⇔x_1 and x(2)⇔x_2 where x is a row matrix. The vector code of the objective function is 3*x(1)^2-7*x(2)^2+12*x(1)*x(2)+2*x(1)-6*x(2)+88. Shown on the upper right side is the implementation applying ongoing function and symbology. The return to O is a two element row matrix corresponding to the independent variables in order.

Linear constraints: Example 2:

Function file needed:

```
function y=f(x)
y=3*x(1)^2-7*x(2)^2+12*x(1)*x(2)+2*x(1)-6*x(2)+88;
```

Calling the optimizing function:

```
>>A=[1 3;-3 1]; B=[4;8]; ↵
>>[O,V]=fmincon('f',[0.5 4],A,B) ↵

O =
    -2    2
     ↑    ↑
    x1   x2
V =
    8   ← Value of f(x1,x2)
```

Example 3:

The function $f(x,y,z)=(-z^2+z)\sin(x-y)$ is to be optimized subject to $x+4y \ge 1.5$, $x+y \le -1$, and $2y-4z \le -0.9$ with the initial guess x =0.1, y =0.1, and z =0.1. It is provided that the optimum value –0.1051 of $f(x,y,z)$ occurs at x =–1.8333, y =0.8333, and z =0.6417 which we intend to get. The independent variables imply $X=\begin{bmatrix}x\\y\\z\end{bmatrix}$ and the codings are as follows: x(1)⇔x, x(2)⇔y, x(3)⇔z, and (-x(3)^2+x(3))*sin(x(1)-x(2))⇔ $(-z^2+z)\sin(x-y)$. Only do we need the first inequality to be rearranged followed by a minus sign hence we have the linear constraints as $\begin{bmatrix}-1 & -4 & 0\\1 & 1 & 0\\0 & 2 & -4\end{bmatrix}\begin{bmatrix}x\\y\\z\end{bmatrix} \le \begin{bmatrix}-1.5\\-1\\-0.9\end{bmatrix}$ or $AX \le B$ (missing variable's coefficient is taken as zero) on that the implementation along with the function file is shown above on the right side applying ongoing function and symbology.

Linear constraints: Example 3:

Function file needed:

```
function y=f(x)
y=(-x(3)^2+x(3))*sin(x(1)-x(2));
```

Calling the optimizing function:

```
>>A=[-1 -4 0;1 1 0;0 2 -4]; ↵
>>B=[-1.5;-1;-0.9]; ↵
>>[O,V]=fmincon('f',[0.1 0.1 0.1],A,B) ↵

O =
    -1.8333   0.8333   0.6417
       ↑        ↑        ↑
       x        y        z
V =
    -0.1051   ← Value of f(x,y,z)
```

◆◆ Only nonlinear constraints

When the constraints C are all nonlinear, they can be subdivided by the terms inequality and equality that is $C=C_{eq}+C_{in}$ for example $3x_1x_2=4$ and $3x_1-x_1x_2 \ge -8$ correspond to C_{eq} and C_{in} respectively. It is strict that we manipulate the given nonlinear constraints to have the form $C_{in} \le 0$ and C_{eq} =0 if they are not so. For multiple nonlinear constraints, the C_{eq} and C_{in} are assumed to be matrices in general. For only nonlinear constraints, we still apply **fmincon** with the syntax **[O,V]=fmincon(**function file name describing only the objective function under quote, initial guess of the independent variables as a row matrix in order,[ ],[ ],[ ],[ ],[ ],[ ],function file name describing only the nonlinear constraints under quote). The six empty input arguments are mandatory (there are some reasons – will be explained latter). More than one nonlinear constraints are put as a column matrix. In the objective function file there are one input and one output arguments – the independent variables (applying aforementioned symbology) and their functional return respectively. In the nonlinear constraint function file, there are two output arguments – one for the inequality part C_{in} and the other for the equality part C_{eq} respectively. We present two examples for only nonlinear constraints in the following.

Example 1:

We intend to optimize the function $f(x_1,x_2)=x_1^2-x_2^2+12x_1x_2-2x_1-6x_2+88$ subject to $0.2x_1x_2=0$, $3x_1x_2-400\le 0$, and $6x_1+8x_2-8x_1x_2\le 88$ with the initial guess x_1=0 and x_2=0. It is given that $f(x_1,x_2)$ has the optimum value −50.24 which occurs at x_1=−1.6 and x_2=4.8 and our objective is to determine them.

Attached on the right side is the complete code for the implementation. There are two independent variables x_1 and x_2 whose code equivalences are x(1)⇔ x_1 and x(2)⇔ x_2. The objective function file writing is similar to that of the previous ones. The nonlinear constraint function file has two output arguments ci and ce, the first and second of which are for the inequalities and equalities respectively. There are one equality and two inequalities given. The first and second inequalities are assigned to c1 and c2 respectively. Latter ci is formed as a column matrix writing ci=[c1;c2];. We named the constraint function file as co. The inequalities and equality are maneuvered to take the form $C_{in}\le 0$ and C_{eq}=0 respectively and given vector code (section 14.2). The names c1, c2, ce, ci, and co are all user-chosen. Both function files have the vector independent set x as the input argument which corresponds to earlier mentioned X. As procedural steps, open a new M-file, type the codes of the objective function file, save the file by the name f, open another new M-file, type the codes of the nonlinear constraint function file, save the file by the name co, and finally call the optimizing function to see the optimal solution as presented above.

Only nonlinear constraints: Example 1:

Objective function file needed:

```
function y=f(x)
y=x(1)^2-x(2)^2+12*x(1)*x(2)-2*x(1)-6*x(2)+88;
```

Nonlinear constraint function file needed:

```
function [ci,ce]=co(x)
c1=3*x(1)*x(2)-400;
c2=6*x(1)+8*x(2)-8*x(1)*x(2)-88;
ci=[c1;c2];
ce=0.2*x(2)*x(1);
```

Calling the optimizing function:

```
>>[O,V]=fmincon('f',[0 0],[ ],[ ],[ ],[ ],[ ],[ ],'co') ↵

O =

   -1.6000    4.8000
      ↑          ↑
      x1         x2
V =

   -50.2400     ← Value of f(x1,x2)
```

Example 2:

Let us optimize the function $f(x,y,z)=(-2z^2+z)\sin(3\pi(y-4x))$ subject to $\frac{x}{y}\le 1$, $2\ge 9xyz$, and $x^3+y^2=0$ with the initial guess x=0.2, y=0.2, and z=0.2. It is given that the optimum value −0.125 of $f(x,y,z)$ occurs at x=−0.1152, y=0.0391, and z=0.25 and our goal is to find these.

On the right side we placed the complete codes. All related symbols have the example 1 mentioned meanings. Because of the involvement of three variables, now we have $X=\begin{bmatrix}x\\y\\z\end{bmatrix}$, x(1)⇔ x, x(2)⇔ y, x(3)⇔ z, x⇔ X, and (-2*x(3)^2+x(3))*sin(pi*3*(x(2)-4*x(1)))⇔ $(-2z^2+z)\sin(3\pi(y-4x))$. There are two nonlinear inequalities, both of which need rearrangement to comply with $C_{in}\le 0$ and which are $\frac{x}{y}-1\le 0$ and $9xyz-2\le 0$ respectively. The code writing of the inequalities takes place after the rearrangement. Execution procedure is similar to that of the example 1.

Only nonlinear constraints: Example 2:

Objective function file needed:

```
function y=f(x)
y=(-2*x(3)^2+x(3))*sin(pi*3*(x(2)-4*x(1)));
```

Nonlinear constraint function file needed:

```
function [ci,ce]=co(x)
c1=x(1)/x(2)-1;
c2=9*x(1)*x(2)*x(3)-2;
ci=[c1;c2];
ce=x(2)^2+x(1)^3;
```

Calling the optimizing function:

```
>>[O,V]=fmincon('f',[0.2 0.2 0.2],[ ],[ ],[ ],[ ],[ ],[ ],'co') ↵

O =

   -0.1152    0.0391    0.2500
      ↑          ↑         ↑
      x          y         z
V =

   -0.1250     ← Value of f(x,y,z)
```

◆◆ Mixed nonlinear and linear constraints

There are instances when the linear and the nonlinear constraints appear simultaneously for which the common syntax is given by [O,V]=fmincon(function file name describing only the objective function under quote, initial guess of the independent variables as a row matrix in order, A_{in}, B_{in}, A_{eq}, B_{eq}, L_B, U_B, function file name describing only the nonlinear constraints under quote). Like the nonlinear constraints, the linear constraints are also separated as inequality and equality components which are given by $A_{in}\ X \le B_{in}$ and $A_{eq}\ X = B_{eq}$ respectively. The L_B and U_B represent the lower and upper bounds of the independent variables of the objective function respectively. Absence of any matrix parameter is notified by an empty matrix [ ]. The other related variables and citation have aforementioned meanings. Let us go through the following examples on the mixed constraints.

Example 1: Optimize the function $f(x_1,x_2)=x_1^3-(x_2-x_1)^3+12x_1x_2-2x_1+57$ over the domain formed by $-1\le x_1\le 2$ and $-2\le x_2\le 3$ subject to $0.09x_1x_2=0.5$, $3x_1x_2-7x_1+2\le 0$, $6x_1+8x_2\le 1$, and $3.6x_1-4x_2=2$ with the initial guess x_1=–1 and x_2=–2. It is given that $f(x_1,x_2)$ has the optimum value 117.1586 which occurs at $x_1=-2.2222$ and x_2=–2.5. Our objective is to determine these data.

We write the code equivalences as follows: $X=\begin{bmatrix}x_1\\x_2\end{bmatrix}$, x⇔$X$, x(1)⇔$x_1$, x(2)⇔$x_2$, Lb⇔$L_B$, Ub ⇔$U_B$, x(1)^3-(x(2)-x(1))^3+12*x(1)*x(2)-2*x(1)+57 ⇔$x_1^3-(x_2-x_1)^3+12x_1x_2-2x_1+57$, 3*x(1)*x(2)-7*x(1)+2⇔$3x_1x_2-7x_1+2\le 0$, 0.09*x(1)*x(2)-0.5⇔ $0.09x_1x_2=0.5$, Ai⇔A_{in}, Bi⇔B_{in}, Ae⇔A_{eq}, Be⇔ B_{eq}, and g⇔initial guess. The solution required domain bounds are –1 and –2 (lower L_B) and 2 and 3 (upper U_B) for the two independent variables respectively. The $6x_1+8x_2\le 1$ and $3.6x_1-4x_2=2$ can be rearranged in matrix form to write $[6\quad 8]\begin{bmatrix}x_1\\x_2\end{bmatrix}\le 1$ and $[3.6\quad -4]\begin{bmatrix}x_1\\x_2\end{bmatrix}=2$ therefrom A_{in}=[6 8], B_{in}=1, A_{eq}=[3.6 –4], and B_{eq}=2. All other symbols and functions have previously mentioned meanings. Attached above on the right side is the implementation of the optimization. As usual, type the objective function file codes in a new M-file, save the file by the name f, type the nonlinear constraint function file codes in another new M-file, save the file by the name co, input all bounds, guess, linear constraint parameters as shown, and eventually call the function fmincon to view the expected solution.

Mixed constraints: Example 1:
Objective function file needed:

```
function y=f(x)
y=x(1)^3-(x(2)-x(1))^3+12*x(1)*x(2)-2*x(1)+57;
```

Only nonlinear constraint function file needed:

```
function [ci,ce]=co(x)
ci=3*x(1)*x(2)-7*x(1)+2;
ce=0.09*x(1)*x(2)-0.5;
```

Calling the optimizing function:

```
>>Ai=[6 8]; Bi=1; Ae=[3.6 -4]; Be=2; g=[-1 -2]; ↵
>>Lb=[-1 -2]; Ub=[2 3]; ↵
>>[O,V]=fmincon('f',g,Ai,Bi,Ae,Be,Lb,Ub,'co') ↵

O =
     -2.2222   -2.5000
        ↑         ↑
        x1        x2
V =
     117.1586     ← Value of f(x1,x2)
```

Example 2: Let us optimize the three variable objective function $f(x,y,z)=(-2z^2+z)\sin(3\pi(y-4x))$ over the intervals $0.1\le x\le 2\pi$, $0.2\le y\le 4\pi$, and $-3\le z\le 3$ with the initial guess x=0, y=0, and z=–3 subject to the constraints $z=3x$, $x-y+6z\le 1$, $2\ge 9xyz$, and $z=2xy$. The optimum value of $f(x,y,z)$ is –0.0971 and happens at x=0.1, y=1.5, and z=0.3 which is what we are after.

Placed on the right side are the implementational codes. Relevant equivalences are as follows: $X=\begin{bmatrix}x\\y\\z\end{bmatrix}$, x⇔$X$, x(1)⇔$x$, x(2)⇔$y$, x(3)⇔ z, Lb⇔L_B, Ub⇔U_B, (-2*x(3)^2+x(3))*sin(3*pi*(x(2)-4*x(1)))⇔$(-2z^2+z)\sin(3\pi(y-4x))$, $[1\quad -1\quad 6]\begin{bmatrix}x\\y\\z\end{bmatrix}$ ⇔

Mixed constraints: Example 2:
Objective function file needed:

```
function y=f(x)
y=(-2*x(3)^2+x(3))*sin(3*pi*(x(2)-4*x(1)));
```

Only nonlinear constraint function file needed:

```
function [ci,ce]=co(x)
ci=9*x(1)*x(2)*x(3)-2;
ce=x(3)-2*x(1)*x(2);
```

Calling the optimizing function:

```
>>Ai=[1 -1 6]; Bi=1; Ae=[-3 0 1]; Be=0; ↵
>>g=[0 0 -3];Lb=[0.1 0.2 -3]; Ub=[2*pi 4*pi 3]; ↵
>>[O,V]=fmincon('f',g,Ai,Bi,Ae,Be,Lb,Ub,'co') ↵

O =
     0.1000    1.5000    0.3000
       ↑         ↑         ↑
       x         y         z
V =
     -0.0971     ← Value of f(x,y,z)
```

$x-y+6z$, Ai⇔A_{in}, Bi⇔B_{in}, Ae⇔A_{eq}, Be⇔B_{eq}, g⇔initial guess, $x-y+6z \le 1 \Leftrightarrow A_{in}\ X \le B_{in}$ so A_{in}=[1 −1 6] and B_{in}=1, $z=3x$ or $-3x+z=0 \Leftrightarrow A_{eq}\ X = B_{eq}$ so A_{eq}=[−3 0 1] and B_{eq}=0, $z=2xy$ or $z-2xy=0 \Leftrightarrow C_{eq}$=0, L_B ⇔all lower interval bounds are 0.1, 0.2, and −3 respectively, U_B ⇔all upper interval bounds are 2π, 4π, and 3 respectively, and all other symbols and functions have previously mentioned meanings.

11.2.5 Multiple objective functions with some goals

So far we exercised the problems of optimization on one objective function. Now we will be having more than one objective functions but all of which are the functions of the same independent variable (s). The built-in function **fgoalattain** (abbreviation for the functional goal attainment) determines the optimum solution for this sort of problem. By the literature term we seek for $\min_{X,\lambda} \lambda$ or $\max_{X,\lambda} \lambda$ such that $F - w\lambda \le G$ where X, F, λ, w, and G are the independent variable vector, multiple objective function as a vector, a scalar, weight vector, and objective functional goal requirement as a vector respectively. The given parameters are F, w, and G and we need to find X. There are many syntaxes seen for the **fgoalattain**, one of which applies as **[O,V]=fgoalattain** (objective function file name under quote which describes the given vector F as a column matrix, initial guess of the independent variables in the F as a row matrix in order, given functional goal values G as a row matrix but in order, given weight values w as a row matrix but in order) where the O and V have previously mentioned meanings. Let us go through the following examples.

◆◆ Example 1

Optimize the functions $f_1(x)=-2x+3$ and $f_2(x)=5x-7$ where the weight and goal attainment values for the two functions are $\begin{Bmatrix}4\\5\end{Bmatrix}$ and $\begin{Bmatrix}23\\28\end{Bmatrix}$ respectively. It is given that the optimal goals of the two objective functions are attained at x=1.3333 with an initial guess x=0 and the optimal values for the two functions are $f_1(x)$=0.3333 and $f_2(x)$=−0.3333 what we are supposed to find.

Multiple objective functions: Example 1:
Objective function file needed:

```
function y=f(x)
y1=-2*x+3;
y2=5*x-7;
y=[y1;y2];
```

Calling the optimizing function:

```
>>G=[23 28]; w=[4 5]; g=0; ↵
>>[O,V]=fgoalattain('f',g,G,w) ↵

O =
    1.3333      ← x at optimum
V =
    0.3333      ← Value of f1(x)
   -0.3333      ← Value of f2(x)
```

Attached on the right side is the implementation of the example 1. Here the $f_1(x)$ and $f_2(x)$ together constitute F and $X \Leftrightarrow x$ because of the single independent variable. Referring to the objective function file, the functional codes for $f_1(x)$ and $f_2(x)$ are assigned to the workspace variables **y1** and **y2** (can be any user-given names) respectively. The **y1** and **y2** are placed as a column matrix by writing **y=[y1;y2];** in which the **y** is any user-given name and it represents the vector function F. The given goal values for the $f_1(x)$ and $f_2(x)$ are 23 and 28 and we enter them as a row matrix in order writing **G=[23 28];** where the **G** is any user-given name. Similarly the given weight values 4 and 5 are also written as **w=[4 5];**. The initial guess x=0 is assigned to **g** by writing **g=0;**. Again the **w** and **g** are user-given names. However we write the objective function file in a new M-file, save the file by the name **f** in our working path, enter all parameters, and finally call the **fgoalattain** to view the optimized solution as presented above. Now the return to the **V** is a two element column matrix holding the optimal values of the functions $f_1(x)$ and $f_2(x)$ respectively.

◆◆ Example 2

We intend to optimize the functions $f_1(x_1,x_2)=-2x_1^{\,2}-3x_2^{\,2}+5$, $f_2(x_1,x_2)=5x_1+6x_2-97$, and $f_3(x_1,x_2)=x_2^{\,2}-x_1^{\,2}-x_1-x_2$ with the initial guess x_1=0 and x_2=0 subject to the linear inequality constraints $x_1+3x_2-7\le 0$ and $5x_1-8x_2\le 7$ and the three objective functions are expected to have the goal values 2, 8, and −7 with the weight values 3, 8, and 5 for $f_1(x_1,x_2)$, $f_2(x_1,x_2)$, and $f_3(x_1,x_2)$ respectively. It is given that the optimal goals for the three functions are achieved at x_1=3.3478 and x_2=1.2174 at which the three functional values are $f_1(x_1,x_2)$=−21.8620, $f_2(x_1,x_2)$=−72.9565, and $f_3(x_1,x_2)$=−14.2911 – that is what we need to find.

Multiple objective functions: Example 2:
Objective function file needed:

```
function y=f(x)
y1=-2*x(1)^2-3*x(2)^2+5;
y2=5*x(1)+6*x(2)-97;
y3=x(2)^2-x(1)^2-x(1)-x(2);
y=[y1;y2;y3];
```

Calling the optimizing function:

```
>>G=[2 8 -7]; w=[3 8 5]; ↵
>>g=[0 0]; Ai=[1 3;5 -8]; Bi=[7;7]; ↵
>>[O,V]=fgoalattain('f',g,G,w,Ai,Bi) ↵

O =
    3.3478      1.2174
      ↑           ↑
      x1          x2        at optimum
V =
   -21.8620   ← Value of f1(x1,x2)
   -72.9565   ← Value of f2(x1,x2)
   -14.2911   ← Value of f3(x1,x2)
```

We did not address all aspects of the **fgoalattain** in the beginning, at least one dozen options are associated in the function. In this example there is some linear inequality constraint like $A_{in}\ X \le B_{in}$ for which the syntax we need is **[O,V]=fgoalattain(**objective function file name under quote which describes the given vector F as a column matrix, initial guess of the independent variables in the F as a row matrix in order, given functional goal values G as a row matrix but in order, given weight values w as a row matrix but in order, A_{in} as a rectangular matrix, B_{in} as a column matrix). Shown at the lower right corner of the last page is the complete coding and solution of the problem. The execution procedure is similar to that of the example 1.

Now we present various correspondences in the implementation as follows: $X = \begin{bmatrix} x_1 \\ x_2 \end{bmatrix}$, x⇔ X , x(1)⇔ x_1, x(2) ⇔ x_2, y1=-2*x(1)^2-3*x(2)^2+5;⇔ $f_1(x_1,x_2) = -2x_1^2 - 3x_2^2 + 5$, y2=5*x(1)+6*x(2)-97;⇔ $f_2(x_1,x_2) = 5x_1 + 6x_2 - 97$, y3=x(2)^2-x(1)^2-x(1)-x(2);⇔ $f_3(x_1,x_2) = x_2^2 - x_1^2 - x_1 - x_2$, y=[y1;y2;y3];⇔ F =[$f_1(x_1,x_2)$ $f_2(x_1,x_2)$ $f_3(x_1,x_2)$], y1⇔ $f_1(x_1,x_2)$, y2⇔ $f_2(x_1,x_2)$, y3⇔ $f_3(x_1,x_2)$, y⇔ F , Ai⇔ A_{in}, and Bi⇔ B_{in}. The inequality $x_1 + 3x_2 - 7 \le 0$ needs rearrangement from which $[1 \quad 3]\begin{bmatrix} x_1 \\ x_2 \end{bmatrix} \le 7$ and the other provides $[5 \quad -8]\begin{bmatrix} x_1 \\ x_2 \end{bmatrix} \le 7$ therefore collectively they become $\begin{bmatrix} 1 & 3 \\ 5 & -8 \end{bmatrix}\begin{bmatrix} x_1 \\ x_2 \end{bmatrix} \le \begin{bmatrix} 7 \\ 7 \end{bmatrix}$ that is how $A_{in} = \begin{bmatrix} 1 & 3 \\ 5 & -8 \end{bmatrix}$ and $B_{in} = \begin{bmatrix} 7 \\ 7 \end{bmatrix}$. The three goal requirements and weights are assigned to **G** and **w** both as a three element row matrix respectively. The **g** holds the two guesses x_1=0 and x_2=0 as a two element row matrix.

Execute **help fgoalattain** to learn more about the other options hidden in the function at the command prompt.

11.2.6 Minimax optimization problems

In the minimax problem, we minimize the maximum of some vector function F where F is in general a multivariable function of X and by the literature term we seek for $\underset{X}{\min} \ \underset{F_i}{\max} \ F_i(X)$ starting with some guess for X . The built-in function **fminimax** helps us determine the optimal solution for the minimax problems. Like the previous optimizing functions, the function has many input argument options, few of which are exercised with the following examples.

♦♦ Example 1

Let us find the minimum of the maximum for the single variable functions $f_1(x) = -5x + 3$, $f_2(x) = 5x - 7$, and $f_3(x) = 3x + 23$ starting from the initial guess x =2. It is provided that the three functions have the optimal values $f_1(x)$=15.5, $f_2(x)$=–19.5, and $f_3(x)$=15.5 and which occurs at x =–2.5 – our objective is to obtain these.

The syntax we need here is **fminimax(**objective function file name under quote which describes the given vector F as a column matrix, initial guess of the independent variable). Applying previous section mentioned symbology and functions, we attached the solution on the right side (y1⇔ $f_1(x)$, y2⇔ $f_2(x)$, y3⇔ $f_3(x)$, F ⇔[$f_1(x)$ $f_2(x)$ $f_3(x)$], and y⇔ F as a column vector).

♦♦ Example 2

We intend to find the minimum of the maximum for the two variable functions $f_1(x_1,x_2) = 2x_1^2 + 3x_2^2 - 5$, $f_2(x_1,x_2) = 5x_1 + 6x_2 + 87$, and $f_3(x_1,x_2) = x_2^2 + x_1^2 + x_1 - x_2$ with the initial guess x_1=0.1 and x_2=2. It is given that the optimal values of the three functions are $f_1(x_1,x_2)$= 50.2188, $f_2(x_1,x_2)$=50.2188, and $f_3(x_1,x_2)$=22.3511 which take place at x_1=–3.7532 and x_2=–3.0026 and our purpose is to have these. We see the solution above applying ongoing functions and symbology (y1⇔ $f_1(x_1,x_2)$, y2⇔ $f_2(x_1,x_2)$, y3⇔ $f_3(x_1,x_2)$, F ⇔[$f_1(x_1,x_2)$ $f_2(x_1,x_2)$ $f_3(x_1,x_2)$], and y⇔ F as a column vector).

Minimax problems: Example 1:
Objective function file needed:

```
function y=f(x)
y1=-5*x+3;
y2=5*x-7;
y3=3*x+23;
y=[y1;y2;y3];
```

Calling the optimizing function:

```
>>[O,V]=fminimax('f',2) ↵

O =
    -2.5000      ← x at optimum
V =
    15.5000      ← Value of f1(x)
   -19.5000      ← Value of f2(x)
    15.5000      ← Value of f3(x)
```

Minimax problems: Example 2:
Objective function file needed:

```
function y=f(x)
y1=2*x(1)^2+3*x(2)^2-5;
y2=5*x(1)+6*x(2)+87;
y3=x(2)^2+x(1)^2+x(1)-x(2);
y=[y1;y2;y3];
```

Calling the optimizing function:

```
>>[O,V]=fminimax('f',[0.1 2]) ↵

O =
    -3.7532  -3.0026
       ↑        ↑
       x1       x2      at optimum
V =
    50.2188   ← Value of f1(x1,x2)
    50.2188   ← Value of f2(x1,x2)
    22.3511   ← Value of f3(x1,x2)
```

◆◆ **Example 3**

In the example 2 suppose we include two linear constraints such as $2x_1 - 3x_2 \le -3$ (inequality $A_{in}\ X \le B_{in}$) and $-x_2 = 3x_1$ (equality $A_{eq}\ X = B_{eq}$). Applying the notations of the previous sections, we have A_{in}=[2 −3], B_{in}=−3, A_{eq}=[3 1], and B_{eq}=0. Subject to the linear constraints, the optimal solution should occur at x_1=−0.2727 and x_2=0.8182 with the functional values $f_1(x_1,x_2)$=−2.8430, $f_2(x_1,x_2)$=90.5455, and $f_3(x_1,x_2)$=−0.3471 and which is what we are after. Now the required syntax is fminimax(F ,initial guess, A_{in} , B_{in} , A_{eq} , B_{eq}). Placed on the right side is the implementation of the problem first entering the constraint parameters and then exercising ongoing functions and symbology.

In order to learn about the other options included in the fminimax, execute help fminimax at the command prompt.

Example 3:
Entering the constraints:

```
>>Ai=[2 -3]; Bi=-3; Ae=[3 1]; Be=0; ↵
>>g=[0.1 2]; ↵
```

Calling the optimizing function:

```
>>[O,V]=fminimax('f',g,Ai,Bi,Ae,Be) ↵

O =
   -0.2727   0.8182
      ↑         ↑
      x1        x2        at optimum
V =
   -2.8430   ← Value of f1(x1,x2)
   90.5455   ← Value of f2(x1,x2)
   -0.3471   ← Value of f3(x1,x2)
```

11.2.7 Help about other optimization problems

From the discussions of previous sections, we guess that the reader has had some idea regarding the computation of the optimization problems in MATLAB. Nevertheless a lot more functions exist in the optimization toolbox (by the name optim) of MATLAB. Comprehensive help about the optimization library is seen by executing the following:

```
>>help optim ↵
 Optimization Toolbox
 Version 3.0 (R14) 05-May-2004

 Nonlinear minimization of functions.
  fminbnd    - Scalar bounded nonlinear function minimization.
  fmincon    - Multidimensional constrained nonlinear minimization.
                        ⋮
```

From the displayed list, select any function and execute help function name for example help fminbnd to see its details at the command prompt. With this clue, we intend to close the chapter.

Chapter 12

Partial Differential Equations

Partial differential equations (PDEs) are receiving enough attention in modeling phenomena in contemporary science and engineering fields for example in quantum mechanics, acoustics, electromagnetic wave propagation, nonlinear optics, and many more. This chapter provides a comprehensive and well-organized treatment of partial differential equations only to the pure mathematics context. Application based partial differential equation demands rigorous treatment which we avoided due to the nature of the text. The theory of partial differential equation is too extensive to fit the context. However our emphasis has been on the following:

- Partial differential equation notations of different orders and way to obtain symbolic solution
- Numerical solution of the partial differential equations with specific examples
- Elaborate discussion on boundary condition, initial condition, PDE coding, and PDE domain
- Visualizing the PDE solution employing the graphics facility of MATLAB

12.1 Partial differential equations

In the ordinary differential equations (chapter 7), the number of the independent variables related to the equation is only one. There are some physical processes and laws which need differential equation involving two or more independent variables. For instance an electromagnetic wave field is a function of distance and time as well. Likewise the dependent variable has more than one derivative thereby requiring the partial derivatives. According to the partial differential notation if z is a function of two independent variables that is $z = f(x, y)$, its different partial derivatives are denoted by $\frac{\partial z}{\partial x}$ (first order w.r.to x), $\frac{\partial z}{\partial y}$ (first order w.r.to y), $\frac{\partial^2 z}{\partial y^2}$ (second order w.r.to y), $\frac{\partial^2 z}{\partial y \partial x}$ (second order w.r.to first y, then x), ...etc. Any differential equation containing the partial derivative is termed as the partial differential equation (PDE). By resemblance with the theory of the ordinary differential equation, the order of a partial differential equation is the highest order partial differential coefficient occurring in it. Thus,

$4y^2\frac{\partial z}{\partial x}+\frac{\partial z}{\partial y}=x+y$ is a first order partial differential equation when z is a function of x and y,

$4v^2\frac{\partial^2 f}{\partial u^2}+\frac{\partial f}{\partial v}+\frac{\partial f}{\partial w}=u\frac{\partial^2 f}{\partial v\partial u}$ is a second order partial differential equation when f is a function of u, v, and w, and

$\frac{\partial^3 g}{\partial p^3}=\left(\frac{\partial g}{\partial q}\right)^2+p+q$ is a third order partial differential equation when g is a function of p and q.

Solutions to the partial differential equations encounter a much more difficult problem than the solutions to the ordinary differential equations do except certain linear or nonlinear partial differential equations. A variety of partial differential equations occurring in physics, chemistry, or engineering can be solved analytically or numerically following the symbology and coding of MATLAB. Briefly we explain the handling of several known types of partial differential equations in the following sections.

12.2 Symbolic solution of PDEs

The master function **pdsolve** (abbreviation for the partial differential equation solve) found in **maple** (section 3.2) solves a lot of partial differential equations symbolically. Different types of PDE need different kinds of input argument which we address in the following. We maintain the font equivalence like **x**⇔x throughout the whole section.

12.2.1 First order partial differential equations

If z is a function of two independent variables – x and y, we write it as **z(x,y)** in **maple**. The first order partial derivative $\frac{\partial z}{\partial x}$ is written as **diff(z(x,y),x)** where the **diff** is the differential operator in **maple** and has two input arguments, dependent and independent variables respectively. In the code writing of the equation, we write the vector code (section 14.2). Let us solve the first order partial differential equation $x\frac{\partial z}{\partial x}+y\frac{\partial z}{\partial y}=3(x+y)z$ whose general solution is given by $z=e^{3(x+y)}h\left(\frac{y}{x}\right)$ where $h\left(\frac{y}{x}\right)$ is an arbitrary function of $\frac{y}{x}$ and which we demand from MATLAB. The vector code of the equation (it is understood that $z=z(x,y)$) is **x*diff(z(x,y),x)+y*diff(z(x,y),y)=3*(x+y)*z(x,y)**. Attached above is the complete solution of the PDE. In the first line we assigned the equation code to the workspace variable **e** (can be any user-given name) within the **maple** where := is the **maple** assignment operator. The **pdsolve** has two input arguments, the first and second of which are the PDE code and required dependent variable respectively. In the second line of the implementation we assigned the **maple** return to workspace **S** (can be any user-given name). The **pretty** of section 3.1 just displays the symbolic form of the string stored in **S** for easy reading in which **_F1(y/x)** indicates $h\left(\frac{y}{x}\right)$. The return to the **S** is the character code which needs using the command **sym** to be mathematical symbol. Let us solve two more examples exercising the same functions and symbology.

Solution for the first order PDE: beginning example:

```
>>maple('e:=x*diff(z(x,y),x)+y*diff(z(x,y),y)=3*(x+y)*z(x,y)'); ↵
>>S=maple('pdsolve(e,z(x,y))'); pretty(sym(S)) ↵
                                   3        3
        z(x, y) = _F1(y/x) exp(x)   exp(y)
```

◆◆ Example 1

Solve the PDE $\frac{\partial u}{\partial \theta}=-5\sin\theta\frac{\partial u}{\partial r}+3\cos\theta$. It is given that $u=3\sin\theta+h(-r-5\cos\theta)$ is the solution of the PDE which we intend to obtain and where h is an arbitrary function. Now the dependent and independent variables are u (function of r and θ) and r and θ respectively. Not having the provision for writing θ, **t** is used instead. Attached above is the solution of the PDE. The equivalences are **u(r,t)**⇔u, **diff(u(r,t),t)**⇔$\frac{\partial u}{\partial \theta}$, **diff(u(r,t),r)**⇔$\frac{\partial u}{\partial r}$, and **_F1(-r - 5 cos(t))**⇔$h(-r-5\cos\theta)$. The command **simple** is used to simplify the mathematical expression stored in the **S**.

First order PDE: Solution to the example 1:

```
>>maple('e:=diff(u(r,t),t)=-5*sin(t)*diff(u(r,t),r)+3*cos(t)'); ↵
>>S=maple('pdsolve(e,u(r,t))'); pretty(simple(sym(S))) ↵
        u(r, t) = 3 sin(t) + _F1(-r - 5 cos(t))
```

♦♦ Example 2

Let us try to find the solution of the PDE $x\frac{\partial z}{\partial x}+\left(\frac{\partial z}{\partial y}\right)^2=3\sin x$ applying ongoing functions and symbology. The solution is displayed on the right side. There is a new partial derivative term in the PDE which is $\left(\frac{\partial z}{\partial y}\right)^2$ and whose code is diff(z(x,y),y)^2. Now we explain the return from the implementation. The **pdsolve** automatically assumes some functional pattern as the solution of the PDE which is $z(x,y)=f(x)+g(y)$ where $f(x)$ and $g(y)$ are the arbitrary functions and indicated by _F1(x) and _F2(y) respectively. As the return appears, there are two ordinary differential equations from which the $f(x)$ and $g(y)$ are obtained. The two ordinary differential equations are $\frac{dg}{dy}=c_2$ and $\frac{df}{dx}=-\frac{c_2^2}{x}+3\frac{\sin x}{x}$ where c_2 is an arbitrary constant and indicated by _c[2]. Within the **maple**, there are some special tools by the name **PDEtools** which finds the close form solution from the previous return. The tools are activated by executing **with(PDEtools)** inside the **maple**. Placed above on the right side is the reexecution of the **pdsolve** but this time we assigned the return from the **pdsolve** to workspace A (can be any name of your choice) within the **maple** in the first line. The **maple** function **build** tries to determine some general solution derived from just mentioned ordinary differential equations which we conducted in the second line of the implementation and assigned to S in MATLAB not in **maple**. Just to see the readable form we applied **pretty** in conjunction with the **sym** as done before. Therefore we read off the general solution as $z(x,y)=-c_2^2\ln x+3Si(x)+c_1+c_2y+c_3$ where each c is some arbitrary constant (_C1⇔c_1 and _C2⇔c_3) and $Si(x)$ is the sine integral (section 6.6) of x. The c_1+c_3 can be replaced by another arbitrary constant of your choice as the theory of PDE says.

First order PDE: Solution to the example 2:

```
>>maple('e:=x*diff(z(x,y),x)+diff(z(x,y),y)^2=3*sin(x)'); ↵
>>S=maple('pdsolve(e,z(x,y))'); pretty(simple(sym(S))) ↵

     (z(x, y) = _F1(x) + _F2(y)) & where
                                                      2
         d                    d                 _ c[2]        sin(x)
    {[{---- _F2(y) = _c[2],  ---- _F1(x) = - --------- + 3 --------}]}
        dy                   dx                  x             x
```

Seeking some close form solution from the PDEtools for the example 2:

```
>>maple('A:=pdsolve(e,z(x,y))'); ↵
>>S=maple('with(PDEtools):build(A)') ↵

S =

z(x,y) = - _c[2]^2*log(x)+3*sinint(x)+_C1+_c[2]*y+_C2
>>pretty(sym(S)) ↵
                  2
   z(x, y) = - _c[2]  log(x) + 3 sinint(x) + _C1 + _c[2] y + _C2
```

12.2.2 Second order partial differential equations

The function **pdsolve** also keeps the provision for solving a second order partial differential equation. Let us go through the following examples regarding this.

♦♦ Example 1

Let us solve the PDE $2\frac{\partial^2 z}{\partial x^2}+7\frac{\partial^2 z}{\partial x\partial y}+6\frac{\partial^2 z}{\partial y^2}+\frac{\partial z}{\partial x}+2\frac{\partial z}{\partial y}=0$ with constant coefficients whose general solution is given by $z=f_1(y-2x)+e^{-\frac{x}{2}}f_2(2y-3x)$. We presented the solution on the right side. The dependent variable z is the function of independent variables x and y i.e. $z=f(x,y)$. Instead of typing **f(x,y)** repeatedly, we assigned that to **z** within the **maple** in the first line of the command. There is smarter way of writing $\frac{\partial^2 z}{\partial x^2}$ in **maple**, which is **diff(z,x$2)**. If we had $\frac{\partial^3 z}{\partial x^3}$, we would write **diff(z,x$3)** and so on. In the second line we assigned the given differential equation code to **e** within the **maple**. Arbitrary function equivalences are _F1(y - 2 x)⇔ $f_1(y-2x)$ and _F2(2 y - 3 x)⇔ $f_2(2y-3x)$. All other functions and symbols have previously mentioned meanings.

Second order PDE: Solution to the example 1:

```
>>maple('z:=f(x,y)'); ↵
>>maple('e:=2*diff(z,x$2)+7*diff(z,x,y)+6*diff(z,y$2)+diff(z,x)+2*diff(z,y)=0'); ↵
>>S=maple('pdsolve(e,f(x,y))'); ↵
>>pretty(sym(S)) ↵
     f(x, y) = _F1(y - 2 x) + exp(- 1/2 x) _F2(2 y - 3 x)
```

Second order PDE: Solution to the example 2:

```
>>maple('e:=4*diff(f(x,y),x$2)-9*diff(f(x,y),y$2)=x^2-y'); ↵
>>S=maple('pdsolve(e,f(x,y))'); ↵
>>pretty(sym(S)) ↵
                                                      2  2
   f(x, y) = _F1(2 y + 3 x) + _F2(2 y - 3 x) + 1/48 x  (x  - 6 y)
```

♦♦ Example 2

It is given that $z = f_1(2y+3x) + f_2(2y-3x) + \frac{1}{48}x^4 - \frac{1}{8}x^2 y$ is the general solution of the nonhomogeneous equation $4\frac{\partial^2 z}{\partial x^2} - 9\frac{\partial^2 z}{\partial y^2} = x^2 - y$ which we wish to compute. The response of MATLAB is shown at the lower right corner of the last page maintaining ongoing functions and symbology. In order to code the nonhomogeneous part $x^2 - y$, we employ the vector string of section 14.2.

♦♦ Example 3

Sometimes user-defined pattern of the dependent functions can be passed to have the general solution. For example the equation $4\frac{\partial^2 z}{\partial x^2} - 9\frac{\partial^2 z}{\partial y^2} - \frac{\partial z}{\partial y} = x$ has the general solution $z(x,y) = f(x)g(y) + \frac{c_1 + c_2 x + c_3 x^3}{24 c_3}$ considering $z(x,y) = f(x)g(y)$ and the functions $f(x)$ and $g(y)$ are the solutions of the ordinary differential equations $\frac{d^2 f}{dx^2} = c_1 f$ and $\frac{d^2 g}{dy^2} = c_1 g - \frac{9}{4}\frac{dg}{dy}$. Attached above is the implementation of the problem maintaining ongoing functions and symbology in which the arbitrary constants are _C1⇔c_1, _C2⇔c_2, and _C3⇔c_3. Now the **pdsolve** has three input arguments, the third of which passes the information about the functions $f(x)$ and $g(y)$ through the reserve word **HINT=** in **maple**. The other two input arguments have the previously mentioned meanings.

Second order PDE: Solution to the example 3:

```
>>maple('e:=4*diff(z(x,y),x$2)-4*diff(z(x,y),y$2)-9*diff(z(x,y),y)=x'); ↵
>>S=maple('pdsolve(e,z(x,y),HINT=f(x)*g(y))'); ↵
>>pretty(sym(S)) ↵
    /                                       3\
    |                   _C1 + _C2 x + _C3 x  |
    |z(x, y) = f(x) g(y) + 1/24 -------------------| & where
    \                           _C3           /

          2                    2
         d                    d                          /d      \
    {[{----- f(x) = _c[1] f(x), ------ g(y) = g(y) _c[1] - 9/4 |---- g(y) |}]}
          2                    2                         \dy     /
        dx                   dy
```

In example 2 of the last subsection we applied the **PDEtools** in order for having some close form solution of the PDE. Let us try to do so here in this example applying the same symbols and functions. Right attached commands help us do that. The only difference is we applied **simple** for the simplification in the last line. Figure 12.1(a) shows the camera snapshot as a solution of the PDE from MATLAB. The next legitimate query should be how to read off the solution, which we provide in the following: $z(x,y) = c_3\, c_1\, e^{-\frac{9}{8}y + \frac{1}{8}a + x\sqrt{b}} + c_3\, c_2\, e^{-\frac{9}{8}y + \frac{1}{8}a - x\sqrt{b}} + c_4\, c_1\, e^{-\frac{9}{8}y - \frac{1}{8}a + x\sqrt{b}} + c_4\, c_2\, e^{-\frac{9}{8}y - \frac{1}{8}a - x\sqrt{b}} + \frac{c_1}{24c_3} + \frac{c_2 x}{24 c_3} + \frac{x^3}{24}$ where the equivalences are _C1⇔c_1, _C2⇔c_2, _C3⇔c_3, _C4⇔c_4, _c[1]⇔b, and %1⇔a⇔ $y\sqrt{81+64b}$.

Seeking some close form solution from the PDEtools for the example 3:

```
>>maple('e:=4*diff(z(x,y),x$2)-4*diff(z(x,y),y$2)-9*diff(z(x,y),y)=x'); ↵
>>maple('A:=pdsolve(e,z(x,y),HINT=f(x)*g(y))'); ↵
>>S=maple('with(PDEtools):build(A)'); ↵
>>pretty(simple(sym(S))) ↵
```

```
                                                 1/2
z(x, y) = _C3 _C1 exp(- 9/8 y + 1/8 %1 + _c[1]     x)

                                               1/2
         + _C3 _C2 exp(- 9/8 y + 1/8 %1 - _c[1]     x)

                                               1/2
         + _C4 _C1 exp(- 9/8 y - 1/8 %1 + _c[1]     x)

                                               1/2                 _C1           _C2 x
         + _C4 _C2 exp(- 9/8 y - 1/8 %1 - _c[1]     x) + 1/24 --- + 1/24 -----
                                                                   _C3           _C3

                   3
         + 1/24 x

                          1/2
%1 := y (81 + 64 _c[1])
```

Figure 12.1(a) Camera snapshot of the example 3 solution

12.3 Numerical solution of PDEs

The symbolic solution of a PDE addressed in the last two sections is not feasible in many practical situations. Very often the numerical solution is sought for the PDEs in those circumstances. But the PDE numerical solution theory is so extensive that we need another book merely for the numerical solution. Besides there is a toolbox and graphical user interface (GUI) dedicated entirely to solving the PDEs. In this short context we intend to remain objective only to the numerical solutions of some PDE examples in the following sections.

12.4 PDE with one space variable and time

The function pdepe finds the numerical solution to a partial differential equation of the form $p\frac{\partial u}{\partial t} = x^{-m}\frac{\partial (x^m q)}{\partial x} + r$ where each of the p, q, and r is a function of four quantities – x, t, u, and $\frac{\partial u}{\partial x}$. The dependent variable is u or $u(x,t)$ which is a function of the single space variable x and time t. In order to code the equation, one needs to know about the function file opening in MATLAB whose reference is seen in section 14.5.

12.4.1 How to write the code of the PDE?

Giving code to a PDE for the numerical solution requires the code writing skills on the given PDE, initial conditions, and boundary conditions, each of which needs writing a function file. Let us not forget that every function file has some input and output which comes from the given PDE descriptions as follows.

❖❖ Coding the PDE

A given PDE must be written in the form $p\frac{\partial u}{\partial t} = x^{-m}\frac{\partial (x^m q)}{\partial x} + r$ in order to utilize the function pdepe for the numerical solution. We intend to discover the p, q, r, and m from some PDEs which pave the way for the code writing in the following:

Given PDE 1. $\frac{\partial^2 u}{\partial x^2} = 4\frac{\partial u}{\partial t}$ or $u_{xx} = 4u_t$

We manipulate to write: $4\frac{\partial u}{\partial t} = \frac{\partial}{\partial x}\left(\frac{\partial u}{\partial x}\right)$ where from p =4, m =0, $q = \frac{\partial u}{\partial x}$ and r =0

Given PDE 2. $t\frac{\partial^2 u}{\partial x^2} = 9t\frac{\partial u}{\partial t} + u + 5$

We manipulate to write: $9t\frac{\partial u}{\partial t} = \frac{\partial}{\partial x}\left(t\frac{\partial u}{\partial x}\right) - u - 5$ where from $p = 9t$, m =0, $q = t\frac{\partial u}{\partial x}$, and $r = -u - 5$

Given PDE 3. $\frac{1}{x^2}\frac{\partial^2 u}{\partial x^2} = 6t\frac{\partial u}{\partial x} + \frac{\partial u}{\partial t}x + u^2$

We manipulate to write: $x\frac{\partial u}{\partial t} = \frac{1}{x^2}\frac{\partial^2 u}{\partial x^2} - 6t\frac{\partial u}{\partial x} - u^2$ or $x^3\frac{\partial u}{\partial t} = \frac{\partial}{\partial x}\left(\frac{\partial u}{\partial x}\right) - 6x^2 t\frac{\partial u}{\partial x} - x^2u^2$ therefore $p = x^3$, m =0, $q = \frac{\partial u}{\partial x}$, and $r = -6x^2t\frac{\partial u}{\partial x} - x^2u^2$

Once we discover the p, q, and r from the given PDE, the next step is to write the function file code for the given PDE which has four input arguments (x, t, u, and $\frac{\partial u}{\partial x}$ respectively) and three output arguments (p, q, and r respectively). Actually we write the functional description of the p, q, and r in terms of x, t, u, and $\frac{\partial u}{\partial x}$ in this function file. We present the function file description for just mentioned three PDEs below:

function file for the PDE 1:	**function file for the PDE 2:**	**function file for the PDE 3:**

function [p,q,r]=eqn(x,t,u,DuDx)
p=4;
q=DuDx;
r=0;
	function [p,q,r]=eqn(x,t,u,DuDx)
	p=9*t;
	q=t*DuDx;
	r=-u-5;
		function [p,q,r]=eqn(x,t,u,DuDx)
		p=x^3;
		q=DuDx;
		r=-6*x^2*t*DuDx-x^2*u^2;

The font equivalence like p⇔ p is maintained in above PDE description. The p, q, r, x, t, u, and DuDx are all user-given names. You could have written them as a, b, c, etc. We named the function file as eqn (can be any name of your choice). Section 14.2 illustrates the functional code writing (vector code) of any expression for example in the third PDE, r=-6*x^2*t*DuDx-x^2*u^2 is equivalent to $r = -6x^2t\frac{\partial u}{\partial x} - x^2u^2$.

♦♦ Coding the initial condition

Initial condition means the condition at $t = t_0$ for all x where t_0 is user-given. We write a function file for the initial condition too which has one input (x) and one output ($u(x,t_0)$) arguments. Let us consider the following example initial conditions (ICs): IC 1. $u(x,t_0) = \sin x$, IC 2. $u(x,t_0) = \begin{Bmatrix} 3x & for\ 0 \le x \le 2 \\ x^2 & for\quad else \end{Bmatrix}$, and IC 3. $u(x,t_0) = \begin{Bmatrix} |1+x| & for\ \ 0 \le x \le 2 \\ -4x & for\ \ 2 < x \le 5 \\ 0 & else \end{Bmatrix}$.

Our objective is to write the function file for each initial condition whose coding is presented on the right side. Operator descriptions are seen in subsection 14.3.1. The conditional statement if-else-end is addressed in the subsection 14.3.4. In the first initial condition there is one expression for all x that is why the code writing is so. There are two expressions for the $u(x,t_0)$ in the second initial condition and you can not fit them in a single expression. We check the x interval using if-else-end syntax and write the code to the corresponding interval. The third initial condition has three intervals for this reason there are three checkings inside the if-end statement. The u0 and x (both can be any name of your choice) refer to $u(x,t_0)$ and x respectively. Any interval like $0 \le x \le 2$ is split as $0 \le x$ and $x \le 2$ and connected by the AND operator &. We named the initial condition function file as ic which can be any name of your choice. Some interval related expressional codes are as follows: sin(x)⇔ $\sin x$, x^2⇔ x^2, abs(1+x)⇔ $|1+x|$, and so forth.

function file for the IC 1:

```
function u0=ic(x)
u0=sin(x);
```

function file for the IC 2:

```
function u0=ic(x)
if (0<=x)&(x<=2)
    u0=3*x;
else
    u0=x^2;
end
```

function file for the IC 3:

```
function u0=ic(x)
if (0<=x)&(x<=2)
    u0=abs(1+x);
elseif (2<x)&(x<=5)
    u0=-4*x;
else
    u0=0;
end
```

♦♦ Coding the boundary condition

Boundary condition means the condition between $x = a$ and $x = b$ for all t if the solution over $a \le x \le b$ is sought where a and b are user-given. The function file for the boundary condition has five input arguments – a, $u(a,t)$, b, $u(b,t)$, and t and four output arguments – $e(a,t,u)$, $g(a,t)$, $e(b,t,u)$, and $g(b,t)$ provided that the given boundary conditions are in the form $e(x,t,u) + g(x,t)q\left(x,t,u,\frac{\partial u}{\partial x}\right) = 0$ both for the $x = a$ and $x = b$ and q has the given PDE equation mentioned meaning (see the PDE description). Symbolically we write different expressions just to grasp the idea but when passed to function file we write the workspace variable for example $e(a,t,u)$ or $e(b,t,u)$ can be written as ea and eb respectively (can be user-given name). We do not write the value of a or b in the input argument of the boundary condition function file instead pass the values on inside the function file. As input and output arguments, we write user-supplied general workspace variable. Let us discover just mentioned parameters for some example boundary conditions (BCs) as follows:

Given BC 1: $u(0,t) = 0$ and $\frac{\pi}{2}e^{-2t} = \frac{\partial u(2,t)}{\partial x}$

Comparing $u(0,t) = 0$ with $e(x,t,u) + g(x,t)q\left(x,t,u,\frac{\partial u}{\partial x}\right) = 0$,

function file for the BC 1:

```
function [ea ga eb gb]=bc(a,ua,b,ub,t)
ea=ua;
ga=0;
eb=pi/2*exp(-2*t);
gb=-1;
```

we have $e(x,t,u) = u(0,t)$ and $g(x,t)$=0 for the lower bound a =0. Again comparing $\frac{\pi}{2}e^{-2t} - \frac{\partial u(2,t)}{\partial x} = 0$ (rearranging) to the same equation, we see $e(x,t,u) = \frac{\pi}{2}e^{-2t}$ and $g(x,t)$=–1 for the upper bound b=2 assuming that $\frac{\partial u(2,t)}{\partial x}$ is related with the previously mentioned q term. Although a =0 and b=2, we seek only the functional relationship for $e(x,t,u)$ and $g(x,t)$ not the value at a or b. Writing ea⇔ $e(x,t,u)$ for a, ga⇔ $g(x,t)$ for a, eb⇔ $e(x,t,u)$ for b, and gb⇔ $g(x,t)$ for b, we attached the function file for the BC above on the right side (also a⇔ a, b⇔ b, ua⇔ $u(a,t)$, ub⇔ $u(b,t)$, t⇔ t, and pi/2*exp(-2*t)⇔ $\frac{\pi}{2}e^{-2t}$).

Given BC 2: $\frac{\partial u(0,t)}{\partial x} = 1 + t$ and $u(3,t) = t - \sin t$

Like the comparison of the BC 1, the $\frac{\partial u(0,t)}{\partial x} = 1 + t$ needs rearrangement i.e. $-1 - t + \frac{\partial u(0,t)}{\partial x} = 0$ so $e(x,t,u) = -1 - t$ and $g(x,t)$=1 (similar assumption). The $u(3,t) = t - \sin t$ also needs to be written as

function file for the BC 2:

```
function [ea ga eb gb]=bc(a,ua,b,ub,t)
ea=-1-t;
ga=1;
eb=-t+sin(t)+ub;
gb=0;
```

$-t+\sin t+u(3,t)=0$ therefore $e(x,t,u)=-t+\sin t+u(3,t)$ and $g(x,t)$=0. Of coarse, we have here a=0 and b=3. However observing ongoing function and symbology, we provided the function file for the BC 2 at the lower right corner of the last page.

Given BC 3: $u(1,t)=t^2$ and $u(3,t)=-8t-7\cos t$

Rearrangement provides $-t^2+u(1,t)=0$ so $e(x,t,u)=-t^2+u(1,t)$ and $g(x,t)$=0 for the lower bound a=1. The other condition needs us to write $u(3,t)+8t+7\cos t=0$ on that $e(x,t,u)=u(3,t)+8t+7\cos t$ and $g(x,t)$=0 for the upper bound b=3. The function file is provided on the right side observing the same function and symbology.

function file for the BC 3:
```
function [ea ga eb gb]=bc(a,ua,b,ub,t)
ea=-t^2+ua;
ga=0;
eb=ub+8*t+7*cos(t);
gb=0;
```

Given BC 4: $5u_x(0,t)+u(0,t)=te^{-4t}$ and $u_x(1,t)=\sinh t$

Writing the conditions in rearranged form, we have $-te^{-4t}+u(0,t)+5\dfrac{\partial u(0,t)}{\partial x}=0$ and $-\sinh t+\dfrac{\partial u(1,t)}{\partial x}=0$ from what cause $e(x,t,u)=-te^{-4t}+u(0,t)$ and $g(x,t)$=5 for the lower bound a=0 and $e(x,t,u)=-\sinh t$ and $g(x,t)$=1 for the upper bound b=1. However its function file code is seen on the right side retaining the same function and symbology.

function file for the BC 4:
```
function [ea ga eb gb]=bc(a,ua,b,ub,t)
ea=-t*exp(-4*t)+ua;
ga=5;
eb=-sinh(t);
gb=1;
```

In all four boundary function files, we named the function file as bc which can be any user-given name.

12.4.2 Model examples on the PDE

In this subsection we intend to solve the following PDE numerically exercising the function pdepe. The pdepe has the syntax pdepe(last subsection mentioned integer m value, function file name describing given PDE under quote, function file name describing the initial condition under quote, function file name describing the boundary condition under quote, required x as a row vector, required t as a row vector). The return of the pdepe is the $u(x,t)$ versus x and t data. It is extremely important that while providing the initial conditions or boundary conditions, data related to bounds on both conditions must be consistent. For instance if we seek for the solution over $1\le t\le 2$, we must provide $u(x,t)$ at t=1 or $u(x,1)$. Let us not forget that $u(x,t)$, x, and t are all continuous but we get the discrete values of $u(x,t)$ for discrete x and t as a solution according to our chosen step size. The return for $u(x,t)$ is just a rectangular matrix. It is assumed that you must have gone through the previous subsections. Let us see the following examples.

♦♦ Example A

Solve the PDE $x+\dfrac{\partial^2 u}{\partial x^2}=4t\dfrac{\partial u}{\partial t}$ over $1\le t\le 2$ and $0\le x\le 2$ with the initial condition $u(x,1)=1-x^2$ and boundary conditions $u(0,t)$=0 and $\dfrac{\partial u(2,t)}{\partial x}=0.5(1-e^{-t})$. Choose the t step as 0.2 and x step as 0.1.

The $x+\dfrac{\partial^2 u}{\partial x^2}=4t\dfrac{\partial u}{\partial t}$ is rearranged to write $4t\dfrac{\partial u}{\partial t}=\dfrac{\partial}{\partial x}\left(\dfrac{\partial u}{\partial x}\right)+x$ so the last subsection mentioned $p=4t$, $q=\dfrac{\partial u}{\partial x}$, $r=x$, and $m=0$ with this we write the function file for the given PDE as shown on the right side. Writing the initial condition function file is straightforward which we also placed on the right side. The first and second boundary conditions say that $e(x,t,u)=u(0,t)$ and $g(x,t)$=0 for the lower bound and $e(x,t,u)=-0.5(1-e^{-t})$ and $g(x,t)$=1 for the upper bound of x. With that we write the boundary function file as attached on the right side. All symbols and functions bear previous subsection mentioned meanings.

Model PDE: Example A:

function file for the given PDE:
```
function [p,q,r]=eqn(x,t,u,DuDx)
p=4*t;
q=DuDx;
r=x;
```
function file for the initial condition:
```
function u0=ic(x)
u0=1-x^2;
```
function file for the boundary conditions:
```
function [ea ga eb gb]=bc(a,ua,b,ub,t)
ea=ua;
ga=0;
eb=-0.5*(1-exp(-t));
gb=1;
```
Calling the pdepe for the solution:
```
>>t=1:0.2:2; ↵
>>x=0:0.1:2; ↵
>>u=pdepe(0,'eqn','ic','bc',x,t); ↵
```

Steps we need:

A. Type the codes of the PDE function file in a new M-file (section 1.3) and save the file by the name eqn,
B. Type the codes of the initial condition in a new M-file and save the file by the name ic,
C. Type the codes of the boundary conditions in a new M-file and save the file by the name bc,
D. Generate the t vector as a row matrix with the given step size (shown above),
E. Generate the x vector as a row matrix with the given step size (shown above), and

F. Finally, call the function pdepe with proper input arguments as shown at the lower right corner of the last page and assign the solution to the workspace u (can be any user-given name).

The solution for the $u(x,t)$ is purely a rectangular matrix which is held in u. In order to know about the u, look at the workspace browser (section 1.4). You must find the variable u in there and doubleclick the u to see its contents (the solution) as shown in the figure 12.1(b) – just a rectangular matrix. Recall that we chose the t step as 0.2 from 1 to 2, there are six points (1, 1.2, 1.4, until 2) corresponding to the vertical direction of the u. Again with 0.1 step from 0 to 2 along x, there are twenty one points (0, 0.1, 0.2, until 2) for this reason the size of the rectangular matrix u is 6×21. It is important to cite that there is no information about the t or x in the u, it is the user who has to remember it. Concerning the figure 12.1(b), the element indexed by (5,3) which is 0.14151 is basically the $u(x,t)$ at $x=0.2$ and $t=1.8$ or $u(0.2,1.8)=0.14151$. Suppose you chose the x and t step as 0.1 and 0.05 respectively, then the u would be of size 11×41.

$x \rightarrow$

Array Editor - u

Stack: Base

$t \downarrow$	1	2	3	4	5	6	7
1	0	0.99	0.96	0.91	0.84	0.75	0.64
2	0	0.21638	0.3997	0.52643	0.58701	0.58418	0.52759
3	0	0.1356	0.25601	0.34829	0.40329	0.41631	0.3867
4	0	0.097791	0.18543	0.25381	0.29567	0.30612	0.28275
5	0	0.07464	0.14151	0.19348	0.22459	0.23048	0.20856
6	0	[illegible]	[illegible]	[illegible]	[illegible]	[illegible]35	0.15485

Figure 12.1(b) Part of the solution of the $u(x,t)$

Sometimes solution at a particular t is required for instance $u(x,1.8)$ it means the whole fifth row of the u and we pick up the fifth row from the u using the command u(5,:) (section 2.6). If you assign that to workspace u1 using u1=u(5,:), u1 holds the $u(x,1.8)$ solution as a row matrix. On the other hand the $u(0.4,t)$ is basically the fourth column in u which is picked up from the u by writing u(:,4).

♦♦ Example B

Let us solve the PDE $6u_t = 35u_{xx}$ for $0 \le x \le 4$ using step 0.2 and $0 \le t \le 1$ using step 0.1 subject to boundary conditions $u(0,t)=2$ and $u(4,t)=5$ and initial condition $u(x,0)=\begin{cases} 2-x & for\ 0 \le x < 2 \\ 6(x-2) & for\ 2 \le x \le 4 \\ 10 & else \end{cases}$.

In example A, we discussed a model PDE in details. In this example we employ the same functions and symbology to solve the PDE.

Given PDE is rearranged as $\frac{6}{35}\frac{\partial u}{\partial t} = \frac{\partial}{\partial x}\left(\frac{\partial u}{\partial x}\right)$ so $p=\frac{6}{35}$, m=0, $q=\frac{\partial u}{\partial x}$ and r=0. Subsection 12.4.1 mentioned programming technique is applied here to write the initial condition. Noticing the boundary conditions, we discover that $e(x,t,u)=u(0,t)-2$ and $g(x,t)$=0 for the lower bound and $e(x,t,u)=u(4,t)-5$ and $g(x,t)$=0 for the upper bound of x. However attached on the upper right side are all necessary codes for solving the PDE. Follow the steps as we did in the example A. On having those implemented, we can say that our required solution of $u(x,t)$ is stored as a rectangular matrix in the workspace u.

Model PDE: Example B:

function file for the given PDE:

```
function [p,q,r]=eqn(x,t,u,DuDx)
p=6/35;
q=DuDx;
r=0;
```

function file for the initial condition:

```
function u0=ic(x)
if (0<=x)&(x<2)
    u0=2-x;
elseif (2<=x)&(x<=4)
    u0=6*(x-2);
else
    u0=10;
end
```

function file for the boundary conditions:

```
function [ea ga eb gb]=bc(a,ua,b,ub,t)
ea=ua-2;
ga=0;
eb=ub-5;
gb=0;
```

Calling the pdepe for the solution:

```
>>t=0:0.1:1; ↵
>>x=0:0.2:4; ↵
>>u=pdepe(0,'eqn','ic','bc',x,t); ↵
```

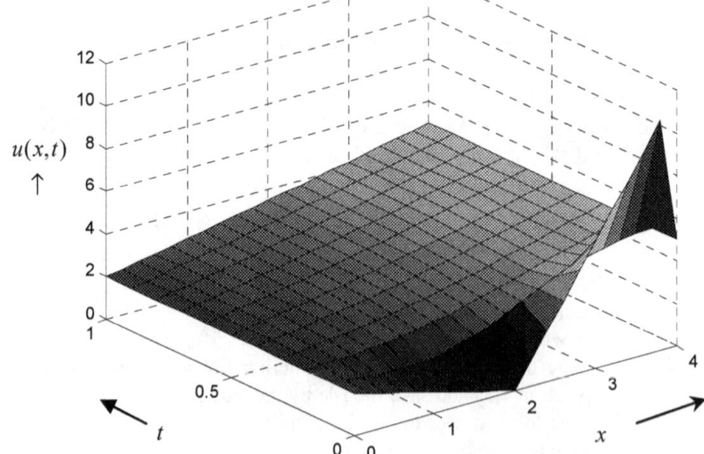

Figure 12.2(a) Surface plot for the PDE solution of example B

♦♦ Example C

The independent variable t does not have to be time. It can be any other variable like y. The example B could have been $6\frac{\partial u}{\partial y} = 35\frac{\partial^2 u}{\partial x^2}$ and would produce the same numerical result. It is just a matter of variable arrangement and naming.

12.4.3 Graphing the PDE solution

It is often of interest that we view the surface plot for the $u(x,t)$ against x and t for which the subsection 13.2.6 mentioned **mesh** or **surf** becomes useful. The solution for $u(x,t)$ over $0 \le x \le 4$ and $0 \le t \le 1$ in the example B is held in the workspace u (as well as the t and x variations as a row matrix in the t and x respectively) in the last subsection and we execute surf(x,t,u) at the command prompt to see the surface plot of the figure 12.2(a). The figure also indicates the variation directions for $u(x,t)$, x, and t.

Another graphing appears in the literature that we plot the $u(x,t)$ for a particular x or t. For instance in the example A of the last subsection, we have u1 holding the $u(x,1.8)$ as a row matrix for $t=1.8$. We intend to plot $u(x,1.8)$ versus x for which the function plot of subsection 13.2.1 is applied. The command plot(x,u1) shows the figure 12.2(b) as the graph. Sometimes for the comparison reason, we may seek the graph for two different t's, let us say the other one is available in u2 and we execute the command plot(x,u1,x,u2) thereafter.

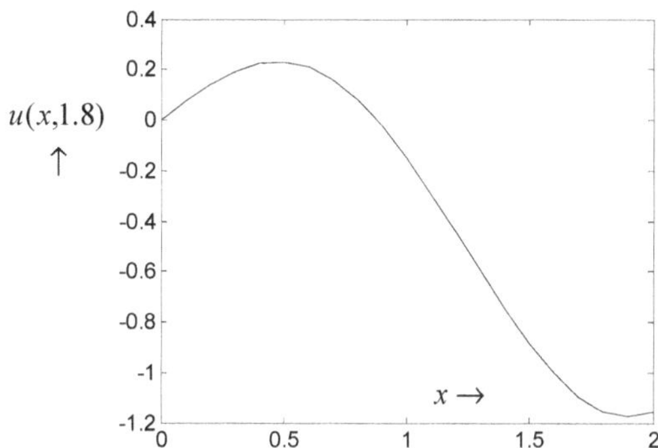

Figure 12.2(b) Plot of $u(x,1.8)$ versus x

Again in the example A, the $u(x,t)$ for a fixed x is addressed as $u(0.4,t)$ which we have exercising u(:,4). The command plot(t,u(:,4)) then brings the graph of the $u(0.4,t)$ versus t for $x=0.4$ in front.

12.5 PDE with two space variables

We can not solve all PDEs in MATLAB because of the complicity of the problem. Some other PDE for example PDE with two space variables is addressed in the following.

12.5.1 Definition of a second order PDE on implementation context

A second order PDE with two independent or space variables which we can solve in MATLAB has the following definition assuming that the a, c, and d are constants for the time being. The dependent variable is $u(x,y)$ or u and the independent variables are x and y. The $u(x,y)$ can also be a function of another independent variable t or time. The MATLAB-defined PDEs (**note that** these definitions differ from the PDE text ones) are classified as follows:

Frequently the operator $\nabla = \overline{a}_x \frac{\partial}{\partial x} + \overline{a}_y \frac{\partial}{\partial y}$ in x - y domain of 2D geometry defines the PDEs as shown below where the $\overline{a}_x$ and $\overline{a}_y$ are the unit vectors towards the x and y directions respectively:

Elliptic PDE:

$-\nabla \circ (c\nabla u) + au = f$ is equivalent to $c\left(\frac{\partial^2 u}{\partial x^2} + \frac{\partial^2 u}{\partial y^2}\right) - au + f = 0$

Parabolic PDE:

$-\nabla \circ (c\nabla u) + au + d\frac{\partial u}{\partial t} = f$ is equivalent to $c\left(\frac{\partial^2 u}{\partial x^2} + \frac{\partial^2 u}{\partial y^2}\right) - au - d\frac{\partial u}{\partial t} + f = 0$

Hyperbolic PDE:

$-\nabla \circ (c\nabla u) + d\frac{\partial^2 u}{\partial t^2} + au = f$ is equivalent to $c\left(\frac{\partial^2 u}{\partial x^2} + \frac{\partial^2 u}{\partial y^2}\right) - au - d\frac{\partial^2 u}{\partial t^2} + f = 0$

Eigenmode PDE:

$-\nabla \circ (c\nabla u) + au = \lambda du$ is equivalent to $c\left(\frac{\partial^2 u}{\partial x^2} + \frac{\partial^2 u}{\partial y^2}\right) - au + \lambda du = 0$ where λ is another scalar (eigenvalue)

It goes without saying that above definitions make use of the basic vector products such as $\overline{a}_x \circ \overline{a}_y = 0$ and $\overline{a}_x \circ \overline{a}_x = 1$. Any given PDE is compared to above types and we determine to which form the given PDE belongs. Let us see the following examples:

Given PDE: $\frac{\partial^2 u}{\partial x^2}+\frac{\partial^2 u}{\partial y^2}=0$ or $\Delta u=0$ indicating elliptic with $c=1$, $a=0$, $f=0$

Given PDE: $\frac{\partial^2 u}{\partial x^2}+\frac{\partial^2 u}{\partial y^2}=6u-2\frac{\partial u}{\partial t}+7$ indicating parabolic with $c=1$, $a=6$, $d=-2$, $f=-7$

Given PDE: $-\frac{\partial^2 u}{\partial x^2}-\frac{\partial^2 u}{\partial y^2}+2u=6\frac{\partial^2 u}{\partial t^2}$ indicating hyperbolic with $c=1$, $a=2$, $d=-6$

From the vector calculus, we know that the operators ∇ and $\nabla\circ$ are called the gradient and divergence and are coded by the grad and div respectively in MATLAB. With this code and font equivalence like u⇔u, the elliptic PDE $-\nabla\circ(c\nabla u)+au=f$ becomes -div(c*grad(u))+a*u=f, which is the entering style of the PDE in MATLAB. Again the $\frac{\partial u}{\partial t}$ or u' and $\frac{\partial^2 u}{\partial t^2}$ or u'' are written as u' and u'' accordingly the parabolic, hyperbolic, and eigenmode PDEs have the MATLAB representations d*u'-div(c*grad(u))+a*u=f, d*u''-div(c*grad(u))+a*u=f, and a*u-div(c*grad(u))= lambda*d*u respectively (lambda⇔λ).

Having defined the PDEs, we see the MATLAB functions assempde, hyperbolic, parabolic, and pdeeig for just mentioned elliptic, hyperbolic, parabolic, and eigenmode PDE solving respectively. Each of the four functions (i.e. assempde, hyperbolic, parabolic, and pdeeig) has many syntaxes providing different options, we will exercise only the problem-specific one latter in this section. You can have command line help executing for example help hyperbolic for the hyperbolic one.

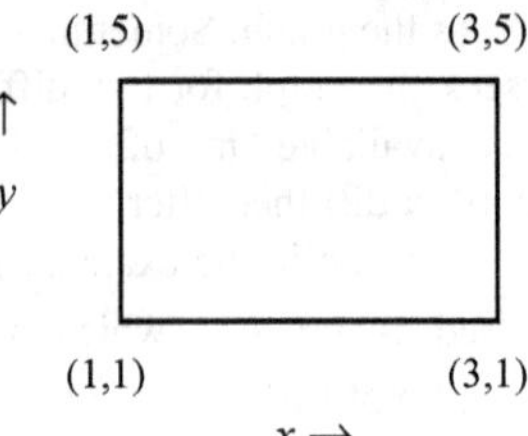

Figure 12.2(c) A closed rectangular domain

12.5.2 Domain description for the PDE solution

The PDE solution is achievable in two space variables (x and y) for any arbitrary closed domain in the x - y plane. There are embedded functions for describing a x - y domain in MATLAB. It is important to point out that the domain must be closed and its edges must be composed of regular curvature like straight line segment, circular arc, or elliptic arc. We present several examples on the domain description in the following.

♦♦ Example 1

The closed domain shown in the figure 12.2(c) is to be described. This is a rectangular domain which we describe using the function pderect with the syntax pderect([minimum x coordinate, maximum x coordinate, minimum y coordinate, maximum y coordinate], user-given domain name under quote). Therefore the domain is entered into MATLAB by writing pderect([1 3 1 5],'R') in which we named the domain as R. Mathematically the command also describes the region defined by $1\le x\le 3$ and $1\le y\le 5$.

♦♦ Example 2

The circular domain in the figure 12.2(d) has the equation $(x-1)^2+(y-1)^2\le 9$ which we describe using the function pdecirc with the syntax pdecirc(center x coordinate, center y coordinate, radius, user-given domain name under quote). The command we need to describe the domain of the figure 12.2(d) is pdecirc(1,1,3,'C') in which we named the circular domain as C.

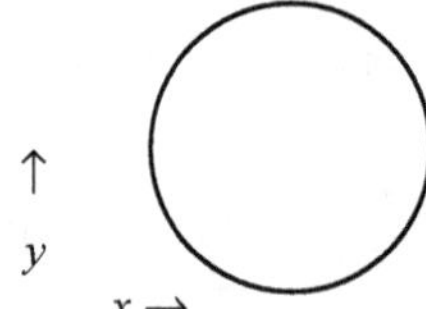

Figure 12.2(d) A circle with the center (1,1) and radius 3

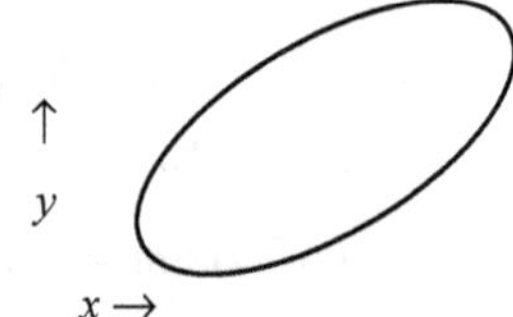

Figure 12.2(e) An ellipse with semi major axis 2, semi minor axis 1, center (2,2), and counterclockwise rotation 30^0

♦♦ Example 3

The function pdepoly with the syntax pdepoly(x coordinates as a row matrix in order, y coordinates as a row matrix in order, user-given domain name under quote) constructs any arbitrary polygon. For example figure 3.4(a) displayed polygon MNOPQ can be formed by writing the command pdepoly([5 8 12 12 15],[5 7 7 10 5],'P') where P is our given name to the polygon. Any triangular domain can also be formed by the pdepoly. The only point is polygonal edges must not intersect. For example figure 3.4(b) displayed ABCDE polygon can not be constructed by the pdepoly.

♦♦ Example 4

The function pdeellip defines an elliptical geometric domain with the syntax pdeellip(x coordinate of the ellipse center, y coordinate of the ellipse center, semi major axis, semi minor axis, counterclockwise rotational angle in radians, user-given domain name under quote). For example the command pdeellip(2,2,2,1,pi/6,'E') constructs the ellipse of the figure 12.2(e) in which the E is our given name to the ellipse.

◆◆ Example 5

Any connected region is also constructable. For example the figure 12.2(f) displayed hollow square indicated by the black region is to be defined. The hollow black area is basically the subtraction of two squares – the outer square minus the inner square. From the given specifications, the inner and the outer squares have the corner points $\left\{\begin{matrix}(-\frac{5}{2},-\frac{7}{2})\\(\frac{1}{2},-\frac{7}{2})\\(\frac{1}{2},-\frac{1}{2})\\(-\frac{5}{2},-\frac{1}{2})\end{matrix}\right\}$ and $\left\{\begin{matrix}(-\frac{7}{2},-\frac{9}{2})\\(\frac{3}{2},-\frac{9}{2})\\(\frac{3}{2},\frac{1}{2})\\(-\frac{7}{2},\frac{1}{2})\end{matrix}\right\}$ respectively. From example 1, the inner and outer squares are defined by the commands pderect([-5/2 1/2 -7/2 -1/2],'I') and pderect([-7/2 3/2 -9/2 1/2],'O') in which the I and O are our given names to the squares respectively. The figure 12.2(f) shown hollow area is formed by writing O-I in the formula bar of the PDE GUI which will be discussed latter.

Figure 12.2(f) A hollow square area with center (−1,−2) and inner side 3

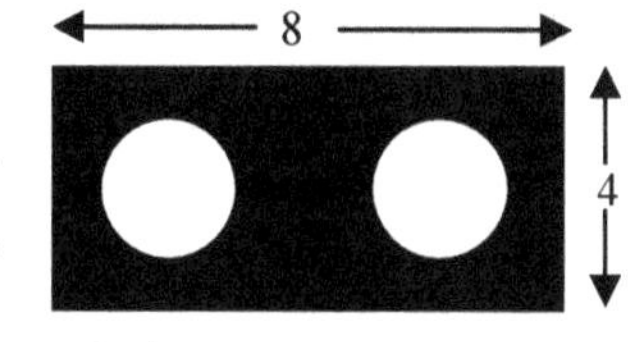

Figure 12.2(g) Two circular holes are made in a rectangular box. Each circle has a radius 1. The left and right circles have the centers at (2,2) and (6,2) respectively

◆◆ Example 6

Multiply connected region such as the black area of the figure 12.2(g) is to be constructed. Referring to the figure, the left and right circles have the codes pdecirc(2,2,1,'C1') and pdecirc(6,2,1,'C2') where C1 and C2 are our given names to the circles respectively (example 2 for circle). From the given dimensions, the outer rectangle in the figure 12.2(g) has the lower leftmost and upper rightmost corner coordinates as (0,0) and (8,4) respectively therefore requiring the code pderect([0 8 0 4],'R') where R is our given name to the rectangle, see example 1. The black area in the figure 12.2(g) is formed from the rectangular area minus the two circular areas therefore we write R-C1-C2 in the formula bar of the PDE GUI which will be discussed latter.

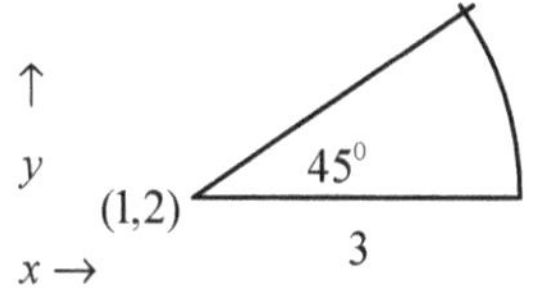

Figure 12.3(a) A circular sector

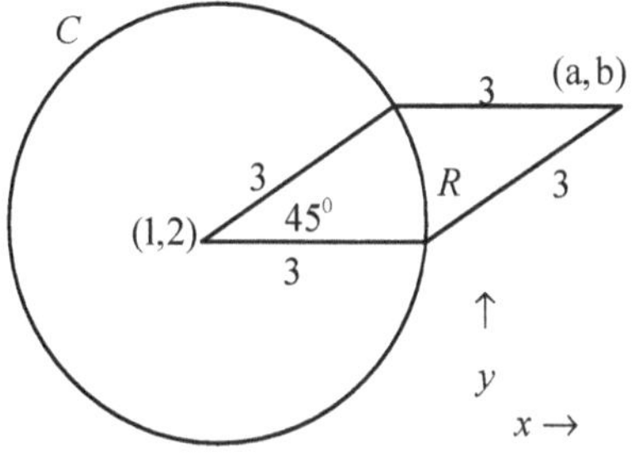

Figure 12.3(b) Circular sector from the product of circle and rhombus

◆◆ Example 7

In this example we wish to construct the circular sector of the figure 12.3(a). We can construct the sector from the product of the circle C and rhombus R as shown in the figure 12.3(b). With the given center and radius, the circle C is composed of using pdecirc(1,2,3,'C') (example 2 mentioned meanings). Our next effort is to find the four corner point coordinates of the rhombus R so that we can use previously cited pdepoly. The arc of the figure 12.3(a) has the end point coordinates (4,2) and $(1+3\cos45^0, 2+3\sin45^0)$. The mid point of the chord

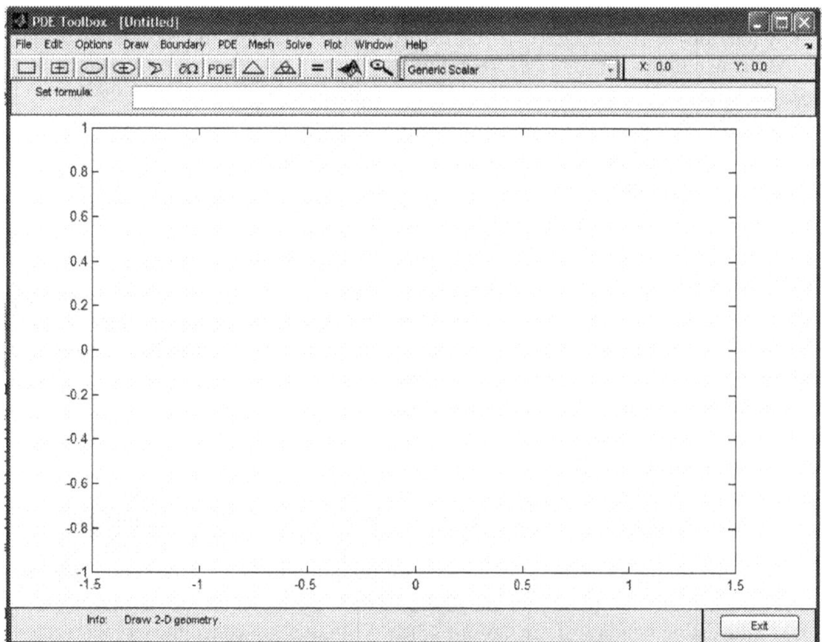

Figure 12.3(c) Firstly opened PDE toolbox graphical user interface (GUI)

related to the arc is ((5+3cos45^0)/2,(4+3sin45^0)/2). The rightmost corner point of the rhombus R is (a,b) (let us say). The midpoint between the circle center (1,2) and the rightmost corner (a,b) is also the midpoint of the chord thereby providing (a,b)=(4+3cos45^0,2+3sin45^0). In counterclockwise direction (which has to be) starting from the circle center, the four corner points of the rhombus are (1,2), (4,2), (4+3cos45^0,2+3sin45^0), and (1+3cos45^0,2+3sin45^0). Having all the corner points available, we are in a position to define the rhombus using pdepoly of example 3 hence the rhombic area is formed on writing pdepoly([1 4 4+3*cos(pi/4) 1+3*cos(pi/4)],[2 2 2+3*sin(pi/4) 2+3*sin(pi/4)],'R'), say the rhombic object is R. The required sector is composed of setting R*C in the formula bar (discussed latter).

We hope that these seven examples will help the reader construct any other closed domain in the x - y plane.

12.5.3 Graphical User Interface (GUI) for the PDE solving

The PDE graphical user interface (GUI) is a gateway between you and PDE toolbox of MATLAB. Figure 12.3(c) shows a firstly opened PDE toolbox GUI. There are scores of features in the PDE GUI. As we have been objective in the problem solving, we plan to concentrate only on the topics that are closed to the model example solving. One can solve PDE numerically writing the code and command line functions but the PDE GUI offers more convenience. Last subsection mentioned all x - y domains can be drawn using the mouse in the PDE GUI. But we do not recommend that you draw the domains using mouse because mouse pointer has some resolution and that may slight shift the corner coordinates of any drawn domain. Primarily we need to be familiar with four procedures – how to enter a PDE specification, how to enter boundary conditions of a given domain, how to enter the initial condition of the PDE, and how to obtain the PDE solution. We attempt to answer all these in the following. One can be efficient in solving a PDE if he employs both the command line functions and the GUI interactive parameters.

⇕⇕ How to reach to the PDE GUI?

There are two ways to reach to the PDE GUI, the first of which is to execute pdetool at the command prompt and the second of which is to follow the clicking sequence Start→Toolboxes→More→Partial Differential Equation → PDETool GUI. This Start is the MATLAB start not the window start. Figure 1.1(a) shows the Start of MATLAB at the lower leftmost corner in the window. Anyhow the figure 12.3(c) presents a firstly opened PDE GUI window.

⇕⇕ How to make the given domain appear in the PDE GUI?

This is the first step of any PDE solving. For instance we intend to bring the hollow square area of the example 5 (subsection 12.5.2) in the PDE GUI. Let us carry out the following at the command prompt:

>>pderect([-5/2 1/2 -7/2 -1/2],'I') ↵ ← Defining the inner square area of the figure 12.2(f), named as I

>>pderect([-7/2 3/2 -9/2 1/2],'O') ↵ ← Defining the outer square area of the figure 12.2(f), named as O

Due to above executions, the PDE GUI appears before you although you did not open the GUI. The GUI x and y axes variation directions also follow to those of the figure 12.2(f). Upper leftmost corner of the figure 12.3(c) holds the formula bar (by the name Set formula:) for designing multiply connected regions. You find I+O (appears automatically for the closed geometric domains present in the GUI) in the Set formula bar as we have given those names. The example 5 also mentions that the hollow area of the figure 12.2(f) is formed from O-I. Bring the mouse pointer over the bar and leftclick the mouse. Therefore we enter O-I deleting I+O using the keyboard in the Set formula bar. The PDE GUI has some default settings for the x and y axes that is why the hollow area of the figure 12.2(f) does not appear completely. The PDE GUI of the figure 12.3(c) contains the Menu Options in the Menu bar. Click Options from the menu bar and then click Axes Limits, the Axes Limit dialog window of the figure 12.3(d) appears. In that window, check Auto for both the X and Y axes range, click Apply, and then Close. You finished entering the figure 12.2(f) mentioned hollow square box in the PDE GUI. You can verify the dimensions of the hollow area by inspection whether they are all okay.

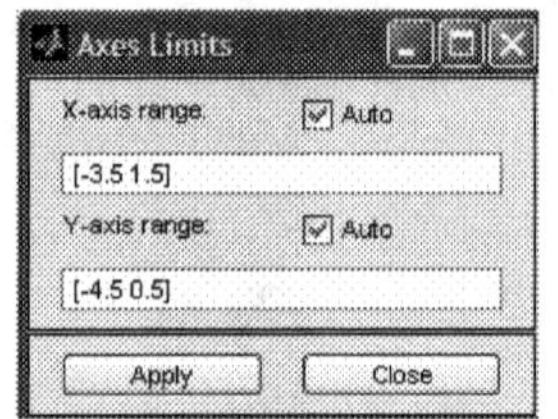

Figure 12.3(d) Axes Limits dialog window of the PDE GUI

At this point you do not see the hollow box, you just see one square is overlapping the other (for space reason we did not include it). The reason is the **PDE GUI is state or mode sensitive**. If you click Draw, Boundary, PDE, or Mesh from the menu bar of the figure 12.3(c), you find Draw Mode, Boundary Mode, PDE Mode, or Mesh Mode in the pull down menu. **Only one mode is activated at a time**. For example if you click Mesh Mode, only the mode will be activated and others are not in action or will not work.

As another example, let us bring the example 7 (last subsection) mentioned circular sector in the PDE GUI for which we execute the following:

>>pdecirc(1,2,3,'C') ↵ ← Defining the circular area of the figure 12.3(b), named as C

>>pdepoly([1 4 4+3*cos(pi/4) 1+3*cos(pi/4)],[2 2 2+3*sin(pi/4) 2+3*sin(pi/4)],'R') ← Defining the rhombus area of the figure 12.3(b), named as R

Go to the Set formula bar of the figure 12.3(c) and enter the formula R*C from the keyboard deleting the default formula in the Ser formula bar. Now click the Options from the menu bar of the PDE GUI, then click the Axes Limits, and set Auto in the dialog window of the figure 12.3(d). With this, we ended the circular sector design in the PDE GUI.

We do not recommend that you play with the mouse pointer over the area you designed. Because for some action if the constructed area is slightly shifted, your PDE solution will not be accurate.

❖❖ How to enter a PDE specification?

In subsection 12.5.1 we defined various PDEs on the implementation context. A PDE specification is nothing but the parameter values (a, c, d, and f – for the time being we assumed them to be constants but they can be functional expressions as well) as defined. In order to enter the PDE specification, there are two options – through the command line functions and through the PDE GUI of the figure 12.3(c). In the same subsection we illustrated that the functions **assempde**, **hyperbolic**, **parabolic**, and **pdeeig** solve different PDEs and just mentioned equation parameters (i.e. a, c, d, and f) appear as the input arguments to these functions (will be discussed latter – this is the command line entering). For the PDE GUI entering, we click the PDE down PDE Specification from the menu bar or the PDE icon in the icon bar of the figure 12.3(c). Either action brings the dialog window of the figure 12.3(e) in which you find all PDE types of subsection 12.5.1 alongside the parameter entering option. Here in this window we enter the values for a, c, d, and f (for example 2 to the slot for a in the figure 12.3(e) when a =2).

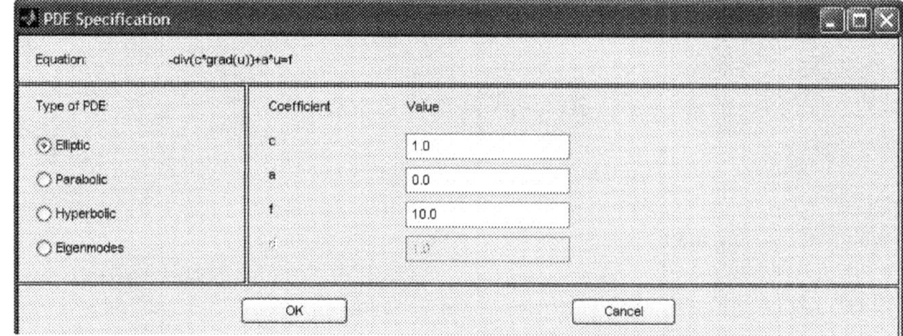

Figure 12.3(e) PDE parameter specification window

❖❖ How to enter the boundary conditions?

The best way to enter the boundary condition is through the PDE GUI. We know that there are two boundary conditions associated with a PDE: namely Dirichlet condition – related to the dependent variable u and Neumann condition – related to the normal derivative on the boundary $\frac{\partial u}{\partial n}$. MATLAB has its own way of describing these two boundary conditions.

For the Dirichlet condition, the general form is $hu = r$ on the boundary $\partial\Omega$ or h*u=r in MATLAB code form. We enter only the coefficients h and r comparing any given value of $u(x, y)$. For example $u(x, y) = 5$ at some boundary is entered as setting h =1 and r =5. As another example of the condition, $4u(x, y) = x$ is written as setting h =4 and $r = x$.

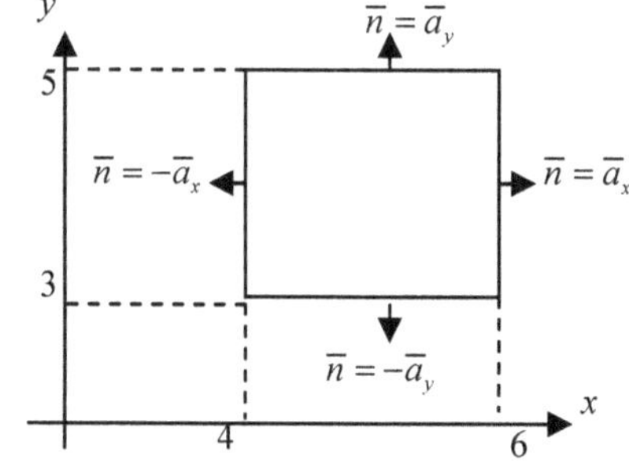

Figure 12.3(f) The perpendicularly outward unit normal $\bar{n}$ in the four sides of a rectangular domain

For the Neumann condition, the general form is $\bar{n} \circ (c\nabla u) + qu = g$ on the boundary $\partial\Omega$ or n*(c*grad(u))+q*u=g in MATLAB code form. The $\bar{n}$, c, ∇u, and u are the formal terms of the PDE and we do not access these terms. These terms are just for the sake of the definition. We only look for q and g on any given boundary $\partial\Omega$. Examples are the best in getting the insight of any ideas. Let us concentrate on the rectangular domain of the figure 12.3(f) which we write as $4 \le x \le 6$ and $3 \le y \le 5$. The right boundary $\partial\Omega$ has the equation x =6 and $\bar{n} = \bar{a}_x$ where $\bar{a}_x$ and $\bar{a}_y$ are the unit vectors towards the x and y directions respectively. The expression $\bar{n} \circ (c\nabla u) + qu = g$ for the right boundary becomes $\bar{a}_x \circ c\left(\bar{a}_x \frac{\partial u}{\partial x} + \bar{a}_y \frac{\partial u}{\partial y}\right) + qu = g$ or $c\frac{\partial u}{\partial x} + qu = g$ applying the dot product of vectors. Suppose the Neumann condition is given as $\frac{\partial u}{\partial n} = 2$ that means c =1, q =0, and g =2 on comparison of the coefficients. For the right boundary of coarse we have $\frac{\partial u}{\partial n} = \frac{\partial u}{\partial x}$. As another example, the Neumann condition $\frac{\partial u}{\partial n} = -\cos y$ indicating c =1, q =0, and $g = -\cos y$. Unless there is some u value in conjunction with the $\frac{\partial u}{\partial n}$ given, the q is always 0. For the top boundary of

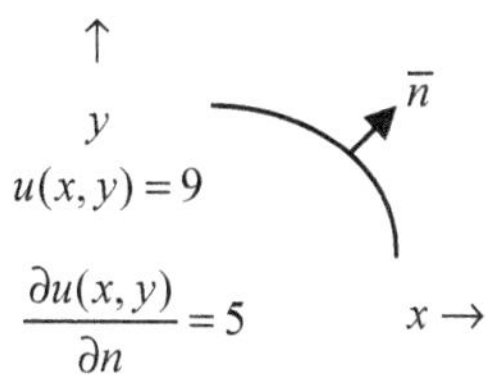

Figure 12.4(a) Two boundary conditions in a circular arc

the rectangle domain in the figure 12.3(f), we have $\frac{\partial u}{\partial n}=\frac{\partial u}{\partial y}$ and the $\partial\Omega$ has the equation y=5. If we have other boundary than straight line like circular arc, the $\bar{n}$ holds both the $\bar{a}_x$ and $\bar{a}_y$ components yet we only look for the q and g not the component. Because the term $\bar{n}\circ(c\nabla u)$ is arc or boundary $\partial\Omega$ adaptive.

Let us say the circular arc (that is our $\partial\Omega$ now) of the figure 12.4(a) holds the attached Dirichlet and Neumann conditions. From ongoing discussions, we discover that h=1, r=9, q=0, and g=5 – that is what we need to enter into MATLAB for the $\partial\Omega$. Also note that for every $\partial\Omega$ in any given domain, we must have these two conditions provided or in other words the values of { h , r , q , g } need to be known for every given boundary.

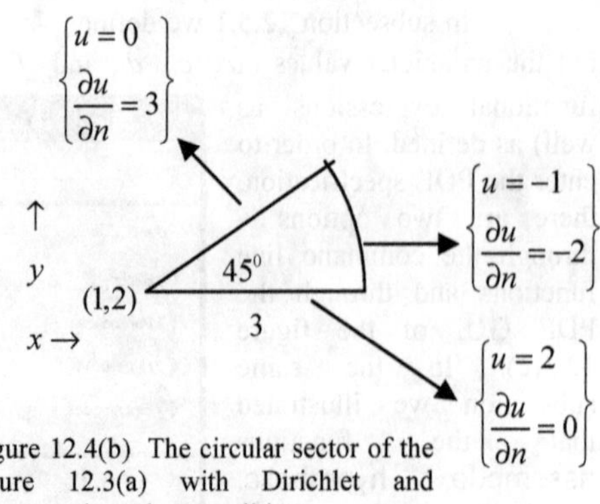

Figure 12.4(b) The circular sector of the figure 12.3(a) with Dirichlet and Neumann boundary conditions

As a consequential query, where should we enter the values of { h , r , q , g }? The first step is to select some domain. Let us consider the 45 degree circular sector of the figure 12.3(a). There are three boundaries and each one's Dirichlet and Neumann boundary conditions are shown using the arrow indication in the figure 12.4(b). From the given values, we write the following; for the horizontal boundary line: { h=1, r=2, q=0, g=0}, for the circular boundary arc: { h=1, r=–1, q=0, g=–2}, and for the inclined boundary line: { h=1, r=0, q=0, g=3}. We intend to enter these boundary conditions into MATLAB.

Earlier in this subsection we cited how one brings the circular sector after setting the **R*C** in the **Set formula** bar and **Auto Axes** Scaling through the **Options** menu in the PDE GUI. Let us not forget that the PDE GUI functions one at a time. That is in order to enter the boundary conditions, the PDE GUI must be set for the boundary mode. Referring to the figure 12.3(c), we find the icon for the symbol $\partial\Omega$ in the icon bar which is right below the menu bar. If you click the $\partial\Omega$ icon, the boundary mode of the PDE GUI becomes activated. Another option is click **Boundary** in the menu bar then **Boundary mode**.

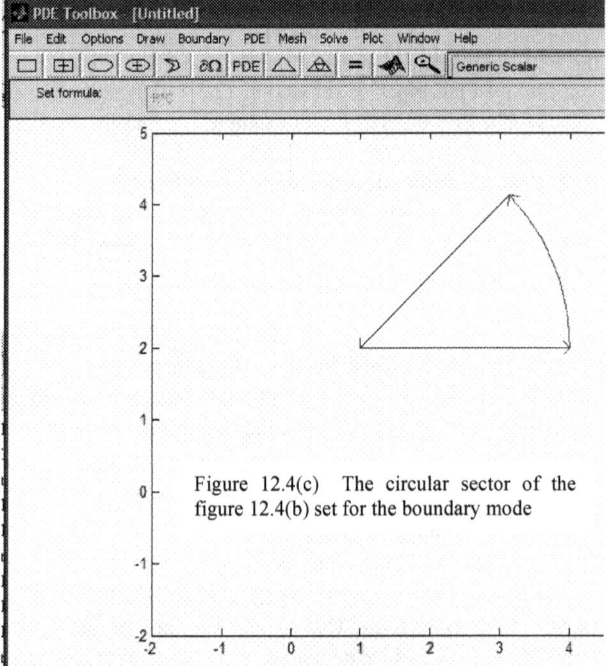

Figure 12.4(c) The circular sector of the figure 12.4(b) set for the boundary mode

However we see the circular sector boundaries as shown in the figure 12.4(c). You can check from the coordinates whether the sector is drawn properly because previously we only set the formula but did not see the drawn sector. Also from the **Options** menu, you can click the **Grid** to see the grid lines for better perception. Bring mouse pointer on any boundary of the sector in the figure 12.4(c), leftclick the mouse (it becomes selected), and doubleclick the mouse. In doing so, the dialog window of the figure 12.4(d) appears for the boundary. We enter the two boundary conditions here in the dialog window but one at a time. For every boundary segment, the **Boundary Condition** dialog window

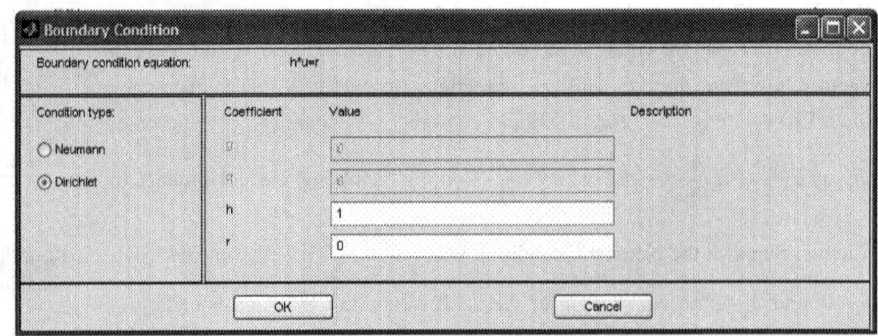

Figure 12.4(d) Dialog window for entering boundary conditions

appears. The **h** of the dialog window corresponds to our h, so does others. As an example, we type 1 and 2 in the slots of the **h** and **r** of the figure 12.4(d) respectively for the horizontal boundary line of the sector and for the Dirichlet condition (default one, Neumann one is deactivated). After that we check the **Neumann Condition** in the **Condition type** of the figure 12.4(d). Since the default values of q and g are 0, there is no need to type anything for the horizontal boundary line of the sector. Thus the other two boundary conditions of the sector can be entered through the **Boundary Condition** dialog window.

The boundary conditions so entered for the sector of figure 12.4(c) are in the PDE GUI. They need to be exported to MATLAB if we intend to work on those in MATLAB. In the pulldown menu of the **Boundary** menu in the PDE GUI, we find the option **Export Decomposed Geometry, Boundary Cond's**. If we click the option, the prompt window of the figure 12.4(e) appears. In the prompt window we see two variable names (reserve variable names) – **g** and **b**. The **g** and **b** hold the complete geometry and boundary condition information (in MATLAB term) for the whole sector of the figure 12.4(c). Click OK in the prompt window of figure 12.4(e) and check at the workspace browser (figure 1.2(d)). You must see the variables **g** and **b** in the workspace browser meaning that they are ready for MATLAB processing.

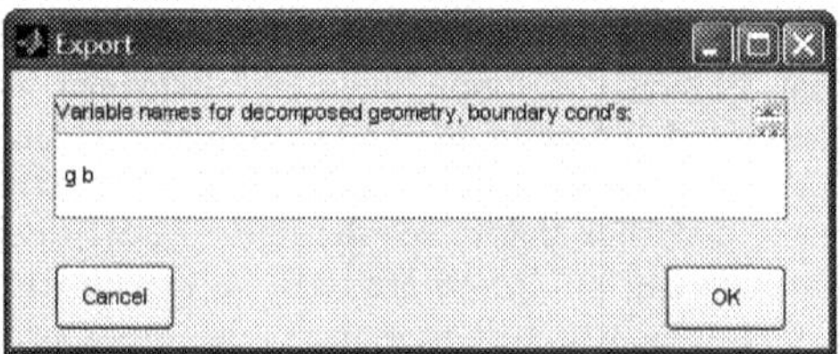

Figure 12.4(e) The dialog window for exporting the boundary conditions

⬥⬥ The basics of the numerical PDE solution

Before we discourse the initial conditions, it is extremely important to mention that the numerical solution conducted in the PDE toolbox is Finite Element Method (FEM) based. There is another method called the Finite Difference (FD) which is used for most numerical computations. The FD and FEM calculating molecules are rectangular and triangular as shown in the figures 12.5(a) and 12.5(b) respectively. The PDE GUI looks for the best triangular mesh representation for any given domain of a PDE solution. Obviously there is some theory behind the triangular molecularization which is beyond the scope of the text. Yet if we intend to obtain the numerical solution of a PDE using the FEM method, we can not bypass their discussions because FEM molecular parameters are involved in the numerical solution finding. Figure 12.5(c) shows the triangular molecularization concept underlying in the PDE solution finding process. Any given domain is decomposed as the three matrices namely point matrix **p**, edge matrix **e**, and triangle matrix **t**. The matrix names **{p,e,t}** are reserved and called the **mesh parameters**.

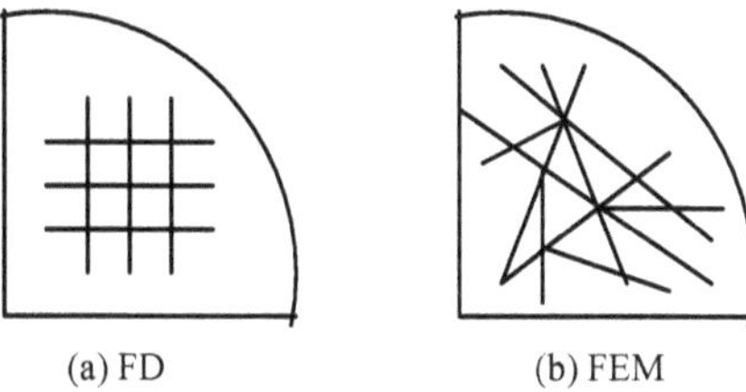

(a) FD (b) FEM

Figure 12.5(a)-(b) Molecules for the calculation based on FD and FEM methods

These three matrices are related with the boundary and initial conditions. Recall that the functions **assempde**, **hyperbolic**, **parabolic**, or **pdeeig** (subsection 12.5.1) finds the numerical solution of a given PDE to which we pass the information about the **{p,e,t}** as the input arguments.

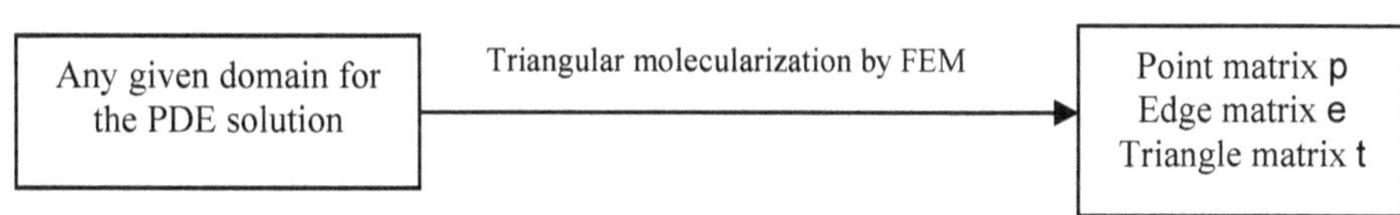

Figure 12.5(c) Triangular molecularization of any given domain to three matrices by the PDE GUI

So now it is essential that we have to have the mesh parameters **{p,e,t}** for any given domain from the PDE GUI. Considering the circular sector of the figure 12.4(c) (we elaborately explained before how to get the sector and make

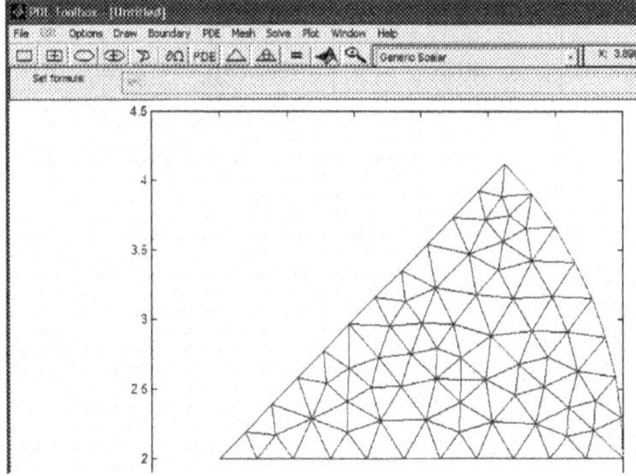

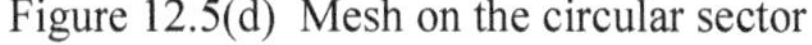

Figure 12.5(d) Mesh on the circular sector

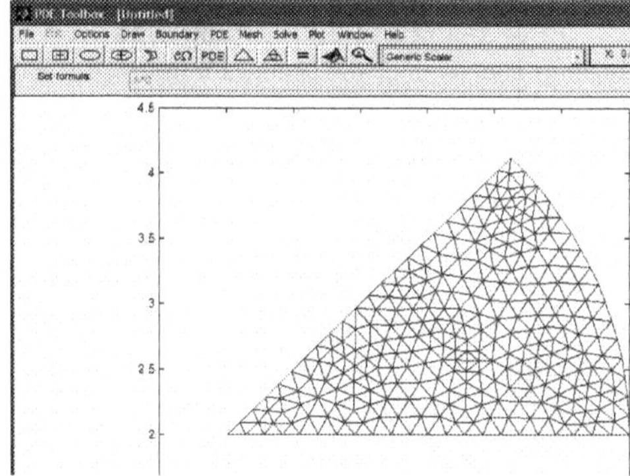

Figure 12.5(e) Refine mesh on the circular sector

it appear like the figure), we intend to get the mesh parameters {p,e,t} of the sector from the PDE GUI in MATLAB.

Once again the PDE GUI becomes activated for one action. In figure 12.3(c) we find one menu called **Mesh** down **Mesh mode** and click the **Mesh mode**. Another option is in the icon bar, we find the icon Δ for the **Mesh mode**. Either way we see the figure 12.5(d) with the mesh formed on the sector. Note that the mesh so formed holds the triangular molecules as we mentioned before in the FEM discussion. Again in the **Mesh** menu of the PDE GUI, we find the **Export Mesh** in the pulldown menu and click that to see the figure 12.5(f) indicating that the mesh parameters {p,e,t} are ready to export. Click OK and this action tells you that you made the mesh parameters {p,e,t} available from PDE GUI to MATLAB. Look at the workspace browser (figure 1.2(d)) and you must see the matrix information (for p, e, and t) there. It indicates that the mesh parameters are ready for MATLAB manipulation.

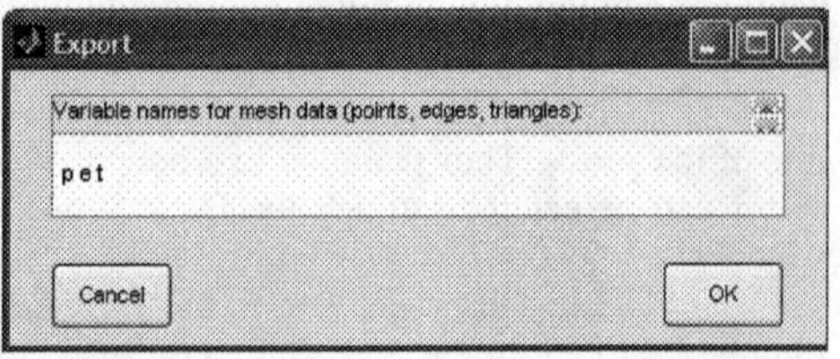

Figure 12.5(f) Mesh parameters {p,e,t} in Mesh export dialog window

At this point better accuracy is achieved in the numerical solution if we reduce the size of the triangle molecule for the FEM analysis – this operation is termed as the mesh refining. The PDE GUI keeps the provision for the mesh refining as well. There are two options in the mesh refining – either click **Mesh** down **Refine Mesh** from the menu bar of the PDE GUI or click the refine mesh icon (figure 12.5(g) shows the icon outlook for mesh refining) in the icon bar of the PDE GUI.

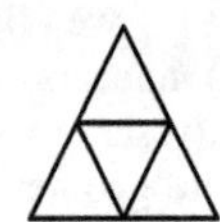

Figure 12.5(g) Icon outlook for the mesh refining

For example, clicking the refine mesh icon once for the ongoing circular sector displays the figure 12.5(e). Do not click the refine mesh icon again and again because over refining may give wrong solution. In most cases refining the domain once or twice is enough. You can also go back to the initial mesh clicking the mesh icon Δ in the icon bar after the refining has been conducted. These all are user-chosen actions. Of coarse with the mesh refining, the matrix size of the mesh parameters {p,e,t} will increase.

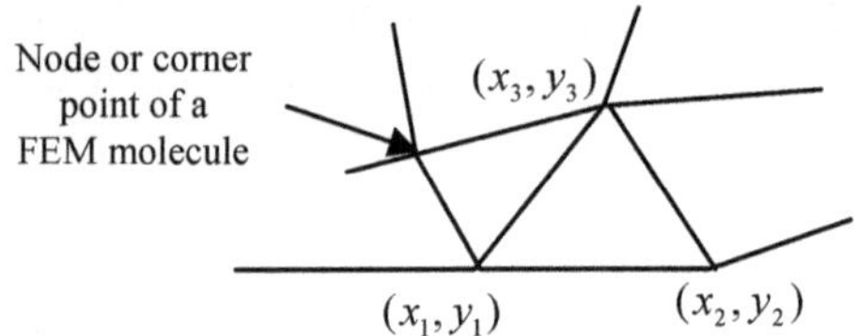

Figure 12.6(a) Three corner coordinates of a triangle molecule within the decomposed domain

❖❖ How to enter initial conditions?

The initial condition means the condition at $t = t_0$ or in other words the value of the dependent variable $u(x, y)$ at $t = t_0$. This is important if a PDE has time or t dependency for example the parabolic one of the subsection 12.5.1. It needs to be stressed that this is the value of $u(x, y)$ for every x and y within the given domain. Just now we finished the discussion of the mesh parameters {p,e,t}. The p as mentioned is the point matrix followed by the FEM triangular molecularization. Well for different geometry or closed domain, we have different p. The p is geometry-based. But one thing is sure that it is a two row matrix indicating all possible nodes or corner coordinates of the FEM triangularized molecules of the given domain. The first and second rows of the p hold corner x and y coordinates in order (or node coordinates) for all molecule triangles (of coarse after mesh decomposition of the given domain) respectively. The number of columns in the p is the number of nodes or corners in the FEM moleularized structure. For example the figure 12.6(a) shows one molecule nodes in some decomposed structure, it should occupy in the p as $\begin{bmatrix} .... & x_1 & x_2 & x_3......... \\ .... & y_1 & y_2 & y_3......... \end{bmatrix}$.

In order to feed the initial condition, we need to access the elements in p. Suppose there are M columns in the p. Any (x , y) coordinates for a single corner in the decomposed domain (or node coordinates) can be reached sequentially through a for-loop (subsection 14.3.3) as follows:

```
>>for k=1:M x=p(1,k); y=(2,k); end
```

The for-loop counter index k changes integerwise from 1 to M. Any x and y coordinates in the p are picked up by x=p(1,k); and y=(2,k); respectively. If we intend to select all x coordinates as a row matrix, we apply the command p(1,:) (section 2.6). Similarly the command p(2,:) picks up all y coordinates of the triangle molecules from p as a row matrix.

The initial condition which is to be entered for the solution must be consistent with the p elements and it is entered as a column matrix. Let us say the column matrix ICu (can be any user-given name) will hold all $u(x, y)$ values at the nodes in the given structure at $t = t_0$ which requires to maintain the following:

ICu(1) is the value of $u(x, y)$ at the first node or in the first column elements in p where x =p(1,1) and y =p(2,1),

ICu(2) is the value of $u(x, y)$ at the second node or in the second column elements in p where x =p(1,2) and y =p(2,2),

ICu(3) is the value of $u(x,y)$ at the third node or in the third column elements in p where x =p(1,3) and y =p(2,3),

and so on until all columns of p are finished.

The same entering style also follows for the $\frac{\partial u(x,y)}{\partial t}$.

Now we intend to set some examples on the initial conditions in the following:

Example 1:

We intend to enter the initial condition $u(x,y)$ =2 for every node (x , y) in some domain at t =0. If we carry out the size of section 2.12 on the point matrix p, we find its matrix size. The execution of [R,C]=size(p); returns R=2 (because p has 2 rows, previously mentioned) and the number of columns (or nodes in the decomposed structure) to C. Whatever be the actual value of (x , y) in p, at which the $u(x,y)$ should be 2 that means a column matrix of 2's where the number of elements will be C and we do so as follows:

>>ICu=2*ones(C,1); ↵ ← Section 2.14 for constant generation, ICu holds $u(x,y)$ =2 for every (x , y) as a column matrix at t =0, where ICu is user-chosen

Example 2:

Enter the initial condition $u(x,y)=\sin x \cos y$ for every node (x , y) in some domain at t =1. Now the $u(x,y)$ has some definitive functional relationship. Under this type of initial condition, we write the scalar code (section 14.2) of the given function but on all (x , y) in the point matrix p. You could ask why did not we write it for the example 1? The answer is any change in (x , y) does not affect value of $u(x,y)$ in the example 1. However let us carry out the following:

>>x=p(1,:); y=p(2,:); ↵ ← All x and y coordinates in p are assigned to x and y respectively where x and y are identical size row matrices

>>ICu=sin(x).*sin(y); ↵ ← Scalar code of $\sin x \cos y$ is assigned to ICu which is also a row matrix

>>ICu=ICu'; ↵ ← The ICu is turned to a column matrix from row one for input argument reason

The ICu holds $u(x,y)=\sin x \cos y$ values for every (x , y) in the p as a column matrix at t =1 where ICu is user-chosen name.

Example 3:

Referring to the circular domain of the figure 12.2(d), the upper right quarter sector of the circle has $u(x,y)$ =2 (as shown by the black zone in the figure 12.6(b)) but the other three quarters have $u(x,y)$ =0 at t =0. We intend to program this initial condition.

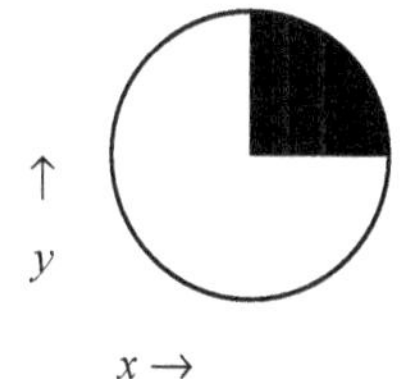

Figure 12.6(b) One quarter of the circle in figure 12.2(d) has constant value 2 at t =0

Here the first step is how to identify the upper right sector starting from the (x , y) coordinates in the circular domain. One way is to check the values of x and y for every (x , y) located in the p. From the given circle specification, the x and y must lie within $1 \le x \le 4$ and $1 \le y \le 4$ for the black sector of the figure 12.6(b). We first find the number of points in p using the size as done in the example 1 (same symbol meanings):

>>[R,C]=size(p); ↵ ← R=2 and C is the number of points in the p or in the whole circle

We then form the initial condition column matrix ICu as all zeroes (this makes $u(x,y)$ =0 for all (x , y) sets in the p) in which the number of zeroes is C and select all x and all y coordinates from p as follows:

>>ICu=zeros(C,1); ↵ ← Section 2.14 for zeros

>>x=p(1,:); y=p(2,:); ↵ ← All x and y coordinates in p are assigned to x and y respectively where x and y are identical size row matrices

After that we form a logical expression (subsection 14.3.1) fulfilling both $1 \le x \le 4$ and $1 \le y \le 4$ intervals for the black sector of the figure 12.6(b) as follows:

>>z=(1<=x)&(x<=4)&(1<=y)&(y<=4); ↵ ← z is any user-given name

The z so obtained is a row matrix of 1s and 0s whose element number is C. In this z, only the 1s correspond to the black sector of the figure 12.6(b) whose integer position index we find employing the find function of section 2.13 in the following. But the fact is the return from find will be a row matrix because the z is a row one (let us assign the return from find to I):

>>I=find(z==1); I=I'; ↵ ← We transposed the integer indexes held in I using I=I'; because ICu is a column matrix

>>ICu(I)=2; ↵ ← Now we set the value 2 to ICu only the integer indexes stored in I making $u(x,y)$ =2 in the black sector

At last the ICu holds the $u(x,y)$ for the whole circle at t =0.

Example 4:

Referring to the example 3, everything is same but $u(x,y)=x^2-y^2$ in the black sector and $u(x,y)=\cos(x+y)$ in the other three quarter sector of the circle at t=0. This initial condition also needs to be programmed.

All execution up to the finding of **z** in the example 3 is due. Now the 1s and 0s in the **z** correspond to $u(x,y)=x^2-y^2$ and $u(x,y)=\cos(x+y)$ respectively. In the case of definitive function, we write the scalar code. Having known that, let us carry out the following:

>>I=find(z==1); V1=x(I).^2-y(I).^2; ICu(I)=V1'; ↵ ← Making $u(x,y)=x^2-y^2$

>>I=find(z==0); V1=cos(x(I)+y(I)); ICu(I)=V1'; ↵ ← Making $u(x,y)=\cos(x+y)$

The x(I) means only the elements in x which are position indexed by the integers stored in the I, so does the y(I). The V1 is any user-given name. The scalar code of x^2-y^2 is x.^2-y.^2 but we need to be index-specific that is why x(I).^2-y(I).^2 is applied in the above execution. The V1 in the above first line holds the values of x^2-y^2 as a row matrix in the beginning. Since the V1 is a row matrix and ICu has to be column one, we transposed the V1 writing V1' during the assigning process. However at the end, the ICu keeps proper $u(x,y)$ for the whole circle at t =0.

Example 5:

In the last four examples, we focused only on $u(x,y)$ initial conditions. The same code writing style follows for the initial condition of the $\frac{\partial u(x,y)}{\partial t}$. For example $\frac{\partial u(x,y)}{\partial t}=x^2-y^2$ in the black sector and $\frac{\partial u(x,y)}{\partial t}=\cos(x+y)$ in the non-black sector of the figure 12.6(b) at t =0 have the example 4 mentioned codes but the variable ICu now corresponds to $\frac{\partial u(x,y)}{\partial t}$ not $u(x,y)$.

12.5.4 Model examples on two space variable PDE

In this subsection we intend to solve various PDEs applying the tools and commands mentioned in the last three subsections. Solving a PDE is nothing but obtaining the value of $u(x,y)$ over the given domain subject to the given boundary and initial conditions. We employ the following steps in order to solve a PDE numerically using the FEM method.

Steps to be observed in solving a PDE:

⇒ Define the domain using the command line functions such as pdepoly, pdecirc, etc

⇒ Make the domain appear in the PDE GUI with proper axes setting

⇒ Set the boundary conditions {h,r,q,g} for every segment or edge of the given closed domain concentrating on the given specification but one at a time

⇒ Export the boundary condition information from PDE GUI to MATLAB for the whole given domain through the workspace variable b

⇒ Triangular molecularize the given domain using the mesh or refine mesh icon and export the mesh parameters {p,e,t} from PDE GUI to MATLAB

⇒ Identify the PDE type in accordance with the subsection 12.5.1 and call the appropriate function for solution

We suggest that you do not play with the mouse to any other icon or actions in the PDE GUI while you are in the process of finding a PDE solution. If you do so, it may corrupt the solution. Only click the icon or perform the action which is absolutely necessary for the solution finding. However let us go through the following model examples.

◆◆ Example 1

Laplace equation is the first example of any two space variable PDE. We intend to solve the Laplace equation $\frac{\partial^2 u}{\partial x^2}+\frac{\partial^2 u}{\partial y^2}=0$ or $\Delta u=0$ over the domain defined by $1\le x\le 3$ and $1\le y\le 5$ subject to the boundary conditions $u(1,y)=u(3,y)=u(x,1)=0$ and $u(x,5)=10$.

The given domain is basically the rectangular domain of the example 1 in subsection 12.5.2. Figure 12.2(c) shows the plot of the rectangle defined by $1\le x\le 3$ and $1\le y\le 5$. As a first step, we enter the domain executing the following at the command prompt:

>>pderect([1 3 1 5],'R') ↵ ← We named the rectangle R, click Options menu and set the Axes limits to Auto

We see the domain in the PDE GUI. In this rectangle and from the given boundary conditions, each of the left, bottom, and right sides of the domain has $u(x,y)$=0 meaning { h =1, r =0, q =0, g =0} for each boundary. Click the boundary icon ∂Ω, doubleclick the left, bottom, and right sides of the domain one at a time, and make sure that these values are set accordingly (fortunately these are the default values). The top side has $u(x,y)$=10 meaning { h=1, r=10, q=0, g=0}. Doubleclick the top side and enter the value of r in the prompt window (others are default). We are done with the boundary condition entering. From the **Boundary** menu, click the **Export Decomposed Geometry, Boundary Cond's** in the pulldown menu and click okay in the prompt window so the **b** holds all boundary information in MATLAB. Click mesh icon Δ once, click refine mesh icon (figure 12.5(g)) twice, click the **Mesh** menu, click the **Export mesh** in the pulldown menu, and click okay in the prompt window. Thus we made the mesh parameters **{p,e,t}** available in MATLAB. Subsection 12.5.1 says that the given Laplace equation fits to the elliptic one with c=1, a=0, f=0. The function **assempde** solves the elliptic equation with the syntax **assempde**(boundary information **b**, mesh point matrix **p**, mesh edge matrix **e**, mesh triangle matrix **t**, given equation coefficient c, given equation coefficient a, given equation coefficient f). We are just one click away from the solution because all parameters are in the workspace now and let us carry out that:

>>u=assempde(b,p,e,t,1,0,0); ↵ ← The **u** can be any name of your choice excluding workspace variables

Consequently we found our expected solution for the $u(x,y)$ numerically from the Laplace equation using the FEM method over the given domain and which is stored in the workspace variable **u**.

♦♦ Example 2

In the example 1 everything is same except the PDE is now a Poisson's equation $\frac{\partial^2 u}{\partial x^2}+\frac{\partial^2 u}{\partial y^2}=-3$. This equation is also an elliptic one with f=3. The functional calling is going to be **u=assempde(b,p,e,t,1,0,3);**.

♦♦ Example 3

We intend to solve the right attached PDE numerically using the finite element method (FEM) over the t variation $0 \le t \le 1$ with a t step 0.2.

$u_t = 2(u_{xx}+u_{yy})$ for $0<x<\pi$, $0<y<\pi$, and $t>0$

$u(x,0,t)=u(x,\pi,t)=1$ for $0 \le x \le \pi$, $t \ge 0$

$u_x(0,y,t)=u_x(\pi,y,t)=-1$ for $0 \le y \le \pi$, $t \ge 0$

$u(x,y,0)=2xy(\pi-y)\cos x$ for $0<x<\pi$ and $0<y<\pi$

The given domain of the equation (in the first line) says that this is a rectangular domain like the figure 12.2(c) in which the four corner coordinates are (0,0), (π,0), (π,π), and (0,π) on that we execute the following:

>>pderect([0 pi 0 pi],'R'); ↵ ← Subsection 12.5.2 mentioned meanings, from **Options** menu of GUI set the **Auto Axes** scaling to make the domain appear

The $u(x,0,t)=u(x,\pi,t)=1$ indicates the top and bottom sides of the rectangle and there is no Neumann condition (i.e. q=0 and g=0 for both sides). The value 1 is the Dirichlet condition therefore h=1 and r=1 for both the top and bottom sides. The condition $u_x(0,y,t)=u_x(\pi,y,t)=-1$ or $\frac{\partial u(0,y,t)}{\partial x}=\frac{\partial u(\pi,y,t)}{\partial x}=-1$ implies the left and right sides of the rectangle and these are the Neumann condition only (see the boundary condition discussion) with the absence of Dirichlet condition (meaning h=1 and r=0 for both the left and right sides). In the Neumann condition, we have { q=0, g=−1} for both the left and right sides of the rectangle. Anyhow we gathered all boundary conditions in the figure 12.6(c) in the PDE GUI term. Now click the boundary icon ∂Ω, set the figure 12.6(c) displayed constants doubleclicking each side but one at a time as done before, and export the boundary information **b** through **Boundary → Export Decomposed Geometry, Boundary Cond's**. Then click the mesh icon Δ once and refine mesh icon once (user-selected), click the **Mesh** menu, and export the mesh parameters **{p,e,t}**. The given PDE $u_t = 2(u_{xx}+u_{yy})$ when compared to subsection 12.5.1 mentioned equations reveals that the match is the parabolic one with c=2, d=1, a=0, f=0. The next concentration is the initial condition $u(x,y,0)=2xy(\pi-y)\cos x$. The required t can be generated by writing **T=[0:0.2:1]**; where **T** is any user-given name. Just not to be mixed up with the mesh triangle matrix **t**, we used **T**. For the initial condition we need to pick up the x and y coordinates of FEM molecule nodes, which happens through **x=p(1,:)'; y=p(2,:)';** as discussed before (we included the transpose operator ' to turn the row matrix to column one because the initial condition input argument needs a column one). From the given specification, the function $2xy(\pi-y)\cos x$ holds true for the whole rectangular domain and the scalar code of the function which is **2*x.*y.*(pi-y).*cos(x)** calculates that. Subsection 12.5.1 cites only the PDE solver name (which is **parabolic**). Until now we did not mention the syntax. The **parabolic** has a syntax **parabolic**(initial

h=1, r=1, q=0, g=0

(0, π) (π,π)

h=1, r=0, q=0, g=−1

h=1, r=0, q=0, g=−1

(0,0) (π,0)

h=1, r=1, q=0, g=0

Figure 12.6(c) The PDE boundary condition in GUI term for the example 3 condition $u(x,y,0)$ as a column matrix, user-required time vector as a row matrix, boundary information **b**, mesh point matrix **p**, mesh edge matrix **e**, mesh triangle matrix **t**, PDE coefficient c, PDE coefficient a, PDE coefficient f, PDE coefficient d). Having known all, we execute the following at the command prompt:

>>T=[0:0.2:1]; x=p(1,:)'; y=p(2,:)'; ↵ ← T holds t vector, x and y all FEM molecule (x, y) coordinates

>>ICu=2*x.*y.*(pi-y).*cos(x); ↵ ← The scalar code of $2xy(\pi - y)\cos x$ is assigned to ICu, ICu⇔ $u(x,y,0)$

>>u=parabolic(ICu,T,b,p,e,t,2,0,0,1); ↵ ← Calling the **parabolic** with the mentioned syntax

Eventually our expected PDE numerical solution is returned to the workspace **u** (can be any name of your choice) which holds $u(x,y,t)$ values on the chosen mesh triangular molecule and t points.

❖❖ Example 4

The wave equation $0.2\frac{\partial^2 u}{\partial t^2} = \frac{\partial^2 u}{\partial x^2} + \frac{\partial^2 u}{\partial y^2}$ needs to be solved using the FEM method over $x^2 + y^2 < 4$ subject to $u(x,y,t)$ =0.2 on the $x^2 + y^2 = 4$. The equation also includes the conditions $u(x,y,1) = \cos x$ and $\left.\frac{\partial u(x,y,t)}{\partial t}\right|_{t=1} = \sin 2ye^{\cos x}$ over $x^2 + y^2 < 4$. The t variation for the solution should be from 1 to 2 with a step 0.2.

The domain described by $x^2 + y^2 < 4$ is a circle with center (0,0) and radius 2. Applying the subsection 12.5.2 addressed function and symbology, we carry out the following at the command prompt:

>>pdecirc(0,0,2,'C') ↵ ← Named the circle as C, click **Options** menu and set the **Axes limits** to **Auto**

This action shows you the circular domain. But with the **Auto** scaling, the minimum and maximum of x or y coordinates are considered for the axis limits which are here −2 and 2 (circle radius) for both the x and y. This makes a problem in viewing the boundaries of the PDE domain. If we set the **Axes limits** slightly more (user-selected), the domain boundaries appear clearly in the PDE GUI. For the circle example at hand, let us make it −2.5 to 2.5 in both the x and y directions. Again click the **Options** in the PDE GUI menu and click **Axes Limits**. The dialog window of the figure 12.3(d) appears, we enter the **[-2.5 2.5]** in both the X and Y – axes limit slots of the prompt window and click **Apply**. Yet due to the aspect ration of the desktop window, the domain might appear elliptic. So again click the **Option** menu of the PDE GUI and click the **Axes Equal** in the pulldown menu. Now you should see a clear circular domain leaving some space around its boundary like the figure 12.6(d). With the click on the boundary mode icon ∂Ω in the PDE GUI, we see the circular boundary appeared as shown in the figure 12.6(d). The figure says that the whole circular boundary $x^2 + y^2 = 4$ is split into four arcs automatically by the PDE GUI. The condition $u(x,y,t)$ =0.2 (meaning the Dirichlet one with $h = 1, r = 0.2$) is equally true for all four arcs. Absence of the Neumann condition makes us write $q = 0$ and $g = 0$ (default ones) for each of the four arcs. Therefore doubleclick each of the four arcs, enter these values in the prompt window of the figure 12.4(d), click the **Boundary** menu, and export the boundary conditions through **b** as done before.

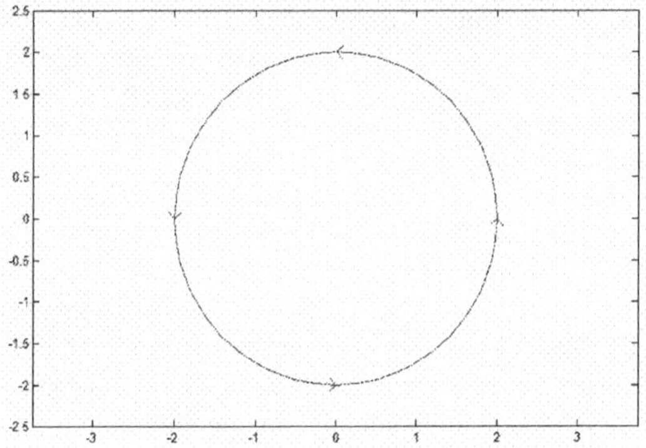

Figure 12.6(d) The circular domain appearance in the boundary mode in the PDE GUI

Now click the Mesh icon Δ and refine mesh icon (figure 12.5(g)) each once, click the **Mesh** menu, and export the mesh parameters **{p,e,t}** as done before.

For the initial conditions $u(x,y,1) = \cos x$ and $\left.\frac{\partial u(x,y,t)}{\partial t}\right|_{t=1} = \sin 2ye^{\cos x}$ over $x^2 + y^2 < 4$, we carry out the following:

>>T=1:0.2:2; x=p(1,:); y=p(2,:); ↵ ←T holds the t vector, x and y are all FEM molecule (x, y) coordinates

>>ICu=cos(x)'; ↵ ←Computation of $u(x,y,1) = \cos x$ and assigned to ICu, ICu⇔ $u(x,y,1)$ as a column matrix

>>ICdu=sin(2*y).*exp(cos(x)); ↵ ← Computation of $\left.\frac{\partial u(x,y,t)}{\partial t}\right|_{t=1} = \sin 2ye^{\cos x}$ through scalar code and assigned to ICdu (user-given name), ICdu⇔ $\left.\frac{\partial u(x,y,t)}{\partial t}\right|_{t=1}$ as a row matrix

>>ICdu=ICdu'; ↵ ← Turning the row matrix ICdu to a column one and again assigned to ICdu

We compare the given equation to the subsection 12.5.1 mentioned equations and it is evident that we have the hyperbolic one with c =1, d =0.2, a =0, f =0. The dedicated function for hyperbolic PDEs also has the name **hyperbolic** which employs a syntax **hyperbolic**(initial condition $u(x,y,1)$ as a column matrix, initial condition $\left.\frac{\partial u(x,y,t)}{\partial t}\right|_{t=1}$ as a column matrix, user-required time vector as a row matrix, boundary information **b**, mesh point matrix **p**, mesh edge matrix **e**, mesh triangle matrix **t**, PDE coefficient c, PDE coefficient a, PDE coefficient f, PDE coefficient d). Having all information in the workspace, it takes no surprise to obtain the solution as follows:

>>u=hyperbolic(ICu,ICdu,T,b,p,e,t,1,0,0,0.2); ↵ ← Calling the **hyperbolic** with the mentioned syntax

The return to the workspace **u** (can be any name of your choice) in the end retains the $u(x,y,t)$ values on the chosen mesh triangular molecule and t points.

♦♦ Example 5

It is given that the PDE $\frac{\partial^2 u}{\partial x^2}+\frac{\partial^2 u}{\partial y^2}=-0.2\lambda u$ over the domain $x^2+y^2<4$ and subject to $u(x,y)$ =0.2 on the $x^2+y^2=4$ is satisfied for multiple λ between 0 and 25. We wish to find those λs and their corresponding $u(x,y)$ solutions.

The given domain is exactly the domain of the example 4 with the exception that there is no t involvement in the Dirichlet condition but the t does not play any role in this PDE. So we obtain the boundary information **b** as we did in the example 4. The same mesh parameters **{p,e,t}** of the example 4 are also applicable here. When we compare the given PDE to the ones in the subsection 12.5.1, we see that this is an eigenmode PDE with c =1, d =0.2, and a =0. We know that the function **pdeeig** solves the eigenmode PDE which uses a syntax **[U,L]=pdeeig**(boundary information **b**, mesh point matrix **p**, mesh edge matrix **e**, mesh triangle matrix **t**, PDE coefficient c, PDE coefficient a, PDE coefficient d, user-required range of the λ as a two element row matrix). But this PDE solver has two output arguments – **U** and **L**, the first and second of which are the $u(x,y)$ solution for all λ as a rectangular matrix and the value of λ as a column matrix respectively. We assume that you did not delete the **b**, **p**, **e**, and **t** of the example 4 on that let us execute the following:

>>[U,L]=pdeeig(b,p,e,t,1,0,0.2,[0 25]); ↵ ← **U** holds $u(x,y)$ solutions for all λ and **L** holds all λ as a column matrix

Some run time message is displayed during the execution, let us ignore those as far as we are interested only on the solution finding. The first column of the **U** holds the values of $u(x,y)$ for the first λ in the **L**, and so on.

12.5.5 Nonlinear PDEs with two space variables

The elliptic PDE coefficients $\{c, a, f\}$ of the subsection 12.5.1 exercised so far are all constants. The definitions of the nonlinear PDE according to the PDE literature and MATLAB term are not the same. Loosely describing, a PDE is said to be nonlinear if the PDE has expression based coefficients $\{c, a, f\}$ and the expressions can be x, y, $u(x,y)$, $\frac{\partial u(x,y)}{\partial x}$, and $\frac{\partial u(x,y)}{\partial y}$ related but with no t involvement. For so mentioned nonlinear PDEs, we employ the solver **pdenonlin** with the syntax **pdenonlin**(boundary information **b**, mesh point matrix **p**, mesh edge matrix **e**, mesh triangle matrix **t**, PDE coefficient c, PDE coefficient a, PDE coefficient f). Let us see three examples on the non-constant coefficient or boundary condition PDE.

♦♦ Example 1

We intend to solve the PDE $(x+y)\left(\frac{\partial^2 u}{\partial x^2}+\frac{\partial^2 u}{\partial y^2}\right)+\frac{\partial u}{\partial x}\frac{\partial u}{\partial y}+3\frac{\partial u}{\partial x}-5\frac{\partial u}{\partial y}+(x+y)u+y=0$ with zero boundary condition over the rectangular domain of the example 1 in the subsection 12.5.2.

If we compare the given PDE to the elliptic one of the subsection 12.5.1, we see that $c=x+y$, $a=-x-y$, and $f=\frac{\partial u}{\partial x}\frac{\partial u}{\partial y}+3\frac{\partial u}{\partial x}-5\frac{\partial u}{\partial y}+y$. We write the scalar code (section 14.2) of the PDE coefficients which requires to write **x+y**, **-x-y**, and **ux.*uy+3*ux-5*uy+y** for the c, a, and f respectively where **x**⇔x, **y**⇔y, **ux**⇔$\frac{\partial u(x,y)}{\partial x}$, **uy**⇔$\frac{\partial u(x,y)}{\partial y}$ and the **ux** and **uy** are reserve words for the partial derivatives. All expressional scalar codes when input argumented to the **pdenonlin** must be as a string that means the code is placed under quote.

>>pderect([1 3 1 5],'R'); ↵ ← Named the rectangle as R, click **Options** menu and set the **Axes limits** to **Auto**

The zero boundary condition means the Dirichlet or Neumann conditions both are 0 or $\{h=1, r=0, q=0, g=0\}$ – these are the default values as well in the window of the figure 12.4(d). Export the boundary conditions through **b** as done before. Now click the mesh icon once and the refine mesh icon twice and export the mesh parameters **{p,e,t}** as done before. Let us assign the scalar codes of the expression coefficients to the like names in the following:

```
>>c='x+y'; a='-x-y'; f='ux.*uy+3*ux-5*uy+y'; ↵
>>u=pdenonlin(b,p,e,t,c,a,f); ↵    ← Calling the pdenonlin for the solution with the mentioned syntax
```

On above execution, the u holds the solution for $u(x,y)$ as a column matrix.

♦♦ Example 2

What if we had the PDE $2xy\left(\frac{\partial^2 u}{\partial x^2}+\frac{\partial^2 u}{\partial y^2}\right)+\left(\frac{\partial u}{\partial x}\right)^2+\left(\frac{\partial u}{\partial y}\right)^2-7\frac{\partial u}{\partial x}-2\frac{\partial u}{\partial y}+8-ux^2=0$ in the example 1? It means the coefficients now we have are $c=2xy$, $f=\left(\frac{\partial u}{\partial x}\right)^2+\left(\frac{\partial u}{\partial y}\right)^2-7\frac{\partial u}{\partial x}-2\frac{\partial u}{\partial y}+8$, and $a=x^2$ and the similar code writing is the following:

```
>>c='2*x.*y'; a='x.^2'; f='ux.^2+uy.^2-7*ux-2*uy+8'; ↵
>>u=pdenonlin(b,p,e,t,c,a,f); ↵←Calling pdenonlin and u holds the solution for u(x,y) as a column matrix
```

♦♦ Example 3

Not necessarily the boundary conditions will be constant always. In this problem we intend to solve a PDE with non-constant boundary conditions. Our objective is to solve the PDE $\frac{\partial^2 u}{\partial x^2}+\frac{\partial^2 u}{\partial y^2}=x^2y^2$ over the rectangular domain of the example 1 in subsection 12.5.2 subject to the boundary conditions $u(1,y)=y^2$, $u(3,y)=\cos y$, $u(x,1)=5x^2-x$, and $u(x,5)=-x$.

First of all if a boundary condition is expression based, we write its scalar code as well. The expressions y^2, $\cos y$, $5x^2-x$, and $-x$ have the scalar codes y.^2, cos(y), 5*x.^2-x, and -x respectively. The $u(1,y)$, $u(3,y)$, $u(x,1)$, and $u(x,5)$ refer to the left, right, bottom, and top sides of the rectangle respectively. There is no Neumann condition in any of the four sides so q =0 and g =0 for each side. We need to enter the following as the boundary condition: {h =1, $r=y^2$, q =0, g =0} for left, {h =1, $r=\cos y$, q =0, g =0} for right, {h =1, $r=5x^2-x$, q =0, g =0} for bottom, and {h =1, $r=-x$, q =0, g =0} for top sides. As usual, we carry out the following to bring the domain in front:

```
>>pderect([1 3 1 5],'R') ↵    ← Click Options menu and set the Axes limits to Auto
```

Now click the boundary icon ∂Ω in the PDE GUI and doubleclick each side of the rectangle to enter just mentioned boundary conditions. For example we enter y.^2 in the slot of the h in the prompt window of the figure 12.4(d), and so on and export the boundary information through b as done before. Given equation comparison with that of the elliptic (subsection 12.5.1) one provides c =1, a =0, and $f=-x^2y^2$ which needs the following execution:

```
>>c=1; a=0; f='-x.^2.*y.^2'; ↵        ← Coefficients are assigned to the like names
```

After that we click the mesh icon Δ once and refine mesh icon (figure 12.5(g)) once and export the mesh parameters {p,e,t} as done before. All input arguments of the pdenonlin are in the workspace so let us execute the following:

```
>>u=pdenonlin(b,p,e,t,c,a,f); ↵←Calling pdenonlin and u holds the solution for u(x,y) as a column matrix
```

12.5.6 Accessibility to and graphing the PDE solution

We know that the numerical solution of a PDE is basically dependent $u(x,y)$ versus x and y data or dependent $u(x,y,t)$ versus x, y, and t data over some given domain. In the last two subsections we solved several PDEs and just found the solution, all of which is assigned to some user-given variable u. Now we explain how the $u(x,y)$, x, y, etc data are organized in the solution.

♦♦ Example 1

From the example 1 of the subsection 12.5.4, we know that the workspace u holds the $u(x,y)$ and the p holds the x and y data for the whole domain defined by $1\le x\le 3$ and $1\le y\le 5$. The u and p are a column and a two-row matrices respectively. Just to see the solution values, let us carry out the right attached command. Since the p is a two-row matrix, transposing the p using p' turns it to be a two-column matrix. In order to see the solution side by side, we employed the command [p' u] (section 2.7). The last element in the display means $u(2.0507,1.6374)$ =0.0558 as shown above by the left arrow, so does the others. Referring to the workspace browser, we find the matrix size of the p and u as 2×1405 and 1405×1

Displaying example 1 variable contents of this subsection side by side:

```
>>[p' u] ↵

ans =

    1.0000    1.0000         0
    3.0000    1.0000         0
    3.0000    5.0000    5.0000
                 :
    2.0126    1.7761    0.0734
    2.0507    1.6374    0.0558 ← u(2.0507,1.6374) =0.0558
      ↑         ↑         ↑
      x         y       u(x,y)
```

respectively. It means when the PDE GUI decomposed the whole domain, there are 1405 nodes covering the FEM triangle molecules like the figure 12.6(a).

♦♦ Example 2

From the example 3 of the subsection 12.5.4, we know that the workspace u holds the $u(x,y,t)$ data, the p holds the x and y data, and the T holds the t data. We wish to see how these data are organized for a t dependent solution.

On the right side we placed all necessary callings to see the contents of T, u, and p. In the first calling of T the contents are just a row matrix holding the t values from 0 to 1 with the step 0.2 – there are six points. When we call the u, we see that the u has six columns corresponding to the six t values. We have shown the indication using the uparrow on the right side. Suppose we wish to have the $u(x,y,0.8)$ values – it means the fifth column of the u. One can use the command u5=u(:,5); to pick up the fifth column from the u where u5 is any user-given name. The u5 then holds the $u(x,y,0.8)$ values as a column matrix. There is no information regarding the x and y in the u. The information about the x and y coordinates is in the mesh parameter p and as a two-row matrix. We transposed that employing p' and placed beside before u using [p' u]. Concerning the above implementation, the last x and y coordinates in the p correspond to the last row in the u or mathematically we say that the last row in the u is actually $u(2.4426,0.5258,t)$. Again the first row in the u corresponds to $u(0,0,t)$ and so on.

Displaying example 2 variable contents of this subsection:

```
>>T ↵          ← Calling T to see its contents

T =
      0    0.2000    0.4000    0.6000    0.8000    1.0000
>>u ↵          ← Calling u to see its contents

u =
     1.0000    1.0000    1.0000    1.0000    1.0000    1.0000
     1.0000    1.0000    1.0000    1.0000    1.0000    1.0000
                            :
    -3.6973   -1.0537   -0.1860    0.2548    0.4962    0.6346
    -5.1432   -2.0205   -0.7531   -0.1018    0.2564    0.4622
       ↑         ↑         ↑         ↑         ↑         ↑
for   t=0      t=0.2     t=0.4     t=0.6     t=0.8      t=1
>>[p' u] ↵  ← Calling p and u side by side to see their contents

ans =
          0         0    1.0000    1.0000    1.0000    1.0000    1.0000    1.0000
     3.1416         0    1.0000    1.0000    1.0000    1.0000    1.0000    1.0000
                                  :
     2.4695    0.3417   -3.6973   -1.0537   -0.1860    0.2548    0.4962    0.6346
     2.4426    0.5258   -5.1432   -2.0205   -0.7531   -0.1018    0.2564    0.4622
       ↑         ↑         ↑         ↑         ↑         ↑         ↑         ↑
       x         y        t=0      t=0.2     t=0.4     t=0.6     t=0.8      t=1
       \_________/        \_____________________________________________/
            p'                                   u
```

♦♦ Example 3

It is very lucid by now that the returned solution for the $u(x,y)$ or $u(x,y,t)$ is in the finite element or triangular molecular element term. What if we need the interpolated data or solution in the finite difference term (figures 12.5(a)-(b))? In the example 2, we see the $u(2.4426,0.5258,t)$ values as the last row of the u. Let us say we intend to compute $u(2.3,0.4,0)$. The t =0 means the first column of the u and we pick it up writing u(:,1). There is a function by the name tri2grid in the PDE toolbox which returns the interpolated value from the FEM domain to the FD domain with the syntax tri2grid(mesh parameter p, mesh parameter t, FEM $u(x,y)$ values as a column matrix, required x coordinate value (s), required y coordinate value(s)). We assume that the p and t are available in the workspace or redo the implementation. However for the example at hand, let us carry out the following:

```
>>tri2grid(p,t,u(:,1),2.3,0.4) ↵

ans =
        -3.3591   ← Meaning u(2.3,0.4,0) =–3.3591 although the PDE solver did not return this value
```

What if we demand for a range of values for example now the x coordinate changes from 2.3 to 2.8 with the step 0.1 (which has the MATLAB code 2.3:0.1:2.8) and the y coordinate and the t are the same? The tri2grid also accepts the range of x and y coordinate values as a row matrix. Let us verify that as follows:

```
>>tri2grid(p,t,u(:,1),2.3:0.1:2.8,0.4) ↵

ans =
        -3.3591   -3.8671   -4.3804   -4.8704   -5.3293   -5.7728
           ↑         ↑         ↑         ↑         ↑         ↑
         x=2.3     x=2.4     x=2.5     x=2.6     x=2.7     x=2.8      ← Value of u(x,0.4,0) at
```

In a similar fashion you can also input the range of the values for the y coordinates. If both the x and y coordinates are a range of values, the output is a rectangular matrix from the tri2grid in which the rows and columns correspond to y and x respectively or you can say the rectangular matrix is basically the $u(x,y)$ values for different x and y coordinates we are familiar with. If we apply the tri2grid on the domain other than formed by horizontal and vertical lines, we find the return as NaN or not a number outside the given FEM decomposed domain. For example the circular domain $x^2+y^2<4$ when applies the FD method, we change the x or y coordinates from −2 to 2 but there will be some area within the rectangle $-2 \le x, y \le 2$ which is beyond the circle. The returns from the tri2grid at those points will be NaN.

◆◆ Graphing the PDE solution

There are two options for graphing the PDE solution. Either you use the PDE GUI option just to see the plot or get the solution data and plot it in your convenience. We intend to solve and graph the Poisson's equation $\frac{\partial^2 u}{\partial x^2}+\frac{\partial^2 u}{\partial y^2}=-3$ over $-2 \le x, y \le 2$ with the zero boundary conditions. Applying ongoing functions and symbology (subsection 12.5.4), we execute the following:

>>pderect([-2 2 -2 2],'R'); ↵ ← Named the rectangle R, click Options menu and set the Axes limits to Auto

Making the domain appear in the PDE GUI, let us go through the both options:

Using the PDE GUI option:

The equation fits in the elliptic one with c=1, a=0, and f=3. Zero boundary conditions mean default setting in the boundary mode. Click the mesh icon Δ once in the icon bar, click the refine mesh icon (figure 12.5(g)) once in the icon bar, click the PDE icon in the icon bar, enter c=1, a=0, and f=3 in the prompt window of the figure 12.3(e), click Solve menu, and click Solve PDE in the pulldown menu of Solve. Performing all these actions, we see the color intensity image plot for the $u(x,y)$ versus x and y (graph not shown for space reason) along with a color scale. The color values are proportional to the $u(x,y)$ values. There is another option for the plotting, which is the surface plot. In the menu bar, we find the menu Plot and Parameters in the pulldown menu of the Plot. A prompt window appears and you find different options for graphing in the prompt window. For a surface plot, check the Height (3D – plot) in the prompt window and click Plot in the prompt window. You must see the surface plot (graph not shown for space reason) of $u(x,y)$ versus x and y.

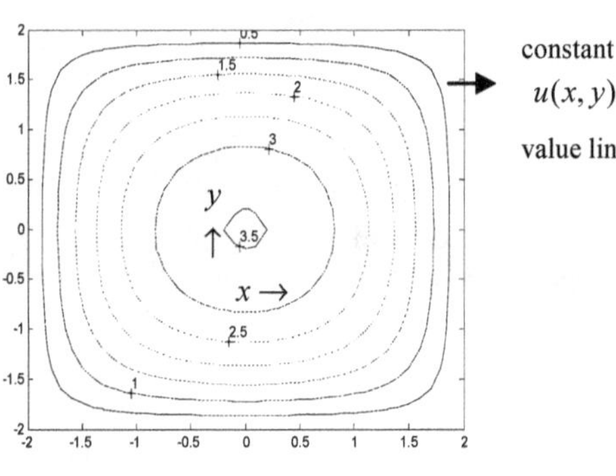

Figure 12.7(a) Contour plot of $u(x,y)$ versus x and y

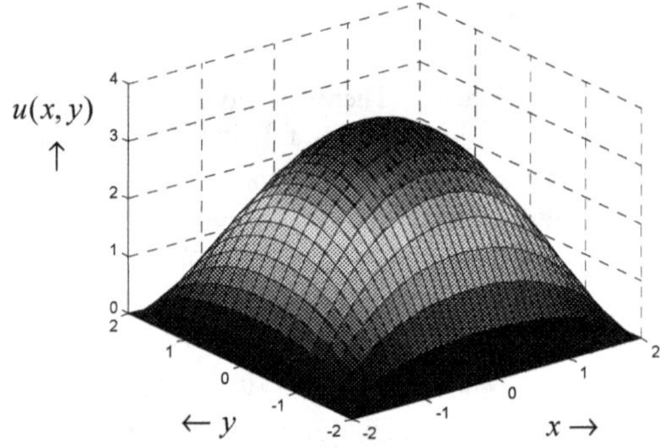

Figure 12.7(b) Surface plot of $u(x,y)$ versus x and y

Graphing after making the data available in the workspace:

Export the boundary information b as done before, export the mesh parameters {p,e,t} as done before, and call the solver as follows:

>>u=assempde(b,p,e,t,1,0,3); ↵ ← Similar to the examples 1 and 2 of the subsection 12.5.4

So our $u(x,y)$ solution is in the variable u but in the FEM triangle molecular domain. If we intend to transform these data in the FD domain, example 3 of this subsection can be seen. Let us say we intend to contour or surface graph the solution over $-2 \le x, y \le 2$ taking a x step 0.1 and y step 0.2 for which we execute the following:

>>x=-2:0.1:2; y=-2:0.2:2; ↵ ← Generating the x and y grid points in the given domain as a row matrix according to the specifications

>>UFD=tri2grid(p,t,u,x,y); ↵ ← Transforming the FEM based values to the FD based values where the UFD is some user-chosen name and the UFD is a rectangular matrix now corresponding to the x and y grid points contrary to the column matrix u

The contour and surface plots of $u(x,y)$ versus x and y need to execute the commands clabel(contour(x,y,UFD)) and surf(x,y,UFD) at the command prompt and whose outputs are the figures 12.7(a) and 12.7(b) (subsections 13.2.5 and 13.2.6) respectively.

We have tried to render some flavor from the PDE toolbox and guess that the reader has had some know-how about the numerical PDE solving employing the package. We intend to bring an end of the PDE discussion with this.

Chapter 13

Graphical analysis is a momentous procedure for visualizing many problems often found in mathematics, scientific, and engineering community. In this chapter we describe how one graphs different functions and data in MATLAB. MATLAB not only computes the toilsome numerical and symbolic problems quickly but also displays the results graphically in a variety of picturesque representations. It is the easy-to-compute and easy-to-plot facility of MATLAB that attracts new users. More and more scientists, researchers, and academicians are becoming affiliated with MATLAB. Broadly speaking, the graphics generated in MATLAB can be classified in two categories – two and three dimensional, and each of which has several forms of representations. We briefly address some of the frequently practiced ones in various disciplines of pure science and engineering. MATLAB is so user friendly that one can even alter the graphics property such as color of lines, axes limiting values, labeling, etc with a single click operation without rigorous programming. However we plan to discuss the following:

- Functional expression based graphing including the implicit, parametric, and polar ones
- Data based graphing in terms of contours or surfaces in two and/or three dimensions
- Multiple plots as well as dissimilar plots over a common axis in a single window
- Split window plots for multiple graphs and special graphs such as scatter point plots
- Graphing in continuous sense accompanying the discrete counterpart and troubleshooting

13.1 Graphing from symbolic functions

Functions of the form $y = f(x)$ or $z = f(x, y)$ are the symbolic functions in two and three dimensions respectively, examples of which can be $f(x) = 2x - 56$, $g(\theta) = \cos\theta - \sin\theta$, $f(x, y) = x^2 + y^2$, $g(u, v) = e^u \cos 2\pi v$, etc. The reader can have MATLAB notion of writing the symbolic functions going through the table 14.A and the section 14.2. The MATLAB functions that graph the symbolic functions are **ezplot** (abbreviation for easy plot), **ezpolar** (abbreviation for easy polar), **ezcontour** (abbreviation for easy contour), **ezsurf** (abbreviation for easy surface), .. etc. We subtitled the problems often found in pure mathematics. Font equivalence of mathematical symbols like x⇔x is maintained throughout the whole chapter.

13.1.1 Functions of the form $y = f(x)$

Let us say we intend to plot the function $y = 2x^2 - 3x + 5$ over the interval $-3 \le x \le 3$. We first give $2x^2 - 3x + 5$ MATLAB vector code (section 14.2) and then assign that to **y** as follows:

```
>>y='2*x^2-3*x+5'; ↵        ← Code under quote
```

To obtain the plot of y in the given interval, we execute the following:

```
>>ezplot(y,[-3,3]) ↵
```

Above command results in the figure 13.1(a). The **ezplot** accepts two input arguments – the first of which is the function code and the second one is the interval description as a two element row matrix over which the graph is to be plotted, the first and second elements are the beginning and ending bounds of the interval respectively (i.e. $-3 \le x \le 3$ is entered by [-3,3]). The **ezplot** graphs $y = f(x)$ in the default interval $-2\pi \le x \le 2\pi$. We attach one more example utilizing the function in the following.

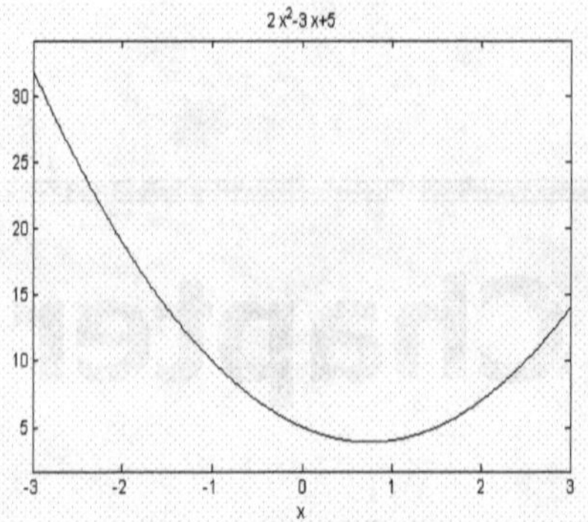

Figure 13.1(a) Plot of $y = 2x^2 - 3x + 5$ versus x over $-3 \le x \le 3$

⬍⬍ Example

Let us plot the damped sine wave $y = e^{-\frac{x}{3}} \sin\left(5x - \frac{\pi}{6}\right)$ over the interval $0 \le x \le 6$ whose execution is the following:

```
>>y='exp(-x/3)*sin(5*x-pi/6)'; ↵
>>ezplot(y,[0,6]) ↵    ← Figure 13.1(b) is the outcome
```

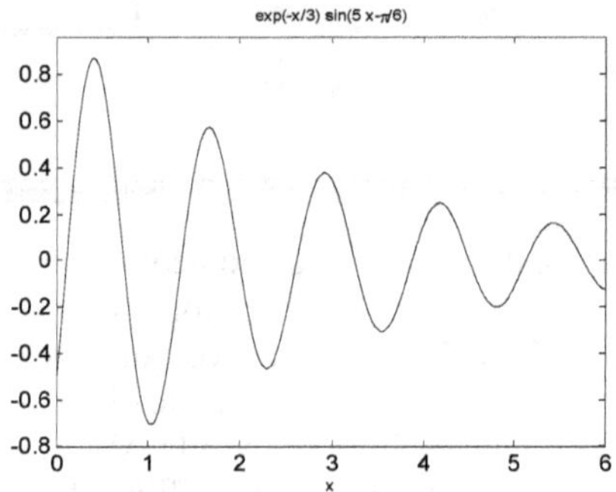

Figure 13.1(b) Plot of $y = e^{-\frac{x}{3}} \sin(5x - \frac{\pi}{6})$ versus x over $0 \le x \le 6$

13.1.2 Implicit functions of the form $f(x, y) = 0$

When the dependent variable y and independent variable x are mingled in an equation $f(x, y) = 0$, we call the equation as an implicit one. We know that the circle having radius 1 and center (0,0) is given by $x^2 + y^2 = 1$. The function **ezplot** is still operational for plotting the implicit function but a little alteration is required in the input argument. The implicit function is rearranged so that the right side of the equation is zero. For the example at hand, the rearranged equation should be $x^2 + y^2 - 1 = 0$. We vector code the left side of the equation and assign that to **E** as follows:

```
>>E='x^2+y^2-1'; ↵    ← Code under quote
```

Two variables (x and y) need insertion of two domain values. The default domains are given by $-2\pi \le x \le 2\pi$ and $-2\pi \le y \le 2\pi$. Let us say we intend the circle to be plotted over $-1 \le x \le 1$ and $-1 \le y \le 1$. The domain is assigned to **D** (any user-given name) as a four element row matrix (where the elements are the lower bound of x, upper bound of x, lower bound of y, and upper bound of y respectively) as follows:

```
>>D=[-1 1 -1 1]; ↵
>>ezplot(E,D) ↵ ← First and second input arguments
                  are the code and domain respectively
```

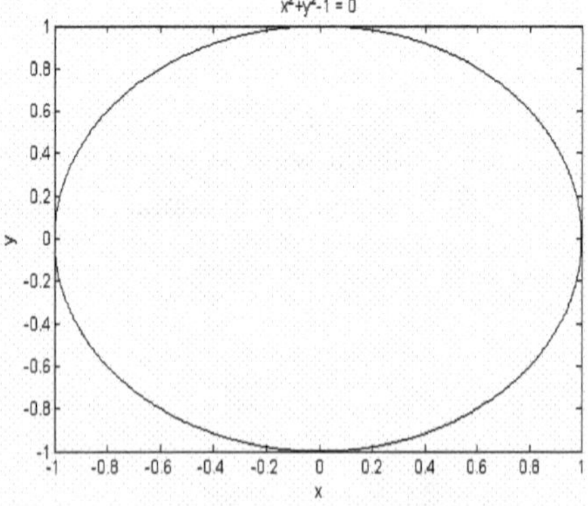

Figure 13.1(c) Plot of $x^2 + y^2 = 1$ over $-1 \le x \le 1$ and $-1 \le y \le 1$

Upon execution of above command you see the graph of the figure 13.1(c). The reader may not agree with the plot because the shape does not appear to be a circle rather an ellipse. The reason for this is the window displayed by MATLAB is not a square window instead a rectangular one (in computer graphics term this is called the aspect ratio). If you resize the window using the mouse to a square one, for sure the graph will look like a perfect circle or you can use the command **axis equal** to obtain the plot in a square window. However two more examples are furnished regarding the implicit function plotting maintaining the same symbology and function as follows:

⬍⬍ Example 1

We plot the implicit function $\frac{1}{y} - \ln y + \ln(x + y - 1) = 1 - y^2$ over the domain $-2.5 \le x \le 5.1$ and $-3 \le y \le 2$ as shown in the following:

```
>>E='1/y-log(y)+log(-1+y+x)+y^2-1'; ↵ ← The equation is rearranged and vector code is assigned to E
>>D=[-2.5 5.1 -3 2]; ↵       ← Domain data is assigned to D as done before
>>ezplot(E,D) ↵              ← Figure 13.1(d) presents the graph following the execution
```

Example 2

The fifth degree curve is not an exception to **ezplot**. Let us prove that for $x^5+8y^5=7x^4y^3-\frac{1}{5}$ over $-5\le x\le 5$ and $-5\le y\le 5$ using the following command:

```
>>E='x^5+8*y^5-7*x^4*y^3+1/5'; ↵ ← The equation is rearranged and its vector code is assigned to E
>>D=[-5 5]; ↵    ← Domain data is assigned to D, writing one is enough for two identical bounds
>>ezplot(E,D) ↵  ← Figure 13.1(e) presents the graph after the execution
```

The assignees can be omitted if we put the whole command in a line like **ezplot('x^5+8*y^5-7*x^4*y^3+1/5',[-5 5])**.

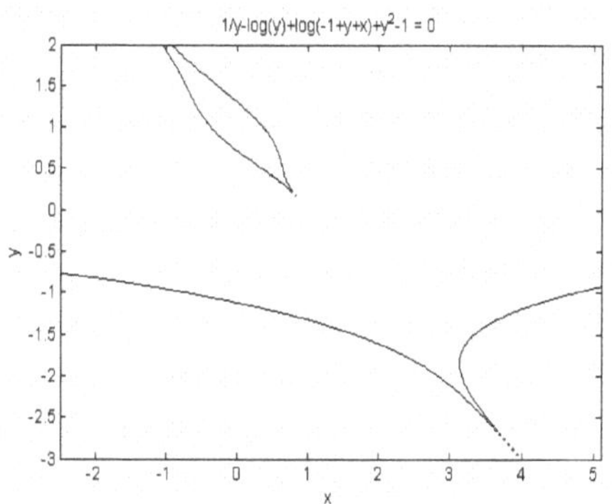

Figure 13.1(d) Plot of $\frac{1}{y}-\ln y+\ln(x+y-1)=1-y^2$ over $-2.5\le x\le 5.1$ and $-3\le y\le 2$

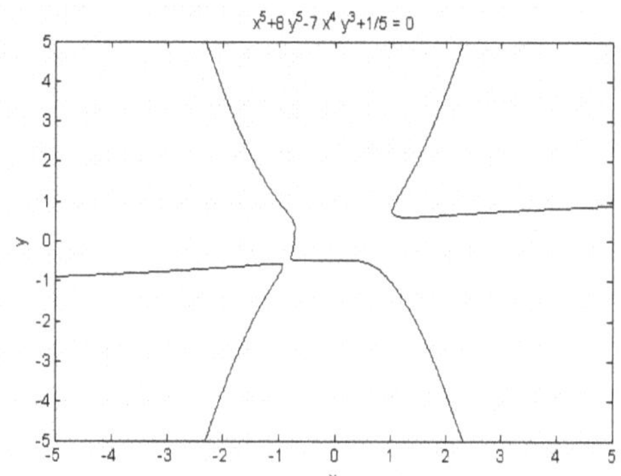

Figure 13.1(e) Plot of $x^5+8y^5=7x^4y^3-\frac{1}{5}$ over $-5\le x\le 5$ and $-5\le y\le 5$

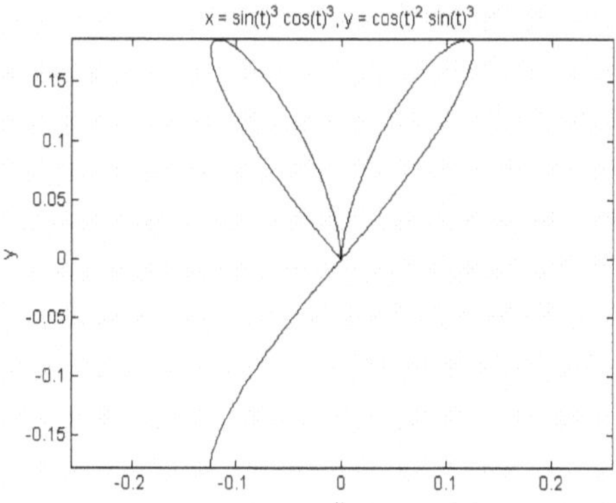

Figure 13.2(a) Plot of $x(\theta)=\sin^3\theta\cos^3\theta$ and $y(\theta)=\sin^3\theta\cos^2\theta$ for $-\frac{\pi}{4}\le\theta\le\pi$

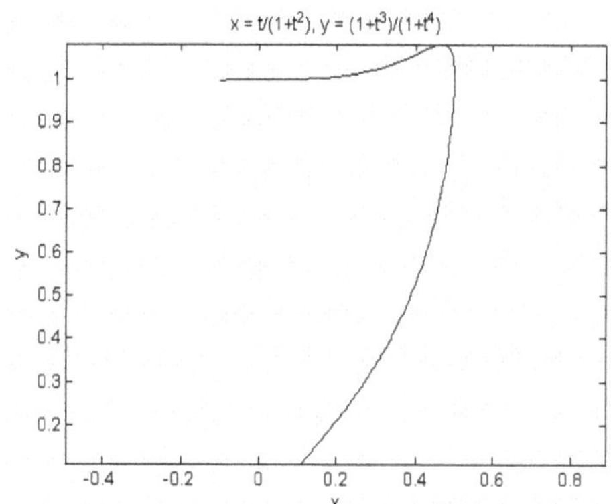

Figure 13.2(b) Plot of $x(t)=\frac{t}{1+t^2}$ and $y(t)=\frac{1+t^3}{1+t^4}$ for $-0.1\le t\le 9$

13.1.3 Parametric equations of the form $x=f(t)$ and $y=g(t)$

In parametric equations, two or more dependent variables are exclusively the functions of some parameters. The simplest example can be an ellipse, the parametric equations of which are given by $x=2\cos t$ and $y=\sin t$. Let us say we intend to plot the equations over the parameter interval $0\le t\le 2\pi$. We again seek help from the function **ezplot** to graph the parametric equations. First we assign the vector codes of the parametric equations under quote to workspace **x** and **y** respectively and then utilize the function as attached on the right side. The execution results a figure very similar to the one in the figure 13.1(c) – for space reason we did not attach it. The **ezplot** now has three input arguments, the first, second, and third of which are the first parametric code, second parametric code, and parameter interval as a two element row matrix respectively. The default parameter interval is $0\le t\le 2\pi$. The first and second parametric codes are assumed to be for the horizontal and vertical axes respectively. Two more examples are presented in the following.

Plotting parametric ellipse:

```
>>x='2*cos(t)'; y='sin(t)'; ↵
>>ezplot(x,y,[0,2*pi]) ↵
```

◆◆ Example 1

Let us plot the parametric equations $x(\theta) = \sin^3\theta\cos^3\theta$ and $y(\theta) = \sin^3\theta\cos^2\theta$ over the parameter interval $-\frac{\pi}{4} \le \theta \le \pi$. Now the independent variable concerns the use of θ but we can not enter θ to MATLAB from the keyboard instead we choose t for θ. The execution (presented on the right side) follows the assignment of $x(\theta)$, $y(\theta)$, and domain of θ to x, y, and D respectively to display the figure 13.2(a). Assignees can be shunned by placing all commands in one line like ezplot('sin(t)^3*cos(t)^3', 'cos(t)^2*sin(t)^3',[-pi/4 pi]).

parametric example 1:

```
>>x='sin(t)^3*cos(t)^3'; ↵
>>y='cos(t)^2*sin(t)^3'; ↵
>>D=[-pi/4 pi]; ↵
>>ezplot(x,y,D) ↵
```

◆◆ Example 2

The rational form expression on the parameter t such as $x(t) = \frac{t}{1+t^2}$ and $y(t) = \frac{1+t^3}{1+t^4}$ over $-0.1 \le t \le 9$ is obtained like the figure 13.2(b) using above command. If the equations were in terms of the parameter u, the command would be ezplot('u/(1+u^2)','(1+u^3)/(1+u^4)',[-0.1 9]) and produce the same graph. Note that the parametric description appears automatically on the top of the graph.

parametric example 2:

```
>>ezplot('t/(1+t^2)','(1+t^3)/(1+t^4)',[-0.1 9]) ↵
```

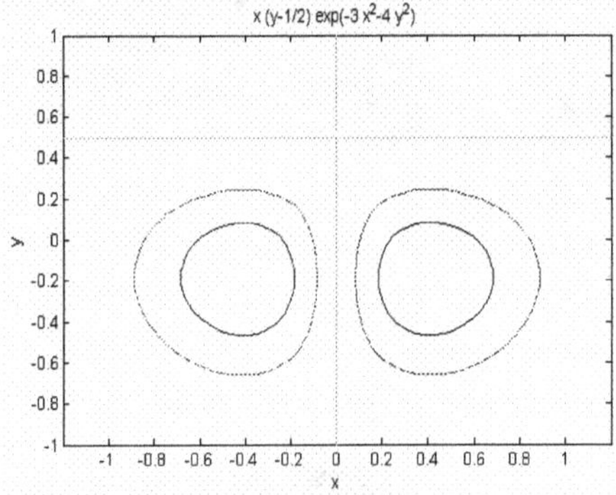

Figure 13.2(c) Contour plot of $x\left(y-\frac{1}{2}\right)e^{-3x^2-4y^2}$ over $-1.2 \le x \le -1.2$ and $-1 \le y \le 1$

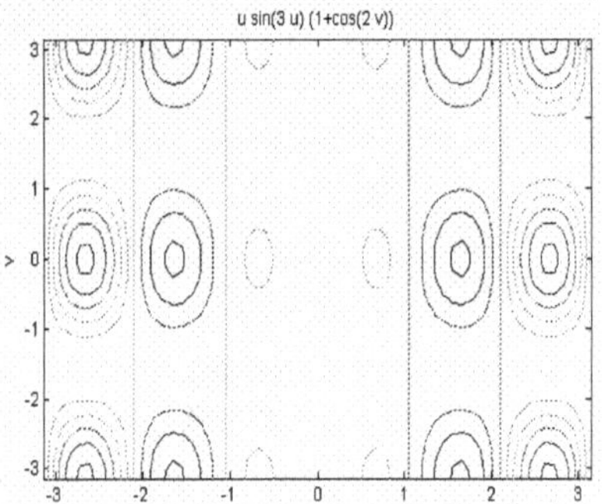

Figure 13.2(d) Contour plot for $f(u,v) = u\sin 3u\,(1+\cos 2v)$

13.1.4 Contour plot from $f(x, y)$

The contour plot of $f(x, y)$ versus x and y is basically a three dimensional plot but graphed on the two dimensional convenience. By mathematical definition, any closed curve is termed as a contour. When a contour is graphed in a computer, curves connected by the lines of the same functional values are called the contour. MATLAB function ezcontour (abbreviation for easy contour) graphs the contour plot from the expression of $f(x, y)$. We intend to graph the contour plot for the function $f(x,y) = x\left(y-\frac{1}{2}\right)e^{-3x^2-4y^2}$ over the domain formed by $-1.2 \le x \le 1.2$ and $-1 \le y \le 1$. The syntax for the plot is ezcontour(vector code of $f(x, y)$ under quote – section 14.2, x interval bounds as two element row matrix, y interval bounds as two element row matrix) on that the necessary command is as follows:

```
>>ezcontour('x*(y-1/2)*exp(-3*x^2-4*y^2)',[-1.2,1.2],[-1,1]) ↵
```
← Figure 13.2(c) presents the graph

Looking into the contour plot, it is very difficult to know the value of the contour (i.e. the functional value of $f(x, y)$). Moreover the contours are displayed in terms of color curves. One needs to know the color scale which should indicate the value of the contour at any x and y, and for which we execute the command colorbar. Upon execution we must find a color bar attached with the contour plot which presents the color code values (not shown for space reason). The default intervals that ezcontour can conceive for the x and y are $-2\pi \le x \le 2\pi$ and $-2\pi \le y \le 2\pi$ respectively. The contours so displayed by the ezcontour are the color curves. Contours filled by various colors are viewed by the function ezcontourf (the last letter is f) as follows (graph is not shown for space reason):

```
>>ezcontourf('x*(y-1/2)*exp(-3*x^2-4*y^2)',[-1.2,1.2],[-1,1]) ↵
```
← Syntax is the same as that of ezcontour

The functional expression automatically appears on the top of the graph. However we include two more examples on graphing a contour in the following.

◆◆ Example 1

Let us contour plot the $f(u,v) = u\sin 3u\,(1+\cos 2v)$ over the domain formed by $-\pi \le u \le \pi$ and $-\pi \le v \le \pi$. Now our independent variables are other than x and y. Following command plots the contour of the figure 13.2(d):

```
>>ezcontour('u*sin(3*u)*(1+cos(2*v))',[-pi,pi]) ↵
```

Alphabetically **u** comes first, and then does **v** which is why **v** and **u** follow the y and x traces respectively. Since the two intervals are identical, mentioning one of them in the input argument is enough.

◆◆ Example 2

Contour the function $f(x,y) = 10+2xy+x^2+y^2-x^2y^2-y-x$ over $-\pi \le x \le \pi$ and $-\pi \le y \le \pi$. Long expression codes can be assigned to some variable (say **f**) first and afterwards the **ezcontour** is employed to obtain the figure 13.2(e) as follows:

```
>>f='10+2*x*y+x^2+y^2-x^2*y^2-y-x'; ↵
>>ezcontour(f,[-pi,pi]) ↵
```

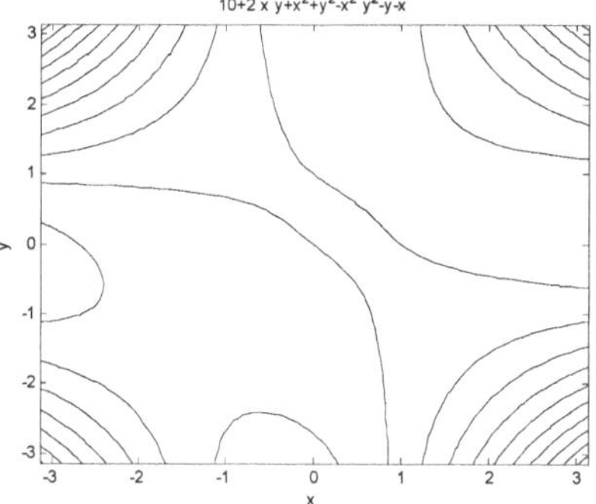

Figure 13.2(e) Contour plot for $f(x,y) = 10+2xy+x^2+y^2-x^2y^2-y-x$

13.1.5 Polar curve of the form $r = f(\theta)$

The symbolic polar function of the form $r = f(\theta)$ can be plotted by the MATLAB function **ezpolar** over the default interval $0 \le \theta \le 2\pi$, example of which can be $r = \sin 5\theta$. The θ function is written in terms of the vector code (section 14.2) and under quote. The variable **t** is used instead of θ because of its unavailability. The command **ezpolar('sin(5*t)')** graphs the figure 13.3(a). We present two more examples pertaining to the polar plots.

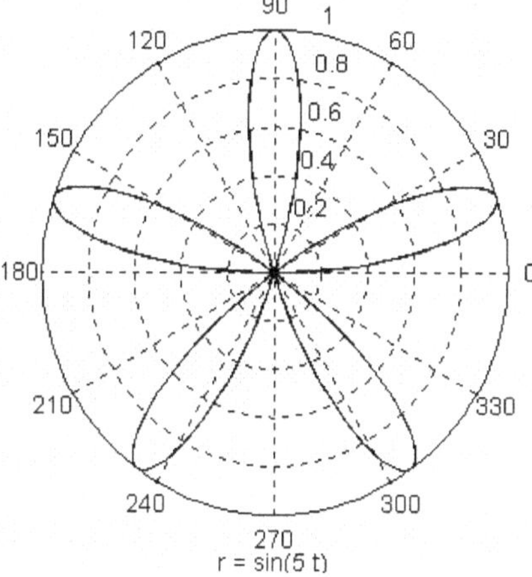

Figure 13.3(a) Polar plot for $r = \sin 5\theta$

◆◆ Example 1

Plot the curve $r = (\theta - \pi)\cos 7\theta$ over $0 \le \theta \le \pi$. The command we need to graph the figure 13.3(b) is **ezpolar('(t-pi)*cos(7*t)',[0,pi])**. The second input argument of the function is the bounds of the required interval as a two element row matrix.

◆◆ Example 2

The **ezpolar** also supports the variables other than θ for example $\frac{1-\sin(\cos^2\phi)}{\sin^2(\phi-\pi)}$. Considering **p** instead of ϕ, the code for the expression is **(1-sin(cos(p)^2))/sin(p-pi)^2** which is graphed over the interval $\frac{\pi}{9} \le \phi \le \frac{\pi}{2}$ using command **ezpolar('(1-sin(cos(p)^2))/sin(p-pi)^2',[pi/9,pi/2])**, graph is not shown for space reason.

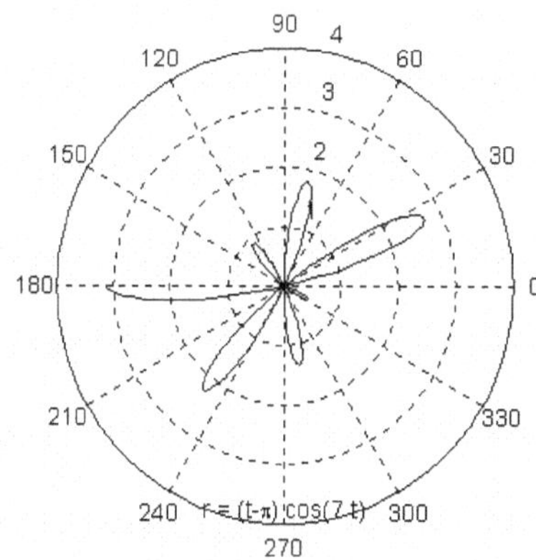

Figure 13.3(b) Polar plot of $r = (\theta - \pi)\cos 7\theta$

13.1.6 Surface plot for $f(x,y)$

Surface plot of $f(x,y)$ versus x and y is a three dimensional one for which we apply the MATLAB function **ezsurf** with the syntax **ezsurf**(vector code of the $f(x,y)$). Considering the function $f(x,y) = -8(x^2+y^2)$, we execute the following to display the figure 13.3(c):

```
>>ezsurf('-8*(x^2+y^2)') ↵
```

The z axis of the figure corresponds to the functional values of $f(x,y)$. The function puts surfaces on the default domain formed by $-2\pi \le x \le 2\pi$ and $-2\pi \le y \le 2\pi$. User-defined domains are entered by a four element row matrix that contains the lower bound of x, upper bound of x, lower bound of y, and upper bound of y respectively. Whatever surface functions are plotted by the **ezsurf** can be plotted by another variant called **ezmesh**. The difference between the **ezsurf** and **ezmesh** is that the former drops a surface and the latter drops a net or mesh proportionately to the z axis or $f(x,y)$ value. Three more examples are included in the following.

◆◆ Example 1

Let us plot the surface of the figure 13.4(a) for different independent variable function $f(m,n) = \frac{m^2(n-1)^2}{\cos^2 m + n^4}$ over the domain formed by $-2 \le m \le 3$ and $-1 \le n \le 5$ as follows:

```
>>ezsurf('m^2*(n-1)^2/(cos(m)^2+n^4)',[-2,3,-1,5]) ↵   ← Bounds of m and n as four element row matrix
```

◆◆ **Example 2**

The parametric surface defined by two parameters u and v takes the form $x = f(u,v)$, $y = g(u,v)$, and $z = h(u,v)$ which can also be plotted by the **ezsurf**. Let us say we have the parametric surface expression $x = 2u - v$, $y = e^{-u-v}$, and $z = \cos(4u + v)$ and we wish to plot the surface over the parameter intervals $-2 \le u \le 3$ and $0 \le v \le \pi$. Let us perform the following:

```
>>x='2*u-v'; ↵            ← Assigning f(u,v) to x
>>y='exp(-u-v)'; ↵        ← Assigning g(u,v) to y
>>z='cos(4*u+v)'; ↵       ← Assigning h(u,v) to z
>>ezsurf(x,y,z,[-2 3 0 pi]) ↵    ← Calling the function
```

The first three input arguments of the **ezsurf** are the parametric equations and the fourth one indicates the parameter interval bound description respectively. Figure 13.4(b) presents the parametric surface plot.

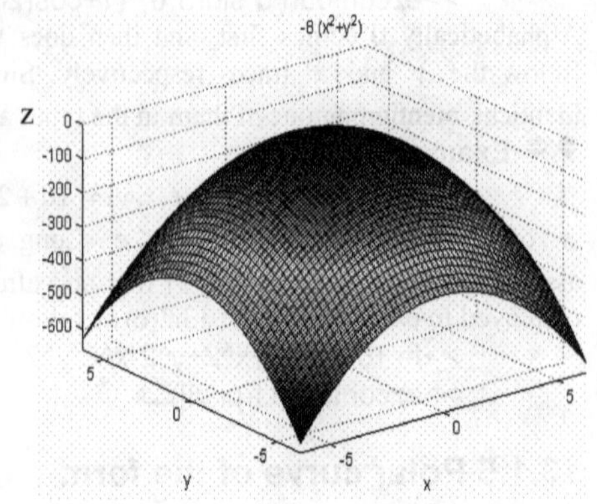

Figure 13.3(c) Surface plot for $-8(x^2 + y^2)$

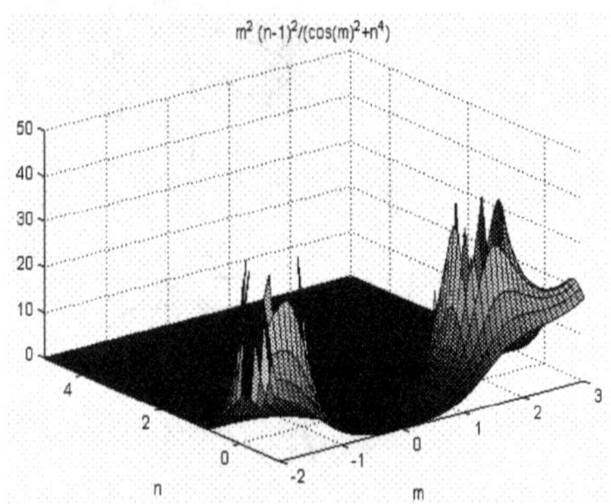

Figure 13.4(a) Surface plot for $\dfrac{m^2(n-1)^2}{\cos^2 m + n^4}$

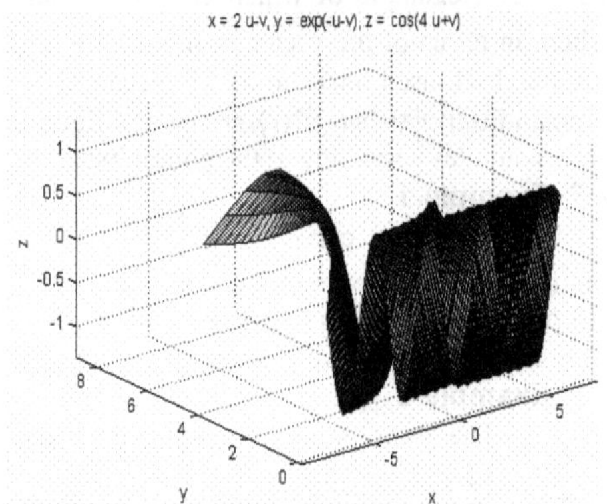

Figure 13.4(b) Surface plot for $x = 2u - v$, $y = e^{-u-v}$, and $z = \cos(4u + v)$

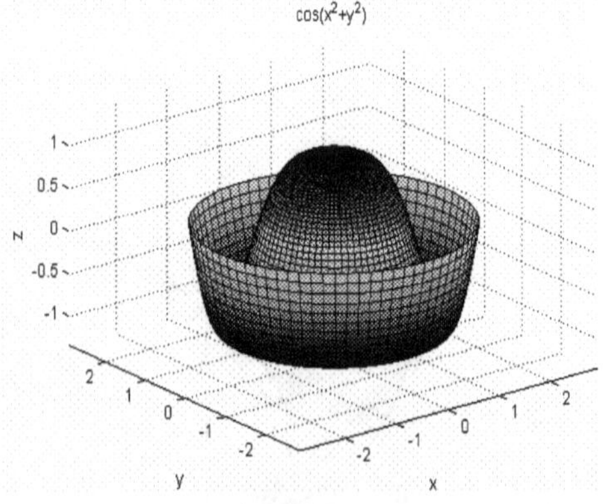

Figure 13.4(c) Surface plot for $\cos(x^2 + y^2)$ on a circular domain regarding x and y

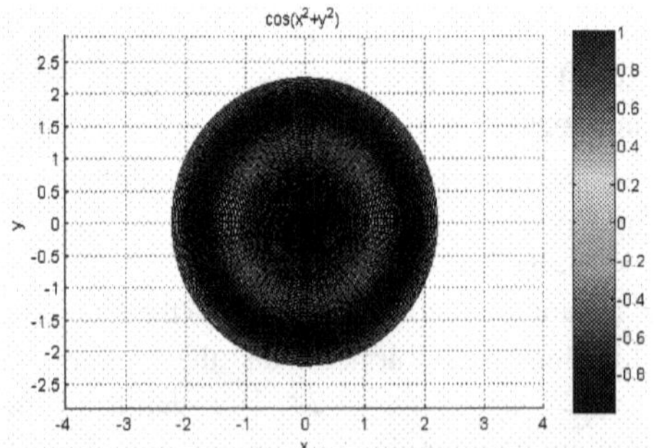

Figure 13.4(d) Top view of the surface plot of the figure 13.4(c) with the gray intensity scale

◆◆ **Example 3**

The examples we mentioned so far consider on the rectangular domains regarding x and y. What if we wish to plot the surface over a circular disc domain on the x and y. Let us plot the surface for the function $f(x,y) = \cos(x^2 + y^2)$ over $-\frac{\pi}{2} \le x \le \frac{\pi}{2}$ and $-\frac{\pi}{2} \le y \le \frac{\pi}{2}$ on a circular disk domain using the following command:

```
>>ezsurf('cos(x^2+y^2)',[-pi/2,pi/2],'circ') ↵
```

We obtain the surface plot like the figure 13.4(c) from above execution. Of the three input arguments, the first, second, and third represent the function $f(x,y)$, the rectangular domain bounds of x and y (since both are identical, coding one is sufficient) as a row matrix, and the reserve word **circ** under quote respectively. Since the surface plot visually represents a three dimensional object on a two dimensional screen, there are infinite views for the three dimensional object depending on the angle you look at. If we want to see the top view of the surface plot with equal axes and intensity scale like the figure 13.4(d), we employ the following commands: **view(0,90)**, **axis equal**, **colorbar**. The command **view** sets the viewing angle for the plot and the angle set **0-90** means the top view.

13.2 Graphing from numerical data

As discussed so far mathematical expressions are easily codeable and executable in MATLAB for plotting. Yet a large variety of scientific and engineering problems demand that numeric data should be plotted in two or three dimension obtained from experiments or simulations. With the availability of faster speed personal computers, the numerical computation and graphing trend is monotonically increasing. We address some of them intending the concept and procedure for data-to-plot illustration. We have some data and we want to plot that – that is all about this section.

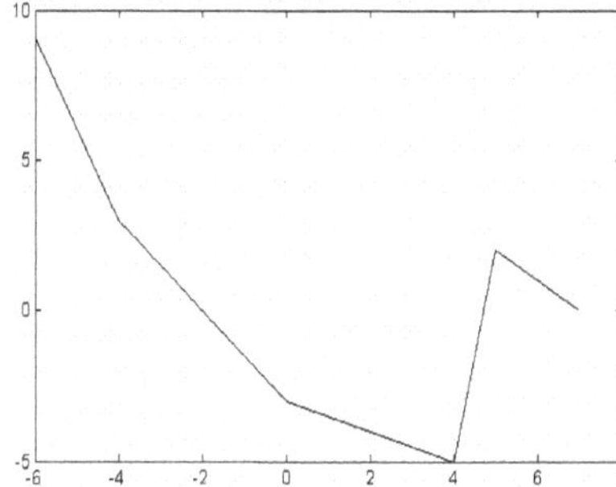

Figure 13.5(a) y vs x plot of the tabular data

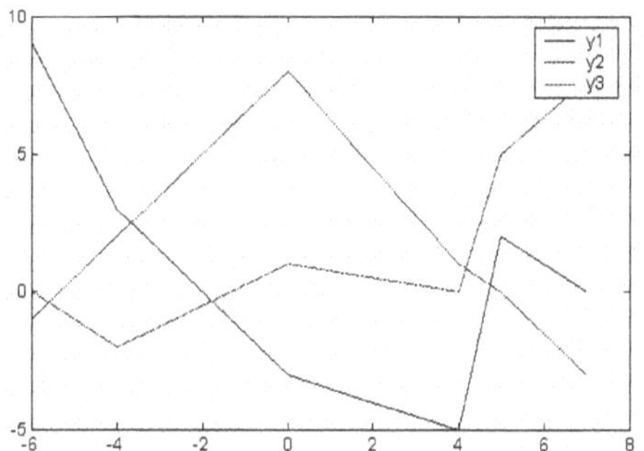

Figure 13.5(b) Multiple y data vs x for the tabular case

13.2.1 y versus x data

The function **plot** graphs y versus x data. Let us say we have the attached (on the right) tabular data. We intend to plot them as y versus x. The command to plot the data is also presented on the right side. First we assign the x and y data to the workspace variables **x** and **y** (any user-given name) respectively and then call the function **plot** to see the figure 13.5(a). The **plot** has two input arguments, the first and second of which are the x and y data both as a row or column matrix of identical size respectively. Our x and y data might be in a matrix form in the workspace. Let us say the matrix is $A=\begin{bmatrix}-2 & 4\\-1 & 7\\0 & -1\\1 & -2\\2 & -3\end{bmatrix}$ and we intend to plot the first and second columns of A as x and y data respectively. The complete code is placed on the right side in which the first line is to assign the matrix A to the workspace **A**. The second line is to pick up the first and second columns from **A** and assign them to workspace **x** and **y** respectively. The third line is to call the function for graphing (graph is not shown for space reason).

Tabular data							**Command to plot y vs x:**
x	-6	-4	0	4	5	7	>>x=[-6 -4 0 4 5 7]; ↵ >>y=[9 3 -3 -5 2 0]; ↵ >>plot(x,y) ↵
y	9	3	-3	-5	2	0	

Graphing from columns of A :
```
>>A=[-2 4;-1 7;0 -1;1 -2;2 -3]; ↵
>>x=A(:,1); y=A(:,2); ↵
>>plot(x,y) ↵
```
Graphing from rows of B :
```
>>B=[-2 4 5 10;-1 7 -3 2]; ↵
>>x=B(1,:); y=B(2,:); ↵
>>plot(x,y) ↵
```

We picked up the x and y data from the column space what if we choose the data to be plotted from the row space for example from $B=\begin{bmatrix}-2 & 4 & 5 & 10\\-1 & 7 & -3 & 2\end{bmatrix}$ in which the first and second rows (section 2.6) are for the x and y data respectively and we intend to plot them. Shown above on the right side is the implementation (graph is not shown for space reason).

In order to plot the mathematical expression using the **plot**, one first needs to calculate the functional values using the scalar code (section 14.2) and then applies the function. During the calculation, computational step selection is mandatory which is completely user-defined. For instance we wish to plot the function $f(x)=x^2-x+2$ over $-2\le x\le 3$. Let us choose some step size say 0.1. The **x** vector as a row matrix is generated by **x=-2:0.1:3;** (section 1.3). At every element in **x** vector, the functional value is computed and assigned to workspace **f** by **f=x.^2-x+2;**. The **f** is any user-given name. Now we call the function writing **plot(x,f)** to see the graph (not shown for space reason). The function **plot** just draws the graph, no graphical features such as x axis label or title are added to the graph. It is the user who is supposed to add these graphical features (section 13.3).

13.2.2 Multiple y data versus common x data

The **plot** keeps many options, one of which is just discussed in the last subsection. We graph several y data versus common x data with the help of the same **plot** but with different number of input arguments. Let us choose the attached table on the right side for the graphing. We intend to plot the y_1, y_2, and y_3 on common x data. To do so,

Tabular data for multiple y versus common x:						
x	-6	-4	0	4	5	7
y_1	9	3	-3	-5	2	0
y_2	0	-2	1	0	5	7.7
y_3	-1	2	8	1	0	-3

>>x=[-6 -4 0 4 5 7]; ↵ ← Assigning x data as row matrix to x
>>y1=[9 3 -3 -5 2 0]; ↵ ← Assigning y_1 data as row matrix to y1
>>y2=[0 -2 1 0 5 7.7]; ↵ ← Assigning y_2 data as row matrix to y2
>>y3=[-1 2 8 1 0 -3]; ↵ ← Assigning y_3 data as row matrix to y3
>>plot(x,y1,x,y2,x,y3) ↵ ← Applying the function plot

The **plot** now has six input arguments – two for each graph, the first and second of which are the common x data and y data to be plotted respectively. If there were four y data, the command would be **plot(x,y1,x,y2,x,y3,x,y4)**. Once the data is plotted for several y, identifying the y traces is obvious and which is carried out by the command **legend**. The command **legend('y1','y2','y3')** puts the distinction among various graphs. The input argument of the **legend** is any user-given name but under quote and separated by a comma. The number of y traces must be equal to the number of input arguments of the **legend**. We gave the names **y1, y2,** and **y3** for the three y traces respectively. In doing so, we end up with the figure 13.5(b). You can even move the legend on the plot area using the mouse. You see all graphics throughout the text as black and white plots because we did not include color graphics in the text (for expense reason). But MATLAB displays figures in color plots, which you can easily identify.

Multiple y trace data can be in a matrix too. Let us say we have
$$A=\begin{bmatrix}-2 & 4 & 5 & 10\\ -1 & 7 & -3 & 2\\ 0 & 4 & -4 & -9\\ -5 & 3 & 7 & -2\\ 4 & -2 & 0 & -3\end{bmatrix}$$
and we intend to plot the first row of A as x data and the rest four rows will be the four consecutive y traces. Its straightforward implementation is shown above (graph is not shown for space reason).

Graphing multiple y data from the matrix A:
>>A=[-2 4 5 10; -1 7 -3 2;0 4 -4 -9;-5 3 7 -2;4 -2 0 -3]; ↵
>>x=A(1,:); ↵ ← Assigning the first row to x
>>y1=A(2,:); ↵ ← Assigning the second row to y1
>>y2=A(3,:); ↵ ← Assigning the third row to y2
>>y3=A(4,:); ↵ ← Assigning the fourth row to y3
>>y4=A(5,:); ↵ ← Assigning the fifth row to y4
>>plot(x,y1,x,y2,x,y3,x,y4) ↵ ← Calling the plot
>>legend('y1','y2','y3','y4') ↵ ← Putting the legend

Another situation can be we have several functions and we intend to plot them on common x variation. For instance we wish to graph $y_1 = x^3 - x^2 + 4$ and $y_2 = x^2 - 7x - 5$ on common $-1 \le x \le 3$. Under these circumstances, the step selection of the x data is compulsory. Without calculating the functional values of the given y curves, we can not graph the functions and for which we use the scalar code (section 14.2). Let us choose the step size as 0.1. We first generate the common **x** vector as a row matrix writing **x=-1:0.1:3;** and then calculate y_1 and y_2 (**y1**⇔ y_1 and **y2**⇔ y_2) writing **y1=x.^3-x.^2+4; y2=x.^2-7*x-5;** and eventually the plot appears executing **plot(x,y1,x,y2)**, graph not shown. Thus you can plot three or more functions. To learn more, execute **help plot** at the command prompt.

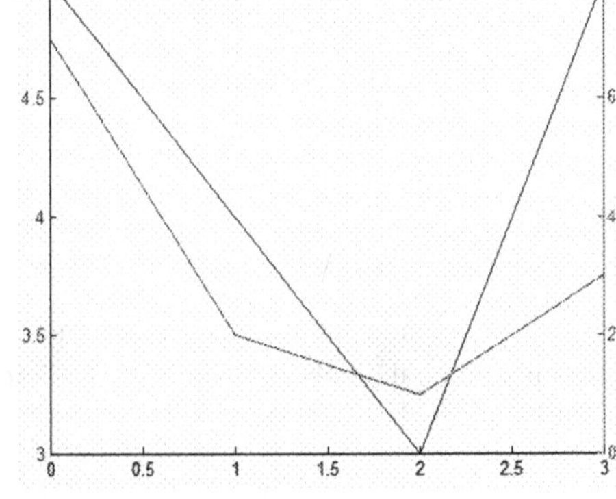

Figure 13.5(c) Two dissimilar y data on common x

13.2.3 Two dissimilar y data on common x

Sometimes two dissimilar y data on common x needs to be plotted. For instance the x, y_1, and y_2 data in
$$\left\{\begin{matrix}x & 0 & 1 & 2 & 3\\ y_1 & 5 & 4 & 3 & 5\\ y_2 & 7 & 2 & 1 & 3\end{matrix}\right\}$$
are in second, meter, and kilogram respectively. Obviously the data in meter and kilogram can not be plotted in a single axis or y trace. For comparison reason one must use two different y axes and which we implement using the function **plotyy** with the syntax **plotyy(** x data as a row matrix, y_1 data as a row matrix, x data as a row matrix, y_2 data as a row matrix). Attached on the right side is the implementation of the function in which the first, second, and third lines are to assign the x, y_1, and y_2 data to the workspace **x, y1,** and **y2** respectively. The

Two dissimilar y data on common x:
>>x=[0 1 2 3]; ↵
>>y1=[5 4 3 5]; ↵
>>y2=[7 2 1 3]; ↵
>>plotyy(x,y1,x,y2) ↵

last line just calls the function to display the graph like the figure 13.5(c). The left and right vertical axes in the graph correspond to the y_1 and y_2 data respectively. The reader is referred to section 13.3 for property addition. But this particular graph needs some other approach. Let us say we intend to include the left and right y axis labels as **Distance in meter** and **Mass in Kg** respectively for which we execute the right side attached commands. In the first line, now we assign the output of the function **plotyy** to some user-given variable which we called **h**. When a graph is plotted, many object properties become associated with the graphics like axes, background, title, text, etc. The **h** is a graphics handle which holds the axes information. The **h(1)** and **h(2)** provide control on the left and right axes respectively. The command **get(h(1),'Ylabel')** looks for the **Ylabel** (reserve word and put under quote) property in the left y-axis. The command **set** writes the user-supplied string or set of characters in the y-axis. The **set** has three input arguments, the first, second, and third of which are the y axis object location (found by the **get**), reserve word **String** under quote, and the user-given words put under quote respectively. Figure 13.5(d) shows the graph following the execution.

Adding y label in dissimilar y plots:

```
>>h=plotyy(x,y1,x,y2); ↵
>>set(get(h(1),'Ylabel'),'String','Distance in meter') ↵
>>set(get(h(2),'Ylabel'),'String','Mass in Kg') ↵
```

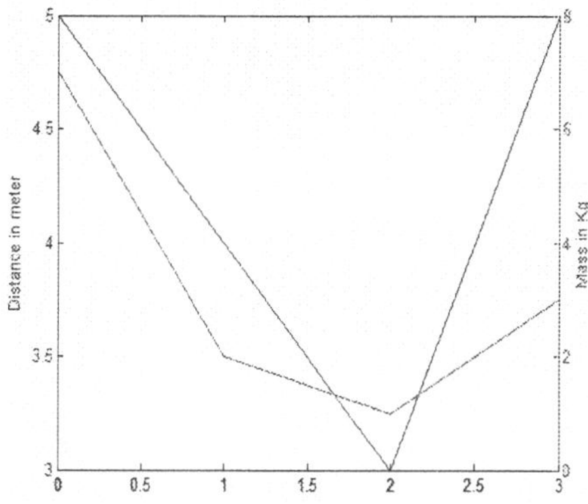

Figure 13.5(d) Labeling the left and right axes of the figure 13.5(c)

As another example, let us say we wish to plot the curves $y_1 = x^3 - x^2 + 4$ and $y_2 = 400(x^2 - 7x - 5)$ on the left and right y axes over the common $-1 \le x \le 3$ with a x step 0.1. We first generate a **x** vector as a row matrix with the given interval and step size using **x=-1:0.1:3;** and then calculate each function using the scalar code (section 14.2) to have the functional values of y_1 and y_2 at the points in **x** in the workspace **y1** and **y2** respectively using the following: **y1=x.^3-x.^2+4; y2=400*(x.^2-7*x-5);**. Eventually the graph appears by the use of the command **plotyy(x,y1,x,y2)**.

13.2.4 Piecewise continuous functions

Two or more functions which are piecewise continuous can be graphed using the **plot** (subsection 13.2.1) too. Let us say we intend to graph the functions $y_1 = 2x^2 - 45$ over $0 \le x \le 3$, $y_2 = -30 + (x-3)^2$ over $3 \le x \le 6$, and $y_3 = -25 + 4(x-3)$ over $6 \le x \le 9$. Let us not forget that the **plot** graphs the functions on numerical data basis so we have to make the data available by first choosing some step size (let us choose 0.1) and then calculating the functions through the scalar code (section 14.2). Attached on the right side is the complete code for graphing the three piecewise functions as shown in the figure 13.5(e). We graph the functions one at a time. After plotting the first graph that is y_1 versus x, we use the command **hold** which retains the last graphics plot. Afterwards it superimposes the subsequent graphs on the same axes settings. We do not have to use the **hold** command again and again.

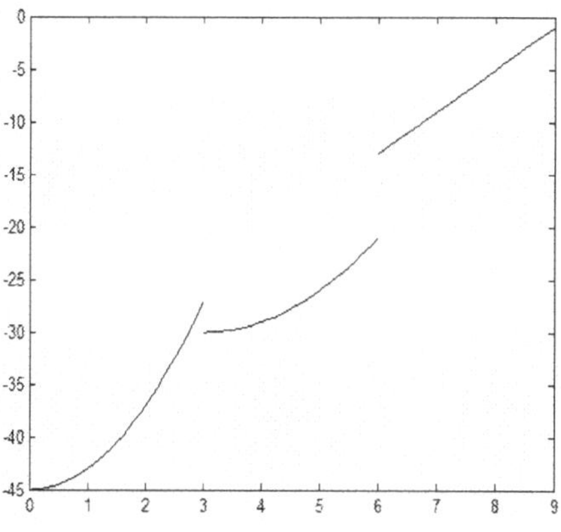

Figure 13.5(e) Plotting three piecewise continuous functions

for graphing the piecewise continuous functions:

```
>>x=0:0.1:3; ↵         ← x holds x points with step 0.1 on 0 ≤ x ≤ 3 as a row matrix
>>y1=2*x.^2-45; ↵← y1 holds y1 functional values as a row matrix
>>plot(x,y1) ↵         ← Graphing only y1 versus x data
>>hold ↵               ← Holding the last graph for subsequent plots
>>x=3:0.1:6; ↵         ← x holds x points with step 0.1 on 3 ≤ x ≤ 6 as a row matrix
>>y2=-30+(x-3).^2; ↵ ← y2 holds y2 functional values as a row matrix
>>plot(x,y2) ↵         ← Graphing only y2 versus x data on previously held graph
>>x=6:0.1:9; ↵         ← x holds x points with step 0.1 on 6 ≤ x ≤ 9 as a row matrix
>>y3=-25+4*(x-3); ↵ ← y3 holds y3 functional values as a row matrix
>>plot(x,y3) ↵         ← Graphing only y3 versus x data on previously held graph
```

13.2.5 Contour plot from sampled $f(x, y)$ data

Not only we can plot the contour plots from the symbolic expressions (subsection 13.1.4) but also one can plot the contours from tabular or matrix data by virtue of the command **contour**. Concerning the right side attached table, it contains the sample values of some function $f(x, y)$ at some x and y. In the table, the x and y vary from -2 to 3 and -1 to 2 respectively. The shaded cell data in the table corresponds to

Tabular data for the contour plot:

$y \downarrow$ \ $x \rightarrow$	-2	-1	0	1	2	3
-1	10	10	10	10	10	10
0	0	2	2	2	2	0
1	-9	-9	-9	-9	-9	0
2	3	3	3	3	3	3

$f(x,y)=f(2,1)=-9$. In order to graph the contour from the data, the x, y, and $f(x,y)$ data must be available in the workspace. We assign the functional values of $f(x,y)$ to some rectangular matrix f as shown below:

```
>>f=[10 10 10 10 10 10;0 2 2 2 2 0;-9 -9 -9 -9 -9 0;3 3 3 3 3 3]; ↵
>>x=-2:3; y=-1:2; ↵      ← Each vector with increment 1
>>clabel(contour(x,y,f)) ↵
```

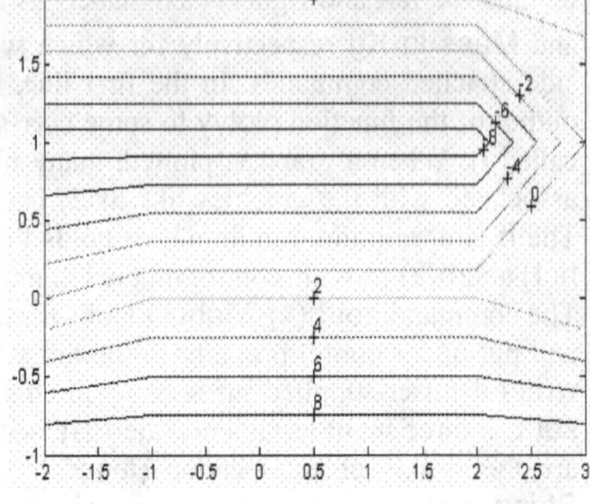

Figure 13.6(a) Contour plot for the tabular data

The x and y variations must be as a row matrix which we assigned to the workspace x and y respectively. The last command line returns the figure 13.6(a). The function contour takes three input arguments, the first, second, and third of which are the x axis variation vector as a row matrix, the y axis variation vector as a row matrix, and the sampled functional values of $f(x,y)$ as a rectangular matrix respectively. The command clabel (abbreviation for contour label) puts the value of the contour curve on the graph which is more indicative.

Recall that in subsection 13.1.4, we contoured the function $f(x,y)=x\left(y-\frac{1}{2}\right)e^{-3x^2-4y^2}$ over the domain formed by $-1.2\le x\le 1.2$ and $-1\le y\le 1$. We wish to do the same using the numerical approach. Again we need to select some step size (let us say 0.1 in each direction) and calculate the functional values of $f(x,y)$ as a rectangular matrix based on the step size through the use of the scalar code (section 14.2). Attached on the right side is the complete code. With the chosen step size, first we generate the x and y vectors both as a row matrix in the given domain of x and y respectively. Two identical size rectangular grid matrices X (only the x coordinates) and Y (only the y coordinates) are generated applying the meshgrid of subsection 3.10.2. We write the scalar code on X-Y not on x-y of the given function which serves the purpose of computation and assign the computed data to f. However the last line in the implementation brings the graph of the figure 13.2(c) with the contour labeling in front (not shown for space reason). To learn more about the function, execute help contour at the command prompt.

Computation and graphing for figure 13.2(c):

```
>>x=-1.2:0.1:1.2; y=-1:0.1:1; ↵
>>[X,Y]=meshgrid(x,y); ↵
>>f=X.*(Y-0.5).*exp(-3*X.^2-4*Y.^2); ↵
>>clabel(contour(x,y,f)) ↵
```

13.2.6 Surface plot from sampled $f(x,y)$ data

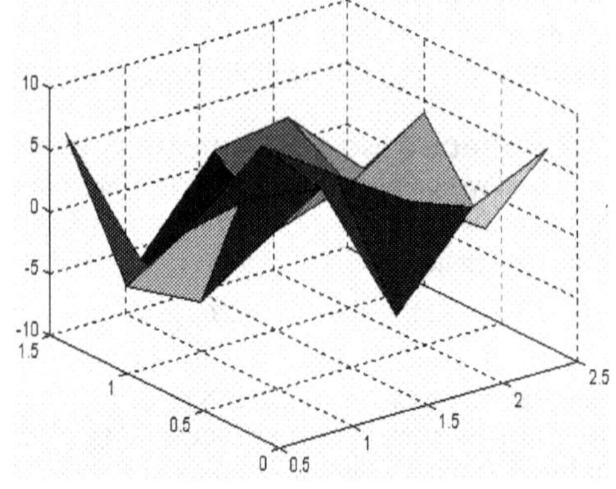

Figure 13.6(b) Surface plot from the sampled $f(x,y)$ data

Like the subsection 13.1.6 mentioned expressional plots, MATLAB also retains the provision for graphing a mesh or surface from the sampled $f(x,y)$ data by means of the function mesh or surf. Both functions accept three input arguments – the x variation vector as a row matrix, the y variation vector as a row matrix, and the sampled $f(x,y)$ data as a rectangular matrix. Let us consider the sampled $f(x,y)$ as $\begin{bmatrix} 9 & 8 & -4 & 3 & 6 \\ 4 & 9 & 5 & 1 & -3 \\ -3 & -6 & -2 & 0 & 4 \\ 7 & -5 & 2 & 3 & -3 \end{bmatrix}$ in which the row and column variations correspond to $0.5\le x\le 2.5$ and $0.2\le y\le 1.4$ respectively. The x and y variation vectors must correspond to the sample values of $f(x,y)$ or the rectangular matrix elements. Since there are 5 columns along the row direction, we must choose 5 points over $0.5\le x\le 2.5$ i.e. the row vector corresponding to x should be [0.5 1 1.5 2 2.5]. Again there are 4 rows in the column direction, the interval $0.2\le y\le 1.4$ must be split as [0.2 0.6 1 1.4]. Placed on the right side is the implementation on the surface plot which results in the figure 13.6(b). The first line is to assign the $f(x,y)$ sample data to f, so is the second line to x and y for the x and y directed vectors respectively. The third line calls the function for graphing. The reader can execute mesh(x,y,f) to see the mesh plot for the problem. The functions merely graph the surface or mesh without labeling. To learn more about the functions, execute help surf or help mesh at the command prompt.

Graphing the surface plot of the figure 13.6(b):

```
>>f=[9 8 -4 3 6;4 9 5 1 -3;-3 -6 -2 0 4;7 -5 2 3 -3]; ↵
>>x=[0.5 1 1.5 2 2.5]; y=[0.2 0.6 1 1.4]; ↵
>>surf(x,y,f) ↵
```

Surface plot is also obtainable from functional expressions. Recall that in subsection 13.2.5, we made the sampled data available for the function $f(x,y) = x\left(y-\frac{1}{2}\right)e^{-3x^2-4y^2}$ to the workspace **f** over the domain on $-1.2 \le x \le 1.2$ and $-1 \le y \le 1$ using the step size 0.1. You need to reexecute the commands to have the **x**, **y**, and **f**. Our objective is to surface graph this function for which the necessary command is **surf(x,y,f)** or **mesh(x,y,f)**, graph is not shown.

13.2.7 Multiple graphs in the same window

The function **subplot** splits a figure window in subwindows based on the user definition. It accepts three positive integer numbers as the input arguments, the first and second of which indicate the number of subwindows in the horizontal and the number of subwindows in the vertical directions respectively. For example 22 means two subwindows horizontally and two subwindows vertically, 32 means three subwindows horizontally and two subwindows vertically, ... and so on. The third integer in the input argument numbered consecutively just offers the control on the subwindows so generated. If the first two digits are 32, there should be 6 subwindows and they are numbered and controlled using 1 through 6. When you plot some graph in a subwindow, as if you are handling an independent figure window.

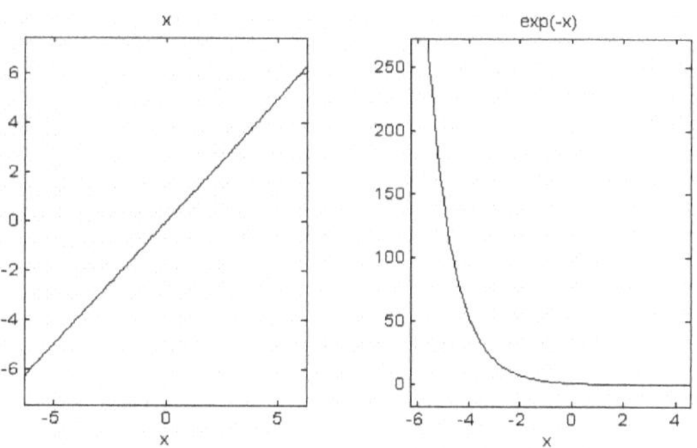

Figure 13.6(c) Plots of $y = x$ and $y = e^{-x}$ side by side in the same window

Let us say we intend to graph $y = x$ and $y = e^{-x}$ side by side as two different plots using the **ezplot** of subsection 13.1.1 but in the same window. If we imagine the subfigures as matrix elements, we have a figure matrix of size 1×2 (one row and two columns). That is why the first two integers of the input argument of the **subplot** should be 12. Attached commands at the lower right corner in this page show the figure 13.6(c). The third integers 1 and 2 give the control on the first and second subfigures respectively.

As another example, we wish to plot $y = x$ and $y = e^{-x}$ in the upper row and only $y = (1-e^{-x})$ in the lower row subfigures in the same window whose implementation needs the lower right side codes and whose final output is the figure 13.6(d). We are supposed to have four figures when the integer input argument of the **subplot** is 22 (two for rows and two for columns). The arguments 221, 222, 223, and 224 provide handle on the four figures consecutively. But the figures could have been plotted on 223 and 224 are absent so we ignore them. The argument 21 creates two subfigures (two rows and one column) handled by 211 and 212, but 211 is absent so we ignore that. Let us see the input arguments of the **subplot** for different subfigures (each third brace set is one subfigure in the following tabular representation) as follows:

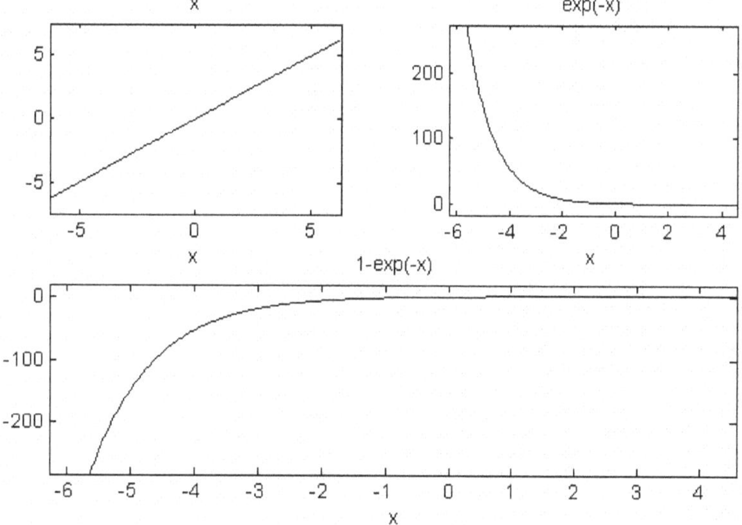

Figure 13.6(d) Plots of $y = x$ and $y = e^{-x}$ in the upper row and $y = (1-e^{-x})$ in the lower row in the same window

Commands for the figure 13.6(c):

>>subplot(121) ↵ ← It handles the first graph
>>ezplot('x') ↵ ← Plotting $y = x$
>>subplot(122) ↵ ← It handles the second graph
>>ezplot('exp(-x)') ↵ ← Plotting $y = e^{-x}$

Commands for the figure 13.6(d):

>>subplot(221) ↵ ← Subfigure selection for $y = x$
>>ezplot('x') ↵ ← Plotting $y = x$
>>subplot(222) ↵ ← Subfigure selection for $y = e^{-x}$
>>ezplot('exp(-x)') ↵ ← Plotting $y = e^{-x}$
>>subplot(212) ↵ ← Subfigure selection for $y = (1-e^{-x})$
>>ezplot('1-exp(-x)') ↵ ← Plotting $y = (1-e^{-x})$

Subfigures needed	First two input integers of subplot	Third input integer of subplot	Commands we need
[] [] [] []	22	[1] [2] [3] [4]	subplot(221) subplot(222) subplot(223) subplot(224)
[] [] [ ]	22 for upper two (lower two remain empty) 21 for the lower one (upper one remains empty)	[1] [2] [2]	subplot(221) subplot(222) subplot(212)
[ ] [] []	21 for the upper one (lower one remains empty) 22 for the lower two (upper two remain empty)	[1] [3] [4]	subplot(211) subplot(223) subplot(224)
[] (tall box) []	22 for the left two (right two remain empty) 12 for the right one (left one remains empty)	[1] 2 [3]	subplot(221) subplot(223) subplot(122)
(tall box) [] []	22 for right two (left two remain empty) 12 for the left one (right one remains empty)	1 [2] [4]	subplot(222) subplot(224) subplot(121)

13.2.8 Scatter data plot using small circles

Scatter plot for the tabular data:

```
>>x=[-6 -4 0 4 5 7]; ↵
>>y=[9 3 -3 -5 2 0]; ↵
>>scatter(x,y) ↵
```

Instead of having a graph as continuous line, it is possible to have the graph in terms of bold dots or round circles like the figure 13.6(e). The function **scatter** returns this sort of graph for which the common syntax is **scatter(** x data as a row matrix, y data as a row matrix, size of the circle, color of the circle). The function also accepts the first two input arguments. The size of the circle is any user-given integer number. The larger is the number, the bigger is the size for example 75, 100, etc. Let us graph the subsection 13.2.1 mentioned tabular data (x and y) as the scatter plot. The command we need is placed on the middle right side in this page. Upon execution of the command, we see the figure 13.6(e). The color of the circle is blue by default but any three element row matrix sets the user-defined color. The three element row matrix refers to red, green, and blue components respectively each one within 0 and 1. Black color means all zero, white means all 1, red means other two components zero, and so on. The circle displayed in the figure 13.6(e) is all empty but one fills the circle using the reserve word **filled** under quote and included as another input argument to the **scatter**. Let us say we intend to scatter graph with circle size 100 and the circles should be filled with black color. The necessary command is **scatter(x,y,100,[0 0 0],'filled')**, graph is not shown.

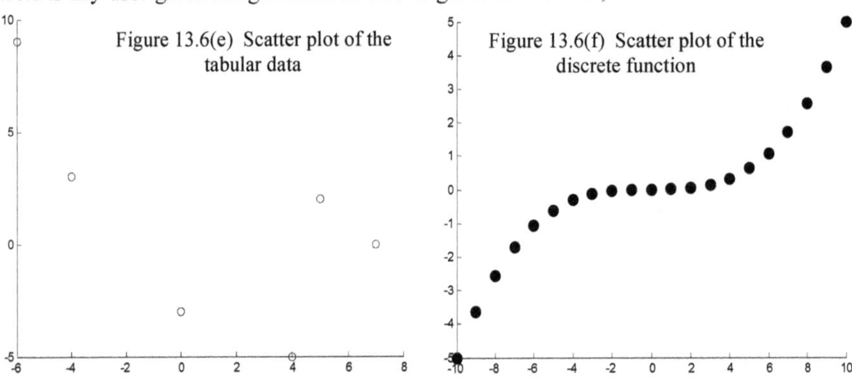

Figure 13.6(e) Scatter plot of the tabular data

Figure 13.6(f) Scatter plot of the discrete function

This type of graph is suitable for representation of the function which is discrete in nature. For instance the discrete function $y[n]=\frac{n^3}{200}$ over $-10\le n\le 10$ is to be plotted with black circles of size 100 where n is integer. As a procedure, we form a row matrix **n** to generate the interval with start value −10, increment 1, and end value 10 writing **n=-10:10;**. The scalar code of section 14.2 computes the $y[n]$ values and assigns those to workspace **y**. However the complete code is placed on the right side which brings about the graph of the figure 13.6(f).

Scatter plot for discrete function:

```
>>n=-10:10; y=n.^3/200; ↵
>>scatter(n,y,100,[0 0 0],'filled') ↵
```

13.2.9 Discrete function or data plotting using vertical lines

In the last subsection we discussed how one graphs the discrete functional data using bold dots. There is another option which graphs any discrete data using vertical lines proportionate to the discrete functional values. A discrete function may exist in two forms – data and expression based. The function that graphs a discrete function is **stem** which has the syntax stem(x data as a row matrix, y data as a row matrix). If we have some expression based discrete function, first the sample values of the discrete function need to be calculated through the scalar code (section 14.2) and after that the graphing is performed. Let us plot the discrete function $f[n]=2^{-n}\cos n$ over the integer interval $-2 \le n \le 5$. Attached above is the implementation of the command which results in the figure 13.6(g). In the implementation, the workspace n and f hold the eight integers from -2 to 5 and sample values of $f[n]$ both as a row matrix. By default the vertical line color of the stem plot is blue. User-defined color of the vertical lines is obtainable adding one more input argument to the stem mentioning the color type but under quote (r for red, g for green, b for blue, c for cyan, m for magenta, y for yellow, k for black, and w for white). If we wish to set the vertical line color as green for the graph of the figure 13.6(g), we exercise the command stem(n,f,'g'). The vertical line head circles can be filled by using the command stem(n,f,'g','filled') where filled is a reserve word placed under quote.

Discrete function plot using vertical lines:

```
>>n=-2:5; ↵
>>f=2.^(-n).*cos(n); ↵
>>stem(n,f) ↵
```

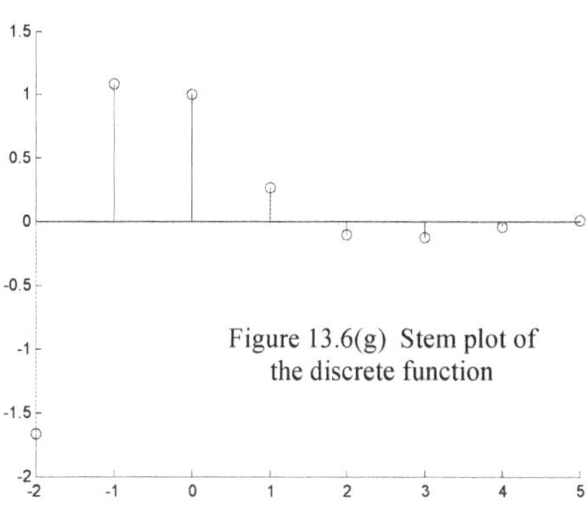

Figure 13.6(g) Stem plot of the discrete function

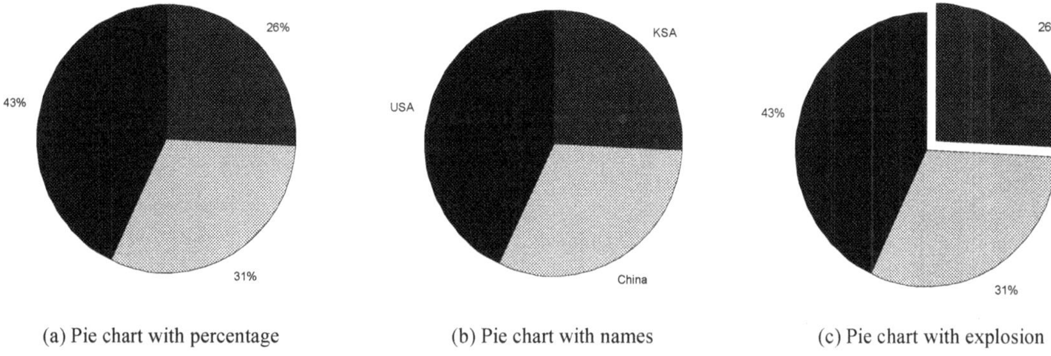

(a) Pie chart with percentage (b) Pie chart with names (c) Pie chart with explosion

Figures 13.7(a)-(c) Different pie charts

13.2.10 Pie chart from some data

Given some data, we graph the pie chart from the data using the function pie (for two dimensional chart) or pie3 (for three dimensional chart) with the syntax pie (given data as a row matrix) or pie3 (given data as a row matrix). Let us say we have the data set x =[78 56.67 46.88] and in percentage it becomes [43% 31% 26%] (from division of each data by the total sum). Executing the command pie([78 56.67 46.88]) returns the figure 13.7(a). Suppose the three data are for the countries USA, China, and KSA respectively and we intend to label them in the chart for which the necessary command is pie([78 56.67 46.88],{'USA','China','KSA'}) and the outcome is shown in figure 13.7(b). There are two input arguments in the last command, the first and second of which are the given data as a row matrix and the user-given string names under second brace respectively. Within the second brace in the second input argument, each name is separated by a comma and placed under quote. If the pie sections slightly come out from the center of the pie, the graph looks better. We intend to do so for the third data in the given set. The intended pie is notified by 1 and the others by 0. The 1s and 0s so mentioned are entered as a row matrix and as the second input argument to the pie. Therefore the command pie([78 56.67 46.88],[0 0 1]) results the figure 13.7(c). If we wanted to explode the first and third pie sections, the command would be pie([78 56.67 46.88],[1 0 1]). Whatever syntax we exercised using the pie can be exercised using the pie3 for the three dimensional chart for example pie3([78 56.67 46.88],[1 0 1]) for the last command (graph is not shown for the space reason).

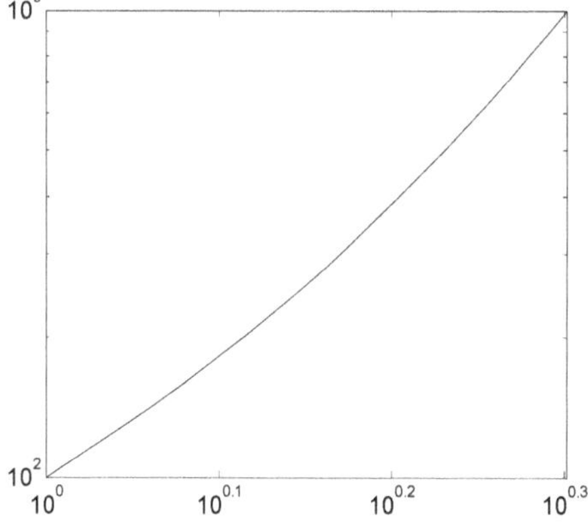

Figure 13.7(d) Log-log plot for the 10×10^{x} versus x

13.2.11 Logarithmic plots

Different types of logarithmic plots are easily graphed in MATLAB. Some of the logarithmic plotters are semilogx, semilogy, and loglog. Suppose we have some function y versus x, then the three functions graph y versus $\log_{10} x$, $\log_{10} y$ versus x, and $\log_{10} y$ versus $\log_{10} x$ respectively. The syntaxes for the three functions are

semilogx(x,y), **semilogy(x,y)**, and **loglog(x,y)** where the input arguments **X** and **y** are the functional data for the x and y respectively but both as a row matrix. If we intend to plot y versus 10^x, 10^y versus x, and 10^y versus 10^x using the three functions respectively, we are supposed to have straight lines from the three graphings.

Suppose $y = 10 \times 10^x$ and we intend to see the log-log plot for the y versus x over $1 \le x \le 2$ with a x step 0.05. For the functional data computation, we write the scalar code (section 14.2) of the given function. First we generate the x data as a row matrix (section 1.3) writing **x=1:0.05:2;** and then the y data is computed by writing **y=10*10.^x;**. Finally the command **loglog(x,y)** results in the graph of the figure 13.7(d). The other two logarithmic plotters also function in a similar fashion. Execute **help loglog** to learn more about the function at the command prompt.

13.2.12 Three dimensional curve plotting

Usually the three dimensional curves are given in terms of the parametric equations. The function **plot3** graphs a three dimensional curve described by the parametric equations $\{x(t), y(t), z(t)\}$ with the syntax **plot3(x,y,z)** where **x**, **y**, and **z** correspond to the $x(t)$, $y(t)$, and $z(t)$ respectively and each of the three input arguments of the **plot3** is a row or column matrix data for the corresponding parametric expression. Let us say we intend to graph the three dimensional curve $x(t) = 4\cos t$, $y(t) = t^2$, and $z(t) = t^2$ over the parameter interval $0 \le t \le 2\pi$. The user needs to decide the parameter step size let us say 0.01. As a first step, we generate the t vector as a row matrix writing **t=0:0.01:2*pi;**. Then, the parametric functional data as a row matrix is made available using the scalar code (section 14.2) and for which we write **x=4*cos(t); y=t.^2; z=t.^2;**. Finally, the command **plot3(x,y,z)** brings forth the graph of the figure 13.7(e) without the grid lines. In order to include the grid lines, just execute **grid** at the command prompt. Execute **help plot3** to see other options in the function.

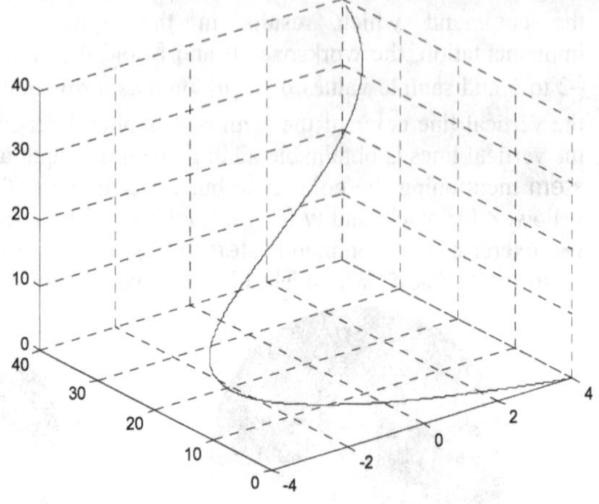

Figure 13.7(e) Plot of the three dimensional parametric curve $x(t) = 4\cos t$, $y(t) = t^2$, and $z(t) = t^2$

The **plot3** we exercised works on data basis. There is another function by the name **ezplot3** for three dimensional curve plotting which works on expression basis without any calculation and with the syntax **ezplot3**(vector code of $x(t)$ under quote, vector code of $y(t)$ under quote, vector code of $z(t)$ under quote, t parameter bounds as a two element row matrix). The parametric function used in the **plot3** is now exercised through **ezplot3** as **ezplot3('4*cos(t)','t^2','t^2',[0 2*pi])** which also shows the graph like the figure 13.7(e).

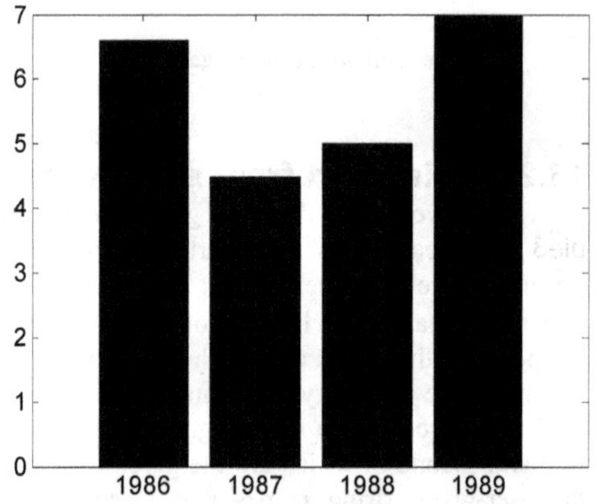

Figure 13.8(a) Bar graph for some x-y data

13.2.13 Bar graph from some x-y data

Suppose we have some year data x =[1986 1987 1988 1989] (four consecutive years) and yield data y =[6.6 4.5 5 7] (percentage yield from some stock) respectively which we intend to use for plotting the bar graph. The command **bar** helps us graph the data with the syntax **bar(** x data as a row matrix, y data as a row matrix). Attached on the right side is the implementation of the graphing (figure 13.8(a)) in which the vertical and horizontal axes correspond to the y and x data respectively. In the first line of the implementation, we entered the x data as a row matrix using the colon operator (section 1.3). The second and third lines of the implementation are to enter the y data as a row matrix and to call the **bar** for graphing respectively. With the same syntax, the function **bar3** displays the three dimensional bar (execute **bar3(x,y)** at the command prompt). Also execute **help bar** to see other options included in the function at the command prompt.

Plotting the bar graph:

```
>>x=1986:1989; ↵
>>y=[6.6 4.5 5 7]; ↵
>>bar(x,y) ↵
```

13.2.14 Intensity image plot of some matrix data

Starting from some matrix data, one may need to display the data as an intensity image plot. Usually in this type of plot we get large dimension matrix like 200×200, 400×400, or more. The intensity plot needs us to know about the data storage of a digital image. First of all a digital image is nothing but a specially arranged data matrix [3]. A digital image element or given matrix element is termed as a pixel and its value must be within predefined range usually as a power of 2 like 64, 256, etc. Any given rectangular matrix data (say **A**) is linearly mapped (minimum and maximum of **A** to 0 and 1 respectively) between 0 and 1 using the function mat2gray (abbreviation for matrix to (2) gray level). After that we map again the 0-1 data to user-defined closest gray level such as 256, 512, etc employing the function im2uint8 (for 256 gray levels), im2uint16 (for 512 gray levels), etc respectively. The function imshow displays the mapped data as a gray image when the matrix is its input argument therefore the command as a whole we need is imshow(im2uint8(mat2gray(A))) for any rectangular matrix A.

As an example let us consider the two dimensional function $f(x,y)=\operatorname{sinc}(x^2+y^2)$ (table 10.A for the MATLAB sinc function) over the domain $-2 \le x \le 2$ and $-1 \le y \le 1$. We intend to show the $f(x,y)$ data as a gray intensity image on the x and y steps 0.02 and 0.02 respectively. The computation of the $f(x,y)$ needs the generation of the rectangular grid points (subsection 3.10.2) as follows:

Figure 13.8(b) Plot of $f(x,y)$ as a gray intensity image

>>x=[-2:0.02:2]; ↵ ← Generating the x grid points as a row matrix over $-2 \le x \le 2$ and given step size 0.02

>>y=[-1:0.02:1]; ↵ ← Generating y grid points as a row matrix over $-1 \le y \le 1$ and given step size 0.02

>>[X,Y]=meshgrid(x,y); ↵ ← X and Y hold only the x and only the y coordinates respectively

>>A=sinc(X.^2+Y.^2); ↵ ← A is a rectangular matrix holding the $f(x,y)$ values at the like positional points of X and Y

>>imshow(im2uint8(mat2gray(A))) ↵ ← Brings the intensity image of the figure 13.8(b) in front

At this point everyone appreciates a color plot specially nowadays. If you say I intend to display the color intensity plot, you have to choose some MATLAB defined color-map (which are reserve and whose names are jet, autumn, bone, colorcube, cool, copper, flag, hot, hsv, pink, spring, and summer). Any one of these color-maps appears as the second input argument of the imshow for example imshow(im2uint8(mat2gray(A)),hsv) for the hsv. Sorry folks, the text is written in black and white form. We could not show you the color image intensity plot certainly MATLAB will not disappoint you if you execute just mentioned command at the command prompt.

13.3 Some troubleshooting while graphing

When you graph some function or data in MATLAB, you may encounter a variety of problems depending on what you plot, insert, or remove. The problems might be related to axes, curves, insertion of some texts, .. etc. We address some frequently occurred problems in the following so that the reader can quickly diagnose the problems and troubleshoots easily while graphing in MATLAB. Following commands can be exercised at the command prompt or in an M-file.

Table 13.A MATLAB codes for various symbols (not in alphabetical order)

MATLAB code	Symbol	MATLAB code	Symbol	MATLAB code	Symbol	MATLAB code	Symbol
\omega	ω	\gamma	γ	\mu	μ	\Xi	Ξ
\Omega	Ω	\Gamma	Γ	\nu	ν	\xi	ξ
\phi	ϕ	\delta	δ	\surd	$\surd$	\oplus	$\oplus$
\Phi	Φ	\Delta	Δ	\in	$\in$	\alpha	α
\zeta	ζ	\epsilon	ε	\chi	χ	\sim	$\sim$
\pi	π	\eta	η	\leq	$\le$	\iota	ι
\Pi	Π	\Psi	Ψ	\geq	$\ge$	\infty	∞
\beta	β	\psi	ψ	\pm	$\pm$	\exists	$\exists$
\theta	θ	\kappa	κ	\int	$\int$	\cap	$\cap$
\Theta	Θ	\Sigma	Σ	\copyright	©	\subset	$\subset$
\lambda	λ	\sigma	σ	\nabla	∇	\ni	$\ni$
\Lambda	Λ	\neq	$\neq$	\upsilon	υ	\oslash	Ø
\partial	∂	\rho	ρ	\tau	τ	\otimes	$\otimes$

♦♦ I do not want axis in my graph

One can remove the axes and boxes of any plot (two or three dimensional) executing axis off.

♦♦ I want to put grid lines in my graph

One can include the grid lines in any figure just executing the command grid at the command prompt or in an M-file. If you work in a figure window, you can select specifically x, y, or z (for three dimensional) grid lines going through Edit ⇒ Axes Properties.

♦♦ I want to put a symbol on the graph

Let us say $r=e^{-2\theta}\sin 2\theta$ is to be plotted over $0 \le \theta \le \pi$. Subsection 13.1.1 mentioned ezplot graphs the function upon the execution of the command ezplot('exp(-2*t)* sin(2*t)',[0 pi]) – t is used for θ and the graph is the figure 13.8(c) without inside text. Now we would like to drop the text The plot of $e^{-2\theta}\sin 2\theta$ on the graph plotted. The command **gtext** gives the provision for dropping a mouse-driven text (written under quote) on the graphics plotted. Let us execute the following at the command prompt:

```
>>gtext('The plot of e^-^2^\thetasin2\theta') ↵
```

Then, go to the figure window and you see that the mouse pointer is activated and a crosshair is appearing. Choose any convenient position in the graph and click the left button of the mouse to see the inside text as in the figure 13.8(c). The symbol θ is written by the command **\theta** in graphics. Any superscript is placed by the command ^, as explanation we can say e^{-} ⇔e^-, e^{-2} ⇔e^-^2, $e^{-2\theta}$ ⇔e^-^2\theta, ... etc. What if we have a subscript (performed by the operator _) for example let us drop the symbolic text $x_{79}y_{12}$ on the last graph for which we execute the command **gtext('x_7_9y_1_2')** at the command prompt. After that go to the figure window, choose any position in the plot to drop the subscript text, and click the left button of the mouse to see the text as in the figure 13.8(c). Multiple subscript writing follows the syntax similar to that of the superscript. The reader may require to know the MATLAB codes for the frequently encountered Greek symbols, which are presented in table 13.A.

Figure 13.8(c) Plot of $r = e^{-2\theta} \sin 2\theta$

Another option can be going through the **Insert** down **Text Box** from the figure window menu as seen in the figure 13.8(d). If you click the **Text Box**, a crosshair appears. Place mouse pointer at your desirable point in the drawn graph and drag the mouse. A box appears and inside the box, you can type anything you like. For example we could have written **e^-^2\theta** without the quote for $e^{-2\theta}$. But the box boundary appears in doing so. Rightclick the mouse on the box and select none as the line style to remove the boundary.

Data Cursor

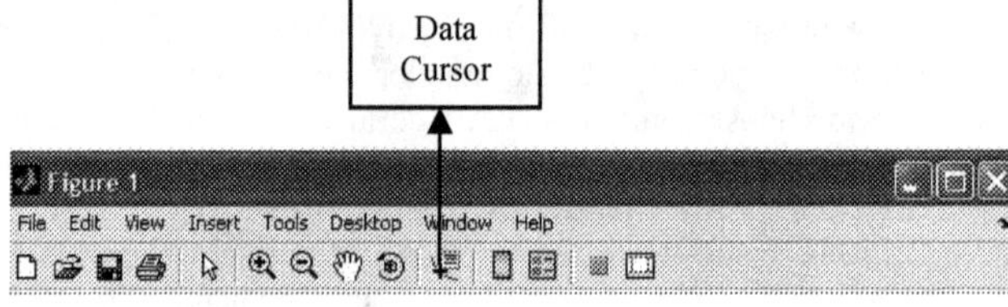

Figure 13.8(d) Menu of the figure window

⬍⬍ I want to see the data statistics of the plot

Statistics of a plot indicate the mean, variance, minimum value, maximum value, ... etc of the plot. The figure window of MATLAB helps us view the x data, y data, or even the multiple y data statistics. Referring to the figure 13.8(d), the clicking sequence is **Tools ⇒ Data Statistics**.

⬍⬍ How can I change the axes settings?

Sometimes adding more or removing unnecessary axis renders a better look of the graph plotted. Let us say we plot the data x=[0 1 1 2] and y=[1 1 0 0] employing the **plot** of subsection 13.2.1 as follows:

```
>>x=[0 1 1 2]; y=[1 1 0 0]; plot(x,y) ↵
```

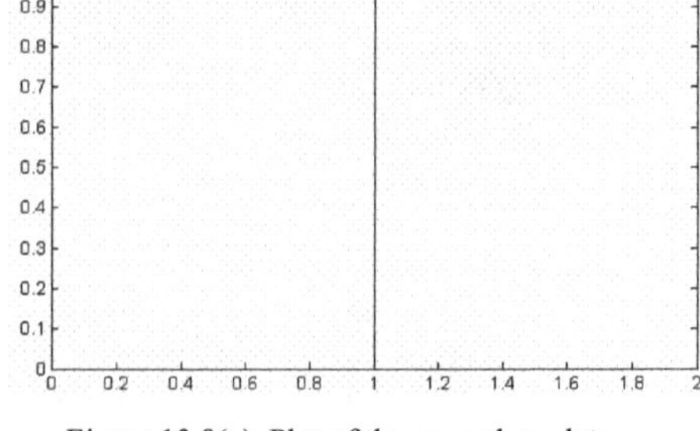

Figure 13.8(e) Plot of the x and y data

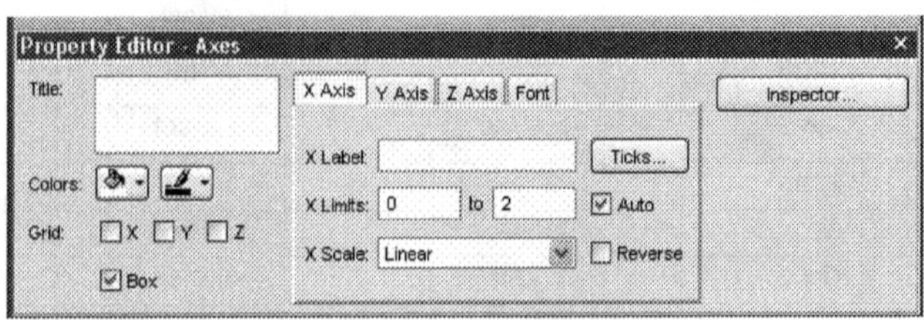

Figure 13.9(a) Property Editor for the Axes of the figure window

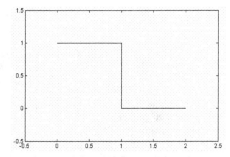

Figure 13.8(f) Replotting the figure 13.8(e) with different axes setting

The resulting graph is shown in the figure 13.8(e). As you see, the upper portion of the graph merges with the upper side of the plot area box. The function **plot** by default graphs the data within the minimum and maximum range. The minimum and maximum values of the x and y data are 0 and 2 and 0 and 1 respectively. Let us change them to −0.5 and 2.5 and −0.5 and 1.5 respectively. To implement that, we go to the figure window menu bar (figure 13.8(d)), click the **Edit** menu, and click **Axes Properties** in the dropdown menu. The Axes Property Editor of the figure 13.9(a) appears. The editor is showing the **X-Axis** selected by default. In the left and right slots beside the **X Limits** of the editor, we enter the –0.5 and 2.5 from keyboard respectively. Then we select the Y-Axis in the editor and enter the y limits similarly. In performing so, we see the figure 13.8(f) – certainly looks better.

♦ ♦ How can I change the figure background or the plot area background color?

The area behind the axes box of any figure window is called the figure background color. If you intend to change the default figure background color, click the Edit in the figure window menu bar and then click the Figure Properties in the drop down menu of the Edit. Figure Property Editor appears and you can choose any color in the Figure Property Editor.

The color in the axes box area is called the plot area background color which is white by default. We can change it from the Axes Property Editor of the figure 13.9(a) (clicking sequence is Edit → Axes Properties).

♦ ♦ I want to put the x label, y label, and tittle to my graph

Let us consider the figure 13.8(e). We intend to include the x label (X Data), y label (Y Data), and title (Plot of Y Data vs X Data) to the drawn graphics like the figure 13.9(b). To include the x label, click Insert menu of the figure 13.8(d), and then click X Label in dropdown menu. Down the x axis, the cursor starts blinking and type X Data at the blinking position of the cursor. Similarly you can include both the y label and title from the Insert menu. Another option is use the command line functions xlabel, ylabel, and title with the quote like xlabel('X Data'), ylabel('Y Data'), and title('Plot of Y Data vs X Data') for the three labeling respectively. For three dimensional graphics, the z axis label is present which also works in a similar fashion. These actions may keep the editing mode in the graphics on. In order to cancel the editing mode, you can click the Edit plot icon (figure 1.2(c)) once or twice looking into the graphics unless the object is deselected.

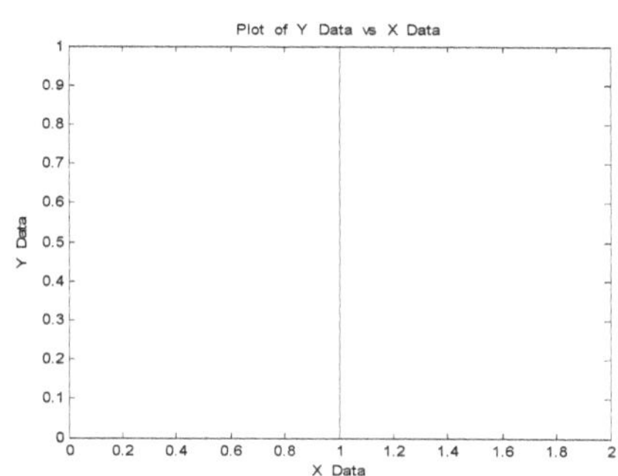

Figure 13.9(b) Plot of the figure 13.8(e) with the x label, y label, and title

♦ ♦ I want to change the line color of my plot

The solution is click the Edit plot icon (figure 1.2(c)), bring the mouse pointer on the line whose color you want to change, click left button of the mouse (the line will be selected), and rightclick the mouse. You see Color option in the popup window and click the Color. Another window prompts, you can select any line color in the prompt window.

♦ ♦ I want to change the x or y label font size to other

The clicking procedure is Edit → Axes Properties. The Axes Property Editor of the figure 13.9(a) appears. In that editor select Font and choose any size in the popup.

♦ ♦ How can I save and open some figure?

The clicking sequence from the figure window menu we need is File → Save or click the Save icon. In clicking so, the save dialog window appears and type any name of your choice in the File name box of the dialog window. The figure is saved with the file extension .fig in the directory or folder displayed in the Current Directory bar of the figure 1.1(a). Remember the figure file name and the directory. Click the File menu of MATLAB Command Window and click Open. Or, click the open file icon in the MATLAB menu bar. The open dialog window appears and select the file name you saved. The default file name is untitled.fig and the path name is C:\MATLAB7\work.

♦ ♦ How can I represent my plot by a dotted or broken line?

The necessary command is click the Edit plot icon (figure 1.2(c)), bring the mouse pointer on the line whose style you want to change, and rightclick the mouse. The popup appears and you find Line Style in the popup. Again from the Line style popup, you can select Solid, Dash, or other.

♦ ♦ How can I move a misplaced text object?

Let us plot the polar curve for the function $r = \sin 2\theta - \cos^2 3\theta$ as shown in the figure 13.9(c) using the subsection 13.1.5 mentioned ezpolar as follows:

>>ezpolar('sin(2*t)-cos(3*t)^2'); ↵ ← t for θ

As you see in the figure, the functional expression for $r = \sin 2\theta - \cos^2 3\theta$ is overlapping with the angular mark of 270. The figure would look better if we were able to move the r expression in other part of the plot area. For doing so, we click the Edit plot icon of the figure 1.2(c), bring the mouse pointer on the r expression, leftclick the mouse to select the object, drag it to any other area of your choice, and finally click the Edit plot icon again to deactivate the editing mode.

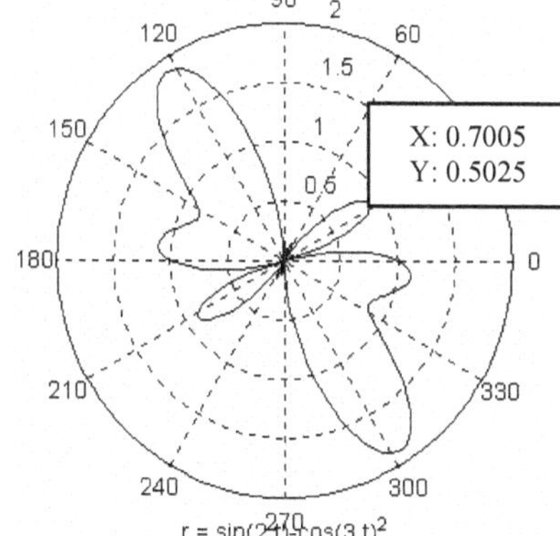

Figure 13.9(c) Plot of $r = \sin 2\theta - \cos^2 3\theta$

⬍⬍ How can I make a line thick in the plot?

Suppose we wish to thicken the line of the figure 13.8(e). For doing so, click the Edit plot icon (figure 1.2(c)), bring the mouse pointer on the line you want to thicken, rightclick the mouse to see the Line Width in the popup, select any width of your choice, and finally click the Edit plot icon again to deactivate the editing mode.

⬍⬍ How can I see the functional x and y values from any drawn curve?

Suppose we have graphed the figure 13.9(c) using the ezpolar. We intend to see the (x, y) coordinates of any point on the curve. Figure 13.8(d) shows the Data Cursor icon in the icon bar of the figure window. Click the icon and bring the mouse pointer on any point on the curve. You find a crosshair activated and leftclick the mouse. A tiny box displays the coordinates as shown in the figure 13.9(c).

Certainly there are numerous graphical feature functions embedded in MATLAB. We do not wish to address all these functions as far as the context is concern. Anyhow we close the graphing chapter with the troubleshooting discussion.

Chapter 14

In most previous chapters, our concentration was to exercise mainly the built-in function for solving pure mathematics problem or visualizing its solution in MATLAB. Many scientific simulations require that an M-file be written for a specific purpose beside the built-in functions. Contents of an M-file are the language codes of MATLAB. Like other high-level structured programming languages such as FORTRAN/C/ PASCAL, MATLAB also has its own code of writing program statements. This chapter highlights commonly used syntaxes of M-file programming and some utility functions. A syntactically correct M-file does not need building an execution file like FORTRAN or C. M-file is accessible to everyone as long as it is executed in the command window of MATLAB. To be an efficient M-file programmer, the thorough knowledge of available command syntax is necessary for which our outline concentrates on the following:

- M-file and frequently used MATLAB coding of mathematical expressions
- Control statements of the programming such as for-looping, if-else logical verifications, etc
- Generally used data organization facilities such as 2D array, cell array, structure array, etc
- User-defined multi-input and multi-output function file writing and data importing-exporting

14.1 What is an M-file?

An M-file is a script or text file that contains a sequence of executable MATLAB statements. If the MATLAB commands are just two or three lines, they can be executed in the command window. But if we have many executable lines, a file is required where we place all commands sequentially so that any modification or editing can be performed according to the user's convenience. Thus the M-files are written externally by the users. Almost all previously mentioned MATLAB functions are written in an M-file. The next consequential query is how one writes and executes an M-file whose answer is provided in chapter 1.

14.2 MATLAB coding of functions

MATLAB executes the codes of a function or expression in terms of a string which is the set of keyboard characters placed consecutively. One distinguishing feature of MATLAB is that the variable itself is a matrix. The strings adopted for computation are divided into two classes – scalar and vector. The scalar computation results the order of the output matrix same as that of the variable matrix. On the contrary, the order for the vector computation is determined in accordance with the matrix algebra rules. Some symbolic functions and their MATLAB counterparts are presented in table 14.A. The operators for the arithmetic computations are as follows:

addition	+
subtraction	–
multiplication	*
division	/
power	^

The operation sequence of different operators in a scalar or vector string observes the following order:

enclosing braces	( )	first,
power operator	^	then,
division operator	/	next,
multiplication operator	*	after that,
addition operator	+	then, and
subtraction operator	–	finally.

The syntax of the scalar computation urges to use .*, ./, and .^ in lieu of *, /, and ^ respectively. The operators *, /, or ^ are never preceded by . for the vector computation. The vector string is the MATLAB code of any symbolic expression or function often found in mathematics. Starting from the simplest one, we present some examples for writing the long expressions for the scalar form and for the vector form as well in MATLAB.

♦♦ *Write the MATLAB codes in scalar and vector forms for the following functions*

$A.\ \sin^3 x\cos^5 x$ $\quad B.\ 2+\ln x$ $\quad C.\ x^4+3x-5$ $\quad D.\ \dfrac{x^3-5}{x^2-7x-7}$ $\quad E.\ \sqrt{|x^3|+\sec^{-1}x}$

$F.\ (1+e^{\sin x})^{x^2+3}$ $\quad G.\ \dfrac{\cosh x+3}{\sqrt{\dfrac{x+4}{\log_{10}(x^3-6)}}}$ $\quad H.\ \dfrac{1}{(x-3)(x+4)(x-2)}$ $\quad I.\ \dfrac{1}{1+\dfrac{1}{1+\dfrac{1}{x}}}$

$J.\ \dfrac{a}{x+a}+\dfrac{b}{y+b}+\dfrac{c}{z+c}$ $\quad K.\ \dfrac{u^2v^3w^9}{x^4y^7z^6}$

In tabular form, they are coded as follows:

Example	String for scalar computation	String for vector computation
A	sin(x).^3.*cos(x).^5	sin(x)^3*cos(x)^5
B	2+log(x)	2+log(x)
C	x.^4+3*x-5	x^4+3*x-5
D	(x.^3-5)./(x.^2-7*x-7)	(x^3-5)/(x^2-7*x-7)
E	sqrt(abs(x.^3)+asec(x))	sqrt(abs(x^3)+asec(x))
F	(1+exp(sin(x))).^(x.^2+3)	(1+exp(sin(x)))^(x^2+3)
G	(cosh(x)+3)./sqrt((x+4)./log10(x.^3-6))	(cosh(x)+3)/sqrt((x+4)/log10(x^3-6))
H	1./(x-3)./(x+4)./(x-2)	1/(x-3)/(x+4)/(x-2)
I	1./(1+1./(1+1./x))	1/(1+1/(1+1/x))
J	a./(x+a)+b./(y+b)+c./(z+c)	a/(x+a)+b/(y+b)+c/(z+c)
K	u.^2.*v.^3.*w.^9./x.^4./y.^7./z.^6	u^2*v^3*w^9/x^4/y^7/z^6

We present some numerical example to quote the difference between the scalar and the vector computations. Let us say we have the matrices $A=\begin{bmatrix}3 & 5\\ 7 & 8\end{bmatrix}$, $B=\begin{bmatrix}5 & 2 & 1\\ 0 & 1 & 7\end{bmatrix}$, and $C=\begin{bmatrix}3 & 2 & 9\\ 4 & 0 & 2\end{bmatrix}$. The scalar computation is not possible between the matrices A and B because of their unequal order nor is between the matrices A and C for the same reason. On the contrary the scalar multiplication can be conducted between B and C for having the same order and which is $B.*C=\begin{bmatrix}15 & 4 & 9\\ 0 & 0 & 14\end{bmatrix}$ (element by element multiplication). Matrix algebra rule says that any matrix A of order $M\times N$ can only be multiplied with another matrix B of order $N\times P$ so that the resulting matrix has the order $M\times P$. For the numerical example of A and B, we have M =2, N =2, and P =3. We obtain the vector-multiplied matrix as $A\times B=$ $\begin{bmatrix}3\times5+5\times0 & 3\times2+5\times1 & 3\times1+5\times7\\ 7\times5+8\times0 & 7\times2+1\times8 & 7\times1+8\times7\end{bmatrix}=\begin{bmatrix}15 & 11 & 38\\ 35 & 22 & 63\end{bmatrix}$, and which has the MATLAB code A*B not A.*B. Similar interpretation follows for the operators * and /. Whenever we write the scalar codes A.*B, A./B, and A.^B, we make sure that both the A and B are identical matrix in size. The 3*A means all elements of matrix A are multiplied by 3 and we do not use 3.*A. Also we do not use A./3 but do A/3. The signs + and – are never preceded by the operator . in the scalar codes. The command 4./A means 4 is divided by all elements in A. The A.^4 means power of all elements of A is raised by 4 and so on.

Table 14.A Some mathematical functions and their MATLAB counterparts

Mathematical notation	MATLAB notation	Mathematical notation	MATLAB notation	Mathematical notation	MATLAB notation
$\sin x$	sin(x)	$\sin^{-1} x$	asin(x)	π	pi
$\cos x$	cos(x)	$\cos^{-1} x$	acos(x)	A+B	A+B
$\tan x$	tan(x)	$\tan^{-1} x$	atan(x)	A–B	A–B
$\cot x$	cot(x)	$\cot^{-1} x$	acot(x)	A×B	A*B
$\cos ec x$	csc(x)	$\sec^{-1} x$	asec(x)	e^x	exp(x)
$\sec x$	sec(x)	$\cos ec^{-1} x$	acsc(x)	A^B	A^B
$\sinh x$	sinh(x)	$\sinh^{-1} x$	asinh(x)	$\ln x$	log(x)
$\cosh x$	cosh(x)	$\cosh^{-1} x$	acosh(x)	$\log_{10} x$	log10(x)
$\sec hx$	sech(x)	$\sec h^{-1} x$	asech(x)	$\log_2 x$	log2(x)
$\cos echx$	csch(x)	$\cos ech^{-1} x$	acsch(x)	Σ	sum
$\tanh x$	tanh(x)	$\tanh^{-1} x$	atanh(x)	Π	prod
$\coth x$	coth(x)	$\coth^{-1} x$	acoth(x)	$\vert x \vert$	abs(x)
10^A	1e *A* e.g. 1e3	10^{-A}	1e- *A* e.g. 1e-3	$\sqrt{x}$	sqrt(x)

* In the six trigonometric functions for example sin(x), the x is in radian. If x is in degree, we use sind(x). The other five functions also have the syntax cosd(d), tand(x), cotd(x), cscd(x), and secd(x) when x is in degree. The default return from asin(x) is in radian, if you need the return to be in degree, use the command asind(x). Similar return is also possible from acosd(x), atand(x), acotd(x), asecd(x), and acscd(x).

14.3 Control statements of M-file programming

Most MATLAB commands utilized in various chapters invoked some built-in M-file functions. These built-in functions are inherently composed of program statements, logical verifications, looping operations, conditional execution of the group statements… etc. There are a number of control statements in MATLAB. The control statements followed by specific syntax observe the sequence of operations, the limit of repetitive computation, and the selection of multiple objective tasks. Understanding of these statements would divulge the insight or the hidden algorithms in a built-in MATLAB function. We are used to seeing the mathematical font such as x but working in MATLAB needs writing some other font such as x – this type of font equivalence is maintained in subsequent discussions.

Table 14.B Equivalence of comparative operators

Comparative operation	Mathematical notation	MATLAB notation
equal to	$=$	==
not equal to	$\neq$	~=
greater than	$>$	>
greater than or equal to	$\geq$	>=
less than	$<$	<
less than or equal to	$\leq$	<=

14.3.1 Comparative and logical operators

The comparative operators are mainly used for the comparison of two scalar elements, one scalar and one matrix elements, or two identical size matrix elements. There are six comparative operators as presented in the table 14.B. The output of the expression pertaining to the comparative operators is logical – either true (indicated by 1) or false (indicated by 0). For example, when A=3 and B=4, the comparisons $A=B$, $A \neq B$, $A>B$, $A \geq B$, $A<B$, and $A \leq B$ should be false (0), true(1), false(0), false(0), true(1), and true(1) respectively. We can implement these comparative operations as presented in the table 14.C. There are two operands A and B in table 14.C, each of which is a single scalar. Each of the operands can be a matrix in general. In that case the logical decision takes place element by element basis on all elements in the matrix. For instance, if A=$\begin{bmatrix} 5 & 8 \\ 5 & 7 \end{bmatrix}$ and B=$\begin{bmatrix} 2 & 1 \\ -2 & 9 \end{bmatrix}$, A>B should be $\begin{bmatrix} 5>2 & 8>1 \\ 5>-2 & 7>9 \end{bmatrix} = \begin{bmatrix} 1 & 1 \\ 1 & 0 \end{bmatrix}$. Again if A happens to be a scalar (say A=4), the single scalar is compared to all elements in the B therefore A≤B should be $\begin{bmatrix} 4\leq 2 & 4\leq 1 \\ 4\leq -2 & 4\leq 9 \end{bmatrix} = \begin{bmatrix} 0 & 0 \\ 0 & 1 \end{bmatrix}$. In a similar fashion B also operates on A however the scalar and matrix related comparative implementation is presented in the table 14.D.

Table 14.C Scalar comparative operation

>>A=3; B=4; ↵ >>A==B ↵ ans = 0 >>A~=B ↵ ans = 1	>>A>B ↵ ans = 0 >>A>=B ↵ ans = 0	>>A<B ↵ ans = 1 >>A<=B ↵ ans = 1

Some basic logical operations are NOT, OR, and AND. The characters ~, |, and & of the keyboard are adopted for the logical NOT, OR, and AND respectively. In all logical outputs the 1 and 0 stand for true and false respectively. All logical operators apply to the matrices in general. For the matrix A=$\begin{bmatrix}0 & 0\\0 & 1\end{bmatrix}$, NOT(A) operation should provide $\begin{bmatrix}1 & 1\\1 & 0\end{bmatrix}$ (see table 14.E). The logical OR and AND operations on the like positional elements of the two matrices A=$\begin{bmatrix}1 & 1\\0 & 1\end{bmatrix}$ and B=$\begin{bmatrix}0 & 1\\1 & 1\end{bmatrix}$ must return $\begin{bmatrix}1 & 1\\1 & 1\end{bmatrix}$ and $\begin{bmatrix}0 & 1\\0 & 1\end{bmatrix}$ respectively. Table 14.E shows both implementations.

Table 14.D Scalar and matrix comparative operation

when A and B are matrices,	**when A is scalar and B is matrix,**
>>A=[5 8;5 7]; ↵ >>B=[2 1;-2 9]; ↵ >>A>B ↵ ans = 1 1 1 0	>>A=4; ↵ >>B=[2 1;-2 9]; ↵ >>A<=B ↵ ans = 0 0 0 1

If A or B is a single 1 or 0, it operates on all elements of the other.

Sometimes we need to check the interval of the independent variable of some function for instance $-6 \le x \le 8$. The interval is split in two parts $-6 \le x$ and $x \le 8$. In terms of the logical statement one can express $-6 \le x \le 8$ as (−6<=x)&(x<=8).

Table 14.E Basic logical operations on matrix elements

for NOT(A) operation,	**for A OR B,**	**for A AND B,**	**for A XOR B,**
>>A=[0 0;0 1]; ↵ >>~A ↵ ans = 1 1 1 0	>>A=[1 1;0 1]; ↵ >>B=[0 1;1 1]; ↵ >>A|B ↵ ans = 1 1 1 1	>>A&B ↵ ans = 0 1 0 1	>>xor(A,B) ↵ ans = 1 0 1 0

There is no operator for the XOR logical operation instead the MATLAB function xor syntaxed by xor(A,B) implements the operation as presented in the table 14.E.

There are two more logical functions by the names any and all found in MATLAB. Both functions in general conceive a rectangular matrix but operate on columns. If any element in the columns of the rectangular matrix is 1, the output returned by any is 1 otherwise 0. If all elements in a column of the rectangular matrix are 1, the output returned by all is 1 otherwise 0. Let us implement that on the last mentioned A as attached above. If we want to perform the operations on the whole rectangular matrix A, two any or all functions are required – one for the columns and the other for the resulting row. Its implementation is also shown above on the right side. There is another option for the whole matrix. We first turn the rectangular matrix A to a column one writing the command A(:) and then use the function writing any(A(:)) or all(A(:)).

any on the matrix A,	**all on the matrix A,**	**on the whole A,**	**on whole A,**
>>any(A) ↵ ans = 1 1	>>all(A) ↵ ans = 0 1	>>any(any(A)) ↵ ans = 1	>>all(all(A)) ↵ ans = 0

14.3.2 Suppressing any execution

Let us assign the row matrix [2 3 4 8 3 8] to the workspace A by the following:

```
>>A=[2 3 4 8 3 8] ↵

A =
        2   3   4   8   3   8
```

MATLAB displays the assignment. Now use the up arrow key from the keyboard to see the last command and type one semicolon at the end of the statement as follows:

```
>>A=[2 3 4 8 3 8]; ↵
>>                    ← Assignment is not displayed due to ;
```

Any MATLAB command ending with a semicolon stops displaying the assignment or contents of a variable. If the user is sure about the command, displaying variable contents in the command window during execution is suppressed by appending one semicolon at the end of each MATLAB statement. It is applicable for the statements written in an M-file too.

14.3.3 For-loop syntax

A for-loop performs similar operations for a specific number of times and must be started with the for and terminated by an end statements. Following the for there must be a counter. The counter of the for-loop can be any variable that counts integer or fractional values depending on the increment or decrement. If the MATLAB command statements between the for and end of a for-loop are few words lengthy, one can even write the whole for-loop in one line. The programming syntax and some examples on the for-loop are as follows:

⬍⬍ Program syntax

for *counter* = starting value : increment or decrement of the counter value : final value

Executable MATLAB command(s)

end

Example 1

Our problem statement is to compute $y = \cos x$ for $x = 10^0$ to 70^0 with the increment 10^0. Let us assign the computed values to some variable y, where y should be [$\cos 10^0$ $\cos 20^0$ $\cos 30^0$ $\cos 40^0$ $\cos 50^0$ $\cos 60^0$ $\cos 70^0$]=[0.9848 0.9397 0.866 0.766 0.6428 0.5 0.342]. In the programming context, y(1) means the first element in the row matrix y, y(2) means the second element in the row matrix y, and so on. The MATLAB code for the $\cos x$ is cosd(x) where x is in degree. The for-loop counter expression should be k=1:1:7 to have a control on the position index in the row matrix y (because there are 7 elements or indexes in y). Since the computation needs 10 to 70, one generates that writing k*10. Following is the implementation:

Executable M-file:

```
for k=1:1:7
        y(k)=cosd(k*10);
end
```

Or, as a one line:

```
for k=1:1:7 y(k)=cosd(k*10); end
```

Steps we need:

Open a new M-file (section 1.3), type the executable M-file statements in the M-file editor, save the editor contents by the name test in your working path, and call the test as shown on the right side.

Interactive sessions with the command window:

```
>>test ↵
>>y ↵

y =
    0.9848 0.9397 0.8660 0.7660 0.6428 0.5000 0.3420
```

Example 2

For-loop sometimes helps us accumulate data (more in section 2.7) consecutively controlled by the loop index. In this example we accumulate some data rowwise according to the for-loop counter index. Let us say for $k = 1$, 2, and 3, we intend to accumulate the k^2 side by side. At the end we should have [1 4 9] assigned to some variable f – this is our problem statement. Let us see the for-loop for the accumulation as attached above (corresponding to the right shifting). The vector code (section 14.2) for k^2 is k^2. The statement f=[ ]; means that an empty matrix is assigned to f outside the loop but at the beginning. An empty matrix does not have any size and completely empty, it follows the null symbol ∅ of the matrix algebra. The k variation in our problem is put as the for-loop counter. How the for-loop accumulates is presented above. The accumulation is happening from the left to the right. A single change provides the shifting from the right to the left which is f=[k^2 f];. The complete code and its execution result are also shown above on the right side (corresponding to the left shifting).

for the right shifting,

```
>>f=[ ]; for k=1:3 f=[f k^2]; end ↵
>>f ↵

f =
      1   4   9
```

for the left shifting,

```
>>f=[ ]; for k=1:3 f=[k^2 f]; end ↵
>>f ↵

f =
      9   4   1
```

When k=1, f=[f k^2]; returns f=[[ ] 1^2]; ⇒ f=1;
When k=2, f=[f k^2]; returns f=[1 2^2]; ⇒ f=[1 4];
When k=3, f=[f k^2]; returns f=[1 4 3^2]; ⇒ f=[1 4 9];

Another accumulation could be columnwise that is we wish to see the output like $\begin{bmatrix}1\\4\\9\end{bmatrix}$. We just insert the row separator of a rectangular matrix (done by the operator ;) in the command f=[f k^2]; as presented on the right side. Again the shifting can happen either from the up to down or from the down to up. Both implementations are shown above.

for the down shifting,

```
>>f=[ ]; for k=1:3 f=[f;k^2]; end ↵
>>f ↵

f =
      1
      4
      9
```

for the up shifting,

```
>>f=[ ]; for k=1:3 f=[k^2;f]; end ↵
>>f ↵

f =
      9
      4
      1
```

Example 3

Many scientific problems need writing multiple for-loops. Usually one loop is for one dimensional function, two loops are for two dimensional function, and so on. One dimensional functional data takes the form of a row or column matrix. Suppose we have the one dimensional data as $y =$[9 6 7 4 6]. We wish to access to every data in y. A single for-loop helps us do that as shown on the right side. First we assigned the data to workspace y as a row matrix. The command length finds the number of elements in the row matrix y. The y(k) means the k-th element in the y which we assigned to workspace v. Every single data in y is sequentially available in v. The contents of y could also be a column matrix.

One dimensional functional data selection:

```
>>y=[9 6 7 4 6]; for k=1:length(y) v=y(k); end ↵
```

A two dimensional functional data takes the form of a rectangular matrix for instance $f[m,n] = \begin{bmatrix}4 & 3 & 5\\9 & 0 & 3\end{bmatrix}$ which has the numbers of rows and columns as 2 and 3 respectively. Our objective is to gain access to every element in the matrix $f[m,n]$. Now we need two for-loops, one for the row and the other for the column. The complete codes are presented on the right side. Because of multiple statements, we write them in an M-file. The first line in the code is to assign the rectangular matrix data to workspace f (can

Executable M-file for two dimensional data selection:

```
f=[4 3 5;9 0 3];
[a,b]=size(f);
for m=1:a
        for n=1:b
              v=f(m,n);
        end
end
```

be any user-given name, here f⇔ $f[m,n]$). In the second line, the command **size** (section 2.12) finds the row and column numbers in the f and puts them to a and b (where a=2 and b=3) respectively. The for-loop counters m (for the row number) and n (for the column number) correspond to any position index (m,n) of $f[m,n]$. The value of $f[m,n]$ at any (m,n) is represented by f(m,n) which we assigned to the workspace v (can be any other name) but the assigned value in v moves rowwise sequentially. Open a new M-file editor, type the statements in the M-file, save the file by the name **test** in your working path, and execute **test** from the command prompt. The outer for-loop gives control on the rows whereas the inner one does on the columns. If you exchange the two **for** command lines, the element selection happens columnwise instead of rowwise.

◆◆ Example 4

Example 2 is the prerequisite before one goes through this example. Employing two for-loops and row-column accumulation computes two independent variable functions. Let us calculate the function $f(x,y)=x+y$ for $-1\le x\le 0$ and $0\le y\le 1$ with the step 0.5 for x or y. The two dimensional computation should be $\begin{bmatrix} f(-1,0) & f(-1,0.5) & f(-1,1) \\ f(-0.5,0) & f(-0.5,0.5) & f(-0.5,1) \\ f(0,0) & f(0,0.5) & f(0,1) \end{bmatrix} = \begin{bmatrix} -1 & -0.5 & 0 \\ -0.5 & 0 & 0.5 \\ 0 & 0.5 & 1 \end{bmatrix}$, and we expect the last matrix from MATLAB as a result of the computation. There are two independent variables hence the use of two for-loop is compulsory. The complete program is shown on the right side. Referring to the executable M-file, the r and f refer to the row and column of the rectangular matrix respectively. The initializations r=[ ]; and f=[ ]; mean that the r and f are empty matrices before entering into the loop. The command r=[r x+y]; places the computed data of x+y on the right side of the last r depending on the for-loop counter until one row placement is finished. The other command f=[f;r]; places the row stored in r down the last f after the first loop. Before the end of the second loop's **end**, the command r=[ ]; is inserted. This is necessary otherwise r would contain all computations in a row matrix. In doing so, a mark of distinction for the consecutive rows of the rectangular matrix is accomplished. However note that the matrix only contains the functional values of $x+y$ and there is no information regarding the x or y. The reader has to keep a mark what these matrix values correspond to. Thus we compute any other two dimensional function (the $x+y$ is too simple, vector code for other functions for example r=[r x^2*y^2]; for $f(x,y)=x^2y^2$) and keep the computational data in a rectangular matrix.

Executable M-file for the example 4:

```
r=[ ];
f=[ ];
for x=-1:0.5:0
    for y=0:0.5:1
        r=[r x+y];
    end
    f=[f;r];
    r=[ ];
end
```

Sessions with the command window: Type left statements in a new M-file, save the file by the name **test**, and execute the following:

```
>>test ↵
>>f ↵

f =
   -1.0000   -0.5000         0
   -0.5000         0    0.5000
         0    0.5000    1.0000
```

14.3.4 Simple if/if-else/nested if syntax

Conditional commands are exercised by the **if-else** statements (reserve words). Also comparisons and checkings need **if-else** statements. We can have different **if-else** structures namely simple-if, **if-else**, or nested-if depending on the programming circumstances some of which we discuss in the following.

Simple if

The program syntax of the simple-if is as follows:

if *logical expression*
    Executable MATLAB command(s)
end

Logical expression usually requires the use of comparative operators whose reference is in subsection 14.3.1. If the logical expression beside the **if** is true, the command between the **if** and **end** is executed otherwise not. In tabular form the simple-**if** implementation is as follows:

Example: If $x\ge 1$, we compute $y=\sin x$. When $x=2$, we should see $y=\sin 2$ =0.9093.	**Executable M-file:**
	x=2;
	if x>=1
	y=sin(x);
	end
		Steps: Save the statements in a new M-file (chapter 1) by the name **test** and execute the following:
		>>test ↵
			Check from the command window after running the M-file:
			>>y ↵
			
			y =
			0.9093

If-else

The general program syntax for the **if-else** structure is as follows:

if *logical expression*
    Executable MATLAB command(s)
else
    Executable MATLAB command(s)
end

If the logical expression beside the if is true, the command between the if and else is executed else the command between else and end is executed. In tabular form, the if-else-end implementation is the following:

Example: When $x=1$, we compute $y=\sin\frac{x\pi}{2}=1$ otherwise $y=\cos\frac{x\pi}{2}=0$.	**Executable M-file:**
	x=1;
	if x==1
	y=sin(x*pi/2);
	else
	y=cos(x*pi/2);
	end
		Steps: Save the statements in a new M-file by the name test and execute the following:
		>>test ↵
			Check from the command window after running the M-file:
			>>y ↵
			
			y =
			1

If we had x=2; in the first line of the M-file, we would see y= $\cos\pi$ =–1.

Nested-if

The third type of the if structure is the nested-if whose program syntax is as follows:

```
if logical expression
        Executable MATLAB command(s)
elseif logical expression
        Executable MATLAB command(s)
                 ⋮
elseif logical expression
        Executable MATLAB command(s)
else
        Executable MATLAB command(s)
end
```

Clearly the syntax takes care of multiple logical expressions which we demonstrate by one example as shown below:

Example: The best example can be taking the decision of grades out of 100 based on the achieved number of a student. The grading policy is stated as if the achieved number of a student is greater than or equal 90, greater than or equal to 80 but less than 90, greater than or equal to 70 but less than 80, greater than or equal to 60 but less than 70, greater than or equal to 50 but less than 60, and less than 50, then the grade is decided as A, B, C, D, E, and F respectively.	**Executable M-file:** N=77; if N>=90 g='A'; elseif (N<90)&(N>=80) g='B'; elseif (N<80)&(N>=70) g='C'; elseif (N<70)&(N>=60) g='D'; elseif (N<60)&(N>=50) g='E'; else g='F'; end	In the executable M-file, the N and g refer to the number achieved and the grade respectively. If the number N is 77, the grade g should be C. Any character is argumented under the single inverted comma. **Steps:** Save the left statements in a new M-file by the name test and execute the following: >>test ↵	**Check from the command window after running the M-file:** >>g ↵ g = C

14.3.5 User input during the run time of an M-file

Sometimes it is necessary to have some input or functional argument from the user when an M-file is being run. It can be accomplished by the command input. Assume that we need any integer from 1 to 10 from the user whose implementation can be conducted without opening an M-file as attached on the right side. The input argument of the function input can be any user-supplied string placed under quote for example we chose the string Enter any integer from 1 to 10: . Upon the execution of the first line, the second line appears and the cursor blinks after :. We typed 5 at the blinking cursor. Whatever input receives the MATLAB prompt is assigned to the variable A in above implementation. Integers are not the only inputs that the function accepts, as another example a column matrix of three decimal numbers (considering $\begin{bmatrix}2.1\\3.2\\1.5\end{bmatrix}$) is to be asked from the user whose implementation is also attached on the right side. The column matrix [2.1 3.2 1.5]' is typed at the blinking cursor following the execution of the first line. Next example shows a string input say the name of a student is needed from the user. Attached on the right side is its implementation as well. The character set or string is

A single scalar input from the user:

```
>>A=input('Enter any integer from 1 to 10: '); ↵
>>Enter any integer from 1 to 10: 5 ↵
>>A ↵      ← To make sure, what is in A

A =
      5
```

A column matrix input from the user:

```
>>A=input('Enter decimal column matrix of 3 elements: '); ↵
>>Enter decimal column matrix of 3 elements: [2.1 3.2 1.5]' ↵
>>A ↵              ← To see the contents of A

A =
      2.1000
      3.2000
      1.5000
```

A string input from the user:

```
>>A=input('What is the name of the student: '); ↵
>>What is the name of the student: 'Rebeca' ↵
>>A ↵              ← To see the contents of A

A =

Rebeca
```

put under quote. For instance we typed Rebeca at the blinking cursor. Now the workspace A is having a character array instead of a numeric one. The A is a user-chosen name. The string can even be a file name with relevant file extension. For easy understanding we executed the input at the command prompt but it can appear in any M-file if some data, string, or file name is required during the execution of the M-file.

14.3.6 Switch-case-otherwise syntax

The switch-case-otherwise syntax provides the programming technique to choose a particular set of executable commands from several sets. The switch requires a key to make the syntax operational and the key is compared to each available case. The syntax executes the set of commands only the case that matches with the key. The basic form for the switch-case-otherwise syntax is shown on the right side in which the words switch-case-otherwise-end are reserve. After the words case and switch, there should be one space gap. The beginning and ending of the syntax are the words switch and end respectively. The right word beside the case can be numeric or character set. If it is a character or string, we put that through quote.

General syntax:

```
switch key for opening the switch
case I
        Executable MATLAB command(s)
case II
        Executable MATLAB command(s)
        ⋮
otherwise
        Executable MATLAB command(s)
end
```

In tabular form, we present example 1 using the charater key in the following:

Example 1: Suppose, a university library has the policy that the teachers, the researchers, and the students can borrow 10, 8, and 5 books respectively. Other people of the university can not borrow a book. The teachers, researchers, and students have the codes T, R, and S respectively. Other than the university staff or student nobody is allowed to issue a book. Our objective is to check how many books one can borrow.	**Executable M-file statements:**
	I=input('Enter your code : ');
	switch I
	case 'T'
	disp('Can borrow 10 books');
	case 'R'
	disp('Can borrow 8 books');
	case 'S'
	disp('Can borrow 5 books');
	otherwise
	disp('Not supposed to borrow')
	end
		Steps: Type the left statements in a new M-file and save the file by the name test.
		Check from the command window after running the M-file:
		>>test ↵
		Enter your code : 'R' ↵
		Can borrow 8 books
		>>test ↵
		Enter your code : 'D' ↵
		Not supposed to borrow

Referring to above M-file statements, the input (for input last subsection) given by the user is assigned to I which serves the purpose of the key to the switch. Whichever is entered to I is checked with all possible cases. We know the three case codes (T, R, and S) from the problem description which we place beside the word case respectively. The command disp displays any user-supplied string under quote in the command window. The example 1 key is a character one, let us see example 2 which applies a numeric key.

Example 2: The numbers −1 and 1 represent the binary digital signal. We are also interested in detecting a 0 value in the digital signal if it exists. Therefore the possible signal values are −1, 0, and 1. If the signal has the value other than the specified three, it is termed as a noise. We enter an unknown signal value and wish to see the type of the signal – problem statement.	**Executable M-file statements:**
	I=input('Enter the signal value : ');
	switch I
	case -1
	disp('Negative digital signal');
	case 0
	disp('Signal value is 0');
	case 1
	disp('Positive digital signal');
	otherwise, disp('This is a noise')
	end
		Steps: Type the left statements in a new M-file and save the file by the name test.
		Interactive session in the command window:
		>>test ↵
		Enter the signal value : 7 ↵
		This is a noise
		>>test ↵
		Enter the signal value : 1 ↵
		Positive digital signal

Its implementation is shown above on the right side. Now the input from the user is not a character therefore we do not need to use the single inverted comma while entering the signal values. The case directives are also numerical and do not use the quote either. You can write the case or otherwise and the executable command in two lines or in one line but separated by a comma (see the otherwise statement).

14.3.7 While-end syntax

The while-end syntax also performs the looping operation similar to the for-loop but having the flexibility to change the counter parameter subject to the logical condition. Inside the while-end syntax, a set of similar commands is carried out until the logical expression beside the while is satisfied. Its general form and implementation are as follows:

General syntax:
while logical expression
Executable command(s)
end
where while and end are the reserve words
	Example: A positive integer greater than 1 will be asked from the user. The sum of the squares from 1 to that integer is required to compute.	**Executable M-file:**
		I=input('Enter integer > 1: ');
		k=0;
		s=0;
		while ~(k>I)
		s=s+k^2;
		k=k+1;
		end
			Steps: Type the left statements in a new M-file, save the file by the name test, and interact like the following:
			>>test ↵
			Enter integer > 1: 7 ↵
			>>s ↵
			s =
			140

Referring to the executable M-file of while-end, the l is not known beforehand and that is the user's choice taken from the command prompt via the command input (subsection 14.3.5). We preset 0 to each of k and s before entering to while-end syntax. The counter index k inside the while-end loop is increased by 1 for each looping operation using the command k=k+1;. The variable s adds consecutively the sum of squares for all integers less than l, which is achieved by s=s+k^2;. Just to have a check, if we input 7 at the command prompt, the output should be $1^2+2^2+..+7^2=140$ that is what is required from the programming. The expression 'k is not greater than l' is written as ~(k>l) in the place of the logical expression of while (sections 14.3.1 and 14.2 for operator and code reference respectively, k, l, ans s are user-chosen).

14.3.8 Comment on executable statements

If an M-file programmer writes some comment beside each executable statement, that helps later or others to go through the program. This is accomplished by the character % which appears at the beginning of each sentence. The commentary sentence can appear at any column of an M-file. For example, we could have explained the contents of l in the subsection 14.3.7 mentioned M-file as follows:

```
l=input('Enter integer > 1: '); % l is the user input
```

The line followed by % does not affect the programming.

14.3.9 Break statement

The break statement is practiced to terminate the loop or iterative operations such as for-loop or while-end loop subject to certain condition. Applying the statement, we present one example in tabular form as follows:

Example: Let us compute the sum of all integer squares from 1 to 20. But as soon as the sum is greater than 400, we terminate the computation and display the sum. The sums of the squares up to 10 and up to 11 are 385 and 506 respectively. As the output, we should see 506.	**Executable M-file:**
	s=0;
	for k=1:20
	    s=s+k^2;
	    if s>400
	        break;
	    end
	end
	disp(s)
		Steps: Type the left statements in a new M-file and save the file by the name test.
		Check from command window after running the M-file:
		>>test ↵
		        506

Concerning attached implementation, the for-loop generates the integer counter index from 1 to 20. We compute the successive sum using the command s=s+k^2; where s=0 before entering to the for-loop. For every k, we check the sum whether s>400 using the if-end of subsection 14.3.4. As soon as s>400, the for-loop is broken and the s returns the last value. The command disp just displays the contents of the variable s. For the multiple or nested loop, the break statement terminates the innermost loop.

14.3.10 String and its related functions

A string is a set of characters that are placed consecutively. Each character as found in the computer keyboard has the unique numeric code stored in MATLAB depending on the character set encoding of a given font. Usually we do not access these values. We work on the characters as they are displayed on the screen. Typical examples of strings include naming a variable or an array, arguments of an M-file, MATLAB codes of a symbolic expression, etc. The strings can be evaluated, compared, or split. Let us execute the following:

```
>>s='MATLAB'; ↵
```

Above command says that we assigned the word or string MATLAB to the workspace variable s. User-provided strings are always entered through quote. Another explanation of the string can be that the string is a character array. For example the s is a character array which has 6 characters. If we know the code of an ASCII character, it can be converted to the character by the function char. For example the characters #, $, %, &, ', (,), *, and + have the numeric codes 35, 36, 37, 38, 39, 40, 41, 42, and 43 respectively. We have them implemented as shown on the right side. The command [35:43] generates a row matrix of integers 35 through 43 and the char finds the character on each element in the row matrix. The input argument of the char can be a rectangular matrix in general. The reverse conversion that is character to number is carried out by the command double. For example the code 35 of # is returned by the command double('#'). If the input argument of the double is a string, the return is a row matrix indicating the element as the integer code of each character.

Code to character:

```
>>char([35:43]) ↵

ans =

#$%&'()*+
```

♦♦ Placing strings horizontally/vertically one after another

Placing the strings one after another is called catenation. There are two types of catenation – horizontal and vertical. For horizontal catenation, the command is strcat (abbreviation for <u>str</u>ing <u>cat</u>enation) and the same for the vertical is strvcat (abbreviation for <u>str</u>ing <u>v</u>ertically <u>cat</u>enated). Let us say we have two strings I love MATLAB, and Do you?. We wish to see them as I love MATLAB,Do you?. Application of the strcat is attached on the right side in which we assigned the two strings in two workspace variables s1 and s2 (can be any user-chosen name) respectively. The strcat has two input arguments, the two string names respectively. The input argument number can be more than two for example strcat(s2,s2,s2) would display the second string three times. We could have assigned the output of strcat to some variable. The string placement is consecu-

Horizontal string placement:

```
>>s1='I love MATLAB,'; ↵
>>s2='Do you?'; ↵
>>strcat(s1,s2) ↵

ans =

I love MATLAB,Do you?
```

tive and there is no space gap between the strings. One blank space is inserted using ' ' if it is necessary.

Sometimes the numeric needs to be converted as strings. Let us say **z** is an integer variable. We intend to form a string in which **value** (some given string) will be followed by the integer assigned to **z**. The function **int2str** (abbreviation for conversion from integers to (2) strings) turns an integer to a string which is performed as attached on the right side. We chose the integer 1000 and assigned it to the workspace **z**. In the second line, the **value** is assigned to **s1**. In the third line we converted the integer to a string and put to **s2**. The last line is to place the **value** and the **1000** as a whole string.

Horizontal placement of value and 1000:

```
>>z=1000; ↵
>>s1='value'; ↵
>>s2=int2str(z); ↵
>>strcat(s1,s2) ↵

ans =

value1000
```

Next we present the vertical catenation of strings. Suppose we have three strings **I love MATLAB**, **Researchers do**, and **Do you?** We wish to see the three strings one after another vertically like $\begin{Bmatrix} \text{I love MATLAB} \\ \text{Researchers do} \\ \text{Do you?} \end{Bmatrix}$. Placed on the right side is its implementation. The first three lines in the implementation are to assign the three strings to the workspace variables **s1**, **s2**, and **s3** (can be any user-given names) respectively. The fourth line is to place the strings vertically through the use of **strvcat** in which the assignees become the input arguments of the function. The function accepts 2, 3, 4, or other number input arguments. If we used the command **v=strvcat(s1,s2,s3)**, **v** would hold all three strings as shown. The second string is having total character number 14 including the intermediate blank space that is why the **v** is a character array of size 3×14 referring to the workspace browser (section 1.2). String that has less number of characters than the maximum one is padded with the blank space.

Vertical placement of the strings:

```
>>s1='I love MATLAB'; ↵
>>s2='Researchers do'; ↵
>>s3='Do you?'; ↵
>>strvcat(s1,s2,s3) ↵

ans =

I love MATLAB
Researchers do
Do you?
```

♦♦ Comparison of strings

If two strings are given, we can compare whether they are identical using the function **strcmp** (abbreviation for string comparison). The function behaves as a logical statement and the return of **strcmp** is either 0 or 1. Let us compare the strings **I love MATLAB** and **I love MATLAb**. The comparison is shown on the right side. The return is 0 since the last letters of the given strings are not having the same case and the function is case sensitive. There is another function called **strcmpi** (abbreviation for string comparison ignoring case) which is not case sensitive. If we used the command **strcmpi(s1,s2)**, we would see 1 as the return.

Comparison of the strings:

```
>>s1='I love MATLAB'; ↵
>>s2='I love MATLAb'; ↵
>>strcmp(s1,s2) ↵

ans =
     0
```

A lot of string related functions are included in MATLAB. To learn about these functions, execute the following at the command prompt:

```
>>help strfun ↵
```

14.4 Three dimensional, structure, and cell arrays

In most chapters, we manipulated the data which is in a matrix form. We call the matrix as a two dimensional array. The matrix-oriented arrangement of data is not convenient for multidimensional and group-related problems. There are three more data arrangement types called the three dimensional, structure, and cell arrays which we address in the following.

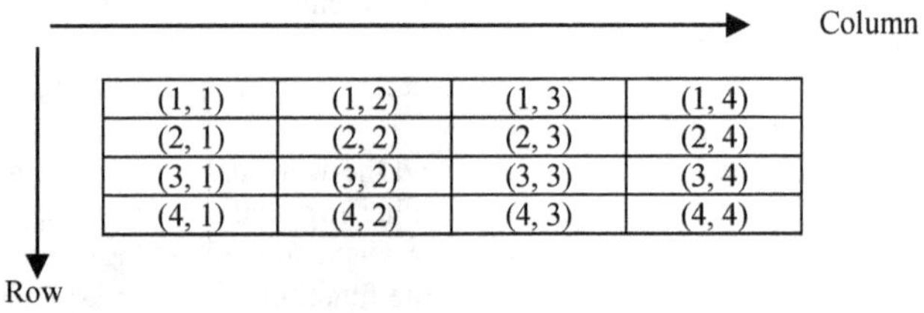

(1, 1)	(1, 2)	(1, 3)	(1, 4)
(2, 1)	(2, 2)	(2, 3)	(2, 4)
(3, 1)	(3, 2)	(3, 3)	(3, 4)
(4, 1)	(4, 2)	(4, 3)	(4, 4)

Figure 14.1(a) Position indexes of a 4×4 rectangular matrix

14.4.1 Three dimensional arrays

A rectangular matrix has two dimensions. The reason we say two dimensions is any element position in the rectangular matrix needs two indexes to describe it – row and column. For example a 4×4 rectangular matrix has the figure 14.1(a) mentioned position indexes in accordance with the MATLAB convention. Note that the left uppermost element is indexed by (1,1) not by (0,0).

Suppose the figure 14.1(a) mentioned 4×4 rectangular matrix fits in one page of a book. If we have two more pages each containing a 4×4 rectangular matrix for some group-related problem or for a single quantity, how can we accommodate the three page data in one variable? This necessitates the use of a three dimensional array. The position indexes of the three 4×4 rectangular matrices in the three pages can be labeled as presented in the figure 14.1(b). We append one more index in the array element position – the third one obviously indicating the page number. For example (4,2,2) means the position index in the second page and the rectangular position index (4,2) in the second page.

If one gathers the three pages one after another, the three dimensional block of the figure 14.1(c) is formed. That is how a three dimensional array is created. One can assign any integer or decimal values to these position indexes.

Let us assume that the three page data is given as follows – page 1: $\begin{bmatrix} 8 & 3 & 6 \\ 2 & 2 & 1 \end{bmatrix}$, page 2: $\begin{bmatrix} 0 & 4 & 4 \\ 5 & 3 & 8 \end{bmatrix}$, and page 3: $\begin{bmatrix} -1 & 2 & 7 \\ -5 & 5 & 6 \end{bmatrix}$.
We wish to enter the three dimensional array to some workspace variable A for which we carry out the following:

```
>>A(:,:,1)=[8 3 6;2 2 1]; ↵
>>A(:,:,2)=[0 4 4;5 3 8]; ↵
>>A(:,:,3)=[-1 2 7;-5 5 6]; ↵
```

Above three line commands assign the three rectangular matrices to the three pages respectively. The A(:,:,1) means all rows and columns of the page 1. Similar explanation applies to the other two pages. In order to see the contents of A, we call the variable:

```
>>A ↵
```

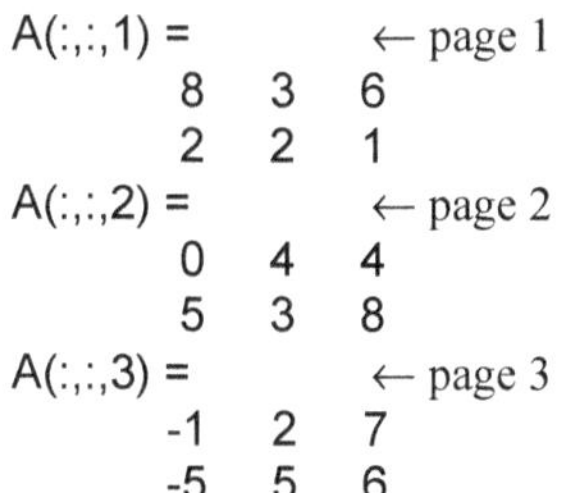

```
A(:,:,1) =          ← page 1
          8   3   6
          2   2   1
A(:,:,2) =          ← page 2
          0   4   4
          5   3   8
A(:,:,3) =          ← page 3
         -1   2   7
         -5   5   6
```

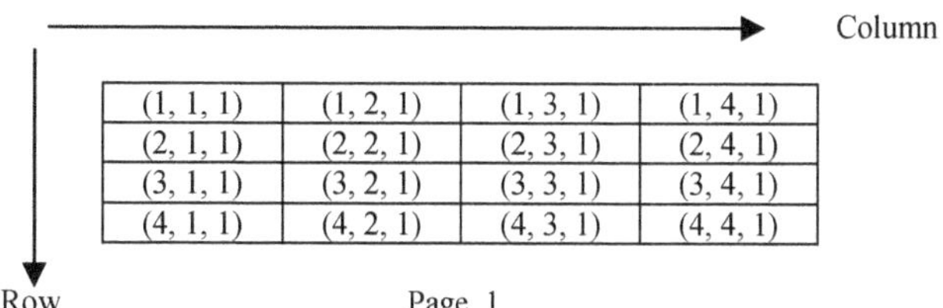

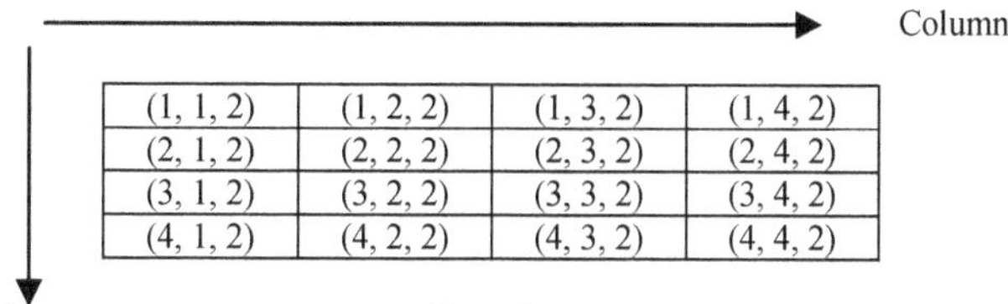

Column

(1, 1, 3)	(1, 2, 3)	(1, 3, 3)	(1, 4, 3)
(2, 1, 3)	(2, 2, 3)	(2, 3, 3)	(2, 4, 3)
(3, 1, 3)	(3, 2, 3)	(3, 3, 3)	(3, 4, 3)
(4, 1, 3)	(4, 2, 3)	(4, 3, 3)	(4, 4, 3)

Row

Page 3

Figure 14.1(b) Position indexes of the three 4×4 rectangular matrices

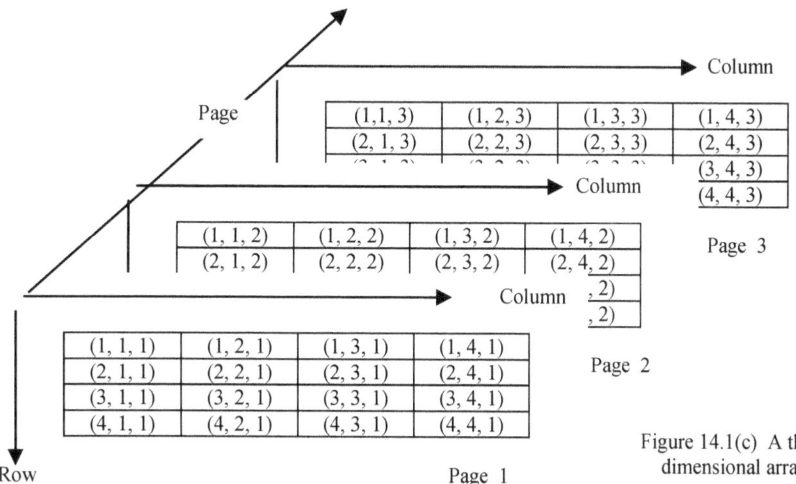

Figure 14.1(c) A three dimensional array

Most manipulations on chapter 2 cited rectangular matrix can be extended for the three dimensional array. Let us see some manipulations on existing workspace A.

The third page element 7 has the first two position index (1,3). It is called by

```
>>A(1,3,3) ↵

ans =
      7
```

We can replace the value say by 10 and have it as follows:

```
>>A(1,3,3)=10; ↵
```

It means 10 is assigned to the three dimensional array A element whose position index is (1,3,3). In order to see the change, we can display only the third page just calling A(:,:,3) at the command prompt. Suppose we intend to remove the third page from A. We assign an empty matrix in the third page writing A(:,:,3)=[ ];.

A long row or column matrix can be converted to a three dimensional array by using the command **reshape** (section 2.10). For example we have R=[1 8 61 11 40 68 34 12 45 32 89 43]. There are twelve elements in R. The product of row, column, and page numbers must be 12. Formation of the three dimensional array is shown on the right side. In the first line we assigned the row matrix to R and in the second line we called the **reshape** with the syntax **reshape**(row or column matrix name,user-given row number,user-given column number,user-given page

Three dimensional array from R:

```
>>R=[1 8 61 11 40 68 34 12 45 32 89 43]; ↵
>>A=reshape(R,2,3,2) ↵

A(:,:,1) =        ← Displays the first page
       1   61   40
       8   11   68
A(:,:,2) =        ← Displays the second page
      34   45   89
      12   32   43
```

number). We chose the row, column, and page numbers to be 2, 3, and 2 respectively. We named the resulting three dimensional array as A (any user-chosen name). Note that the conversion is columnwise.

Again a three dimensional array A can be converted to a column matrix by using the command A(:). The A from the last execution holds $\begin{bmatrix} 1 & 61 & 40 \\ 8 & 11 & 68 \end{bmatrix}$ and $\begin{bmatrix} 34 & 45 & 89 \\ 12 & 32 & 43 \end{bmatrix}$ as the two pages. The command A.^2 performs squares of all elements in each page of A. One can add one more page assigning a 2×3 matrix to A(:,:,3). Adding some scalar say 5 to each element of A is accomplished by A+5. Multiplication of a three dimensional array is not defined. Pages of the array can be multiplied according to the rules of matrix algebra for example page 2 with page 3 by A(:,:,2)*A(:,:,3). For simplicity we have shown the manipulations considering integer elements but the elements can be decimals, characters, or even symbolic variables.

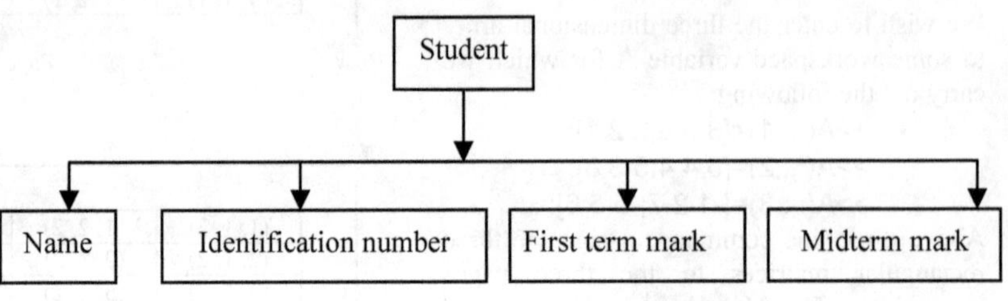

Figure 14.2(a) Hierarchy of a structure array

14.4.2 Structure arrays

All elements of an ordinary array are identical data. Data can be integers, decimal numbers, complex numbers, or symbolic variables. A structure array has mixed type of arrays as individuals and the individuals are termed as members. The composition of the structure array will be illustrated from the following example. Suppose a physics teacher teaches two classes. For each class, he wants to keep the examination records for all students applying the hierarchy of the figure 14.2(a). Let us consider that the names, identification numbers, first term marks out of 30, and midterm marks out of 30 are $\begin{bmatrix} \text{Reza} \\ \text{Shameem} \\ \text{John} \\ \text{Rebeca} \\ \text{Richard} \end{bmatrix}$, $\begin{bmatrix} 91 \\ 92 \\ 89 \\ 96 \\ 95 \end{bmatrix}$, $\begin{bmatrix} 23.5 \\ 29.7 \\ 23 \\ 9 \\ 12 \end{bmatrix}$, and $\begin{bmatrix} 25.5 \\ 27.7 \\ 21 \\ 20 \\ 19 \end{bmatrix}$ respectively. The data we have is of mixed type for instance the names and the identification numbers are characters and integers respectively. In order to understand the composition of the structure array, we enter the four arrays as shown on the upper right side. In the first line the names are entered as a character array using strvcat (subsection 14.3.10) and assigned to N. Each row in the N is the name of students. We entered the identification numbers, first term marks, and midterm marks all as a column matrix (section 1.3) to I, F, and M in the second and third lines in the execution respectively. The N, I, F, and M are all user-chosen names. The command struct composes a structure array from various members. The members are called fields to the context of structure array. Field names are also user-chosen, let us name various fields of the structure array as Name, ID, Fgrade, and Mgrade respectively. Shown above on the right side is the formation of the structure array. During the formation, the field names are put under quote. Every field name is followed by the assignee name containing the data of the individual array for example Name is the field name and its data is held in N regardless of character or numeric. Similar explanation goes for the other three members. The input arguments of the struct are separated by a comma. The placement order of the members of the structure array is user-defined. The constructed array we assigned to S which can be any user-given name. Whenever we call S, all information about its members appears as shown above.

Entering the individual arrays:

```
>>N=strvcat('Reza','Shameem','John','Rebeca','Richard'); ↵
>>I=[91 92 89 96 95]'; F=[23.5 29.7 23 9 12]'; ↵
>>M=[25.5 27.7 21 20 19]'; ↵
```

Forming the structure array from the individual arrays:

```
>>S=struct('Name',N,'ID',I,'Fgrade',F,'Mgrade',M) ↵

S =

     Name: [5x7 char   ]
       ID: [5x1 double ]
   Fgrade: [5x1 double ]
   Mgrade: [5x1 double ]
```

To invoke the particular field ID:

```
>>S.ID ↵

ans =
    91
    92
    89
    96
    95
```

To invoke the particular field Name:

```
>>S.Name ↵

ans =
Reza
Shameem
John
Rebeca
Richard
```

To invoke a particular member from the structure S, we execute the syntax S.member for instance only the identification numbers (which has the field name ID) are seen by S.ID, execution is shown above. Note that the field name is invoked not the data holding variable name. Again the field Name content is also shown above.

A specific element of the field ID (say the second one, which is 92), can be accessed by S.ID(2) as follows:

```
>>S.ID(2) ↵

ans =
        92
```

Since the field Name is a two dimensional (5×7) character array, the maximum number of characters in a row can be 7. The second name Shameem is addressed by:

```
>>S.Name(2,:) ↵

ans =

Shameem
```

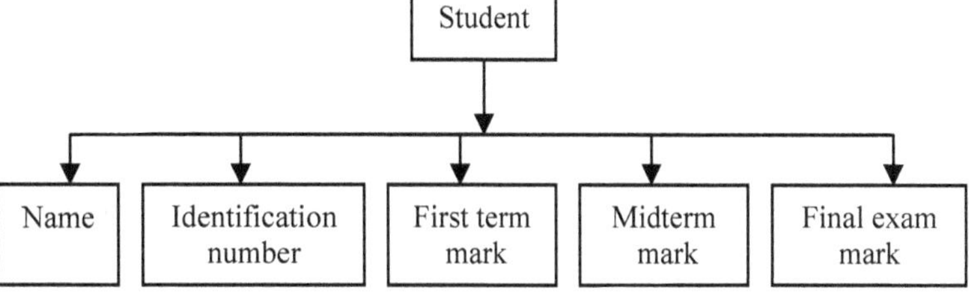

Figure 14.2(b) Adding a field final exam mark to the existing hierarchy

Adding the field Final in existing S:

```
>>FN=[35.5 37.7 24 30 23]'; ↵
>>Physics1=setfield(S,'Final',FN) ↵

Physics1 =
      Name: [5x7 char  ]
        ID: [5x1 double]
    Fgrade: [5x1 double]
    Mgrade: [5x1 double]
     Final: [5x1 double]  ← Final is here
```

Removing a field from S:

```
>>rmfield(Physics1,'Final') ↵

ans =

      Name: [5x7 char  ]
        ID: [5x1 double]
    Fgrade: [5x1 double]
    Mgrade: [5x1 double]
```

Suppose the final examination marks out of 40, which are $\begin{bmatrix}35.5\\37.7\\24\\30\\23\end{bmatrix}$ for the respective students, are available at the end of the semester. The hierarchy is pictured in the figure 14.2(b). The teacher now wants to include the final mark field with the existing structure array S. Let us name the field as Final. The function setfield adds a field to the existing structure S whose implementation is presented above. In the implementation we assigned the given final examination marks to workspace FN (can any user-given name). The setfield has three input arguments, the first, second, and third of which are the existing structure array name (S), user-given new field name under quote (Final), and variable name in which the data is available (FN) respectively. We assigned the outcome to another assignee Physics1 (any user-given name) which is a new structure array. The leftarrow in above implementation shows the addition of the field Final.

Sometimes removal of a field may be required. We conduct that on using the function rmfield (abbreviation for <u>re</u>move <u>field</u>). Let us remove just added field Final from Physics1 as shown above on the right side. The rmfield has two input arguments, the first and second of which are the structure array name (Physics1) and field name (Final) respectively. There is no need to mention the variable name.

Finally let us aggregate all marks to have the total grades out of 100 and put them to another field Total as presented on the right side. We removed the field Final from Physics1 but did not assign to any variable so the Physics1 is still having all fields. We assigned the summation of all grade fields to T (any user-given name). In the second command line we appended the field Total and again assigned to Physics1 as done before. The total marks out of 100 should be [84.5 95.1 68 59 54] which we verified calling the field Total (in the third command line).

Adding all marks to find the total out of 100:

```
>>T=Physics1.Fgrade+Physics1.Mgrade+Physics1.Final; ↵
>>Physics1=setfield(Physics1,'Total',T); ↵
>>Physics1.Total ↵

ans =
       84.5000
       95.1000
       68.0000
       59.0000
       54.0000
```

14.4.3 Cell arrays

A cell array is composed of cells where the cells can contain previously discussed ordinary arrays (of real, integer, or complex numbers), structure arrays, multidimensional arrays, character arrays…etc. The cells of a cell array are indexed like a rectangular matrix but using the second brace {..}. For example A{3,4} indicates that A is a cell array and we are addressing the cell with the coordinates (3,4) – third row and fourth column. If we build a cell array A of order 2×3, the position indexes of different cells are A{1,1}, A{1,2}, A{1,3}, A{2,1}, A{2,2}, and A{2,3} rowwise respectively.

As an example, we assign the matrices $\begin{bmatrix}1+2i & 2-3i\\4+6i & 9+3i\end{bmatrix}$, $\begin{bmatrix}7 & 2\\4 & 9\end{bmatrix}$, [2.34 34.5 4.6], $\begin{bmatrix}\text{Shameem}\\\text{Shimul}\\\text{Richard}\end{bmatrix}$, $\begin{bmatrix}x^2-4x+56\\3x+7\end{bmatrix}$, and a three dimensional array T with three pages $\begin{bmatrix}2 & 3\\4 & 5\end{bmatrix}$, $\begin{bmatrix}11.1 & 30.3\\12.2 & 51.9\end{bmatrix}$, and $\begin{bmatrix}19 & 36\\2.2 & 55\end{bmatrix}$ respectively to the different cells of a 2×3 cell array. Schematic representation for different cell contents is shown in the figure 14.2(c).

We assume that the reader has gone through the array mentioned sections on which the implementation (let us name the cell array as A) is presented in the following:

```
>>A{1,1}=[1+2i 2-3i;4+6i 9+3i]; ↵
```
← Assign the complex matrix $\begin{bmatrix} 1+2i & 2-3i \\ 4+6i & 9+3i \end{bmatrix}$ to cell(1,1)

```
>>A{1,2}=[7 2;4 9]; ↵
```
← Assign the integer matrix $\begin{bmatrix} 7 & 2 \\ 4 & 9 \end{bmatrix}$ to cell(1,2)

```
>>A{1,3}=[2.34 34.5 4.6]; ↵
```
← Assign the decimal element matrix [2.34 34.5 4.6] to cell(1,3)

```
>>A{2,1}=strvcat('Shameem','Shimul','Richard'); ↵
```
← Assign the two dimensional character array $\begin{bmatrix} \text{Shameem} \\ \text{Shimul} \\ \text{Richard} \end{bmatrix}$ to cell (2,1)

```
>>syms x, A{2,2}=[x^2-4*x+56;3*x+7]; ↵
```
← Assign the symbolic matrix $\begin{bmatrix} x^2-4x+56 \\ 3x+7 \end{bmatrix}$ to cell(2,2)

```
>>T(:,:,1)=[2 3;4 5]; ↵                ← Assign the first page of T
>>T(:,:,2)=[11.1 30.3;12.2 51.9]; ↵    ← Assign the second page of T
>>T(:,:,3)=[19 36;2.2 55]; ↵           ← Assign the third page of T
>>A{2,3}=T ↵                           ← Assign the three dimensional array T to cell(2,3)

A =
        [2x2 double]    [2x2 double]    [1x3      double ]
        [3x7 char   ]   [2x1 sym    ]   [2x2x3    double ]
```

Instead of displaying the contents, A is showing the type of the component cells. Let us see some maneuverings of the cell array in the following. The cell(1,2) has the 2×2 integer matrix. Element having the position index (2,1) of this matrix is 4. We access the element as follows:

```
>>A{1,2}(2,1) ↵

ans =
          4
```

Placing cell inside cell is also possible. Suppose another cell array B of order 1×2 is to be built where the cell(1,1) and the cell(1,2) of B contain the just mentioned 2×3 cell array A and a row matrix [47 31] respectively (figure 14.2(d)). It is just the matter of assignment as follows:

```
>>B{1,1}=A; ↵
>>B{1,2}=[47 31]; ↵
>>B ↵

B =

    {2x3 cell}    [1x2 double]
```

Cell indexing similar to an ordinary array (chapter 2) accesses to the subset of a cell. For instance the cells of the cell array A taken from the intersection of the first and second rows and the second column which are shown in the figure 14.2(e) are invoked as follows:

```
>>A(1:2,2) ↵
```

Cell(1,1): $\begin{bmatrix} 1+2i & 2-3i \\ 4+6i & 9+3i \end{bmatrix}$	Cell(1,2): $\begin{bmatrix} 7 & 2 \\ 4 & 9 \end{bmatrix}$	Cell(1,3): [2.34 34.5 4.6]
Cell(2,1): $\begin{bmatrix} \text{Shameem} \\ \text{Shimul} \\ \text{Richard} \end{bmatrix}$	Cell(2,2): $\begin{bmatrix} x^2-4x+56 \\ 3x+7 \end{bmatrix}$	Cell(2,3): A three dimensional array, T 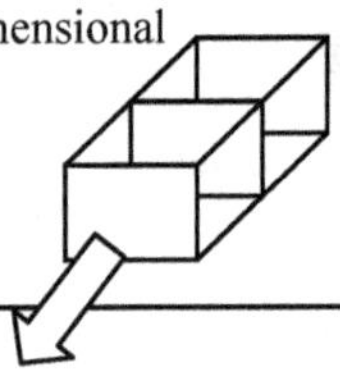

Three pages of the three dimensional array corresponding to cell(2,3) are $\begin{bmatrix} 2 & 3 \\ 4 & 5 \end{bmatrix}$, $\begin{bmatrix} 11.1 & 30.3 \\ 12.2 & 51.9 \end{bmatrix}$, and $\begin{bmatrix} 19 & 36 \\ 2.2 & 55 \end{bmatrix}$ respectively.

Figure 14.2(c) Two dimensional cell array A of order 2×3

Cell(1,1): A	Cell(1,2): [47 31]

Figure 14.2(d) 1×2 cell array B showing cell inside cell

Cell(1,2): $\begin{bmatrix} 7 & 2 \\ 4 & 9 \end{bmatrix}$
Cell(2,2): $\begin{bmatrix} x^2-4x+56 \\ 3x+7 \end{bmatrix}$

Figure 14.2(e) Subset of cell array A

```
ans =
            [2x2   double]
            [2x1   sym    ]
```

Let us delete the cell(1,3) and the cell(2,3) from A as follows:

```
>>A{1,3}=[ ]; ↵
>>A{2,3}=[ ] ↵
```

2 deleted cells ↓

```
A =

[2x2 double ]     [2x2 double ]     [ ]
[3x7 char    ]     [2x1 sym     ]     [ ]
```

Reshaping, catenating, and forming three dimensional arrays of the cell arrays can be accomplished too. Some functions, which handle different types of arrays, are supplied in table 14.F.

Table 14.F Some functions regarding multidimensional, structure, and cell arrays

Purpose	Function	Purpose	Function
To concatenate arrays	cat	To see structure field names	fieldnames
To know the number of array dimensions	ndims	To check whether a field is in a structure array	isfield
To permute array dimensions	permute	To display contents of a cell array	celldisp
To shift array dimensions	shiftdim	To convert a numeric array to cell array	num2cell
To remove singleton dimensions	squeeze	To convert a cell array to structure array	cell2struct
To check whether an array is a structure array	isstruct	To convert a structure array to cell array	struct2cell
To create a cell array	cell	To check whether an array is a cell array	iscell

14.5 Creating a function file

A function file is a special type of M-file which has some user-defined input and output arguments. Both arguments can be single or multiple. The first line in a function file always starts with the reserve word **function**. The function file must be in your working path or its path must be defined in MATLAB. Depending on the problem, a function file is written by the user and can be called from the MATLAB command prompt or from another M-file. For convenience, long and clumsy programs are split into smaller modules and these modules are written in a function file. However the basic structure of a function file is as follows:

MATLAB Command Prompt → function file

$>> g =$call f ⟹ $\underbrace{g(y_1, y_2, \ldots. y_m)}_{\text{output arguments}} = \underbrace{f(x_1, x_2, x_3, \ldots x_n)}_{\text{input arguments}}$

We present the following examples for illustration of the function files keeping in mind that the arguments' order and type of the caller function and the function file are identical.

Example 1

Let us say computation of $f(x) = x^2 - x - 8$ is to be implemented as a function file. When $x = -3$ and $x = 5$, we are supposed to have 4 and 12 respectively. The vector code (section 14.2) for the function is x^2-x-8 assuming x is a scalar. We have one input (which is x) and one output (which is $f(x)$). Open a new M-file editor (chapter 1), type the codes of the figure 14.3(a) exactly as they appear in the M-file, and save the file by the name f. The assignee y and independent variable x can be any name of your choice and which are the output and input arguments of the function respectively. Again the file and function name f can be any user-chosen name only the point is the chosen function or file name should not exist in MATLAB. Let us call the function to verify the programming as shown on the right side. You can write dozens of MATLAB executable statements in the file but whatever is assigned to the last y returns the function f(x) to g. Writing the = sign between the y and f(x) in the function file is compulsory.

Calling for example 1: for $x = -3$,

>>g=f(-3) ↵ ← call $f(x)$ for $x = -3$

```
g =
      4
```

for $x = 5$,

>>g=f(5) ↵ ← call $f(x)$ for $x = 5$

```
g =
      12
```

Example 2

Example 1 presents one input-one output function how if we handle multiple inputs and one output? The input argument names are separated by commas in a function file. A three variable function $f(x_1, x_2, x_3) = x_1^2 - 2x_1x_2 + x_3^2$ is to be computed from a function file. The input arguments (assuming all scalar) are x_1, x_2, and x_3 and the output argument is the functional value in the function file. The x_1 is written as x1, and so is the others. Follow the procedure of the example 1 but the code should be as shown in the figure 14.3(b). Let us inspect the function (with the specific x_1=3, x_2=4, and x_3=5, the output value of the three variable function must be $f(3,4,5) = 3^2 - 2\times3\times4 + 5^2 = 10$) as presented above.

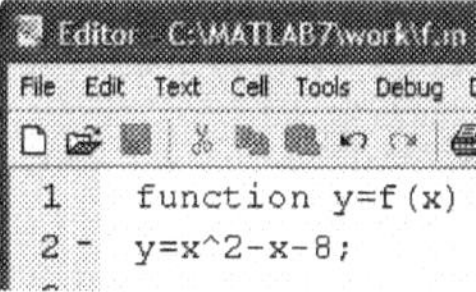

Figure 14.3(a) Single input – single output function file

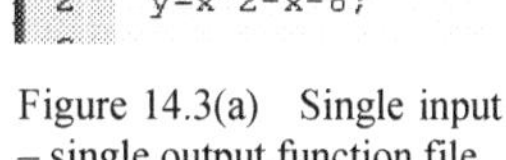

Editor - C:\MATLAB7\work\f.m

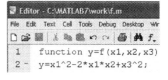

```
1   function y=f(x1,x2,x3)
2 - y=x1^2-2*x1*x2+x3^2;
```

Figure 14.3(b) Multiple inputs – single output function file

Calling for example 2: when input arguments are all scalar:

>>g=f(3,4,5) ↵ ← calling $f(x_1, x_2, x_3)$ for x_1=3, x_2=4, and x_3=5

```
g =
      10
```

The **function** not only works for the scalar inputs but also does for matrices in general for example a set of input argument values are $x_1 = \begin{bmatrix} 2 \\ 3 \\ 4 \end{bmatrix}$, $x_2 = \begin{bmatrix} -2 \\ 2 \\ 5 \end{bmatrix}$, and $x_3 = \begin{bmatrix} 1 \\ 0 \\ 3 \end{bmatrix}$ for which the $f(x_1, x_2, x_3)$ value should be $\begin{bmatrix} 13 \\ -3 \\ -15 \end{bmatrix}$. The computation needs the scalar code (section 14.2) of $f(x_1, x_2, x_3)$ regarding x_1, x_2, and x_3. The second line modified statement of the figure 14.3(b) now should be y= x1.^2-2*x1.*x2+x3.^2;. On making the modification and saving the file, let us carry out the right attached commands. If it is necessary, the output can be assigned to user-given workspace variable v writing v= f(x1,x2,x3) at the command prompt. The return from the function file follows the input matrix order. If input arguments are rectangular matrix, so is the output. The input arguments of the function file do not have to be the mathematics symbol. Suppose x_1=ID, x_2=Value, and x_3=Data, one could have written the first and second lines of the function file in the figure 14.3(b) as **function y=f(ID,Value,Data)** and y=ID.^2-2*ID.*Value+Data.^2; respectively.

Calling for the example 2: when input arguments are all column matrix:

```
>>x1=[2 3 4]'; ↵   ← x1 values are assigned to x1 as a column matrix
>>x2=[-2 2 5]'; ↵  ← x2 values are assigned to x2 as a column matrix
>>x3=[1 0 3]'; ↵   ← x3 values are assigned to x3 as a column matrix
>>f(x1,x2,x3) ↵    ← calling f(x1, x2, x3) using column matrix input arguments

ans =
    13
    -3
   -15
```

Example 3

To illustrate the multi-input and multi-output function file, let us consider that p_1 and p_2 are to be found from three variables x_1, x_2, and x_3 (all are scalars) employing the expressions $p_1 = x_1^2 - 2x_1x_2 + x_3^2$ and $p_2 = x_1 + x_2 + x_3$ whose function file (type the codes in a new M-file editor and save the file by the name f) is presented in the figure 14.3(c). Choosing x_1=4, x_2=5, and x_3=6, one should get p_1=12 and p_2=15 for which the right side attached commands are conducted at the command prompt. More than one output arguments (which are here p_1 are p_2 and represented by p1 and p2 respectively) are separated by commas and placed inside the third brace following the word **function** of the figure 14.3(c). When we call the function from the command prompt, the output argument writing is similar to that of the **function** file (that is why we write [p1,p2] as output arguments at the command prompt). The output argument variable names do not have to be p1 and p2 and can be any name of user's choice. If there were three output arguments p_1, p_2, and p_3, the output arguments in the function file would be written as [p1,p2,p3] and their calling would happen in a like manner.

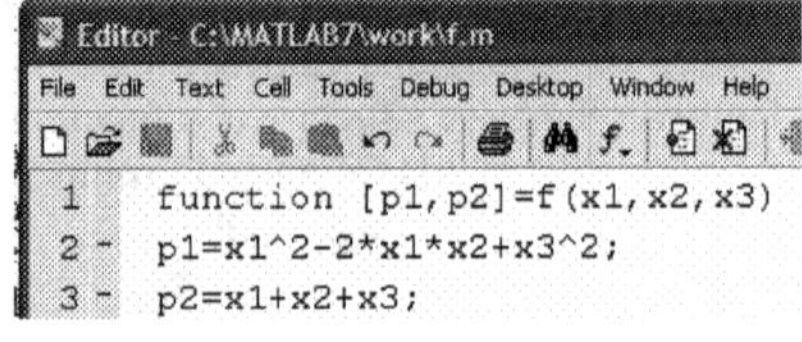

Figure 14.3(c) Function file for three input and two output arguments

Function file calling for the example 3:

```
>>[p1,p2]=f(4,5,6) ↵ ← calling the function file f for p1 and
                       p2 using x1=4, x2=5, and x3=6

p1 =
    12
p2 =
    15
```

14.6 Saving, importing, and exporting data

User can save workspace variables or data in a binary file (called MAT file) having the extension .mat and the command **save** allows us to carry out that with the syntax **save** [user-given file name] [variable names seperated by one space gap]. Suppose the two matrices A= $\begin{bmatrix} 3 & 4 & 8 \\ 0 & 2 & 1 \end{bmatrix}$ and B= $\begin{bmatrix} -2 & 5 \\ 9 & 3 \end{bmatrix}$ are to be saved in a MAT file by the name data.mat. First we enter the matrices into the workspace of MATLAB as follows:

```
>>A=[3 4 8;0 2 1]; B=[-2 5;9 3]; ↵
```

In order to save the matrices A and B in the file data.mat, we execute the following:

```
>>save data A B ↵        ← One space gap among save, data, A, and B
```

We do not write the file extension while saving (only the data). In order to see the file existence, we exercise dir *.mat at the command prompt to display all MAT files present in the current directory. The contents of A and B do not have to be number. Any array or variable of the section 14.4 can be saved this way. If the workspace contains many variables, it is not feasible that we save all typing the names. We save the whole workspace just executing **save data** as done for the two matrices. No matter how many variables are present, all of which remain in the file data.mat. You can quit MATLAB and work later on the variables stored in the data.mat.

There is another option for the data file saving. Whatever workspace variable we have is displayed in the workspace browser (section 1.4, figure 1.2(d)). Using the mouse pointer and Shift key of the keyboard, we can select any variable present in the workspace. For the matrix example, bring the mouse pointer on **A** in the workspace browser, click on **A**, hold the Shift key, and click on **B**, the two matrices are selected. Then rightclick the mouse to see the **Save As** option in the popup window. Once we click the option in the popup window, the save dialog window prompts and we type the file name **data** there in the prompt window.

The reverse operation that is the retrieval of the data takes place through the command **load**. Just now we saved the matrices A and B in the file **data.mat**. The matrices A and B are existing in the MATLAB workspace. We remove them from the workspace using the command **clear** at the command prompt. Then we execute the command **who** at the command prompt to check whether A and B exist. Or if we look at the workspace browser, we do not find any variable there. But you are sure that the MAT file **data.mat** contains the matrices A and B in the current directory or folder (section 1.4). To import the file **data.mat** in the workspace, the commad **load** is used as follows:

>>load data ↵ ← File extension **.mat** is not necessary, one space gap between **load** and **data**

We perform the same action through clicking from the menu **File** → **Import Data** → Select data file name and folder in the prompt window (figure 1.1(b)). Either way the variables A and B become available in the workspace. Execute **who** at the command prompt or look at the workspace browser to ascertain the data loading.

Importing and exporting data

Intersoftware data exchange is achievable in MATLAB. Suppose we have data $C=\begin{bmatrix} 23.4 & 12.5 \\ 2.4 & 23 \\ 2.5 & 12 \end{bmatrix}$ in Microsoft Excel and intend the data to be imported in MATLAB. We assume that Microsoft Excel is installed in your system. Open the Excel and type the matrix data as shown in the figure 14.4(a). Figure 1.1(a) shows the directory (look at the Current Directory) you are in or execute **cd** at the command prompt to know the working directory. When you save the typed data in Excel, make sure you save it in the same folder where your MATLAB prompt is in. When you try to save the Excel file, save dialog window appears, select the path (for example **C:\MATLAB7\work** for our case), and provide a data file name (the default one is **Book1**) in there. However we saved the matrix C in Excel file **Book1**.

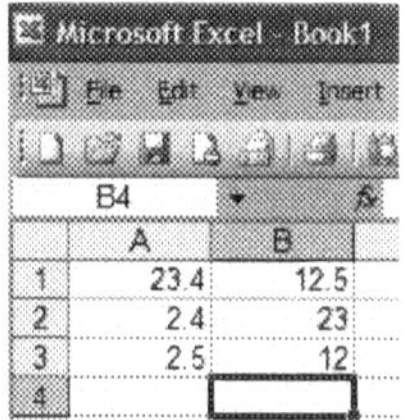

Figure 14.4(a) Matrix C is typed in Microsoft Excel

Now we wish to get the matrix in MATLAB. Click the **File** menu down the **Import data**, file opening dialog window appears, select **Book1** (file type option should be all file), and try to open the file. In doing so, the data **Import Wizard** window appears and click **Finish** in the window. In the **Import Wizard** window, you find the variable information and its data content as a sheet. The default name of the variable is **Sheet1**. Now go to MATLAB command prompt and call the variable as follows:

>>Sheet1 ↵ ← **Sheet1** holds the C contents

```
Sheet1 =
        23.4000    12.5000
         2.4000    23.0000
         2.5000    12.0000
```

Microsoft Excel - data

	A	B
1	2.60E+01	5.60E+01
2	2.60E+01	9.30E+01
3	2.70E+01	8.20E+01

Figure 14.4(b) Matrix D is opened in Excel

If we use **C=Sheet1**, the matrix C becomes available in **C** in MATLAB. Instead of going through all these, say we have the data file in Excel by the name **Book1.xls**. The function **xlsread** reads the data file and assigns the result to the workspace **C** employing the command **C=xlsread('Book1.xls')**. You can verify that from the example data we just mentioned.

The reverse data exchange i.e. from MATLAB to Microsoft Excel occurs through some data format like ASCII code. Let us say we have the matrix $D=\begin{bmatrix} 28 & 56 \\ 26 & 93 \\ 27 & 82 \end{bmatrix}$ and intend to open it in Excel. The first step is to save the matrix as a data file **data.mat** in MATLAB as follows:

>>D=[28 56;26 93;27 82]; ↵ ← Just entering the matrix to D

>>save data D -ascii -double -tabs ↵ ← One space gap among the MATLAB words

The command **save data D** has previously mentioned meanings (regarding the **save**). The reserve words **-ascii**, **-double**, and **-tabs** indicate that ASCII code saving, double precision data format, and tab separated respectively. We saved the file **data.mat** in **C:\MATLAB7\work**. Now open the file in Microsoft Excel from just mentioned folder which shows you the data as shown in the figure 14.4(b). During the opening, you need to select **All File** type option in the open dialog window and click **Finish** in the **Import Wizard** window of Excel. The displayed data is in exponential format but that does not change the value. The reason for adopting exponential format is it can accommodate higher digit numbers with better accuracy.

This sort of data exchange not only happens between MATLAB and Excel but also does between MATLAB and any other package like Microsoft Word, Fortran, C, etc.

MATLAB resources for the technical programming are plentiful. The software is the outgrowth of professional activities of many practicing engineers and scientists. We should not expect that all features of MATLAB will be known in one manuscript. Application dependent programming such as graphical user interface, simulink modeling, etc is not covered in the text because that is beyond the scope of the text. We are confined to the scheme of delineating the introductory computing, visualizing, and programming. Once the preliminary steps and tactics of computations and visualizations are understood, the advanced programming techniques can facilely be developed. The easy accessible graphics and numerous built-in functions have made the software more versatile. We hope our easy-to-exercise examples will inspire the reader to work out his or her scientific and technical problems in MATLAB.

Appendix A

MATLAB functions exercised in the text

Function name	Purpose	Page
adj	finds the adjoint of a square matrix in maple	53
algsubs	performs algebraic substitutions in mathematical expressions	33
all	checks whether all elements are nonzeroes in a row or column matrix	24
altitude	finds the altitude from a vertex to a triangle	47
any	checks whether any element is nonzero in a row or column matrix	24
ArcLength	computes the arc length of a curve from an expression	80
area	computes the area of 2D geometric objects in maple	42
AreConcurrent	decides whether three straight lines are concurrent	47
AreConcyclic	decides whether four points are concyclic	47
AreOrthogonal	decides whether two nonconcentric circles are orthogonal	48
AreTangent	decides whether a line is tangent to a circle	47
assempde	solves a second order MATLAB-defined elliptic PDE numerically	187
assume	passes on some variable condition in maple	43
band	generates a band matrix from user requirement	67
bar	graphs a bar graph from some y and x data	216
bar3	graphs a three dimensional bar graph from some y and x data	216
basis	finds the basis of some vector set in maple	56
besselj	returns the value of the Bessel function of the first kind	91
beta	returns the functional value of the beta function	90
betastat	returns the beta statistics from the parameters of the distribution	140
binocdf	computes cumulative function for binomial distribution	140
binomial	returns the binomial coefficients (located in the mfun library)	148
bisector	finds the angular bisector of an angle in a triangle	47
centroid	computes the centroid of a 2D polygon	49
char	displays the ASCII character from integer code	229
charmat	finds the characteristic matrix of a square matrix in maple	55
cholesky	performs the Cholesky factorization of a square matrix	64
circle	defines a 2D geometric circle in maple	41
circumcircle	finds the circumcircle of a triangle in maple	49
compan	generates a companion matrix from user-given polynomial	66
completesquare	forms complete square of a quadratic expression in maple	34
cond	determines the condition number of a rectangular matrix	57
cond	finds the geometric object condition in maple	47
conv	computes the convolution of two discrete functions	29
convert	the name of a maple library in which many conversion functions are affiliated	31
coordinates	returns the coordinates of points defined in maple	43
corrcoef	finds the correlation coefficients as a matrix for several random variables	137
cosint	returns the functional value of the cosine integral function	90
cov	finds the variance and covariance matrix of some random variables	137
crossprod	computes the cross product of two vectors in maple	80
cumsum	performs cumulative sum of elements in a row or column matrix	141
curl	computes the curl of a vector function in different coordinate systems in maple	79
dblquad	integrates an expression numerically for double integration	87

Continuation of the last table...

Function name	Purpose	Page
deconv	computes deconvolution from polynomial coefficients	30
det	computes the determinant of a square matrix	54
detail	provides the description of a geometric object in maple	42
diag	forms diagonal matrix	51
diff	differentiates any expression symbolically	71
distance	finds the geometric distance between two points in maple	45
diverge	computes the divergence of a vector function in different coordinate systems in maple	78
double	turns any symbolic data to double precision value or decimal	35
dsolve	returns analytical solutions for a variety of differential equations	94
eig	returns the eigenvalues and eigenvectors of a square matrix	55
elmat	displays elementary matrix operations available in MATLAB	8
Equation	shows the equation of any geometric object in maple	40
erf	returns the functional value of the error function	90
erfc	returns the functional value of the complementary error function	90
eval	evaluates any coded expression	38
excircle	finds the excircle of a triangle in maple	49
expand	expands any expression algebraically or trigonometrically	29
expcdf	returns the cumulative density functional value for the exponential distribution	140
expint	returns the functional value of the exponential integral function	90
expinv	returns the inverse value of the cumulative distribution function for the exponentially distributed random variable	141
expm	finds the matrix exponential of a square matrix	62
eye	forms identity matrix from user-required order	51
ezcontour	graphs contour from two dimensional expression	206
ezmesh	graphs surface using mesh from two dimensional expression	207
ezplot	graphs a y versus x expression without any calculation	6
ezplot3	graphs a three dimensional curve from expression	216
ezpolar	graphs a polar curve from an expression	207
ezsurf	graphs surface from two dimensional expression	207
factor	factorizes an integer or a mathematical expression	29
ffgausselim	performs fraction free Gaussian elimination in maple	53
fftshift	flips any row or column matrix data about the half index	14
fgoalattain	performs goal attainment optimization for vector objective functions	176
find	finds the position indexes of the elements in a matrix subject to logical condition	24
FindAngle	finds the angle between two straight lines in maple	45
fix	discards the fractional part from a decimal number	22
fliplr	flips the data of a row or rectangular matrix from left to right	13
flipud	flips the data of a column or rectangular matrix from up to down	13
fminbnd	determines numerical minimum from one variable function	82
fmincon	performs M-file based constraint optimization	172
fminimax	solves minimax optimization problems	177
fminunc	performs M-file based unconstraint optimization	172
FunctionAverage	computes the functional average from an expression in maple	80
gamma	returns the functional value of the gamma function	90
gausselim	performs Gaussian elimination of a rectangular matrix in maple	53
gcd	finds the greatest common divider of integers or expressions	33
geneqns	generates equations from matrix data in maple	68
genmatrix	generates matrix from linear equations in maple	68
geomean	finds the geometric mean of a row or column matrix data	133
grad	computes the gradient of a scalar function in different coordinate systems in maple	78

Continuation of the last table...

Function name	Purpose	Page
gtext	drops any mouse-driven text on any graphics	218
hadamard	generates a Hadamard matrix from user given dimension	65
hankel	generates a Hankel matrix from user requirement	67
harmmean	computes the harmonic mean of some data in a row or column matrix	134
help	shows the description of a function or word followed by help	8
hessian	computes the Hessian matrix from some scalar function in maple	77
hilb	generates a Hilbert matrix from user given dimension	65
hsv	a built-in color map which is the abbreviation for the hue saturation value	217
hyperbolic	solves a second order MATLAB-defined hyperbolic PDE numerically	187
im2uint8	transforms a 0-1 matrix data to unsigned 8-bit integer	217
implicitdiff	finds the derivative from some implicit equation but in maple	75
imshow	displays a MATLAB-held data matrix as a digital image	217
incircle	finds the incircle of a triangle in maple	49
inline	constructs an expression based object in the command widow	87
input	accepts data from the user during the run time of an M-file	227
int	integrates any expression symbolically	83
intersection	returns the intersecting points of two geometric objects in maple	48
inv	computes the square matrix inverse in numeric, rational, or symbolic form	54
IsOnCircle	checks whether a point is on a circle in maple	46
IsOnLine	checks whether a point is on a line in maple	46
jacobian	computes the Jacobian matrix from some vector function	77
jordan	performs the Jordan form decomposition of a square matrix	64
laplacian	computes the Laplacian of a scalar function in different coordinate systems in maple	80
lcm	finds the least common multiplier of integers or expressions	33
length	finds the number of elements in a row or column matrix	23
limit	computes the limit of a function in rational form	69
line	defines a 2D geometric line in maple	40
linprog	performs linear programming optimization	169
linspace	generates linearly spaced vector from user requirement	59
load	loads the saved data file from binary format in MATLAB	236
loglog	plots a log in y direction versus log in x direction curve from some x-y data	215
logspace	generates logarithmically spaced vector from user requirement	59
lookfor	searches for possible matches of a function or word followed by lookfor	8
lu	performs LU triangular factorization of a square matrix in numeric form	63
LUdecomp	performs LU triangular factorization of a square matrix in maple	62
mad	computes the mean absolute deviation of some data	135
mahal	computes the Mahalanosis distance	145
MakeSquare	defines a 2D geometric square in maple	41
mat2gray	transforms a matrix data between 0 and 1	217
matrix	enters a matrix in maple	62
max	finds the maximum element from a row or column matrix	20
maximize	finds the maximum symbolically from a user-given function	81
mean	finds the mean of a row or column matrix data	134
mean2	finds the mean of a rectangular matrix data	134
medial	finds the medial triangle of a triangle in maple	49
median	computes the median from some data	135

Continuation of the last table...

Function name	Purpose	Page
median	finds the median from a vertex to a triangle	46
meshgrid	generates rectangular grid points from user-requirement	39
mfunlist	displays the mfun library contents of classical functions	147
min	finds the minimum element from a row or column matrix	20
minimize	finds the minimum symbolically from a user-given function	81
minor	finds the minor of a matrix	52
minpoly	finds the minimal polynomial of a square matrix in maple	62
mmax	finds multiple maxima numerically (author-written)	82
mmin	finds multiple minima numerically (author-written)	82
moment	computes the moment on user-given order in some data	135
mzero	finds multiple zeroes or roots from a function numerically (author-written)	36
nnz	finds the number of nonzero elements in a matrix	23
nonzeros	finds nonzero elements from a matrix	23
norm	determines various matrix norms	58
normrnd	generates Gaussian random numbers from user-supplied mean and standard deviation	132
null	finds the basis of the null space on some vectors	56
numden	separates the numerator and denominator from an expression	32
ode23	solves a differential equation numerically on the order 2-3	99
ode45	solves a differential equation numerically on the order 4-5	103
ones	generates matrix of ones from user-defined dimension	25
OnSegment	finds the division point on a line segment from user-given ration	45
orth	finds the orthonormal basis of some vectors	61
orthocenter	finds the orthocenter of a triangle	48
orthog	checks the orthogonality of a square matrix in maple	61
padarray	extends a rectangular matrix size from user-supplied elements	26
parabola	defines a 2D geometric parabola in maple	42
parabolic	solves a second order MATLAB-defined parabolic PDE numerically	187
parfrac	finds the partial fraction in maple symbolically	30
pdecirc	describes a circular domain for numerical PDE solution	188
pdeeig	solves a second order MATLAB-defined eigenmode PDE numerically	187
pdeellip	describes an elliptic domain for PDE numerical solution	188
pdepe	finds the numerical solution of a PDE with one space variable	185
pdepoly	describes a polygonal domain for PDE numerical solution	188
pderect	describes a rectangular domain for PDE numerical solution	188
pdsolve	finds the symbolic solution of a PDE in expression form	180
PerpendicularLine	finds the perpendicular line from a point to another line	44
pie	graphs a pie chart from some data	215
pie3	graphs a three dimensional pie chart from some data	215
pinv	computes the pseudoinverse of a rectangular matrix	60
pivot	performs the pivoting of a matrix about a user-required element in maple	52
plot	graphs y versus x data for single or multiple traces	209
plot3	graphs a three dimensional curve from parametric function data	216
point	defines a 2D geometric point in maple	39
poisstat	returns the Poisson statistics from the parameters of the distribution	140
poly	forms a polynomial from its roots	28
poly	computes the characteristic polynomial of a square matrix	55
poly2str	displays polynomial coefficients as mathematical polynomial form	27
polyarea	returns the polygonal area	42

Continuation of the last table...

Function name	Purpose	Page
polyder	computes the polynomial derivative in coefficient form only	70
polyfit	fits the data into user-chosen polynomials	141
polyval	evaluates a polynomial at some user-given point	29
pretty	displays any coded expression in mathematical form	28
princomp	computes the principal components of some data	144
prod	multiplies all elements in a row or column matrix	19
projection	finds the projection of a point on a line	45
qr	performs Q-R factorization of a matrix in numeric form	63
QRdecomp	performs Q-R factorization of a matrix in rational form	63
quad	integrates an expression numerically for single integration	87
quadprog	performs quadratic programming optimization	170
quo	finds the quotient expression from polynomial division in maple	30
randint	generates random integers from user-requirement	132
randsrc	generates a random number from user-supplied set	133
range	finds the range of some data in a row or column matrix	134
rank	determines the rank of a matrix	53
reflection	returns a reflected 2D geometric object about a point or line in maple	44
regress	computes the regression coefficients from user data	143
rem	finds the remainder expression from polynomial division in maple	30
rem	finds the remainder after integer division	23
repmat	forms repetitive matrices from the same matrix	22
reshape	reshapes a given matrix in user-defined dimension	21
residue	finds the residue from some rational form expression	31
rmfield	removes a field from an existing structure array	233
roots	returns the roots of a polynomial from its coefficients	28
rotation	rotates a geometric object defined in maple	43
round	rounds a fractional number towards the nearest integer	22
rref	returns the reduced row echelon form of a matrix	52
save	saves any workspace data	236
scatter	graphs discrete y versus x data using dots or circles	214
semilogx	plots a y versus log in x direction curve from some data	215
semilogy	plots a log in y direction versus x curve from some data	215
setfield	appends an extra field to an existing structure array	232
simplify	simplifies any expression which is in coded form in MATLAB or in maple	47,74
sinc	computes the sinc functional values	159
sinint	returns the functional value of the sine integral function	90
size	finds the row and column dimensions of a matrix	23
solve	solves algebraic equations mainly in symbolic form	34
sort	sorts the data in a row or column matrix in ascending order	20
std	computes the standard deviation from some data	134
stem	graphs a discrete functional data using vertical lines	214
strcat	catenates or places string horizontally	229
strcmp	compares strings	230
struct	composes structure array from user-definition	232
strvcat	catenates or places string vertically	229
subs	substitute the value of some variable in an expression	77
sum	sums all elements in a row or column matrix	19
SurfaceOfRevolution	computes the surface of revolution of a curve in maple	89
svd	performs the singular value decomposition of a rectangular matrix	57
sym	declares independent variables of an expression	10
sym2poly	returns the polynomial coefficients from a symbolic polynomial	28

Continuation of the last table...

Function name	Purpose	Page
syms	declares independent variables of an expression	10
syms or sym	describes any variable in symbolic or rational sense	10
symsum	performs the summation of a series in rational form	88
tabulate	prepares a frequency table of data only for positive integers	133
Tangent	finds the tangent to a polynomial curve in maple	80
taylor	finds the Taylor series polynomial approximation of some function	75
taylortool	displays a graphical user interface for the Taylor series finding from user definition	77
toeplitz	generates a Toeplitz matrix from user requirement	66
trace	computes the trace of a matrix	59
triangle	defines a 2D geometric triangle in maple	40
triplequad	integrates an expression numerically for triple integration	88
unifpdf	returns the functional value of the probability density function for the uniformly distributed random variable	139
unifrnd	generates uniformly distributed random number in continuous sense	132
vander	generates a Vandermonde matrix from user requirement	66
var	computes the variance from some data	134
vector	forms a vector in maple	56
VolumeOfRevolution	computes the volume of revolution of a curve in maple	89
xcorr	computes the cross correlation of two random processes	146
zeros	generates matrix of zeroes from user-defined dimension	25

Appendix B

Some symbols presented in the text

Symbol	Meaning
$\Leftrightarrow$	which is equivalent to
↵	pressing the Enter key from the keyboard
$\rightarrow$	clicking sequence of mouse
$\Rightarrow$	clicking the mouse sequence or provides
$\leftarrow$	short explanation of the MATLAB execution
>>	MATLAB's command prompt
[ ]	empty matrix
i or j	imaginary number
$\langle X,Y \rangle$	inner product of two identical size matrices X and Y
λ	eigenvalue of a square matrix
I	identity matrix
∇^2	Laplacian operator
∇	gradient operator
$\nabla \circ$	divergence operator
$\nabla \times$	curl operator
σ	standard deviation of some data
σ^2	variance of some data
μ	mean of some data
ρ	correlation coefficient
T	transposition operator
H_N	Hadamard matrix of order $N \times N$
$f[m]$, $f[n]$	any one dimensional discrete function
$f[m,n]$	any two dimensional discrete function
2D	two dimensional
3D	three dimensional
CDF	cumulative probability density function
DFT	discrete Fourier transform
PDF	probability density function

References

[1] Mohammad Nuruzzaman, "*Tutorials on Mathematics to MATLAB*", 2003, AuthorHouse, Bloomington, Indiana.

[2] Mohammad Nuruzzaman, "*Modeling and Simulation in SIMULINK for Engineers and Scientists*", 2005, AuthorHouse, Bloomington, Indiana.

[3] Mohammad Nuruzzaman, "*Digital Image Fundamentals in MATLAB*", 2005, AuthorHouse, Bloomington, Indiana.

[4] Duffy, Dean G., *"Advanced Engineering Mathematics with MATLAB"*, Second Edition, 2003, Chapman & Hall, CRC, Boca Raton.

[5] Hanselman, Duane C. and Littlefield, Bruce R., "*Mastering MATLAB 5: A Comprehensive Tutorial*", 1998, Prentice Hall, Upper Saddle River, New Jersey.

[6] Shampine, Lawrence F. and Reichelt, Mark W., *"The MATLAB ODE Suite"*, 1996, The Math-Works, Inc., Natick, MA.

[7] Rafael C. Gonzalez, Richard E. Woods, and Steven L. Eddins, *"Digital Image Processing Using MATLAB"*, 2004, Pearson Prentice Hall, Upper Saddle River, New Jersey.

[8] Peter V. O'Neil, "*Advanced Engineering Mathematics*", Third Edition, 1991, Wadsworth Publishing Company, Belmont, California.

[9] Ali S. Hadi, "*Matrix Algebra - As A Tool*", First edition, 1996, Wadsworth Publishing Company.

[10] Serge Lang, "*Calculus of Several Variables*", Second Edition, 1979, Addison–Wesley Publishing Company.

[11] Rogers, Gerald Stanley, "*Matrix Derivatives*", 1980, M. Dekker, New York.

[12] Marcus, Marvin, "*Matrices and MATLAB - A Tutorial*", 1993, Prentice Hall, Englewood Cliffs, N. J.

[13] Ogata, Katsuhiko, "*Solving Control Engineering Problems with MATLAB*", 1994, Englewood Cliffs, N. J. Prentice Hall.

[14] Part-Enander, Eva, "*The MATLAB Handbook*", 1998, Harlow: Addisson Wesley.

[15] Prentice Hall, Inc., "*The Student Edition of MATLAB for MS-DOS Personal Computers*", 1992, Prentice Hall, Englewood Cliffs, N. J.

[16] Saadat, Hadi., "*Computational Aids in Control Systems Using MATLAB*", 1993, McGraw-Hill, New York.

[17] Gander, Walter. and Hrebicek, Jiri., "*Solving Problems in Scientific Computing Using MAPLE and MATLAB*", 1997, Third Edition, Springer Verlag, New York.

[18] Biran, Adrian B and Breiner, Moshe, "*MATLAB for Engineers*", 1997, Addison Wesley, Harlow, Eng.

[19] D. M. Etter, "*Engineering Problem Solving with MATLAB*", 1993, Prentice Hall, Englewood Cliffs, N. J.

[20] Shahian, Bahram. and Hassul, Michael., "*Control System Design Using MATLAB*", 1993, Prentice Hall, Englewood Cliffs, N. J.

[21] Prentice Hall, Inc., "*The Student Edition of MATLAB for Macintosh Computers*", 1992, Prentice Hall, Englewood Cliffs, N. J.

[22] Ogata, Katshuiko, "*Designing Linear Control Systems with MATLAB*", 1994, Prentice Hall, Englewood Cliffs, N. J.

[23] Bishop, Robert H., "*Modern Control Systems Analysis and Design Using MATLAB*", 1993, Addsison Wesley, Reading, MA.

[24] Moscinski, Jerzy and Ogonowski, Zbigniew., "*Advanced Control with MATLAB and Simulink*", 1995, E. Horwood, Chichester, Eng.

[25] Gene Howard Golub and Charles F. Van Loan, "*Matrix Computations*", 1983, Johns Hopkins University Press, Baltimore.

[26] Alberto Cavallo, Roberto Setola, and Francesco Vasca, "*Using MATLAB Simulink and Control Systems Toolbox - A Practical Approach*", 1996, Prentice Hall, London.

[27] I. Gohberg, P. Lancaster, and L. Rodman, "*Matrix Polynomials*", 1982, Academic Press, New York.

[28] Jackson, Leland B., "*Digital Filters and Signal Processing with MATLAB Exercises*", Third Edition, 1996, Kluwer Academic Publishers, Boston.

[29] Kuo, Benjamin C. and Hanselman, Duanec., "*MATLAB Tools for Control System Analysis and Design*", 1994, Prentice Hall, Englewood Cliffs, N. J.

[30] Chipperfield, A. J. and Fleming, P. J., "*MATLAB Toolboxes and Applications for Control*", 1993, London, New York: Peter Peregrinus on Behalf of the Institute of Electrical Engineers.

[31] Math Works Inc., "*MATLAB Reference Guide*", Math Works Inc., 1993, Natick, Massachusetts.

[32] Cleve Moler and Peter J. Costa, "*MATLAB Symbolic Math Toolbox*", User's Guide, Version 2.0, May 1997, Natick, Massachusetts.

[33] R. Braae, "*Matrix Algebra for Electrical Engineers*", 1963, I. Pitman, London.

[34] Lokenath Debnath, *"Nonlinear Partial Differential Equations for Scientists and Engineers"*, 1997, Birkhäuser, Boston.
[35] Peter V. O'Neil, *"Beginning Partial Differential Equations"*, 1999, John Wiley & Sons, Inc., New York.

Subject Index

A

2D curve 204
2D parametric curve 205
2-norm 58
3D array 230
3D curve 216
3D parametric curve 216
absolute value 223
accumulation 225
acos 223
acosec 223
acot 223
adjoint of a matrix 53
appending columns 16
appending elements 16
appending rows 17
area 42
area finding 42
array 15
array extension 26
array field 232
array manipulation 15
array size 23
ASCII code 229
asec 223
asin 223
asinh 223
atan 223
average 80
axis removal 217

B

bar graph 216
basis 56
basis of null space 56
basis of vectors 56
Bessel equation 90
Bessel function 90
Bessel function of the first kind 91
Bessel function of the second kind 91
best fit curve 141
best fit line 141
beta function 90
bilinear form 60
binary number 154
binomial coefficient 148
boundary condition 191
break 229
break statement 229

C

cdf 140
cell array 233
character code 229
characteristic polynomial 55
Chebyshev polynomial 156
Cholesky decomposition 64
circle 41
coding 221
collinear 45
coloning 15
command prompt 2
command window 2
comment statement 229
companion matrix 65
comparative operator 223
complementary error function 90
complex computation 152
complex form Fourier series 106
complex grid 153
complex number 149
complex number computation 150
complex number division 151
complex number logarithm 151
complex number multiplication 150
complex to real 149
constants 25
continuous Fourier transform 111
contour 206,211
contour graph 206
contour graph of data 211
control statements 223
conversion of numbers 154
convolution 29
correlation 136
correlation coefficient 136
cos 223
cosec 223
cosh 223
cosine integral 90
cot 223
creating a function file 235
cross correlation 145
cross product 154
cumulative distribution function 140
cumulative sum 141
curl 79
curve intersection 48
curve tangent 80

D

data accumulation 225

data exchange 236
data export 236
data flipping 13
data import 236
data load 236
data maximum 20
data minimum 20
data plot using dots 214
data save 236
data sorting 20
decibel plot 115
definite integration 85
deleting elements 16
determinant 54
determinant of a matrix 54
DFT 116
diagonal matrix 51
difference equation 130
differential equation 93
dimension 23
dimension finding 23
discrete Fourier transform 116
discrete function plot 214
discrete plot 214
dissimilar y versus x graph 210
divergence 78
domain construction 188
dot product 154
double integration 84
double numerical integration 87

E

editing elements 16
eigenmode PDE 187
eigenvalue 55
eigenvector 55
element check 23
element reshaping 21
element summation 19
elliptic PDE 187
error function 90
exponential distribution 138
exponential integral 90

F

factor 29
factorial 149
finding area 42
finding elements 23
first order ode 94
first order PDE 183
flipping 13
for-loop accumulation 225
for-loop syntax 224
forward Fourier transform 112
forward Laplace transform 121
forward Z transform 126
Fourier reconstruction 110
Fourier series 105
Fourier spectrum 114
Fourier transform 112
Fresnel cosine integral 148
Fresnel sine integral 148
full rectified wave 163
function file 235
function file generation 235
function generation 159
function graphing 203
function plot 203
functional average 80
functional code 221
functional inverse 155
functional zeroes 36

G

gamma function 90
Gaussian elimination 53
geometric mean 134
geometry package 39
goal optimization 176
gradient 78
graph from data 209
graph from function 203
graph of bar graph 216
graph of discrete function 214
graph of dissimilar y data 210
graph of multiple y data 210
graph of parametric curve 205
graph of pie chart 215
graph of piecewise function 211
graph of three dimensional curve 216
graph of y vs x data 209
graphing a function 203
graphing Fourier series 109
graphing ODE solution 104
graphing parametric equation 205
graphing PDE solution 187
graphing spectrum 114
grid generation 38
grid lines 217

H

half index flipping 14
half rectified wave 163
Hankel function 91
Hankel matrix 67
harmonic mean 134
help 8
Hessian 77
hexadecimal number 154
higher order differential equation 101
higher order ode 101

Hilbert matrix 65
horizontal catenation 229
horizontal string 229
hyperbolic PDE 187

I

identity matrix 51
if-end syntax 226
imaginary number 149
imaginary part 149
implicit equation 75
implicit function graphing 204
impulse function 112
indefinite integration 84
indexing 15
infinity norm 58
initial condition 194
inner product 25
input 227
input during run time 227
integer division 22
integral calculus functions 90
integration 83
integrodifferential equations 125
intensity image plot 216
intersection of curves 48
inverse DFT 116
inverse discrete Fourier transform 116
inverse Fourier transform 113
inverse Laplace transform 124
inverse of a complex matrix 152
inverse of a function 155
inverse of a matrix 54
inverse Z transform 128

J

Jacobian 77
Jordan decomposition 63
Jordan form 63

L

L_2 norm 58
Laplace transform 121
Laplace transform of derivatives 121
Laplace transform of integrals 123
Laplacian 80
large matrix 19
left limit 70
length 23
length of a vector 23
limit 69
linear constraint 173
linear equality constraint optimization 173
linear optimization 169
linear plot 209
linear programming 169
linear vectors 59
logarithmic plot 215
logarithmic vectors 59
logical operator 223
log-log plot 215
LU decomposition 62

M

magnitude spectrum 114
Mahalanobis distance 144
maple 30
MAT file 236
MATLAB 1
MATLAB coding 221
matrix addition 9
matrix algebra 51
matrix arithmetic 12
matrix coloning 15
matrix determinant 54
matrix dimension 23
matrix extension 26
matrix inverse 54
matrix manipulation 15
matrix multiplication 10
matrix norm 58
matrix of constants 25
matrix of ones 25
matrix of zeroes 25
matrix padding 26
matrix rank 53
matrix reshaping 21
matrix subtraction 9
matrix trace 58
matrix transposition 4
maximum 20
maximum from a function 81
maximum with index 20
mean 133
mean absolute deviation 135
median 135
mesh plot 207,212
M-file 221
M-file function 162
M-file maxima 82
M-file minima 82
M-file optimization 171
minimax optimization 177
minimum 20
minimum from a function 82
minimum with index 20
minor of a matrix 52
Modified Bessel function 91
moment 135
multi-input function file 235
multi-output function file 235
multiple graph 213
multiple if 226
multiple maximum 82
multiple minimum 82

multiple objective function 176
multiple zeroes 25

N

nested-if 226
nonlinear constraint 173
nonlinear optimization 173
nonzero element 23
norm 58
norm of a matrix 58
normal distribution 132
normal random numbers 132
normalization 60
n-th root 152
null space 56
number conversions 154
numeric optimization 172
numerical integration 87
numerical PDE 182
numerical solution to an ODE 98
numerical solution to a PDE 193

O

octal number 154
ode 98
ones 25
operator 222
optimization 167
ordinary differential equation 98
orthogonal polynomial 156
orthonormalization 61
outer product 25

P

padding 26
parabola 42
parabolic PDE 187
parametric curve 205
parametric equation graphing 205
partial differential equation 179
partial fraction 30
PDE 179
PDE boundary condition 191
PDE domain 188
PDE GUI 189
PDE initial condition 194
PDE solution 196
pdf 139
periodic function 163
perpendicular line 44
phase angle 149
pie chart 215
piecewise continuous function 156
piecewise function 156
pivoting 52
pivoting about an element 52
plot 209
point formation 39
Poisson distribution 138
polar graph 207
polar plot 207
polar to rectangular 151
polynomial division 30
polynomial interpolation 155
polynomial multiplication 29
polynomial roots 28
position index 24
power law fitting 142
power of a matrix 54
power operation 14
power operations 14
principal component 143
probability density function 139
product 19
producting elements 19
programming 229
projection 45
pseudoinverse 60

Q

QR decomposition 63
quadratic form 60
quadratic programming 170

R

ramp function 159
random integers 132
random numbers 132
rank 53
real form Fourier series 106
real part 149
real spectrum 116
real to complex 152
reciprocal 12
rectangular to polar 151
rectified wave 163
reflection 44
regression analysis 143
regression coefficients 143
relational operator 223
remainder 22
replacing elements 16
reshaping 21
residue 31
right limit 70
roots of a polynomial 28
rotation 43
rounding elements 22

S

sawtooth wave 165
scalar addition 12

scalar code 221
scalar coding 221
scalar division 12
scalar multiplication 10
scatter 214
scatter plot 214
sec 223
second order ode 100
second order PDE 187
semilog plot 215
series 75,88
series summation 88
set complement 158
set difference 158
set functions 157
set intersection 157
set union 157
similar triangle 45
simple if 226
sin 223
sinc function 159
sine integral 90
sine wave 163
single integration 84
single numerical integration 87
singular value decomposition 57
sinh 223
sinusoidal wave 163
size 23
size of a matrix 23
sort 20
sorting with index 20
special matrices 65
square wave 164
standard deviation 134
statistical toolbox 146
stem plot 214
string 229
string catenation 229
string comparison 230
structure array 230
submatrix 15
subwindow plot 213
successive differentiation 73
sum 19
summation of a series 88
summing elements 19
surface graph 207
surface graph of data 212
surface of revolution 89
surface plot 207,212
switch-case syntax 228
symbolic integration 83
symbolic optimization 167
symbolic partial fraction 31
symbolic PDE solution 180
system of differential equations 96,102

T

tan 223
tangent 80
Taylor series 75
three dimensional array 230
three dimensional curve 216
trace 58
transpose of a matrix 4
transposition 4
triangle 40
triangular wave 165
triple integration 85,88
triple numerical integration 88
troubleshooting 217
troubleshooting in graphing 217

U

uniform random numbers 131
unit step function 112
user-input 227

V

Vandermonde matrix 66
variance 134
vector code 221
vector coding 221
vector function optimization 176
vector multiplication 11
vector outer product 25
vector size 23
vertical catenation 229
vertical string 229
volume 89
volume of a solid 89
volume of revolution 89

W

while-end syntax 228
workspace browser 3,6

Y

y versus x graph 204

Z

Z transform 126
zeroes 25

www.ingramcontent.com/pod-product-compliance
Lightning Source LLC
Chambersburg PA
CBHW060533060326
40690CB00017B/3479

* 9 7 8 1 4 2 5 9 7 7 3 8 2 *